Herbs and Spices
Proceedings of the Oxford Symposium on Food and Cookery 2020

Herbs and Spices

Proceedings of the Oxford Symposium on Food and Cookery 2020

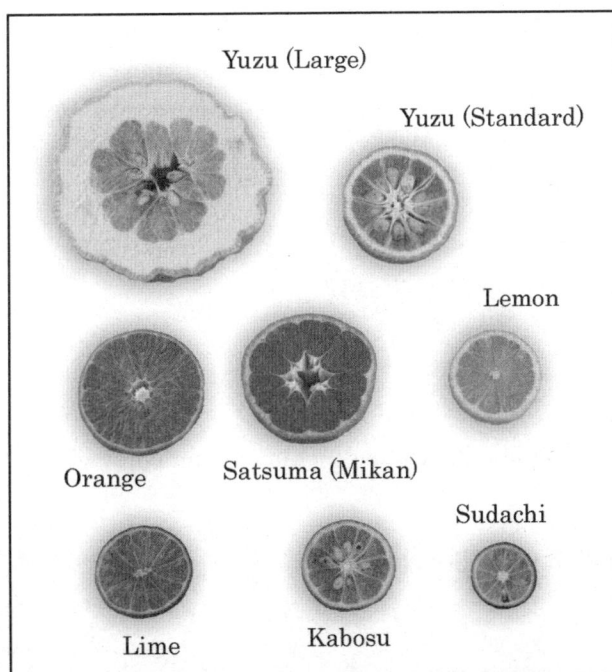

Yuzu (Large)

Yuzu (Standard)

Lemon

Orange   Satsuma (Mikan)

Sudachi

Lime   Kabosu

Edited by Mark McWilliams

Prospect Books
2021

First published in Great Britain in 2021 by Prospect Books, 26 Parke Road, London SW13 9NG.

The image on the title page is a comparison of yuzu to other citrus fruits, showing the thickness of the peel and oversized seeds.

ISBN 978-1-909-248-72-4

Design and typesetting in Gill Sans and Adobe Garamond by Catheryn Kilgarriff and Brendan King.

Printed and bound in Great Britain.

Contents

Herbs and Spices

Herbs and Spices

Foreword

No one expected intimacy. When the Oxford Food Symposium announced, at the beginning of this long pandemic year, that the 2020 gathering would be a virtual event, many anticipated missing the magical spaces of St Catherine's College: the filled-to-capacity Bernard Sunley lecture hall, the packed foyer and book stand during tea breaks, the overstuffed – and overly stuffy – session rooms, the bar with symposiasts too amped to end the day's discussions spilling out into the grounds, and most of all the dining room with its sea of faces turning excitedly from each to the next over spectacular meal after spectacular meal. Those spaces were integral to the Symposium, weren't they, and while the move online was understandably necessary, almost everyone anticipated their loss. It just wouldn't be the same, would it, but we'd carry on.

It was not the same, of course, and yet after what came to be called the V-Symp was over, the word "intimate" kept turning up in symposiasts' survey responses. That would have been shocking to the organizers if we had not all felt that intimacy ourselves. The Symposium is a famously welcoming gathering, and yet there was something even more levelling about meeting in Zoom breakout rooms, where perceived differences in reputation or experience seemed lost in the virtual shuffle of suddenly finding a group of interested faces peering out of our screens. And, too, there was something unexpectedly unifying in seeing each other not in the shared venues of St Catz but instead in our own spaces, in our own living rooms and offices and kitchens.

That intimacy surprised me too. I always had confidence we could pull off the academic exchanges of the Symposium somehow. When we gathered in Borough Market's kitchen for the annual editorial meeting – at what turned out to be the last trip any of us took until vaccinations came months later – the Symposium's Chair pulled me aside and quietly asked what we could do if we had to cancel. It seemed immediately clear that the papers, at least, could be successful: at worst we could exchange comments via email or a website, and we could end with the usual volume of published papers.

What an impoverished imagination I had. Instead of some emailed comments, we ended up with, by some expert accounts, the most interactive online scholarly conference yet. We decided very early on that there would be no webinars: all the symposiasts would have live mics. And we also decided that we would, as far as possible, sacrifice nothing. We'd even figure out how to host the Symposium's legendary meals virtually, and we'd find some way to share a celebratory drink afterwards. The papers remained at the Symposium's core, with our authors showing off new Zoom recording skills.

And those papers – most featured in this volume – were fabulous. This year's theme was Herbs and Spices, and the range of topics and depth of analysis was as impressive as ever. We worried this was a particularly bad year to be online, where there seemed no way to feel the heft of a quill of Alba-grade cinnamon or the roughness of stone-flower, to taste the subtlety of annatto or stinging nettle, but we quickly realized that the V-Symp solved a long-standing problem: with presentations recorded and panel discussions spread out over almost two weeks, symposiasts no longer had to choose which panel to attend: we could see them all! And the V-Symp solved trickier problems too: dramatically lowering the cost and completely eliminating travel expanded access, with more symposiasts participating from farther away, particularly from across the Global South. Going online offered new opportunities to Change the Conversation, Expand the Table, and Improve the Plate.

In the middle of the V-Symp, Barbara Wheaton, leading a late-night discussion of The Sifter, the amazing food studies database she's been building for years, looked away from her camera, paused, then turned back: "I just looked out my window to see the trees here in Massachusetts, but I thought I was at St Catz." The Symposium, it turns out, is wherever symposiasts gather. This year that will again be online, in our now-trusty spaceship, but in 2022 we will have to face the challenge of keeping all we have gained in the virtual space while also returning physically to St Catz. We will have to accomplish that without hierarchy, without one group or another feeling like mere observers. But we'll figure it out. After all, the magic is not in the spaces: it is in us.

Here I would like to thank some of the magicians: Elisabeth Luard, Cathy Kaufman, Naomi Duguid, Jessica Seaton, Carolyn Steel, and especially Ursula Heinzelmann and David Matchett, who kept us building the V-Symp through good humour and the force of absolute optimism, and Gamze İneceli, who performed never-before-seen tricks with our still-shared meals. I'd also like to recognize those who helped this volume – the tenth under my editorship! – make it to publication: Catheryn Kilgarriff, Brendan King, Jake Tilson, Peter Hertzmann, and all the authors whose papers brought à virtual symposium to real life.

Mark McWilliams
Editor, Oxford Symposium on Food and Cookery

Gastrophysics: The Psychology of Herbs and Spices

Opening Plenary Address

Charles Spence

Introduction: Herbs and Spices

According to the US Food and Drug Administration (FDA), spice can be defined as an 'aromatic vegetable substance in the whole, broken, or ground form, the significant function of which in food is seasoning rather than nutrition' and from which 'no portion of any volatile oil or other flavoring principle has been removed'. Indeed, it is not uncommon in the industry to group herbs and spices under the header of the latter. Nowadays, herbs are defined as the leafy parts of a plant including stalks and flowers, whether fresh or preserved.[1] Spices are usually, but not always, used in dried form, acting as the fragrance carriers derived from every other part of the plant including seeds, arils, bark, flower-buds, stigmas, roots, and resins (Freedman 2020: 78).[2]

While more than one hundred different herbs and spices have been identified, only a relatively small number are in common usage today.[3] As Colquhoun notes:

> For those of us whose use of culinary herbs is restricted, say, to parsley, coriander, sage, thyme and basil, the cornucopia in use in the late sixteenth century is striking:

> Thyme, Savourie, Hyssop, Pennyroyal [...], sage, Garden Clary [a kind of sage], baulme, Mints, Costmary and Maudeline, tansie, Burnet, Monkes Rubarbe, Bloodwort [dock], sorel (much used in sawses), langdebeef [lamb's lettuce], arrach [similar to spinach], blites, beetes, Alisanders, Smallage, Parsley, fennel, Dill, chervil, mallows, Succourie [curly chicory] and Endive, spinach, lettice, purslane, tarragon, cresses, rocket, mustard, asparagus' (2008: 115-16).

The popularity of different herbs and spices has undoubtedly changed over time, with ancient and medieval cooking distinguished by a heavy hand with herbs and spices (Bellamy and Pfister 1992; Freedman 2020). Wake summarizes various sources documenting a massive increase in pepper and other spice imports into Europe in the sixteenth century (1979). The incorporation of locally-grown herbs and spices in recipes in Europe decreased after the arrival of pepper and certain other spices in large volumes. So, for example, the use of cinnamon, cloves, and saffron is way down in the UK nowadays as compared to what it was in the medieval period.[4] By contrast, sales of pepper, garlic, and chilli pepper have risen dramatically (e.g. Spence 2018a; Wake 1979).

To put this into perspective, according to Cordell and Araujo, one in every four people on the planet ate chillies on a daily basis by the 1990s (1993).[5] Meanwhile, according to Tainter and Grenis, in 1991, 87 million pounds of pepper were imported into the US alone (1993). According to data from Parker, the amount spent by Australians on sales of fresh herbs and spices in major supermarkets suggests that the most popular three by weight are garlic, ginger, and chilli, followed by basil, coriander, and parsley (2004). Chives, lemon grass, rosemary, oregano, dill, and thyme were also popular amongst Australian consumers, according to Parker (see also McGee 2004: 418; Paivia 2018). Survey results published in 1995 suggested that individual consumers in Australia and New Zealand were consuming an average of about 1 gram of herbs and spices per day (Williams 2006).

One of the recent worldwide trends in the food sector has been the increased use of herbs and spices as flavourings (Sloan 2005). For instance, just take the 20-30% growth in sales of herbs and spices reported over the opening five years of the twenty-first century in both the United Kingdom and the United States (Global Information, Inc. 2005).

Galangal was also a surprisingly popular ingredient in recipes in the UK until a few hundred years ago.[6] The emergence of the French style of cooking in the early 1700s led to the decline in the use of spices in many western cuisines (Freedman 2015, 2020; Pinkard 2009). Notice here how many spices are now relegated to traditional puddings (especially in British cuisine). It is perhaps worth noting that nowadays, spices are mostly associated with desserts (Freedman 2015, 2020).

On the Historical Use of Herbs and Spices

At various times in history, certain herbs and many spices were incredibly expensive, rare, and exotic. The marked difference in shelf-life has meant that herbs and spices have played quite different roles on the world stage, despite the fact that botanists (and many in the industry) make no distinction between an herb and a spice. Herbs, not traditionally seen as a trade-item, when used fresh, and often available for foraging, would once have helped sustain the rural poor. Herbs were widely used in the UK up until the Industrial Revolution. Spices, by contrast, were once considered exotic Veblen goods that were offered to guests to display one's wealth (e.g. Schivelbusch 2005a, b).[7] What is more, the introduction of spices into recipes for cooking meat appear more related to aspirational desires linked to the East. Medieval trade (not to mention the Crusades) also played an important role in bringing a number of exotic spices to Europe (Dalby 2000; Lopez and Raymond 1955; Mintz 1985; Parry 1953; Spence 2021a).[8] Spices also played a role in early religious rituals too (see Bradley 2015; Spence 2021a).

Over the millennia, many spices have had medicinal uses (e.g. Bellamy and Pfister 1992; Block 1986; Hemphill and Cobiac 2006; Laudan and Pilcher 1999; Monardes 1577; Steiner 1985).[9] Still today, many people consume herbs and spices for their beneficial psychological effects (e.g. on well-being). This, for example, is likely to be the case for many who consume the more than one million cups of chamomile tea drunk every day (Srivastava, Shankar, and Gupta 2010; see also Herz 2009 on the use of essential oils from various herbs and spices, such as peppermint, lavender, lemon balm, and cinnamon, in aromatherapy). Or think of all the mint/peppermint used in chewing gum and as a dominant flavour (and antimicrobial agent) in toothpaste (Bernstein 2019: Smolarek and others 2015). The medicinal use of herbs and spices also played some role in their popularity in the Middle Ages (Freedman 2015).[10] However, while acknowledging the medicinal and psychological use of herbs and spices, this does not really help to explain their seemingly ubiquitous incorporation into our cuisine nowadays.[11]

What, Exactly, Are Herbs and Spices Doing in Our Food?

If herbs and spices innately tasted good (like sugar, say), then the question of what they are doing in our food and drink would likely not arise. However, this is simply not the case. Rather, the majority of herbs and spices actually taste pretty unpleasant, at least initially. As Sherman and Flaxman put it: 'Pungent spices like garlic, ginger, anise and chilies are initially distasteful to most people' (2001: 146). Indeed, it was precisely the unpleasant sensation associated with pepper pungency, what Harry Lawless once described as 'the forgotten flavour sense' (1989; see also Nilius and Appendino 2013), that led Pliny the Elder to wonder: 'Who was the first to try it (pepper) with food? Who was so anxious to develop an appetite that hunger did not suffice? Pepper (he continues) is neither sweet nor beautiful, merely pungent' (Freedman 2020: 80).[12] Isabella Mary Beeton, author of the hugely popular *Mrs. Beeton's Book of Household Management*, was certainly no fan of garlic, describing its smell as 'offensive' and continuing that 'it is the most acrimonious in its taste of the whole of the alliaceous tribe' (1861: 190).[13] There is, in other words, a sense in which we need to learn to like herbs and spices. And many people come to like the painful burning sensation associated with chilli a great deal (Calvino 2009; Gonzalez-Crussi 1989; Gorman 2010). Hence, the question of what, exactly, herbs and spices are doing in our food and drink, and why, at certain points in history, people have been willing to pay so much to possess them remains.

Generally speaking, herbs and spices provide little in the way of nutrition (though there are exceptions, such as the chilli fruit which provides a useful source of vitamins A and C (Rozin 1987; see Spence 2018a), and parsley is also a rich source of vitamin C (Valšíková and others 2016)). Herbs and spices do not serve to bulk out foods, with an average of just 0.25-3g of spice typically being added per kilogram of primary ingredients, according to an analysis conducted by Sherman and Hash (2001).[14] Herbs and spices do not intrinsically act as generalized flavour enhancers either (e.g. in the way that salt, a mineral rather than a spice, and umami are thought to do (Breslin and Beauchamp 1997; Halim and others 2020; Suwankanit and others 2013; though also see Yang and others 2021)). However, as we will see later, they can take on this role as a result of associative learning.

13

What is more, the majority of herbs and spices do not innately taste or smell good either. Rather, they often taste bad, that is, bitter, irritating, pungent, or burning (Carstens and others 2002).[15] Herbs and spices contain various secondary plant compounds, known as phytochemicals, that are expressed by plants to prevent predation (Fraenkel 1959). Put simply, herbs and spices 'don't want to be eaten', at least not by us![16] Here, one might consider only how the capsaicin in chilli peppers generally helps to deter ground-based mammals from consuming this literally low-hanging fruit because they find the associated burning sensation innately unpleasant. Birds, by contrast, are insensitive to capsaicin (Jordt and Julius 2002; Tewksbury and Nabhan 2001; Tewksbury and others 1999), hence effectively facilitating the transmission of the seeds of this fruit – and perhaps providing an explanation for the Victorians' penchant for feeding their pet parrots chilli peppers (see Spence 2018a).

Many herbs and spices evolved to taste bad: think here only of the bitterness, oral irritation, pungency, the electric tingle of the sanshool in Szechuan peppercorns or electric daisies (Hagura, Barber, and Haggard 2013), and the pain of chilli (Caterina and others 1997; Spence 2018a).[17] We were not born liking such unusual/intense taste sensations (Rozin 1980), and early exposure (e.g. during pregnancy), which can sometimes help to build up familiarity and hence liking (Mennella 1995), is likely low for many herbs and spices due to their teratogenic properties (Flaxman and Sherman 2000; Profet 1992; exceptions here include garlic and vanilla; Mennella and Beauchamp 1991, 1994a, 1994b). Or, as the title of one article put it: 'Psychology of Chemesthesis – Why Would Anyone Want to be in Pain?' (Dalton and Byrnes 2016; see also Boddhula and others 2018).[18] So, the question becomes one of how (and when) we 'learn' to like the taste, aroma, and/or flavour of herbs and spices (Birch 1999; Dalton and Byrnes 2016; Rozin 1990; Rozin, Ebert, and Schull 1982; Ventura and Worobey 2013). What are the key factors governing the particular combinations of herbs and spices, not to mention the wide variety, that are used to season foods in different parts of the world?

Why Are Herbs and Spices such a Ubiquitous Feature of Our Cuisine?

According to the dominant evolutionary (or Darwinian) gastronomy account, known as the antimicrobial hypothesis, that has prevailed over the last couple of decades or so, the ultimate reason why herbs and spices are added to foods is to help kill microbes and thus provide some degree of protection against a range of food-borne illnesses (Sherman and Billing 1999; Sherman and Flaxman 2001; Sherman and Hash 2001; see Breslin 2013 on the evolutionary approach to taste). At the outset, it is worth noting that a large and growing body of scientifically credible evidence has demonstrated just how effective the bioactive compounds found in many different herbs and spices are in terms of their antimicrobial properties (e.g. Beuchat 1994; Billing and Sherman 1998; Ceylan and Fung 2004; Cichewicz and Thorpe 1996; Hargreaves and others 1975; Liu, 1996; Marini and others 2015; Molina-Torres, García-Chávez, and Ramírez-Chávez 1999; Omolo and others 2014; Shelef 1984; Tajkarimi, Ibrahim, and Cliver 2010).

According to the antimicrobial hypothesis, herbs and spices are added to help cleanse food of parasites and pathogens. Importantly, the antimicrobial hypothesis makes a number of testable predictions. First, a greater use of spices should be found in meat-based recipes than in vegetable-based recipes, given the greater risk of parasites and pathogens in the former.[19] Second, the antimicrobial hypothesis predicts that there should be a greater use of spices as the ambient temperature increases, as this also increases the likelihood of parasites and pathogens (especially prior to the widespread availability of refrigeration).[20]

Billing and Sherman have helpfully highlighted the antibacterial function of thirty spices (1998: see Figure 1). Intriguingly, the graph shows that all of the listed spices inhibit some species of food-spoilage bacteria they have been tested on, and about half inhibit 75% of bacteria. Sherman and Flaxman argue that the most commonly used spices are, in fact, potent inhibitors of bacterial growth (2001). What is more, the four most potent herbs and spices, namely garlic, onion, allspice, and oregano – killed all of the bacterial species frequently implicated in food-borne illness that Billing and Sherman were able to find data on. Gottardi and others provide an updated review of the research underpinning the antimicrobial properties of 99 different herbs and spices (2016; see also Ceylan and Fung 2004). Meanwhile, according to an analysis of meat- and vegetable-based recipes from a wide variety of countries by Sherman and Hash, it would indeed appear to be the case that the mean number of herbs and spices are noticeably higher in meat- than in vegetable-based recipes (2001: see Figure 2).

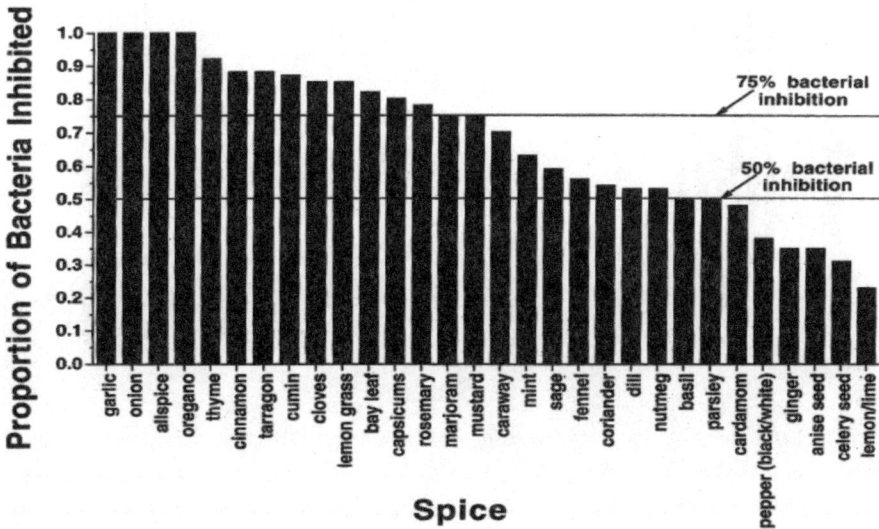

Figure 1. Antimicrobial properties (inhibition of growth or killing) of 30 herbs and spices for which appropriate data were available, arranged from greatest to least inhibition. [Graph represented from Billing and Sherman, 1998).][21]

Of course, from a culinary perspective, one might argue that it is not sufficient simply to show that fresh herbs and spices contain bioactive compounds that can kill a range of potentially harmful microbes. What one would also need to know, for the antimicrobial hypothesis to have legs, is that the amount, or concentration, of bioactive compounds typically present in recipes is sufficient to achieve this 'sterilizing' function. Rough calculations from Sherman and Hash suggest that 'recipes generally [contain] 0.25–3g spice/kg of primary ingredients (i.e., 250-3000 ppm)' which appears sufficient to either kill or inhibit food-borne bacteria in the laboratory (2001: p. 149; Hirasa and Takemasa 1998; Ismaiel and Pierson 1990).

Additionally, one would also want to be sure that these bioactive compounds retained their antimicrobial capabilities after cooking. While, as far as I am aware, there has been less research directly addressing this question, what evidence there is would certainly appear to support the thermostability of many phytochemicals, thus ensuring that their antimicrobial effects are preserved during cooking (e.g. Diebel and Banawart 1984; Moyler 1994; however, on others, e.g. cumin, see Chen, Chang, and Chang 1985; Srinivasan, Sambaiah, and Chandrasekhara 1992). Interestingly, those herbs and spices that are not thermostable, such as parsley and cilantro, are typically added after a dish has been cooked, hence meaning that their antimicrobial effects are not lost either

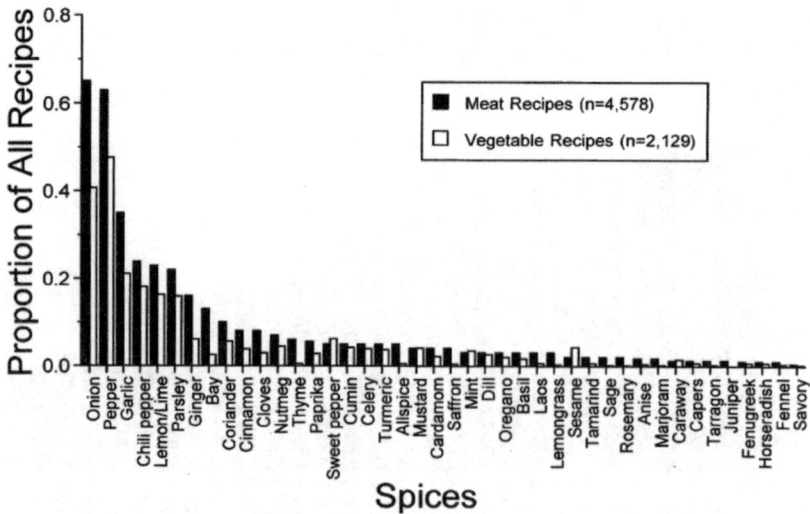

Figure 2. Graph showing the proportion of 4578 meat-based recipes (filled bars) and 2129 vegetable-based recipes (open bars) from traditional cookbooks of 36 countries calling for each of 41 herbs and spices. But are onions (leeks, shallots), lemon/lime juice, and capers really spices? (Note that, for somewhat different reasons, Sherman and Billing also question whether onions – chives, leeks, and shallots – and chillies should be counted as spices, given that they are sometimes served as main dishes (1999).) Summer 'savory' on the right of the graph, refers to Satureja hortensis. [Graph represented from Sherman and Hash (2001).]

– though whether sprinkled herbs just prior to consumption is an effective means of inhibiting the growth of food-borne bacteria is not so clear.[22] Another relevant issue here concerns how the antimicrobial function of herbs, such as bay leaf (*Laurus nobilis* L), might be affected by drying. Should there be a significant difference, then this would lead to further predictions about their use in recipes. Relevant here, research from Algabri, Doro, Abadi, Shiba, and Salem has shown that ground dried bay leaf offers significant antibacterial and antioxidant activity (2018). Meanwhile, in contrast, Valšíková and others have reported a dramatic reduction in vitamin C in parsley and celery that has been either frozen or dried (2016).

Sherman and Hash have also provided convincing evidence consistent with the predictions of the antimicrobial hypothesis concerning the greater use of herbs and spices in meat- than in vegetable-based recipes from traditional cookbooks from 36 countries (2001: see Figure 2).[23] The mean number of spices per meat-based dish of 3.9 compares to 2.4 for vegetable-based ones (see Sherman and Hash 2001: 153). Intriguingly, one doesn't see the same trend (or ambient temperature-dependence) for those herbs and spices (e.g. black and white pepper, and lemon and lime juice) that do not have such an antimicrobial function – though while these have low antimicrobial activity they can help to potentiate the antimicrobial effects of other spices. Indeed, parsley and dill were the only two herbs to show a negative relationship, meaning these herbs were more common in the cuisine of cooler climes, according to Sherman and Billing's own analysis (1999).

In one example, engagingly titled 'Chicken with Latitude', Sherman and Hash compared chicken recipes from the two countries with one of the highest and lowest mean annual temperatures, respectively (2001). In Norway, the mean annual temperature is just 2.8°C, and the average meat recipe includes just 1.6 herbs and spices. By contrast, in India, where the mean annual temperature is 26.9°C (Thailand is higher at 27.6°C), there are an average of 9.3 spices per meat recipe. Sherman and Billing's results highlighted a robust correlation between ambient temperature and the number of spices in meat-based recipes (1999). What is more, in those cultures spanning different climatic zones (such as, for example, China and the US), the same relationship between ambient temperature and the use of spices in meat-based recipes has also been observed. Specifically, lower latitude and lower altitude parts of the country tend to use a greater variety of spices, and more spices, on average.

Analysis of recipes from cookbooks in a wide range of countries supports both of these hypotheses. Namely, the average, and total, number of spices in recipes turns out to be correlated with the national mean average temperature for that country (see Figure 3a and 3b). What is more, the average number of spices included in meat dishes is significantly higher than for vegetable dishes (see Figures 2 and 3). Another finding that is also in line with the antimicrobial hypothesis is that as the average national temperature increases, the number of spices present in recipes increases more rapidly for meat- than for vegetable-based dishes (see Figure 3c). Sherman and Flaxman note

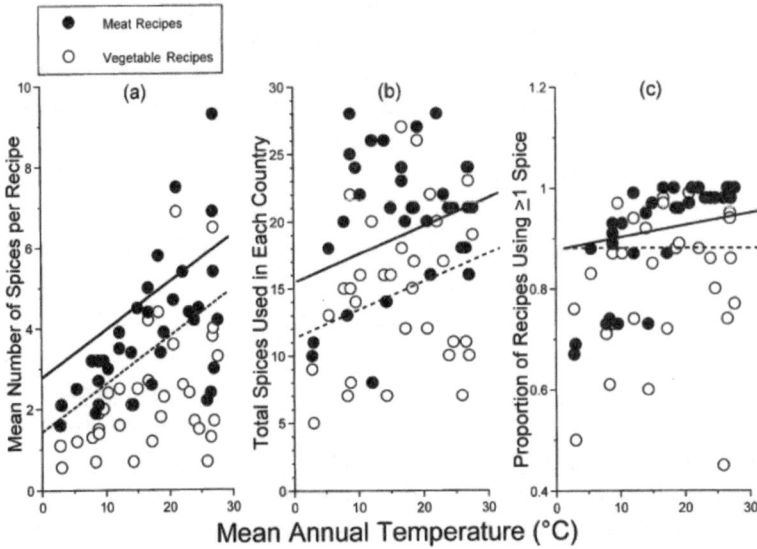

Figure 3. Graphs highlighting the relationship between mean annual temperatures and spice use in traditional meat-based (filled circles) and vegetable-based recipes (open circles) from 34 non-regional countries (i.e. excluding China and the United States). (a) Mean number of spices per recipe; (b) Total number of spices used in each country; and (c) Proportion of recipes in each country that used at least one spice. [Figure reprinted from Sherman and Hash, 2001).]

that the trends for increased use of spice with temperature was especially strong for the most effective, or inhibitory, of spices, i.e. 'those that reduced the growth of 75 per cent or more of bacterial species tested – including chilli peppers, garlic, onion, cinnamon, cumin, lemongrass, bay leaf, cloves and oregano' (2001: 144).

While Sherman and his colleagues' research is undoubtedly intriguing, not to mention convincing, I can't help but wonder whether the story (or findings) would change should a more broadly accepted definition of herbs and spices be adopted (i.e. one that excluded the questionable categories of onions, leeks, shallots, and lemon/lime juice, given that they contributed much of the data). One challenge to the antimicrobial hypothesis comes from the results of a study by Zhu and others (2013). These researchers analyzed various online databases documenting recipes (N=8498, comprising 2911 ingredients) from Chinese regional cuisines (N=20). They were able to show that geographical proximity overrode climatic proximity in terms of determining the similarity of regional cuisines. More importantly for present purposes, these researchers failed to find any evidence of a relationship between the mean annual temperature of a region and the number of spices per meat-based recipe used there (see Figure 4).

It might be suggested that Zhu and others' null results reflect the limits associated with studying a single country with a narrower variation in temperature than the many

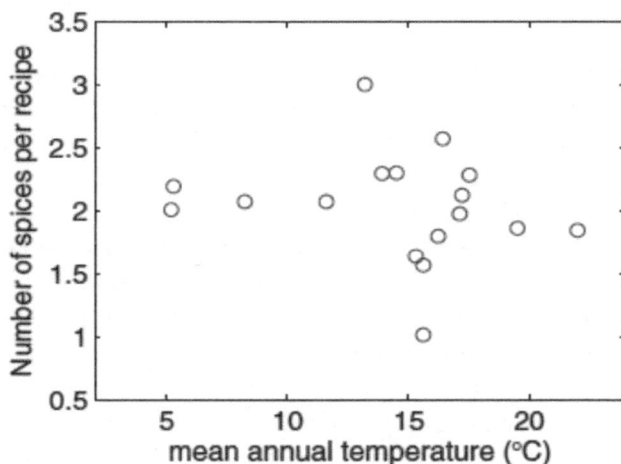

Figure 4. Graph plotting average number of spices per recipe as a function of the mean annual temperature in 17 of the 20 regions in China (represented by circles) as studied by Zhu and others (2013). The correlation was insignificant (p-value is 0.238). [Figure reprinted from Zhu and others (2013: Figure 7) <http://doi.org/10.1371/journal.pone.0079161.g007>.]

countries studied by Sherman and colleagues. However, given that Sherman and Flaxman reported such a temperature-spice relationship when comparing the culinary traditions of North and South China, this would seem unlikely to explain the difference (2001). One other point to consider is how, exactly, spices were defined in Zhu and others' study.

Interim Summary

Taken together, the results of several studies published over the last couple of decades or so have provided clear support for the key predictions of the antimicrobial hypothesis. The antimicrobial hypothesis is also consistent with the use of herbs like parsley and coriander (but not cumin), which lose their antimicrobial function on cooking, being added at the end of meal preparation (see Srinivasan, Sambaiah, and Chandrasekhara 1992). It is also consistent with the prominent role played by herbs and spices in the context of food preservation (for a review see Gottardi and others 2016).[24] However, at this point one might be tempted to wonder just how robust the temperature-spice correlation is to the particular definition of herbs and spices used in Sherman and colleagues' research. At the same time, one might wonder why the most antimicrobially effective spices (e.g. allspice, alliums, (onion,) and oregano; see Figure 1) aren't the ones called for most frequently in recipes? And why is it that modestly antimicrobial spices such as pepper (lemon/lime juice) are so popular?[25] In other words, the antimicrobial hypothesis fails to provide any explanation for which particular combination of spices are found (M=3.9 spices per meat-based recipe in the international selection of cuisines by Billing and Sherman 1998, as mentioned in Sherman and Billing 1999: 455).

It is tempting to consider the antimicrobial account to have been more relevant prior to modern food production and preservation. However, arguing against this position, it is worth bearing in mind that it has been estimated that one in ten North Americans are affected by bacteria-related food poisoning every year (Hui and others 1994). The real challenge for humans is that there is simply no way of determining whether a food contains food-borne microorganisms, nor whether they are more or less dangerous to our health, based on either the appearance or smell of a dish (Sherman and Hash 2001: 157).

Given that the antimicrobial hypothesis fails to explain why we add the particular combinations of herbs and spices that we do, we can ask what role taste plays in our decision to season our food in quite the way that we do. As Sherman and Flaxman note: 'What accounts for the enduring value of spices? The obvious answer is that they enhance the flavor, color and palatability of food. This *proximate*, or immediate-cause, explanation is true, but it does not address the *ultimate*, or long-term, questions of why people find foods more appealing when they contain pungent plant products' (2001: 142). However, spice use does not seem to be correlated with availability as the taste-good account would predict. Sherman and Hash raise the possibility that the flavour of herbs and spices may have played a role in their initial use (and incorporation in our cuisine): 'We speculate that people initially used pungent plant materials either because their flavors were appealing (e.g., cinnamon, basil) or they caused pleasurable psychological sensations' (2001: 158). Meanwhile, Billing and Sherman write that 'flavors of many widely used spices are not immediately appealing' (1998: 29). At the same time, however, Sherman and Billing claim that 'some spices are initially appealing (e.g. cinnamon, basil, and thyme)' (1999: 460). However, it is worth mentioning that no evidence is provided in support of any of these claims. Furthermore, the latter suggestion goes against the negatively-valanced response that so many of us have when first exposed to many herbs and spices.

The antimicrobial hypothesis also fails to provide a satisfactory explanation for the changing patterns of consumption that have been documented in Europe, say, over the last 800 years (e.g. Schivelbush 2005a, 2005b; Wake 1979), which likely has as much to do with expense and availability as anything else. That all being said, let us now turn to the proximal causes for the consumption of herbs and spices.

Proximate Perceptual Explanations for the Use of Herbs and Spices in Recipes

Masking Tainted Meat
At this point, it is worth mentioning an alternative (proximate) account for why herbs and spices may have been incorporated into our cuisine. According to one popular suggestion, they may originally have been added to help mask the taste/aroma/flavour of spoiled food, especially in the days prior to widespread refrigeration (e.g. Cole 2007; Govindarajan 1985). This account also predicts greater use of herbs and spices in meat

than vegetable dishes, and greater use in the cuisines of hotter countries. However, it has been argued that this particular account is unlikely to be valid (e.g. Colquhoun 2008; Sherman and Billing 1999; Sherman and Hash 2001). Specifically, the learned taste aversion that rapidly follows eating foods that we believe made us ill (e.g. Bernstein 1978; Gustavson 1977; Milgram, Krames, and Alloway 1977). That is, our predecessors would presumably soon have acquired a dislike for the tastes, aromas, and/or flavours of those spices that happened to be commonly associated with dishes that had made them ill (though there are exceptions: think here only how not everyone who has been poisoned by oysters necessarily gives them up).[26]

Freedman has also questioned the widespread assumption that fresh meat was in short supply in the medieval era and that was why spices were once such a popular feature of the cuisine (2008).[27] If one goes back to the Middle Ages, when the desire for spices was at its peak, at a time when only the very richest members of society would have been able to afford them, those who were rich enough to afford spices would presumably also have had no problem affording sufficient fresh meat for the table. At the same time, however, there is a stage where meat starts to deteriorate, when it starts to smell/taste foul, without it necessarily making one ill should one consume it. In such cases, seasoning the tainted meat to mask the taste/flavour likely helps make the food more palatable. Under such conditions, perhaps it does not matter too much what that taste is other than it is capable of masking the off taint. Note that we are unable to discern the presence, nor the danger posed by, food-borne microorganisms through either appearance or smell (Sherman and Hash 2001: 157).

Masking Undesirable Tastes

At the same time, there is presumably no reason why herbs and spices might not have been used to help mask other undesirable tastes/notes (such as the boar taint that many people used to find off-putting prior to the contemporary practice of castrating male pigs; Wysocki and Beauchamp 1984). Beyond the masking of one flavour by another, the addition of herbs and spices can sometimes result in the emergence of new flavours (e.g. as when lemongrass is added while cooking cauliflower). In support of this version of the masking account, the latest research has shown how cooking cruciferous vegetables with herbs and spices can help children who are supertasters, and hence who may find vegetables taste particularly bitter, to eat more greens (Carney and others 2018). (Since the food is not off, but simply has an unagreeable taste, learned taste aversion is presumably not a relevant concern here.) It should, though, be borne in mind that even this version of the masking account still doesn't necessarily explain how the taste, aroma, and flavour of herbs and spices came to be liked in the first place.

Relieving Boredom and Adding Complexity to a Meal

Could it also be, though, that the incorporation of herbs and spices into our cuisine once helped to relieve the monotony and boredom of mealtimes (on the notion of sensory boredom, see Piqueras-Fiszman and Spence 2014)? For example, it has been suggested that the early cultivation of chilli in the coastal regions of Northern South America may have been based on the desire to liven-up the taste of an otherwise boring, maize-based diet (Perry and others 2007; cf. Martínez 1992; Yang and others 2021; though see also Kraft Brown and others 2014). Note here also how chilli has always been part of the Holy Trinity of the Mexican diet: corn, beans, and chilli (Martínez 1992: 218). At the same time, however, one should not forget that herbs and spices have, for centuries, been added to make food look more visually appealing too (e.g. Woolgar 2018). It is, after all, presumably saffron's ability to add a golden red colour to food (perhaps even more than for the delicate flavour it imparts to a dish; Freedman 2020: 79) that helps to explain why it is often ranked as the most expensive naturally-occurring spice (e.g. Chartier 2012: 131; Crossley 2014). Saffron, note, does not come high on the antimicrobial scale (e.g. see Figure 1; though see also Sethi and others 2013).

It has also been suggested that herbs and spices might sometimes have been added to a dish to enhance the perceived complexity of its taste/flavour. Just take Chartier's suggestion that 'In Europe, cloves are used mainly to enhance the taste of desserts, while in most other parts of the world they serve to render meat's flavour more complex' (2012: 113). At the same time, however, while many different spices are typically combined in an Indian curry, there is a sense that the chef has failed if one is able to detect individual spices (see Spence and Wang 2018). The blending of multiple botanicals in a well-balanced gin such as Bombay Sapphire would also seem to presuppose that the drinker is unable to distinguish the elemental flavours. In the latter case, the botanicals include coriander, grains of paradise, angelica, liquorice, cassia bark, orris root, cubeb, lemons, juniper, and almonds. These examples hint that physical/chemical complexity does not necessarily equate to perceived complexity (see Spence and Wang 2018 for a review of the relationship between the two concepts).

Importantly, as yet, we have no means of predicting the perceived complexity of flavours in the context of food and drink. Mixing multiple flavourful elements is, in other words, a complex business. Nevertheless, it would at least seem reasonable to assume that, on average, adding herbs and spices will, if anything, increase the complexity of a dish (even if, in any particular instance, that outcome cannot be guaranteed). After all, the alternative would seem to be that adding herbs and spices elicits no change in the perceived complexity of the taste/flavour, while it would seem far less likely that adding distinctive volatile compounds would reduce the perceived complexity of a mixture.[28]

Interim Summary
This section suggests that herbs and spices may, in part at least, have been incorporated into our cuisine in order to help mask those tastes, aromas, and flavours that are less desirable while, at the same time, possibly helping to increase perceived complexity and interest/variety in cuisine. The traditional role of certain herbs and spices in helping to

22

add an attractive colour to dishes should not be neglected either, such as the addition of chopped spinach or parsley to many dishes (see Woolgar 2018). Spice use might also be linked to their ability to help tenderize meat and possibly also to improve digestion (Bellamy and Pfister 1992; Bober 1999; Spence 2018a).[29] As Freedman puts it, 'Spices had an important place in ancient and medieval cooking. Medical theories about diet and health overlapped with taste preferences' (2020: 77).

However, there are at least two key questions that we still do not have an answer to: first, why is it that different combinations of herbs and spices are used in different recipes within a given food culture, and second, why it is that different combinations of herbs and spices are found across food cultures (Rozin 1983)?[30]

Can Computational Gastronomy Help Explain the Use of Herbs and Spices?

In terms of the use of herbs and spices to help enhance, or mask, flavour, it is tempting to ask whether the emerging science of computational gastronomy can help to explain why different combinations of herbs and spices may be found in different dishes and/or different cultures (Ahnert 2013; Bhattacharya 2020). Computational gastronomy builds on the food pairing hypothesis that '[i]f two ingredients share important flavor compounds, then they will go well together' (Ahn and Ahnert 2013). Or take de Klepper's slightly more nuanced definition: 'The more aromatic compounds two foods have in common, the better they taste together. This effect is particularly strong when two foods share aromas that make up their characteristic flavour' (2011: 55). One finds just this kind of explanation in the work of Chartier, who writes at one point that 'thymol – the volatile compound responsible for the most important aromatic characteristic of thyme – is also the principal sapid (flavour) molecule contained in lamb. This explains the age-old use of thyme in lamb recipes' (2012: 92).

Should the food pairing hypothesis be valid, then it might indeed help to explain, at least in part, which particular combination of herbs and spices we use for particular dishes. Unfortunately, however, it has been found wanting by those who have rigorously put the theory to the test. For instance, Kort and others found no support for food pairing whatsoever. They conclude that 'food pairings with more aroma overlap did not taste better than food pairings with less overlap. For example, chocolate and tomato (43% overlap) did not taste better than cauliflower and pear (no overlap) [.... F]ood pairing based on aromatic overlap is not a guaranteed recipe for success. Balancing flavors is what does the trick' (2010; see also Blumenthal 2010; Bredie and others 2015 for a similarly pessimistic take on the flavour pairing hypothesis). Balancing flavours perceptually, therefore, depends on psychology and cannot be predicted chemically.

While flavour pairing fails to provide a plausible explanation for why specific herbs and spices are incorporated in particular dishes, the flavour network analysis of food pairing has identified an intriguing cultural element to how flavours are combined. Specifically, it has been shown that ingredients that co-occur in Western cuisines tend to share more similar flavour compounds than expected by chance. By contrast, analysis of more than

23

2500 online regional Indian recipes revealed that ingredients (N=7 in an average recipe) tend to be combined because they are dissimilar (Jain, Rakhi, and Baglerb 2015b). That is, ingredients with dissimilar flavour compounds appear to be combined more frequently than would be expected by chance. Similar trends have subsequently been reported in several other Asian countries, for example South Korea (see Ahn and others 2011; Ahn and Ahnert 2013).[31] While this kind of network analysis (and data mining approach) has undoubtedly highlighted some intriguing differences between Eastern and Western recipes, it is important to stress that the analysis of flavour networks tells us nothing about what underlies such cross-cultural differences. It would all make much more sense if the flavour pairing hypothesis were to have been supported. However, as we have just seen, that is not the case (though see also Simas and others 2017).

One other potentially important consideration to bear in mind is that the sensory properties of herbs and spices may well have changed over the centuries and likely differ as a function of climate, *terroir*, and selective breeding (cf. Bell and others 2017). For instance, consider only what the latter has achieved in terms of elevating the Scoville value of chilli plants by many orders of magnitude in recent years (see Boddhula and others 2018; Bodkin 2017; Bosland, Coon, and Reeves 2012; da Silva 2011; Davis 2018; Gorman 2010; Pavia 2018; Spence 2018a). Or consider only how the one descriptor 'chilli' describes (or rather encompasses) a very wide range of different taste/flavour profiles as, for example, used in Mexican cuisine (e.g. see Miller and Harrisson 1991). Just take the Mexican dish known as *sopa de medulla* (spinal cord): It incorporates chilli pasilla for colour, guajillo for flavour, pique for heat, and chipotle for smokiness.

24

Learning to Like the Taste of (Many) Herbs and Spices

According to Jain and others, the '[m]olecular composition of food dictates the sensation of flavour' (2015a: 3). This is the strong claim behind much of the computational gastronomy research. However, it is important to stress that our perceptual/hedonic response to the taste, aroma, and/or flavour of the majority of herbs and spices (just like so many other flavours) is likely learned as a result of associative learning/conditioning (cf. Rozin and Zellner 1985; Zellner and others 1983). For instance, a growing body of empirical research has demonstrated the importance of acquired taste (e.g. Blank and Mattes 1990; Jones, Roberts, and Holman 1978; Stevenson and Boakes 2004). In particular, those novel food aromas that are typically experienced together with a particular taste in food (e.g. sweet, sour, bitter, salty) come to take on, and become more perceptually similar to, whichever taste that they are commonly associated with. Hence, the smell of vanilla, caramel, and strawberries becomes sweet (despite vanilla pods actually tasting very bitter). What is more, learning to like the taste/aroma/flavour of the majority of herbs and spices likely takes place later than for other flavours, given their teratogenic properties (Shilling and Feldman 2001; see also Cooper and Cooper 1996). Indeed, it has been reported that pregnant mothers tend to avoid 'spicy' foods during the first trimester (Flaxman and Sherman 2000; Profet 1992).[32]

It can be argued that it is the acquired taste properties of aromas that are key to explaining their contemporary incorporation in dishes.[33] It may also help to explain some of the cultural/historical differences in the taste for herbs and spices that have been documented (Logue and Smith 1986; Williams and others 2016). The aroma of a given herb or spice associated with savoury dishes in one culture might be associated with sweet foods in another (cf. Breslin and other 2003; Spence 2008). Here, one might only consider how, in India, cinnamon tends not to be used in sweets but rather in savoury dishes, whereas the association of cinnamon with sweetness is much stronger currently in the West (e.g. see Blank and Mattes 1990). The latter researchers also highlight some differences between white and black North Americans in terms of the relative sweetness that they associate with spices such as nutmeg and anise.[34] According to Reed and Knaapila, there may also be a heritable component to the pleasantness of the smell of cinnamon (2010).

The key point to note here, though, is that the perceived sensory and hedonic properties of herbs and spices (as is the case for many other flavours) do not rely solely on their chemical composition but change as a function of exposure – or rather, of repeated co-exposure – in our diets. Hence, any attempt to explain why it is that herbs and spices work well together, and why specific combinations of herbs and spices are found in particular dishes, based solely on the chemical composition of the constituent ingredients is unlikely to succeed, despite the undoubted appeal of this kind of approach (see Spence, Wang, and Youssef 2017). As such, it can be argued that the molecular composition of herbs and spices certainly does not dictate the associated flavour sensation, contrary to the claim made by Jain and others (2015a). At the same time, it is important to stress that the chemical composition of herbs and spices is critically important in terms of giving rise to particular trigeminal sensations such as the oral pungency of pepper, the burning sensation of chilli, the tingling of Szechuan, the cooling of mint, the anesthetizing effect of cloves, etc.

Conclusions

While the antimicrobial hypothesis provides a reasonably satisfactory ultimate (evolutionary) answer to the question of what herbs and spices are doing in our food, proximal explanations for why we choose to season food as we do (e.g. to enhance the taste/flavour and/or appearance) are much more complicated, especially when the issue is addressed in a historical context. A key point to bear in mind here, though one seemingly often ignored by those working in the field of Darwinian, and especially computational, gastronomy, is that we learn to like the sensory properties and physiological consequences of consuming many of the herbs and spices that are incorporated into our diets (e.g. think only of learning to like the burn of capsaicin in chilli; Billing and Sherman 1998; Breslin 2013). We were most probably not born perceiving vanilla to be sweet (Stevenson and Boakes 2004).[35] Ultimately, therefore, providing an answer to the why question likely requires explanations at multiple levels, evolutionary/Darwinian gastronomy as well as a historical/anthropology approach (Sutton 2010), and even in terms of gastrophysics (Spence 2017). The latter is especially important when considering the use of herbs and spices to add colour (e.g. Woolgar 2018), or the green herbs that can help to add 'freshness' to a dish (Spence 2019). There is also a sense in which the ubiquity of black pepper on the dining table in many countries also allows for 'personalization' of the taste profile of a dish (see Spence 2017). While we can probably live with the industry shortcut to place both herbs and spices under the header of spices, there nevertheless remains something of an unresolved question as to what exactly counts as a spice. Consider here only how a few centuries ago sugar was commonly considered a spice (see Freedman 2020; Mintz 1985).[36] While no one would classify sugar as a spice nowadays (though see Blank and Mattes 1990, for one relatively recent exception), the inclusion of onions and lemon/lime juice as spices, as in the work of Sherman and colleagues, would, to this author at least, seem somewhat more debatable (Sherman and Billing 1999; Sherman and Flaxman 2001; Sherman and Hash 2001). It will therefore remain for future research to determine the extent to which support for the antimicrobial hypothesis depends on the particular definition (or rather inclusion criteria) for herbs and spices that is used (cf. Zhu and others 2013).

As we have seen, neither the antimicrobial hypothesis nor the computational gastronomy approach (built as it is on the food pairing hypothesis; Varshney and others 2013) can explain why it is that specific combinations of herbs and spices are found in particular dishes, nor why different combinations of herbs and spices are such distinctive features of the cuisine of different cultures (Rozin 1983). In terms of the specific combination of herbs and spices in dishes, they may play different roles in terms of adding colour, masking a variety of less pleasant tastes, as well as adding complexity/variety. The synergistic role of combining different herbs and spices in a dish should not be forgotten either (Sherman and Billing 1998).[37]

Herbs and Spices: Contemporary Usage

Having studied a number of the historical drivers behind the incorporation of herbs and spices into our food and drink, I would like to conclude by considering some of their contemporary and possible future uses. The use of herbs and spices to help colour food is rather less common these days than once it was (see Woolgar 2018). Not that colouring our foods is any less common, but rather that numerous cheaper synthetic and natural alternatives have come onto the market in recent years (see Hisano 2019; Spence 2018c). There is, though, continued interest in the natural antimicrobial properties of spices such as chilli (Omolo and others 2014). Herbs (think mint, parsley, dill, Sorrel Roberta, coriander leaf, and various kinds of basil) are also increasingly popular additions to leafy green salads (see Spence 2020b for a review).

One might consider whether the recent rise in popularity of fusion foods would act as a driver of increased contemporary exposure to unusual (novel) herbs and spices. However, a closer analysis of contemporary fusion foods suggests that this is not obviously the case (Spence 2018b), perhaps because most consumers may not be all that familiar with the flavour principles underlying different styles of cuisine (see Rozin 1983) – thus meaning that 'con-fusion' would likely be the result instead (see Stano 2014, 2016).

The rise in gastrotourism in recent years, especially when combined with an increasingly adventurous approach to food, is likely to play a role in exposing many consumers to a wider range of herbs and spices than might otherwise have been the case formerly (Amey, 2015; and e.g. Ullrich and others 2004; see also Mukherjee, Kramer, and Kulow, 2017). The growing interest in flavour pairing might also be seen as something of a driver for interest in the varied flavours offered by herbs and spices (see Spence 2020a for review). At the same time, one should probably not forget to highlight the contemporary role of celebrity endorsers in helping to popularize specific herbs and spices. For instance, just take the pronounced increase in sales of cinnamon attributed to Delia Smith (Singh 2009; see also Nolan 2013). Back in 1990, the British chef apparently had the cinnamon sticks flying off the shelves after incorporating this particular spice into one of her TV recipes (Singh 1990). Meanwhile, a few years later, a TV advert from Jamie Oliver was held responsible for a fourfold increase in sales of nutmeg (see Anon. 2005). That being said, such influences tend not to extend beyond national boundaries, and so the effects are perhaps limited in scope (though see also Farrimond 2018 and Feldmar 2020 on the recent culinary popularization of spices).

The role of herbs and spices in helping to personalize a dish, and of green herbs to add 'freshness' to a dish look set to continue (Spence 2017, 2018d, 2019). Looking to the future, herbs and spices will likely continue to be used to help mask unpleasant tastes (e.g. such as the bitter taste of cruciferous vegetables amongst supertasting children; e.g. Carney and others 2018). At the other end of the age spectrum, it has been suggested that the trigeminal sensory (or chemesthesis) stimulation associated with chilli, black pepper, etc. may also help to enliven food experiences for the growing number of elderly individuals suffering from a profound loss of their senses of taste and smell (Schiffman and Warwick 1989; Spencer and Dalton 2020). This will likely become an increasingly important issue in the years ahead as more of us live past the age of 60 or 70 years, for this is when the inevitable decline in gustatory and olfactory perception really start to take their toll (see Spence and Youssef 2021).

27

Herbs and spices can be used to help provide a healthy replacement for salt (Tapsell and others 2006), or sugar (Fial 1978), and/or as a generalized flavour enhancer (Williams 2006; Yang and others 2021). Such seasoning functions are likely based on the phenomenon of acquired taste, whereby the aromas of specific herbs and spices come to be associated with specific tastes through being commonly associated in an individual's prior tasting experience. Elsewhere, it has been suggested that 'sweet' aromas (e.g. of vanilla) may help to enhance the perceived sweetness of foods without the need to add so much sugar (Blank and Mattes 1990; Stevenson and Boakes 2004).

Beyond their ability to mask, and/or add, taste, aroma, and/or flavour to foods, the public's awareness of the health benefits of various herbs and spices has also been growing in recent years (Craig 1999; Krishnaswamy 2008; Moyers 1996; Spencer and Dalton 2020; Tapsell and others 2006). Consider here only the enhanced longevity recently documented in heavy users of chilli (American Heart Foundation 2020; Chopan and Littenberg 2017; Lv and others 2015; Mosley, 2017), or the widespread excitement around the benefits of consuming turmeric (e.g. Singletary 2010) as but two relevant examples.[38] Ginger also has a well-established role as an anti-inflammatory and purportedly helps to counteract motion sickness too (Grzanna, Lindmark, and Frondoza 2005).[39] As such, we may increasingly see a return to a more medicinal, or neutraceutical, approach to the use of herbs and spices in our cuisine in the years ahead (linked to the rise in functional foods and dietetics; Sloan 2005; Tapsell and others 2006).[40]

Finally, it is worth highlighting how the emerging field of crossmodal correspondences research has recently started to demonstrate the various crossmodal associations that exist between the aroma, taste, and flavour of various herbs and spices, and everything from colours to shapes, and from sounds to textures (e.g. Biggs, Juravle, and Spence 2016; Crisinel and others 2013; Gil-Pérez and others 2019; Spence 2018e; Wang, Keller, and Spence 2017; Seo and others 2010; Shermer and Levitan 2014; Xu and LaBroo 2014). Such correspondences are increasingly being incorporated into the design of multisensory experiential marketing, and advertising, campaigns (e.g. see 'The Sound of Taste' campaign from Schwartz Flavour Shots; Dunne 2014). The latter hopefully will help to attract the general public's attention to what, as we have seen, constitutes both a ubiquitous and healthy part of our diet.

28

Acknowledgements

Many thanks to the audience of the Oxford Food Symposium who provided such thoughtful and helpful comments on my presentation. They have helped to enrich my thinking about herbs and spices substantially.

Notes

1   Traditionally, the term applied to all green crops.
2   As Sherman and Billing note, 'spice' is a culinary term and not a specific botanical category (1999; Farrell 1990).
3   The typical herbarium in the UK in Anglo Saxon times would list as many as 500 herbs. Some, like the Roman favourite, Silphium, which grew in Libya and was never domesticated, disappeared altogether in the first century AD (see Freedman 2020). Meanwhile, we have simply no idea what others were (or were similar to), like *vescovo* (literally 'bishop'; Lopez and Raymond 1955: 109-14), mentioned by the Florentine author of a medieval manual of commerce (*La practica della mercatura* from c. 1340, see Pegolotti 1936).
4   Freedman notes that 70% of English medieval recipes in a modern adaptation of *Pleyn Delit* involved some sort of spice, often, in fact, a spice mixture (2020: 85). In contrast, 27% of present day recipes call for cinnamon. Meanwhile, a Catalan cookbook written a little before 1500 contains around 200 recipes, of which 125 call for cinnamon, 76 for ginger, 54 for saffron, and 48 for pepper.
5   As Tu, Yang, and Ma note, 'in China, spicy foods are sold ubiquitously in street stalls, restaurants, grocery markets and convenience stores. This near universal preference for spicy food is summed up in

the Chinese proverb: "Without chilli peppers, a dish just can't be delicious"' (2016: 52).

6   Freedman notes that 'Many Asian spices such as zedoary, long pepper, and galangal, all familiar to medieval cooks, were discarded. Modern cuisine and its turn away from spices began in seventeenth-century France' (2020: 84). Other formerly popular spices such as cubeb, cassia, and grains of paradise (African *malagueta*) have also fallen out of fashion in the recent era (Laurioux 1989: 40). One relevant question here is why that should be so.

7   According to the food historians, the desirability of spices in the medieval period actually has more to do with their being exotic (Eastern), mysterious, and precious (e.g. Freedman 2015; Schivelbush 2005a, 2005b; Woolgar 2001). For example, during the European Middle Ages, Freedman describes how spices were 'elite consumer products' imbuing those who could afford them with status (2015: 47). He continues, 'But much of the attraction of spices to medieval taste-makers and elites was due to factors beyond gastronomy' (Freedman 2015: 48). Bober (1999) and Mead (1967), meanwhile, talk of the consumption of spices as a means of allowing the guests at courtly banquets to taste the bounty of princely magnificence (see Cole 2007). And, going further back in history, the Roman Emperor, Nero, once ordered that saffron be scattered on all roads leading to Rome for his triumphal entry (Walker 1972).

8   In the Middle Ages, spices were sometimes offered to guests as 'Veblen goods', long before the term had even been invented (Colquhoun 2008; Veblen 1992). For instance, Henisch talks of the conspicuous consumption of spices amongst the increasingly rich inhabitants of medieval Europe (1976: 103-04). This would presumably count as a psychological motivation for the consumption of spices in a historical context. By 1400, there was extensive use of pepper, ginger, sugar and cinnamon, so what distinguished the wealthy was the provision of rare and expensive spices such as nutmeg, cloves, and grains of Paradise (Freedman 2015).

9   In fact, as Freedman has noted recently, in many languages the same word is used for 'recipe' and 'prescription' (2020: 84).

10   One should probably not forget garlic's purported role in helping to ward off vampires either (Maas and Voets 2014). This myth is thought to have originated in the Balkans in the medieval era, when garlic was used medicinally to help fight various diseases, including diseases of the blood (see Block 1986).

11   The medicinal role of chilli consumption was already being discussed by the middle of the sixteenth century. As Lauden and Pilcher note, 'By 1577, Nicholas Monardes, a Spanish physician who wrote one of the first treatises on New World plants, enthused that "It dooeth comforte muche, it dooeth dissolve windes, it is good for the breaste, and for theim that bee colde of complexion: it dooeth heale and comforte, strengthenyng the principall members"' (1999: 64).

12   Note that the Romans used *piper longum* (long pepper) which is more floral than *piper nigrum* (black pepper), but it has a tendency to go mouldy and doesn't keep as well.

13   Sometimes, of course, there may be a resistance to certain herbs and spices because they are associated with 'otherness', the flipside of the exoticism that has attracted people to spices at certain points in history. Indeed, it has been suggested that the British have treated garlic with suspicion ever since the Romans left. Intriguing, though, there is little mention of onions in Apicius (1936), appearing in only seven recipes (Potter 2015). Meanwhile, Buddhist objections to alliums and such were originally grounded in problems of ritual purity.

14   Spice blends with powdered grains make thickening agents in Indian regional cuisines. It is claimed that ground cinnamon can also add a gelatinous/viscous texture when added to water.

15   Cloves also thought to have an analgesic function, hence presumably the eugenol smell that so many of us associate with a trip to the dentist.

16   The story is very different when it comes to vegetables such as tomatoes, though (see Goff and Klee 2006). Of course, some herbs and spices, such as onions, leeks, garlic, and chives are also classed as vegetables, thus complicating the story somewhat.

17   Or consider only coriander leaf. This aromatic herb tastes unpleasantly soapy to something like a third of the population (e.g. Eriksson and others 2012; Mauer and El-Sohemy 2012; McGee 2010). How, then, is one to explain this herb's ubiquity in global cuisine?

18 Or, as Paul Bloom puts it in his best-selling book *How Pleasure Works*, 'Man is the only animal that likes Tabasco sauce' (2011: 52).

19 Certainly, in hot climates, meat products are associated with more outbreaks of food-borne illnesses than are vegetables (Sockett 1995; Todd 1994).

20 One might also wonder whether in those countries with a marked seasonal change in temperature/ cuisine, more herbs and spices would be present in the recipes for those dishes typically prepared/ consumed in the warmer months of the year (cf. Giese 1994; Spence 2021b).

21 It is perhaps strange to see no mention of turmeric in this chart, given its renown for that property in the Indian subcontinent.

22 One might also think here how *garam masala* powder, which contains cumin and coriander seed, is often added after cooking a curry.

23 Here, one might wonder whether it is simply the fact that the majority of spices are grown in warmer climates that explains their more widespread use in warmer countries. However, the evidence argues against this being the explanation. Note also how many spices are not consumed in the same countries where they grew or originated. For example, black pepper only grows in a relatively small number of tropical countries but, according to Sherman and Hash, is the world's most widely used spice (2001: 148). Billing and Sherman counterintuitively found no relationship between a country's mean annual temperature and the number of spice plant species that grow there (1998).

24 The use of herbs and spices to help preserve foods, especially meats, has also been suggested in a historical context (Küster 2000). However, the food preservation account does not explain why spices became so popular in the Middle Ages when the desire for spices in Europe was at its peak. There are a number of other more effective, and undoubtedly much cheaper, means of preserving meat, such as smoking, drying, pickling, and salting, which were all in widespread use (e.g. Peterson 1980: 317-320; Sass 1981: 7-13; Scully 1995: 56-57, 84).

25 While lemon/lime juice is highly acidic, many bacteria are resistant to pH-mediated destruction (e.g. see Kim and others 2019). One answer to the latter question is in terms of the possible synergistic effects that sometimes emerge when specific herbs and spices are combined in a dish (Sherman and Billing 1999). As one example of just such a synergy, it has been suggested that pepper enhances the bioavailability of many vitamins, such as vitamin C (Fernández-Lázaro and others 2020; Srinivasan 2007; see also Johri and Zutshi 1992). Meanwhile, citric acid has been shown to potentiate the antibacterial effects of other spices because low pH disrupts bacterial cell membranes (Booth and Kroll 1989). Salad dressings containing herbs and spices have been shown to increase the antioxidant capacity of salad. In one study, for example, adding 3g marjoram to a 200g salad increased the antioxidant capacity by 200% (Ninfali and others 2005). However, the reverse can also occur, as when the addition of rosemary oil reduces the absorption of non-haem iron.

26 Intriguingly, however, in their early paper, Sherman and Billing actually used the phenomenon of taste aversion learning to suggest that spice use may initially have been used to help transform the taste/ flavour of meats that had made us ill (and which we thus became averse to), while, at the same time, making it safe to eat, and hence over time spiced tastes would have become more liked (1998: 30).

27 Of course, the exoticism of spices, and their status as Veblen goods, are probably rather more relevant to explaining the historical popularity of spices in Europe, in particular.

28 Assuming, that is, one does not reach the very specific conditions giving rise to so-called 'olfactory white' (Weiss and others 2012).

29 Indeed, the use of herbs and spices in therapeutic recipes for settling the stomach, improving the digestion, killing parasites, etc., should not be downplayed here. These semi-medicinal recipes, and their physiological effects, may have been more important than the antimicrobial properties of herbs and spices (Freedman 2015; though see Cichewicz and Thorpe 1996). It is presumably possible that some recipes may have started out as interventions to deal with various health problems and then gradually, over time, have been sought out for their unique flavours. Ginger and rhubarb migrated from the pharmacy to the kitchen in the not-too-distant past (cf. Segnit 2010). Indeed, many spices,

30

like ginger, would once have been sold in the UK at the apothecary, spicers, or pepperers, rather than at the grocers from the twelfth century onward (e.g. Matthews 1980; Whittet 1968).

30 One might also wonder why it is that New World spices such as allspice and chilli became popular around the globe, whereas achiote and epazote did not (Freedman 2020: 87). A difference in antimicrobial prowess, perhaps?

31 When thinking about the overlapping versus distinct use of flavour compounds in Eastern versus Western recipes, one might wonder whether there is a link to agricultural practice which, or so it has been claimed, influences local versus global information processing (Talhelm, Zhang, Oishi, Shimin, Duan, Lan, and Kitayama, 2014; though see Laudan, 2014)?

32 Herz notes: 'The fact that maternal diet can influence a newborn's flavor preferences also means that cultural differences in response to foods and aromas can set their roots prior to birth. A culture with a diet rich in spices will produce babies wanting curry with their mashed bananas, whereas a culture in which the diet is relatively spice free will produce babies who snub foods with seasonings' (2007: 40).

33 Are herbs and spices, because of their aromatic role, special vehicles for acquired taste?

34 To me, Dugan's description of marjoram as a 'sweet' spice in the Early Modern era in the British Isles also speaks to historical differences in the acquired tastes that may have been associated with fragrant herbs and spices (2008).

35 At the same time, the fact that vanillin is found in both breast milk and vanilla might perhaps bias us towards finding this aroma pleasurable (see Jebreili and others 2015; Kanbur and Balci 2019; Mennella and Beauchamp 1996).

36 According to Freedman, anything exotic and expensive was once considered a spice, thus including sugar, perfume, and ambergris (2020: 80); ambergris was apparently once eaten with eggs in England (Macaulay 1849). So, sugar, because of its expense, even though it is not aromatic, functioned as a spice – expensive, imported, and credited with both medicinal and gastronomic uses.

37 As Hooker, a North American herb specialist, noted half a century ago: 'thyme is essential to every kitchen because of its abilities to enhance combinations of herbs' (1971: 21).

38 At the same time, the literature on the health and wellness benefits of various natural products (including herbs and spices) often tends to be conflicting and statistically underpowered. In part, this presumably reflects the fact that there is simply insufficient financial motivation to adequately test the health claims for those products that (unlike pharmaceuticals) are difficult to protect commercially.

39 In fact, *Ga*, the word for ginger in Ghana, is the same as the word for medicine.

40 There is likely also a fruitful line of research linked to the use of herbs in ancient Ayurvedic medicine (Govindarajan, Vijayakumar, and Pushpangadan 2005; Thatte and Dahanukar 1986). For instance, according to Hemphill and Cobiac: 'Examples of Ayurvedic use of herbs and spices for health effects include turmeric for jaundice, basil to protect the heart, mace for stomach infections, cinnamon to stimulate circulation, and ginger as the universal medicine, in particular for relieving nausea and indigestion' (2006: S5).

References

Ahn, Y.-Y., and S. E. Ahnert. 2013. 'The Flavor Network', *Leonardo*, 46: 272-73.

Ahn, Y.-Y., and others. 2011. 'Flavor Network and the Principles of Food Pairing', *Scientific Reports*, 1.196: 1-6.

Ahnert, S. E. 2013. 'Network Analysis and Data Mining in Food Science: The Emergence of Computational Gastronomy', *Flavour*, 2.4.

Algabri, S. O., and others. 2018. 'Bay Leaves Have Antimicrobial and Antioxidant Activities', *Journal of Pathogen Research*, 11: 3.

American Heart Association. 2020. 'People who Eat Chilli Pepper May Live Longer?' *ScienceDaily*, 9 November <www.sciencedaily.com/releases/2020/11/201109074114.htm> [accessed 31 March 2021].

Amey, K. 2015. 'Food for Thought! One-fifth of Brits Admit that Local Cuisine Is the Most Important Factor when Choosing a Holiday Destination,' *Daily Mail Online*, 4 August <https://www.

dailymail.co.uk/travel/travel_news/article-3184743/Food-thought-One-fifth-Brits-admit-local-cuisine-important-factor-choosing-holiday-destination.html> [accessed 31 March 2021].

Anon. 2005. 'Sector Insight: Seasonings – Added Spice', *Marketing*, 16: 36.

Apicius. 1936. *Cooking and Dining in Imperial Rome* (c. 1st century), trans. by J. D. Vehling (Chicago: University of Chicago Press).

Beeton, I. M. 1861. *Household Management* (London: Ward, Lock. and Co).

Bell, L., and others 2017. 'Analysis of Seven Salad Rocket (*Eruca sativa*) Accessions: The Relationships between Sensory Attributes and Volatile and Non-Volatile Compounds', *Food Chemistry*, 218: 181-91.

Bellamy, D., and A. Pfister. 1992. *World Medicine: Plants, Patients and People* (Oxford: Blackwell Publishers).

Bernstein, I. L. 1978. 'Learned Taste Aversion in Children Receiving Chemotherapy', *Science*, 200: 1302-03.

Bernstein, N. 2019. 'How Your Minty Toothpaste Gets so Minty Fresh', *Forbes,* 26 November <https://www.forbes.com/sites/nadiaberenstein/2019/11/26/how-your-toothpaste-gets-so-minty-fresh/?sh=453d19b94327> [accessed 31 March 2021].

Beuchat, L. R. 1994. 'Antimicrobial Properties of Spices and Their Essential Oils', in *Natural Antimicrobial Systems and Food Preservation*, ed. by V. M. Dillon and R. G. Board (Wallingford, UK: CAB International), pp. 167-79.

Bhattacharya, T. 2020. 'The Indian Academic Making the World Look at Flavours and Food in a Fresh Way', *The National*, 25 April.

Biggs, L., G. Juravle, and C. Spence. 2016. 'Haptic Exploration of Plateware Alters the Perceived Texture and Taste of Food', *Food Quality and Preference*, 50: 129-34.

Billing, J., and P. W. Sherman. 1998. 'Antimicrobial Functions of Spices: Why Some Like It Hot', *Quarterly Review of Biology*, 73: 3-49.

Birch, L. L. 1999. 'Development of Food Preferences', *Annual Review of Nutrition*, 19: 41-62.

Blank, D. M., and R. D. Mattes.1990. 'Sugar and Spice: Similarities and Sensory Attributes', *Nursing Research*, 39: 290-93.

Block, E. 1986. 'Antithrombotic Agent of Garlic: A Lesson from 5000 Years of Folk Medicine', in *Folk Medicine, the Art and the Science*, ed. by R. P. Steiner (Washington, DC: American Chemical Society), pp. 125-37.

Bloom, P. 2011. *How Pleasure Works: Why We Like What We Like* (London: Vintage).

Blumenthal, H. 2010. 'Naivety in the Kitchen Can Lead to Great Inventions, but Too Much Can Take You to Some Strange Places', *The Times*, 19 August, p. 45.

Bober, P. P. 1999. *Art, Culture, and Cuisine, Ancient and Medieval Gastronomy* (Chicago: University of Chicago Press).

Boddhula, S. K., and others. 2018. 'An Unusual Cause of Thunderclap Headache after Eating the Hottest Pepper in the World – "The Carolina Reaper"', BMJ *Case Reports* <https://www.doi.org/10.1136/bcr-2017-224085>.

Bodkin, H. 2017. 'Hottest Chilli Pepper in the World Accidentally Created by Welsh Farmer', *The Telegraph*, 17 May <http://www.telegraph.co.uk/news/2017/05/17/welsh-grown-hottest-ever-chilli-line-chelsea-flower-show-prize/> [accessed 31 March 2021].

Booth, I. R., and R. G. Kroll. 1989. 'The Preservation of Foods by Low pH', in *Mechanisms of Action of Food Preservation Procedures*, ed. by G. W. Gould (London: Elsevier), pp. 119-60.

Bosland, P.W., D. Coon, and G. Reeves. 2012. '"Trinidad Moruga Scorpion" Pepper Is the World's Hottest Measured Chile Pepper at More than Two Million Scoville Heat Units', *Horticultural Technology*, 22: 534-38.

Bradley, M. 2015. 'Introduction: Smell and the Ancient Senses', in *Smell and the Ancient Senses*, ed. by M. Bradley (London: Routledge), pp. 1-16.

Bredie, W. L. P., and others. 2015. 'Flavour Pairing of Foods: A Physical-Chemical and Multisensory Challenge for Health Promotion', *European Sensory Network* <http://www.esn-network.com/index.php?id=1034> [accessed 31 March 2021].

Breslin, P. A. S. 2013. 'An Evolutionary Perspective on Food and Human Taste', *Current Biology*, 23: 409-18.

Breslin, P. A. S., and G. K. Beauchamp. 1997. 'Salt Enhances Flavor by Suppressing Bitterness', *Nature*, 387: 563.

Breslin, P. A. S., and others. 2003. 'Learned Flavor Congruency: The Importance of Experience in the Sub-Threshold Integration of Tastant/Odorant Pairings', paper presented at the 5th Pangborn Symposium, Boston.

Calvino, I. 2009. *Under the Jaguar Sun*, trans. by W. Weaver (London: Penguin).

Carney, E. M., and others. 2018. 'Increasing Flavor Variety with Herbs and Spices Improves Relative Vegetable Intake in Children who Are Propylthiouracil (PROP) Tasters Relative to Nontasters', *Physiology and Behavior*, 188: 48-57 <https://doi.org/10.1016/j.physbeh.2018.01.021>.

Carstens, E., and others. 2002. 'It Hurts So Good: Oral Irritation by Spices and Carbonated Drinks and the Underlying Neural Mechanisms', *Food Quality and Preference*, 13: 431-43.

Caterina, M. J., and others. 1997. 'The Capsaicin Receptor: A Heat-Activated Ion Channel in the Pain Pathway', *Nature*, 389: 816-24.

Ceylan, E., and Fung, D. Y. C. 2004. 'Antimicrobial Activity of Spices', *Journal of Rapid Methods and Automation in Microbiology*, 12: 1-55.

Chartier, F. 2012. *Taste Buds and Molecules: The Art and Science of Food, Wine, and Flavor*, trans. by Levi Reiss (Hoboken, NJ: John Wiley and Sons).

Chen, H. C., M. D. Chang, and T. J. Chang. 1985. 'Antibacterial Properties of Some Spice Plants Before and After Heat Treatment', *Chinese Journal of Microbiology and Immunology*, 18: 190-95.

Chopan, M., and B. Littenberg. 2017. 'The Association of Hot Red Chilli Pepper Consumption and Mortality: A Large Population-Based Cohort Study', *PLoS ONE*, 12.1 <https://www.doi.org/10.1371/journal.pone.0169876>.

Cichewicz, R. H., and P. A. Thorpe. 1996. 'The Antimicrobial Properties of Chile Peppers (Capsicum species) and Their Use in Mayan Medicine', *Journal of Ethnopharmacology*, 52: 61-70.

Cole, D. E. 2007. 'Feasting and Festivity in Early Tudor Entertainment', in *The Senses in Performance*, ed. by S. Banes and A. Lepecki (New York: Routledge).

Colquhoun, K. 2008. *Taste: The Story of Britain through its Cooking* (London: Bloomsbury).

Cooper, R. L., and M. M. Cooper. 1996. 'Red Pepper-Induced Dermatitis in Breast-Fed Infants', *Dermatology*, 193: 61-62.

Cordell, G. A., and O. E. Araujo. 1993. 'Capsaicin: Identification, Nomenclature, and Pharmacotherapy', *Annual Pharmacotherapy*, 27: 330-36.

Craig, W. J. 1999. 'Health-Promoting Properties of Common Herbs', *American Journal of Nutrition*, 70.3 (Suppl): 491S-99S.

Crisinel, A.-S., and others. 2013. 'Composing with Cross-Modal Correspondences: Music and Smells in Concert', *Chemosensory Perception*, 6: 45-52 <https://www.doi.org/10.1007/s12078-012-9138-4>.

Crossley, L. 2014. 'How an Ounce of Saffron is More Expensive than Gold: Cultivation of Exotic Spice returns to Essex for the First Time in 200 Years', *Daily Mail Online*, 6 November <http://www.dailymail.co.uk/news/article-2823029/How-ounce-saffron-expensive-gold-Cultivation-exotic-spice-returns-Essex-time-200-years.html> [accessed 31 March 2021].

Dalby, A. 2000. *Dangerous Tastes: The Story of Spices* (Berkeley: University of California Press).

Dalton, P., and N. Byrnes. 2016. 'Psychology of Chemesthesis – Why Would Anyone Want to be in Pain?', in *Chemesthesis: Chemical Touch in Food and Eating*, ed. by S. T. McDonald, D. A. Boilliet, and J. E. Hayes (Oxford: Wiley-Blackwell), pp. 8-31.

da Silva, M. 2011. 'World's Hottest Chilli Grown by Aussies', *Australian Geographic*, 12 April <https://www.australiangeographic.com.au/topics/science-environment/2011/04/worlds-hottest-chilli-grown-by-aussies-1/> [accessed 31 March 2021].

Davis, N. 2018. 'Competitive Eater Taken to Hospital after Eating World's Hottest Chilli Pepper', *The Guardian*, 9 April <https://www.theguardian.com/science/2018/apr/09/competitive-eater-taken-to-hospital-after-eating-worlds-hottest-chilli-pepper> [accessed 31 March 2021].

De Klepper M. 2011. 'Food Pairing Theory: A European Fad,' Gastronomica: *The Journal of Food and*

33

Culture, 11: 55-58.

Diebel, K. E., and G. J. Banawart. 1984. 'Effects of Spices on Campylobacter jejuni at Three Temperatures', *Journal of Food Safety*, 6: 241-51.

Dugan, H. 2008. "Scent of a Woman: Performing the Politics of Smell in Early Modern England', *The Journal of Medieval and Early Modern Studies*, 382: 229-52.

Dunne, C. 2014. 'Watching These Spice Bags Explode Is the Most Satisfying Thing You'll Do Today', *Fast Company*, 15 January <http://www.fastcodesign.com/3024922/watching-these-spice-bags-explode-is-the-most-satisfying-thing-youll-do-todayc4bc30d66beab_7135000.webm> [accessed 31 March 2021].

Eriksson, N., and others. 2012. 'A Genetic Variant near Olfactory Receptor Genes Influences Cilantro Preference', *Flavour*, 1: 22.

Farrell, K. T. 1990. *Spices, Condiments, and Seasonings*, 2nd ed. (New York: Van Nostrand Reinhold).

Farrimond, S. 2018. *The Science of Spice: Understand Flavour Connections and Revolutionize Your Cooking* (New York: DK Publishers).

Feldmar, J. 2020. 'Stock Your Spice Rack with These Chef-Recommended Essential Spices', *Eater*, 18 May <https://www.eater.com/21562799/best-cooking-spices-seasonings-recommended-by-chefs> [accessed 31 March 2021].

Fernández-Lázaro, D., and others. 2020. 'Iron and Physical Activity: Bioavailability Enhancers, Properties of Black Pepper (Bioperine®) and Potential Applications', *Nutrients*, 12.6: 1886 <https://doi.org/10.3390/nu12061886>.

Fial, A. Z. 1978. 'Adding Spice to Sugar-Reduced Diets', *Journal of the American Dietetic Association*, 85: 961-65.

Flaxman, S. M., and Sherman, P. W. 2000. 'Morning Sickness: A Mechanism for Protecting Mother and Embryo', *Quarterly Review of Biology*, 75: 113-48.

Fraenkel, G. S. 1959. 'The Raison D'être of Secondary Plant Substances', *Science*, 129: 1466-70.

Freedman, P. 2008. *Out of the East: Spices and the Medieval Imagination* (New Haven: Yale University Press).

Freedman, P. 2015. 'Health, Wellness and the Allure of Spices in the Middle Ages', *Journal of Ethnopharmacology*, 167: 47-53.

Freedman, P. 2020. 'History of Spices', in *Handbook of Eating and Drinking*, ed. by H. Meiselman (Cham, Switzerland: Springer), pp. 77-91.

Giese, J. 1994. 'Spice and Seasoning Blends: A Taste for All Seasons', *Food Technology*, 48: 87-90, 92, 94-95, 98.

Gil-Pérez, I., and others. 2019. 'Hot or Not? Conveying Sensory Information on Food Packaging through the Spiciness-Shape Correspondence', *Food Quality and Preference*, 71: 197-208.

Global Information, Inc. 2005. *Seasonings – UK* (Mintel International Group Ltd.), August [As reported in Williams 2006.]

Goff, S. A., and H. J. Klee. 2006. 'Plant Volatile Compounds: Sensory Cues for Health and Nutritional Value?', *Science,* 311: 815-19.

Gonzalez-Crussi, F. 1989. *The Five Senses* (New York, NY: Harcourt, Brace, Jovanovich).

Gorman, J. 2010. 'A Perk of Our Evolution: Pleasure in Pain of Chillies', *The New York Times,* 20 September <http://www.nytimes.com/2010/09/21/science/21peppers.html?pagewanted=all> [accessed 31 March 2021].

Gottardi, D., and others. 2016. 'Beneficial Effects of Spices in Food Preservation and Safety', *Frontiers in Microbiology*, 7: 1394 <https://www.doi.org/10.3389/fmicb.2016.01394>.

Govindarajan, R., M. Vijayakumar, and P. Pushpangadan. 2005. 'Antioxidant Approach to Disease Management and the Role of "Rasayana" Herbs of Ayurveda', *Journal of Ethnopharmacology*, 99: 165-78.

Govindarajan, V. S. 1985. 'Capsicum Production, Technology, Chemistry, and Quality. Part I: History, Botany, Cultivation, and Primary Processing', *CRC Critical Reviews in Food Science and Nutrition*, 22: 109-76.

Grzanna, R., L. Lindmark, and C. G. Frondoza. 2005. 'Ginger – an Herbal Medicinal Product with Broad Anti-Inflammatory Actions', *Journal of Medicine and Food*, 8: 125-32.

Gustavson, C. R. 1977. 'Comparative and Field Aspects of Learned Food Aversions' in *Learning Mechanisms in Food Selection*, ed. by L. M. Barker, M. R. Best, and M. Domjan (Waco, TX: Baylor University Press), pp. 23-43.

Hagura, N., H. Barber, and P. Haggard. 2013. 'Food Vibrations: Asian Spice Sets Lips Trembling', *Proceedings of the Royal Society B* <https://doi.org/10.1098/rspb.2013.1680>.

Halim, J., and others. 2020. 'The Salt Flip – Sensory Mitigation of Salt (and Sodium) Reduction with Monosodium Glutamate (MSG) in "Better-for-You" Foods', *Journal of Food Science*, 85.9: 2902-2914 <https://www.doi.org/10.1111/1750-3841.15354>.

Hargreaves, L. L., and others. 1975. 'The Antimicrobial Effects of Spices, Herbs and Extracts from These and Other Food Plants', *British Food Manufacturing Industries Research Association*, 88: 1-56.

Hemphill, I., and L. Cobiac. 2006. 'The Historical and Cultural Use of Herbs and Spices', *Medical Journal of Australia*, 185(S4): S5.

Henisch, B. 1976. *Fast and Feast: Food in Medieval Society* (College Park: Pennsylvania State University Press).

Herz, R. 2007. *The Scent of Desire: Discovering Our Enigmatic Sense of Smell* (New York: William Morrow).

Herz, R. S. 2009. 'Aromatherapy Facts and Fictions: A Scientific Analysis of Olfactory Effects on Mood, Physiology and Behavior', *International Journal of Neuroscience*, 119: 263-90.

Hirasa, K., and Takemasa, M. 1998. *Spice Science and Technology* (New York: Marcel Dekker).

Hisano, A. 2019. *Visualizing Taste: How Business Changed the Look of What You Eat* (Cambridge: Harvard University Press).

Hooker, A. 1971. *Herb Cookery* (San Francisco: 101 Productions).

Hui, Y. H., and others (eds.). 1994. *Foodborne Disease Handbook: Diseases Caused by Bacteria, vol. 1* (New York: Marcel Dekker).

Ismaiel, A. A., and M. D. Pierson. 1990. 'Inhibition of Growth and Germination of Clostidium Botulinum 33A, 40B, and 1623E by Essential Oil of Spices', *Journal of Food Science*, 55: 1676-78.

Jain, A., N. K. Rakhi, and G. Bagler. 2015a. 'Spices Form the Basis of Food Pairing in Indian Cuisine <http://arxiv.org/ftp/arxiv/papers/1502/1502.03815.pdf> [accessed 31 March 2021].

Jain, A., N. K. Rakhi, and G. Bagler. 2015b. 'Analysis of Food Pairing in Regional Cuisines of India', *PLoS ONE*, 10.10 <https://www.doi.org/10.1371/journal.pone.0139539>.

Jebreili, M., and others. 2015. 'Comparison of Breastmilk Odor and Vanilla Odor on Mitigating Premature Infants' Response to Pain During and After Venipuncture', *Breastfeed Medicine*, 10.7: 362-65 <https://www.doi.org/10.1089/bfm.2015.0060>.

Johri, R. K., and U. Zutshi. 1992. 'An Ayurvedic Formulation "Trikatu" and Its Constituents', *Journal of Ethnopharmacology*, 37: 85-91.

Jones, F. N., K. Roberts, and E. W. Holman. 1978. 'Similarity Judgments and Recognition Memory for Some Common Spices', *Perception and Psychophysics*, 24: 2-6.

Jordt, S.-E., and D. Julius. 2002. 'Molecular Basis for Species-Specific Sensitivity to "Hot" Chilli Peppers', *Cell*, 108: 421-30.

Kanbur, B. N., and S. Balci. 2019. 'Impact of the Odors of Vanilla Extract and Breast Milk on the Frequency of Apnea in Preterm Neonates', *Japan Journal of Nursing Science*, 2019: 1-7.

Kim, C., and others. 2019. 'Influence of Prior pH and Thermal Stresses on Thermal Tolerance of Foodborne Pathogens', *Food Science and Nutrition*, 7.6: 2033-42 <https://doi.org/10.1002/fsn3.1034>.

Kort, M., and others. 2010. *Food Pairing from the Perspective of the 'Volatile Compounds in Food' Database*, pp. 589-92 <https://home.zhaw.ch/~yere/pdf/Teil146%20-%20Expression%20of%20Multidisciplinary.pdf>.

Kraft, K. H., and others. 2014. 'Multiple Lines of Evidence for the Origin of the Domesticated Chilli Pepper, Capiscum annuum, in Mexico', *Proceedings of the National Academy of Sciences of the USA*, 111: 6165-70.

Krishnaswamy, K. 2008. 'Traditional Indian Spices and Their Health Significance', *Asia Pacific Journal of Clinical Nutrition*, 17 (Suppl 1): 265-68.

Küster, H. 2000. 'Spices and Flavorings', in *The Cambridge World History of Food*, ed. by K. F. Kiple and K. C. Ornelas (Cambridge: Cambridge University Press), vol. 1, p. 436.

Laudan, R. 2014. 'Do Those who Cultivate Rice Paddies Think Holistically and Lag Industrially?', *Rachel*

Laudan, 9 May <https://www.rachellaudan.com/2014/05/do-those-who-cultivate-rice-paddies-think-holistically-and-lag-industrially.html> [accessed 31 March 2021].

Laudan, R., and J. M. Pilcher. 1999. 'Chiles, Chocolate, and Race in New Spain: Glancing Backward to Spain or Looking Forward to Mexico?', *Eighteenth Century Life*, 232: 59-70.

Laurioux, B. 1989. *Le moyen âge à table* (Paris: A. Biro).

Lawless, H. 1989. 'Pepper Potency and the Forgotten Flavor Sense', *Food Technology*, 11: 52, 57-58.

Logue, A. W., and M. E. Smith. 1986. 'Predictors of Food Preferences in Adult Humans', *Appetite*, 7: 109-25.

Lopez, R., and I. Raymond. 1955. *Medieval Trade in the Mediterranean World* (New York: Columbia University Press).

Lv, J., and others. 2015. 'Consumption of Spicy Foods and Total and Cause Specific Mortality: Population Based Cohort Study', *BMJ (Clinical Research Ed.)*, 351: h3942.

Maas, R. P. P. W. M., and P. J. G. M. Voets. 2014. 'The Vampire in Medical Perspective: Myth or Malady?', *QJM: An International Journal of Medicine*, 107.11: 945-46 <https://doi.org/10.1093/qjmed/hcu159>.

Macaulay, T. B. 1849. *The History of England from the Accession of James II*, vol. 1 (London: Longman, Brown, Green and Longmans).

Martínez, Z. 1992. *Food from my Heart: Cuisines of Mexico Remembered and Reimagined* (New York: MacMillan).

Matthews, L. 1980. *The Pepperers, Spicers, and Apothecaries of London during the Thirteenth and Fourteenth Centuries* (London: Society of Apothecaries).

Mauer, L., and A. El-Sohemy. 2012. 'Prevalence of Cilantro (Coriandrum sativum) Disliking among Different Ethnocultural Groups', *Flavour*, 1: 8.

McGee, H. 2004. *On Food and Cooking: The Science and Lore of the Kitchen*, rev. ed. (New York: Scribner).

McGee, H. 2010. 'Cilantro Haters, It's Not Your Fault', *The New York Times*, 13 April <http://www.nytimes.com/2010/04/14/dining/14curious.html?_r=0> [accessed 31 March 2021].

Mead, W. 1967. *The English Medieval Feast* (London: George Allen and Unwin).

Mennella, J. A. 1995. 'Mother's Milk: A Medium for Early Flavor Experiences', *Journal of Human Lactation*, 11: 39-45.

Mennella, J. A., and G. K. Beauchamp. 1991. 'Maternal Diet Alters the Sensory Qualities of Human Milk and the Nursling's Behavior', *Pediatrics*, 88: 737-44.

Mennella, J. A., and G. K. Beauchamp. 1994a. 'Early Flavor Experiences: When Do They Start?', *Nutrition Today*, 29: 25-31.

Mennella, J. A., and G. K. Beauchamp. 1994b. 'The Infant's Responses to Flavored Milk', *Infant Behavior and Development*, 17: 819

Mennella, J. A., and G. K. Beauchamp. 1996. 'The Human Infants' Response to Vanilla Flavors in Mother's Milk and Formula', *Infant Behavior and Development*, 19: 13-19.

Milgram, N. W., L. Krames, and T. M. Alloway (eds.). 1977. *Food Aversion Learning* (New York: Plenum Press).

Miller, M., and J. Harrisson. 1991. *The Great Chile Book* (Berkeley: Ten Speed Press).

Mintz, S. 1985. *Sweetness and Power: The Place of Sugar in Modern History* (New York: Penguin).

Molina-Torres, J., A. García-Chávez, and E.Ramírez-Chávez. 1999. 'Antimicrobial Properties of Alkamides Present in Flavouring Plants Traditionally Used in Mesoamerica: Affinin and Capsaicin', *Journal of Ethnopharmacology*, 64: 241-48.

Monardes, N. 1577. *Joyfull newes out of the new founde worlde*, trans. by J. Frampton. Ed. by S. Gaselee (London, 1925), I, 48.

Mosley, M. 2017. 'Why Hot Chillies Might Be Good for Us', *Daily Mail Online*, 10 March <http://www.bbc.co.uk/news/health-39217603> [accessed 31 March 2021].

Moyers, S. 1996. *Garlic in Health, History, and World Cuisine* (Venice, FL: Suncoast Press).

Moyler, D. A. 1994. 'Spices – Recent Advances', in *Spices, Herbs, and Edible Fungi*, ed. by G. Charalambous (Amsterdam: Elsevier), pp. 1-71.

Mukherjee, S., T. Kramer, and K. Kulow. 2017. 'The Effect of Spicy Gustatory Sensations on Variety Seeking', *Psychology and Marketing*, 34.8: 786-94.

Nilius, B., and G. Appendino. 2013. 'Spices: The Savory and Beneficial Science of Pungency', *Reviews of Physiology, Biochemistry and Pharmacology*, 164: 1-76 <https://www.doi.org/10.1007/112_2013_11>.

Ninfali, P., and others. 2005. 'Antioxidant Capacity of Vegetables, Spices and Dressings Relevant to Nutrition', *British Journal of Nutrition*, 93: 257-66.

Nolan, S. 2013. 'The Heston Effect? List of Food Trends Moves Away from the Traditional and Embraces the Unusual', *Daily Mail Online*, 2 April <http://www.dailymail.co.uk/news/article-2302999/The-Heston-effect-List-food-trends-moves-away-traditional-embraces-unusual.html> [accessed 31 March 2021].

Omolo, M. A., and others. 2014. 'Antimicrobial Properties of Chilli Peppers', *Journal of Infectious Diseases and Therapy*, 2: 145 <https://www.doi.org/10.4172/2332-0877.1000145>.

Parker, J. 2004. 'Culinary Herbs', in *The New Crop Industries Handbook*, ed. by S. Salvin, M. Bourke, and T. Byrne, RIRDC Publication No. 04/125 (Canberra: Rural Industries Research and Development Corporation), pp. 236-43.

Parry, J. W. 1953. *The Story of Spices* (New York: Chemical Publishers).

Pavia, W. 2018. 'Diners Must Sign Waiver before Eating Chilli Pizza', *The Times*, 19 January, p. 30.

Pegolotti, F. B. 1936. *La pratica della mercatura*, ed. by A. Evans (Cambridge, MA: Medieval Academy of America).

Perry, L., and others. 2007. 'Starch Fossils and the Domestication and Dispersal of Chilli Peppers Capsicum spp. L.) in the Americas', *Science*, 315: 986-88.

Peterson, T. 1980. 'The Arab Influence on Western European Cooking', *Journal of Medieval History*, 6: 317-40.

Pinkard, S. 2009. *A Revolution in Taste: The Rise of French Cuisine* (Cambridge: Cambridge University Press).

Piqueras-Fiszman, B., and C. Spence. 2014. 'Colour, Pleasantness, and Consumption Behaviour within a Meal', *Appetite*, 75: 165-72.

Pliny the Elder. 1968. *Natural History, ed. by H. Rackham*, vol. 4 (Cambridge: Harvard University Press).

Potter, D. 2015. 'The Scent of Roman Dining', in *Smell and the Ancient Senses*, ed. by M. Bradley (London: Routledge), pp. 120-32.

Profet, M. 1992. 'Pregnancy Sickness as Adaptation: A Deterrent to Maternal Ingestion of Teratogens', in *The Adapted Mind: Evolutionary Psychology and the Generation of Culture*, ed. by J. H. Barkow, L. Cosmides, and J. Tooby (Oxford: Oxford University Press), pp. 327-65.

Reed, D. R., and A. Knaapila. 2010. 'Genetics of Taste and Smell: Poisons and Pleasures', *Progress in Molecular Biology Translational Science*, 94: 213-40.

Rozin, E. 1983. *Ethnic Cuisine: The Flavor-Principle Cookbook* (Brattleboro, VT: Stephen Greene Press).

Rozin, P. 1980. 'Acquisition of Food Preferences and Attitudes to Foods', *International Journal of Obesity*, 4: 356-63.

Rozin, P. 1987. 'Psychobiological Perspectives on Food Preferences and Avoidances', in *Food and Evolution: Toward a Theory of Human Food Habits*, ed. by M. Harris and E. B. Ross (Philadelphia: Temple University Press), pp. 181-205.

Rozin, P. 1990. 'Getting to Like the Burn of Chilli Pepper: Biological, Psychological, and Cultural Perspectives', in *Irritation*, ed. by B. G. Green, F. R. Mason, and M. R. Kare, *Chemical Senses*, vol 2 (New York: Dekker), pp. 217-28.

Rozin, P., L. Ebert, and J. Schull. 1982. 'Some Like It Hot: A Temporal Analysis of Hedonic Responses to Chilli Pepper', *Appetite*, 3: 13-22.

Rozin, P., and D. Zellner. 1985. 'The Role of Pavlovian Conditioning in the Acquisition of Food Likes and Dislikes', in *Experimental Assessments and Clinical Applications of Conditioned Food Aversions*, ed. by N. S. Braveman and P. Bronstein (New York: New York Academy of Sciences), pp. 189-202.

Samman, S., and others. 2001. 'Green Tea or Rosemary Extract Added to Foods Reduces Nonheme-Iron Absorption', *American Journal of Clinical Nutrition*, 73: 607-12.

Sass, L. J. 1981. 'Religion, Medicine, Politics and Spices', *Appetite*, 2: 7-13.

Schiffman, S. S., and Z. S. Warwick. 1989. 'Use of Flavor-Amplified Foods to Improve Nutritional Status in Elderly Persons', *Annals of the New York Academy of Sciences*, 561: 267-76.

Schivelbusch, W. 2005a. *Tastes of Paradise: A Social History of Spices, Stimulants, and Intoxicants,* trans. by David Jacobson (New York: Pantheon).

Schivelbusch, W. 2005b. 'Spices: Tastes of Paradise', *The Taste Culture Reader: Experiencing Food and Drink*, ed. by C. Korsmeyer (Oxford, UK: Berg), pp. 123-30.

Scully, T. 1995. *The Art of Cookery in the Middle Ages* (Woodbridge, Suffolk: Boydell and Brewer).

Segnit, N. 2010. *The Flavour Thesaurus: Pairings, Recipes and Ideas for the Creative Cook* (London: Bloomsbury).

Seo, H.-S., and others. 2010. 'Cross-Modal Integration between Odors and Abstract Symbols', *Neuroscience Letters,* 478: 175-78.

Sethi, S., and others. 2013. 'Antimicrobial Activity of Spices against Isolated Foodborne Pathogens', *International Journal of Pharmacy and Pharmaceutical Science,* 5: 260-62.

Shelef, L. A. 1984. 'Antimicrobial Effects of Spices', *Journal of Food Safety*, 6: 29-44.

Sherman, P. W., and J. Billing. 1999. 'Darwinian Gastronomy: Why We Use Spices. Spices Taste Good Because They Are Good for Us', *BioScience*, 49: 453-63.

Sherman, P. W., and Flaxman, S. M. 2001. 'Protecting Ourselves from Food', *American Scientist,* 89: 142-51.

Sherman, P. W., and G.A. Hash. 2001. 'Why Vegetable Recipes Are Not Very Spicy', *Evolution and Human Behavior*, 22: 147-63.

Shermer, D. Z., and C. A. Levitan. 2014. 'Red Hot: The Crossmodal Effect of Color Intensity on Perceived Piquancy', *Multisensory Research*, 27: 207-23.

Simas, T., and others. 2017. 'Food-Bridging: A New Network Construction to Unveil the Principles of Cooking', *Frontiers in ICT,* 4: 14 <http:www.doi.org/10.3389/fict.2017.00014>.

Singh, A. 2009. 'Delia Effect has Cinnamon Sticks Flying Off the Shelves', *Daily Telegraph*, 3 December, News p. 3.

Singletary, K. 2010. 'Tumeric: An Overview of Potential Health Benefits', *Nutrition Today,* 45.5: 216-25.

Sloan, A. E. 2005. 'The Top 10 Functional Food Trends', *Food Technology*, 59: 20-32.

Smolarek, P. C., and others. 2015. 'In Vitro Antimicrobial Evaluation of Toothpastes with Natural Compounds', *European Journal of Dentistry*, 9.4: 580-86 <https://doi.org/10.4103/1305-7456.172632>.

Sockett, P. N. 1995. 'The Epidemiology and Costs of Diseases of Public Health Significance, in Relation to Meat and Meat Products', *Journal of Food Safety*, 15: 91-112.

Spence, C. 2008. 'Multisensory Perception', in H. Blumenthal, *The Big Fat Duck Cook Book* (London: Bloomsbury), pp. 484-85.

Spence, C. 2017. *Gastrophysics: The New Science of Eating* (London: Viking Penguin).

Spence, C. 2018a. 'Why Is Piquant/Spicy Food So Popular?', *International Journal of Gastronomy and Food Science*, 12: 16-21.

Spence, C. 2018b. 'Contemporary Fusion Foods: How Are They to be Defined, and When Do They Succeed/Fail?', *International Journal of Gastronomy and Food Science*, 13: 101-07.

Spence, C. 2018c. 'What Is so Unappealing about Blue Food and Drink?', *International Journal of Gastronomy and Food Science*, 14: 1-8 <https://www.doi.org/10.1016/j.ijgfs.2018.08.001>.

Spence, C. 2018d. 'The Psychology of Condiments: A Review', *International Journal of Gastronomy and Food Science*, 11: 41-48.

Spence, C. 2018e. 'Crossmodal Contributions to the Perception of Piquancy/Spiciness', *Journal of Sensory Studies*, 34: e12476 <https://www.doi.org/10.1111/joss.12476>.

Spence, C. 2019. 'Fresh Thinking', *Class Magazine*, June/July, 62-64.

Spence, C. 2020a. 'Flavour Pairing: A Critical Review of the Literature on Food and Beverage Pairing', *Food Research International*, 133: 109124 <https://www.doi.org/10.1016/j.foodres.2020.109124>.

Spence, C. 2020b. 'Gastrophysics: Nudging Consumers toward Eating More Leafy (Salad) Greens', *Food Quality and Preference*, 80: 103800 <https://www.doi.org/10.1016/j.foodqual.2019.103800>.

Spence, C. 2021a. 'Scent in the Context of Live Performance', *i-Perception,* 11.6: 1-28 <https://www.doi.org/10.1177/2041669520985537>.

Spence, C. 2021b. 'Explaining Seasonal Patterns of Food Consumption', *International Journal of Gastronomy

& Food Science, 24: 100332 <https://www.doi.org/10.1016/j.ijgfs.2021.100332>.

Spence, C., and Wang, Q. J. 2018. 'On the Meaning(s) of Complexity in the Chemical Senses', *Chemical Senses*, 43: 451-61.

Spence, C., Wang, Q. J., and Youssef, J. 2017. 'Pairing Flavours and the Temporal Order of Tasting'. *Flavour*, 6: 4 <https://www.doi.org/10.1186/s13411-017-0053-0>.

Spence, C., and Youssef, J. 2021. 'Aging and the Chemical Senses: Implications for Food Behaviour amongst Elderly Consumers', *Foods*, 10.1: 168 <https://www.mdpi.com/2304-8158/10/1/168> [accessed 31 March 2021].

Spencer, M., and Dalton, P. 2020. 'The Third Dimension of Flavor: A Chemesthetic Approach to Healthier Eating (a Review)', *Journal of Sensory Studies*, 35.2: 12551 <https://www.doi.org/10.1111/joss.12551>.

Srinivasan, K. 2007. 'Black Pepper and Its Pungent Principle-Piperine: A Review of Diverse Physiological Effects', *Critical Reviews in Food Science and Nutrition*, 47: 735-48 <https://www.doi.org/10.1080/1040 8390601062054>.

Srinivasan, K., K. Sambaiah, and N. Chandrasekhara. 1992. 'Loss of Active Principles of Common Spices during Domestic Cooking', *Food Chemistry*, 43: 271-74.

Srivastava, J. K., E. Shankar, and S. Gupta. 2010. 'Chamomile: A Herbal Medicine of the Past with Bright Future', *Molecular Medicine Reports*, 3.6: 895-901 <https://doi.org/10.3892/mmr.2010.377>.

Stano, S. 2014. 'Con-fusion Cuisines': Melting Foods and Hybrid Identities', *Proceedings of the World Congress of the IASS/AIS 12th WCS Sofia 2014 New Semiotics between Tradition and Innovation* <http://www.iass-ais.org/proceedings2014/view_lesson.php?id=134> [accessed 31 March 2021].

Stano, S. 2016. 'Lost in Translation', *Semiotica*, 211: 81-104.

Steiner, R. P. (ed.). 1985. *Folk Medicine: The Art and the Science* (Washington, DC: American Chemical Society).

Stevenson, R. J., and R.A. Boakes. 2004. 'Sweet and Sour Smells: Learned Synaesthesia between the Senses of Taste and Smell', in *The Handbook of Multisensory Processing*, ed. by G. A. Calvert, C. Spence, and B. E. Stein (Cambridge: MIT Press), pp. 69-83.

Sutton, D. E. 2010. 'Food and the Senses', *Annual Review of Anthropology*, 39: 209-23.

Suwankanit, C., and others. 2013. 'Umami: Suppressed by All Other Tastes but Itself an Enhancer of Salty and Sweet Perception', poster presented at 10th Pangborn Sensory Science Symposium, 11-15 August 2013, Rio de Janeiro, Brazil.

Tajkarimi, M. M., S. A. Ibrahim, and D. O. Cliver. 2010. 'Antimicrobial Herb and Spice Compounds in Food', *Food Control*, 21: 1199-1218 <https://www.doi.org/10.1016/j.foodcont.2010.02.003>.

Tainter, D. R., and A. T. Grenis. 1993. *Spices and Seasonings* (New York: VCH Publishers).

Talhelm, T., and others. 2014. 'Large-Scale Psychological Differences within China Explained by Rice versus Wheat Agriculture', *Science*, 344: 603-08.

Tapsell, L. C., and others. 2006. 'Health Benefits of Herbs and Spices: The Past, the Present, the Future', *Medical Journal of Australia*, 185.4 (Suppl): S1-S24.

Tewksbury, J. J., and G. P. Nabhan. 2001. 'Seed Dispersal – Directed Deterrence by Capsaicin in Chillies. *Nature*, 412: 403-04.

Tewksbury, J. J., and others. 1999. 'In Situ Conservation of Wild Chillies and Their Biotic Associates', *Conservation Biology*, 13: 98-107.

Thatte, U. M., and S. A. Dahanukar. 1986. 'Ayurveda and Contemporary Scientific Thought', *Trends in Pharmacological Sciences*, 7: 247-51.

Todd, E. C. D. 1994. 'Surveillance of Foodborne Disease', in *Foodborne Disease Handbook. Diseases Caused by Bacteria*, ed. by Y. H. Hui and others (New York: Marcel Dekker) vol. 1, pp. 461-536.

Tu, Y., Z. Yang, and C. Ma. 2016. 'The Taste of Plate: How the Spiciness of Food Is Affected by the Color of the Plate Used to Serve It', *Journal of Sensory Studies*, 31: 50-60.

Ullrich, N. V., and others. 2004. 'PROP Taster Status and Self-Perceived Food Adventurousness Influence Food Preferences', *Journal of the American Dietetic Association*, 104: 543-49.

Valšíková, I., and others. 2016. 'Changes of Vitamin C Content in Celery and Parsley Herb after

Processing', *Potravinarstvo*, 10.1: 637-42 <https://www.doi.org/10.5219/687>.

Varshney, K. R., and others. 2013. 'Flavor Pairing in Medieval European Cuisine: A Study in Cooking with Dirty Data', *Proceedings of the International Joint Conference on Artificial Intelligence Workshops*, pp. 3-12.

Veblen, T. 1992 [1899]. *The Theory of the Leisure Class* (New Brunswick, NJ: Transaction Publishers).

Ventura, A. K., and J. Worobey. 2013. 'Early Influences on the Development of Food Preferences', *Current Biology*, 23.9: R401-R408.

Wake, C. H. H. 1979. 'The Changing Patterns of Europe's Pepper and Spice Imports, ca. 1400-1700', *Journal of European Economic History*, 8: 361-403.

Walker, E. H. 1972. 'The History Back of the Name Walden', *The Concord Saunterer*, June (Supplement No. 2).

Wang, Q. (J.), S. Keller, and C. Spence. 2017. 'Sounds Spicy: Enhancing the Evaluation of Piquancy by Means of a Customised Crossmodally Congruent Soundtrack', *Food Quality and Preference*, 58: 1-9.

Weiss, T., and others. 2012. 'Perceptual Convergence of Multi-Component Mixtures in Olfaction Implies an Olfactory White', *Proceedings of the National Academy of Sciences of the USA*, 109: 19959-64.

Whittet, T. D. 1968. 'Pepperers, Spicers and Grocers: Forerunners of the Apothecaries', *Proceedings of the Royal Society of Medicine*, 61: 801-06.

Williams, J. A., and others. 2016. 'Exploring Ethnic Differences in Taste Perception', *Chemical Senses*, 41: 449-56.

Williams, P. G. 2006. 'Public Health', *Medical Journal of Australia,* 185 (S4): S17.

Woolgar, C. 2001. 'Fast and Feast: Conspicuous Consumption and the Diet of the Nobility in the Fifteenth Century', in *Revolution and Consumption in Late Medieval England,* ed. by M. Hicks (Woodbridge, Suffolk: Boydell and Brewer), pp. 7-25.

Woolgar, C. 2018. 'Medieval Food and Colour', *Journal of Medieval History*, 44.1: 1-20.

Wysocki, C. J., and Beauchamp, G. K. 1984. 'Ability to Smell Androstenone is Genetically Determined', *Proceedings of the National Academy of Sciences USA*, 81: 4899-902.

Xu, A. J., and A. A. Labroo. 2014. 'Incandescent Affect: Turning on the Hot Emotional System with Bright Light', *Journal of Consumer Psychology*, 24: 207-16.

Yang, N., and others. 2021. 'Impact of Capsaicin on Aroma Release and Perception from Flavoured Solutions', *LWT – Food Science and Technology*, 138: 110613.

Zellner, D. A., and others. 1983. 'Conditioned Enhancement of Humans' Liking for Flavour by Pairing with Sweetness', *Learning and Motivation*, 14: 338-50.

Zhu, Y. X., and others. 2013. 'Geography and Similarity of Regional Cuisines in China', *PLoS One,* 8.11: e79161.

'Half-Coloured with Turmeric': The Visual Function of Spices in Early Modern Britain

OFS Rising Scholar Award Winner

Julia Fine

'If you will have a pleasant colour for your frute,' this manuscript from *c.* 1688 begins, 'do thus for a Red boyle[:] Brasil, Turne Soyle or Sanders and for a Yellow use Saffaron or Turmerack.' It then goes on to describe how to give these colourful fruits 'a dainty taste and smell', instructing the reader to 'beat Cloves Mace Cinamon and Nutmegs to powder'.[1] For this seventeenth-century author, then, colour was an essential part of the eating experience. Indeed, that the manipulation of colour was discussed before the manipulation of taste and smell perhaps even suggests the primacy of colour as an influencer of early modern food consumption.

In the past forty years, colour in the early modern world has emerged as an important locus for exploration among both historians of art and historians of science.[2] These 'early modern color worlds', as Tawrin Baker has called them, are critical to understanding how different engagements with and conceptualizations of colour were shaped and practiced in the period.[3] And yet, despite the demonstrated and pervasive importance of colour in early modern life, scholars of food studies have given less study to the importance of colour to food, instead privileging taste and smell in studies of consumption. However, as the above excerpt on colouring fruit demonstrates, early modern eaters were particularly concerned with the colour of their foods, explicitly manipulating the colour through the addition of particular spices. This paper explores the intersection between 'color worlds' and 'foodways' and demonstrates how a focus on one particular colour can deepen our understanding of these two intertwined facets of early modern life.

In this paper, I probe the 'early modern color worlds' of one particular spice: turmeric. Despite the relative ubiquity of turmeric in early modern manuscript recipe books and herbals, as well as the relatively high rate at which it was imported to London during the early modern period, turmeric has received comparatively little attention as an important spice during this era.[4] I explore turmeric as a food colouring agent within the 'contact zone' of early modern Britain. I draw on Catherine Molineux's understanding of this term, in which not only the 'colonial periphery' represented a 'contact zone' between white British subjects and the empire, but also the metropole itself, due, in part, to popular representations of colonial topics and subjects in a wide range of metropolitan spaces, from coffee houses and tobacco shops to private art collections. These representations engendered spaces within the metropole which nurtured imperial fantasies and which allowed Britons to conceptualize a racial other.[5] I extend her argument by demonstrating that what she has called the 'fantasy' of British empire was not only forged through the visual arts but also through food – and, in particular, through spices. I also seek to demonstrate how these fantasies included ideas about Asia as well as the African continent. Through analyzing how turmeric was employed in this 'contact zone' of the metropole, I seek to uncover how this specific spice helped create and perpetuate the fantasies of empire.

My focus is mainly on manuscript receipt books, which, unlike printed cookbooks, give a clearer understanding of how the spice was being used and imagined by Britons.[6] My evidence focuses particularly on the early modern English manuscript recipe books held by the Folger Shakespeare Library, the largest such collection in the world, and is supplemented by holdings elsewhere. These manuscript cookbooks, as scholars have shown, represented 'tools of empire' through which global foodways were 'appropriate[d], translate[d], and transmit[ted]'.[7] Through the exploration of these tools of empire, I argue that the descriptions of and fascination with turmeric in manuscript receipt books reveal the ways in which spices as consumed in the early modern British isles, particularly through description and use of their colours, were understood as an aesthetic experience through which ideas about empire and imperialism could be defined.

The Role of Colour in Early Modern England

Before delving into how the colour of spices contributed to the 'fantasy of empire', we must understand how colours were understood broadly in early modern Britain writ large. The period that this paper treats represents a moment of great change for understandings of colours. In the pre-Newtonian world, colours in Britain were understood not only in a shade-focused sense, but also in regard to their reaction, consistency, and brightness.[8] However, it was not until the seventeenth century that the most profound shift in the European conception of colour occurred. During that period, a 'unified theory of light and colour' took hold, which focused on the prismatic refraction of light.[9] It was then that our present-day understanding of optics-based colour emerged.

It was into this early modern European world, with its newly developed theories about light and colour, that turmeric entered. Turmeric, a plant native to South and Southeast Asia, was and continues to be deeply embedded within those cultures as a yellow dyeing agent. Indeed, in the *Atharva Veda*, a Vedic book of healing recipes from *c.* 1200-1000 BCE, the herb is referred to in the verse, 'O colorer, do thou color this leprous spot and what is pale. The leprous spot, what is pale, do thou cause to disappear.'[10] Similarly, in certain marriage rites in the subcontinent, bright yellow turmeric paste has long been bedaubed on the bridal couple, in order to protect the couple from evil and bring them favour.[11]

When turmeric was brought to Europe, most likely at first via Arab trading routes and then via European colonialism in the seventeenth and eighteenth centuries, the importance of its colour was retained, albeit in different cultural contexts. Prominently, turmeric was understood as a powerful dyeing agent. In the cookbook of Jane Dawson from the late seventeenth century, the author noted that to make a dye for cloth, 'for a lemon coler Turmerick & spannish broun should be employed'.[12] Similarly, in a manuscript cookbook from *c.* 1700-1775, the author gave a recipe for how to 'dye [clothes] French yellowes,' which called for 'Turmerick finely beaten'.[13] And a popular artist's paint pigment in Europe was called 'Indian yellow', tying the colour of yellow directly to the Indian subcontinent.[14] These sources demonstrate how turmeric was explicitly prized for the colour it could impart to other goods in the contexts of art and fashion.

The importance of turmeric's colour extended to its use in early modern medicine. In the period, Paracelsus championed the idea that 'health must grow from the same root as disease, and whither health goes, thither also disease must go'.[15] In other words, early modern cures often mirrored the symptoms of their diseases. In the early modern English manuscript receipt books held by the Folger, turmeric often appears as a cure for yellow jaundice. For instance, in an anonymous late-seventeenth or early-eighteenth-century manuscript receipt book, the author gives a cure specially for 'yellow Iandise' containing 'powder Turmerick'.[16] This book contains many other cures for jaundice, but only in the case of yellow jaundice is turmeric employed. Here, we can see that, for this anonymous author, turmeric was specifically understood as a medicinal agent laden with the properties of the colour yellow.

Turmeric in Foodstuffs

While turmeric's ability to dye medicine and clothing was clearly significant, its application as a dye to foodstuffs was critical to the ways that early modern people thought and learned about the world around them. Turmeric's colour was understood as a means through which British people could enact the fantasy of empire, taking in the supposedly 'exotic' aspects of this ingredient while simultaneously translating foods into British contexts.

Turmeric was heavily associated with both foreignness in general and the Indian subcontinent in particular, as a recipe for '*Frangas incapadas*' demonstrates. Presented in an anonymous recipe book created sometime between 1690 and 1750, '*Frangas incapadas*' most likely refers to a corruption of the Portuguese term for chicken soup. This recipe suggested the cook should 'half colour' the rice in the soup with turmeric. The focus on colour, rather than flavour, demonstrates how turmeric was an important food-dye, particularly in recipes thought of as 'exotic', as demonstrated by the non-English title. Indeed, it does not seem like a stretch to say that the Portuguese-language title, which was a rarity in manuscript receipt books, could have called to mind for its readers the Portuguese colonization of

43

Indian Ocean worlds. Here, then, turmeric as a food-dye demonstrates the ways British eaters could experience 'exotic' foods from their own homes.

The importance of turmeric's colour as a way to allow Britons to participate in the spoils of empire from their own homes is made even more explicit by the prominence of two types of recipes in particular. Excluding its uses as a fabric dye and as a cure for yellow jaundice, the Folger recipe corpus shows that turmeric was mainly employed in two types of recipes: for various types of pickles and curry powder.[17] In both of these examples, turmeric appeared in recipes marked as Indian both explicitly and implicitly. Early modern pickles were often described using the eponym of 'Indian'. Both pickles and curry suggest that, through its very colour, turmeric allowed Britons to participate in the imperial project from their own homes.

First, pickles. Indian pickles as translated into British cuisine, later sometimes referred to as 'piccalilli', were a preserved condiment characterized by the use of ginger, garlic, and, especially, turmeric. One prototypical recipe for Indian Pickles from an anonymous manuscript cookbook from *c.* 1700-1775, for instance, gives the recipe as such: '1 pound of peeled, Garlick, 1 pound of raced Ginger cut thin, 2 ounces of long pepper 4 ounces of the best flour of mustard 3 ounces of Turmarick in powder, six quarts of Crab vinegar, put all into the vinger, it must be cold'. Mrs. White of Stoney Lane, England, in her 1700s recipe book, gave a similar recipe, 'To make Indian pickle':

> Take four Gallons of the best Vinegar and one lb of Ginger; lay it in Salt & Water night, take it out & cut it in thin Slices & lay it in dry salt for 3 days; then take it out & put it in the Sun to dry, & when ready put it in the vinegar; a lb of Garlic; pickle it & lay it in dry Salt 3 Days; then take it out & wash it & lay it in dry salt for 3 Days more; then put it in the Sun to dry; long Pepper & turmerick 1 ½ oz.; 1 lb of white Mustard Seed; cut Cabbage in Quarters & put it in dry Salt for 3 Days, then put it in the Sun for 3 days more; cut Cucumbers in large Slices & do the same Way.[18]

These recipes for Indian pickles almost all call for turmeric and emblematize how the spice was utilized in dishes associated with South Asia.

The broader significance of turmeric, though, is suggested in one seventeenth-century recipe for 'The Pickle'. This recipe calls for Capsicum, noting that 'either green or Red' was appropriate. In a manuscript cookbook that tended towards specificity, why the intentional lack of instruction as to which capsicum would work? One possible answer lies in the next line of the recipe, which notes that the pepper should be covered with ½ an ounce of 'Turmeric root powder.'[19] Perhaps the colour of capsicum did not matter because the flavour was not of primary importance: rather, the colour of the turmeric took primacy, which would cover up either the red or green of the pepper.

Pickled mangoes, a popular dish at the time, also demonstrates the ways Britons participated in the larger empire through food colouring. This condiment became popular during the colonial period, as British imperial agents came across novel fruits like the mango and sought to recreate such fruits upon their return to the British isles. 'Pickled mangoes' made out of a variety of non-mango ingredients soon proliferated in the pages of cookbooks written by people not necessarily directly associated with the colonization of India. For example, one late eighteenth-century recipe, 'To Pickle Mellons like Mangoes', calls for small melons, and instructs that after 'par[ing] off the green Rine', 'take an oz & half of Tumerick' and 'rub it over Mellon with your finger'.[20] It is unclear what colour melon would have been used for this recipe. However, perhaps it did not matter: the fact that the melons were covered in turmeric suggests how the melon would have been dyed a bright, mango-esque yellow.[21] Thus, Britons who most likely had never eaten a mango could participate in eating these 'exotic' foods from their homes half a world away. Melon wasn't the only food used to emulate mangoes: other early modern recipes call for cucumber and turnips to be pickled 'like Indian mangoes'.[22] Turmeric – and, in particular, its colour – thus represented an instrument of empire, that is to say, a means through which Britons could imaginatively participate in the spoils of imperialism through means of culinary 'translation'.

Early modern people used turmeric not only to translate foods, but also to mark them as visually different.[23] This becomes clear in the case of curry powder. Most curry powder recipes in early modern Britain were laden with turmeric. Indeed, one curry powder recipe from a *c*. 1700 English cookbook called for a full pound of turmeric, alongside only four ounces of ginger and white pepper, two ounces of cayenne, and one ounce of fenugreek and coriander. This immense amount of turmeric would have imbued what food it met with a vivid orange hue. In Susanna, Elizabeth, and Mary Kellet's printed 1780 recipe book, the authors give a recipe for 'A Curry of Chickens'. In this recipe, 'a small table spoonful of curry powder', which, as scholars have noted, presumably contains turmeric is added. However, at the end of the recipe the authors call for an additional 'two small teaspoonfuls of turmerick' to be added, specifically 'to colour' the curry.[24]

It was important for curry powder and curry recipes to contain so much turmeric because colouring the food made it distinctly 'foreign' and 'exotic', as an alternative to 'traditional' English food.[25] A similar trope emerges in manuscript cookbooks. For instance, in one 1700s receipt book, the author Mrs. White gives a recipe 'To Make Curry'. She calls for the fowls in the curry to be seasoned with 'a little Pepper, Salt, & Turmeric, Coriander Seed & a little Ginger sliced & a clove of Garlic'. However, at the end, she writes, 'if you think it is not yellow enough put in a little Turmerick Juice.'[26] Turmeric thus becomes a tool to deem a foodstuff as 'foreign', allowing Britons to participate in the orientalized exoticism of empire from the 'imperial metropole'.

Conclusion

By analyzing recipes for pickles and curries, it becomes evident that turmeric served many functions in early modern Britain. It was a flavouring agent. It offered its metropolitan users a sense of exoticism. But primarily, it was a colouring agent: in paints, in fabric

45

dyes, and most especially in foods. Turmeric helped Britons to 'translate' foods from abroad.[27] As scholars and food writers such as Susan Zlotnick, Uma Narayan, and Nupur Chaudhuri have shown, when Victorian Britons consumed foods from India, they participated in a 'domestication of empire' which allowed upper-class women and men to exploit their connection to the empire and reimagine an exoticized India safely within their own British homes.[28] As this essay has shown, a different, but no less critical, process took place when turmeric's golden hue was employed in early modern British kitchens. The history of turmeric in early modern Britain suggests the ways in which these women and men participated in imperialism in ways that were small but significant: through this golden-yellow hue, early modern Britons could create an imaginary 'contact zone' with India inside of their own British kitchens.

Notes

1   Washington, DC, Folger Shakespeare Library, Anon., Miscellaneous collection of receipts, 1688?, Bd.w.A1767.

2   See, for instance, Tawrin Baker and others, *Early Modern Color Worlds* (Leiden: Brill, 2015); Robert L. Feller and others, *Artists' Pigments: A Handbook of Their History and Characteristics* (Washington, DC: National Gallery of Art, 1986); Jenny Boulboullé, 'Seasonality and the (Re)Creation of Early Modern Color Worlds', *The Recipes Project* <https://recipes.hypotheses.org/9359> [accessed 3 May 2020]; Henry Guerlac, 'Can There Be Colors in the Dark? Physical Color Theory before Newton', *Journal of the History of Ideas*, 47.1 (1986), 3-20; Magdalena Bushart and Friedrich Steinle, *Colour Histories: Science, Art, and Technology in the 17th and 18th Centuries* (Berlin; Boston: De Gruyter, 2015).

3   Baker and others.

4   For a glimpse at the rate at which turmeric was imported to England by the East India Company, see Washington, DC, Folger Shakespeare Library, East India Company Cargo Sheets, 1700s, 214215.

5   Catherine Molineux, *Faces of Perfect Ebony: Encountering Atlantic Slavery in Imperial Britain*, Harvard Historical Studies (Cambridge: Harvard University Press, 2012), pp. 12-17.

6   For a brief overview on methodologies for reading manuscript recipe books, see Elaine Leong, *Recipes and Everyday Knowledge: Medicine, Science, and the Household in Early Modern England* (Chicago: University of Chicago Press, 2018), pp. 11-16.

7   Jack B. Bouchard and Amanda E. Herbert, 'One British Thing: A Manuscript Recipe Book, ca. 1690–1730', *Journal of British Studies*, 59.2 (April 2020), 396.

8   I am grateful to Bénédicte Miyamoto for pointing this out to me.

9   John Gage, *Colour and Culture: Practice and Meaning from Antiquity to Abstraction* (London: Thames and Hudson, 1994), p. 153.

10   Charles Rockwell Lanman, *Atharva-Veda Saṁhitā* (Cambridge: Harvard University Press, 1904), p. 24.

11   Urvija Banerji, 'How Turmeric Became a Cure-All Product in India', *Atlas Obscura* <http://www.atlasobscura.com/articles/how-turmeric-became-a-cureall-product-in-india> [accessed 3 May 2020]

12   Washington, DC, Folger Shakespeare Library, Jane Dawson, Cookbook of Jane Dawson, late seventeeth century, p. 52, V.b.14.

13   Washington, DC, Folger Shakespeare Library, Anon., Cookbook, *c.* 1700-*c.* 1775, p. 8, W.a.317.

14   Feller and others, p. 18.

15   Paracelsus, *Selected Writings* (Princeton: Princeton University Press, 1988), p. 78.

16   Washington, DC, Folger Shakespeare Library, Anon., Receipt book, late seventeenth-early eighteenth century, p. 37, V.b.400.

17   For recipes on curry powder, see, for example, Washington, DC, Folger Shakespeare Library, Jane

Staveley, Receipt book of Jane Staveley, 1693-1694, fol. 1, p. 35 and 37, V.a.401; see also Iowa City, University of Iowa Special Collections (Iowa), Anon., English cookbook, 1700-1710, Szathmary Culinary Manuscripts and Cookbooks. For recipes on Indian Pickles, see Washington, DC, Folger Shakespeare Library, Mrs. Knight, Mrs. Knight's Receipt Book, 1740, W.b.79; Washington, DC, Folger Shakespeare Library (Folger), Anon., Medicinal, Household, and Cookery Receipts, seventeenth-eighteenth centuries, V.a.563; Iowa City, University of Iowa Special Collections (Iowa), Anon., Recepts [*sic*] in cookery, copied from a M.S. Book belonging to Mrs. White of Stoney Lane, etc., 1700/1799, p. 36, Szathmary Culinary Manuscripts and Cookbooks.

18 Iowa, Recepts [sic] in cookery, copied from a M.S. Book belonging to Mrs. White of Stoney Lane, etc., p. 36.

19 Folger, V.a.563, p. 1.

20 Iowa, Anon., English Cookbook, 1750-1780, p. 129.

21 For more on the types of melons that proliferated by the late medieval period, see Harry S. Paris, Zohar Amar, and Efraim Lev, 'Medieval Emergence of Sweet Melons, *Cucumis melo* (Cucurbitaceae)', *Annals of Botany*, 110.1 (2012), 23-33.

22 Iowa City, University of Iowa Special Collections, Miss Caldwell, Miss Caldwell cookbook, 1757/1790, p. 67, Szathmary Culinary Manuscripts and Cookbooks; Iowa City, University of Iowa Special Collections, Anon., Yorkshire cookbook, 1799-1837, p. 305, Szathmary Culinary Manuscripts and Cookbooks.

23 This process mirrored the way the imperial gaze created a racialized other in the 'contact zone' of the metropole. For more on this, see Molineux.

24 Susanna Kellet, Elizabeth Kellet, and Mary Kellet, *A Complete Collection of Cookery Receipts* (Newcastle-upon-Tyne: T. Saint, 1780), 28-29. See also Stephanie R. Maroney, '"To Make a Curry the India Way": Tracking the Meaning of Curry Across Eighteenth-Century Communities', *Food and Foodways: Food Globality and Foodways Localities*, 19.1-2 (2011), 130.

25 Maroney, p. 130.

26 Iowa, Recepts [sic] in cookery, copied from a M.S. Book belonging to Mrs. White of Stoney Lane, etc., p. 65.

47

27 For more on the idea of 'translation' in foodways, see Marcy Norton, *Sacred Gifts, Profane Pleasures: A History of Tobacco and Chocolate in the Atlantic World* (Ithaca: Cornell University Press, 2008).

28 Susan Zlotnick. 'Domesticating Imperialism: Curry and Cookbooks in Victorian England', *Frontiers*, 16.2 (1995), 51-68; Nupur Chaudhuri, 'Shawls, Jewelry, Curry, and Rice in Victorian Britain', in *Western Women and Imperialism: Complicity and Resistance*, ed. by Nupur Chaudhuri and Margaret Strobel (Bloomington: Indiana University Press, 1992); Uma Narayan. 'Eating Cultures: Incorporation, Identity and Indian Food', *Social Identities*, 1.1 (1995), 63-86.

The Rise and Fall of Certain Herbs

Ken Albala

This paper begins with a question that inevitably arises with historic cooking and sourcing ingredients for old recipes. Why do some herbs become popular in some periods and then virtually disappear from the culinary landscape? Why do others replace them in historic cookbooks seemingly out of nowhere?

The fate of herbs is different historically than spices which rise and fall in popularity due to changing trade routes, patterns of colonial exploitation, and, perhaps most importantly, social connotations that shift with the changing winds of rarity and cost. An expensive spice imported from the other side of the globe, in limited supply, serves as a marker of social status. When imported in greater quantities and at a lower price, and precisely because those of middling ranks can afford it as a means of imitating their superiors, the spice then goes out of fashion. Even if it remains popular, it is marginalized to the dessert course, as happened to cinnamon, and you could argue sugar too when it became cheap and ubiquitous after the seventeenth century.

Herbs are a different matter. They are mostly locally grown, are almost always inexpensive, and almost never have explicit social connotations for the elite or the poor. They are usually ubiquitous flavouring agents, and logically there is no good reason why any should disappear or become obscure.

By herb, I mean leaves grown locally and used fresh or dried as seasoning, as opposed to imported dried spices which are roots, bark, buds, stamens in the case of saffron, nuts in the case of nutmeg, and sometimes oils like spikenard, resins like mastic, and berries like sumac. Herbs should not have been subject to the same vagaries of fashion compared to spices, and yet they were. With the exception of the likely extinction of silphium, there is no logical reason why a plant once popular and used frequently in a cookbook should disappear a few centuries later.

That tastes radically shift over time so that we actually can't appreciate the flavours our forebears enjoyed seems unlikely. Preferences of course change, and flavour combinations shift dramatically, but that is a much bigger question than why a few dozen herbs come and go.

Another possibility is the commercialization of seasonings as agricultural commodities. Some will fetch a good price in the market, and others simply don't sell well and are relegated to the status of weeds. They may still be growing wild everywhere until revalorized as a new discovery by gastronomes. Sorrel is a good illustration of this process, or dandelion in the US which grows in everyone's lawn but can also be purchased in exclusive groceries. Those aren't exactly culinary herbs though: they're leafy greens. Or it may simply be a process of distribution, an herb like basil may have had a limited range but was transplanted slowly over time and then remains in the culinary repertoire thereafter.

I think expansion in knowledge of medicinal or even potentially toxic properties of particular herbs may have caused them to fluctuate between culinary use and the pharmacopoeia. This is the case with spices like cubebs, grains of paradise, and galangal which were popular in the Middle Ages but only appear in apothecary lists thereafter. It may also explain why tansy disappears after the Middle Ages – because of potentially toxic properties, real or supposed. Artemisia species suffer this fate. Directly relevant to the topic of herbs is how at a certain point rue and pennyroyal were both classified as abortifacients – and in fact they still are and are labelled with warnings if you buy them online. Such warnings rarely dissuade people from using these herbs, but it may at some point in the past have persuaded cookbook authors to stop using them. How important these dangerous properties may have been in the centuries between late antiquity and the later Middle Ages, when rue disappears, is impossible to know.

Before we can say anything meaningful about the changing fortune of specific herbs, we need to count their frequency of use in key cookbooks. Recognizing that cookbooks are not necessarily an accurate measure of how people actually cook, at least they give a decent glimpse of what the cookbook author thought the audience would like and what they in all likelihood could find. If rue appears often in an ancient cookbook, it seems safe to assume people were familiar with it. Because it practically never appears in a modern cookbook, the opposite is true, at least from a culinary standpoint.

Another consideration in choosing which cookbooks to examine is that we shouldn't be comparing apples to oranges. In other words, a cookbook from England will probably not contain the same herbs as one from Southern Europe simply because of climate difference. However, over time climate change might have influenced the distribution of herbs and where they could be grown in the past. What could be grown during the warming cycle of 1000-1300 might actually not be comparable to the exact same place during the so-called little ice age. But if that were the case, we would expect botanical authors and herbals to mention it, as happened in the case of the limits of viticulture. With perhaps a few exceptions it seems safe to say that the majority of herbs were not subject to climate change unless we were talking about the periphery, where global warming would suddenly make cultivation or even spontaneous wild growth possible or not.

For this reason, I chose to stay within one area of Europe and compare three cookbooks both separated by many centuries and representative of eras that had little culinary knowledge of those preceding them. In other words, they represent completely distinct cuisines even though they were composed on the same soil. The first book is the fourth-century compilation associated with Apicius which gives us a good idea of ancient

Roman use of herbs. The second is from the fifteenth century – *De honesta voluptate*, which is partly a cookbook written by Martino of Como, stuffed into a larger book about food properties by Bartolomeo Sacchi (who was known as Platina) that was published around 1470. Finally, there is Pellegrino Artusi's *La Scienza in Cucina e l'arte di mangiar bene* (*Science in the Kitchen and the Art of Eating Well*) first published in 1891, which reflects Italian cuisine of the era from many different regions where Artusi collected recipes. That is, there is no one single cookbook author behind any of these books – even the Martino that makes its way into Platina is more of a compilation of late medieval cuisine than something reflecting the individual preferences of a single author.

Starting with Apicius, it is easy to be distracted by the overall flavour combinations in ancient Roman cooking: think immediately of pepper, fish sauce, honey, vinegar, oil, and a few other seasonings. These are ubiquitous and in fact salt is rarely used, and sugar never. What is perhaps less apparent is the heavy use of fresh and dried herbs. With the exception of pepper and cumin, this is not a cuisine that uses many spices. Rather it is a combination of the sweet, sour, spicy, salty flavours mentioned above with predominantly bitter herbs.

Moreover, the range of herbs used is very surprising. There are 455 recipes in the entire book, assuming that we count every 'Aliter' or another version within each heading as a separate recipe. Since there is no index to the ingredients in any edition, I had to just count their frequency.

Of the 455 recipes, 163 contain lovage, which at 36% is the most popular herb by a wide margin. It almost always follows pepper and is crushed along with it, often with other herbs and seasonings as a sauce for vegetables, poultry, fish, and meat dishes. In terms of flavour, lovage is reminiscent of celery leaves. It is markedly bitter, and it seems this was the flavour the Romans were after in combination with other primary flavours.

The next most popular herb in Apicius, used in 16.4% of all recipes, is rue. There is nothing quite so bitter in the entire repertoire of modern cuisine. It has an alluring aroma, but on its own it definitely overpowers everything else. However, with the umami saltiness of fish sauce and sweetness of honey it balances nicely with any other savoury ingredients. That is, there is no particular type of dish where rue appears: it is scattered evenly throughout the recipes as the second most popular herb.

Following on the heels of rue is mint in 15% of all recipes. This is somewhat surprising, partly because in modern European cuisines it appears mostly with sweet dishes or in mint sauce for lamb. But there is no real logic to where mint appears. It is never used as a garnish but is rather pounded together with other flavourings. To my sensibilities it always stands out, but that's presumably a culturally learned phenomenon.

A few herbs appear at roughly the same frequency, and these waver relatively less in popularity through the ages. There is oregano in 11% of recipes; coriander leaf or cilantro in 10%, although that's rarely used in Italian cuisine today; parsley in 6.5%; thyme in 6.4%, savory in 5.7%; and dill in 5%. Except for dill, which is not used often, none of these is uncommon in Italian cooking in general today.

The real surprise comes with those herbs barely mentioned in Apicius – or not at all. Basil is only mentioned once in Apicius, along with hyssop, wormwood, and catmint. The infamous silphium is only mentioned in 2.4% of recipes, but that may be because it came in several forms including laser (resin and root), which is mentioned as a separate seasoning. Even more popular, however, is pennyroyal which is included in 13 recipes or 3%. It has a brash minty flavour and like rue carries a warning that it may induce abortion today. It can easily be bought online though.

The other herbs mentioned are bay leaf; chamomile; elecampane; fennel fronds; hazelwort (though I think this may be misidentified); malabathrum, which may be cinnamon leaf so maybe that should be considered a spice; and just a few recipes include saffron or safflower. None of these is very important though.

What is completely missing from Apicius, surprisingly, are sage, rosemary, tarragon, chervil, lavender, and many other lesser herbs which were common in the Middle Ages if not today. In the case of tarragon, we know it was only introduced from Asia in the Middle Ages, and herbalists for some reason believed it was an invented plant made by putting a flax seed in a radish root. While the Romans didn't have tarragon, they certainly knew most of these other herbs, but apparently they had little interest in cooking with them.

By the late Middle Ages and Renaissance the herbal landscape had completely changed. Here, it is important to note that we are looking at two different texts stuffed together. First is Platina, who had an interest in recording every common herb he could think of, its natural history mostly via Pliny, and its medical uses taken from a variety of sources. So not surprisingly, his work has a much longer list of herbs. But inside his book is stuffed Martino of Como's cookbook which actually uses far fewer herbs. Complicating any statistical survey is that Martino often just calls for aromatic herbs without specifying. Nonetheless I think we can get a very good picture of how the use of herbs changed in the millennium between these two texts.

Let's start with the printed book that includes both texts. Parsley has shifted into first place with 53 uses in the text, mint follows next with 28, then sage at 17 with marjoram running neck and neck. Far behind is a mass of other herbs which appear only in Platina's sections, so we still briefly see pennyroyal, basil makes a sudden appearance, oregano is only mentioned 5 times in the text, and then dill, chervil, elecampane, southernwood, hyssop, pimpernel, and wormwood only appear in the botanical section, primarily for medical reasons. The Roman standby rue is only mentioned 4 times in the entire text, and lovage is nowhere. But we have a brief entirely new appearance from tarragon.

To ascertain percentage of usage among the recipes, one must consult the Martino manuscript, and here the patterns of culinary usage become much clearer. Out of 262 recipes parsley is in first place with 65 appearances, or 25% of all the recipes. Here marjoram and sage are each used in 25 recipes or 9.5% of the recipes, neither of which was used in Apicius, and mint is slightly behind with 22 recipes or 8.3 %. Rosemary makes a sudden appearance in 13 recipes, or 4.9%. Thyme is still unusual in only

3 recipes. More interestingly, lovage, rue, and hyssop, found frequently in Apicius, have now disappeared. Cilantro or green leaf coriander completely disappears as well.

As we move ahead four centuries, there are many other interesting changes. In Pellegrino Artusi, parsley is still king. Out of 790 recipes (which he very conveniently numbers) there are 153 that include parsley. That is 19.3% which means that, counter to what we might have guessed, the modern Italian cook uses far fewer herbs than medieval or ancient cookbook writers. Now it may be that as a decidedly bourgeois author he wanted to distance himself from what he perceived as rustic peasant foodways, but that might be reading too much into his intentions. Whatever the reason, sage appears in 40 recipes, which is 5%; rosemary, or ramerino as he calls it, has suddenly become relatively popular with 26 recipes or 3.3%; and basil suddenly appears in 22 recipes or 2.7%. These low numbers may reflect that fact that Artusi has many more recipes, including desserts that would rarely include herbs, so these might not reflect common usage well, but compared to earlier cookbooks the herbal profile has simply narrowed. Mint is no longer anywhere; only calamint appears 9 times. Thyme only makes a cameo appearance in what seems to be a Frenchified *bouquet garnis*, and even oregano is only in 9 recipes, with marjoram, its close relative, in just one. Dill appears in 6 recipes, though Artusi makes a point of mentioning that it is completely unheard of in Tuscany. Rue, lovage and pennyroyal are gone, along with savory.

From a purely statistical standpoint, most herbs, with the exception of parsley, completely come in and out of fashion in cookbooks of the Italian peninsula. Here is a brief table of the major herbs listed alphabetically with percentage of use. (And keeping in mind that some herbs are mentioned in Platina but not in Martino's recipes, like basil, dill and rue.)

Herb	Apicius	Martino	Artusi
Basil	.2	0	2.7
Cilantro	10	0	0
Dill	5	0	.7
Lovage	36	0	0
Marjoram	0	9.5	.1
Mint	15	8.3	0
Oregano	11	0	1.1
Parsley	6.5	25	19.3
Pennyroyal	3	0	0
Rosemary	0	4.9	3.3
Rue	16.4	0	0
Sage	9.5	5	5
Savory	5.7	0	0
Thyme	6.4	1.1	.2

Making sense of these patterns is another matter entirely. I decided upon an experimental approach. If there were no obvious economic or social factors that could explain the rise and fall of particular herbs, then perhaps there was some internal logic. Perhaps the flavour profiles contained some gastronomic coherence that explained why lovage would go better with ancient food and parsley with modern.

Remaining objective about flavour is of course impossible, but I thought there might be revealing flashes of insight, like discovering how artichokes and wine taste terrible together. But I thought it has to be more than simply throwing various herbs together. Perhaps rather than a combination of herbs on their own it was more a matter of the preparatory combinations, cooking methods, and final garnish. Here it was easy to see regular patterns. For example, in the majority of recipes Apicius has us grind pepper and lovage, moisten with fish sauce, and then combine with more fish sauce and wine – often with the addition of more herbs, honey, or raisin wine. These make a basic flavour combination as common as say soy, ginger, garlic, and sesame in Chinese cooking. Apicius almost always finishes with a flourish of pepper, just as parsley is used in Artusi's modern cooking, and sugar and cinnamon is used in Martino. I thought that it was more complex than certain flavours going together, but rather the entire ensemble of flavours and technique.

To illustrate this point metaphorically, three woodwinds together: flute, clarinet, and oboe (like any three herbs) will sound very nice together, but if you combine flute with tuba and cello, you simply won't hear the flute, or the sound combination will be objectively discordant.

Try a pinch of rue in a tomato sauce to get a sense of this cacophony. The acid accentuates the bitterness and makes it completely unpalatable. However, salty fish sauce and sweet honey does balance pleasantly – much the same way you find fish sauce, sugar, cilantro, and chilli in Southeast Asian cooking. Gastronomically, it is surprisingly similar to Apicius's universal oenogarum sauce.

Here are the results of the practical experiments. I took one classic flavour combination from each of the three historical periods. And I switched out the major herb with other herbs not common to that cuisine, to see whether it radically changed the flavour combination in a negative way. This was a classic taste test. I was not able to use subjects but I invite anyone to try these at home and would be very grateful for feedback, using either these trials or any other.

The first experiment involved what is called oenogarum, which in its simplest form means a wine and fish sauce combination, but usually involves herbs and other seasonings and importantly is cooked. I began with the instructions in countless Apicius recipes: grind pepper and lovage; moisten with fish sauce; add rue, honey, wine, and oil; and heat. There are several variations with other herbs, but I wanted to keep it simple. The original classic was strange to the modern palate, but very pleasantly balanced. There was significant heat from the pepper, saltiness and funk from the fish sauce, and a deep brooding undercurrent of bitter herb, balanced by the sweetness of the honey in a basic oil and wine sauce. Vinegar would have been a viable option too, as would be raisin wine or reduced wine. This sauce goes on pretty much anything: vegetables, fish, meat. I tasted it on its own, on bread, on leftovers. It's a remarkable sauce, like nothing in the modern repertoire. But was the lovage essential to the final flavour profile?

I tried it again replacing lovage with oregano, which is not used often in Roman cuisine. Same proportions, roughly equal, same technique, same heating in a pan. And this was pretty good. Not quite as rich as the original, but it would certainly work in a pinch. And this may explain why oregano is there in ancient cuisine, but not so prominently. It goes with this flavour combination but sticks out a little – oddly, it may be too aromatic.

The third ancient test involved rosemary, which is known in the ancient world but not called for in the cookbook anywhere. And using the original technique it was decidedly dreadful. The piney resiny flavour took over the entire sauce, it became acrid when cooked. It completely makes sense, given the techniques used in Apicius, that rosemary just doesn't work in the recipes.

For the next round of taste tests, I went to the nineteenth century and tried Pellegrino Artusi's classic Salsa di Pomodoro (#125) which he says is seen everywhere. It's a very simple cooked sauce that starts with a battuto of onion, garlic, and celery flavoured with basil and parsley cooked in olive oil until it breaks down and then sieved. It takes maybe 10-15 minutes to make. This classic version is exquisite with ripe Roma tomatoes. Artusi says it goes on boiled meat, and with cheese and butter on pasta and in risotto.

I wanted to see what would happen if I switched out the herb, instead using cilantro – which Italians now seem to abhor – and dill. Both were commonly used among ancient Romans. This sauce was good but not quite balanced. It tasted Mexican, and a chilli pepper would have been good, along with a corn tortilla or enchilada. That's just my projection of what I know to be Mexican food today, but it really doesn't taste Italian.

But to see how tomatoes may have been the big game changer, try mint and fennel fronds. The sauce turned dark, and tasted like toothpaste or gum had been melted in the sauce. The herbs totally take over – in a way that they don't in Roman sauces with strong sweet and sour and fishy flavours. But with tomato it's just bad. Again, this supports my idea that there is some kind of internal gastronomic logic to why certain herbs go in and out of favour.

With medieval sauces the experiment becomes more complicated because we have to factor in spices as well. I intentionally chose a sauce that emphasizes herbs over spices – the *salsa verde* which includes parsley, serpillum (wild thyme), a little beet greens (Swiss chard) or other good herb, a little pepper, ginger (dried), and salt – pounded, mixed with strong vinegar, and passed through a sieve. The sauce can include a frond of little garlic if you like, which I added. The classic version was remarkably hot and spicy, very surprisingly so. It would make a perfect foil for meat and seems to be exactly what medieval gastronomy was after.

The experimental versions included dill and mint in one, which I assumed would work well, since dill and vinegar certainly go nicely and so does mint in a pounded mint sauce. It was all right, but the garlic and ginger really threw it off. I can see why a medieval cook wouldn't want to use these herbs.

Then I used lovage and rue, assuming this would work something like the ancient moretum, which is a powerhouse of a sauce, but this version with spices was pretty unappealing, certainly compared to the others. I also tasted all three with pasta and none actually worked well; in technique they're like a modern pesto, but the pasta needs the fat from cheese, nuts, and oil. These are lean, and I think would only work with meat.

In conclusion, I think my theory held up fairly well, that is the internal gastronomic logic and the common cooking techniques, and perhaps new ingredients like the tomato, explain why certain herbs come in and out of fashion over time. I believe that it is only with systematic tastings can we come nearer to understanding the fate of not only herbs but all food enjoyed in the past.

Bibliography
Apicius, trans. by Christopher Grocock and Sally Grainger (Totnes, Prospect Books, 2006)

Pellegrino Artusi, *La Scienza in Cucina e l'arte di mangiar bene* (*Science in the Kitchen and the Art of Eating Well*), trans. by Murtha Baca (Toronto: University of Toronto Press, 2003)

Platina, *De honesta voluptate*, trans. by Mary Ella Milham (Tempe, AZ: Medieval and Renaissance Texts and Studies, 1998)

A Visual History of Basil

Lauren Allen

This paper is based on an illustrated map that presents a tour through history with basil as the driving force. The map is a physical work of art that spans twelve feet by three feet. I explore the use of illustrations to better understand the geography and history of basil. Through a thorough exploration, viewers experience the history of basil and its adaptation into different societies. The map allows viewers to begin at any point, going backwards or forwards in time, or starting in various geographical locations. Visual geography helps us learn about the history of food in different cultures by showing how a common ingredient takes different forms in recipes, medicines, and religions. Of course, these forms frequently overlap. This geographical angle encourages a deeper understanding of basil's importance in human history, and it may help us think about the future of that food differently. Visual geography manifests a storied past in order to understand the lateral migrations of basil across the world (and perhaps into outer space).

The map creates a holistic exploration to help viewers understand how basil's relationship with humanity has evolved. This approach avoids a linear storyline, providing room for expansion as more research accumulates. Following this illustration of basil's global history visually explains the complex nuances of its movements and cultural significance through varied spaces and peoples.

While interpretation of the research is ongoing, I express ideas visually to help better understand and organize the data. Basil's migration was intentional – it did not travel around the globe accidentally – and it was important for people to take with them as they migrated.

Etymology and Taxonomy

While information about the etymology of basil is often conflicting or inconsistent, it is worth mentioning that the genus of basil is *Ocimum*, derived from the Greek *ozo*, meaning 'to smell', likely related to the strong odour that the plant emits. Basil is often referred to as the 'king of herbs', relating to the Greek word for 'king', *basileus*.[1] This could also be related to basil's historical uses in medicine or perfumes for royalty. The word 'basilica' derives from the same roots, and basil is frequently associated with cultures of conquest.[2]

Basiliscus in Latin and *basiliskos* in Greek are commonly associated with the basil plant through symbolism and lore, translating directly to 'little king', but also referring to the serpent or the basilisk, because of the crown-like features on its head.[3] In Latin, it could also mean 'dragon', and this may explain basil's symbolic associations with scorpions and serpents in folklore, medicine, and religion.[4] Basil was said to attract basilisks if carried in travellers' pockets when leaving India.[5] The legend of the basilisk told that it could cause death with a single glance.[6] In Hinduism, basil is associated with Vishnu, who is frequently depicted sitting on a seven-headed serpent, a creator god named Shesha.[7]

One thing that categorizes the genus *Ocimum* is the great variability in both its morphology and chemical composition.[8] Scholars disagree on exactly how many species of basil exist. While several sources estimate from 60 to 65 species, other estimates suggest there are up to 150. This may be due to taxonomic miscategorization.[9] *O. basilicum* refers to sweet basil and its cultivars, but there are many different types that are referred to by different taxonomic names, some of them hybrids.[10] The sweet basil cultivars include, but are not limited to: Genovese basil, large leaf, lettuce leaf, and mammoth basil. Cultivars of purple basils within the sweet basil taxonomy include dark opal, purple ruffles, red rubin, and osmin basil.[11] *O. sanctum* is otherwise known as holy basil, or tulsi.[12] *O. americanum* refers to lemon or lime basil, and *O. xcitriodorum* to a type of lemon-Thai basil.[13] Aroma compounds vary throughout the species, cultivars, and hybrids, to the extent that some cultivars produce cinnamon, anise, liquorice, or camphor fragrances.[14] While different varieties, cultivars, and hybrids of basil exist worldwide, sweet basil has naturalized itself nearly all over the globe.[15]

Medicine and Prescriptive Literature

Some of the oldest uses of basil in medicine are included in the Rigvedas, Ayurvedic texts which date to 3500-1600 BCE.[16] In Ayurvedic medicine, basil was used to treat many ailments including snake bites, warts, cancer, and coughs.[17] One medicinal Ayurvedic recipe calls for black peppercorns wrapped in basil leaves to be taken in the morning as a treatment for malaria. According to a medical journal, this recipe has been found to relieve the symptoms of the parasitic disease.[18]

A Chinese herbal from 1060 CE mentions basil as a remedy for stomach spasms and kidney ailments.[19] In ancient Egypt, Dioscorides recorded that basil was used to treat scorpion stings.[20] Other medicinal uses of basil in folk remedies treat insanity, nausea, impotency, epilepsy, deafness, gout, hiccup, and boredom.[21] Basil is commonly believed to have febrifugal properties in West Africa, where basil is known as the 'fever-plant' and used to make fever-breaking tea; in Japan, basil is used as a remedy for colds.[22]

An early English book from 1596, *A Rich Store-House or Treasury for the Diseased*, included instructions for 'A most excellent remedy to ease the raging paine of the teeth': 'Take a little balme and basill, and rub them both together in the palme of your hand, untill such time as they come almost to a iuice [juice], and then put it into your eare on the same side that the paine is on, and it will help you presently. This hath holpen many.'[23]

The 'Preservatives Against the Plague' chapter of *Queen Elizabeths Closset of Physical Secrets, with Certain Approved Medicines Taken out of a Manuscript Found at the Dessolution of One of Our English Abbies* included a recipe entitled 'A Quilt for the Heart'. What is interesting about this recipe is that the author, presumably an alchemist, used basil in a way in which it was neither ingested nor used to make a balm. It seems to take the role of symbolic protector and healer in a sack that is placed over the heart of the sick while they sweat. Here 'ana' means 'of each an equal quantity' and was used in writing prescriptions.[24]

> Take the floures of Nenuphare, Burrage, Buglofs, *ana*, a little handfull: Floures of Balm, Rosemary, *ana* 3 iii. Red fanders, Red corall, *Lignum aloes*, Rinde of a citron, *ana* 3i. Seeds of Basil, Citrons, *ana* 3 i. Leaves of Dittander, Berries of Juniper, *ana* 3 i. Bone of a Stags Heart, half a scruple, Saffron, four grains.
>
> Mix all these in grosse powder, and put them in a bag of crimson Taffetie, or Lincloth, and lay it to the heart, and there let it remain. All these things being done, then procure him to sweat, having a good fire in the chamber, and windowes close shut, and so let him sweat three or four houres more or lesse, or according as the strength of the sick body can endure, and then dry the body well with warm clothes, taking great care that the sick catch not cold in the doing thereof, and then give him some of this Julep following, and apply the aforesaid quilt or bag to the heart.[25]

(I wonder if the heat from the room or body could have released oils from the herbs in the sack, creating a vapor that was inhaled?)

The basil plant and its varieties contain monoterpenes, sesquiterpenes, and phenylpropanoids – organic compounds that make up essential oils.[26] These compounds protect the plant from predators, such as insects and herbivores, by creating an astringent flavour, while also protecting the plant from pollutants, UV rays, and other plant stressors.[27] These same compounds are what lend themselves to the scientific basis that the basil plant possesses antiseptic, anti-inflammatory, antimicrobial, antiparasitic, and antiviral properties. Other aroma compounds in basil, such as estragol, eugenol and linalool, also possess antiseptic, anti-inflammatory, and insecticidal properties.[28] Derivatives of basil are used in modern-day pharmacology and further research is underway.[29]

Basil in Religion and Death

Tulsi, also known as the tulasi plant or holy basil, is perceived as the place where heaven and earth meet in Hindu myth, folklore, and literature.[30] Tulsi is strongly associated with Krishna, Vishnu, and one of Vishnu's wives, Lakshmi.[31] It is said that another creator god, Brahma, lives on the branches of the tulsi plant.[32] Followers of Vishnu are often characterized as ones 'who bear Tulasi round the neck', wearing necklaces, rosaries, or wreaths made from basil leaves, stems, and roots.[33]

The Puranas, writings of Hindu legends and folklore, say that all things associated with the tulsi plant are holy, including the water given to it, the soil in which it grows, and all of its parts.[34] The writings also say that a guilty person has their sins absolved if they are cremated with tulsi twigs.[35] Basil is held in the hands of those making pilgrimages, known to repel the lord of death, protect against evil and impurity, and drive away demons.[36] Sprigs of tulsi are placed on the chests of those that are dying, as a viaticum, and often placed in the mouths of the recently deceased.[37] Mortuary practices often involve bathing bodies in tulsi water, which ensures the soul enters into heaven, reinforcing the idea that tulsi is the place where heaven and earth meet.[38]

Some of these symbolic interpretations of basil overlap with other religious traditions, likely in part due to Alexander the Great having brought basil to Greece from Iran, Afghanistan, or Western India.[39] Roman historian Elizabeth Pollard notes that 'religious ideas, detached from original social contexts, flowed east and west on the silk roads and gained ritual power'.[40] Early Christians believed that basil grew on Christ's grave. Today, basil is used in funerals in Iran, where it is planted on graves, and in Crete it is used as a symbol of mourning. The ancient Greeks also regarded basil as a sign of mourning.[41]

A symbol of conquest and kingliness, basil is used to make holy water in Greek Orthodox Christianity. Instructions from the Saint George Greek Orthodox Church in Chicago say that in order for a priest to bless your new home, he will need water to bless, and a sprig of basil to dip into the water, to sprinkle it into the corners of the home.[42] Poet George Kalogeris's 2001 poem 'Basil' mentions a weekly Sunday ritual in which his father blesses their home in a similar fashion.[43]

Culinary Basil

The culinary uses of basil vary greatly. Due to its naturalization on every continent except Antarctica (where, however, it is grown in greenhouses by scientists experimenting with space farming techniques), it is a common ingredient in many cultural foodways.[44] In a study of Los Angeles restaurants, of all types of restaurants, 79% used basil, whether fresh, frozen, or dried.[45] Basil seeds are also used. *Falooda*, a chilled dessert drink, is made with water-soaked basil seeds, strawberry or raspberry jelly, vermicelli noodles, ice cream, rose syrup, and nuts.[46] This recipe from culinary historian Pushpesh Pant involves soaking the seeds as well:

59

Tulasi Sherbet Sweet Basil Sherbet
Origin: Awadh
Preparation time: 20 minutes, plus soaking and cooking time
Serves: 8-10
4 tablespoons of sweet basil seeds
120 g / 4 oz (½ cup) sugar
1 teaspoon kewra water or rosewater
500 ml / 18 fl oz (2 ¼ cups) cold milk

Put the seeds in a large bowl, pour in 750 ml / 1 ¼ pints (3 ¼ cups) water and soak for about 1 hour, or until they swell up. Drain off any excess liquid.

Heat 1 litre / 1 ¾ pints (4 ¼ cups) water in a large heavy-based pan over low heat, add the sugar and stir until dissolved. Remove from the heat and cool.

Add the basil seeds and stir until well blended, then stir in the kewra water and milk before serving.[47]

Other recipes of interest are turtle soup, pistou, pesto, and fetter lane sausages. Basil has also been used as a preservative for meat and fish before refrigeration. Historically, pesto preserves basil for winter use and can be used as a concentrated seasoning.[48]

Future recipe research will include using archaeological methods to better understand how basil was used in preservation and food storage. This research may be able to integrate contextual, social, historical, economic, and societal clues to help gain broader insights about the value and meaning of basil in people's lives and cultures. Using experimental archaeological approaches to recreate historical recipes and cooking techniques may also help to understand the relationships between basil and its users.

The distinction between food and medicine rarely exists in quotidian life. Food and ingredients can simultaneously be recognized as both, either in dishes or on their own. I have considered them separately here to bring light to the science behind why and how basil possesses medicinal properties.

Sinister Basil?

For all its perceived benefits and majestic qualities, some thought that basil had a darker side. In the 70s CE *Natural History,* Pliny the Elder emphasized that basil should be planted 'with the utterance of curses and imprecations, the result being that it grows all the better for it; the earth too, is rammed when it is sown, and prayers offered that the seed may never come up'.[49] Boccaccio included basil as a central component in his story of Lisabetta and Lorenzo, with its major themes of jealousy, intrigue, and madness, in the *Decameron*.[50] Merely smelling the herb could breed scorpions on the brain, thought sixteenth-century French physician Hilarius.[51] Herbalist Nicholas Culpeper thought basil was dangerous, straying from historical opinions of Arabian physicians that preceded him. In *The English Physician*, Culpeper wrote:

> And away to Dr. Reason went I, who told me it was an herb of Mars, and under the Scorpion, and perhaps therefore called Basilicon; and it is no marvel if it carry a kind of virulent quality with it. Being applied to the place bitten by venomous beasts, or stung by a wasp or hornet, it speedily draws the poison to it; *Every like draws his like.* Mizaldus affirms, that, being laid to rot in horse-dung, it will breed venomous beasts. Hilarius, a French physician, affirms upon his own knowledge, that an acquaintance of his, by common smelling to it, had a scorpion bred in his brain. Something is the matter; this herb and rue will not grow together, no, nor near one another: and we know rue is as great an enemy to poison as any that grows.
>
> To conclude; It expels both birth and after-birth; and as it helps the deficiency of Venus in one kind, so it spoils all her actions in another. I dare write no more of it.[52]

Basil in Poetry/Art

> With Basil then will I begin,
> Whose scent is wondrous pleasing.
> Michael Drayton, *Poly-Olbion* (1612)[53]

Literature, poetry, and art can show us what things were culturally important. The sensorial aspects of basil are often present in its description, such as in this excerpt from Drayton's poem.

As mentioned above, Boccaccio's fourteenth-century *Decameron* includes a story of the lovers Lisabetta (also known as Isabella) and Lorenzo. Lorenzo is murdered by Lisabetta's brothers. She dreams of his burial site, exhumes the body, cuts off his head, takes it home, puts it in a pot, plants basil over it, and waters it with her tears:

> Moreover she took wont to sit still near the pot and to gaze amorously upon it with all her desire, as upon that which held her Lorenzo hid; and after she had a great while looked thereon, she would bend over it and fall to weeping so sore and so long that her tears bathed all the basil, which, by dint of long and assiduous tending, as well as by reason of the fatness of the earth, proceeding from the rotting head that was therein, waxed passing fair and very sweet of savour.[54]

The story ends with her brothers stealing the pot, and Isabella dying from the grief of losing her lover, twice. This story further inspired a narrative poem by John Keats, 'Isabella, or the Pot of Basil', in the early nineteenth century; it mentions basil twelve times.[55] Keats's poem inspired two nineteenth-century paintings by the same name, *Isabella and the Pot of Basil*, by William Holman Hunt and John White Alexander, and a symphonic poem by Frank Bridge in 1907.[56]

We find mentions of basil in contemporary poetry as well. Sandra Gilbert's 1997 poem alludes to several of the themes represented in my research:

'Basil'

A question the box of earth
still asks the kitchen,

as in green blades
of Liguria, green

spears of the watery
forests of Thailand,

peppery keen
airs of August,

as in wise king

do not fade,

as in a pot of,
where the lover's head

explodes into new
ideas, *as in*

chop the loss finely,
add salt and stew

and halo the old charred
grandmother stove,

as in what to do
with the last

three stained tomatoes
hung on the vine.[57]

Other contemporary poets, such as Ilya Kaminsky and James Davis May, include basil as a symbol of normalcy and goodness, contrasting broader narratives about police brutality and domestic abuse within their poems.[58]

Miscellaneous Uses of Basil

Henry VIII employed a strewer, Thomas Tusser, who compiled a list of sixteen essential sweet-smelling herbs and flowers, including basil, that were to be spread across the floor of the castle, creating a sweet aroma from being crushed by people's feet.[59] That practice sought the pleasant smell, but elsewhere basil is used to rid places of pests. In Kenya, it is used to make brooms to sweep chicken coops to rid them of fleas and as an insecticide on maize cobs.[60] Basil is commonly used ornamentally to drive away flies and mosquitoes.[61]

In many countries throughout Europe, basil has been, or is, considered to be a token of love. In Tuscany, it goes by the name *amorino*, 'little love'. In the Chieti Province of Italy, the smell of basil is thought to create instant attraction.[62] In Sicily a pot of basil on a balcony could signal that a daughter is of marriageable age, similar to the fifteenth-century story by Gentile Sermini, where removal of a pot of basil from a window served as a signal between lovers that the coast was clear for a meeting.[63] In Romania and Moldova, a sprig of basil is given as a love token.[64] In Iran, a person who consumes a dry mixture of basil and olives is certain to be loved. Ayurveda and Pliny refer to basil as being an aphrodisiac.[65] Basil was also seen as a symbol of chastity and virginity. In Vogtland, Germany, a sprig of basil was given as a test to young girls – if it withered in her hands, she was not chaste.[66]

In Hinduism, basil may be placed over the ear to keep a person from telling a lie.[67] During British colonial rule of India, tulsi was used in lieu of a Bible, sworn upon by

Indian citizens taking an oath in a court of law.[68]

Humanity's journey with basil is ongoing. In 1998, NASA had plans to build a space garden. Of the thirty plants to go in the garden, basil was important enough to be included.[69] That effort explains basil's cultivation by scientists in Antarctica. Future generations may see basil growing on Mars or the Moon.[70]

Conclusion

Basil has had numerous meaningful applications throughout human history. By tying together pieces of basil's history, using visual history and geography, and other multidisciplinary methods as research tools, we can discover more about basil's role in different aspects of human life from interacting with others to engaging with the divine. Basil is an object that has been sensorially experienced and ingested by people all over the world across time. It has impacted our health and longevity: cured our ailments, broken our fevers, eased our raging pains, and its derivatives are still used in modern pharmacology. It has preserved our foods and provided flavour for winter months. It has been stepped on to freshen rooms or drive away insects; it has been carried in people's pockets across deserts and oceans. Basil's multiple uses and interpretations – its lore, myth, creed, power, symbolism – are modes of metaphorical expression of cultures.[71] By further compiling and synthesizing this information, I aim to express the importance of basil in our global history and perhaps create a point in which to better understand the significance of its role in our future.

63

Notes

1   Margaret Grieve, 'Basil, Sweet', *A Modern Herbal*, ed. by C.F. Leyel (New York: Harcourt, Brace, 1931), *Botanical.com* <https://botanical.com/botanical/mgmh/b/basswe18.html>; Christopher Sullivan, 'Basil (*Ocimum basilicum*)', *Herbs for Thought: The Science, Culture, & Politics of Food*, 2009, p. 1-3 (p. 1) <https://academics.hamilton.edu/foodforthought/our_research_files/herbs.pdf> [accessed 1 May 2020]

2   Douglas Harper, 'Basil', in *Online Etymology Dictionary* <https://www.etymonline.com/search?q=basil> [accessed 2 May 2020]; Grieve, 'Basil, Sweet'; Sullivan, p. 1.

3   Harper.

4   Grieve, 'Basil, Sweet'; Sullivan.

5   Gregory Mcnamee, 'Basil', in *Moveable Feasts: The History, Science, and Lore of Food* (Westport, CT: Praeger Publishers, 2007), pp. 38-42.

6   Grieve, 'Basil, Sweet'; Mcnamee.

7   Wendy Doniger, 'Vishnu', *Encyclopedia Britannica* <https://www.britannica.com/topic/Vishnu> [accessed 3 May 2020]

8   *Basil*, ed. by Raimo Hiltunen and Yvonne Holm (Milton Park: Taylor and Francis, 2006), p. 42.

9   *Basil*, p. 1-2.

10   *Basil*, p. 27.

11   *Basil*, p. 42.

12   *Basil*, p. 126.

13   Gary Allen, *Herbs: A Global History* (London: Reaktion Books, 2012), p. 81; *Basil*, p. 18.

14   *Basil*, p. 42.

15   *Basil*, p. 39.

16   P. Prakash and Neelu Gupta. 'Therapeutic Uses of Ocimum Sanctum Linn (Tusli) with a Note on Eugenol

and its Pharmacological Actions: A Short Review', *Indian Journal of Physiology and Pharmacology*, 49.2 (2005), 125-31 (p. 126) <https://ijpp.com/IJPP%20archives/2005_49_2/125-131.pdf> [accessed 24 May 2020].

17 Margaret Grieve, 'Basil, Bush', *A Modern Herbal*, ed. by C.F. Leyel (New York: Harcourt, Brace, 1931), *Botanical.com* <http://botanical.com/botanical/mgmh/b/basbus17.html>; McNamee, pp. 38-42; Prakash and Gupta, p. 126; Sullivan, p. 3.

18 Prakash and Gupta, p. 127.

19 *Basil*, p. 113.

20 Grieve, 'Basil, Bush'; McNamee, pp. 28-42.

21 Sullivan, p. 3.

22 Grieve, 'Basil, Bush'.

23 A.T., 'A Most Excellent Remedy to Ease the Raging Paine of the Teeth', in *A Rich Store-House Treasurey for the Diseased* (1596), image 78, in *Early English Books Online* <https://search-proquest-com.ezproxy.bu.edu/eebo/docview/2240941206/Seco357/D5EFFFF523164353PQ/1?accountid=9676> [accessed 26 May 2020].

24 'ana', in *Merriam-Webster* <https://www.merriam-webster.com/dictionary/ana#h1>

25 A.M., 'A Quilt for the Heart', in *Queen Eizabeths Closset of Physical Secrets, with Certain Approved Medicines Taken out of a Manuscript Found at the Dessolution of One of Our English Abbies* (1656), pp. 30-31, Image 60 in *Early English Books Online* <https://search-proquest-com.ezproxy.bu.edu/eebo/docview/2248509556/Seco255/DB9A0A7464554008PQ/1?accountid=9676> [accessed 26 May 2020] (italics in original).

26 *Basil*, p. 77.

27 L. Korkin and others, 'Plant Phenylpropanoids as Emerging Anti-Inflammatory Agents', in *The National Library of Medicine Database*, 2011 <https://www.doi.org/10.2174/138955711796575489>

28 C.F. Bagamboula, M. Uyttendaele, and J. Debavere, 'Inhibitory Effect of Thyme and Basil Essential Oils, Carvacrol, Thymol, Estragol, Linalool and P-cymene towards Shigella sonnei and S. flexneri', *ScienceDirect*, 21.1 (2004) <https://www.doi.org/10.1016/S0740-0020(03)00046-7>; *Basil*, pp. 113-30.; Prakash and Gupta, pp. 128-29.; A.B. Sell and E.A. Carlini, 'Anesthetic Action of Methyleugenol and Other Eugenol Derivatives', *Karger International*, 14.4 (1976) <https://www.doi.org/10.1159/000136617>

29 Bagamboula and others; Marc Maurice Cohen, 'Tulsi – *Ocimum sanctum*: A Herb for all Reasons', *Journal of Ayurveda and Integrative Medicine*, 5.4 (2014), 251-59 <https://www.doi.org/10.4103/0975-9476.146554>; Prakash and Gupta, pp. 128-29.

30 Frederick J. Simoons, *Plants of Life, Plants of Death* (Madison: University of Wisconsin Press, 1998), p. 9.

31 Grieve, 'Basil, Sweet'; Simoons, pp. 14-17.

32 Simoons, p. 9.

33 Simoons, p. 14.

34 Simoons, p. 28.

35 Simoons, p. 31.

36 Simoons, pp. 23, 28.

37 *Hinduism, Nursing Management*, 12.6 (2005), 8-10 <https://search-proquest-com.ezproxy.bu.edu/docview/236939937?accountid=9676.> [accessed 30 May 2020]; Simoons, p. 30.

38 Simoons, p. 30.

39 Simoons, p. 37.

40 Elizabeth Ann Pollard, 'Indian Spices and Roman "Magic" in Imperial and Late Antique Indomediterranea', *Journal of World History*, 24.1 (2013), 1-23 (p. 23), in *JSTOR* <www.jstor.org/stable/43286244> [accessed 30 May 2020]

41 Simoons, p. 38.

42 Department of Internet Ministries of the Greek Orthodox Archdiocese of America, 'Blessing of the Home', Saint George Greek Orthodox Church <http://stgeorgegoc.org/pastors-corner/house-blessing-stheophany> [accessed 10 May 2020]

43 George Kalogeris, 'Basil', *Literary Imagination*, 3.2 (2001), 277 <https://www.doi.org/10.1093/litimag/3.2.277>

44 *Basil*, p. 39.; Menaka Wilhelm, 'Antarctic Veggies: Practice For Growing Plants On Other Planets', NPR: *The Salt*, 18 April 2018 <https://www.npr.org/sections/thesalt/2018/04/18/601654780/antarctic-

veggies-practice-for-growing-plants-on-other-planets> [accessed 10 May 2020]

45 *Basil*, p. 57.

46 Sailu, 'Falooda recipe', *Sailu's Food: Deliciously Indian* <https://www.sailusfood.com/falooda-recipe/> [accessed 1 May 2020]

47 Pushpesh Pant, 'Tulasi Sherbet', *India Cookbook* (London: Phaidon Press, 2010), p. 722.

48 Nancy Arrowsmith, 'Basil', *Essential Herbal Wisdom: A Complete Exploration of 50 Remarkable Herbs* (Woodbury, MN: Llewellyn Publications, 2009), pp. 82-83.

49 Allen, pp. 36-37.; Elizabeth Ann Pollard, 'Pliny's Natural History and the Flavian Templum Pacis: Botanical Imperialism in First-Century CE Rome', *Journal of World History*, 20.3 (2009), 309-38 (p. 311), in *JSTOR* <https://www-jstor-org.ezproxy.bu.edu/stable/40542802?seq=1#metadata_info_tab_contents> [accessed 30 May 2020]

50 Rich, p. 12.

51 Nicholas Culpeper, 'Garden Bazil, Or, Sweet Bazil', in *The English Physitian* (1653), pp. 24-25, in *Early English Books Online*, <https://search-proquest-com.ezproxy.bu.edu/eebo/docview/2240956895/fulltext PDF/9E34CB3891F7483APQ/15?accountid=9676> [accessed 25 May 2020]

52 Culpeper, p. 24-25.

53 Qtd. by Arrowsmith, p. 79.

54 Giovanni Boccaccio, *The Decameron*, trans. by John Payne, IV. 5, passages 217-219, in Project Gutenberg <https://www.gutenberg.org/files/23700/23700-h/23700-h.htm#THE_FIFTH_STORY4> [accessed 25 May 2020].

55 John Keats, 'Isabella; Or the Pot of Basil', *Genius Media Group* <https://genius.com/John-keats-isabella-or-the-pot-of-basil-annotated> [accessed 20 May 2020].

56 William Holman Hunt, *Isabella and the Pot of Basil*, 1868, Laing Art Gallery, Newcastle Upon Tyne, England <https://www.college.columbia.edu/core/content/decameron-iv5-isabella-and-pot-basil-william-holman-hunt-1868>; John White Alexander, *Isabella and the Pot of Basil*, 1897, oil on canvas, 192.09 × 91.76 cm, Museum of Fine Arts Boston <https://collections.mfa.org/objects/31098>; Frank Bridge, *Isabella*, BBC National Orchestra of Wales, cond. by Richard Hickox (Chandos, CHAN9950, 2001); Jeremy Dibble, 'Isabella (1907)', *American Symphony Orchestra* <https://americansymphony. org/concert-notes/isabella-1907/> [accessed 12 May 2020]; Gunnar Frederikson, *Frank Bridge, Isabella, Symphonic Poem after Keats*, YouTube, 27 June 2019 <https://www.youtube.com/watch?v=dTS-Foleq2Q> [accessed 20 May 2020].

57 Sandra Gilbert, 'Basil', *Poetry*, October 1997, 28 <https://www.poetryfoundation.org/poetrymagazine/ browse?volume=171&issue=1&page=28> [accessed 22 May 2020].

58 Ilya Kaminsky, 'In a Time of Peace', *Poets.org* <https://poets.org/poem/time-peace> [accessed 23 May 2020]; James Davis May, 'Basil', *storySouth*, 36 (Fall 2013) <http://storysouth.com/stories/basil/> [accessed 23 May 2020].

59 Allen, p. 35.

60 *Basil*, p. 113.

61 Arrowsmith, p. 86.

62 Simoons, p. 37.

63 Simoons, p. 38.

64 Arrowsmith, p. 90.

65 Simoons, p. 37.

66 Rich, p. 15; Simoons, p. 38.

67 Simoons, p. 30.

68 Sullivan, p. 1.

69 Susan Lang, 'For Out-of-this-World Space Habitat Menus, Cornell Experts Develop Plant-Based Foods, such as Tofu Cheesecake and Carrot 'Drumsticks'', *Cornell Chronicle*, 19 January 1998 <https:// news.cornell.edu/stories/1998/01/extraterrestrial-cuisine-cooking-cornell-lab> [accessed 23 May 2020]

70 Wilhelm.

71 Christine Hastorf, *The Social Archaeology of Food* (Cambridge: Cambridge University Press, 2017), p. 14.

Season to Measure: Measurements in Early Culinary Recipes and their Relation to Medicine

Volker Bach

When we read pre-modern recipes, we are frequently struck by what seems like an unconscionable carelessness about quantities, proportions, and balances. We see this from the earliest sources onward, such as surviving Babylonian recipes: 'Leg of mutton broth: With fresh meat from the leg of mutton. Other meat is also used. Prepare water; add fat; salt, to taste; bread crumbs, (?); onion, *samidu*; leek and garlic, mashed with *kisimmu*.'[1]

Apicius, of course, is famous for this habit, and giving ingredients without quantities and proportions accounts for many misconceptions about the nature of Roman cookery. A recipe like Apicius 4.3.5 is hard to interpret without additional guidance:

> *Minutal* of apricots: put oil, *liquamen* and wine in a pan, chop in dried ascalonian onions and diced cooked shoulder of pork. When all this is cooked, pound pepper, cumin, dry mint, dill; pour on honey, *liquamen*, *passum*, a little vinegar, some of the cooking liquor; balance the flavours. Put in stoned apricots, bring them to a simmer until they are thoroughly cooked. Crumble a *tracta* and thicken with some of it. Sprinkle with pepper and serve.[2]

Such a recipe is easier to follow in the case of Roman cooking because we have a better understanding of the ingredients and cooking methods than we do in the case of Ancient Mesopotamia, but even with a better knowledge of the terminology and available kitchen equipment, it is hard to reconstruct the flavour that was aimed for here. This recipe, like many others of its kind, is intended for an audience already knowledgeable in the ins and outs of cookery. That is what most European culinary recipes continue to look like until the Renaissance, when quantities begin to appear more frequently in written sources.

However, every now and then a modern cook trying to find clues on how to reconstruct the tastes of our ancestors will come across a much more instructive source. One such case is Anthimus' famous sixth-century recipe #3 for beef stew:

> Beef which has been steamed can be used both roasted in a dish and also braised in a sauce, provided that, as soon as it begins to give off a smell, you put the meat in some water. Boil it in as much fresh water as suits the size of the portion of meat; you should not have to add any more water during the boiling. When the

meat is cooked, put in a casserole about half a cup of sharp vinegar, some leeks and a little pennyroyal, some celery and fennel, and let these simmer for one hour. Then add half the quantity of honey to vinegar, or as much honey as you wish for sweetness. Cook over a low heat, shaking the pot frequently with one's hands so that the sauce coats the meat sufficiently. Then grind the following: 50 pepper corns, 2 grammes (*quantum medietatem solidi*) and 1.5 grammes (*quantum pensat tremissis* I) of cloves. Carefully grind all these spices together in an earthenware mortar with the addition of a little wine. When well ground, add them to a casserole and stir well, so that before they are taken from the heat, they may warm up and release their flavour into the sauce. Whenever you have a choice of honey or must reduced by either a third or by two thirds, add one of these as detailed above. Do not use a bronze pan, because the sauce tastes better cooked in an earthenware casserole.[3]

This is something that, despite uncertainties about the type of beef used, the intensity of flavour in the spices, and the quantities of some ingredients, we can feel confident to approximate reasonably closely. Yet this is not a matter of the author's personal style. Anthimus does not always give instructions this detailed. His recipe for hare (#13) is much more typical: 'Hare, if young, can be eaten in a sweet sauce made with pepper, a little clove and ginger, costmary, and spike or leaf of nard.'[4]

If, as is generally assumed, recipe collections of this kind are collected from various sources, it is reasonable to think that recipes including such detailed instructions may share a common origin. Tempting though it is to imagine a Q of the culinary corpus, that is probably not a single document, but it may be a tradition. Specifically, the tradition of pharmaceutical recipes.

The connection between food and medicine was strong in the ancient world. Many medical writers made detailed suggestions on foods to seek out or avoid in a given situation. Prevailing medical theory held that the body's balance depended on four bodily fluids, the humours, each with its own specific qualities, and that outside influences, including food and drink, could strengthen or weaken these qualities. The very word 'diet' originally goes back to the Greek word *diaita* and referred to all aspects of life that an individual could control. It was how physicians approached many diseases.

Yet in addition to such overarching remedies, there was a rich tradition of pharmaceuticals promising more immediate relief. These were prepared by apothecaries, specialists in the growing and preserving of medicinal plants, the sourcing of often expensive imported ingredients, and their combination. Since, unlike those used in cookery, medicinal ingredients were often potentially hazardous, apothecaries required more stringent and precise guidelines. A mistake with foxglove or hellebore could ruin far more than a meal. Most medicinal recipes were for 'simples', single plants used for a given purpose. These rarely required detailed instructions. The more demanding 'compounds', of several ingredients, though, needed exact proportions and procedures.

As we would expect, there is a good deal of attention to measures in surviving recipes. This example from Dioscorides (1.99.3) is unusually precise even for ancient medical literature: 'So-called *rhodides* (rose pastilles) are made thus: 40 drachms of green, unmoistened roses, 5 drachms of Indian nard and 6 drachms of myrrh are ground up, shaped into balls the weight of three obols, and dried in the shade. Then, they are kept in a closed ceramic vessel that admits air. Some also add 2 drachms of costmary and orrisroot mixed with honey and Chian wine.'[5]

Several centuries later, roughly contemporaneous with Anthimus, the herbal of Apuleius (15.3) gives instructions for aiding virility: 'If one cannot [perform] with a woman: Orchis root, the right bulb of the root [the Latin uses the word *testiculum*] which is larger. You grind it with 47 peppercorns and four ounces of honey. Dissolve the drug in the best wine and take the weight of 9 scruples for three days.'[6] This comes remarkably close in diction and practice to Anthimus' beef stew: counting out peppercorns, weighing ingredients, and taking procedures step by step. It is a form we will find again and again in the more detailed recipes from the culinary corpus of pre-modern Europe, and it distinguishes these examples clearly from the majority.

It is noteworthy that recipes involving precise measurements in the earliest sources almost always involve spices. This, too, is not surprising. Spices were rare and expensive, and often associated with apothecaries due to the concentrated qualities they were thought to possess. Adding them to food was thought of as a good way of shifting its humoral balance. They were weighed out in small quantities both for practical reasons – portions were small – and because of their value. The Formulary of Marculphus dating to Merovingian times lists pepper, cloves, costmary, spikenard, and cinnamon among the supplies given to royal emissaries.[7] Unfortunately it does not preserve quantities, but the form of the placeholder (*tantum* for pepper, singular *tanto* as opposed to plural *tantos* for the others) suggests a measure. No unit is given, as it is for other supplies measured in pounds and *modii*. Peppercorns are counted, other spices weighed – the picture is consistent.

For a considerable period after the works of Anthimus and Vinidarius, almost no culinary recipes survive from medieval Europe. Medicinal recipes do, though not in large numbers. Many continue in the tradition of the ancient world, not least in preserving the specific system of measurement used by apothecaries. An exact standardization was never achieved, but the Roman subdivision of the pound into ounces, drachms, and grains was universally understood and used. This is not to say that all medicinal recipes were precise. We find many that rarely bother with measurements beyond what is to hand in a kitchen, as in this example from the tenth-century Bald's Leechbook: 'For headache, take blossoms of dill, seethe in oil, smear the temples therewith. [...] For the same, take a vessel full of leaves of green rue, and a spoon-full of mustard seed, rub together, add the white of an egg, a spoon full, that the salve may be thick. Smear with a feather on the side which is not sore.'[8] This looks a lot like culinary recipes do when they surface in written sources.

The association of spices with apothecaries continues through the Middle Ages. This is not necessarily because they were commonly used for medicinal reasons. The eleventh-century 'Macer Floridus', a didactic poem on medicinal plants, states clearly that pepper, though part of many compound medicines, is *notius ipsa coquina quam medicina* – more renowned through the kitchen than through medicine (l 2060).[9] In many places, apothecaries simply were the main source of spices for private customers. In German cities especially, they enjoyed a legal monopoly on their retail well into the modern age. A chance survival of the 1564 inventory shows the privileged apothecary of Hamburg held – among other goods – 6 lbs. of cassia, 12 lbs. of ginger, 9 lbs. of cinnamon, 4 lbs. of cardamom, and 12 lbs. each of nutmeg and saffron, along with 1727 lbs. of sugar, 2½ tuns of various honeys, and 15 *stöveken* (about 60 litres) of olives.[10] Both the quantities and the product range suggest that the goods were intended for culinary purposes.

Meanwhile, culinary recipe collections continue to offer the odd example of highly specific, detailed instructions along with more general descriptions. In the Harpestreng collection which may date to the thirteenth century, we have a good example of using proportion rather than quantity to determine the amount of spices:

> How to prepare a sauce for the lords and how long it lasts: One takes cloves and nutmeg, cardamom, pepper, cinnamon – that is canel – and ginger, all in equal amounts, except that there should be as much canel as all the other spices; and add twice as much toasted bread as of everything else, and grind them all together, and blend with strong vinegar, and place it in a cask. This is a lordly sauce, and it is good for half a year.[11]

The German cookbook of Meister Hans, a collection of courtly recipes dating to around 1460, gives instructions for reconstituting dried ginger roots to simulate preserved ones (recipe #153):

> Also if you want to make good green ginger, almost like they bring it from Damascus. Take warm water and place the ginger into it overnight. Let the water stand by the embers overnight. This way it becomes quite soft during the night. Take it then and peel it with a knife. Keep and dry the skin and grind it to a powder. Then take honey and clear it, so that the scum goes away from it. With four *lot* take one *lot* ground white ginger, two *lot* cloves, three *lot* ground sugar, and one *lot* cinnamon bark. Put all of this into a pan with the white ginger and let it boil nice and long. That way the syrup is good. Then take glazed jars, which must be glazed inside and out, and place twelve pieces into each. Pour the syrup into them until they are full, then it is good.[12]

This recipe is interesting for several reasons. First, it indicates ginger preserved in sugar syrup was a familiar trade item; second, it gives precise quantities of spices to reconstruct a flavour combination; and, third, it gives them in *lot*, a fraction of the pound used by merchants, not apothecaries. The item itself is something one could easily see an apothecary selling.

69

In fact, many of the culinary recipes we find giving exact quantities or proportions are of this kind. Often, they are spice mixes and seasoned wines, products people would normally have purchased from apothecaries or spicers. Since the ability to source raw materials in bulk and have them processed in the household was one of the distinguishing marks of wealth in pre-modern European society, such recipes would have represented valuable knowledge. One can see why they were entered into collections.

The Menagier de Paris (recipe 273) preserves instructions for preparing Ypocras powder used to make a popular variety of spiced wine: 'take an *once* of *cinamonde*, known as long tube cinnamon, a knob of ginger, and an equal amount of galangal, pounded well together, then take a *livre* of good sugar; pound this all together and moisten it with a gallon of the best Beaune wine you can get, and let it steep for an hour or two. Then strain it through a cloth bag several times so it will be very clear.'[13] This was also used as a spice mixture known as Duke's powder (which may be a misreading of *poudre doux* – sweet powder). In a fourteenth-century Italian recipe collection, we find other, more robust blends: 'Fine spices for all foods: Take an *onza* of pepper and one of cinnamon and one of ginger, and half a quarter of cloves and a quarter of saffron. [...] Black, strong spices to make sauces: take half a quarter of cloves and two *onze* of pepper, and take the same amount of long pepper and two nutmegs; this will serve for all spices.'[14]

Sweet mixtures remained especially popular, and we find them returning in many Renaissance collections. One of the very rare Low German recipe collections, the *klene Kakeboeck* printed in Hamburg in the late sixteenth century, records two (recipes 28 and 29) by the name of Salsament: 'Half a pound of sugar, one *lot* of ginger, one *lot* of cinnamon, a *quentin* of mace, a *quentin* of galingale, those shall be taken and ground up small and mixed together. [...] Two pounds of sugar, three *lot* of cinnamon, two *lot* of ginger, two *lot* of galingale, one *lot* of mace, a *quentin* of cardamom, a *quentin* of pepper, grind that to powder etc.'[15]

Balthasar Staindl's South German cookbook records a very similar mix by the more familiar name *triget* and adds a more complex spice mixture for fish:

> To make a *species*: For fish, take cinnamon tubes four *lot*, ginger one and a half *lot*, pepper one *lot*, grains of paradise half a *lot*, galingale, cloves, costmary and nutmeg each the weight of a guilder, whole saffron, rue, and sanicle each the weight of two guilders. Soak the saffron and sanicle in good brandy for an hour or two. Cut the cinnamon tubes, galingale, ginger and nutmeg into pieces and leave the other things uncut. Put it all together into a mortar and take eight *lot* of sugar with it. Then pour in the saffron and sanicle together with the brandy and pound it until it is very small. Do not sift it until the saffron and sanicle is mixed in very well with all the rest. Then sift it. But if it will not pass, let it stand to dry in the sieve, or in the sun, or in the (heated) room until it is dry. Then pound it, sift it and mix it thoroughly. You may add little (less) sugar or none, as you wish.[16]

In all these cases, the majority of recipes in the source give few or no quantities.

We frequently encounter references to 'sweet spices', '*triget*', or 'strong spices' in other recipes, and they may well refer to such mixes. It is likely they could be bought ready-made, though some cooks may have preferred to blend their own or combine spices anew every time. Certainly they were luxury goods and the knowledge how to produce them was marketable. Getting the proportions right would have been important in order to approximate a familiar flavour, a kind of brand identity that allowed for variation, but could not be abandoned. The cognoscenti knew what Ypocras or *triget* were supposed to taste like.

None of this shows with certainty that the medicinal tradition is the source of these precise ingredient measures. Another possible origin is the Arabic tradition, where precise measures in recipes go back much farther than in the West. However, the fact that the mode of measuring is often that used in contemporary medicinal texts and that it is almost always spices – medicinally potent and expensively traded – that were thus measured suggests it.

The Arabic tradition approaches the question from a different perspective. Here, precise instructions are intended to ensure a replicable experience, holding cooks to exacting standards and conveying the craft in a measure of detail that would not be seen in Western recipes until the Renaissance. An example of this is a recipe for sweet rice porridge from the *Treasure Trove of Benefits and Variety at the Table* dating to the fourteenth century:

> Grind the rice, and for each *qadah* (2 ¼ pounds) of it, use one *jarwi ratl* (2 pounds) of sugar syrup or sugar cane molasses. Cook the syrup until it boils, and then gradually add the rice and gently stir it. Continue adding hot water whenever you see it becoming dry, until it is done.
>
> Colour it with saffron, using ½ *dirham* (¼ teaspoon) for each *qadah*. Season it with camphor, musk, and rosewater. Keep the pot on the remaining heat to simmer, and serve.[17]

By the sixteenth century, recipes more frequently included quantities and detailed instructions. This tradition spread from Italy, where more and more cookery texts began including such detail as a matter of course. Whether this was due to influence from the Arabic tradition remains to be studied, but it is certainly possible. As texts became cheaper to reproduce with the advent of paper and print, it was even feasible to become chatty. In Germany, several large volumes were produced in the late sixteenth century that would go on to define the genre for almost a hundred years. Among them, the *New Kochbuch* by the personal cook to the Archbishop-Elector of Mainz, Marx Rumpolt, is the most interesting source historically. However, the one that stands out for its attention to quantities, proportions, and processes is the 1597 *Köstlich New Kochbuch* by Anna Wecker, the first printed cookbook authored by a woman. The author was the widow of a renowned physician and dedicated her work to invalid cookery. This was the kind of thing to which medical professionals legitimately paid attention. Her description of making a simple pear tart is instructive:

> Cook sliced pears well, make them thin in fat the way you would otherwise cook a spoon dish of pears [*Birnenmus*] so that they have a nice cooking liquid, whether of their own or made, and so that they stay white. The slices should be very thin and broad.
>
> Prepare the pastry crust. Take ginger, cinnamon, nutmeg, and sugar according to how sweet the pears are by themselves, and strew of this in the bottom of the crust together with raisins. Then lay the pears on it well and orderly so that you cannot see the bottom. Then strew it again with the above stuff [spices] and make another layer [of pears] in the middle. Lay it a little thicker than at the edges. Strew it well again on top.
>
> No pastry crust for any tart should be thicker than a finger. Not only does that make them common [*paeurisch* – literally peasant style], but they also do not turn out as nicely as they should.
>
> Place a nicely cut lid on top, brush it with beaten egg and bake it crisp, but not too dry. Pour in the cooking liquid the pears had at the top when the crust has hardened. Nutmeg is very useful in spices with pears.[18]

This is an entirely different mode of communicating cooking instructions. Anna Wecker has exact quantities in some recipes – interestingly, often those that deal with a large variety of spices – but most of her detail is put in terms that made sense in a kitchen of her time. It is also a tradition of her own. Her husband published medicinal recipes in his lifetime, and they use the traditional apothecaries' measures and vocabulary. One example of this is:

> A noble and proven aqua vitae or golden water for many illnesses as follows hereafter:
> Take cinnamon 20 *lot*
> paradise wood v *quintlin*
> cardamom, cubebs, cloves each 4 ½ *quintlin*
> galingale root 3 *quintlin*
> yellow sanders 3 ½ *quintlin*
> dried red roses 4 ½ *quintlin*
> nutmeg and mace each half a *quintlin*
> castoreum 1 *quintlin*
> ambergris 15 grains

> Grind each ingredient separately to a powder and mix it all together in a large glass container. Then pour over it 12 pounds good distilled liquor [*Branntenwein*] that has been distilled frequently in glazed vessels, lemon syrup of the peel, and quince juice [known as Mina Cidoniorum] each one pound. Close the glass container and leave it standing for one month. Then pour it carefully into another glass container and keep it. For this water is good for all diseases that

originate from coldness. It causes good memory, strengthens the senses and the heart, dries the brain, makes you joyful, destroys superfluous bad moisture in the stomach, causes good digestion, and protects people from stroke and pestilence; taken every morning, one tablespoon on an empty stomach.[19]

This is already quite close to the diction and organization of modern culinary recipes, which is not a surprise. However, it would not have been useful to most cooks. Only large and well-appointed kitchens were normally equipped with scales or measuring cups before the nineteenth century. Pounds and their fractions, units known from market sales, the volume of familiar containers, and counts of things like eggs and fruit are the quantities we find used in cookery instructions more frequently in the seventeenth and eighteenth centuries. A typical example (recipe 430) comes from Marcus Looft's successful *Niedersächsisches Kochbuch* of 1786:

> An applecake. A good part of apples are peeled, the cores removed and cut into thin slices before the hand. Further, you make one and a half quarter pounds of beaten butter, stir eight egg yolks into it, eight pennies' worth of grated white bread, ¼ lb pounded sugar, lemon peel, cleaned raisins and pounded cinnamon. The egg whites are beaten to a foam and also stirred in, and then this is mixed very strongly with the cut apples. The cake is best baked in a hoop prepared for the purpose.[20]

Recipes like these still required interpretation, but they were – and still are – easy to follow for experienced cooks. Spices, however, were now mostly left to the cook's discretion even in recipes where the intended balance and quantity would matter. German cooking never abandoned spices to the degree French court cuisine did, but German cookbooks readily omitted any guidance as to how to apply them even in a recipe calling for bay leaves, lemon peel, thyme, parsley, pepper, cloves, and mace.[21]

By the time exact measures became common in recipes, spices had lost their medicinal standing and their social status. Largely viewed as superfluous fripperies, they were frequently ignored by nineteenth-century cookbook writers. Instances of precision in seasoning are rare and usually aimed at cooks of the lower classes who were generally discouraged from using spices at all. Meta Adam, writing a mass-market cookbook in Germany's darkest half-century, suggested simplifying the process to a *Gewürzdosis*, a spice dose of four peppercorns, two grains of allspice, one clove, and half a bay leaf that is either included in a recipe, or not.[22] It was practical, but hardly appealing. Today, with spicing once more the hallmark of a good cook and still depending on individual judgement, experience, and unspoken agreement, there are books and websites dedicated to teaching this art. In their way, they sell valuable secrets just as medieval recipe collections did in laying out the composition of spicing mixtures. Whether they, too, come to introduce a new tradition to the genre of recipe writing and what this might be remains to be seen.

Notes

1 Qtd. in Jean Bottéro, *The Oldest Cuisine in the World: Cooking in Mesopotamia* (Chicago: University of Chicago Press, 2004), p. 28. Tablet A, recipe 18.

2 *Apicius. A Critical Edition with an Introduction and English Translation*, ed. and trans. by Christopher Grocock and Sally Grainger (Totnes: Prospect Books, 2006), p. 197.

3 *Anthimus de obseruatione ciborum. On the Observance of Foods*, ed. and trans. by Mark Grant (Totnes: Prospect Books, 1996), p. 51.

4 *Anthimus*, p. 55

5 *Pedanius Dioscurides aus Anazarba: Fünf Bücher über die Heilkunde,* ed. and trans. by Max Aufmesser (Hildesheim: Olms Verlag, 2002), p. 72 (English translation mine).

6 *Apuleius Heilkräuterbuch Herbarius*, ed. and trans. by Kai Brodersen (Wiesbaden: Marix Verlag, 2015), p. 66 (English translation mine).

7 *Monumenta Germaniae Historica, Leges V: Formulae Merowingici et Karolini aevi* (Hanover: Hahniani, 1886), p. 49 <https://www.dmgh.de/mgh_formulae/index.htm#page/(II)/mode/1up> [accessed 08 May 2020]

8 *The Leechdoms, Wortcunning, and Starcraft of Early England*, ed. and trans. by Oswald Cockayne (London: Longman, 1863), vol. II, p. 20 <https://archive.org/details/leechdomswortcun02cock/page/n11/mode/2up> [last accessed 08 May 2020].

9 *Kräuterbuch der Klostermedizin. Der Macer floridus. Medizin des Mittelalters*, ed. and trans. by Johannes Gottfried Mayer and Konrad Goehl (Leipzig: Verlag, 2003), p. 248.

10 Volker Bach, *The Kitchen: Food and Cooking in Reformation Germany* (Lanham, MD: Rowman and Littlefield, 2016), p. 92.

11 Rudolf Grewe and Constance B. Hieatt, *Libellus de arte coquinaria: An Early Northern Cookery Book* (Tempe, AZ: Arizona Center for Medieval and Renaissance Studies, 2001).

12 *Maister Hannsen des von Wirtenberg Koch*, ed. and trans. by Trude Ehlert (Frankfurt: Tupperware, 1996) (English translation mine).

13 Qtd. in Odile Redon, Francoise Sabban, and Silvano Serventi, *The Medieval Kitchen* (Chicago: University of Chicago Press, 1998), p. 221. The *once* is about 30 grammes and the *livre* about 480 grammes in the Paris measure.

14 Qtd. in Redon, Sabban, and Serventi, p. 22. The exact weight of the *onza* (*oncia*) is uncertain.

15 Qtd. in Nicole Brunzel, '"Lat klene Kakeboeck..." Eine Untersuchung zur mittelniederdeutschen Fachprosa' (unpublished master's thesis, University of Hamburg, 1994), p. 41 (English translation mine). The most likely measure used here, the Hamburg pound, is 484 grammes, the *lot* is 15 grammes, the *quentin* about three.

16 Balthasar Staindl, *Ein sehr künstlichs und nutzlichs Kochbuch* (Augsburg: 1569), p. 43 v. (English translation mine).

17 Qtd. in Nawal Nasrallah, *Treasure Trove of Benefits and Variety at the Table: A Fourteenth-Century Egyptian Cookbook* (Leiden: Brill, 2017), recipe 67.

18 Anna Wecker, *Ein Köstlich New Kochbuch* (Amberg: 1598), p. 114 f (English translation mine).

19 Johann Jacob Wecker, *Ein Nützliches Büchlein von mancherleyen Künstlichen Wassern* (Basel: 1605), p. 15 (English translation mine).

20 Marcus Looft, *Zweytes Niedersächsisches Kochbuch oder Bemerkungen und Zusätze zu Marcus Looft's Niedersächsischem Kochbuche* (Göttingen: 1786), p. 327 (English translation mine).

21 *Das Brandenburgische Koch-Buch* (Berlin: 1723), recipe 22 for cold rolled beef.

22 Meta Adam, *Hamburger Kochbuch* (Hamburg: Broschek Verlag, 1949), p. 11.

Melegueta or Grains of Paradise: To be 'pepperish'

Scott Alves Barton

Introduction

'Emi to o je ata, emi yepere ni.'
('The spirit that doesn't eat pepper is a feeble one')

The context is Nigerian; our food is ideally always pepperish. The Yoruba have disdainful words for those who don't eat pepper, those who can't eat it, and a categorical declaration of where pepper goes when it is eaten. All the spheres that it touches, especially the spirit.

– Yemisi Aribisala (2015)

'A Preta do Acarajé	'The Black Bean Fritter Vendor'
... Dez horas da noite,	Ten o'clock at night
na rua deserta	On a deserted street
A preta mercando	The black [woman] street vendor
parece um lamento	Sounds a lament
É o abará!	There is *abará*!
Na sua gamela	In her wooden bowl
tem molho cheiroso	She has an aromatic sauce
Pimenta da costa, tem acarajé	With spicy peppers from the coast
Ô, acarajé e cor	The *acarajé* is coloured (*from palm oil*)*
[…] Todo mundo gosta de acarajé	Everyone loves *acarajé*

– Dorival Caymmi (1930)

'Atarere èwọ ọbbẹ': melegueta 'is never used in sauce', although present in ritual offerings (Crowther 1843). This arcane aphorism explicitly states that melegueta peppers are not for cooking. This claim is diametrically opposed to Caymmi's anthem to the black-eyed pea fritter vendor, who seasons her food with melegueta. And to Yemisi Aribisala's desire to walk with melegueta/chillies whenever leaving Nigeria to make food 'pepperish'. Melegueta and kola nuts are thought to be indispensable in a Nigerian home, much as salt and black pepper may be to Western Europeans. Lydia Cabrera and William Bascom identify several *ebós* (sacred offerings to Orixá) requiring melegueta: 'For Orixá Oxossi: Offer a sacrifice; guinea peppers. What should he do to be able to have magical power? Father should offer 80 guinea peppers […] he had medicine that

he was using. Orixá says that this person has a medicine. Orixá says that he should use guinea pepper; he should eat lots of it, eagerly. Orixá has spoken. The deities ordain it' (Bascom 1993: 340-43).

Ethnobotanist Robert Voeks identifies melegueta as a colonial export to Brazil, where it has 'magical use', as well as honouring the deity Èsù (the trickster figure) as a disruptive force (Voeks 1997: 45, 113, 125-28, 214). Chinua Achebe's *Things Fall Apart* also links melegueta to magic as we meet protagonist Okonkwo's father Unoka: 'lazy improvident and incapable of thinking about tomorrow'. When neighbour Okoye calls on Unoka to talk and divine, Unoka fetches his *opon ifá* (divining tray), kola nuts, *pemba* (diviner's chalk), and melegueta, saying, 'I have kola nuts.' Okoye replies, 'He who has kola, brings life [...] With kola [and melegueta] we have life. We should all live. We pray for life, children and a good harvest' (Achebe 1959: 3-14).

Within West African religious cosmology there exists a symbiosis between melegueta and *obi/orobô,* kola nuts. Purification and breath rituals, like the initiation rites of priests who celebrate the ancestral dead, utilize melegueta. Mastication of melegueta renovates one's energy, particularly in community or in celebration of Èsù, Ogum, and Xangô. Kola nuts fight malevolent forces and are oracles themselves: demonstrating divine loyalty and fidelity. Joceval, Candomblé *Ogã* (a male priest; guardian of altars), and Claudio, *Ojé* (Egúngún priest) described melegueta's role in ritual sacrifice and Èsù rituals. Èsù guards the crossroads and acts as an interlocutor between mortals and deities (Barton 2020).

76

Taste and Agency

'Guinny Pepper is not plentifull, it groweth in the Woods wilde, a small plant like Privet or Pricke-wood' (Hair and Kelling 1607/1981).

This piece is challenging; naming varies – varies widely – predicated on African ethno-linguistic distinctions and taxonomical variations, including cross-references to cardamom. Names created to market melegueta exports fostered more variations, as did melegueta exchanged as currency. This essay engages with power/agency, flavour, culture, and circulation of melegueta (Hepper 1967; Limborch 1679:100; Stokes 1812: 71-2; Van Wyk 2013; Krondl 2008).

Melegueta pods were gathered from wild-foraged bushes flourishing in West African coastal forest zones and savannah woodlands from Sierra Leone, Guinea, Ivory Coast, and Ghana, from the Gulf of Guinea to Nigeria and the Benue river delta. It is found sparsely further south in Cameroon, Gabon, and Angola. Melegueta's pre-contact name came from cognates, potentially, of *wiza*: *awisa* or *awusa* (Ewe), *wisa* or *wusa* (Fante), *wie* (Gã-Daŋbe), *citta* (Hausa), *Atarere èwọ ọbbẹ, atarere, ata, ata-re, ose-oji,* or *ata kekere* (Yoruba), *ossame* (Angolares and Forros of the São Tomé/Principe islands), and *eza* (Nzema); for North African Arabs and Berbers *tin al-fil,* 'pepper fruit', and a condensation, *itrifil;* 'African pepper' in Turkish. *Alligator pepper* or *Guinea pepper* are bastardized nomenclatures, 'alligator' being a wholly different spice. Spellings include *milleguetta, melegette/melegete, malagueta/malaghetta, menegetai* stemming from Romance language linguistic variations, *meléga* or *meligo* related in size to millet in archaic Italian, *malagua* or the jellyfish's sting, and Phoenicia's (Andalusian) ancient port, Málaga. *Malagueta 'mala fide'* ('bad faith') are chillies that were exported to Latin America with the enslaved; Brazil's melegueta is *pimenta da costa*, West African 'coastal peppers' (SNNPR 2017; Barth 2019: 8).

Agency, the power to assert and galvanize energy, existed for all parties. Flavour's agency is distinct since fashion fluctuates for cultural, ethnic, or national groups. Culture is apparent in Caymmi's song of the lonely Bahian African-Brazilian street-food vendress. Authenticity and taste anchor the wares of this *ur-Baiana de acarajé* (bean-fritter vendress). Melegueta gave her hot sauce its memorable punch. *Acarajé,* fried to order and slathered with this zesty hot sauce, secured her clientele's devotion.

Paula Wolfert reveres tastes, distinguishing *Ras el hanout,* Morocco's iconic spice blend, as 'a spice merchant's top selections'. Her ideal had twenty-six spices, including melegueta (1973: 24-26). Tunisian *Qâlat/Gâlat Dagga* is a 'sweet-n-warm' blend of cloves, nutmeg, cinnamon, peppercorns, and melegueta (Sambar 2003:

77

*Figure 1. Grains of paradise (*Aframomum melegueta *pods), and husked seed (slightly larger quinoa/millet). Roça São João dos Angolares in São Tomé Island, São Tomé/Príncipe (Moody 2006).*

175). The University of Iowa's Silk Routes Research Project posits that melegueta's reddish-brown lachrymiform pods (+/-2 inches), which hold sixty-one hundred seeds, fostered West Africans' 'predilection for tiny, fiery chiles' (Figure 1). Vaguely reminiscent of black pepper's (*piper nigrum*) woodiness, it's characterized by concurrent numbing and piquancy. Related to ginger (*Zingiberaceæ*), melegueta's gingerols and essential oils define its flavour chemistry: 'peppery, spicy, hot, gingery, and pleasantly bitter, with an aftertaste of lemon, cardamom, camphor, and cloves' (2015-2020). Prized for its flavour, use as a stimulant, and medicine, Africans chew it with kola nuts. It is medicinally used for dysentery and stomach disorders, and as an antibacterial, antiviral, antifungal, and anti-inflammatory for animals and humans (Macfoy 2013).

Transnational Trade

Fifteenth-century Venetian slave trader Alvise Cadamosta, sponsored by Dom Henrique, o Navegante, twice sailed West Africa's coast tracing the Gambia River to its mouth. From Cadamosta's journal, *Navigazioni* (1508):

> On this coast there grows a species of *melegete*, extremely pungent like pepper, and resembling the Italian grain called *sorgo*. It produces likewise a species of pepper of great strength, not inferior to any of that which the Portuguese bring from Calicut, under the name of *Pimienta del rabo*, or *Pepe dalla coda*, and which African pepper resembles *cubbebs*, but so powerful that an ounce will go farther than a pound of the common sort; but its exportation is prohibited, lest it should injure the sale of that which is brought from Calicut (Kerr 1811: 270).

In the 1660s, German pastor Wilhelm Johann Müller described its cultivation and taste: 'this African spice is sharp and hot enough, but East Indian pepper is far superior' (Brooks 1993: 54-57).

Along the Maghreb, Berber, Arab, and Jewish merchants traded melegueta with farmers along the 'Pepper Coast/Grain Coast'; named for 'grains of paradise', not cereals/legumes (Figure 2). Tuareg caravans ferried it up the Sahel, and across the Sahara through to the Sudan and Ceuta. 'Melegetae' appears in a mock battle at an elite festival in Treviso, Italy, in 1214 as a spice in the 'faux fortress' that one dozen ladies protected from invading knights. Another vestige of sub-Saharan trade routes referenced between melegueta and the Levant and the Arabian Peninsula are *jouz as-Sudan* and *gawz al-Sudan,* thus broadly: Sudanese nuts (Van Harten 1970).

The Iberian Reconquista and its resultant expulsion of the 'Moors' provided potential for trading, wealth, and power that would not only subvert Islam (and Judaism) but also the monopoly Genovese and Venetian city-states had had for years. Christian Iberians sought a direct route to India to establish and exploit the trade in spices. Dom Henrique encouraged maritime prowess, technology, and exploration. Portugal's caravels and magnetic compasses were a boon to colonial successes. King Alfonso granted Fernão

Figure 2. 'Grains of Paradise'.

Gomes a trade monopoly along West Africa's coast. He travelled south to Morocco, then Mauritania and onto the Grain Coast; followed by Pedro de Sintra. Cadamosta lost his coastal claims following Dom Henrique's death in 1460. By 1487 King João II, Henrique's brother, enlisted Pero da Covilha and Alfonso de Pavia, bilingual in Portuguese and Arabic and posing as Moors, to scout out foreign spice markets and trade routes. They identified Calicut (Kozhikode; Kerala) having travelled by land through Egypt and East Africa en route to India, hastening the need for fast sailing routes from Iberia to India. Portuguese Bartolomeu Dias rounded South Africa's Cape of Good Hope (1487-1488), and Vasco da Gama identified sea lanes between West Africa and India (1496), opening the fifteenth century's 'Age of Discovery/Imperialism', as a lucrative period for Portugal's melegueta trading. Europeans accepted the flood of melegueta since the Romans had previously popularized pepper, reflected in Apicius's first century cookbook (Barth 2019: 34-42).

Key political economy challenges for farmers, traders, and merchant/slave traders began with access. Contact frequently took place onboard ship due to the lack of navigable waterways, topographical threats, the paucity of trading posts and urban centres, and an overall sparse population. Ascertaining fair value was abstract when gold, ivory, and melegueta were traded for European textiles, brass and copper bangles, and domestic tools ostensibly exotic in a subtropical culture. Many traders were also enslavers: doing business might cost someone their freedom. Additional threats to local are evidenced by how European ethnocentric mariners described the Africans. Pereira's *Esmeraldo de situ orbis* (1505-1508) corroborates the derogation of indigenous populations in narratives centred on navigational and exploitative descriptions of Grain Coast traders (Hilling 1969):

> There is very large dense forest that extends 2 leagues from Cabo Mesurado to Santa Maria where the malagueta trade begins and extends forty leagues along the coast [...]

Eighteen leagues down between Rio do Junco to Rio dos Cestos received its names (junk and wicker-basket) since this is where the negroes come to the ships to sell their plentiful good quality pepper. Ships should anchor in 10-12 fathoms for safety where the bottom is muddy, not at 20 [...]

Three leagues from Rio dos Cestos near Ilha da Palma, [...] one could buy a bushel of peppers for a half-pound brass bracelet, and a slave for 2 of barber's basins; now a bushel is worth 5-6 bracelets, a slave 4-5 basins [...]

The best trading months are from October to April before the tempests arrive and pepper is plentiful...from Cabo Fermoso to Resguate do Genoês pepper and slaves are easily obtained. Anchor at 15 fathoms [...]

3 leagues to Rio de Sao Vicente it is rocky, but SE by E and NW by N for 15 leagues there is pepper [...] 4 leagues along the coast to Praya dos Escravos runs for 2 leagues you can find more pepper than slaves [...]

Seven leagues from Praya dos Escravos to Lagea WNW and ESE is marked by a huge rock (Druta), more than a bowshot long and half wide, ¼ league from

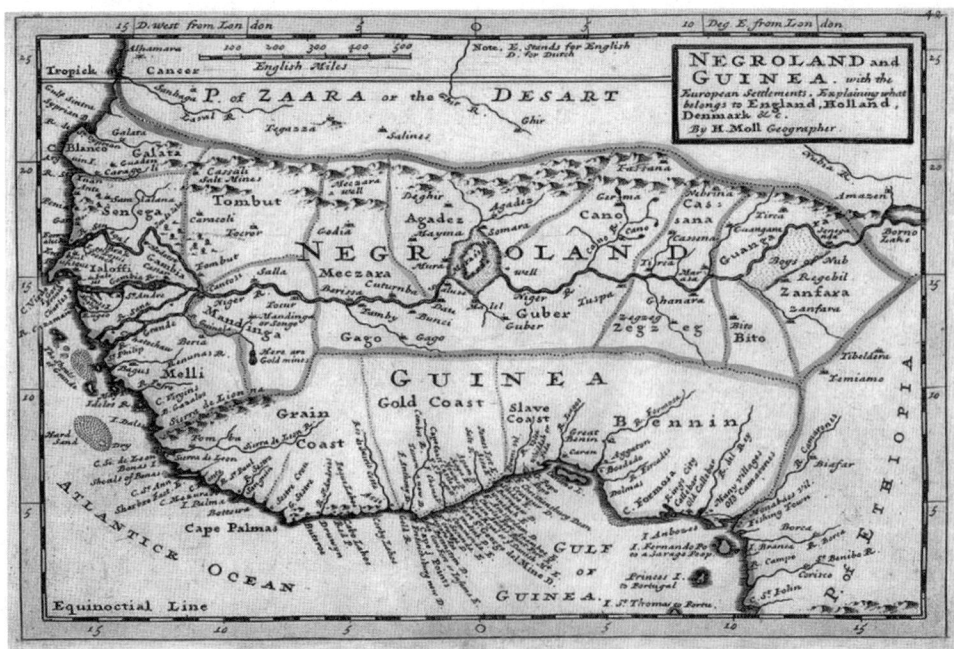

Figure 3. 'Negroland and Guinea with the European Settlements, explaining what belongs to England, Holland, Denmark, et cetera'. H. Moll Geographer (printed and sold by T. Bowles next ye Chapter House in St. Paul's Church yard, & I. Bowles at ye Black Horse in Cornhill, 1729, originally published in 1727).

shore. […] the best place along the whole coast for pepper […]

Use the rock […] as your landmark. The negroes of this coast bring pepper for barter to the ships in the fishing canoes. […] naked and not circumcised, they are idolators, being heathens […]

These negroes are idolators, not circumcised, vicious people, seldom at peace…A hundred leagues upstream […] is a negro country called Opuu, here there is much pepper, ivory, and slaves. 70 latitude north to Equator (Kimble 2016).

Sixteenth-century British annals of trade in bodies/commodities reiterate the desire for pepper, gold, and ivory. On Towerson's voyages, 'his men could barter with the negroes for malagueta pepper'. On Lok's 1554-1555 Mina voyage, Eden reports that the crew gathered 'foure hundred-pound weight and odde of gold, of two-&-twentie carrats, one graine in finenesse; sixe-&-thirtie buts of graines [of paradise: malagueta pepper]; about two hundred fifty elephant's teeth'. During William Towerson's second Guinea voyage in 1556-1557, 'they had bene six weekes upon the coast, and had gotten but three tunnes of graines [malagueta pepper]' that they wanted to bring to the Mina market before the Portuguese. King Philip II, in a letter to Count de Feria in Brussels dated 20 January 1559, mentioned 'the English ships, that had arrived in Portsmouth, laden with gold and pepper, which they had brought from the coast of Mina, to a greater amount than was covered by their sureties for 1,500 crowns' – approximately $150,000.00 dollars (Blake 1942: 257, 335, 395, 433).

These transnational profiteering monopolies stopped at nothing to realize greater financial success even when taking a toll on the economics of their trading partners or more egregiously on human life, whether African or European. Slaver William Hawkins's second Sierra Leonese voyage, seeking goods not slaves for the Company of Merchant Adventurers, gathered over four hundred pounds of gold, thirty-six butts (holding 2016 pounds each) of 'Guinea grains', and approximately two hundred fifty ivory tusks (1553). Forty years later in 1593, Dutch slaver Barent Erickson made his second West African voyage, returning in March 1594 with a valuable Gold Coast cargo of gold, ivory, and 'grain' – pepper. Successive expeditions sourced these three products (McLaughlin 2014; University of Iowa 2015-2020; Kup 1961: 40; Brooks 1993; Marees 1987).

French slaver Jean Barbot's journals (1678-1679) described the highly organized market structure where vendresses controlled trade. Whether Barbot intended to be culturally relativistic, his journals clearly show the industry, knowledge, skill, and order inherent in these market women:

Apart from the peasants who bring palm wine and sugarcane to market every day, there are no men who stand in public markets […] The goods always sold there are the following: sugarcane, plantains (*bananes*), bananas (*baccovens*), [sweet] potatoes, yams, lemons, oranges, rice, millet, maize, maniguette [pepper], bread, cakes, fish (raw, boiled, or fried), palm oil, eggs, pumpkins, purslane, the beer called *pitou*, fire-wood, roofing material, and country tobacco in untreated leaves […]. (Rönnbäck 2015: 122).

In oblique hindsight *Despatch* crewmember John Stubbs's journal appears darkly humorous. He understands how their 'trifling, valuable' cargo may be lost to pirates. When, the Royal African Company's 1719 *Despatch* was captured near the Canary Islands, Stubbs, 'a witty, brisk fellow' ingeniously argued with pirate Howel Davis:

'Pray, Gentlemen, […] if this Ship is burnt, you will thereby greatly serve the Company's Interest. […] The Vessel has been out these two years on her Voyage, being old and crazy, and almost eaten to pieces by the Worms; besides, her Stores are worth little; and as to her Cargoe, it consists only of a little Redwood and Melegette-pepper [Malaghetta]; so if she should be burned, the Company will lose little; but the poor People […] will lose all their Wages, […] three times the Value of the Vessel, and of her trifling Cargoe; so that the Company will be greatly obliged to you for destroying her.' The rest of the Crew being convinced by these Reasons, the Vessel was spared, and delivered again to Captain Wilson (Breverton 2004: 50).

A Danish-British register from 1785-1786 lists goods exported from an English factory on Bence/Bunce island, including ivory, hides, wax, indigo, cotton, rice, millet, tamarinds, pepper of different kinds, cassia canes, other chemical drugs, tortoise shell, […] spermaceti, ambergrease, and gold sold to Captain Basteresse for $1,400,00.00, or about $3,700,500 today (Kup 1961: 118). Such accounts detail trade, consumption,

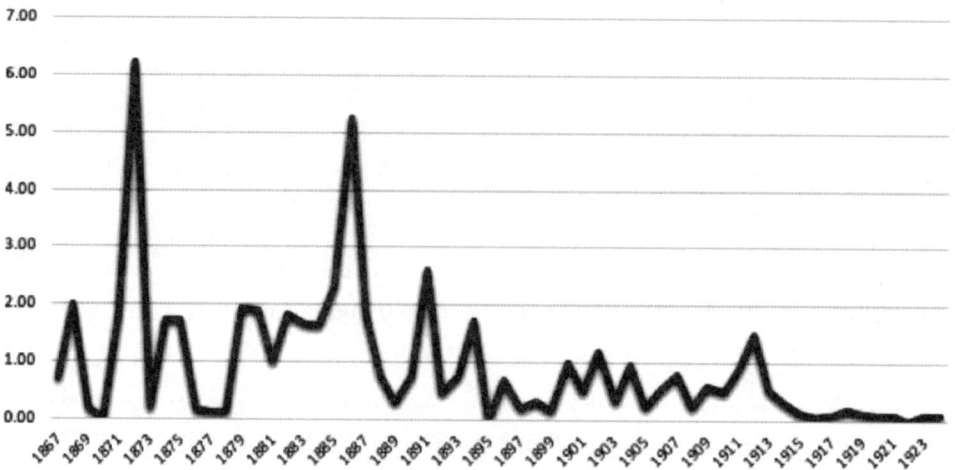

Figure 4. Gold Coast Colony Melegueta Exports 1867-1924 in lbs. x 10⁵. British Library Online: Gold Coast Colony Blue Book Statistics.

and profiteering patterns for melegueta. The spice enthralled consumers and sustained coffers across Europe to the detriment of the West Africans who had transformed a wild plant into a commodity. This production-distribution chain centred Africans as peripheral, the least return from the most arduous labour, along with the threat of enslavement. Dominant European core metropoles, urban middlemen, and financiers gained the majority profits from this spice trade.

...What's Cooking?

Flooding Europe with melegueta can be evidenced through four early cookbooks, *The Forme of Cury* (c. 1390), *Le Viandier* (1300/1486), *Liber de coquina* (1304-1314) and *De re coquinaria* (1541). *Pouldre fine/douce*, 'fine spice' (powder), was commonly found in noble Medieval French pantries. A 'labour-saver', cooks ground the 'big four' spices – ginger, cinnamon, cloves and grains of paradise – together and stored *pouldre* in leather pouches (Scully and others 2002: 55). *The Forme of Cury* lists *'greynes de Parys'* in *Sawse Noyre for Capouns Yrosted. XX.VI.XVII* and *PUR FAIT YPOCRAS [1]. XX.IX. XI.*, (Capons with Black Sauce, and, To Make Spice Wine). Each use of melegueta was not noted, yet these recipes indicate how it was used in bread-thickened sauces for roasted and boiled poultry, pork, or fish and in 'mulled' or spiced wine. The wine's spices were both for taste and digestion (Brander and Pegge 1780; Krondl 2008). Apicius advocates for pepper, which ambiguously may reference melegueta: 'that in this case the term [pepper] probably stands for some other kind of aromatic seed less pungent than the grain known to us as "pepper" and one more acceptable to the fine flavor of   *83*

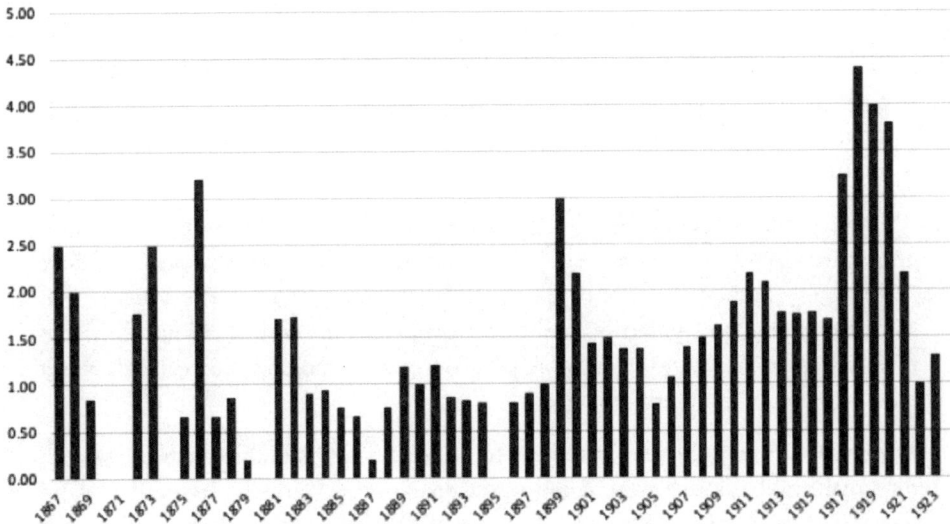

Figure 5. Gold Coast Colony Melegueta Export Value in £ x 10⁵ 1867-1924. British Library Online: Gold Coast Colony Blue Book Statistics.

Year	£ x 10,000
1875	2.95
1891	1.87
1900	2.39
1910	1.70

Figure 6. Price of black pepper (piper nigrum) *per tunne at London auction. British Library Online: Gold Coast Colony Blue Book Statistics.*

fruit, namely pimiento, allspice for instance, or clove, or nutmeg, or a mixture of these. "Pepper" formerly was a generic term for all of these spices' (Apicius and Vehling 1977).

Liber de coquina uses melegueta for camelina, a Saracen (Arab/Muslim) style sauce, Candied Relish, Ash Gray Sauce for a Wild Boar Civet, Ambroyno (sweet food), and in a spiced almond/almond milk thickened sauce for sautéed chicken. Camelina produced a spiced drink as a digestive aid with vinegar, and/or breadcrumbs (Möhren 11).

Le Viandier has the largest volume of recipes with melegueta (including some with offal) including partridge *trimolette,* capons, hare and rabbit civet, *porc du mer* (porpoise), *Ung rozé a chair* (a pink dish for meat days), lamprey, fish/meat *en gelée,* civet of veel [sic], shredded mutton, hasty pork menu with vinaigrette, potage *lians,* and sauces, including *gravé de loache* (gravy), sauce 'to preserve fish', boiled sauces, cameline sauce, *Brouet Rousset* (a broth), and crayfish gravy. As with *The Forme of Cury,* these bread- or nut-thickened sauces often complemented proteins subjected to two or more cooking methods. Sauces are spiced with ginger, cinnamon, cloves, long pepper, saffron, and verjuice/vinegar in addition to melegueta. Two headnotes summarize the spice mixtures:

> A hot, dry spice such as pepper is appropriate for a cold, moist meat such as pork, and particularly for its viscera; […] For the *Menue haste de porc* prepared here in Recipe 17, rather than the pepper used by the *Enseignments,* the *Viandier* has substituted grains of paradise, melegueta pepper. "Plus connu aujourd'hui sous le nom de *maniguette.* On l'emploie pour donner du montant aux eaux-de-vie et aux vinaigres […]" (Scully 1988: 62)

> Both almonds and chicken were held to be particularly suitable for persons with digestive problems and were relied upon regularly to form the bases of a bland diet. Ginger—reinforced here by grains of paradise, a relative of pepper—is the predominant spice and is likewise a favorite 'digestive' (Scully 1988: 66).

Legal Limitations

Dutch taxation records from 1358 levied import duties on '*Greyn Paradijs*'. From the period as a wild cultivar to a key transnational commodity, economics and trade along with regional and personal tastes changed, allowing *pipers nigrum*, *longum*, and *cubeba* to usurp its position in food and beverages in the mid-twentieth century. Additionally, cacao's rise in international popularity and cultivation as a commodity overtook lands previously dedicated to melegueta. Official Blue Book statistics cite 191,011 pounds exported from the Gold Coast (Ghana) in 1871. In 1919 combined British imports from the Ivory Coast, Ghana, and Sierra Leone into Liverpool totalled 30 'tonnes' (imperial long tonnes of 2240 pounds each, as opposed to 2000 pounds for US tons, or 67,200 pounds total); and 19,857 pounds were imported to the US in 1940 (Figures 4-6). Yet, after several centuries of a run in popularity melegueta fell under legal edict, a harbinger of its nadir.

Melegueta was added to European beers, gin, aquavit, and flavoured wines as an adulterant: 'To obtain the appearance of a good quality porter – to get "a fine frothy head," iron sulphate, alum, salt, capsicum and grains of paradise improved weak and insipid beer'. Although foods were flavoured with melegueta during Queen Elizabeth I's reign, and she added it to her beer, in 1816 it was banned in the UK for use in strengthening or revitalizing beer. Parliamentary Act 56 Geo. 3. C.58 forbade the use of adulterants including melegueta, resulting in the levying of heavy financial penalties and/or revocation of licensure thereby forbidding brewers, chemists, and publicans to possess or use grains of paradise to make beer (£200 fines); druggists found selling to brewers were fined £500. Chemists are a significant addition since melegueta was also seen as a digestive aid. *The Domestic Chemist* also identified melegueta as a key adulterant to beer and ale in 1831 (Van Harten 1970; Hart 1952; McCulloh 1839:8-13; British Online Archives; Ashworth 2004).

Contextualizing these gastronomic decisions against the West African traditions that today are sacralized suggests certain commonalities, despite highly disparate applications. Consider the concurrent chewing of melegueta and kola nuts as a physical and spiritual stimulant. This practice focuses one's sense of taste and heightens flavours on the tongue as well as aiding digestion. Or consider its use in Candomblé ceremony, where its bracing flavour is shared in a group activity to bring reverence to ritual offerings and directly engage with specific deities in Bantu and Yoruba traditions. Metaphorically, these uses compare to the *Le Viandier* claim that melegueta – and/or the '*pouldre fine*', the fine spices of the *ur-quatre épice* – contributes to uplifting the spirits. Can we then link the visceral desire to enliven a moment, a gustatory or a sacred experience that transformed a wild perennial cultivar into a global commodity, as having a shared resonance between Europeans and the African Diaspora? This possibility further enhances the agency and deleterious effects of a pepper that contributed to the enslaving of Africans, elevated European political economy, and became an abstract substitute or simulacra for the inhumane trade in bodies. This product could be valued by pirates and privateers and destroyed by bacterial moulds or invasive pests, but it was much easier to manage than enslaved chattel. Carried as a provision on Middle Passage slave ships, melegueta was 'given to our Negroes in their messes to keep them from the flux and dry belly-ach, which they are incident to' (Phillips [1693-1694]: 394). Onboard rations for the enslaved consisted mainly of horse beans boiled to a pap, boiled yams, and rice, with the possible sailor's leavings of beef or pork. To this was added a condiment, dubbed 'slabber sauce', made by mixing palm oil, wheat flour, water, and melegueta pepper. Even vile and or rancid victuals were enhanced by melegueta. To understand 'pepperishness' may provide an insight into West African culinary cultural epistemologies, underscoring the value of their knowledge systems and dogma, both in their own right and in relation to European epistemes, which historically have always been seen as more advanced.

References

Achebe, Chinua. 1959. *Things Fall Apart: The Story of a Strong Man* (New York: Anchor Books)

Apicius and Joseph Dommers Vehling. 1977. *Apicius, Cookery and Dining in Imperial Rome: A Bibliography, Critical Review and Translation of the Ancient Book Known as 'Apicius de re coquinaria'* (New York: Dover Publications)

Aribisala, Yemisi. 2015. "For the Love of Peppers", *Okra*, 23 October <https://medium.com/@YemisiOkra/for-the-love-of-peppers-52b675deaaeb> [accessed 20 April 2021]

Ashworth, William J. 2004. 'Practical Objectivity: The Excise, State and Production in Eighteenth Century England' *Social Epistemology*, 18.2-3, 181-97.

Barth, Joe. 2019. *Pepper: A Guide to the World's Favorite Spice* (Lanham, MD: Rowman & Littlefield)

Barton, Scott Alves; Joceval Santos, and Claudio Alves. 2020. "Sacred foods and rituals," *Personal communication with a Candomblé Ogá and Egungun Ojé.*

Bascom. William R. 1993. *Sixteen Cowries: Yoruba Divination from Africa to the New World* (Bloomington: Indiana University Press)

John W. Blake. 1942. *Europeans in West Africa, 1450-1560: Documents to Illustrate the Nature and Scope of Portuguese Enterprise in West Africa, the Abortive Attempt of Castilians to Create an Empire There, and the Early English Voyages to Barbary and Guinea*, vol. II, 2nd series, no. 87 (London: Hakluyt Society)

Brander, Gustavus and Samuel Pegge. 1780. *The forme of cury, a roll of ancient English cookery: compiled about A.D. 1390 by the master-cooks of King Richard II, presented afterwards to Queen Elizabeth by Edward Lord Stafford and now in the possession of Gustavus Brander, Esq.* (London: J. Nichols)

Breverton, Terry. 2004. *Black Bart Roberts: The Greatest Pirate of Them All* (Gretna, LA: Pelican)

British Online Archives. 1846-1953. 'Ghana (Gold Coast Colony), Blue Book', *Colonial Africa in Official Statistics* (London: British Foreign & Commonwealth Office) <https://microform.digital/boa/collections/39/volumes/230/ghana-gold-coast-1846-1939> [accessed 20 April 2021]

Brooks, George E. 1993. *Landlords and Strangers: Ecology, Society, and Trade in Western Africa, 1000-1630* (New York: Routledge).

Caymmi, Dorival and others. 1930. *A Preta do Acarajé. Scena Typica Bahiana* (Odeon)

Crowther, Samuel. 1843. *Vocabulary of the Yoruba language* (London: Printed for the Church Missionary Society [by] Watts)

The domestic chemist: comprising instructions for the detection of adulteration in numerous articles employed in domestic economy, medicine, and the arts, to which are subjoined, the art of detecting poisons in food and organic mixtures, and a popular introduction to the principles of chemical analysis. 1831. (London: Bumpus & Grifin)

Hair, P.E.H. and William Keeling. 1981. *Sierra Leone and the English in 1607: Extracts from the Unpublished Journals of the Keeling Voyage to the East Indies* ([Freetown]: Institute of African Studies, University of Sierra Leone)

Hart, F. Leslie. 1952. 'A History of the Adulteration of Food Before 1906', *Food, Drug, Cosmetic Law Journal*, 7.1 (January), 5-22.

Hepper, F. N. 1967. 'The Identity of Grains-of-Paradise and Melegueta Pepper (Aframomum, Zingiberaceae) in West Africa', *Kew Bulletin*, 21.1, 129-37.

Hilling, David. 1969. 'The Evolution of the Major Ports of West Africa', *The Royal Geographical Society*, 135.3 (September), 365-78.

Kerr, Robert. 1811. *General History of Voyages and Travels* (Edinburgh: J. Ballantyne & Co.), ed. by Frances Pritchett, 2004-2008, vol 2, chapter 5, section 2 <http://www.columbia.edu/itc/mealac/pritchett/00generallinks/kerr/vol02chap05.html#section02> [accessed 19 May 2021]

Kimble, George H.T. (trans. and ed.). 2016. 'The Second Book: Describing the Discoveries of King Alphonso V of Portugul', *Esmeraldo de Situ Orbis, by Duarte Pacheco Pereira* (London: Routledge [London: Hakluyt Society, 1937]), pp. 103-38

Krondl, Michael. 2008. *The Taste of Conquest: The Rise and Fall of the Three Great Cities of Spice* (New York: Ballantine Books)

Kup, Alexander Peter. 1961. *A History of Sierra Leone, 1400-1787* (Cambridge: Cambridge University Press)

van Limborch, Gulielmus. 1679. *Vade Mecum, sive Lexicon Vegetabilium usualium.*

Lock, J. M., J. B. Hall, and D. K. Abbiw. 1977. 'The Cultivation of Melegueta Pepper (Aframomum melegueta) in Ghana', *Economic Botany*, 31.3 (July-September), 321-30

Macfoy, Cyrus. 2013. *Medicinal Plants And Traditional Medicine In Sierra Leone* (Bloomington, IN: iUniverse)

de Marees, Pieter. 1987. *Description and Historical Account of the Gold Kingdom of Guinea* (1602) (Oxford: Oxford University Press)

McCulloch, J. R. 1839. 'Ale and Beer', *A Dictionary, Practical, Theoretical, and Historical, of Commerce and Commercial Navigation: Illustrated with Maps and Plans* (London: Longman, Orme, Brown, Green, and Longmans), pp. 8-13

McLaughlin, Raoul. 2014. *The Roman Empire and the Indian Ocean: The Ancient World Economy and the Kingdoms of Africa, Arabia and India* (Barnsley: Pen and Sword, 2014)

Moody, Inna. 2006. 'Roça São João dos Angolares, São Tomé: Naturmort: "grains of paradise" or "Guinea pepper"', *Moody World-Flickr* <https://www.flickr.com/photos/moodyworld/252197885/> [accessed 21 April 2021]

Möhren, Frankwalt. n.d. *Il libro de la cocina: Un ricettario tra Oriente e Occidente* (OAPEN: Heidelberg University Publishing)

Phillips, Thomas. [1693-1694]. 'A Journal of a Voyage made in the Hannibal of London, Ann. 1693-1694', in *Documents Illustrative of the History of the Slave Trade to America, Vol. I: 1441-1700*, ed. by Elizabeth Donnan (New York: Octagon, 1969), pp. 392-410

Rönnbäck, Klas. 2015. *Labour and Living Standards in Pre-Colonial West Africa* (Abington: Taylor and Francis)

Sambar, Alexia. 2003. *La Saveur des Roses* (Paris: Éditions Le Manuscrit)

Scully, Eleanor D., Terence Scully, and J. David Scully. 2002. *Early French Cookery: Sources, History, Original Recipes and Modern Adaptions* (Ann Arbor: University of Michigan Press)

Scully, Terrence. 1988. *The Viandier of Taillevent: An Edition of All Extant Manuscripts* (Ottawa: University of Ottawa Press)

SNNPR, FEWSNET, and DPPA/B. 2006-2017. '19: Basketo-Melo Coffee and Root Crop Livelihood Zone', *Southern Nations Nationalities and Peoples Region (SNNPR) Livelihood Profiles – Regional Overview* (Washington, DC: USAID)

Stokes, Jonathan. 1812. *A botanical materia medica; consisting of the generic and specific characters of the plants used in medicine and diet, with synonyms, and references to medical authors* (London: Johnson), pp. 71-72

87

Toussaint-Samat, Maguelonne. 2008. 'Bochet', *A History of Food* (Hoboken, NJ: John Wiley & Sons), pp. 30-35

University of Iowa. 2015-2020. "Melegueta Pepper/Grains of Paradise," *Silk Routes* (University of Iowa: International Writing Project) <https://iwp.uiowa.edu/silkroutes/melegueta-pepper-grains-paradise> [accessed 21 April 2021]

Van Harten, A.M. 1970. 'Melegueta Pepper', *Economic Botany*, 24.2 (April-June), 208-16

Van Wyk, Ben-Erik. 2013. *Culinary Herbs & Spices of the World* (Chicago: University of Chicago Press), pp. 32, 52

Voeks, Robert A. 1997. *Sacred Leaves of Candomblé: African Magic, Medicine, and Religion in Brazil* (Austin: University of Texas Press)

Wagner, Mark. 1981. 'The Introduction and Early Use of African Plants in the New World', *Tennessee Anthropologist*, 6.2 (Fall), pp. 112-23

Wolfert, Paula. 1973. *Couscous and Other Good Food from Morocco* (New York: Harper & Row), pp. 24-26

Cheating the Senses

Nina Bauer

The history of spice adulteration is both a history of deceit and falsification, and a history of detection and the fight for food safety. It is a tale of ingenuity and perseverance on both sides. Spice adulteration has been one of the more common forms of food fraud since the global spice trade began and is still today a major problem. Spices are especially vulnerable to adulteration and fraud. Spices travel through many countries and through many hands before they arrive in the kitchen, and spices are often in powder form which makes adulteration hard to determine. This paper explores the theme of spice fraud and its different incarnations in the nineteenth century, during the Second World War, and in today's global food market.

Any kind of food fraud, no matter what food it involves, affects more than just the food on our plates. It has an enormous impact on society and the way we think about food. Food scandals take away our trust in the food we eat and in the safety measures installed to counter fraud. Because of this diminishing of trust in our food supply and in our society's ability to keep us safe from fraud, no food scam is truly innocent and without consequences.

This is not a new issue. In 1820 the famous chemist Friedrich Accum (1769-1838) stated that 'of all possible nefarious traffic and deception, practised by mercenary dealers, that of adulterating the articles intended for human food with ingredients deleterious to health, is the most criminal, and, in the mind of every honest man, must excite feelings of regret and disgust'.[1]

One kind of spice adulteration cheats the senses but leaves most of us blissfully unaware that someone might have been tampering with the content of our spice racks. This effect is exacerbated by the fact that most people do not know much about spices beyond how to cook with them. How many of us are completely sure how they are supposed to look, smell, and taste at their best, especially when looking down into a jar full of aromatic powder? It is tempting to choose the ones with the brightest colours, but beware: the spices may have been touched up with synthetic dyes, and short of scientific analysis it is impossible to be sure that what you're looking at is pure spice. This uncertainty rises when there are multiple spices at play. With the popularity of readymade spice mixes and seasonings from garam marsala to pumpkin pie mix, the potential for fraud is high.

Spices travel through many countries and through many hands before they arrive in the kitchen, and adulteration can happen at any stage. Some swindlers look to deceive the next link in the long chain, and some are not even overly concerned with hiding their fraud. Though adulteration can be quite crude, and sometimes even poisonous or harmful to humans or the environment, more often spice fraud involves a lot of bulking and padding to increase the weight of wares. In fact, the most common type of fraud across all foods is the use of water to increase the weight of the product. But while it is easily possible to soak fresh herbs in water before weighing them, or even to pump water into chicken breasts, spices and water do not go well together. Instead, swindlers have looked to other powdery substances to increase their lot. Through history these materials have included flour, ground rice, arrowroot powder, ground coconut shells, gypsum, sand, brick dust, ground seed husks, and many other things.

Dried herbs are not safe from adulteration either. According to the European Spice Association and the American Spice Trade Association only two species of the genus *Origanum* may be sold as oregano: *Origanum vulgare hirtum* and *Origanum onites*. But that restriction does not prevent adulteration with dried leaves from other plants like rockroses, myrtle, and European hazelnut.[2]

When the fraud targets the consumer directly, the swindlers are often banking that the shame felt by the tricked person is big enough to forestall any backlash against them and their business. A hapless customer who buys fake saffron from a market stall might be too embarrassed to return and make a fuss. Tourists on holiday browsing spice markets are obvious targets for this type of fraud. Very often the adulteration is discovered too late: only when the buyers are back in their own countries and cook with the spices do they realize something is wrong.

To further muddy the waters, some spices are not only adulterated but are also used as adulterants themselves. For example, turmeric can be used instead of saffron to give dishes the rich yellow colour but not the taste of saffron. This practice, of course, is only fraud if the product claims to use saffron, and not turmeric, in its ingredients. Spanish paella has a long history of being made with saffron, but now it has become more accepted to use turmeric instead, and many might not even know that it is supposed to contain saffron. This form of ingredient displacement may not be fraud, but it still deprives the paella of a part of its history and cultural significance.

The history of food adulteration shows that, with few exceptions, the methods of swindling have changed from rather crude and often dangerous methods, like boiling sour wine in lead vessels to sweeten it or using heavy metal compounds to colour sweets, to very sophisticated methods today. As a result, adulterated food, while being almost undetectable in some cases, is most often not as dangerous to consume as it was in earlier times. However, poisonings caused by adulterants can still occur today, as the scandals like the discovery in the early 2000s of the carcinogenic azo dye Sudan 1 (or Sudan Red) in food products, among others, in chilli powders across Europe.

Counterfeit Pepper and Food Scares

In the nineteenth century there were cases of adulteration that had fatal consequences for some consumers, while other food scams merely cheated people into paying more money than a product was worth. The industrial revolution's wide-ranging changes to the world's foodways considerably widened the gap between producer and consumer. As Jeffrey Pilcher argues:

> the meaning of "wholesome" changed fundamentally as foods began arriving by railroad and steamship from around the world. The freshness of meat was no longer determined by the health of the animal or how recently it had been slaughtered but rather by its packaging and refrigeration. Shoppers, who could formerly judge the quality of foods for themselves by smell and touch, increasingly had to trust the label on a can.[3]

With more links in the supply chain, swindlers had more opportunities to cheat. However, this century also saw scientists, chiefly chemists and doctors, emerge as food detectives to battle adulteration. Using scientific methods to meticulously examine commodities, they sought to expose widespread adulteration and educate consumers to avoid getting swindled.

Scientists in London were at the forefront of this development, but for reasons that might involve more than Britain's status as a centre for science and industrialization. Considered through the lenses of adulteration and food safety, the state of English food was appalling. In 1850, the French chemist Alphonse Normandy (1809-1864), living in London, lamented:

> If one of the principal characteristics of our epoch, in a commercial point of view, is the immense progress which every department of productive industry has achieved, it must be admitted that the arts of adulteration and sophistication have more than kept pace with that progress. [… A]ll that can be mixed, hackled, twisted, ground, pulverized, woven, pressed – all articles of consumption in trade, in manufactures, in the arts, in a word, all that can be made matter of commerce and be sold, is adulterated, falsified, disguised, or drugged.[4]

In response to this mire of adulteration and fraud, in 1820 Accum took it upon himself to expose the swindlers and educate the public about the dangers lurking in the shops and kitchens. With his treatise, he intended to 'exhibit easy methods of detecting the fraudulent adulterations of food, and of other articles, classed either among the necessaries or luxuries of the table; and to put the unwary on their guard against the use of such commodities as are contaminated with substances deleterious to health'.[5] Accum's treatise not only detailed chemical tests for exposing adulteration but also listed the names and businesses which had been charged and prosecuted for adulteration, so as to serve as a warning to both swindlers and consumers. The book became a bestseller, with one thousand copies sold within the first month.

It is almost impossible to overstate the importance of Accum's work not just for Britain but for the entire Western World. 'In the history of adulteration,' writes Bee Wilson, 'there are two stages: before 1820 and after 1820; before Accum and after Accum.'[6] With Accum, the topics of adulteration and food safety gained attention both in the international scientific community and among the public.

At the time, most adulteration of spices was crude and unsophisticated, but the swindlers showed surprising ingenuity and creativity when it came to adulterants. Anything that could be pulverised and, perhaps with the help of colorants such as red lead or naphthol yellow, achieve the look of ground spices, might be used.

The simplest way to adulterate spices was to substitute a good part of the spice with another substance similar in looks but not necessarily in taste. While many would not be able to distinguish between pure cinnamon and cinnamon mixed with cassia, cumin seeds adulterated with grass seeds that had been coloured with charcoal dust would make most people suspicious.[7]

At the other end of the spectrum was the manufacturing of counterfeit peppercorns. Through the centuries pepper has been adulterated with anything even remotely pepperlike, in the nineteenth century some pepper sellers made artificial peppercorns using linseed oil cakes, clay, and a bit of cayenne pepper as a gesture toward flavouring. To make the counterfeit look like real peppercorns, the mixture was pressed through a sieve and then rolled in a cask to form little spheres. Fortunately, this fraud could be detected quite easily. 'It is only necessary to throw a sample of the suspected pepper into a bowl of water,' wrote Accum, 'the artificial pepper-corns fall to powder, whilst the true pepper remains whole.'[8]

Ground pepper was another story. It could be adulterated with anything from cayenne and rape seeds to burned potato scraps and gypsum. Often these unsavoury mixtures were bolstered with the floor sweepings from pepper warehouses that came to be known as 'pepper dust'.[9] All over Europe pepper was adulterated with whatever was locally available. In France, for instance, the use of ground olive stones was widespread.[10]

Adulteration did not end with Accum, but his work spurred other scientists to take up the cause. One of them was the physician and chemist Arthur Hill Hassall (1817-1894), and he too would revolutionize the way adulteration was detected. With the use of a microscope, Hassall could reveal the components of even the most finely ground spices. Before he turned to the subject of food adulteration, Hassall had made headlines with his examinations of the London water supply that helped bring on water reforms.

The focus of Hassall was on the scope of adulteration. In collaboration with the founding editor of *The Lancet*, Thomas Wakley (1795-1862), he purchased samples of products from shops all around London and used his trusty microscope to examine them. He then reported on how many samples were pure and how many adulterated, as well as the nature of the adulterants. According to Hassall's analyses the extent of spice adulteration in London was great, but maybe not as dire as the citizens feared. It was possible to find pure spices among the falsified. Hassall showed that among nineteen samples of ground cinnamon, three turned out to be cassia, 10 were padded with materials such as flour and arrowroot, and six were pure cinnamon. However, while mace seemed to be only rarely adulterated, it was impossible for Hassall to find pure mustard anywhere.[11]

As Accum had done before him, Hassall also strove to publicize the shops and manufactures involved in the adulteration of food: 'Experience has shown, that any merely general exposure of the nature of the adulterations practiced on the public through their food is not sufficient to deter from a repetition of them, and that the only way in which it can be hoped that such fraudulent practices can be stayed, and the public protected, is by such proceedings as will entail personal discredit and probable loss.'[12]

Hassall became known far and wide, and his analyses became a guarantee for the quality of products. A Danish producer of chocolate, Elisabethsminde, proudly stated in their announcements in 1889 that '[t]he famous English analysts Arthur Hill Hassall and Edwyn Godwin Clayton say about Elisabethsminde's cocoa powder: it is evident from the analysis, that this preparation is pure cocoa, finely pulverised [...]. Elisabethsminde's cocoa powder is in this regard very favourable, compared to the other countless preparations we have examined'.[13]

The purity of spices was not just a problem in Europe. When the American chemist Harvey Washington Wiley (1844-1930), who would later be known as the 'Father of the Pure Food and Drugs Act', was testing spices and other foods in his laboratories in the 1880s, he and his team were horrified to find how much adulteration was going on. They found that the most common spices to be adulterated were pepper, mustard, cloves, cinnamon, cassia, allspice, nutmeg, mace, and ginger.[14] Some American spice sellers developed sophisticated recipes for imitating their chosen spices, while others found one type of adulterant and stuck with it. One story goes that a New York purveyor of pepper, mustard, cloves, cinnamon, cassia, allspice, nutmeg, and mace adulterated them all with ground coconut shells, of which the firm purchased five thousand pounds a year.[15]

As in Europe, spice adulteration showed both great creativity and contempt for food safety. Chemist Clifford Richardson (1856-1932) stated, in a chapter on pepper producers in America, that '[s]pecimens from Baltimore mills of very low-quality goods were found to contain but little pepper, and that of the worst quality, being made up of cracker dust, yellow corn, cayenne, and charcoal in so disgraceful a way as to be visible to the unassisted eye on close examination'.[16] It was no wonder that consumers treated spices with trepidation when such findings were made public.

The fear of adulteration and fraud persists even when food safety measures are put in place that improve food quality. As Bee Wilson has shown, there were fewer scandals of adulterated food in Britain in the 1880s as opposed to earlier in the century, but the fear of adulteration remained at an all-time high.[17] Food scandals can easily lead to scaremongering and the demonization of an entire industry, and the fear of adulteration takes on a life of its own even though it can be proved that not everyone is adulterating their products. In some cases, this fear can lead to people becoming distrustful of food in general, and demands for pure and untainted food free of any adulterants and additives can become extreme. In the United States, Ella Eaton Kellogg (1853-1920), wife of John Harvey Kellogg of the famous Battle Creek Sanatorium, rallied the Women's Christian Temperance Union to fight for abstinence in a broader sense than mere liquor, and to only eat pure and unadulterated food. However, according to her, 'stimulating' condiments as pepper and mustard were equally contaminated and should be avoided at all cost.[18]

Substitutes and Sawdust in Denmark

During the Second World War adulteration became almost normalized in the form of ersatz products. With rationing and all the other restraints on daily cooking brought on by the war, ersatz products became an important part of keeping the meals as close to peacetime recipes as possible. But, at the same time, the war gave rise to new forms of adulteration that played on the fact that it became harder to differentiate between illegally adulterated products and legal ersatz products. The term *authenticity* came to have many different meanings during this period.

In Denmark food adulteration had not had the same attention as in Britain, but Accum's treatise and Hassall's examinations had not gone unnoticed. Denmark had had a general food safety legislation dating back to 1701, when the police were tasked with ensuring that no harmful or spoiled wares or harmful substances were sold as food. In 1836 came the first positive list of colourants for cakes, after a series of cakes coloured with heavy-metal-based paints were discovered by the police in Copenhagen.[19] Spices do not seem to have been seen as especially vulnerable to adulteration in nineteenth century Denmark, but this changed during the twentieth century.

Throughout the Second World War many Danish ersatz spices were found to consist of little genuine spice and a great deal of sawdust. The use of sawdust was not a new thing: it had been used as an adulterant in ground spices for hundreds of years, and the means of detecting it was with the microscope. Clifford Richardson had noted in 1887 that 'sawdust of various woods may be recognized by the fragments of various spiral and dotted vessels and fibrous materials which are not found in the spices or other adulterants'.[20] In 1937, the Danish authorities expressed concern over the many cases of ground cinnamon adulterated with a high percentage of 'crushed cigar boxes' (Spanish cedar, *cedrela odorata*).[21]

With the Nazi occupation of Denmark in April 1940, the country was suddenly cut off from a lot of the countries it normally traded with. Half of all Denmark's imports stopped abruptly, and the other half was controlled by the German Wehrmacht. This meant that many spices abruptly became unavailable. The Danes had a love of spices, especially cinnamon and pepper. Before the war Denmark imported about half a million kilos of spice each year.[22] This meant that people were hungering for spices and ready to accept substitutions of a quality that today would be viewed as unacceptable.

The idea behind using sawdust, or 'tree flour' as it was officially named to make it seem more palatable, in ersatz spices was to have a cheap and available receptor for flavour and aroma. Essential oils extracted from real spices or artificial flavourings would be added to very finely ground sawdust, primarily from beech trees though oak was also used. Through this process the sawdust would absorb the flavour and aroma of the original spice. However, spice flavours proved to be quite volatile using 1940s techniques, and many ersatz spices lost their taste when heated during cooking. As chef Richard Oest-Larsen lamented: 'We do not have pepper and all the other glorious flavours, and ten cents' worth of sawdust in the meatballs, will not make them taste better.'[23]

Ersatz cinnamon could be made by adding cinnamaldehyde to sawdust and then colouring it at the end to make it look more like real cinnamon. 'Many will perhaps find this distasteful to use sawdust for this purpose,' wrote one newspaper, 'but fairly considered, it may well be the same whether one uses bark from the cinnamon tree or another tree.'[24]

But even in ersatz products the sawdust content could be too high to be anything other than a counterfeit spice. In 1942 Steins Laboratorium, which handled food testing for the state, publicised the test results of 4400 samples of all kinds of food including spices, and the results were not good. Several samples of cardamom proved to be made of 'a waste product, which was completely worthless as a spice', while especially cinnamon seemed to be made up of the ever-present sawdust mixed with starch, cocoa shells, and ochre.[25] One pepper sample was made almost entirely of crushed dried peas, and two samples of cloves had so much sawdust that they were stamped as falsifications. All in all, 310 samples of the 4400 were found so badly adulterated or spoiled that there were official reprimands and large fines.[26]

The demand for spices also revived an older method of swindling. This fraud involved selling spent spices as fresh. Spices such as cinnamon could be boiled to remove its essential oils and then re-dried and sold, while the essential oils could be used to flavour sawdust for ersatz spices. Back in the 1850s Hassall had illustrated how spent spices could be detected, through looking at the starch granules that change shape after being boiled.[27]

With all the dubious ersatz products and falsified exotic spices on the market it is no wonder that many Danish housewives instead turned to other means of flavouring their meals. A very popular book in Denmark during the Second World War was Herluf Petersen's *Spisekammeret paa Grøftekanten* (*The Larder on the Edge of the Ditch*). It described in detail several edible wild plants growing in Denmark, how to cook with them and their flavour profile. Gråbynke (mugwort, *Artemisia vulgaris*), for instance, could be used as a seasoning for roasts.[28]

The Danish newspapers were also quick to offer advice on foraging and gardening; one local newspaper stated that 'such home-grown spices, as we ourselves grow, dry and grind, are without any danger of being falsified'.[29]

Spice Adulteration Today

Before the 1970s a lot of food legislation around the world was concerned with labelling to prevent false branding, like the marketing of margarine as butter, rather than the labelling of ingredients we see today. For many products, the ingredients were shrouded in trade secrets and not disclosed to the public, so consumers could easily be misled in the jungle of colourants, additives, and artificial flavourings that had come into use in the post-war decades. Developments in food science had made it possible to create nature-identical substances, and food adulteration had thereby entered a new era. Legitimate spice brands could now be 'natural', 'nature-identical', and 'artificial'.

One of the best-known cases is the different vanilla flavourings. Vanilla is the second most expensive spice on the market, so adulteration happens frequently. The chemical compound which is mostly responsible for giving the vanilla bean its flavour is vanillin. The chemical structure of vanillin had been known since the late 1850s, and vanillin had been synthesized and manufactured as a flavouring on a large scale from the 1870s. The use of synthetic vanillin can be characterized as nature-identical, since vanillin also occurs in nature, while another vanilla-substitute, ethyl-vanillin, does not and is therefore an artificial flavouring.

The 1970s became a ground-breaking decade for food safety legislation with several new food safety measures being introduced and older food laws updated around the world. In 1973, the first comprehensive Danish *positivliste* (positive list) listed approved food additives using the European Union's E-number system. Introduced in 1962, the e-number system laid the groundwork for better regulation of food production and promoted openness and transparency within the food industry. During the research that led to the list, food producers were interviewed about their use of additives, and their answers were codified into the list. Thus, it gave an almost complete view of food production in Denmark and its use of additives.[30] However, as the history of adulteration shows, both scientific and legislative breakthroughs in food safety and production give rise to new forms of swindling.

Food adulteration has evolved with the times and there is big money involved in an ever-growing international market, so more and more resources and manpower are needed to combat food fraud which is now more than ever a global issue.

96

When the Danish Food Authorities established a flying squad in 2006, the team consisted of six people; today there are thirty-one employees. When asked about the scope of adulteration and fraud in October 2019, the leader of the team, Michael Rosenmark, stated, 'With icebergs you know that you have to multiply by ten. When it comes to food fraud, I do not know whether to multiply by two or ten.'[31]

Food scandals still happen frequently, and they shock and outrage us, just as they did in Accum's time. And, while today's adulteration is overall less harmful to human health than the fraud in the nineteenth century, poisonous substances can still find their way into our food.

In the early 2000s the growing use of azo dyes, especially Sudan Red, to adulterate chilli powder came under scrutiny by food authorities in Europe, and in 2003 the EU issued a directive requiring all dried and ground chilli entering the EU to be certified free of Sudan Red. At first it was thought that the adulteration only occurred amongst producers in India, but the list rapidly grew to include other chilli producing countries such as China, Pakistan, South Africa, and Turkey. Sudan dyes are usually used to colour waxes, solvents, polishes, and certain fabrics, and they have not been legal for food use in the EU since 1997 because of their potential carcinogenic properties. Swindling chilli producers had used Sudan Red to colour chilli powder adulterated with stems, seeds, and other bulking material, so that the characteristic bright red nuance could be achieved. This scandal culminated in 2005 with the recall of more than 350 products in the UK because contaminated chillies had been used as ingredients in a variety of products like Worcestershire sauce, which had in turn been used as ingredients in processed foods.[32]

Today we no longer see counterfeit peppercorns made from floor sweepings and linseed oil cakes, but that does not mean that fraud with pepper has disappeared. Today's preferred pepper adulterant is dried papaya seeds. The seeds are only a little bit smaller than real peppercorns and are readily available. Spices are still one of the most vulnerable foods when it comes to fraud, and, since they are integral to food cultures all around the globe, spices will continue to play a part in the future story of adulteration.

97

Notes

1   Friedrich Christian Accum, *A Treatise on Adulteration of Food, and Culinary Poisons, Exhibiting the Fraudulent Sophistications of Bread, Beer, Wine, Spirituous Liquors, Tea, Oil, Pickles, and Other Articles Employed in Domestic Economy. And Methods of Detecting Them*, 2nd ed. (London: Longman, Hurst, Rees, Orme, and Brown, 1820), p. IV <https://archive.org/details/treatiseonadulteooaccurich> [accessed 20 April 2021].

2   Ezra Bejar, 'Adulteration of Oregano Herb and Essential Oil', *Botanical Adulterants Prevention Bulletin* (Austin, TX: ABC-AHP-NCNPR Botanical Adulterants Prevention Program, 2019), pp. 1-10.

3   Jeffrey M. Pilcher, *Food in World History* (New York: Routledge, 2006), p. 55.

4   Alphonse Normandy, *The Commercial Hand-Book of Chemical Analysis: Or, Practical Instructions for the Determination of the Intrinsic or Commercial Value of Substances Used in Manufactures, in Trades, and in*

the Arts (London: George Knight and Sons, 1850). p. iii.

5 Accum, p. III.

6 Bee Wilson, *Swindled from Poison Sweets to Counterfeit Coffee the Dark History of the Food Cheats* (London: John Murray, 2009), p. 1.

7 Richard Evershed and Nicola Temple, *Sorting the Beef from the Bull: The Science of Food Fraud Forensics* (London: Bloomsbury, 2017), p. 210.

8 Accum, p. 285.

9 Accum, p. 286.

10 Clifford Richardson, *Foods and Food Adulterants. Second Part. Spices and Condiments* (Washington, DC: Government Printing Office, 1887), p. 133 <https://archive.org/details/foodsfoodadulter13rich> {accessed 20 April 2021].

11 Wilson, p. 127.

12 Arthur Hill Hassall, *Food and Its Adulterations: Comprising the Reports of the Analytical Sanitary Commission of 'The Lancet' for the Years 1851 to 1854 Inclusive* (London: Longman, Brown, Green, and Longmans, 1855), p. 1.

13 'Engelsk Udtalelse om 'Elisabethsminde's' Kakaopulver', *Den til Forsendelse med de Kongelige Brevposter privilegerede Berlingske Politiske og Avertissementstidende* 29 (4 February 1889), 1 (all translations by the author unless otherwise noted).

14 Richardson, p. 131.

15 Deborah Blum, *The Poison Squad: One Chemist's Single-Minded Crusade for Food Safety at the Turn of the Twentieth Century* (New York: Penguin, 2018), p. 31.

16 Richardson, p. 144.

17 Wilson, pp. 93-150.

18 Wilson, p. 164.

19 Helle Blomquist, 'Kager og legetøj: første positivliste for levnedsmidler', *Fortid og nutid* (1992), pp. 2-15.

20 Richardson, p. 164.

21 'Cigarkassetræ som Kanel og Sand som stødt Peber!', *Demokraten*, 55.90 (3 April 1937), 6.

22 'Erstatningsindustrien blomstrer som aldrig før', *Landbrugernes Dagblad. Maribo*, 11.121 (29 May 1942), 5.

23 'Husmoderforeningens eneste mandlige Medlem giver gode Raad', *Ribe Stifts-Tidende*, 159.211 (14 September 1944), 4.

24 'Krydderier af Bøgetræ', *Thisted Amtsavis*, 119.194 (24 August 1942), p. 8.

25 'Ikke al vor Mad taaler at blive set igennem en Lup', *Horsens Social-Demokrat*, 54.203 (3 September 1942), 1.

26 'Savsmuld, Kakaoskaller og Borsyre som Menneskeføde!', *Demokraten*, 59.2323 (26 August 1941), 6.

27 Hassall, p. 401.

28 Herluf Petersen, *Spisekammeret paa Grøftekanten: vilde danske Planter, der kan anvendes i Husholdningen* (Slagelse: Poul Carit Andersen, 1940), p. 12.

29 'Krydderurter', *Ærø Avis*, 84.140 (21 June 1941), 4..

30 Jan Krag Jacobsen, 'Adulteration as part of Authenticity', *Authenticity in the Kitchen: Proceedings of the Oxford Symposium on Food and Cookery 2005*, ed. by Richard Hosking (Totnes: Prospect Books, 2006) pp. 252-61 (p. 254).

31 Kristoffer Lottrup, 'Falsk føde', *Weekendavisen*, 24 October 2019, p. 53 <http://www.weekendavisen.dk/content/item/23176> [accessed 21 April 2021].

32 Steven Jaffee and others. *The Safe Food Imperative: Accelerating Progress in Low- and Middle-Income Countries* (Washington, DC: World Bank, 2018), p. 51.

Travelling with a Hairy Heart, or Where Cooking with Annatto Can Take You

Janet Beizer

Gastronomy is a narrative.
— Richard Sennett[1]

Origins

Like many stories, this one opens with a recipe. And recipes are always already stories; they unfold in time and space, open embedded narratives, and branch into tangential chronicles as they do so.[2] In what follows, I will be guided by the trajectory of a seed through a recipe and beyond.

Bò Kho is a Vietnamese braised beef dish I had been eager to turn my hand to for a good while. A product of the French colonization of Indochina, the stew infuses a traditional French *ragoût* with no less traditional Vietnamese spices and herbs. A cold snap last winter offered a compelling prompt for experimentation. I combed through two recipes, one from David Tanis and another from Andrea Nguyen, and then prepared for my venture by collecting star anise, five-spice powder, cinnamon sticks, ginger root, carrots, shallots, scallions, tomatoes, and garlic from my larder.[3] A supermarket sweep produced most of the remaining ingredients: beef chuck, fresh lemongrass, basil, cilantro, and tiny, fiery Thai red peppers. Neither home nor grocery shelves yielded annatto seed, however. After scouring the spice racks of a number of Boston-area markets to no avail, I turned to various books about herbs and spices, as well as the internet, to find images of this spice whose name I knew but had never seen, nor, to my knowledge, smelled or tasted.

Annatto, I learned, was the crimson, heart-shaped seed of a shrubby tree whose leaves are also formed like hearts. The seeds are borne in similarly red, heart-shaped pods covered with spikey hairs that make them resemble a cross between a porcupine and a hirsute strawberry. Each pod reportedly contains ten to fifty seeds, likening them visually to a bursting pomegranate. But not a single one of these seeds was to be found in any of my ordinarily well-supplied local grocery stores. Though the ingredient was in fact bracketed as optional in my recipes, by the time I had reached this point of the quest, my curiosity was piqued by every single one of the bristles on the surface of each fruit of the densely-podded bushes in the multitudes of images I had uncovered, and I would not give up; nor could I resign myself to buy the spice online and await delivery. The moment was ripe (as were the other ingredients in my refrigerator). And so I began a series of phone inquiries. By early evening, I was closer. Formaggio, my local purveyor of cheese and fine food, actually carried them – but was temporarily out of stock. Finally I hit pay dirt: there was a stash of annatto seeds not on the shelf, but sequestered in the basement of Savenor's (appropriately, Julia Child's favourite butcher shop in Cambridge), as if they were a secret treasure trove, the beating red heart of the establishment. The shop was closing for the day but promised them for the morning.

Waiting for Annatto: Background

Meanwhile, in the hours before my annatto pickup, I continued to read about the science and folklore of the spice, not always able to discern where to draw the line between the two. Cultivated throughout history for its culinary uses as both a colourant and an aromatic, but also for its nutritional and medicinal properties, the annatto seed reads on paper as on the internet as a botanical miracle. Originating in the Amazonian rainforest, it has long been used by indigenous peoples for ritual body paint; dye for feathers, rugs, and pottery; insect repellent; and sunscreen – though paradoxically, in South America today it is often combined with monoï oil as a tanning agent. It is also used in cosmetics such as eyeshadow and lip colour (the annatto shrub is commonly called 'lipstick tree' in a number of languages). It is a good source of vitamin A (it is one hundred times higher in beta-carotene than carrots, though to eat even one carrot's weight in annatto seed would be a feat); it is also a source of calcium, selenium, and vitamin E. It is reputed to have healing powers that aid in the formation of scar tissue; it neutralizes free radicals and boosts the immune system; it regulates the oxidation of blood lipids, benefiting cardiac health; it is reputed to be an anti-inflammatory, an antiseptic, an antifungal agent, an emollient. More specifically, it is touted as an antivenin (an antidote for snake bite), an eyewash, an acne treatment, an expectorant, a laxative, and an aphrodisiac.[4]

Into the Kitchen

I was not prepared for the sheer loveliness of the seeds. Mounded tightly in the clear-topped container in which they were delivered, the flinty, blood-red shards looked like infinitesimal arrowheads, so many tiny, hardened hearts rattling thinly when shaken. When ground to a powder in my spice mill, the seeds turned a dusty, earthy pinkish-red, something glowing and crepuscular, reminiscent of the colour of the ochre cliffs of Roussillon in the south of France. The taste was not close to anything I had imagined after reading numerous descriptions that ranged from 'practically no flavour' to 'lightly peppery with a note of nutmeg', to 'smooth, fruity, reminiscent of passionfruit [...] smooth giving way to bitter', to 'slightly sweet and peppery'.[5] Taste tends to be subjective, of course; for me, the seeds, both whole and ground to a dust, have an earthy, slightly horseradish-like flavour that is deep and mellow, if subtle. I therefore increased the quantity suggested by my recipe by one and a half. The result was spectacular in a muted, complex way; the powdered annatto gave depth to the pungency of the ginger, garlic, shallots, and hot peppers and the acidity of the tomatoes, gently lacing through them the sweet richness of the star anise and cinnamon. Its background warmth balanced the fresh sharpness of the cilantro, scallions, and Thai basil that are showered on the finished stew in the serving bowl. Contrary to culinary commentary I'd read about the spice, I found that it added more to the general flavour profile of the dish than to its colour. The tomatoes worked more powerfully to redden the rusty brown of the beef, and the annatto powder seemed only to impart a very faint dusky tinge to the reddish-brown sauce against the striking orange contrast of the carrot chunks.

Bò Kho recipes mostly call for chunked chuck, considered to be one of the less noble cuts of beef; it often is marinated, and stands up to long slow cooking. Lengthy braising time of course breaks down fat and gristle. When I turned to Julia Child to see what cuts she recommended for traditional French recipes based on similar techniques of browning and then braising (fricassees and ragoûts), I noted that she liked rump pot roast or sirloin tip as well or better, and counselled: 'the better the meat, the better the stew'.[6]

Yet Julia's advice to Americans seeking to master French cooking has little to do with the socioeconomic reality of what today might be called Vietnamese-French 'fusion cooking'. Let me stop for a moment to consider the fusional nature of *Bò Kho*: it combines French cooking techniques, as in a *boeuf aux carottes*, for example, or other braised dishes, and Southeast Asian flavours. But let's take a second look at 'fusion cooking' as it happened in late nineteenth-century Indochina, where *Bò Kho* originated under the French colonialist regime, though decidedly not at the hands of the French masters. There was no question of French chefs or their masters' wives adapting French recipes to assimilate Vietnamese spices and herbs; on the contrary, they were 'purists', as Monique Truong puts it succinctly in her novel, *The Book of Salt*. Head chefs were classically trained in France, and the rallying cry of the imperial households in which they worked was 'As if in France!'[7]

The hierarchy that reinforced French domination in Indochina extended to diet, so much so that the colonists would eat canned goods imported from France rather than fresh local products.[8] *Bò Kho* and other dishes we often think of as traditionally Vietnamese (such as *Phò*) were instead created by indigenous cooks to whom devolved the dregs of French kitchens. Prior to French conquest, buffalo rather than cows provided meat in Indochina (in addition to pork, poultry, and fish): they were the beasts of burden used in rice farming, and were sourced as food when they became 'injured or sick'.[9] It was only after the French had established sovereignty and residence in the colony and insisted on eating as if at home in the hexagon that beef cattle began to be imported, first from neighbouring Cambodia, and by the end of the century from Brittany, Normandy, and Switzerland. While prime cuts of beef were unaffordable to most of the local population, they took advantage of the discarded remains. Nguyen reports that 'resourceful Vietnamese cooks, left with only a carcass after the colonialists carved off their beef steaks, used the scraps to create popular dishes like *bò kho* [...] and *phò bò*'.[10]

And Peters elaborates: 'Beef broths had not been common in either Vietnamese or Chinese cooking, but during colonialism French consumption of beef left the bones and other scraps available [...] Networks of Chinese and Vietnamese who cooked or butchered meat for the French most likely diverted beef remnants to street soup vendors.'[11]

While much ink has been spilled of late in discussions of the demerits of fusion cooking as a form of cultural appropriation and exploitation, the case of *Bò Kho* suggests that culinary fusing is at least sometimes a bottom-up rather than a top-down process. While the forces of hierarchy and hegemony do not change, the direction of borrowing and the source of creativity do.

Translations

But what ship, what wind of trade or conquest carried annatto halfway around the world to Southeast Asia from its origins in the South American rainforest? Though I cannot trace the specific routes that took annatto to Vietnam, it is commonly (if vaguely) thought to have been introduced to warm regions across the globe by the Spanish over the course of the seventeenth century. It does well in tropical or subtropical zones with heavy rainfall, and is now heavily cultivated in Asia, Africa, and Central America as well as its South American homeland.

Linguistic as well as spatial translations have been helpful to me in understanding annatto's pathways through history and story as well as geography. Its Latin botanical classification, *Bixa orellana*, combines the word for the plant in the aboriginal Taino language, *bixa*, with the modifier taken from the name of the sixteenth-century explorer and conquistador Francisco de Orellana, who claimed much of the Amazon region for Spain. One might say that the history of the world is contained in this microcosmic botanical pod, summed up in the double name that tacitly acknowledges a pattern of indigenous origination and foreign annexation.

Annatto is perhaps best known today by its Spanish name *achiote* and its culinary applications under that name in Mexican and other Central American cuisines (*recado rojo* or *achiote* paste, *empanandas, tamales*, and *tascalate*, the spiced chocolate-roasted maize drink – to name just a few). It is widely used in meat marinades all over South America. In the Philippines, where it is known as *atsuete*, it is used widely in the preparation of *adobo* and other dishes. It is common as well in Jamaica, in the Antilles, and in Cuba and Puerto Rico, where it is an ingredient of *sofrito*. Globally, it tends to be substituted, when necessary, for the more expensive saffron. In French, annatto is variously known as *le roucou, le rocou, le raucourt* (all deformations of the word used in Portuguese, *urucú*, which in fact is taken from the indigenous Tupi language name for the spice, which means 'red'.)

Underground Butter: *Les Halles*

As I followed the translations of the seed across languages and topographies, I realized that I had already 'met' annatto under its French identity in Zola's 1873 marketplace novel, *The Belly of Paris* (*Le Ventre de Paris*). Zola's revelation of the sordid activities of the underground spaces of *Les Halles* (the central market of Paris) ranges from the mouth-to-mouth force-feeding of pigeons moments before slaughter, to the sorting and re-assembly of partially consumed meals for re-sale, to the cosmeticizing treatment of inferior butter with *le raucourt*, now known to me alternatively as annatto.

In the cellar of the butter pavilion, we find the *marchande de beurre*, Mme Lecoeur, with her bare arms plunged to the elbows in the mountain of fat she is kneading in order to meld different mounds of sundry origin together, like a winemaker seeking to minimize the flaws and mediocrities of certain varietals.[12] In the case of this particular *caviste*, some of the varietals are not merely substandard, but blatantly rancid, and her well-pounded amalgam is chalky white, perhaps because she has already processed the spoiled butter with lime chloride (a bleaching powder), as one common method prescribed (p. 329).[13] For the next step, Mme Lecoeur has at the ready on her table 'a small pot full of a kind of red dye', which, Zola explains, will give the mass of butter a 'nice yellow colour'. He adds that the vendors 'believe they are keeping the dye a strict secret, though its source is simply the seed of the annatto tree; it is true that they also make such dye from carrots and marigolds'. We are led to wonder if the frugal Mme Lecoeur may in fact have substituted one of these second-rate colourants, or if she simply skimped on the annatto seed, for her niece, a former butter vendor herself, mutters, when she peers into the crock of dye: 'your annatto is too pale' (pp. 330-31).

Annatto was not a particularly rare ingredient at this point in late nineteenth-century Paris, however, and was likely not costly. My research suggests that at the time Zola was writing his marketplace novel, it was in fact plentiful, imported mainly from the French colonies of Guiana and Guadeloupe – and primarily from French Guiana, until its cultivation there dramatically declined after 1880.[14] Since Guadeloupean annatto was found to be more bitter, the Guianese source was preferred, especially for culinary uses.[15] In France at this time it was used to dye silk as well as to colour butter, margarine (first made in 1869), cheese, and more. *103*

Zola says nothing in his novel about the origins of the dye Mme Lecoeur uses to prepare her blended butter for sale. This in itself might be attributable to oversight or ignorance on his part, or even just to a decision to streamline his narrative (though spare, sleek expositions are certainly not his custom, and his food scenes are barded with minutely researched information). What is odd about his origin-less presentation of *le raucourt* in the otherwise intricately detailed butter scene of *Belly of Paris* is that French Guiana (referred to most often in metonymic shorthand by the name of its capital, Cayenne) otherwise plays a crucial, insistent – if shadowy – role throughout his novel.[16]

In the Penal Colony: French Guiana[17]

Florent, the antihero of *The Belly of Paris*, enters the novel – and re-enters Paris – in the spring of 1859, after an absence of eight years. During this interim period, initiated by his arrest as a political dissident and his sentencing to the prison colony on Devil's

Island in French Guiana, he was confined there for several years before escaping to make his long, tortuous way back to Paris first by land, through Dutch Guiana (today Surinam), and then by sea.[18]

Florent's fraught return to Paris, outfitted with false papers and consumed by a dread of detection, is studded with nightmarish flashbacks to his years in the penal colony: a diet of maggot-infested rice and spoiled meat; ever vigilant guards with raised whips; relentless mosquito attacks; dangerous ocean swells; forest floors swarming with venomous snakes; alligator-infested waters and quicksand pathways; boa constrictors as thick as tree trunks; a reunion with a companion turned corpse, his extremities mauled and his gaping belly crawling with crabs; the tantalizing lure of poisonous berries to starving men (pp. 140-52). Notwithstanding all this local lore, there is not one annatto tree reference, not one blood-red *graine de rocouyer* (annatto seed) in Zola's Guiana. And this despite the fact that one of his principal sources for the Guiana passages of the novel, the writer Eugène Sue, describes the chief of a local tribe painted red head-to-toe with an annatto-derived dye, in an 1840 novel set in Dutch and French Guiana, *The Adventures of Hercules Hardy or Guiana in 1772* (*Aventures d'Hercule Hardi ou la Guyane en 1772*).[19]

France's South American colony seems to be important to Zola's novel as a dramatic counterpoint to his complacent Paris eaters, a way to imply to his readers the depths of metropolitan savagery and predation by analogy with the exotic examples of distant rainforest jungles metaphorically present in the laws of the Parisian marketplace. But he prefers to confine realist detail to Paris spaces, leaving unspoken the derivation of the dye, and the seeds, and the tree he names in his detailed exposition of butter making. To describe the French Guiana origins of the red seed would mean engaging with a story of plantations, slavery, and post-slavery, indentured labour, freed slaves, covert settlements of escaped slaves, and a lingering population of indigenous tribes. And that part of empire would be beside the point of his Second Empire novel.[20]

Food in a Time of Corona

When I started thinking about this paper in January of 2020, we lived in a different world. Had I moved on to research and writing then, the paper would doubtless have unfolded differently. This is true on a very pragmatic level. As I turned to the writing of the paper in May of that same year, I had access only to what was available on my home bookshelves or what branched into my home office from the web. This meant having recourse to what my graduate students call 'pantry writing', an appropriate metaphor for this venue, but in reality a somewhat limiting one.

On a more metaphysical level, I recognize that the passage from January to May put me, like most of us, in a place of confinement with no known hour of exit. It changed the experience of time, and so necessarily altered the kind of narrative I could write. Both factors, the material and the abstract, fused to turn this paper into a more personal, even on some perhaps not entirely perceptible level, a more intimate one.

Where I live, as in much of the world, flour is now almost unattainable, and butter is hard to find. We all seem to be cooking more. The Sunday *New York Times* now includes an 'At Home' section that suggests recipes and recommends books to read. We need stories to feed our socially isolated bodies and recipes to nourish our conversationally segregated minds. If food is good to think with, as Claude Lévi-Strauss famously observed, so are stories, and stories about food may be especially helpful. I made a second rendition of *Bò Kho* as I started to write this paper, for some reason that escapes me but that probably has to do with confinement. I'm not sure I would have been propelled to rehearse a beef stew I had already prepared, photographed, and mentally annotated in far more appropriate winter climes, in the 80-degree temperatures of a summer heatwave, if life had been flowing in its regular channels.

In the country where I am now embarrassed to live, the pandemic has been irrevocably laced with racial and social injustices, as many have powerfully commented and explored. Otherwise said, the pandemic has brought into clear focus the extreme racial and social hierarchies inherent in our political structures that help to determine who lives and who dies, and how living and dying are differently experienced. That the murder of George Floyd in Minneapolis, the racist accusations against black bird-watcher Christian Cooper by a white woman in New York's Central Park, the arrest of black-latino CNN reporter Omar Jimenez in Minneapolis, the killing of Breonna Taylor in Louisville, and the shooting of Ahmaud Arbery in South Georgia have been backlit by the Covid 19 virus – and vice versa – has served to highlight the deeper and more entrenched viruses raging among us.[21]

Writing about the global circuit of annatto in the light of Coronavirus, which I take to mean as well in the shadow of the racial and economic pandemic that is harrowing the US today, I have tended to see the spice in the stark terms of hierarchy, conquest, and domination. This is not the whole picture, but it is surely a viable angle of perception. Looking again at my little vial of densely packed annatto seeds tonight as I finish this coda, I cannot help but see them realigned in the now-familiar formation of the electron microscope image of the virus, with the fiery red seeds positioned as spikes on the outer surface of the virus, like the flare of a corona surrounding the virion.

Notes

1   Richard Sennett, *The Craftsman* (New Haven: Yale University Press, 2008), p. 189.

2   My thanks to Barbara K. Wheaton for introducing me to the world of storied recipes in her seminar at the Schlesinger Library of Harvard University several years back.

3   Andrea Quynhgiao Nguyen, *Into the Vietnamese Kitchen: Treasured Foodways, Modern Flavors* (Berkeley: Ten Speed Press, 2006), pp. 151-52; David Tanis, 'Vietnamese Braised Beef Stew (*Bo Kho*)', *NYT Cooking* <https://cooking.nytimes.com/recipes/1019891-vietnamese-braised-beef-stew-bo-kho> [accessed 18 January 2020].

4   This is a very brief compendium of a much longer list of uses and properties widely ascribed to annatto. For the most complete scientific paper compiling these, see Catherine Ulbricht and others, 'An Evidence-Based Systematic Review of Annatto (*Bixa Orellana* L.) by the Natural Standard Research

Collaboration', *Journal of Dietary Supplements*, 9.1 (2012), 57-77. For broad-ranging folkloric accounts – which interestingly often overlap with scientific indications – follow the numerous internet entries for the name of the tree in as many languages as possible.

5   Ben-Erik Van Wyk, *Culinary Herbs & Spices of the World* (Chicago: University of Chicago Press, 2013), pp. 82-83; N.A. 'Roucou: *Bixa orellana*' in Wikipédia <https://fr.wikipedia.org/wiki/Roucou> [accessed 27 May 2020]; N.A., 'Graines de Rocou' <https://ileauxepices.com/epices/368-1379-rocou.html> [accessed 19 January 2020]; Ulbricht, p. 58. All translations from the French throughout this paper are mine.

6   Julia Child, Louisette Bertholle, and Simone Beck, *Mastering the Art of French Cooking*, 2 vols. (New York: Knopf, 1983 [1961]), vol. I, p. 314. In a second rendition I used sirloin tips; the finished beef was slightly more tender but didn't hold together very well.

7   See Monique Truong, *The Book of Salt* (New York: Houghton Mifflin, 2003), pp. 42, 46. I take the liberty of citing this novel and giving it evidentiary value because it corroborates starkly and forcefully what I have read elsewhere in more documentary accounts of Vietnamese cuisine (see Nguyen, and Peters, below).

8   See Ericka J. Peters, *Appetites and Aspirations in Vietnam: Food and Drink in the Long Nineteenth Century* (Plymouth, UK: AltaMira Press [Rowman and Littlefield], 2012), pp. 154-55. She makes the interesting distinction between military and civilian French settlers, on the one hand, and missionaries, on the other, who understood the symbolic importance of alimentary acceptance and assimilation and consumed the local diet to a greater or lesser extent (pp. 39-42, 155).

9   Peters, p. 163.

10 Ngyuen, p. 9.

11 Peters, p. 204.

12 Émile Zola, *Le Ventre de Paris*, ed. by Henri Mitterand (Paris, Gallimard [Folio], 2002 [1873]), pp. 329-31. Subsequent references are cited in the text.

13 See Rosalie Blanquet, *La Cuisinière des ménages ou manuel pratique de cuisine et d'économie domestique pour la ville et la campagne* (Paris: Théodore Lefèvre et Cie, 1881), pp. 493-94; cited in Marni Reva Kessler, *Discomfort Food: The Culinary Imagination in Late Nineteenth-Century Art* (Minneapolis: University of Minnesota Press, forthcoming, 2021), p. xx. See Kessler's chapter 2, 'Clarifying and Compounding Antoine Vollon's *Mound of Butter*' for more details on the various methods of disguising rancid butter.

14 See Serge Mam Lam Fouck, *La Guyane française au temps de l'esclavage, de l'or et de la francisation (1802-1946)* (Petit Bourg, Guadeloupe: Ibis Rouge Editions, 1999). Mam Lam Fouck gives cotton, sugarcane, and annatto as the dominant crops in French Guiana beginning in the eighteenth century, though they each evolved differently over the course of the nineteenth century: cotton production declined, as did that of sugarcane, faced with competition from the developing production of beetroot sugar in France, while annatto production, 'benefitting from a near-monopoly on the metropolitan market, managed to maintain itself in spite of depreciating values' (pp. 141-42). Even after the abolition of slavery, the production of annatto held fast and then rose to a high in 1869 and a near-high in 1878 (pp. 219, 229). Intermittent lulls in cultivation and exportation were responsive to lowered prices, suggesting that the spice was plentiful and easily available in France, which purchased eighty percent of its colony's exports. It was only in the 1880s that annatto plantations began to undergo massive abandonment, as French Guiana ceased to be an agricultural colony, largely due to the discovery of gold; it would progressively shift in the direction of mining and penitentiary establishments (p. 230).

15 This distinction is reported in an entry under the title, 'Annatto (*Bixa Orellana*, L.)' of the Kew *Bulletin of Miscellaneous Information, Royal Gardens* no. 7, July 1887 (London: Eyre and Spottiswode, 1887), p. 6.

16 Zola borrowed heavily for this butter tableau as for many background details of his novel from his friend Maxime du Camp's massive documentary work, *Paris, ses organes, ses fonctions, et sa vie jusqu'en 1870* (Monaco: G. Rondeau, 1993 [1869-75]).

17 I note in passing that it is widely assumed that the unnamed French Caribbean island site of Franz Kafka's short story, 'In the Penal Colony', published in 1919, was French Guiana.

18 While France had established a colony at Cayenne as early as 1664, and chose French Guiana as a

place to banish counter-Revolutionaries in the 1790s, the first penal colony per se was instituted in 1852, intended initially primarily for political dissidents, but shortly thereafter for convicts as well. The principle of *doublage*, which obliged those sentenced to fewer than eight years to spend an equivalent time in the colony once freed, yoked penalization to colonization, a policy that was instrumental to the imperial project following the abolition of slavery in 1848. See Charles Forsdick, 'Postcolonializing the Bagne', *French Studies*, 82.2 (2018), 237-55, and Miranda Spieler, *Empire and Underworld: Captivity in French Guiana* (Cambridge, MA: Harvard University Press, 2012).

19 In fact Sue writes '*l'arnoka*', which does not exist in any dictionary I have found, but the very similar '*l'arnotta*', diverging by a mere phoneme, is given as another word for annatto (attributed to Native American) by Ulbricht, p. 57: 'The chief of the tribe [...] had his entire body painted bright red, by means of annatto seed mixed with castor oil' ('*le chef de la tribu* [...] *avait le corps entièrement teint en rouge vif, au moyen de la semence d'arnoka mélangée dans de l'huile de castor*') (*Aventures d'Hercule Hardi ou la Guyane en 1772* in *Deux Histoires* (Paris: Librairie Internationale, 1869 [1840]), p. 24). Sue's Guianese novel is a compendium of tropical exotica, a picture of forests swarming with escaped slaves and native tribes set against renditions of rampant flora and fauna that seem to anticipate in words the paintings of the *Douanier* Rousseau.

20 See Jennifer Yee, *The Colonial Comedy: Imperialism in the French Realist Novel* (Oxford: Oxford University Press, 2016) for some excellent pages on how Zola confronts and avoids French colonialism in *Le Ventre de Paris* (pp. 137-43)

21 As I revise this essay some months after its initial drafting, I resist – both to remain faithful to my timeline and to keep my narrative from overflowing – the impulse to add to the list of acts of racist violence those that have followed since then. It is banal but necessary nonetheless to add that the violence continued – continues – to flood our American lives.

Shichimi: The Spice, its Trade, and Centuries of Food Business Survival in Japan

Voltaire Cang

Introduction

Japanese cuisine is not known for its spiciness, and its flavour descriptions are often confined to 'subtle', 'mild', and 'natural', sometimes 'bland', but almost never 'hot' or 'spicy'. Spices, however, have been in use in Japan from its early history: the *Kojiki* ('Records of Ancient Matters') from 712, the country's oldest extant literary and historical text, includes several references to *sanshō* (Japanese pepper or prickly-ash), which is indigenous to the Japanese archipelago, as well as ginger. Texts from later eras also describe other spices and condiments such as black pepper, sesame, and wasabi. And the Shosoin Repository, the treasure house in the ancient capital of Nara that stores valuable arts and crafts of the ancient imperial court from the eighth century, includes actual spices like cloves, cinnamon, and black pepper in its vast collection; these would have been brought into the country from Southeast Asia through mainland China.[1]

Most of these ancient spices and condiments, however, were used for purposes other than cooking, as in the treatment of various ailments, as aphrodisiacs, or as incense for burning in shrines and temples. Only much later during the Edo period (1603-1868) did spices begin to regularly appear in food preparation, as various cookbooks from the period recommended their use. For example, *Shirōtobōchō,* one of the most referenced cooking manuals from the eighteenth century, lists scallions and red chilli pepper among the main ingredients for *taimeshi* (sea bream rice), a dish that is still eaten today but is generally prepared without chilli.

Spices' late entry into the culinary repertoire may account for their relative obscurity in Japanese cuisine today, even as many so-called 'traditional' Japanese dishes do call for the addition of certain spices to 'complete' their preparation, such as the sprinkle of powdered *sanshō* over grilled eel and the dab of wasabi between raw fish and rice in sushi. Several spices feature regularly in Japanese cuisine, if one just knows where to look. Among these different spices, the most widely used and, thus, prominent would be *shichimi tōgarashi*, or simply, *shichimi*.

Shichimi is actually a spice blend that is made with seven ingredients (*shichi*=seven; *mi*=taste). Its main component is coarsely ground red chilli pepper (*tōgarashi*), into which are added any six of the following: roasted chilli pepper, *sanshō*, hemp seeds, black sesame seeds, white sesame seeds, *chimpi* (dried tangerine peel), dried green *shiso* (perilla) leaves, dried purple *shiso* leaves, poppy seeds, nori seaweed, rapeseeds, and ginger. Recent blend variations incorporate dried yuzu peel and powdered wasabi, as well as 'non-traditional' ingredients such as garlic, basil, oregano, cloves, and cumin, among others.

Like *sanshō* for eel and wasabi for sushi, *shichimi* is usually added as a final touch to the food, especially since its complex but delicate flavours can get lost during the cooking process. In many cases, it is sprinkled on food just before it is consumed, by the person eating the dish, and not by its cook. And there are many such dishes *shichimi* is sprinkled onto: *udon* and soba noodles served in broth, ramen, *oyakodon* (chicken and eggs over rice in a bowl), *gyūdon* (beef over rice in a bowl), *yakitori* (grilled chicken on skewers), grilled fish and seafood, various soups and hotpot dishes, *tsukemono* pickles, and all kinds of boiled vegetables. With *shichimi*, one would say that Japanese food can be hot and spicy.

The recent global boom in Japanese food, and especially that of ramen and other noodle dishes, has resulted in the growing popularity of *shichimi* worldwide. In early 2019, Bloomberg devoted one news report solely to *shichimi*, calling it 'the Japanese spice blend slowly taking over America'. The article described American chefs' fascination with the spice and the novel ways it is used in their restaurants and bars all over the country, such as in salads, on eggs Benedict, in Mexican-inspired dishes, over fried chicken, and in cocktails (*shichimi*-spiced Bloody Mary, anyone?).[2]

While new to American food culture, *shichimi* significantly predates the United States, having been produced and marketed in its country of origin since the early seventeenth century. There are three main producers of *shichimi* in Japan today: Yagenbori, established in 1625 in Tokyo; Shichimiya Honpo, c. 1655, in Kyoto; and Yawataya Isogoro, the youngest, from 1736, in Nagano. All three engage solely in the *shichimi* trade and continue to do brisk business in the present. They are also among the oldest businesses in Japan, which currently boasts more than 1400 companies aged at least two hundred years, the majority of them producing food, including condiments and confectionery, and drinks like sake.[3]

This paper considers *shichimi* and utilizes the spice's trade among its major purveyors as a lens for looking into relevant issues that help explain the reasons for the longevity of food business enterprises in Japan. For background, a brief history of *shichimi* is offered immediately below, as gleaned from the few sources available.

Shichimi: A Short History

The story of *shichimi* must begin with the story of its chief ingredient, the red chilli pepper, and its arrival in Japan. While historical sources on the chilli pepper in Japan are much easier to find than accounts dealing only with *shichimi*, available texts have not settled debates on the routes by which the red chilli pepper came to the country. Historians generally subscribe to one of three narratives, as follows.

One: *Shichimi* first arrived in Japan through a Portuguese Jesuit mission led by one Balthazar Gago that landed in Bungo Province (most of Oita Prefecture today) in the southern island of Kyushu in 1552. They had brought pumpkin and chilli pepper seeds among their gifts for the *daimyō* (provincial lord), Ōtomo Sōrin.[4] Regarding this story, web and print articles, including some scholarly literature, place the year 1542 as the date the chilli pepper – perhaps its seeds – was first brought by the Portuguese. This date is erroneous, as will be explained immediately below, but it is widely cited since it comes from the *Sōmoku rikubu kōshuhō*, a thirty-volume encyclopedia from 1829 published by famed Edo-period farmer-philosopher (and physician) Satō Nobuhiro (1769-1850). This highly-regarded work explains the cultivation of nearly 300 useful plants – including chilli pepper – in scientific detail that was unprecedented in its time. In this work, Satō explicitly mentions that Portuguese visitors first brought chilli seeds to Japan from Brazil (then already occupied for several decades by Portugal), emphasizing the date 1542 as the year the travellers paid their respects to Sōrin.[5]

While there is little doubt today about the Brazilian connection – the chilli pepper is after all indigenous to Central and South America – the date could only be a typographical error, especially since other diaries and travel logs from the era expressly indicate the first visits to Bungo by the Portuguese as occurring in the 1550s, with a few expressly dating Gago's visit in 1552.[6] In any case, Sōrin would have only been twelve years old in 1542, a fact that is curiously neglected in some accounts on the chilli pepper's history in Japan. At this time Sōrin was yet to succeed his father as *daimyō*, which he did eight years later in 1550. He could not have received the Portuguese mission in the manner detailed by Satō in his treatise. As for the actual journey of the chilli pepper from South America to Japan, the consensus is that it followed a circuitous route, from Brazil to Portugal, then to Goa in the Indian subcontinent through to Southeast Asia and Macao, perhaps southern China, too, and finally southern Japan.[7]

Two: The second route concerns the famous and powerful ruler, Toyotomi Hideyoshi. Not a few histories credit Hideyoshi as the actual person to have brought chilli pepper to Japan in 1592, during the first of his two invasions of the Korean peninsula. The source for this origin story is, again, another famed writer, the botanist-philosopher Kaibara Ekiken (1630-1714). While Ekiken today is better known for his teachings on etiquette and moral behaviour, he had also published *Yamato Honzō* (1709), a sixteen-volume masterwork on medicinal plants – including references to a few other useful animals and minerals – that is considered the first botanical and agricultural science text in Japan. In this work, Ekiken explicitly states that 'Japan did not have chilli pepper, but when Hideyoshi struck that country [Korea], he brought back the seeds of what we now call Koryo [Korean] pepper'.[8]

This thesis is plausible, especially when one considers the looming presence of chilli in kimchi and other distinctive dishes in Korean cuisine today. However, Korean culinary historian and scientist Chong Dae-song asserts the reverse, declaring the chilli pepper as having been imported into the Korean Peninsula from Japan. He cites Yi Su-gwang's *Jibong Yuseol* from 1614, considered the earliest Korean encyclopedia, which also contains the oldest reference to chilli pepper in Korean literature. The *Jibong Yuseol*, says Chong, calls the chilli pepper 'Japan mustard/pepper' from its place of origin. (In this case, then, granting that Hideyoshi did bring chilli into Japan from Korea, he could just as well have inadvertently re-imported it back into the country.[9]) As for the chilli pepper's indispensability to kimchi, Chong also states this was to come much later: none of the Korean cookbooks written before the late seventeenth century included it in any of the recipes for what is now the Korean national dish, he notes.[10]

Historians who engage in the Japan-or-Korea debate generally maintain that the chilli pepper came to either country by the Pacific route: through Mexico to the Philippines and other islands of Southeast Asia, then on to the Asian continent and/or Japan. It bears mentioning that neither Ekiken in Japan nor Yi in Korea describes the culinary uses of the chilli pepper. The former refers to it as an ornamental plant that could be used to cure headaches and chills, while Yi determines it to be poisonous.[11]

Three: Still another historical encyclopedia, the *Wakan sansai zue* (literally, 'Japan-China Illustrated Encyclopedia') compiled by Terajima Ryōan and published in 1712, forms the source for the third professed route taken by the chilli pepper to Japan. Ryōan's work is even more voluminous than the two multiple-volume anthologies mentioned above, comprising 105 volumes of facts about daily life in Japan and China, including the constellations and weather, daily life and activities, flora and fauna, etc. The *Wakan sansai zue* includes a brief description of the chilli pepper as a plant normally grown in Southeast Asia that was then brought to Japan by Portuguese traders together with tobacco at the end of the sixteenth century, specifically in the Keicho era (1596-1614).[12] Whether or not the chilli pepper came from elsewhere before Southeast Asia is not explained in the work.

Whichever of the three versions of history one accepts, the general conclusion is that the chilli pepper was already in Japan by the turn of the seventeenth century, having arrived by way of the Asian mainland or through Southeast Asia, most likely having been brought in by Portuguese traders or missionaries. After chilli's introduction to the country, it did not take long for it to evolve into *shichimi*. And concerning the origins of *shichimi*, we can but only turn to yet another encyclopedia, *Morisada mankō*.

Morisada mankō was written during a thirty-year span from 1837 by historian Kitagawa Morisada (pseudonym, 1810-unknown). The collection is composed of thirty-five comprehensive volumes that describe the history and development of daily life, including manners, customs, and material culture, in Japan's three major cities of Edo, Kyoto, and Osaka. For the purposes of this paper, it is also the earliest work in the literature that indicates the origin of the *shichimi* trade. Morisada states that it was one Nakajima Tokuemon who was the first person to produce and sell *shichimi*, in his shop in the downtown district of Ryogoku in Edo, in 1625. The shop's name was Yagenbori. From Ryogoku, the shop's location has since been moved to the Asakusa temple district in present-day Tokyo, where it still sells *shichimi* and is run by the tenth-generation owner.

Yagenbori was originally an herbalist's shop: the term *yagen* in its name refers to the chemist's mortar. According to the shop's official history, the first owner conceived of *shichimi* through advice from 'many herbalists and apothecaries who plied their trade in the area, [whereby] he created a new blend of spices that was not only tasty, but also healthful.

*Figure 1. Shichimi seller (*Kinsei akinai zukushi kyō utaawase, *1852), National Diet Library collection.*

Tokuemon called his blend *shichimi-togarashi* (seven-flavoured capsicum), and it gained such popularity with the citizens of Edo that the Yagenbori name became synonymous with the seven-flavoured spice itself'.[13] The historical text *Morisada mankō* states that from its early beginnings, the *shichimi* produced by Yagenbori was used as a flavouring for many kinds of food by the people of Edo. Tokuemon's shop sold its signature product in bamboo tube containers, as did other shops and itinerant street vendors.[14]

There is one existing illustration with accompanying text from the late Edo period, reproduced from earlier sources, that depicts an itinerant *shichimi* seller and his merchandise in very clear visual and textual detail (see figure 1). The illustration is from an 1852 publication named *Kinsei akinai zukushi kyō utaawase* (literally, 'Modern merchants' poetry collection'); its text, read from top to bottom, right to left, is translated as follows:[15]

Seven-Coloured Chilli Pepper

Come, let us talk of the
Very useful Yatsufusa chilli,[16] *the famous product from Naito in Yotsuya* [in Edo]

Here we have black sesame
to reinvigorate the spirit and give lustre to your hair
Then chimpi *that is made from mikan tangerine peel*
Its fruit is poisonous, but its skin is potent enough to cure colds
Poppy seeds
are [health] *supplements to help increase your body heat*
Hemp seeds
are good for curing sexually transmitted diseases
Sanshō
is a pungent medicine
Roasted chilli pepper
is pungent, fragrant, and delicious
Watch me fill up this bag, adding extra from all the bits that fall out
More, more, more, more

He says more; this is a short version
[Brief note at the end] *Finally, you add shiso and nori seaweed.*[17]

The seven ingredients of *shichimi* described in the text – red chilli pepper, black sesame, *chimpi,* poppy seeds, hemp seeds, *sanshō,* roasted chilli pepper – are the exact same ingredients that compose the signature *shichimi* product sold by Yagenbori in Tokyo today.

As mentioned above, Yagenbori is one of three major producers of traditional *shichimi* in Japan today. All three have different and distinct recipes for their flagship products, all of which have also remained unchanged since their establishment three centuries or more earlier. The table below lists the ingredients for each of the three major producers' flagship *shichimi* (Table 1). For Shichimiya Honpo in Kyoto, the blend includes dried chilli pepper, nori seaweed, *sanshō,* black sesame, white sesame, *shiso,* and hemp seeds. In the case of Yawataya Isogoro, it is composed of dried chilli pepper, ginger, *sanshō,* black sesame, *chimpi,* green *shiso,* and hemp seeds.

113

Yagenbori	Shichimiya Honpo	Yawataya Isogoro
Red chilli pepper	Dried chilli pepper	Dried chilli pepper
Sanshō	Sanshō	Sanshō
Black sesame	Black sesame	Black sesame
Hemp seeds	Hemp seeds	Hemp seeds
Chimpi	White sesame	Chimpi
Poppy seeds	Green Shiso	Green Shiso
Roasted chilli pepper	Nori seaweed	Ginger

Table 1. List of ingredients for shichimi from the three major producers

The *Shichimi* Trade and Company Longevity in Japan

As this paper is also an investigation of Japanese company longevity utilizing the *shichimi* food business as its lens, detailed descriptions of each of the three major producers would be ideal, if not imperative. Space constraints prevent a discussion of all three, however. The author had also initially planned to conduct an ethnographic study of Yagenbori, as it is the originator of *shichimi* and its main shop is easily accessible from the author's location in Tokyo. However, the current (early 2020) pandemic and resulting restrictions in movement prevented any such ethnographic study to even be initiated. In lieu of ethnographic information, this paper instead uses data from an oral history on the *shichimi* business of Shichimiya Honpo in Kyoto by its current head. This oral history was compiled from an interview conducted under the auspices of Kyoto Hyakumikai, an association of traditional businesses based in Kyoto.[18] Selected passages from the oral history describe aspects of the traditional *shichimi* trade that are relevant to the present discussion; these passages are interspersed with research information and explanation, as follows.

> Shichimiya Honpo (SH): *Our shop was established 350 years ago in the Meireki years [1655-1658] of the early Edo period [...]. Initially, we opened as a tea shop along the main road that leads to the Kiyomizu Temple, where travelling worshippers and the faithful could stop for tea and rest their legs on their way to the temple.*

Along with Yagenbori, which is found near the entrance to Asakusa Temple, and Yawataya Isogoro, which is within striking distance of the main gate to Zenkōji Temple in Nagano, all three shops are located near Japan's biggest and most famous Buddhist temples. The shops' prime location assures them of a constant stream of walk-in customers in addition to their regular clients (restaurants, food service establishments, individual customers, etc.). Their proximity to major religious institutions also accords their products a certain level of prestige – through implicit sanction from the temples – and enhanced desirability – with the temple's endorsement, the product could only be good for you – that may not be obtained in other locations.

> SH: *From the time red chilli pepper came to Japan during the Azuchi Momoyama period [1573-1603], people have known that chilli warms the body [...]. In our tea shop, we used to serve* karashi-yu, *hot water that contained a pinch of chilli, for worshippers to warm their bodies with. Our shop always stocked up on chilli for our customers. Before we knew it,* karashi-yu *became our best-seller, and in 1818, we changed our name to* Shichimiya ['Shichimi Shop'] *and sold shichimi exclusively.*

A great majority of Japan's longest-lived companies are famous for a single product, many that are tradition-oriented and possess historical and cultural cachet. Kyoto and Tokyo especially are home to many companies providing such culturally important products; these companies have been referred to by one author as 'living heritage industries'.[19] By tenaciously specializing in a single but top-of-its-class product, that is, its 'core competency', these heritage industries survive through generations, and throughout social and technological change.[20]

> SH: *We refer to our product using only one word,* shichimi tōgarashi, *but each of the seven ingredients put into it is different from the others because of the characteristics of the land and place it came from, its history, and other reasons...Still, shichimi is just a blend of seven ingredients, so that the blending process becomes very critical...*
>
> *All seven ingredients are organic products. They change according to the weather, whether there is rain or sunshine, and to changes in the temperature; all seven are influenced by that day's conditions. So even if you use the same composition from the previous day, the colour could be different, the spiciness, too, and you would not be able to make the same blend. For consistency in taste, you must blend the ingredients using all the senses of your body, noticing the changes with your eyes, nose, mouth, and adjust the recipe according to the day's conditions.*

The Japanese term for traditional shops or companies is *shinise* (literally, 'old shop'), many of which engage in food production or service. In his proclamations above, the head of Shichimiya Honpo expresses his shop's dedication and commitment to quality, a characteristic that is automatically ascribed to *shinise* by its customers and the general public. In Japan, the term *shinise* connotes sophisticated taste and premium quality, which grants the establishment high social standing and prestige. This image of the *shinise* as a provider of quality and luxury often translates into fierce brand loyalty among its clients. As one academic explains: 'Japan has its love for luxury-brand shoes and bags, which exists in the West as well, but in Japan it extends to food – a desire to eat famous things. As a result, there are lots more companies considered *shinise* in Japan'.[21]

The prestigious image of the *shinise* coupled with fervent loyalty from its clients can sometimes act as insurance to protect the company and ensure its long-term survival, even during times when it is seen to have transgressed its commitment to quality. The 2007 scandal surrounding Akafuku, a confectionery founded in 1707, tells of this special and selective protection that is afforded to *shinise* food establishments.

Akafuku's flagship product is the Akafuku mochi, a simple glutinous rice ball (mochi) that is covered in red bean paste formed in the shape of water ripples, which the company explains was originally designed in the image of water lapping at the banks of the Isuzu River. The Isuzu River is the body of water that flows in Mie Prefecture and, most significantly, through the Ise Grand Shrine, Japan's most important Shinto shrine, bar none. Akafuku's main store is on the main road to the Inner Shrine of Ise, where worshippers and tourists throughout the past several centuries have frequently stopped before or after their visit to the shrine; here, they may enjoy Akafuku mochi with tea in the shop's premises or buy these as gifts to take home. Akafuku's shop has been a landmark associated with the Ise Grand Shrine from its establishment in the same location at the turn of the eighteenth century, and the Akafuku mochi, whose recipe and appearance have remained largely unmodified since, has sold in the millions all these years.

However, a government investigation in what would have been the company's 300th anniversary in 2007 revealed that Akafuku had been tampering with its expiration-date labels for years, if not a few decades. Among several irregularities, it was discovered that the company consistently reused unsold and sometimes expired products by freezing and later selling these as freshly made sweets, with new expiration dates, after they had been thawed. (Frozen mochi can keep long.) In some cases, unsold sweets were refashioned into other confections and sold to other shops and unsuspecting customers.

The scandal roped in officials from the highest levels of the government. The then Minister of Agriculture, Forestry, and Fisheries – the ministry in charge of looking after the nation's food production and supply – revealed to news reporters that he himself recently had Akafuku mochi at home two weeks before news of the anomalies broke, and that he found the sweets to be delicious as always. He did end his confession with a warning to Akafuku, at the same time expressing his disappointment with the company, saying that he 'never imagined a *shinise* of this level to be involved in label-tampering illegalities. As they [Akafuku] are a highly-trusted *shinise* manufacturer, this is a very serious problem'.[22]

The government promptly ordered Akafuku to cease operations in mid-October (2007), and at the end of the month, its chairman, the tenth-generation head, resigned from his post. At the height of the scandal, several media sources thought that it spelled the end of Akafuku. A report in the *New York Times* that compared Akafuku's troubles with those of other famous confectioners also involved in scandals of their own declared that '[s]taging a comeback may be more difficult for Akafuku, whose transgressions are far more serious.'[23]

Akafuku, however, ostensibly cleaned up its act, reformed its manufacturing and sales systems, and established a 'Corporate Social Responsibility' panel to oversee its overall operations. Although it remained closed in the 2008 New Year season, when sales would have been at their peak, the government lifted its business cessation orders at the end of January 2008, and Akafuku resumed operations from the beginning of February. The chairman was also reinstated. Today in 2020, it is business as usual at its main shop near the Ise Grand Shrine, and Akafuku mochi continues to be sold – freshly made, it is quietly claimed and assumed – in great quantities in department stores, train stations, souvenir shops, and other establishments in and around Mie Prefecture and beyond.

> SH: *I think it is impossible to put our blending techniques into writing. The* [unwritten] *recipe for our shichimi is handed down as a family secret, and the blending process is passed on according to* isshi sōden [literally, 'one child, all inheritance'].

This is perhaps the essential characteristic of long-lived companies in Japan, that is, that they have from the beginning been family-owned and -run businesses assiduously guarding secrets that are passed only to selected successors across generations. *Isshi sōden*, as mentioned in the above comment, is the practice found in many art and cultural traditions that refers to the 'transmission of all learning by one teacher to only one disciple or heir'.[24] The practice is commonly followed in Japan's art traditions to preserve their 'true' teachings and, consequently, ensure their legitimacy and reputation across generations. *Shinise* food businesses engage in the same practice, as their 'emphasis [is] on sustainability, rather than quick maximization of profit' in order for the business to last as long as is possible. 'In Japan, it's more: how can we move [the company] on to our descendants, our children, our grandchildren?' and keep it in the family by all means necessary. At the same time, 'closing a company or selling it is also considered something of a failure and shame in Japan, and this feeling goes back centuries. So these cultural issues also seem to encourage families to keep firms going'.[25]

Shichimiya Honpo is currently headed by the fifteenth-generation 'spice master', while Yawataya Isogoro, eight decades younger, is still on its ninth generation of doing business. Astonishingly, Yagenbori, the oldest of them all, has had only ten generational changes in its history. The latter's provenance and historical continuity are particularly emphasized in the names taken by or granted to each generation head, beginning with its founder Nakajima Tokuemon. As the shop explains:

> Tokugawa Iemitsu, the third Tokugawa Shogun, was so enamoured of [Yagenbori's] spice that he granted all succeeding generations of Yagenbori spice masters permission to use the character 徳 (*toku*) in their name, a tradition that lives on with the current tenth-generation spice master, Tokuaki.[26]

In his book, *The Living Company*, business theorist Arie de Geus investigated long-lived companies in several countries worldwide, including a significant number in Japan. He outlined the reasons for their longevity, most of which align with the characteristics of the *shinise* discussed here. In his summation, de Geus observed: 'Companies die because their managers focus on the economic activity of producing goods and services, and they forget that their organizations' true nature is that of a community of humans.'[27] It may be said that the *shichimi* purveyors described in this paper and many of their counterpart *shinise* all over Japan have never shed this 'true nature' throughout their centuries of existence.

Notes

1   Kazuhiko Kojima, '*Nihon no shokubunka: kōshinryō to shokubunka* [Japanese Food Culture: Spices and Food Culture]', *Vacuum and Surface Science*, 62.8 (2019), 522-24.

2   Larissa Zimberoff, 'The Japanese Spice Blend Taking Over America', *Bloomberg: Food* <www.bloomberg.com/news/articles/2019-02-19/shichimi-togarashi-spice-takes-over-america-what-is-it-recipes> [accessed 15 May 2020].

3   '*Zenkoku shinise kigyō chōsa* [Nationwide Survey of Traditional Companies]', Tokyo Shoko Research, 2016 <www.tsr-net.co.jp/news/analysis/20161202_01.html> [accessed 15 May 2020].

4   Japanese names in the main text appear in the conventional order, that is, surname (Ōtomo) first, followed by the first name (Sōrin). Ōtomo Sōrin was a powerful Christian *daimyō* who established control over a large swathe of Kyushu.

5   In volume 17 ('*Kagaku Zenshū*') of *Sōmoku rikubu kōshuhō*. See Hitomi Enokido, '*Edo jidai no tōgarashi* [The

Chilli Pepper in the Edo Period]', *International Japanese Studies Research* (Tokyo: Hosei University, 2010).

6   See Rui Manuel Loureiro, 'Jesuit Textual Strategies in Japan Between 1549 and 1582', *Bulletin of Portuguese-Japanese Studies*, 8 (2004), 39-63.

7   Chihiro Kato, *Ra no michi* [Spice Journey] (Tokyo: Heibonsha, 2014).

8   Ekiken Kaibara, *Yamato Honzō* (Tokyo: Ariake Shobo, 1975), p. 158.

9   Toshio Asakura, *Sekai no shokubunka: Kankoku* [World Food Culture: South Korea] (Tokyo: Nosangyoson Bunkakyokai, 2005).

10   See Chong Dae-song, '*Kimchi no chōrigaku* [Kimchi Cookery]', *Science of Cookery*, 27.4 (1994), 302-07.

11   Chong.

12   *Wakan sansai zue*, ed. by Ryōan Terajima (Tokyo: Heibonsha, 1990).

13   'About Yagenbori Shichimi-Togarashi, *Yagenbori* <http://yagenbori.jp/about/english/> [accessed 15 May 2020].

14   Morisada Kitagawa, *Morisada mankō* (Tokyo: Iwanami Bunko, 1996).

15   Translation by the author.

16   The Yatsufusa ('eight-cluster'), *Capsicum annuum* variety of chilli pepper was developed in Japan and is also known as 'chile(s) Japones'. The Japanese name is from the appearance of the fruit, which grow upright in bright-red clusters of usually five or six. Yatsufusa are also grown as ornamental plants today.

17   Translated as written in the original text.

18   Kyoto Hyakumikai published some of the oral histories, including Shichimiya Honpo's, in a book titled *Kyoto shinise: hyakunen no kodawari* [Kyoto's Traditional Shops: Centuries of Commitment] (Kyoto: Gentosha, 2004).

19   Yuzo Murayama, *Heritage Culture and Business, Kyoto Style,* trans. by Juliet Winters Carpenter (Tokyo: Japan Publishing Industry Foundation for Culture, 2019), p. 10.

20   Bryan Lufkin, 'Why So Many of the World's Oldest Companies Are in Japan', *BBC Worklife,* 13 February 2020 <www.bbc.com/worklife/article/20200211-why-are-so-many-old-companies-in-japan> [accessed 15 May 2020].

21   Yuri Kageyama, 'Why Japan Has the Most Old Companies in the World', *Associated Press*, 27 April 2015 <www.businessinsider.com/how-japan-has-more-old-businesses-than-any-other-developed-nation-2015-4> [accessed 15 May 2020].

22   'Akafuku Tampered Manufacturing and Expiry Dates from Thirty Years Ago', *Tenkannichijō*, 10 December 2007 <http://iori3.cocolog-nifty.com/tenkannichijo/2007/10/30_99e9.html> [accessed 15 May 2020].

23   Norimitsu Onishi, 'Wait, Don't Eat That: Candy Scandal Stuns Japan', *New York Times,* 30 October 2007 <www.nytimes.com/2007/10/31/world/asia/31iht-31japan.8123604.html> [accessed 10 May 2020]

24   Voltaire Cang, 'Preserving Intangible Heritage in Japan: The Role of the *Iemoto* System', *International Journal of Intangible Heritage*, 3 (2008), 71-81 (79).

25   Lufkin.

26   Yagenbori.

27   Arie de Geus, *The Living Company* (Cambridge, MA: Harvard Business School, 1997), p. 3.

From Acapulco to Manila, Culinary Spices to Medical Supplies: Useful Plants Introduced to the Philippines in the Age of the Galleons

Marianne Jennifer Datiles, Francesca Scotti,
Vivienne Lo, and Michael Heinrich

...they presented fish, a jar of palm wine, which they call *uraca*, figs more than one *palmo* long, and others which were smaller and more delicate, and two cocoanuts [...]. The king had a plate of pork brought in and a large jar filled with wine. At every mouthful, we drank a cup of wine [...]. We ate with such ceremonies and with other signs of friendship. I ate meat on holy [Good] Friday, for I could not help myself.[1]

When the Magellan-Elcano crew landed in the Philippines in March 1521, Antonio Pigafetta recorded his impressions of the hospitality of the local people, various foods served, as well as flora, fauna, gold, and other items the locals possessed. Magellan's fleet, the *Armada de Molucca*, had, after all, come in search of the Spice Islands, and direct access to Asian resources, goods, and trade was central to the Spanish empire's ambitions of conquest in the Pacific. Magellan was killed in battle a month later by the forces of Lapulapu and the datus of Mactan, but the Philippine archipelago eventually fell to colonial rule. For the next three centuries the islands served as the Spanish empire's foothold in Asia, an international trade hub where Asian, American, and European cultures crossed and exchanged goods, metals, and ideas. This was made possible by Urdaneta's discovery of a direct route between the Philippines and the west coast of Mexico, a route that ran from 1565 to 1815 and came to be known as the Manila-Acapulco Galleon Trade.

In early European accounts like Pigafetta's, we read descriptions of the 'Spanish East Indies' teeming with natural resources to rival Dutch and Portuguese supplies. Even now the term 'green gold' perhaps conjures images of fragrant and precious cargo such as tea, cacao, nutmeg, and cloves, all shipped by the tons from Asia and the Americas to satiate a growing European appetite during the early modern period.[2] Less attention, however, has been paid to the movement in the other direction. What plant materials were being carried into Asia-Pacific?

Numerous food plants of tropical and subtropical American origin are ubiquitous in the Philippines today. The potato (*Solanum tuberosum* L.) and corn (*Zea mays* L.) are staple ingredients, and Doreen Fernandez writes that the tomato (*Lycopersicon esculentum* Mill.) is 'as indispensable to Philippine cooking as it is to Mexican cuisine'.[3] Pineapple (*Ananas comosus* (L.) Merr.), papaya (*Carica papaya* L.), and guava (*Psidium guajava* L.) have likewise found their place on the Pinoy dinner table. These plants are Filipino food because they have become so. However, their assimilation into Filipino culture was not necessarily immediate or straightforward, and use-knowledge likely changed over time.

This paper explores the changing use-knowledge of two culinary plants in the Philippines, *atsuete* (*Bixa orellana* L.) and *pasotes* (*Dysphania ambrosioides* (L.) Mosyakin and Clemants, better known by its synonym *Chenopodium ambrosioides* L.). Our ongoing research utilizes medical botanical works, understudied sources in Filipino food history, in order to investigate how plants introduced to the Philippines during the 'Age of Empire' were used over time as both food and medicine. Doing so can reveal a richer historical context for these foodstuffs that, despite being material evidence of a dark colonial past, still find appreciation on plates today.

Case Study I: *Bixa orellana* L., 'Achiote', 'Achiotl' (Mexico) / 'Atsuete', 'Achuete', 'Chotis' (Philippines)

Bixa orellana L. is a shrub or small flowering tree originating from the tropical regions of the Americas with hairy red pods containing red seeds dusted in red powder. These seeds are usually sold in the UK and US by the names *annatto* or *achiote*, and in the Philippines names include variations of *atsuete* and *chotis*. The names derive from *achiotl*, the classical Nahua name for the tree.

Early Records of Atsuete: A Food Spice with Medicinal Qualities

Atsuete was well known among the Aztecs to colour the froth of the *xochiaya cacahuatl*, one of several types of cacao beverages used for religious and social purposes.[4] Cacao mixed with *atsuete* may have symbolized blood, and white maize bones, in Mayan stories of birth, rebirth, and creation.[5] In addition to the use of its bark for rope-making and wood for fire, its seeds were also used to make red body paint and were traded as a dye among the Aztecs and Mayans, the Incas and Mohicas, as well as the Chaco.[6] By the time the Spaniards set foot in what is now Mexico, *atsuete* was a well-established spice plant in Tenochtitlan, the capital of the Aztec empire. The plant's medicinal uses were described in the *Libellus de medicinalibus indorum herbis*, the oldest known surviving American herbal written in Nahuatl by Martín de la Cruz, a member of the young Aztec nobility, and translated into Spanish by Franciscan friar Juan Badiano. Here as a medicine, *atsuete* was recorded as an ingredient in an astringent wash to treat genital infection and in a mixture for urinary problems.[7]

Atsuete was actively cultivated across the Americas prior to European contact. In 1526 Oviedo wrote in his *Historia general y natural* that the tree was both wild and cultivated across Nueva España and Terra Firme, the northern Spanish territory of South Americas.[8]

Hernández also reported that *atsuete* was widely esteemed and planted around houses during Spain's first royal scientific expedition (1570-1577).[9] While there is a possibility *atsuete* reached the south of Asia and Africa through the Portuguese trade that linked Brazil to Goa in India, the earliest documented uses for *atsuete* in the Philippines closely mirror those of Nueva España, to which it was directly linked.[10] Association of *atsuete* with its origin is suggested by the phonetic similarities we see today between the Nahuatl word *achiotl* and names in the Philippine lexicon such as *atchiti, chotes,* and *sotis*.[11]

Atsuete *in the Philippines*

By the end of the sixteenth century the Spanish empire had access to *atsuete* plantations across the Americas, and the plant was recorded in the Philippines by 1611. It would have been cultivated for domestic use only, however, and not for export to Europe; valuable cargo space on ships leaving Manila would have been reserved for the lucrative goods found exclusively in Asia, and fresh *atsuete* supplies could be obtained when ships passed through the Americas on the return journey to Europe.[12] Furthermore, the Philippines' primary role was as a colonial trade hub rather than a spice source; the few well-known attempts at Spanish cultivation efforts were thwarted by lack of local leadership, communication, and funding, as in the case of the eighteenth-century commercial cinnamon failure in Mindanao.[13] Indeed, in 1628 Carmelite friar Antonio Espinosa wrote that *atsuete* was commonly exported from Nueva España to China, 'where it sells very well for dyeing silk and for other purposes'.[14]

Atsuete was listed in the Philippines' earliest surviving medico-botanical work, *El libro de medicinas caseras* by friar Blas de la Madre de Dios in 1611, for its use in treating burns, boils, scabies, and swellings. These uses are included in *El libro de medicinas de esta tierra*, written between the 1660s-1680s by Augustinian friar Ignacio Mercado, called the first Filipino-born botanist. Both Madre de Dios' and Mercado's manuscripts were intended as practical manuals for other missionaries' use and focused on locally available plants to treat both Spaniards and the various *indios* of the Philippines.[15] This is in contrast with the more general *relaciones*, ethnographic accounts such as Pigafetta's, and academic-oriented works, such as what is considered the first flora of the Philippines, *Herbarium aliarumque stirpium in insula Luzone Philippinarum*, written by Jesuit Georg Josef Kamel and published in 1704 as an appendix to the famous *Historia plantarum* of English physician John Ray.[16] Mercado was a self-taught botanist, but he had access to the major writings that shaped the early modern European medical tradition. In his work he cited Laguna's recent translation of Dioscorides and drew from the well-known European accounts of 'New World' plants from the sixteenth to seventeenth centuries, such as those of Carolus Clusius and Francisco Hernández.[17]

This influence is evident in Mercado's description for *atsuete*:

> It is cold in the third degree, and has some astringency [...] it severely quenches thirst and burning fever, and it is useful for fevers, caused by heat, and it dissolves

growths and swellings. Hence, it can and should be used, with very good success [...] in drinks and syrups, and in delicacies when it is intended to cool and refresh. Add achiote to cocoa for hot tooth aches: it clenches and fortifies teeth, quenches thirst, and is good for the poor instead of saffron [.... It] comforts the stomach, increases milk and restricts the chambers. Mixed with resin, it cures the scabies, and other sores. Poured into cocoa, it makes it possible to drink more than usual, without harm or damage to health because it helps digestion and never causes disgust.[18]

This appears to be derived from Hernández's *Historia natural*:

[It is] cold in the third degree and with some dryness and astringency [...] it calms the burning of fevers, relieves dysentery and makes tumours disappear, for which reason it can be conveniently mixed with [...] any [cool] foods or medications. It is added to cacáoatl as a refresher and to enhance its colour and flavour. It removes tooth pain caused by heat, and strengthens them; it causes urine, quenches thirst, and among certain people acts as saffron [...] mixed with resin it cures scabies and ulcers; strengthens the stomach, stops the flow of the belly, and increases [breast] milk. Mixed with cacáoatl shells, makes it harmless whatever the amount in which it is taken, as it is usually digested with its help without any discomfort.[19]

122   Hernández's descriptions influenced many botanical works during this time. Robert Lovell in Oxford, for instance, published a nearly identical description in 1665 in English, although no source was mentioned:

It's cold third degree and somewhat dry and binding. The seed drunk helps the heat of feavers, and dysenteries, and applied repelleth tumours, and is mixed with remedies for the like purposes. It helpeth the toothache of a hot cause, it corroborareth, and evacuates urine, it helpeth thirst, and is used instead of saffron. The gaines being boiled in water, and mixed with [resin] it helps the scab and ulcers: it corroborates the stomack, stops the belly, and causeth milke.[20]

Such plant description parallels exemplify how the circulation of medical knowledge of 'New World' plants directly impacted the works of scientists and missionaries who were sent to the Philippines, and, in turn, shaped the colonial Philippine botanico-medical tradition.[21]

Atsuete and Colour: Across and Beyond the Food-Medicine Interface
In Europe, *atsuete* appears to have been generally considered an insignificant culinary spice in the early modern global trade in comparison to spices like nutmeg, cloves, cinnamon, and pepper. It did, however, constitute a regular part of the pigment trade that rose in the mid-sixteenth century and continued through at least the end of the eighteenth.

Hernández had described it as producing a dye 'so tenacious that a mere dab will not wash out', and the spice was imported as a colourant for yellow silks, a finishing dye, and a red pigment alternative to the one produced by the far more costly cochineal.[22] In 1665, Lovell had called it 'dyers-tree', and we know *atsuete* was listed among the cargo being shipped from the Spanish West Indies to Europe in Woodes Rogers' famous 1708-1711 voyage.[23] In 1766 the Spanish ship *Nuevo Constante* was reportedly carrying about 5000 pounds of *atsuete* bound for Cadiz when it wrecked off the coast of Louisiana, along with over 40,000 pounds of other dye products.[24] In late eighteenth-century England *atsuete* was recorded as 'for the use of the dyers, principally'; 'the preparation [was] made by the druggist, both in England and in the country [...] the pigment, it is said, was formerly collected in Jamaica: but has of later years been brought there (in seproons, or bags made of undressed hides) from the Spanish settlements.'[25]

The import of *atsuete* to Europe for textile purposes from the sixteenth century onwards may have encouraged a new use for it in food: cheese. Realizing they could skim the cream off and sell it separately, European cheesemakers used *atsuete* as a 'trick' to colour the resulting low-fat cheese, since the natural yellow colour of a full-fat cheese served as a measure for its quality.[26] Surveyor William Marshall complained in 1789 that the 'crime of colouring cheese' had 'long been practiced by the Gloucestershire dairywomen', and that, 'such cheese having been found to bear a better price [...] than cheese of a paler palor, they set about *counterfeiting nature*'; he also noted that the practice was done in other countries.[27] This cheese colouring practice continues today; *atsuete* is used to colour many cheddar cheeses and Gloucester cheese, and it is responsible for the signature colour of Leicester Red.[28]

In the Philippines, *atsuete*'s association with colour caused a shift in its perceived medicinal use. The Dominican Fernando de Santa Maria, operating in the Philippines between 1730 and 1774, wrote *Manual de medicinas caseras*, a missionary manual with the explicit intention of assisting '*pobre Indios*' in places where '*no hay médicos ni botica*'.[29] First published in 1768, Santa Maria's work groups *atsuete* as one of four *azafrins* (saffrons): saffron (from stigma and styles), turmeric (from a root), *atsuete* (from seed pods), and safflower (from flower petals). These different spices were reportedly interchangeable to an extent and used for the same purposes as saffron, signalling that its basis as a medical spice in colonial Philippines had by this point altered to include association with a particular pigment. Santa Maria's manual was reprinted at least nine times between 1768 and 1905, indicating its influence persisted beyond Spanish rule and into the American colonial period.

If *atsuete* had been first introduced to the Philippines for medicinal use, it was as a food colouring substitute for saffron that *atsuete* achieved its role in Filipino culture that it maintains today. As food historian Felice Prudente Sta. Maria and Filipino chefs Amy Besa and Romy Dorotan write, today you will find *atsuete* in many cherished Filipino foods including 'fiesta dishes' like *kare-kare* (peanut-based oxtail stew); in sauces for noodles as in *pancit palabok, pancit luglug,* and *pancit malabon* (rice noodle dish variations); and comfort foods like chicken *inasal* (basted chicken) and *adobong pula* (red adobo).[30]

123

Case Study 2: *Dysphania ambrosioides* (L.) Mosyakin and Clemants, 'Epazotl', 'Epazote' (Mexico) / 'Pasotes', 'Apasote', 'Pasotis' (Philippines)

Pasotes is a common plant in its native Mexico, where it is known as *epazote* or *epozote* and used extensively as a culinary herb in foods like corn stews and fried beans dishes. When crushed, its leaves give a distinctive aroma that some have described as akin to gasoline; the name *epazote* is said to derive from the Nahuatl word *epatl*, for skunk. The flavourful leaves serve a double function in bean dishes, since they are believed to reduce stomach gas, and the essential oil has long been known among Native peoples of the Americas to be an effective vermifuge. It easily disperses and has become an invasive species in many regions of the world, usually growing along roadsides and rocky areas as a weed.[31]

Pasotes as Food and Medicine

In Mesoamerica, the ubiquitous plant was interestingly not mentioned in the de la Cruz-Badiano manuscript of 1552. Hernández, however, described it in detail in his *Historia natural* (1570-1577):

> It is a herb with branched roots, from where stems of a long elbow with oblong, crenelated and reddish leaves, and seed with spikes. It is pungent, odorous, and calorific in the third degree; It is eaten raw or cooked, and added to meals strengthens, relieves asthmatics and breast sufferers, and provides pleasant food. The decoction of roots contains dysentery, removes inflammations and [expels harmful worms] from one's stomach.[32]

124

In the Philippines, *pasotes* is considered a galleon introduction, either as a medicinal food plant intended for cultivation which subsequently escaped into the wild, or an accidental introduction which was then recognized and put to use.[33] European-trained missionaries in the Philippines would have been familiar with it from studying 'New World' plants and medicines.

In his seventeenth-century description for *pasotes*, Mercado again chose to draw from Hernández with a near-identical description as the one above. However, he included another use: an infusion of its seeds in wine 'dulls the senses in such a way that those who are flogged do not feel the lashes and those put in torment do not feel it'.[34] While Nicolas Moñardes, a contemporary of Hernández, had also mentioned the use of *pasotes* for pain in Nueva España, the specificity of this use, Mercado asserted, was based on his personal observation of Filipino patients.

In 1837 Franciscan friar Manuel Blanco, in his landmark botanical work *Flora de Filipinas*, copied Mercado's descriptive use as an anaesthetic and wrote, 'this is what has been written in the Islands', supporting Mercado's claim that this was not an imported use for an imported plant, but something new based on experience in the Philippines.[35] Some fifty years later noted Filipino physician and historian Trinidad Pardo de Tavera also quoted Mercado's description in his *Plantas medicinales de Filipinas* (1892) and commented, 'these properties, if true, make this plant one of the most useful in the Philippines.'[36]

Adapted Dishes, New Uses in Philippine Food

Today, *pasotes* does not appear to be well known as a medicine, much less an anaesthetic, possibly linked to its inconspicuousness, its smell which is often seen as undesirable, or concerns of its toxicity. It is, however, still used in regional cuisine, with two notable examples.

In the Ilocos region, the Filipino dish *pipian* was adapted from the Mexican dish of the same name and calls for both *pasotes* and *atsuete*. Besa and Dorotan write that 'in Mexico, *pipian* is a sauce thickened with ground toasted *pepitas* (pumpkin seeds); in the Philippines, ground toasted rice is used instead [.... T]he main flavouring agent is the *pasotes*, called *pasotes* in Ilocos'.[37] Besa and Dorotan suggest that it is only found in Ilocos Sur, in northern Luzon. While the plant is found elsewhere in the Philippines, it should be noted that Vigan, the capital city of Ilocos Sur, is a UNESCO world heritage centre located near the northwest tip of Luzon Island and, as a major commercial port for the galleons, traded directly with China throughout the colonial period.[38] It is fitting that Vigan, known for its colonial Spanish architecture, would have retained such plant knowledge and blending of traditions that resulted from this period.

In the Visayan region of Cebu, *pasotes* is the secret ingredient in a local version of what Anthony Bourdain once called 'the finest pig' and 'the best of the best': Cebu *lechón*, a fire-roasted whole-pig fiesta dish.[39] *Lechón* deserves its own place in Filipino food history, as its Spanish-given name conceals its likely pre-colonial indigenous Filipino origins. There are many varieties across the islands which are often stuffed with various local herbs, and *pasotes* is used to make the Carcar City, Cebu version. Doreen Fernandez writes that foreign dishes like Spanish *paella* and Chinese *batsui* were 'adjusted to the Filipino palate' when they were incorporated into Filipino cuisine.[40] Conversely, Carcar *lechón* exemplifies how a foreign ingredient was incorporated to an indigenous dish and contributed to a flavour that is celebrated as uniquely Filipino.

Notes on Taxonomic Changes and Vernacular Names

Tracing plant uses across contexts is often complicated by taxonomic classification, which is based on both morphological and phylogenetic features and may not always reflect how plants are grouped with others as traditional foods and medicines. In the case of *pasotes*, cultural distinctions between plants have been reported based on morphology, specifically colour. Among Zapotec, for example, *bitia morad* (purple-stemmed *pasotes*), and *bitia nol* (white-stemmed *pasotes*) are reportedly somewhat interchangeable and used when cooking beans, whereas young leaves of the green *bitia z* should be used exclusively in corn stews.[41]

Taxonomically, the species was previously a member of the *Chenopodium* genus until it and several other species were moved to the Australian genus *Dysphania* following phylogenetic studies in the 2000s. In testing, the essential oil of *D. ambrosioides* var. *ambrosioides* was found to be much lower in ascaridole, and thus less toxic, than *D. ambrosioides* var. *antihelminticum*.[42] This taxonomic change may be highly relevant from a plant systematic perspective, but it is problematic for traditional uses and names of the plant, especially for those studying use-histories. It also does not seem to correlate with local plant taxonomies. With the Rarámuri people of Chihuahua, Mexico, for example, it is one of three plants with similar uses, called *chuá*; the other two plants are *Chenopodium album* and *C. graveolens*, which are also used like spinach among indigenous groups of North America but have other uses for medicine and in rituals, and possess different chemical constituents from *D. ambrosioides*.[43]

Common names can also cause confusion when citing uses from historical literature. Several plants unrelated to *pasotes* share the name 'Mexican tea', such as *Ephedra* spp., which has a long history of use in many medical systems including Chinese medicine and are of pharmacological interest.[44] Another name for *pasotes*, 'wormseed', has been applied to various plants with perceived vermifugal properties, such as those of the genus *Artemisia*; and the name for *pasotes*, 'Jesuits tea', is perhaps most known in the context of *mate*, the caffeinated drink made from *Ilex paraguariensis* A. St.-Hil, a member of the holly family.

Final Thoughts

The cases of *atsuete* and *pasotes* demonstrate the nonlinear journeys across and beyond the food-medicine interface that spice plants, and any useful plant, can take as they are introduced into a new environment. Intentional botanical introductions often come with existing use-knowledge attached which are enforced in the new cultural landscape, and over time are continued, rejected, forgotten, or transformed into new uses. *Atsuete* was used for centuries as a food, medicine, and pigment source before the European expansion. It traversed all three of these spheres as it was introduced to Europe in the sixteenth century and traded as a pigment, inserted into Spanish Philippine medicine, and found a permanent place as a food colouring. Similarly, *pasotes* was recognized early on by European missionaries in the Philippines and entered into written tradition as a medicine and leafy vegetable. Eventually, both these uses fell out of practice, and today you may know it as a regional herb for a traditional Ilocano dish and in a tasty, tourist-attracting Cebuano roasted pig.

The year 2021 marks 500 years since Magellan and Elcano landed in the Philippines. The first circumnavigation was a significant milestone in botanical exploration and had profound effects on the peoples of Asia and the Pacific world that altered their courses forever. While we confront the detrimental history of colonialism and reflect on the impact non-native plants cause on new environments, may we also find ways to look forward to the future and celebrate the healing and nurturing power of foods that bind our world together.

Acknowledgements

We thank the organizers, Laura Romuroso, Paz Nolasco, and Consuelo David for sharing their time and knowledge, and Raf Ignacio at Filipino Food Crawl. In memory of Dr. Manuel B. Datiles III, MD.

Notes

1   Antonio Pigafetta, *Primo viaggio intorno al mondo* (Original Text of the Ambrosian MS, with English Translation), ed. and trans. by J. A. Robertson (Cleveland: Arthur H. Clark Co, 1906), pp. 103-04, 119.

2   See, e.g., Daniela Bleichmar, *Visual Voyages: Images of Latin American Nature from Columbus to Darwin* (New Haven: Yale University Press, 2017); Harold J. Cook, *Matters of Exchange: Commerce, Medicine, and Science in the Dutch Golden Age* (New Haven: Yale University Press, 2007); Paula de Vos, 'The Science of Spices: Empiricism and Economic Botany in the Early Spanish Empire', *Journal of World History*, 17.4 (2006), 399-427; Stephanie Ganger, 'World Trade in Medicinal Plants from Spanish America, 1717-1815', *Medical History*, 59.1 (2015), 44-62.

3   Doreen Fernandez, *Tikim: Essays on Philippine Food and Culture*, 2nd ed., (Leiden: Brill, 2020), p. 147.

4   R.A. Donkin, '*Bixa orellana*: The Eternal Shrub', *Anthropos*, 69.1/2 (1974), 33-56; Marcy Norton, 'Tasting Empire: Chocolate and the European Internalization of Mesoamerican Aesthetics', *The American Historical Review*, 111.3 (2006), 672; *The Mexican Treasury: The Writings of Dr. Francisco Hernández*, ed. by Simon Varey (Stanford: Stanford University Press, 2000), p. 19.

5   Michael J. Coe, 'The Hero Twins: Myth and Image', in *The Maya Vase Book*, ed. by Justin Kerr (New York: Kerr Associates, 1989); Michael Grofe, *The Recipe for Rebirth: Cacao as a Fish in the Mythology and Symbolism of the Ancient Maya* (2007), pp. 34-35.

6   Donkin, 1974; Varey, pp. 242-43.

7   Martín de la Cruz and Juan Badiano, *The Badianus Manuscript, Codex Barberini, Latin 241, Vatican Library; an Aztec Herbal of 1552*, trans. by Emily W. Emmart (Baltimore: Johns Hopkins Press, 1940), pp. 287-89.

8   Gonzalo Fernández de Oviedo y Valdés, *Historia general y natural de las Indias, islas y tierra-firme del mar oceano*, ed. by José Amador de los Rios (Madrid: Impr. de la Real Academia de la Historia, 1851), Bk 8 Ch VI.

9   Francisco Hernández, *Historia natural de Nueva España*, Vol. I (México: Universidad Nacional de México, 2015), Ch XCVIII.

10 Alphonse de Candolle, *On the Origin of Cultivated Plants* (New York: D. Appleton and Co, 1885), pp. 401-02.

11 Paloma Albalá, 'Hispanic Words of Indoamerican Origin in the Philippines', *Philippine Studies*, 51.1 (2003), 125-46.

12 For more on the galleon trade, see, e.g., de Vos, Ganger, Reyes, and Schurz.

13 Bleichmar, pp. 123-48; Francisco Mallari, 'The Mindanao Cinnamon', *Philippine Quarterly of Culture and Society*, 2.4 (1974), 190-94.

14 Antonio Vásquez de Espinosa, *Compendium and Description of the West Indies,* trans. by Charles Upson Clark (Washington DC: Smithsonian Miscellaneous Collections 102, 1942), p. 238.

15 Anagnostou; Blas Sierra de la Calle, 'El P. Ignacio Mercado (1648-1698) *y las plantas medicinales filipinas*', *Archivos Agustinos*, 100 (2016), 331-492 (372-74). See also Sabine Anagnostou, Florike Egmond, Christoph Friedrich, eds., *A Passion for Plants: Materia Medica and Botany in Scientific Networks from the 16th to 18th Centuries* (Stuttgart: Wissenschaftliche Verlagsgesellschaft, 2011).

16 Anagnostou, Egmond, and Freidrich; Sebastian Kroupa, 'Georg Joseph Kamel (1661-1706): A Jesuit Pharmacist at the Frontiers of Colonial Empire' (unpublished doctoral thesis, University of Cambridge, 2019).

17 Anagnostou; Sierra de la Calle; Celestino Fernando-Villar, '*Apuntes para servir á la Biografía del P. Fr. Ignacio de Mercado*', in *Flora de Filipinas Gran Edición Cuarto Tomo*, ed. by Manuel Blanco (Manila: Establecimiento Tipográfico de Plana y Citia, 1880-1883), pp. 33-36.

18 Ignacio de Mercado, '*Libro de Medicinas de Esta Tierra*', in *Flora de Filipinas Gran Edición Curato Tomo*, p. 20.

19 Francisco Hernández, *Historia natural de Nueva España*, Vol. II (México City: Universidad Nacional de México, 2015), Ch XCVIII.

20 Robert Lovell, *Pambotanologia* (Oxford: printed by W.H. for Ric. Davis, 1665), p. 502.

21 Anagnostou; Varey. See also Kroupa, pp. 156-59.

22 Varey, p. 197; Elena Phipps, 'Textile Colors and Colorants in the Andes', in *Colors between Two Worlds: The Florentine Codex*, ed. by Gerhard Wolf and Joseph Connors (Florence: Kunsthistorisches Institut, 2011), pp. 272-75.

23 Edward Cooke, *Voyage to the South Sea and Round the World* (London: 1712), Vol II, xvii.

24 Charles E. Pearson and Paul E. Hoffman, *El Nuevo Constante* (Anthropological Study No 4) (Baton Rouge: Louisiana Archaeological Survey and Antiquities Commission, 1998), pp. 8-9, 27.

25 William Marshall, *The Rural Economy of Gloucestershire, Including its Dairy, Vol I* (London: printed by R. Raikes, for G. Nicol, 1789), pp. 289-93.

26 Allison Aubrey, 'How 17th Century Fraud Gave Rise to Bright Orange Cheese', *The Salt* (2020) <https://www.npr.org/sections/thesalt/2013/11/07/243733126/how-17th-century-fraud-gave-rise-to-bright-orange-cheese> [accessed 18 May 2020]. See also Paul Kindstedt, *Cheese and Culture: A History of Cheese and its Place in Western Civilization* (White River Junction, VT: Chelsea Green Publishing, 2012).

27 Marshall, pp. 289-93.

28 Thomas Arthur Layton, *The Cheese Handbook: Over 250 Varieties Described, with Recipes* (Mineola, NY: Dover Publications, 1973), pp. 108-10.

29 Fernando de Santa María, *Manual de medicinas caseras* (Manila: University of Santo Tomas Press, 1768), p. vi.

30 Amy Besa and Romy Dorotan, *Memories of Philippine Kitchens* (New York: Stewart, Chobani, and Chang, 2006), pp. 17, 55, 78-79, 175; Felice Sta. Maria, *The Governor-General's Kitchen: Philippine Culinary Vignettes and Period Recipes, 1521-1935* (Pasig City: Anvil Publishing, 2006), p. 81. See also Fernandez, p. 81.

31 Julissa Rojas-Sandoval and Pedro Acevedo-Rodríguez, *Dysphania ambrosioides* (Mexican tea), *CABI Invasive Species Compendium* (2014) <https://www.cabi.org/isc/datasheet/113977> [accessed 10 Jan 2020]

32 Hernández, Vol I, Ch XL.

33 Rojas-Sandoval and Acevedo-Rodríguez.

34 Mercado, p. 15.

35 Manuel Blanco, *Flora de Filipinas* (Manila: Santo Tomás por D. Candido Lopez, 1837), pp. 200-01.

36 Trinidad Pardo de Tavera, *Plantas medicinales de Filipinas* (Madrid: Bernardo Rico, 1892), p. 251.

37 Besa and Dorotan, p. 119.

38 UNESCO, *Historic City of Vigan* (2020) < https://whc.unesco.org/en/list/502/> [accessed 16 Aug 2020]

39 Joel Binamira, 'It's the Best of the Best', *Market Manila* (2009) <http://www.marketmanila.com/archives/its-the-best-of-the-best> [accessed 28 May 2020]; 'Recap of the Anthony Bourdain related posts on Marketmanila.com', *Market Manila* (2018) <http://www.marketmanila.com/archives/a-recap-of-the-anthony-bourdain-related-posts-on-marketmanila> [accessed 28 May 2020]; IMDB, 'Philippines "Land of the Lechon"', *Anthony Bourdain: No Reservations*, S5E7 (2020) <https://www.imdb.com/title/tt1566957/> [accessed 28 May 2020]

40 Fernandez, p. 173.

41 Fructuoso Irigoyen-Rascón and Alfonso Paredes, *Tarahumara Medicine: Ethnobotany and Healing among the Rarámuri of Mexico* (Oklahoma City: Oklahoma University Press, 2015), p. 323.

42 Rovert Tisserand and Rodney Young, *Essential Oil Safety: A Guide for Health Care Professionals* (Edinburgh: Elsevier, 2014), pp. 470-71.

43 Robert Bye, 'Medicinal Plants of the Sierra Madre: Comparative Study of Tarahumara and Mexican Market Plants', *Economic Botany*, 40 (1986), 103-24; Irigoyen-Rascón and Paredes.

44 Yuntao Dai and others, 'Quality Marker Identification Based on Standard Decoction of Differently Processed Materials of *Ephedrae Herba*', *Journal of Ethnopharmacology*, 237 (2019), 47-54; Ernest Small, *Culinary Herbs*, 2nd Edition, National Research Council of Canada Monograph Series (Ottawa: NRC Research Press, 2006).

Grass Fed: Cannabis Cooking in the United States

Rebecca Federman and Jessica M. Pigza

At the New York Public Library, most of the newly released cookbooks arrive on our shelves from publishers automatically. Cooking, baking, any and all food-related books are hugely popular with patrons, so we tell the book vendors our budget and then watch as the books trickle in, month by month. With such a large collection, it's easy to spot trends: Atkins, South Beach, keto, gluten-free, sourdough – and you notice the regular players, too: Martha, Jamie, Alton, Chrissy. But a few newcomers have joined the table in the last few years, bringing with them a new ingredient which until just a few years ago wasn't even legal. Their new cookbooks are not just cookbooks. They're guides to getting well, or high, or both. Not so long ago, the most infamous cookbook to cover cannabis was *The Anarchist Cookbook*. Today's cookbooks, with their locked-down prescriptive approaches to serving sizes and safety, are a far cry from promoting anarchy in the kitchen.

Would-be cannabis cooks and diners in today's post-prohibition world have a wealth of choices among glossy cookbooks, magazines, and wellness guides all showcasing this herb, many produced by content creators intent on selling new audiences on the role weed can play in enlightened self-care, dining, and entertaining. What about half a century earlier, when *The Anarchist Cookbook* first appeared and a turned-on generation imagined a future in which the herb was legal? Did the countercultural cannabis palate extend beyond the ubiquitous pot brownie? Yes, it did, as we found by reading cookbooks and periodicals from the 1960s and 1970s. The psychedelic dishes from that period provide an informative counterpoint to today's recipes and remedies.

Cannabis as an Herb

Cannabis is an annual flowering herb which has been valued for thousands of years by humans both for its strong fibres (good for rope and canvas) as well as its psychoactive and pain-relieving cannabinoids (including THC and CBD). It also has an extensive history as an ingredient in dishes around the world. In India, *bhang*, a milk-based drink with cannabis, spices, and seeds, is consumed during Hindu rituals and celebrations. In Morocco, one can find *majoun*, a sweet, rolled ball filled with honey, nuts, cannabis, and dried fruit.[1]

In the United States, cannabis has long been subject to polarizing debates. Is it toxic or medicinal? A multipurpose plant or a dangerous weed? A food or a drug? Groovy or scary? Cannabis shifted from being the source of common legal tinctures and candies to become classed as a dangerous drug, prohibited in the United States first in 1937 – targeting African Americans and Mexicans – and then again in 1970.[2] But cannabis and medical rights activists were ultimately successful in changing many state governments' laws to legalize the herb. As of this writing, thirty-three states allow cannabis use for medical purposes and eleven states permit it for recreational use.[3] Prior to the measured and deliberate lifting of prohibition, cannabis went underground for decades.

Counterculture's Kitchens

Evelyn Schmevelyn, Deena Shupe, and the True Light Beavers may not have the same name recognition as Fannie Farmer or Irma Rombauer in kitchens today. But these authors were among many writers, gardeners, activists, and alternative living experimentalists who wrote cookbooks, pamphlets, and articles on cannabis. They each championed the herb's culinary potential in their own ways by writing cookbooks and articles in underground newspapers (although sometimes using pseudonyms). The dishes they presented in those freewheeling days of the 1960s and 1970s mirror the changing food culture of that moment in time, but with the addition of weed. Readers could find weed-heightened versions of homey dishes like meatloaf as well as more ambitious surprises like frogs' legs. Some cannabis recipes depended on convenient boxed and canned foods, while others incorporated fresh garden produce. And some writers seemingly offered grass-forward adaptations of recipes from their own childhood comfort food memories.

New York-based conceptual designer Deena Shupe aimed to help 'transform your kitchen from a place for traditional concoctions into a new place to turn on' with *The High Art of Cooking*.[4] One imagines Shupe in her Greenwich Village apartment, trying out recipes on fellow artists (like Hannah Wilke, whose works illustrate *The High Art*) while her new puppy Fawn (also featured in her cookbook) looks on. *The High Art* feels personal and welcoming, and it draws cooking inspiration from a variety of culinary corners. Shupe's own Jewish family recipes, including dairy borscht and chopped herring, share space with Japanese *zensai* chicken bits and golden bats (deep fried weed-stuffed frogs' legs). Shupe also includes recipes influenced by the emerging organic movement in the United States. 'Natural foods heighten your sensory appetite, and so does that natural weed,' she explains when introducing a chapter focusing on whole grains and fresh vegetables and fruits.[5] But even a recipe for something as wholesome as a double batch of whole wheat bread includes one cup of grass and this sly note: 'Each raised bread highs 10.'[6]

One hundred miles north of Greenwich Village, the members of a Woodstock, New York-based commune called the True Light Beavers were busy at work on *Eat, Fast, Feast*, a rambling cookbook and memoir that reveals its authors' priorities through the life they describe. Recipes mingle with discussions of composting, feeding babies, wine making, food preservation, using insects in agriculture, fasting, foraging, and butchering, accompanied by short fiction ('pornography of the palate') and art.[7] In a chapter promising 'to turn your mind on through your mouth', they offer psychoactive recipes which include two for the fruit-nut-cannabis paste they call 'marjoome': the 'authentic' version makes use of cannabis, oil, chickpea flour, dates, and almonds, while the 'Europeanized' recipe replaces chickpea flour with 'flour (or brownie or chocolate cake mix)' and suggests including raisins.[8]

The whimsically pen-named author Evelyn Schmevelyn, recognizing that for some, eating cannabis would require a bit of orientation, provides it in *Cooking with Marijuana*. She sprinkles her breezy advice among recipes and trippy line drawings of dancing bananas, human-sized mushrooms, and loads of grinning hippies. Schmevelyn teaches you to pre-cook and grind up the herb to avoid its 'awful gritty feeling' and 'acrid unforgettable flavor', and she offers wise words about the delayed high that comes from eating weed: 'Give it a chance before you eat another helping or you may find yourself deeply engrossed in the stitches on your saddle shoes.'[9] Because she finds 'food that is very spicy and flavorful is best able to accommodate pot', she includes 'pot Italiano' recipes as well as 'delicacies with a Mexican flavor'.[10] A chapter called 'Having Fun with Bananas' features 'Farouk's dick', a dish of bacon-wrapped mini-bananas dusted with sugar and hashish.[11] And although she doesn't lean heavily on processed food ingredients, Schmevelyn kindly provides the following tips on improving brownies made from a mix: pre-cook and grind weed to a fine powder, and stir in extras like wheat germ, chocolate chips, or coconut flakes.[12]

It was hard to avoid brownie talk in publications from that period, and cannabis cookbooks today often include brownies as well – nodding to their place in history while at the same time reinventing them completely for twenty-first-century tastes. *Quicksilver Times*, an underground newspaper based in Washington, DC, reported in 1971 that the brownie 'has become the traditional method of cooking with grass in the United States' in an article about the herb. The unnamed author provided a few beginner recipes as well – for infused butter, honey slides (fried weed suspended in warm honey), and 'cop-out brownies', noting, 'We recommend Betty Crocker Mix because it has the strongest brownie flavor and thus best masks the grass flavor.'[13]

Another dessert, wiggley weed, is featured in an 'all-weed meal' in *The Fifth Estate*, a Detroit, Michigan-based paper that made weed their cover story in April 1973. Their cannabis dining article is one of a series of pieces about the herb, including its health benefits and how to 'avoid that bust' by police when at home, in your car, or while hitchhiking. To make wiggley weed, readers are advised to first make a batch of weed tea by boiling cannabis leaves, stems, and seeds in water for at least four hours ('the longer the better'). The resulting liquid, once strained, is used 'instead of water with any fruit jello'.[14] Simple, portable, and sweet. One might consider wiggley weed's place among other spiked gelatin-based sweets like cannabis-infused gummies so popular today and candy-coloured alcohol-infused jello shots.

Cannabis cooking formed part of larger conversations about politics, race, and

131

cultural change taking place in underground newspapers. The *Los Angeles Free Press*, regularly answered readers' cannabis questions via 'Dr Hip Pocrates' and ran advertisements for mail-order weed cookbooks. Readers could also find out about the struggles faced by the local Black Panther Party when opening their free medical clinic.[15] In the same issue of *The Fifth Estate* that featured wiggley weed is news of workshops hosted by the city's Women's Health Project for women who 'want to learn about their bodies and want to begin developing alternatives to the way women are treated in traditional medical settings'.[16] That imperative to understand, control, and care for one's own body would be echoed in the actions of those who would soon lead the fight to legalize cannabis for medical use, as well as, much later, in the motivation of readers in 2016 turning to *The Medical Marijuana Dispensary*. In the March 1974 issue of *The Lesbian Tide*, Sudi Mae, 'friend of maryjane', argued that women should support an upcoming 'reeferendum' decriminalizing possession and use of weed in California to ensure control over 'our own lives & bodies', outlining 'parallels between the state's laws against gay love & against grass'.[17] Mae also included a culinary argument for supporting decriminalization: although it took more weed to get high by eating than by smoking, the referendum would allow prices to drop and people to grow their own, so that 'we could afford baked marijuana instead of roasted lung'.[18]

Sudi Mae wasn't alone in considering the culinary benefits of growing one's own. *The Primo Plant: Growing Sinsemilla Marijuana* provides far more cultivation guidance than kitchen advice, but its author, Carolyn 'Mountain Girl' Garcia, indulged readers with two foundational infusion recipes (for marijuana butter and for Barney's tequila verde).[19] Dedicated to J. I. Rodale (a publisher whom the *New York Times Magazine* called 'the guru of the organic food cult' in 1971), *The Primo Plant* outlines Garcia's cultivation method that succeeds without use of chemical fertilizers, which she states may be injurious to plants and 'affect the taste'.[20] One can trust Garcia's advice on taste, as she has been both an influential figure in cannabis legalization efforts as well as a countercultural celebrity long associated with musician Jerry Garcia and his band, the Grateful Dead.

The anonymous author of *A Guide to the Complete Enjoyment of Pot* also includes instructions on growing and preparing your own plants. But half of this slender volume is devoted to recipes, including one for 'glorified high', a cannabis-laced spin on a conventional dish called glorified rice.[21] A dessert of rice, cream, canned or fresh fruit, and marshmallows, glorified rice was promoted to homemakers across the United States through advertisements placed by the Southern Rice Industry's Home Economics Department in *Good Housekeeping Magazine* in the early decades of the twentieth century.[22] Another well-established American recipe, shrimp wiggle, also gets a cannabis makeover thanks to the anonymous creators of *Supermother's Cooking with Grass*, a collection of twelve printed recipe cards sold as a set. A classic chafing dish recipe that had a place in *Joy of Cooking* for decades, shrimp wiggle was only removed from that book in 2019 with the publication of *Joy's* ninth edition.[23] *Supermother's* weedy version

132

largely follows that of *Joy*'s first edition, but it uses more butter (which would, one imagines, be soaked up by the ⅛ cup of grass).[24]

Weed as a Medical Necessity

Despite the continued presence of cannabis recipes in counterculture newspapers and cookbooks, and the creative ways their authors suggested incorporating the herb into one's diet, cannabis was not as enthusiastically received by the US government. In 1970, President Nixon – violently opposed to both cannabis and people who used it, especially people of colour – signed the Controlled Substances Act, which classified drugs by different schedules based on medicinal value and potential for abuse.[25] Cannabis fell alongside LSD and heroin under Schedule I, drugs with high potential for abuse and no currently accepted medical use.[26] In the years that followed the signing of the CSA, many medical rights activists took issue with the schedule designation or ignored it completely. And one in particular made edible cannabis the cornerstone of her work.

In the 1980s and 1990s, Mary Jane Rathbun became an icon in San Francisco for her commitment to supplying AIDS patients, or her 'kids' as she called them, with free cannabis-laced brownies to help ease pain and increase appetite. This seemingly innocuous white lady became the poster child – or rather, poster grandmother – for medical rights and cannabis legalization in the form of her 'magically delicious' edibles. But Rathbun, who became known as 'Brownie Mary', didn't start baking with charity in mind. Upon arriving in San Francisco from the Midwest, she started her weed-spiked brownie business to supplement income from her waitressing job. By the late 1970s, she was selling up to fifty dozen brownies a day in her Castro neighbourhood, until leaflets advertising her goods gave her away to the police. As part of her court-mandated community service, she volunteered with the AIDS outpatient wing of the San Francisco General Hospital just as the AIDS crisis was gaining national attention. Despite her brush with the law, she brought cannabis brownies every day to the patients in paper bags, and within a few years, her charitable baking was famous throughout the city.[27] While her commitment to helping her 'kids' through baking didn't stop the arrests, it did stop the police from pressing charges. In August 1992, just a month after her third arrest, the Board of Supervisors proclaimed August 25th 'Brownie Mary Day' for the city of San Francisco.[28]

Four years later, due in part to the notoriety of Brownie Mary and the work of many others, California became the first state to legalize cannabis for medical use.[29] And in doing so, that state put into motion a wave of medical and recreational legalization throughout the country that is still moving forward today.

Eating Weed Today

Since so many states have begun lifting prohibitions, today's home cooks can choose from a glut of new cannabis cookbooks. Unlike counterculture titles that were published by underground presses or available only via mail order, today's titles are

133

proudly displayed on the shelves of bookstores, purchased by public libraries, and used as promotional and retail platforms for their authors. But like cannabis itself, there are many strains to these cookbooks, each one approaching the herb through a different lens and for particular audiences. Some promote cannabis as an elixir to be prescribed as part of a larger wellness program, while others look to cannabis as an ingredient to enhance flavour and expand consciousness. And still others, but a smaller number to be sure, just want to get you high.

Perhaps not surprisingly, *The Official High Times Cannabis Cookbook* falls under the latter category. The cookbook is a celebration of the years of recipes published in its namesake magazine, *High Times*. It features dishes from former writers and editors, such as the long-standing *High Times* Psychedelic Kitchen columnist Chef Ra (his great ganja pumpkin pie graces the cover), and other canna-friendly chefs – some famous (Eddie Huang's Cheeto fried chicken), and others less so (Ganja Granny's smoked mac 'n' cheese).[30] While *High Times* was founded in 1974 alongside other counterculture publications, it's outlasted them all, garnering mainstream appeal with a name that has become synonymous with cannabis culture. The *High Times* cookbook was the first cannabis cookbook released by a major commercial publisher, Chronicle Books, in 2012, when cannabis was legal for medical use in about a dozen states and on the verge of legal recreational use.[31] And while the recipes do nod to 'medibles' by offering two dosing measurements – the medical dosing is more than twice the recreational amount – the cookbook openly promotes a 'stoner-style cuisine' with irreverence, humour, and willingness to experiment using one's 'stash' in food.[32] Instead of serving sizes, the recipes in *High Times* boast the number of people who can get properly stoned from each dish. Fat joints and cold beer are the suggested accompaniments to the Willie Nelson-inspired Texas cannabis chilli recipe.

Despite its conventional appearance and the concessions it makes to adjust recipes for medical use, the *High Times Cannabis Cookbook* is a throwback. Its authors wholeheartedly embrace a cannabis high and in doing so align themselves more with their counterculture predecessors than with their commercialized and often health-conscious successors.

Laurie Wolf is one of the new breed of wellness-focused guides. Called 'the Martha Stewart of marijuana edibles' by the *New Yorker*, Wolf is half of the mother-daughter-in-law team Laurie & Maryjane, an Oregon-based business whose aim is to provide high-quality and reliable edibles to those seeking the healthful benefits of cannabis.[33] She's also the author of four cookbooks, including the *Medical Marijuana Dispensary* which, like its title suggests, dispenses thorough and exacting advice for first-time users. Wolf goes into great detail explaining dosing, cannabis strains, and the best methods of cannabis intake based on physical limitations. It's a prescription bottle in book form, where you'll find recipes for cannabis cough syrups, lozenges, salves, and suppositories. The food-based recipes here are secondary – a hodgepodge of mostly hearty, many gluten-free, somewhat bland foods (besides cannabis, few other herbs make an appearance): rice and bean bowl, stuffed sweet potato, stewed prunes. Will readers of Wolf's book, new to edibles and potentially suffering from illness, whip up a canna-compound to add to their overnight French toast? Perhaps, but far more likely is now that they trust Wolf's cautious expertise, they'll buy her line of small batch edibles and CBD granola by mail.

While *High Times* and Laurie Wolf might look at ingesting cannabis as a one-time high or as a dose of medicine, author Cedella Marley promotes a more holistic and spiritual approach to cannabis. It's the tradition she grew up with as the child of reggae royalty, Bob and Rita Marley. In 2017, she published *Cooking with Herb*, a collection of low-dosage recipes that incorporate the herb seamlessly into all the facets of one's life, 'from teas and tonics to soups and soaks'.[34] The seventy-five recipes include many Caribbean dishes and Marley family favourites, like jerk chicken and green juices, healthful breakfasts, tonics and teas, and scrubs and masks. Legalization, Marley points out, now allows for the herb to be present throughout one's daily life with a reverence that she grew up with: 'The ways that my family uses Herb are as diverse and varied as the colors of the ocean. It is really a part of the fabric of our lives'.[35]

Andrea Drummer's 2017 book *Cannabis Cuisine: Bud Pairings of a Born Again Chef* represents a different cannabis strain altogether, although, like *Cooking with Herb*, it is a post-prohibition cookbook by a black woman in an industry with few faces of colour. Drummer is a formally trained chef, a Cordon Bleu graduate and head chef of the country's only cannabis restaurant, the Original Cannabis Cafe (née Lowell Cafe), in West Hollywood. Drummer writes about her childhood, family, food, cooking, and her reacquaintance with cannabis as an adult. Her recipes reflect her thoughtfulness: they're creative, bold, modestly dosed – Drummer calls for approximately one quarter of the cannabis *High Times* uses in a similar recipe – and yet, although all her recipes call for cannabis oils and butters, the herb is secondary to both her narrative and to her dishes.[36] The recipes in *Cannabis Cuisine* stand out far more for their flavour combinations and culinary complexity than for the potentially brow-raising inclusion of weed. For Drummer, cannabis is yet another ingredient among a list you can add to, or swap out completely, as you wish.

135

> I've gleefully brought in an exciting new concept and ingredient to the repertoire – cannabis. But wait, it is actually no different from the fresh corn that my father used to bestow upon us as kids, or the ripened berries, peaches, and crab apples that we'd pick along the roadside. I dissect cannabis as I do everything else: carefully and consideringly. I smell and taste its potential as a full-bodied ingredient, honoring the integrity of the various strains and perfectly pairing them with other ingredients, flavors, textures, and tastes.[37]

Drummer hones in on the food itself, with dishes like quail confit with balsamic blueberry barbecue sauce (one tablespoon cannabis oil for eight servings) or blood orange sorbet (half a gram for six servings).[38] This is deliberate. Unlike other cookbook authors whose business model often relies on website sales of cannabis infusions and edibles, Drummer's cooking stands on its own – without the bud – because it has to: the menu of the Original Cannabis Cafe does not yet feature infused dishes (it's not legal). Instead, *Cannabis Cuisine* demonstrates Drummer's culinary range and talent in elevating cannabis to an ingredient that can be incorporated into a fine dining experience.

Due to the limited number of online consumption licenses, Drummer's Original Cannabis Cafe is the first, and thus far, only restaurant specializing in cannabis in California.[39] While the hospitality industry is one that offered the most promise for cannabis-friendly chefs and restaurateurs, it has also proven to be one of the most challenging to penetrate due to strict local and state-wide licenses and regulations. Cookbooks, then, offer one of the few ways for chefs and edibles experts to market themselves, their brands, and their products without having to muscle through a confusing system of compliance rules and regulations.

It's unclear whether Brownie Mary, a woman whose very identity is linked to cannabis brownies, followed a recipe besides the one she whipped up on her own. But likely not. Rathbun didn't start baking brownies because a cookbook published an especially enticing recipe, but because there was a market for them – legal or not – that she easily tapped into. Her home-baked brownies both supplemented her income and comforted AIDS patients, so much so that with both projects, she instituted waiting lists for her treats.[40] And she didn't feel compelled to leave a recipe behind either. Even the 1993 cookbook she and fellow activist Dennis Peron co-authored, *Brownie Mary's Marijuana Cookbook and Dennis Peron's Recipe for Social Change*, slyly left out that very sweet so many readers were hoping to recreate on their own. 'When and if they legalize it', she told the *New York Times* in 1996, 'I'll sell my brownie recipe to Betty Crocker or Duncan Hines and take the profits and buy an old Victorian for my kids with AIDS'.[41] When she died in 1999, she took her brownie recipe to the grave.

The Future of the Herb

For all the discussion around the popularity of cannabis and its inclusion in recent cookbooks, one is not likely to see Betty Crocker's Brownie Mary Mix at the local Safeway anytime soon. Major food manufacturers like Kraft and General Mills will likely wait until cannabis is removed from the Schedule I classification and becomes legal throughout the United States. But even without federal legalization, there is reason for cannabis advocates to worry about the intrusion of Big Canna.

Legalization has produced many of the benefits advocates have been campaigning for, but it has not ameliorated longstanding injustices. Many cannabis chefs and producers are left out of the legal marketplace due to prohibitions against those with prior arrests. And for people of colour, who are nearly four times more likely than whites to be arrested for cannabis despite similar usage rates, these laws perpetuate the inequities.[42] Additionally, 'the reluctance of banks to supply credit to marijuana entrepreneurs for fear of being seen as enabling a business still illegal under federal law' leaves licenses open only to wealthy individuals and, of course, to Big Canna.[43]

136

Small growers are also concerned by the threat of Marlboro Man suddenly rolling a joint and patenting it. Mountain Girl may have imagined a future of individual gardeners nurturing and enjoying their own herb gardens, but today huge agricultural companies like Scotts Miracle-Gro have been buying up the means of cannabis production.[44] And there are worries that Monsanto will develop a genetically modified strain of cannabis and corner the market – once it becomes legal.[45] In other words, there are many cannabis advocates who are understandably nervous that the future of cannabis legalization will continue to entice large corporate interests, who, like Big Pharma, see the monetary gain in the herb's medicinal value. As former *High Times* editor David Bienenstock said, 'Prohibition, for all of its evils, acted in a way to protect the underground economy from capitalism'.[46]

Cannabis culture in 2020 continues to be rooted in opposing worlds: legal and outlawed, counterculture and mainstream, essential and recreational, and homespun and corporate. And questions remain about what lies ahead: What is the future of cannabis cooking? And who will be welcome at the table?

Notes

1   Robyn Griggs Lawrence, *Pot in Pans: A History of Eating Cannabis* (London: Rowman & Littlefield, 2019), 'bhang' p. 37; 'majoun' p. 167.

2   Martin A. Lee, *Smoke Signals: A Social History of Marijuana – Medical, Recreational, and Scientific* (New York: Scribner, 2012), '1937' p. 53; '1970' p. 118.

3   Jeremy Berke and Skye Gould, 'States where Marijuana Is Legal', *Business Insider,* 1 Jan 2020 <https://www.businessinsider.com/legal-marijuana-states-2018-1> [accessed 31 May 2020].

4   Deena Shupe, *The High Art of Cooking* (San Francisco: Synergisms, 1971), p. [3].

5   Shupe, p. 80.

6   Shupe, p. 95.

7   True Light Beavers, *Eat, Fast, Feast: A Tribal Cookbook* (Garden City: Doubleday, 1972), p. xii.

8   True Light Beavers, 'to turn' p. xiii; marjoome recipes pp. 244-46.

9   Evelyn Schmevelyn, *Cooking with Marijuana* (Seattle: Sun Magic Publishing, 1977), 'awful' and 'acrid' p. 2; 'give it a chance' p. 42.

10   Schmevelyn, 'food that is very spicy' and 'pot Italiano' p. 24; 'delicacies' p. 17.

11   Schmevelyn, pp. 37-38.

12   Schmevelyn, p. 10.

13   [Anon.], 'Gobble Grass', *Quicksilver Times*, 31 December 1971, p. 7.

14   [Anon.], 'A Meal with Weed', *Fifth Estate*, 28 April 1973, p. 6.

15   Dennis Levitt, 'Black Panthers Open Free Clinic', *Los Angeles Free Press*, 2 January 1970, p. 3.

16   Miriam Frank, 'Women's Health', *Fifth Estate*, 28 April 1973, p. 7.

17   Sudi [Mae], 'Women for Weed', *The Tide*, March 1974, p. 5; this was the first of five successive issues printed in 1974 when editors of *The Lesbian Tide* temporarily removed the word 'lesbian' from the journal title.

18   Mae, pp. 20-21.

19   Mountain Girl, *The Primo Plant: Growing Sinsemilla Marijuana* (Berkeley: Wingbow; Bolinas: Leaves of Grass, 1977), pp. 94-95.

20   Wade Greene, 'Guru of the Organic Food Cult', *New York Times Magazine*, 6 June 1971; Mountain Girl, p. 22.

21 [Anon.], *A Guide to the Complete Enjoyment of Pot; or, Moments of Pleasure with Cannabis Sativa* (San Francisco, CA: Enterprise Unlimited, [1966(?)]), p. 18.

22 Southern Rice Industry, [display advertisement], *Good Housekeeping Magazine,* December 1936, p. 200.

23 Aimee Levitt, 'What the Hell Was Shrimp Wiggle?' *The Takeout,* 23 Oct 2019 <https://thetakeout.com/what-is-shrimp-wiggle-joy-of-cooking-1839236691> [accessed 31 May 2020].

24 Irma S. Rombauer, *The Joy of Cooking: A Compilation of Reliable Recipes with a Casual Culinary Chat* (St. Louis: A.C. Clayton, 1931), p. 49; [Anon.], *Supermother's Cooking with Grass* (San Francisco: Flash Transactions International, 1971).

25 Lee, p. 119.

26 United States Drug Enforcement Administration, *The Controlled Substances Act*, s. 201 <https://www.dea.gov/controlled-substances-act> [accessed 31 May 2020].

27 Lawrence, pp. 105-08.

28 Cary Goldberg, '"Brownie Mary" Fights to Legalize Marijuana', New York Times, 6 July 1996, p. 6.

29 Lawrence, p. 109.

30 Elise McDonough and the Editors of *High Times Magazine, The Official High Times Cannabis Cookbook* (San Francisco: Chronicle Books, 2012), 'pumpkin pie' p. 285; 'fried chicken' p. 189; 'mac n cheese' p. 175.

31 Lawrence, p. 100.

32 McDonough, 'medibles' p. 22; 'dosing' p. 52.

33 Lizzie Widdiecombe, 'High Cuisine', *New Yorker,* 24 April 2017, p. 48.

34 Cedella Marley, *Cooking with Herb* (New York: Pam Krauss Books/Avery, 2017), p. 17.

35 Marley, p. 26.

36 Canna-butter dosing comparison in macaroni and cheese recipes in Drummer, p. 128, and McDonough, p. 175.

37 Andrea Drummer, *Cannabis Cuisine: Bud Pairings of a Born Again Chef* (Coral Gables: Mango Publishing, 2017), p. 17.

38 Drummer, 'quail' p. 172; 'sorbet' p. 271.

39 Marla Cimini, 'What It's Like to Go to the First Cannabis Cafe in the United States', *USA Today,* 6 Feb 2020 <https://www.10best.com/interests/food-culture/original-cannabis-cafe-first-united-states-los-angeles/> [accessed 31 May 2020].

40 Lawrence, p. 106-07.

41 Goldberg, p. 6.

42 American Civil Liberties Union, *The War on Marijuana in Black and White* (New York: ACLU, 2013), p. 4.

43 Steven Bender, 'The Colors of Cannabis: Race and Marijuana', *U.C. Davis Law Review,* 50 (2016), p. 705.

44 Max A. Cherney, 'Scotts Miracle-Gro to Acquire Hydroponics Supplier Sunlight Supply', *Market Watch,* 17 April 2018 <https://www.marketwatch.com/story/scotts-miracle-gro-to-acquire-hydroponics-supplier-sunlight-supply-2018-04-17> [accessed 31 May 2020].

45 Paul Roberts, 'The Bayer-Monsanto Deal Won't Eat the Cannabis Industry...Yet', *Leafly,* 15 September 2016 <https://www.leafly.com/news/industry/bayer-monsanto-deal-wont-eat-cannabis-industry-yet> [accessed 31 May 2020].

46 Lawrence, p. 148.

The Savoury Course at Oxford and Cambridge Colleges

Paul Freedman

The savoury survives in a few odd corners, but its glory years were from the 1870s until the Second World War. A small spicy or salty course served between the sweet and dessert, it is uniquely British. Typical savouries are Welsh rarebit, devils on horseback (which are prunes wrapped in bacon), angels on horseback (oysters wrapped in bacon), Scotch woodcock (scrambled eggs and anchovy paste on toast) and herring roes on toast. Curry and other piquant flavours are popular. In the authoritative *Répertoire de la cuisine*, Saulnier and Gingoire say that all savouries should be highly spiced with cayenne, but this admittedly within a context of disapproval as they include the course only because the English and Americans persist in serving them.[1]

Many savouries were presented on toast (*en croûte*) or as canapés (bread trimmed of crusts and toasted or fried). From 1904 to 1932 the Reform Club created no less than 46 *croûtes* including *croûte Indienne* (curried shrimp and chutney) and more mysteriously *croûte Alexandre le Grand* and *croûte Murrumundi* (the latter is a place in New South Wales, Australia).

Savoury as an identifying course name dates from the 1870s, by which time Mrs de Salis could entitle the first cookbook devoted to the subject *Savouries à la Mode* (1877).[2] A penultimate course mixing sweet and savoury, essentially a medieval invention, had persisted in Britain well into the Victorian period. What was new, the innovation which took place between 1850 and 1870, was separating the savoury to form a service of its own. Rather than accompanying pastry and pudding, now it followed them. In *What Shall We Have For Dinner?* (published in the 1850s) Catherine (Mrs Charles) Dickens offers possibilities for winding up the dinner that reflect a transitional moment in which one occasion might see cold lemon pudding served simultaneously with bloaters, while another menu suggested tarts and puddings followed by dressed crab.[3]

The emergence of a distinct savoury course out of what had been previously a miscellaneous assortment of *entremêts* was facilitated by the gradual adoption of Russian service. If instead of having dozens of dishes brought to the table simultaneously, with only two or three courses, Russian service could accommodate six, eight, fourteen successive services, so why not present an amusingly unexpected small but sharp-flavoured last or nearly-last course? Other factors favouring the savoury's origination include the occasional cheese course and serving dessert wines, particularly port, after the meal and coffee – all relatively new forms of prolonging the meal. Naturally this does not explain why no one outside Britain thought the savoury a good idea.

We cannot identify one single moment when the savoury was 'invented', nor did anyone claim credit for it. By 1886, however, Mary Allen, author of *Savouries and Sweets Suitable for Luncheons and Dinners,* could pronounce without the likelihood of contradiction that these 'piquant little dishes' were 'universally served between the sweets and the dessert'.[4]

The prolific journalist and gourmand George Augustus Sala disapproved of the savoury because it spoiled appreciation of dessert fruit. Oddly, he blamed the innovation on women. In *The Thorough Good Cook* (1885), he affected to concede ruefully, 'I know perfectly well […] that when a lady has made up her mind to anything, that the thing has got to be done; and so I have carefully selected some recipes for savouries.'[5] Apart from this eccentric instance, it was generally agreed that the savoury was a male preference. Women were always regarded as fond of sweets, and men were at least sometimes thought partial to robust and spicy flavours. Whatever the truth of this as a general observation, the true home of the savoury, much more than household or restaurant, was the male association: clubs, livery companies, Inns of Court, and Oxford and Cambridge colleges. What follows is devoted to the colleges, appropriate to our conference's home in Oxford even if in this disastrous year 2020 we are meeting in virtual exile.

Oxford and Cambridge

In terms of which savouries were favoured and the chronology of their rise and decline, the Oxford and Cambridge colleges do not differ greatly from London clubs or similar fellowships. As with clubs, the older male foundations were more splendid than the newer and less generously endowed women's institutions. My impression, and it is preliminary rather than assured, is that female clubs and colleges did not have savouries. In *A Room of One's Own,* Virginia Woolf famously compared the luxurious dining of a nameless male college with an indifferent dinner at Fernham, a women's college. True, a going-down song at Somerville (sung to the tune of the 'Skye Boat Song') recalls sybaritic prewar pleasures:

> Potatoes galore, chicken and beef
> Cake every day for tea,
> Biscuits for lunch, and chocolate too;
> Saturday savoury.[6]

One would like to know what that Saturday savoury was, but it is unlikely to have been a dinner course. Menus from the Somerville archives have nothing to say about savouries.

Oxbridge colleges are distinct from clubs and livery companies in that the fellows and guests leave the Hall for a cosier and more informal Common or Combination room in order to take dessert, post-prandial wines, and coffee. This reverses what used to be the dinner-party convention of ladies leaving the table for the men to drink port and then re-joining for coffee. Moving the concluding acts reflects a desire for a less formal phase of dinner going back to late-medieval conventions of the banquet, originally a kind of supper during which women and men could converse.[7]

Colleges' archives preserve different chronological ranges for reports of their meals and somewhat different types of documentation. Trinity College, Cambridge, has a large run of menus from 1890 to the 1930s, and many are for routine dinners rather than special feasts. Christ Church records cover the same period and beyond, but only for gaudies and other festive events. All Souls preserves few menus but numerous 'menu books' and 'dinner books', records kept by the kitchen and service staff that also list the expenses.

A Trinity menu for Ascension Day, 22 May 1884, gives a sense of the splendid level of dining as well as a context for the embryonic savoury, not yet a course of its own.[8] The first course consists of two soups (*consommé à l'Archiduchesse* **and** *à la Mongol*) followed by three fish (turbot, salmon, and fried fillets of sole). The entrées are fried sweetbreads *à l'impériale* and leveret timbale with *sauce chasseur*. Four joints (*relevés*) come next: spring chickens with tarragon, tongue, chine of lamb with cucumber sauce, and sirloin of beef. The roast course is green geese and quails, served with peas. Finally, *entremêts*, consisting of a pudding (*à la Leopold*), strawberry jelly, an assortment of ice-cream 'boats', and *diablotins de gruyère*, usually a canapé with Béchamel sauce, grated cheese, and cayenne pepper sprinkled with Parmesan and browned on top.

Shortly thereafter, the savoury, although unnamed, was clearly a separate course. For a Trinity Vice-Master's Dinner in 1888, the bill of fare lists three '*Entremêts*': *poudings soufflés à l'Ananas, gelées au Kirsch*, and Maids of Honour. Then another sweet, *bombes à l'Indienne*, and finally, set off from the rest, cheese straws (*pailles au Parmesan*). At the Feast of the Audit on December 1, 1898, we see for the first time what would become the *141* pattern: a sweet course labeled *Entremêt* (including 'Hindostan pudding'), Ice (brown bread and Curaçao), and a specifically entitled savoury course consisting of two items: bloater roe and minced haddock toasts.

Beginning somewhat earlier than at Trinity, All Souls meals often concluded with a savoury.[9] Because of its special nature as a college without resident undergraduates, All Souls meals were small. The dinner book for 1878 notes five for a meal on 12 October at which the following were served:

> Vermicelli Soup
> Turbot, Shrimp Sauce
> Curried Rabbit
> Leg of Mutton
> Windsor Pudding
> Salad
> Bloaters

Fourteen fellows and guests were present on 17 November, a Sunday nine-course affair at which, after a game service of snipe, there was a sweet consisting of jelly and plum pudding and finally haddock.

Before the First World War, a savoury was common if not inevitable at Oxbridge colleges. In the interwar period, All Souls seems have let the savoury lapse, but Trinity maintained its enthusiasm and even presented its own invention, 'Champignons Alma Mater'. Jesus College similarly saw a consistent inclusion of savouries once the Great War was over, particularly at dinners for student groups such as 'The Natives' (symbol: two oysters) and 'The Rooster', a debating society. The Roosters favoured comical names for savouries such as 'roosters on horseback' or 'wizzard gizzards', but these alternated with conventional devils on horseback and *coquilles au fromage*. Bump Suppers at Jesus College between 1920 and 1937 always included savouries in what were rather simple meals, usually of four courses only. A supper on 23 February 1935 began with whitebait, followed by roast ducks with potatoes and peas, a sweet course of *bombe Venitienne,* and *croûtes de Lyon* to conclude.[10]

Although interwar dinners were less ostentatious than in the past – the days of a separate *relevé* and multiple-dish *entremêts* were over – feasts retained their earlier distinction and generally included a savoury course. The 1937 Commemoration dinner at St Catharine's, Cambridge, began with oysters, offered thick and clear soups, and continued with sole, mutton, suckling pig, a Champagne sorbet, roast teal as a game course, and, after two sweets, two savouries: lobster pancakes and *fines herbes* toast.

War and Postwar

War rationing put an end to luxury dining, and, as regulations limited how many courses could be served, the savoury almost everywhere disappeared. Exceptionally, boat race dinners at St Catharine's, Cambridge, between 1941 and 1945 still included savouries – some examples are egg and anchovy *croûtes*, egg and kipper *croutes*, and stuffed tomatoes.[11]

Records for festive meals at Magdalene College, Cambridge, show both the grim effect of the War on dining and the persistence of the savoury course.[12] The annual dinner in honour of Samuel Pepys in 1939 had eight courses with the same number of wines. The menu is accompanied by three apposite passages from Pepys' diaries:

Huitres
(Champagne nature Château de Mesnil)

Tortue Claire
(Sherry Amontillado)

Saumon et concombre
(Hock Oestricher 1934)
'This day Sir W. Batten tells me that Mr. Newburne is dead of eating cowcumbers, of which the other day I heard another' – August 22, 1663

Agneau printanier roti
(Champagne Perrier Jouet 1928)

Game Pasty
(Burgundy Richebourg 1923)

142

'A pie of such pleasant variety of good things, as in all my life I never tasted'

Pêches Richelieu
Mousse Madrid

Aiguillettes de mer

Dessert

Wines:
Port Cockburn 1896
Claret Château Haut Brion 1929
Clos de la Barangerie 1934
'…here drank a sort of French wine called Ho Bryan, that has a good and most particular taste that I never met with' – April 10, 1663

The savoury here, *'aiguillettes de mer'*, is made with strips of sliced fish. Four years later, the 1943 Pepys commemoration offered only three courses, but the last was 'nabobs' which I take to be a vaguely Anglo-Indian savoury.

During the first postwar years, Magdalene College, Cambridge, was among the few plucky colleges that refused to allow the savoury to fade. It offered surprisingly elaborate, five-course feasts for its patron saint's day and *croûtes* appeared in 1946, 1947, and 1949: haddock *croûtes*, Ivanhoe *croûtes* (haddock puréed with mushrooms), and Harlequin *croûtes* respectively. Harlequin *croûtes* were multi-coloured, typically with strips of tongue, truffle, smoked salmon, and gherkin. The 1945 Peckard Feast (in honour of an eighteenth-century Master of the College, later University Vice-Chancellor) included Ivanhoe *croûtes*. Mushrooms Lucullus were presented in 1948.

Most of the colleges whose menus I have examined revived the savoury by the mid-1950s. They differ as to when they abandoned the course. Consider Christ Church. Its 1946 Gaudy was meagre, but it did feature a savoury of small salmon pastries. In 1947 there was a turtle soup, a tomato hors d'oeuvre, and a fish course of salmon trout *meunière*, roast chicken, and a meringue sweet. The savoury was mushroom *croûtes*. The 1953 Gaudy was commemorated with six courses, including salmon and saddle of mutton, and ending with fried Parmesan pastries (*aigrettes de Parmesan*). Thereafter, for a time, Gaudies and Censer's Dinners include savouries such as mushroom *croûtes*, cauliflower au gratin, tartines, and cassolettes. By the late 1970s, the savoury died out at Christ Church. There was an attempt to revive it in the 1980s, but it was unsuccessful.[13]

Hertford College too consistently favoured savouries on its Gaudy menus from the 1950s to the late 1970s. *Champignons Bordelaise* was nearly inevitable for Gaudy dinners at Hertford (the savoury usually preceded by *fraises Romaines* or *gâteau Hertford*). Regular meals also routinely included savouries. From 1950 until 1973 savouries alternated among several kinds of *croûte*, devilled lobster, cheese items, and something referred to as 'gondolas of haddock'.[14]

143

Post-Postwar

What ended the era of the savoury was not post-war austerity but rather prosperity and the internationalization of British taste beginning in the late 1950s. The slowness of the economic recovery intensified the impression that British food was impoverished and dreary – canned soup, frozen *gâteau,* dollops of Marmite or HP Sauce, and locally described by cheery but not very inviting terms such as 'fry up'. Rupert Croft-Cooke in his 1960 call to arms, *English Cooking: A New Approach*, bemoaned the nation's culinary mediocrity, imposed as it was by indifference, forgetfulness, and tasteless affluence rather than by excusable dearth. Such writers aimed to combat decline by restoring Britain's real food traditions. Croft-Cooke, as it happens, was opposed to the savoury because its piquant or sharp tastes interfered with the appropriate pairing of wines.[15] An American author, Audrey Alley Gorton, wrote a cookbook with the spirited title *In Defense of British Cooking* and this too appeared in 1960. Unlike Croft-Cooke, she was fond of savouries, considering them typical and appropriate for her campaign and provided recipes for thirteen classics, from caviar pancakes to cod's roe on toast.[16]

These were losing efforts, however, and, for several decades after 1960, sophisticated dining was Continental or Mediterranean. As we all know, it took a while for European standards of freshness, craftsmanship, and *terroir* to be applied to Britain.

Recently the savoury has experienced a modest revival, although it has lost its place in the order of courses, so that Welsh rarebit or Scotch woodcock might be an hors d'oeuvre, a side dish, or offered in lieu of dessert. At Cambridge, St John's College still approximately once a week presents savouries such as devils on horseback, canapé Cadogan (oysters and spinach with *sauce Mornay*), canapé Ivanhoe, and Welsh rarebit.[17] Feasts at Magdalene College, Cambridge, have preserved savouries consistently since the end of the Second World War. They continue to appear in recent annual commemorations such as Pepys dinners and especially the feast in honour of St Mary Magdalen, from haddock *sur croûtes* in 1946 to angels on horseback in 1969 and 1970, to sliced mushrooms on toast in 2013 and 2014.[18]

I hesitate to ask for savouries to be adopted as *de rigueur* at future Oxford Food Symposium dinners, contenting myself with the hope that we will meet again over those wonderful collations, whatever their bills of fare.

Acknowledgements

Although this is a short communication, I have many people to thank, based as it is on several archives and libraries that required guidance to navigate. I would like to express my gratitude to the following: For Somerville College, Dr Alice Prochaska, former Principal, and the Librarian Dr Anne Manuel. For the Cambridge colleges Trinity, Jesus and Gonville & Caius, I was greatly aided by Paul Aste, a student at Caius and archival intern there. At All Souls, Professor Julia Smith kindly introduced me to Dr Norma Aubertin-Potter, Clerk to the Archives of the Codrington Library. The late Peter Linehan, Fellow of St John's College, Cambridge, introduced me to the librarians and archivists of the College. Judith Curthoys, Archivist at Christ Church College helped me with that collection. Two former Yale students who subsequently studied in Britain, one at Oxford, the other at Cambridge, looked up material for me: Joshua Evans at Hertford College, Oxford, and Christina Stankey at Magdalene College, Cambridge. Finally my gratitude to Professor Nora Berend of St Catharine's College, Cambridge, and Dr Colin Higgins, Librarian and Fellow of St Catharine's.

Notes

1   L. Saulnier and Th. Gringoie, *Le Répertoire de la cuisine*, 3rd. ed. (Paris, 1923), p. xiv: '*Les savouries (ou bonnes-bouchés) decraient être supprimées radicalement; nous en indiquon cependant des recettes, parce qu'un grand nomvre d'Anglias et d'Américains leur sont demeurés fidèles.*'

2   Mrs de Salis [Harriet Anne Bainbridge de Salis], *Savouries à la Mode* (London: Longmans Green & Co., 1877).

3   'Lady Clutterbuck' [Catherine Dickens], *What Shall We Have For Dinner? Satisfactorily Answered for Numerous Bills of Fare for from Two to Eighteen Persons*, 2nd ed. (London, Bradbury & Evans, 1856), reprinted with an introduction by Susan M. Rossi-Wilcox, *Dinner for Dickens: The Culinary History of Mrs Charles Dickens* (Totnes, Prospect Books, 2005), pp. 1, 18, 27, 37. See also Rossi-Wilcox, 'Saucing the Dish of Authenticity: Mrs. Charles Dickens's Menus and Her Husband's Writings', in *Authenticity in the Kitchen: Proceedings of the Oxford Symposium on Food and Cookery 2005*, ed. by Richard Hosking (Totnes: Prospect Books, 2006), pp. 368-78.

4   Mary L. Allen [also known as Macaire Allen], *Savouries and Sweets Suitable for Luncheons and Dinners* (London: J. S. Virtue and Co. Ltd., 1886), p. [ii].

5   George Augustus Sala, *The Thorough Good Cook: A Series of Chats on the Culinary Art and Nine Hundred Recipes* (London: Cassell and Co., 1885), pp. 43-44.

6   Oxford, Somerville College Archive. Unclassified.

7   Yann Morel, '*Le banquet à la cour de Bourgogne au XVe siècle: essai de définition*', in *Le Banquet: Manger, boire et parler ensemble (XIIe-XVIIe siècles)*, ed. by Bruno Laurioux and others (Florence: Sismel, Edizioni del Galluzzo, 2018), pp. 185-203; Thalia Brero, '*Soirées festives et vie nocturne à la cour de Savoie*', pp. 229-59 in the same collection.

8   Cambridge, Trinity College Archive, Hall menus, 22 May 1884.

9   Oxford, All Souls College, Codrington Library, Undated Menu Book (datable to the 1870s or 1880s).

10 Cambridge, Jesus College Archives, Student Societies, 1905-1962, Series 4, JCCA/C5/4/6, Dinners and Events

11 Cambridge, St Catharine's College Archive, U/S/6/5, a total of seven menus from June 7, 1941 to March 4, 1944.

12 Cambridge, Magdalene College Archives, E/A/3, Box 1, folder 5, Pepys Dinner 1905-1993.

13 Oxford, Christ Church College Archives. The menus are kept in a section that includes information of Gaudies and other festive dinners. I thank Professor Carolyne Larrington, now at St John's College, Oxford, for telling me about the failed attempt to revive savouries at Christ College.

14 Oxford, Hertford College Archive, menus.

15 Rupert Croft-Cooke, *English Cooking: A New Approach* (London: W. H. Allen, 1960), pp. 24-25, 189.

16 Audrey Alley Gorton, *In Defense of British Cooking: 200 Wonderful Recipes That Prove the English CAN Cook* (Brattleboro, VT: Stephen Greene Press,1960), pp. 80-85.

17 I thank Mr. W. A. Brogan, kitchen manager at St John's College.

18 Magdalene College Archives, E/A/3, Box 1, folder 5, Pepys Dinners, 1905-1993; Box 3, folder 8, St Mary Magdalene Feast, from 1935.

Vodka in Early Modern Muscovy: Foreign Doctors, Travelling Herbalists, and the Tsar's Kitchen

Alexandr Gorokhovskiy

Russian vodka is arguably the most gastronomic spirit in the world. Throughout its history it was – and still is, at least in its home country – mainly consumed as part of a hearty meal or accompanied by numerous *zakuski* (appetizers). But how did this come about? Why is vodka such an integral part of Russian culinary culture? In this paper I will briefly review what we know about the beginnings of vodka and look at how Western medical practice, local herbalist traditions, and gastronomic needs and preferences of the Muscovite court have all contributed to early identity formation of Russia's national drink.

The origins of vodka are obscure, and very little historical material is currently available from which we can safely ascertain when the inhabitants of what is now European Russia started to produce distilled alcoholic beverages, and whether this was the result of a technology transfer or a purely domestic development. The earliest mention of spirit making in Muscovy is found in *Tractatus de duabus Sarmatiis*, a popular treatise on the geography, history, and culture of Eastern Europe composed by Polish scholar and physician Maciej Miechowita and printed in Cracow in 1517. In a chapter dedicated to Muscovy he writes: 'They frequently use warming spices, and often sublimated spices and honey [*sublimatis de aromatibus de melle*] or other calefactory [beverages], this way, and [also] by making from oats burning water [*aquam ardentem* …] and drinking [it], they repulse and drive away the cold and chill, otherwise from the coldness they will freeze.'[1]

Aqua ardens ('burning water') was one of the Latin terms commonly applied to distilled alcohol since late medieval times. The name probably referred either to the burning sensation appearing in the mouth and throat after drinking a spirit, or to the fact that it contained enough alcohol to burn. The term could also have been derived from the actual process used to heat and vaporize the base liquid during distillation. Another popular medieval term related to spirits, *vinum adustum* (or *vinum crematum*), makes it clear what this base liquid originally was – literally, this means 'burnt wine'. However, in those countries where grapevines did not grow and wine was too expensive an ingredient for distilling, it was a mash of fermented grains that eventually became the principal raw material for making strong liquor.[2] Muscovy was one of such places and it seems that spirits were produced there from cereals right from the onset of Russian distilling (even though not necessarily in all cases, as we will see).

The author of *Tractatus de duabus Sarmatiis* never visited Muscovy, but according to some witnesses Miechowita's informants were Russian prisoners of war taken at the Battle of Orsha.[3] We can therefore assume that his account is still accurate to some degree, although its emphasis on the role played by distillates in keeping Muscovites warm in freezing weather raises suspicions of stereotyping. Having said that, it is true that during the same period other nations living in similar temperatures were also consuming distilled liquor not for intoxication but rather to fight the effects of the cold climate: in sixteenth-century Germany, for example, spirits were normally drunk in the morning – just as coffee is today – for warmth and 'strength', and mainly during winter months.[4]

That Russians were already familiar with distilled alcohol in the first quarter of the sixteenth century finds confirmation in the writings of a Habsburg diplomat, Sigismund von Herberstein, who visited Moscow twice, in 1517 and 1526 – his first trip occurring during the same year Miechowita's book was published. An energetic and capable ethnographer, he left rich and objective descriptions of Muscovy based mainly on personal observations. (Herberstein was born and grew up in the Duchy of Carniola, now in Slovenia, which meant that when he came to Russia his knowledge of a Slavonic language allowed him to communicate freely with the locals.)

While waiting for an audience with the Grand Prince after his arrival in Moscow in April 1517, Herberstein resided in a house allocated to him by the authorities that had food and beverages brought in daily. Among the supplies were beef, pig fat, rabbit meat, chicken, live sheep, fresh and smoked fish, cheese, salt, spices such as saffron and pepper, mead, and two types of beer. In his autobiography, written in German, Herberstein mentions that a small jug of 'burnt wine' (*pranndt Wein* in the original text) was also delivered and claims that 'they [the Muscovites] always drink it at the table before a meal'.[5]

The notion that Russians always consume spirits before taking their food can once again be found in a description of a ceremonial dinner that Herberstein attended at the Grand Prince's palace during his second visit to Moscow, given in his *Rerum Moscoviticarum Commentarii* – a detailed eyewitness ethnography of Russia, originally published in Latin in 1549: 'Finally, the stewards went out for food, [...] first they brought in *aqua vitae*, which they always drink at the commencement of the dinner; then they brought roasted swans, which it is almost always their custom to lay before their guests for the first dish whenever they eat meat.'[6] *Aqua vitae* ('water of life') was another generic term for distilled alcohol in late medieval and early modern times, the name implying that back in the day it was used mainly for medicinal purposes. It has been replicated in many languages, from French *eau-de-vie* to Gaelic *uisce beatha*, and in some countries even became the appellation of the national spirit – like *akvavit*, the Scandinavian grain distillate flavoured with a variety of herbs, the principal ones being caraway and dill seed.

Herberstein does not mention if the *aqua vitae* that he encountered in Russia was infused or distilled with herbs or spices, but this is entirely possible – as Miechowita's account suggests, some of the beverages popular among Muscovites did contain spices. The very fact that spirits were consumed in Muscovy before meals may itself mean that the local liquor could well have been herbed and/or spiced: one of the reasons why distilled beverages in the early modern period were seen as something that can both arouse appetite and promote digestion laid in the properties attributed to plant extracts that they often contained.

In Western Europe distillation was applied to herbal material as early as in the fourteenth century, and by the middle of the fifteenth century extracting flavours and medicinal value from plants by boiling them in water or wine and then condensing the vapours became common practice – to such an extent that from the early sixteenth century onwards many manor houses had a stillroom where herbal preparations were made and stored for future use.[7] Such a stillroom was often combined with the kitchen since distilling required a reliable source of heat.

The dissemination of distillation technology across the continent during the second half of the fifteenth and the first half of the sixteenth centuries accelerated with the invention of the printing press. One of the earliest and most comprehensive printed manuals on the distillation of herbal 'waters' and their medical applications was *Liber de arte distillandi de simplicibus* by Hieronymus Brunschwig, written in German (despite its Latin title) and first published in 1500 in Strasbourg.[8] Having been immensely successful in Germany both in its original format and as a revised, longer version called *Liber de arte distillandi de compositis* (1512), as well as eventually becoming an integral part of popular herbal compendiums, it remained in print for more than a century and was translated into other languages, including Dutch (1517), English (1527), and Czech (1559).

There are several (at least six) known manuscript copies of what appears to be the Russian translation of Brunschwig's treatise, the earliest of which dates to the last quarter of the sixteenth century. It is called *Skazanie o propushchenii vod* and has a Muscovite origin, even though translation itself might have been done either in Pskov or Novgorod, or by someone originating from there.[9] *Skazanie*'s emergence was most probably linked to the creation in Moscow of the Apothecary Chancery (*Aptekarskiy prikaz*) – the medical department of the tsar's palace.

We don't know when the Apothecary Chancery was formed, but it seems to have been fully operational by 1582.[10] This institution grew out of the Russian monarch's private pharmacy and initially cared only for the royal household, but eventually ended up serving also the needs of the tsar's close courtiers, the nobility more generally, the higher clergy, and the army. The Chancery was staffed by imported – Dutch, English, German – doctors and apothecaries, and relied in large part on Western medical texts, many of which were brought from Europe by the foreign specialists themselves. A number of important medical books were translated into Russian in this period, and *Liber de arte distillandi* must have been one of them.

148

The extent of *Skazanie*'s circulation is not clear, and its emersion by no means antedated Russian distilling as such. As we saw, alcohol distillation was practiced in Muscovy well before Brunschwig's work got translated (unless a much earlier copy of this translation is waiting somewhere to be discovered), with grain spirits being produced at least since the early sixteenth century.[11] However, the appearance of this and similar books and transmission into Russia of the medical know-how that they manifested undoubtedly contributed to further development of the apparently already existing local practice of distilling with herbs and spices.

Since most, if not all, early modern medicines were derived from herbs (including by way of preparing medicinal distillates, as described in *Liber de arte distillandi*), herb collection and processing was one of the key functions of the Apothecary Chancery. Various plants of the *materia medica* were grown in its own apothecary gardens, and starting from at least 1630s collecting herbs and berries – such as juniper, for example – for the Chancery became an official seasonal obligation born by peasant communities in some parts of Muscovy. In addition, special herb-gathering expeditions were organized all around the tsardom.[12]

As can be seen from the available documents, Apothecary Chancery's staff herbalists (*travniki*), who normally led such expeditions, were almost always accompanied in the field by *pomyasy*, drafted from the tsar's kitchen (*Kormovoy dvorets*).[13] The meaning of the word *pomyas* is not very clear. According to *Dictionary of Church Slavonic and Russian Language* (1847), *pomyas* is a person who is responsible for 'watching over the meat supplies'. Izmail Sreznevsky in his *Materials for a Dictionary of the Old Russian Language* (1902) also defines it, albeit not very confidently, as 'meatman'. In *Dictionary of the Russian Language of XI-XVII Centuries* (1991), *pomyas* is 'someone who kneads dough or mixes ingredients during cooking'.[14] Such difference in suggested meanings can be explained by the similarity between the Russian words *myaso* ('meat') and *mesit'* ('to knead', also 'to mix'). Regardless of its etymology, it seems that the term was used to refer to a person involved in food (most likely, meat) storage and/or preparation. What is not clear is why of all the available personnel it was *pomyasy* who were regularly dispatched by the palace to assist *travniki* in collecting medicinal plants all over Muscovy.

The answer may be that in medieval and early modern cooking herbs and spices were not only used to help digestion or enhance food flavour; they also played an important role in the preservation of meat products due to their natural antimicrobial and antioxidant properties. It is not only imported Asian spices that possess such qualities – compounds that can be found in plants native to Europe, such as fennel, parsley, rosemary, thyme, sage, mustard, etc., are also able to eliminate or delay the action of pathogenic microorganisms that attack meat if it is stored at room temperature for more than few hours. Moreover, many herbs exhibit greater antibacterial potency when they are blended together than when used alone.[15] It could be that the 'ingredients' which *pomyasy* were supposed to be mixing in their kitchens were herbs and spices, and the main reason for them to be sent along with *travniki* on herb-collecting expeditions organized by the Apothecary Chancery was their expertise of working with herbal material.

Herbs, roots, flowers, and berries collected in the field by *travniki* and *pomyasy* were used by the Chancery's *alkhemisty* (at Muscovite court this word denoted pharmacists and staff distillers, not alchemists in a philosophical or scientific sense) for the preparation of vodkas and essential oils, which would then be supplied to the tsar's courtiers and servicemen on special request. The earliest known approval of such a request was reported in November 1581: 'By order of *oruzhnichiy* [the tsar's armoury keeper] Bogdan Yakovlevich Belskiy, doctor Ivan took for *lovchiy* [master of hounds] Ivan Mikhailovich Pushkin endive vodka and ribwort vodka – a cup of each.'[16] The assortment of vodkas produced by the Apothecary Chancery was impressive, as demonstrated by a humble petition made to Tsar Mikhail Romanov by his courtier Ivan Mikhailovich Katyrev-Rostovsky in February 1630: 'Order, Sire, to give me for my headache from your state apothecary [...] vodkas [made with]: rose hip, buckwheat, dill, mint, fennel. Your Majesty, have mercy, please!'[17]

Judging by their frequent appearance in the surviving records, anise and wormwood vodkas were by far the most popular ones. Perhaps not coincidentally, both of these herbs were considered as 'warm', being able to comfort and aid the digestive system (according to the medical theory of the time, overeating as well as bad appetite were caused by the loss of internal heat, resulting in a 'cold stomach' – one that cannot generate enough warmth to be able to digest food). Coriander, hyssop, laserwort, mezereon, strawberry, cornflower, and linden blossom vodkas are also regularly mentioned in the materials related to the Apothecary Chancery's functioning. Imported spices such as cloves, galangal root, and cinnamon were used for vodka making, too.

It wasn't just vodkas made with individual plant species that were produced: various herbal mixtures were also quite common. Here is, for example, a seventeenth-century Russian recipe for *vodka Apoplectica*, which was considered to be a good remedy for migraines and paralysis:

> Take cinnamon, cloves, ginger, wormseed, mastic, frankincense, 20 *zolotniks* each. Nutmeg, peony root, sweet flag, olive pits, lemon zest, thyme, saw-wort, 12 *zolotniks* each. Juniper berries, white mustard, coriander, ground cardamom, lavender, rosemary, marjoram, ¼ of a pound. Sage, hyssop, mint, betony, lemon balm – a handful of each. [Add] a pound of lily of the valley blossom, crush all this coarsely, cut the herbs, pour in two *vedros* of simple *vino* [double-distilled grain spirit], or half-and-half with *romanennaya vodka* [brandy made from *romaneya* sweet wine], and steep for two weeks; after it's infused, distil in a pot still – there will come out a *vedro* of vodka [....][18]

Just like most of Brunschwig's 'waters', many early Russian vodkas probably did not contain any alcoholic enhancement. However, as can be seen from this recipe, pre-distilled alcohol was sometimes used as a basis for some of the concoctions made

150

by the Apothecary Chancery. These more potent vodkas must have been held in much greater esteem: not only is ethanol a better solvent for phytochemical compounds present in herbs, it also helps to keep the shelf life of the end product for longer by acting as a preservative. The inebriating qualities of alcoholic vodkas were surely noticed, as well, contributing to their rising popularity.

It is interesting to see brandy (*romanennaya vodka*) being mentioned as one of the ingredients in the *Apoplectica* recipe. Sweet wines from Greece were very popular at the Muscovite court, and sometimes they were distilled – either on their own or with herbs and spices added. In the latter case it was often done for the production of vodkas intended for the royal consumption, such as the one mentioned in the following document from 1645: 'By the order of His Majesty the Tsar and Grand Prince of all Rus' Mikhail Fedorovich, command *boyarin* [highest rank of Russian aristocracy] Fedor Ivanovich Sheremetev to distil in the Apothecary Chancery for *Sytnoy dvorets* for His Majesty's usage cinnamon vodka from four *vedros* of *romaneya*.'[19] The fact that this cinnamon vodka was to be distilled for *Sytnoy dvorets* clearly indicates that as early as in 1640s vodka was already used at the Russian court not only for medicinal purposes, but also as a gastronomic drink. *Sytnoy dvorets* (or *Sytnoy dvor*, sometimes called *Sytennoy*) was a subdivision of the catering administration of the tsar's palace overseeing the provision of beverages, including mead (hence the name, as the Russian verb *sytit'* was used to describe the process of diluting honey with water), kvass, beer, and wines.[20] Since the Apothecary Chancery also was a branch of the royal household, it was natural for the palace's food and drink department to expect *alkhemisty* to meet the court's demand in spirits – the same way the royal kitchen had to regularly provide its *pomyasy* for the Chancery's seasonal herb-gathering expeditions.

151

During the course of the second half of the seventeenth century vodka once and for all ceased to be considered solely as a medicine and became a drink purely for pleasure and enjoyment. This change is very well illustrated by an entry in the palace register books, describing a royal banquet held by Tsar Alexey Mikhailovich in October 1674:

> After dinner the Great Tsar deigned to amuse himself with various games. And the Great Tsar was entertained, the pipe organs were played, the foreigner [*nemchin*] played the organ, *surny* [shawm-like instruments] and trumpets were blown, and *surenki* [small *surny*] were played, and all the drums and timpani were beaten. And the Great Tsar granted his archpriest, the Great Tsar's confessor, and his *boyars* and *duma dyaks* [members of the tsar's council], who attended the evening meal, with *votkas* [sic], Rhenish and *romaneya* wine and different other drinks, bestowing his grace upon them: and got them all drunk.[21]

Distilled alcohol seems to have already been known in Muscovy in the beginning of the fifteenth century, and judging by a well-documented Muscovite custom of drinking spirits before meals it was initially employed mainly to increase hunger and improve digestion. Western doctors, who started to come to Moscow in the second half of the sixteenth century in increasing numbers, used herbal 'waters' for the treatment of a variety of diseases as well as in therapeutic purposes, including appetite stimulation, thereby contributing to a further endorsement of distilled liquor as a digestive. Eventually, this led to the development of a whole category of compound alcoholic beverages known collectively as *vodki*. Interestingly, it is this meaning – a cordial distilled with local herbs or foreign spices – that the term 'vodka' implied in Russia well into the nineteenth century, while the drink itself became firmly established as an important part of the local gastronomic culture.

Notes

1   Maciej Miechowita, *Tractatus de duabus Sarmatiis Asiana et Europiana et de contentis in eis* (Cracow: Johannes Haller, 1517), *Tractatus secundus libri secundi, Capitulum primum de Moscouia*. It is tempting to assume that *sublimatis de aromatibus de melle* in Miechowita's account is also a reference to distillates, but what he describes is most likely a traditional Russian beverage called *vzvar* or *sbiten'* – a honey broth brought to boil (i.e. 'sublimated') with spices such as hypericum, saffron, pepper, bay leaf, cinnamon, etc., mixed in.

2   In many such countries, the term 'burnt wine' was applied to any spirit, regardless of whether it was based on grapes or cereals. Muscovy was no exception – a product of distillation (with no herbs or spices added) in early modern Russia was called *goryachee vino* ('burnt wine'), somewhat later shortened to simply *vino* ('wine'). Not surprisingly, this creates a lot of confusion among historians.

3   *Trattamento di pace tra il Serenissimo Sigismondo Re di Polonia, et Gran Basilio Prencipe di Moscovia, Hauuto dalli Illustri Signori, Francesco da Collo, Cauallier, Gentil'huomo di Conegliano, et Antonio de Conti Cauallier, Gentil'huomo Padouano, Oratori della Maestra di Massimilian, Primo Imperatore L'anno 1518* (Padua: Lorenzo Pasquato, 1603), p. 56.

4   B. Ann Tlusty, 'Water of Life, Water of Death: The Controversy over Brandy and Gin in Early Modern Augsburg', *Central European History*, 31.1–2 (1999), 1–30 (p. 14).

5   'Selbst-Biographie Siegmunds Freiherrn von Herberstein, 1486-1553', in *Fontes Rerum Austriacarum*, vol. I, ed. by Th. G. von Karajan (Vienna, 1855), pp. 67-396 (p. 121). In German-speaking countries the product of burning, that is, distilling wine (as well as distilled ale or beer – see n. 2) was called *geprannter Wein*, or *prannt Wein* for short (also *branntwein*). The English word 'brandy' was coined in the seventeenth century from the Dutch *brandewijn*, itself derived from the German contraction.

6   *Rerum Moscoviticarum Commentarii Sigismundi Liberi Baronis in Herberstain, Neyperg et Guettenhag: Russiae, et quae nunc eius metropolis est, Moscouiae, breuissima descriptio* (Basel: Johannes Oporin, 1556), p. 128. In 1557, Herberstein's own translation of his book into German was published in Vienna (*Moscovia der Hauptstat in Reissen, durch Herrn Sigmunden Freyherrn zu Herberstain, Neyperg und Guetenhag obristen Erbcamrer und öbristen Erbtruckhsessen in Kärntn, Römischer zu Hungern und Behaim Khü. May. Etc. Rat, Camrer und Presidenten der Niderösterreichischen Camer zusamen getragen* (Vienna: Michael Zimmerman, 1557)). In the German version, the distillate that the author came across in Muscovy is once again referred to as *Prandtwein* or *Prantwein*.

7   R.J. Forbes, *A Short History of the Art Distillation from the Beginnings Up to the Death of Cellier Blumenthal* (Leiden: E.J.Brill, 1948), pp. 62-66. On the ubiquity of household distilling in Britain in Tudor times see C. Anne Wilson, *A History of Wine-Distilling and Spirits, 500 BC – AD 2000* (Totnes: Prospect Books, 2006), pp. 169-88.

8   *Liber de arte distillandi de simplicibus: Das Buch der rechten Kunst zu distilieren die eintzige Ding von Hieronymo Brunschwig* (Strasbourg: J. Grüniger, 1500). It was not the first printed book on distillation – Michael Puff von Schrick's *Von den ausgeprannten Wassern* was published in 1477 in Augsburg and seems to have been rather popular, undergoing forty-four editions by 1500 (Gregory A. Austin, *Alcohol*

in Western Society from Antiquity to 1800: A Chronological History (Oxford: Clio Press, 1985), p. 122). Brunschwig's book, however, became much more influential and was instrumental in spreading the practice of distillation across Europe.

9   N.A. Bogoyavlensky, *Drevnerusskoe vrachevanie v XI-XVII vv.* (Moscow: Medgiz, 1960), pp. 72-83. For a more recent overview of *Skazanie* and its surviving copies see K.I. Kovalenko, '"*Skazanie o propushchenii vod*" *kak leksikograficheskiy istochnik*' in *Acta linguistica Petropolitana. Trudy Instituta lingvisticheskikh issledovaniy RAN*. Vol. XIII, Part 2 (St Petersburg: Nauka, 2017), pp. 416-72; and O.S. Sapozhnikova, '*Vklad drevnerusskikh knizhnikov XVII veka v otechestvennuyu meditsinu* (Dionisiy Zobninovskiy, Ivan Nasedka, Sergiy Shelonin)', in *Materialy i soobscheniya po fondam otdela rukopisey BAN*, Issue 7, ed. by Podkovyrova V.G. (St Petersburg: BAN, 2019), pp. 249-73.

10   According to the inventory of the Russian royal household from 1582/83, a herbal belonging to the palace had been kept in Aptekarskaya izba – literally, 'Apothecary House' (*Vremennik Imperatorskogo Moskovskogo obschestva istorii i drevnostey rossiyskih*, vol. VII (Moscow, 1850), pp. 1-46 (p. 6). From the 1540s to the 1590s the word *izba* was used in the Muscovite state to designate permanent administrative offices with fixed location and specialization. Unkovskaya's claim that the aforementioned inventory related to 1572 (M. V. Unkovskaya, 'Learning Foreign Mysteries: Russian Pupils of the Aptekarskii Prikaz, 1650-1700,' *Oxford Slavonic Papers*, 30 (1997), 1-20 (p. 5)) must be a result of her miscalculation of the year corresponding to '7090 from the creation of the world' in the original document.

11   The earliest reference to distilled alcohol in a Muscovite document is found in the instructions given by Joseph Volotsky, a Russian Orthodox theologian and abbot of a monastery at Volokolamsk, to his brethren not to drink or store any liquor, dated between 1479 and 1515 (*Dopolneniya k Aktam istoricheskim*, Vol. 1, no. 212 (Saint Petersburg, 1846), p. 360). The term used by Joseph was *goryachee vino* (see n. 2 above).

12   I. Ya. Gurliand, *Mozhzhevelovaya povinnost': Materialy po istorii administratsii Moskovskogo gosudarstva vtoroi poloviny XVII veka* (Yaroslavl: Tipogragiya Gubernskogo Pravleniya, 1903).

13   *Pomyasy* start to appear in the surviving Apothecary Chancery materials beginning in 1632, while the first document mentioning their affiliation with the tsar's kitchen dates to April 1645. From another record recorded in June 1645, we learn that some of the *pomyasy* drafted from the royal kitchen a couple of months earlier had to be replaced due to their drunkenness and lack of zeal (see K.S. Khudin, '"*Travniki*" *i* "*pomyasy*". *K vorposu o deyatelnosti Aptekarskogo prikaza* (1629-1645 gg.)' in *Tret'i Chteniya pamyati akademika RAN L.V.Milova 'Rus', Rossiya. Srednevekovye i Novoe vremya'* (Moscow, 2013), pp. 423-27). For a good overview in English of both *pomyasy* and *travniki*, as well as a recapitulation of the juniper obligation in Muscovy, see Rachel Koroloff, '*Travniki, Travniki*, and *Travniki*: Herbals, Herbalists and Herbaria in Seventeenth-Century and Eighteenth-Century Russia', *Vivliofika*, 6 (2018), 58-76.

14   *Slovar' tserkovno-slavyanskago i russkago yazyka*, Vol. III (St Petersburg: Tipografiya Imperatorskoy Akademii Nauk, 1847), p. 331; I.I. Sreznevskiy, *Materialy dlya slovarya drevne-russkago yazyka po pis'mennym pamyatnikam*, Vol. II (St Petersburg: Tipografiya Imperatorskoy Akademii Nauk, 1902), p. 1176; *Slovar' russkogo yazyka XI-XVII vv.*, Issue 17 (Moscow: Nauka, 1991), p. 45.

15   See Paul W. Sherman and Jennifer Billing, 'Darwinian Gastronomy: Why We Use Spices: Spices Taste Good Because They Are Good for Us', *BioScience*, 49.6 (1999), 453-63; Marija M. Škrinjar and Nevena T. Nemet, 'Antimicrobial Effects of Spices and Herbs Essential Oils', *Acta Periodica Technologica*, 40 (2009), 195-209; and Davide Gottardi and others, 'Beneficial Effects of Spices in Food Preservation and Safety', *Frontiers in Microbiology*, 7 (2016), 1-20.

16   G. Zharinov, '*Zapisi o raskhode lekarstvennykh sredstv, 1581-1582 gg.*', *Arkhiv russkoy istorii*, Issue 4 (Moscow, 1994), pp. 103-25. Bogdan Belskiy, Ivan IV's bodyguard and minion, was the first head of the Apothecary Chancery – such choice being explained by the tsar's ever-present fear of poisoning. 'Doctor Ivan', who is also mentioned, is most probably the court physician, Dutchman Johan Eylof.

17   *Akty istoricheskie, sobrannye i izdannye Arkheograficheskoyu kommissieyu*, Vol. 3 (St. Petersburg: Tipografiya II-go Otdeleniya, 1841), p. 289.

18   V. M. Florinskiy, *Russkie prostonarodnye travniki i lechebniki. Sobranie meditsinskikh rukopisei XVI*

i XVII stoletiia (Kazan: Tipografiya Imperatorskago universiteta, 1879), p. 213. *Zolotnik* was an old Russian unit of weight equal to 4.266 grams; a Russian pound, or *funt*, was equal to 409.5 grams; *vedro* ('bucket') was a liquid measure equal to 12.3 litres. *Romaneya* (*romney* or *rumney* in English, *romenier* or *rumenier* in German, *roemeni* in Dutch and *vino di Romania* in Italian) was a sweet wine originally from the Peloponnese and the Ionian islands, traded in northern Europe by Italian merchants. One of the three major wines exported from Greece in medieval and early modern times (the other two were malvasia and bastard), it was named after *Romania* ('land of the Romans') – the term applied to the regions that constituted the core of the former Byzantine empire, whose inhabitants continued to identify themselves as 'Romans' until modern times. The author would like to thank Mariella Beukers for valuable information related to the identification of *romaneya* as a Greek wine, kindly shared by her during the Symposium.

19 *Akty istoricheskie*, p. 472. Fedor Sheremetev was the head of the Apothecary Chancery in 1638-1639 and 1645-1646 (D.V. Liseytsev, N.M. Rogozhin, Yu.M. Eskin, *Prikazy Moskovskogo gosudarstva XVI-XVII vv. Slovar-spravochnik* (Moscow: Tsentr gumanitarnykh initsiativ, 2015), p. 34).

20 According to Grigoriy Kotoshikin, a Russian diplomat and high-ranking official at the Ambassadorial Chancery who in 1664 defected first to Poland and then to Sweden and later wrote a treatise on the Muscovite state, *Sytennoi dvor* had more than thirty cellars with various drinks stored on ice, as well as a separate cellar for imported wines (G. Kotoshikhin, *O Rossii, v tsarstvovanie Alekseya Mikhailovicha* (St Petersburg: Tipografiya Eduarda Pratza, 1840), p. 60).

21 *Dvortsovye razryady*, Vol. III (St Petersburg, 1852), p. 1081.

Foraged Food of Nepal: A Short History of Stinging Nettle

Binti Gurung

In the early months of the evolving COVID-19 pandemic in Nepal, many urban poor and migrant workers were caught in the lockdown measures imposed by the government. People's mobility was abruptly frozen, and in the days that followed different sections of the Nepali public were caught in the COVID-19 situation.[1] A rising concern was felt for the segment of the public affected by this crisis who might be unable to meet their basic needs. This situation required a return to subsistence farming and to older indigenous practices of food gathering.

The Rural Population of Nepal and Their Lifestyles

Nepal is an agrarian society, and its identity is strongly tied to the land. Nearly a third of its thirty million population continue to live in rural areas. People in these remote regions rely heavily on forest resources and agriculture for their sustenance and livelihood.[2] Nepal's unique biodiversity and geographical topography of high mountains, gorges, river valleys, and low flatlands allow for an abundance of crops, edible plant species, unique herbs, and food grains.[3] Publications on the connection of rural life and food security highlight the contribution of forest resources as a crucial source of rural diet and livelihood. While these views have been examined and continue to be explored, most research papers on the role of the forest and foraging activities, especially in context of nettle, are often written from a lens that limits or fails to take account of the cultural and spiritual consciousness of the Nepali people. The attestations in religious and spiritual texts indicate that the practice of foraging for nettle was not just a means of livelihood for the Nepali people.

The concept of foraging as practiced in rural Nepal provides us with an insight about Nepali social and cultural life. The timing of its significance in the midst of the current COVID-19 situation also calls for an exploration from a Nepali perspective, which can help us to understand its cultural meanings and connection to food security. The act of gathering and collecting food items from the local environment in Nepal has a recorded history that dates back many centuries. Within the broad historical landscape, spiritual figures within the Tibetan Buddhist tradition have made use of herbs almost a thousand years ago; then the Gorkhalis make their presence in the eighteenth century; and the practice is still seen among the rural and indigenous people of Nepal in more recent times. Therefore, the culture of accessing food items and medicinal herbs from the local surroundings is not a new practice. In fact, it can be argued that it has always been a way of life continued on by a large section of the indigenous and non-indigenous rural people of Nepal.

Among the Gurungs, an indigenous group that comprises of 3% of Nepal's population, the use of medicinal herbs from the forest is traditionally practiced. Broughton Coburn attributes much of this tradition as being unique only to them.[4] However, it is possible to assert that this way of food practices goes beyond the indigenous group of Gurungs; Om Gurung, an anthropologist based in Kathmandu, mentions that other indigenous communities such as the Chepangs, Rautes, and Kusundas have always lived through foraging practices, although wild hunting practices are more pronounced among the Gurungs.[5] Stan Mumford's exploration of the Tibetan Lamas and Gurung Shamans in Nepal in the 1970s seems to support this view because wild deer sacrifices are frequently narrated in the Gurung shamanic ritual discourses.[6] This type of practice is explained within the larger spiritual worldview behind the ancient ritual practices of the Gurungs, the specifics of which, however, are beyond the focus of this paper.

When we view the history of foraging such food items as nettle, oral knowledge is an important source for the historical enquiry of the ethnic food practices of Nepal. The Nepalese historian Pratyoush Onta calls for a pluralist approach to a historical enquiry of Nepali society, emphasizing the need to use oral knowledge as a method of research in the social history of Nepal.[7] This approach is useful as a guide in supporting some of the often-heard oral knowledge related to the Gurung origins. The view that this ethnic group ventured out from Tibet has long been known from the oral accounts and the modern literature on the Gurungs. Alan MacFarlane has presented two pathways of migration of the Gurungs, one of them being the direct route of Gurungs as wandering shepherds from Tibet through Mustang to their present settlement. Another account, which lends towards a Hindu-influenced description, claims the migration from northern India.[8] In yet another account, written of Tibetan Lamas and Gurung Shamans as Mumford has described, it is the figure of Jomo, whose name is the Tibetan term for the female head of a noble household, who stands at the origin of the Gurungs in Nepal: after giving birth to two children in a cave in Tibet, she arrived in the northern regions of Nepal with her two sons.[9] In a village near Ngawal in Manang district, remnants of this historic site still exist as material proof of this early Gurung settlement. The locals who have been living there for many generations believe that the Gurung kings have settled and dispersed from this site, migrating further south towards Lamjung and beyond. One of the sons of Jomo, Timu, is believed to have conquered the people of Nar in Manang and to have become a king, while the other son Dong went further towards Gorkha with his mother. The recent findings by Tek Bahadur Gurung dispel the southerly origin of the Gurungs. In his doctoral research, he locates the confirmed point of origin, on the basis of historical research and DNA-testing, in the triangular zone of Kokonor, comprising the upper reaches of the Yellow River, the Lokha area, and southwest China. His innovative use of scientific tracing has been heralded as having far-reaching implications for the ethnic indigenous communities in Nepal and India.[10] So it is with this confirmed knowledge of the nomadic roots and ancient cultural practices of the Gurungs that the idea of foraging can be placed in a wider context for this ethnic group. I will now further explore the following two themes: (1) the perception of the ancient foraging practices existent in rural Nepal and its connection with rural cuisine, and (2) pressure on this cultural practice due to the changes imposed by new social forces.

Foraging and the Position of Stinging Nettle within this Culture

A large number of medicinal herbs and forest food resources exist within the foraging system in Nepal.[11] Among these items, stinging nettle will be taken as an example because of its long recorded historical and cultural connection, and, despite Nepal's social hierarchies, it can be seen to transcend class and caste barriers. Amongst the two varieties of nettle, *sisnu* (*Urtica Parviflora* Roxb.) is strongly identified as a rural cuisine. By contrast, the Himalayan Giant Nettle (*Girardinia diversifolia*), locally known as *puwa* or *allo* and found at an altitude between 1300m and 3000m, is predominantly used for items of utility, especially among certain indigenous communities. Gurung and others have explored this context within the framework of traditional knowledge of the Gurung community, where the *puwa* fibre is extracted to produce household items such as grain sacks, mats, ropes, and functional wear.[12]

I was able to observe this traditional method of processing from *puwa* in the village of Kavre, a sparsely populated Gurung settlement north of Pokhara, where I witnessed an elderly woman (*bajyai*), one of the last persons in the village to hold the skill, weaving a traditional Gurung costume of *bhangra*, a cross between a vest and a backpack, which is commonly used by local shepherds. This process of handicraft involved an elderly Gurung man (*baje*) from the village who was responsible for collecting the fibre from the wild forest. He had to identify the site of the nettle and strip the bark from the nettle stalks by hand. Once the extraction process was complete, it was passed on to the *bajyai*, who completed the rest of the process by following a series of steps that took several days. In the evening, over a conversation and visit by another elderly female neighbour, the green fibre was boiled together with ashes, and then washed with fresh water the next day. According to the *bajyai*, traditionally this part of the activity is performed near a stream or by the riverbanks. The fibre is washed and beaten frequently using a *bhogu*, a wooden hammer, to soften the fibre until the white fibre for textile is produced. As no drying technology in the processing of *puwa* is available, having a sunny day helps to dry the fibre until the nettle yarn is ready for weaving. Gurung and others have also documented this process in detail.[13] Now I will turn to the other variety of nettle, *sisnu* (*Urtica parviflora* Roxb.), to explore its historical place in Nepali cuisine.

157

The Origins of Nettle and Its Depiction in Nepali History

The earliest record of nettle as a food item in Nepal is found in the accounts of Tibetan Buddhist masters who descended into the Himalayan regions that now form part of Nepal. The spiritual texts and visual materials of the Tibetan Buddhist tradition depict nettle (*tser-ma* in Tibetan) as a crucial part of the life story of Milarepa, a renowned yogi from the eleventh century. Meditating in the isolated caves of Tibet and northern Nepal, he famously ate nothing but nettle, and as a result, his skin turned completely green, taking the colour of the herb. Milarepa's life generates profound interest not only for his spiritual attainment, but also for his life account prior to becoming a yogi. Cheated of his fortune by his uncle and aunt, he committed himself to take revenge by learning the powers of sorcery, by means of which he stirred hailstorms that destroyed the crops in his village and killed the people who had wronged his family. However, in the wake of these actions, he was overcome by remorse and the profound feeling that he had to purify himself from the negative karma that he had acquired, by entering the Buddhist path of liberation. After a long struggle for spiritual instruction, he applied himself fully, with complete disregard to his bodily needs and subsisting on nettle alone, and he finally attained supreme awakening. His life is thus one of great symbolic achievement, with Milarepa going from the lowest of lows to the highest awakening within one lifetime.

While it is not only Milarepa who has a connection with nettle in the Tibetan Buddhist tradition – lesser known than Milarepa, but no less powerful, is the Tibetan master Duwang Tenzin – it is due to its significant role in the transformative life story of Milarepa that nettle is still held in veneration within the Tibetan community. In the *Life of Milarepa*, Tsangnyon Heruka has traced the spiritual journey of the yogi, and he has recorded the sites of his meditation in Tibet and Nepal.[14] Near a village of Brakha, a Gurung settlement in Manang district, a cave named after the yogi still remains, and the locals have informed me that a gathering is held every year to celebrate the life of Milarepa. In such isolated settings, the yogi sustained himself on nettle during his long meditative practices. However, on occasion there are also other food items that feature in this narrative. Food items such as *tsampa*, prepared from roasted barley grains and still popular in Tibetan life today, feature consistently in the diet of the yogi. And it was only after he had run out of the food items of meat, barley, and cheese that he started to live off nettle, which Lambert in *Portraits of the Himalayas* has pointed to as showing how attuned the yogi was with his surroundings, where nettle was readily found. Lambert also points out that nettle has numerous nutritional properties such as calcium, iron, magnesium, chlorophyll, vitamins D and K, and amino acids and so on.[15] With such nutritional elements contained in the herb it is easy to see why over the centuries nettle has figured so prominently. Moreover, in some rural and ethnic food cultures of Nepal, nettle is also mentioned as a winter food due to its ability to generate heat in the body. As a result, it is greatly consumed in the winter months, along with food grains such as millet.

Walking along the trekking routes in Manang, in the northern region of Nepal, nettles are seen growing abundantly, and in contemporary Nepal nettle is not only encountered in the accounts and visual depictions of the past but also in the present-day Tibetan diet.[16] A conversation with a hotelier from the Tibetan community in Kathmandu led to how it is consumed in contemporary times. The method of preparing the soup involved adding a small quantity of powdered leaves of nettle into boiled water with garlic, salt, and diced beef meat and *tsampa*. In contrast to the vegetarian version of the nettle soup of *sisnu ko khole*, which is served as a replacement for *dal* (lentil soup) in the rural Nepali cuisine, the Tibetan version differs by its inclusion of meat and *tsampa*. Tamang and Kailasapathy have described the inclusion of meat in the Tibetan diet as a geo-climatic influence, with the dependency on meat being a necessity in a landscape that lacks plant sources of protein.[17]

If nettle is depicted as an embodiment of the spiritual values of the eleventh-century Milarepa, towards the mid-eighteenth century it is mentioned in an entirely different historical context. Placed between the two different polarities of political and social discourses, the nature of nettle as a magical superfood and its social function raises some questions for further exploration. It is well known that the Gorkhali rulers with King Prithvi Narayan Shah at the political helm led the formation of modern Nepal. In 1767, as the process of the Gorkhali project to annex the smaller principalities took place in central Nepal, the entry of the East India Company into the political scene of Nepal and their subsequent military defeat remain important to the modern history of Nepal. Threatened by the increasing encroachment of the Gorkhalis, Kathmandu-based King Pratap Malla had sought the military assistance of the East India Company to counter the Gorkhali forces. But Captain Kinloch's expedition from the northern region of Patna in India was fraught with problems that hindered the expedition from the start, so when they arrived via Janakpur to Sindhuli, where the confrontation with the Gorkhalis took place, they lacked not just food grains and supplies, but also reliable knowledge of the hostile landscape through which they were marching.[18] The outcome of this failed expedition can be attributed to the lack of information of the surroundings and the specific conditions created by the Gorkhalis. The Gorkhali narrative of the events shows their strategic knowledge of the local environment, which they used to their advantage. The Gorkhalis of that time were adept at using ancient knowledge in their warfare, and some of these methods were adopted even before the confrontation in Sindhuli. Among these tactics that the Gorkhalis adopted was the *mauri ko gola* (round-shaped beehives) that served as a booby trap, and as soon as the approaching invaders drew near, a shot at the hives would trigger the release of the bees attacking the opponents.[19] Another tactic involved making makeshift nettle frontiers along the forts, which served the dual purpose of providing sustenance for the marching Gorkhali soldiers, as well as a trap for the approaching enemies. Local historian Nirmal Shrestha highlights that wherever nettles are planted, *titepati* (mugwort) can also be found, and this is arranged so that the mugwort would serve as an antidote to the nettle stings.

Unlike today, the transport of food supplies and grains was carried out manually at the time of the Gorkhali expansion. According to Shrestha, portable food items such as *sattu* (a mixture of pounded grains), *khatte* (roasted brown rice eaten as a Nepali snack), *sakkhar* (jaggery), and *malpuwa* (sweet fried bread) were made by the provision and logistics team of Dakre, who were enlisted for just this purpose. And it is only after the Gorkhalis had run out of these items that the nettle, which was abundantly available in the area, became part of their food as well as a tactic to avert the incoming East India Company troops.

Such stories reveal how interwoven nettle is within the fabric of Nepali society. Yet, today, it is clearly a neglected and underutilized wild herb.[20] The public perception of nettle within mainstream society is also conflicting. This view can be said to have developed from the perceived notions attached to those at the lower end of the social hierarchy of rural Nepal. Traditionally, nettle is prepared as *khole* or *bhyatal* (nettle curry), and consumed with *dhido* (a thick porridge prepared with corn, millet, or buckwheat flour). The ingredients used to prepare the curry can vary slightly but the method remains the same in most rural regions. The fresh nettle leaves are boiled in water, and salt and chilli are added to the nettle broth. This mixture could undergo a further process of frying in oil or ghee (clarified butter), and in some cases garlic and *timur* (Nepali pepper) could also be included in the dish for flavouring. This way of preparing nettle in combination with traditional *dhido* has been the diet of many rural and hill communities and for those tending to the fields: it is a filling and nutritious meal. It could be argued that nettle prepared in this way does not appeal to the changing taste of the modern urban Nepali. To some, even the culinary description can sound unappealing, as it has a resonance of a certain kind of imagined impoverished rural life. The idea that nettle falls within the poor household diet has been perpetuated because it continues to be a foraged food for many rural people who have no private land for their own cultivation.

Considered as bland and earthy in taste, nettle is additionally viewed as an impure food by higher-caste Nepali Brahmins, which certainly does not generate a positive perception. This view has social and religious consequences, especially within devout Hindu households, even though in my personal view the religious lines in many Nepali household tend to be fluid or not very strict. This understanding of nettle determined by caste hierarchy sits differently when seen in contrast to the writings of Laxmi Prasad Devkota, a celebrated poet of Nepal, who belonged to a high-caste of Brahmin. In his widely recognized poem 'Muna Madan', he depicts the herb in the following way:

Sacks of gold, what use are they?
Like dirt of the hand,
It is better to eat nettles with a content heart.[21]

In this portrayal of nettle, it is depicted as a food of simplicity against the background of the character going off to Tibet leaving his wife and family in the hope of gaining wealth. As a Brahmin, Devkota advocates the consumption of nettle, which can leave the reader with the implication that it can be part of a cuisine for anyone, irrespective of caste. The description of nettle in his poem sits on this parameter – that, regardless of wealth, the issue is how to lead a happy life rather than one defined along the caste-based hierarchy. While Devkota's portrayal of nettle can be seen as an attempt to disassociate the herb, knowingly or unknowingly, from the restrictions of the caste system, its cultural perception as an impoverished rural cuisine continues to prevail within Nepali society.

Although nettle can have this negative association for the contemporary urban Nepali, it can also be a food of nostalgia, a yearning for a rural way of life whose food system is considered to have a deep connection with the land and forests. The new urbanites of Kathmandu with rural leanings and connections can often be seen foraging nettle, which was observed even more during the early part of the COVID-19 crisis. Dr Debendra Shrestha, a researcher in agriculture science, shares the indigenous food culture of the Kumal ethnic group, located in the region of Gulmi in mid-west Nepal. Foraging activity for the Kumals consists of collecting *khole saag* (watercress) from the riverbanks, and each year members of the community, after harvesting the plants, barter the spinach for food items such as *chiura* (beaten rice), tobacco, or sugar with the local neighbours. In recent years the changing socio-economic forces have put these kinds of practices at risk, as more people move to towns and no longer value these practices. In his writings on the Gurung way of foraging life during the 1970s, Coburn already noted the observation of elderly Gurungs and field workers that foraged herbs are decreasingly used within the community.[22] Likewise, within the context of returning Gurkhas from the Gurkha regiment, Caplan mentions an ongoing trend among the ex-servicemen to divert their resources towards consumption of urban foods and services as they move away from their earlier rural roots and lifestyles.[23]

Conclusion

It is clear from these accounts that nettles occupy a unique position in the history of food in Nepal. The narratives of nettle provide a window through which we glimpse the inspiring spiritual paths of the Tibetan Buddhist masters, but most of all, what makes it so compelling as a foraged cuisine in all of these narratives is an understanding of its superfood qualities. In some sense, it may have served a practical purpose for survival, but the historical records indicate to us the important place that nettle occupied at a certain time and space within Nepal's food repository. Some of the negative perception that it later gained can be interpreted as an outcome of specific social, political, and religious thoughts that became predominant in Nepali society.

The decline of some of these foraging practices was briefly mentioned in the 1970s by Coburn. Similarly, Caplan also observed a trend of a significant population migration from the villages to towns. This movement has resulted in the loss of food practices and traditions, since resources are shifted away from the earlier settled lifestyle. However, within modern Nepali society, as much as foraging is longingly spoken of by people in the city who are disconnected from the land, it is not to say that foraging is not fraught with physical dangers and difficulties. Occasionally, there have been reports of fatalities when a wild plant was incorrectly identified as edible and wrongly consumed. Although these skills can be gained from practicing foraging and living in rural settings, at least within the context of modern times, the practical dangers of foraging do exist. Still, nettle, with its many nutritional benefits, continues to be part of Nepali cuisine and sustenance, and its cultural meanings may further evolve over time.

Acknowledgements

I would like to express my appreciation to Dr Om Gurung at Tribhuvan University; Dr Daniel McNamara at the Rangjung Yeshe Institute; Dr Megan Clayton at Lincoln University in New Zealand; and Thomas Cruijsen, who provided extensive editorial comments on the final draft.

Notes

1   Nisha Bhandari, 'The Long March: Travails of Men who left Solukhumbu for Kailali on Foot', *Setopati*, 13 April 2020.
2   Arun Khatri-Chhetri and Keshar Lal Maharjan, 'Role of Forest in Household Food Security: Evidence from Rural Areas in Nepal', *Annual Report of Research Center for Regional Geography*, 15 (2016), 41-67 (p. 41).
3   Bal K. Joshi and others, *Neglected and Underutilized Species (NUS), and Future Smart Food (FSF) in Nepal* (Kathmandu: Nepal National Agriculture Genetics Resource Centre, 2019), pp. 1-60.
4   Broughton Coburn, 'Some Native Medicinal Plants of the Western Gurung', *Kailash, A Journal of Himalayan Studies*, 11, 1984, pp. 1-34.
5   Om Gurung, private correspondence.
6   Stan Royal Mumford, *Himalayan Dialogue: Tibetan Lamas and Gurung Shamans in Nepal* (Wisconsin: University of Wisconsin Press, 1989), pp. 63-79.
7   Pratyoush R. Onta 'Rich Possibilities: Social History in Nepal', *Contributions to Nepalese Studies*, 21 (1994), 1-43.
8   Alan MacFarlane, 'Some Background Notes on Gurung Identity in a Period of Rapid Change', *Kailash, A Journal of Himalayan Studies*, 15.3-4 (1989), 179-90.
9   Mumford, p. 64.
10 Tek Bahadur Gurung, 'Understanding the Ethnic History of Nepal: A Case Study of the Gurungs' (unpublished doctoral thesis, Sichuan University, 2019).
11 Joshi and others, pp. 16-22.
12 Anup Gurung and others, 'Traditional Knowledge of Processing and Use of the Himalayan Giant Nettle (Girardinia diversifolia Friis) Among the Gurung of Sikles Nepal', *Ethnobotony Research and Applications*, 10 (2012), 167-174.
13 Gurung and others.
14 Tsangnyon Heruka, *Life of Milarepa*, trans. by Andrew Quintman (New York: Penguin, 2010).
15 John Lambert, *Portraits of the Himalayas* (Leicester: Scripsi, 2006), p. 69.
16 'Teacher (Lama) – Milarepa', Himalayan Art Resources, 2021 <https://www.himalayanart.org/items/11173> [accessed 1 May 2020].
17 Jyoti Prakash Tamang and Delwen Samuel, 'Dietary Cultures and Antiquity of Fermented Foods

and Beverages', in *Fermented Foods and Beverages of the World*, ed. by Jyoti Prakash and Kasipathy Kailasapathy (Florida: CRC Press, 2010), 1-31 (p. 2).

18 Samuel Mark Ellis, 'Neither the Hills nor Rivers will Obstruct': Revisiting the East India Company's 1767 Expedition to Nepal' (unpublished doctoral thesis, University of Leeds, 2019), pp. 64-72.

19 Nirmal Shrestha, private correspondence.

20 Joshi and others, p. 16.

21 Laxmi Prasad Devkota, *Muna Madan*, trans. by Padma Devkota (New Delhi: Adarsh Books, 2018), p. 60.

22 Coburn.

23 Lionel Caplan, *Warrior Gentlemen: 'Gurkhas' in the Western Imagination* (New York: Berghahn, 1995), p. 67.

Perils of Popularity: How Popularization Leads to Ultimate Degradation

Ian Hemphill

The Oxford English Dictionary describes the attributive meaning of 'popular' thus: 'Intended for or suited to the taste, understanding, or means of the general public, rather than specialists or intellectuals'. Therefore, as authored by a herb and spice specialist, this paper does focus on 'popular' as defined above. (Full Disclosure: The author is the owner of an artisan herb and spice business in Australia, has worked in the herb and spice industry in Australia and overseas for fifty years, and has authored award-winning books on herbs and spices.[1] His points of view expressed here should be taken in acknowledgement of this context.)

An Ancient Trade

A jocular salesman once told me that the only thing older than herbs and spices is sex, and the world's second oldest profession is the spice trade, with as many rogues in it as in the first. True or not, herbs and spices have been a part of our culinary heritage for thousands of years. Now in 2020 herbs, spices, and spice blends have achieved unprecedented popularity, and the widest distribution and availability in history. But, we have to wonder, at what cost? And who – or what – are the spice rogues of today?

Long before the advent of social media, popularity has always been desirable. There are instances where a chef, Australian David Thompson for example, becomes passionate about tracing original methods and ingredients. David's obsession to replicate an authentic Thai cuisine raised his profile, and he became an adored and respected celebrity. What follows is an expectation that the general consumer can recreate his masterpieces using a supermarket jar of Thai Green Curry paste. Thus the original artisan ideal is bastardized.

Does popularity and widespread acceptance necessarily lead to a devaluation of the true intrinsic qualities in something? What are the risks of losing quality and accuracy of information? Is a herb, spice, or spice blend, based on cultural traditions evolved over thousands of years, in danger of losing its identity? Or, with the modern supermarket trend of including seasonings in the herbs and spices category, is the meaning of just what are herb and spice blends being devalued?

Awakening

As a boy, my parents started a herb nursery that developed into an artisan herb and spice business. My father made Pot-Pourri from scratch with artisanal care. He harvested and dried the fragrant flowers and herbs, blended essential oils with spices, and mixed all the ingredients by hand. Sadly, commercial Pot-Pourri is now made with coloured wood shavings, and you can even purchase a chemical room freshener, offensively named Pot-Pourri.

My first-hand experiences in all sides of the herbs and spices industry have given me an in-depth appreciation of this industry's dynamics. Interactions with farmers, traders, distributors, manufacturers, marketers, retailers, chefs, caterers, and consumers, from the respectable to the downright dishonest, continues to raise three disturbing issues.

Misinformation

Many cooks, writers, and food professionals, who no doubt are skilled in their use of spices and have undertaken extensive research, repopulate incorrect information about many of the basics. An example is stating that sumac is the ground seeds of the tree (*rhus coriaria*).[2] In fact, most deep purple sumac, rich in malic acid, is the flesh and skin of the berry, which is rubbed off from the hard seed. In another example of misinformation, an in-flight magazine several years ago used photos of poison sumac (*R. vernix*) in an article on culinary sumac! Other examples abound, such as brands of smoked paprika that contain 'Paprika and Natural Identical Smoke Flavour (Salt used as a carrier)'.[3] True smoked paprika is produced by smoking paprika pods as part of the drying and curing process.[4] Many journalists and spice companies confuse Sri Lankan cinnamon (*Cinnamomum zeylanicum*) with cassia (*C. burmanii*) in writing about Sri Lankan cinnamon but showing photos of cassia bark.[5] One is not simply being pedantic here, as these two cinnamons have different flavours, and using cassia instead of cinnamon may ruin a recipe.

Journalists tend to be unrealistically zealous in their descriptions of many spices when exposed to a new commodity, especially when the experience is in an exotic and welcoming environment. One of my favourite examples is an article on fennel pollen that appeared in October 2000.[6] The writer gushed that fennel pollen is one hundred times more intense than ground fennel seeds. Really? This hyperbole is simply incorrect. Others have often described a spice they've seen as 'the best in the world' despite many producers of the same spice making the same claim. A more honest appraisal should focus on the intensity of the aroma, the brilliant colour, or more realistic attributes to give readers a better understanding of that particular spice. I have seen many excellent spices, and some are the best I've seen, but that does not categorically mean that they are the best in the world.

Adulteration and Food Fraud

Instances of adulteration are nothing new. White pepper was adulterated with rice flour, and black pepper with burnt bread in Victorian times, according to Mrs Beeton, in her *Book of Household Management*.[7] Most of us will remember the case of Sudan Red in chilli powder in the UK and USA.[8] Consider that many traders sell ground white pepper adulterated with corn and/or rice flour, naming it spuriously 'Manufacturer's Pepper'.[9] Is it any wonder that food fraud is on the increase? Major retailers of food products constantly gouge suppliers on cost, discounts, and promotional deals. Suppliers are then forced to reduce their manufacturing costs, so they have to search for cheaper input commodities. Due to their relative high value, herbs and spices are often the first casualty. One independently verified example of food fraud was in 2016, when oregano from Turkey was found to be adulterated with olive leaves.[10] More disturbing, due to the high cost, is the manufacture of fake saffron stigmas, made from a dissolvable gelatine-like material, artificially coloured and flavoured with sandalwood.[11]

There are further common examples of adulteration. In 1919, in investigating twenty-five samples of cloves, H. Harald in Stockholm found clove stems, fruits of cloves, rice, white pepper, sand, earth, and spent cloves (material after extraction of clove oil). Cinnamon was found with components of powdered beechnut husks aromatized with cinnamic aldehyde and marketed as 'pure powdered cinnamon'. Pepper, the most traded spice in the world until overtaken in volume terms by chillies in the last decade, was commonly adulterated with pawpaw seed, olive kernels, palm-kernel meal, and light berries (empty peppercorns, also called pin-heads).[12]

The list is long, and one can understand the urge to adulterate given the value involved. Red beet powder and brick dust in chilli powder, turmeric, and paprika; safflower petals, sandalwood, annatto, and corn silk passed off as saffron.[13] Even coal tar dye in turmeric! Bulking out the genuine article with a cheap additive, which may or may not be harmful, has been the common practice for centuries, and details of such adulteration and its history have been well documented.[14]

Although most developed countries have strict food laws that should ideally negate these practices, many traders lack sufficient product knowledge to properly evaluate their imports, and herbs and spices are rarely tested for adulterants that sit under the radar. Cost cutting to achieve low prices generally has serious consequences for the credibility of the herb and spice industry. A common misconception is that one is advised to seek out items such as saffron in specialty ethnic markets.[15] However, this author's experience has tended to be the reverse, where white peppercorns have been dyed green and pink, safflower petals and fake saffron sold as the genuine article, and spices like ground cumin seed adulterated with the cheaper and milder ground coriander seed. Let the buyer beware has never been more relevant!

Devaluation of Spice Blends

Herb and spice blends fall into two main categories; those based on traditional combinations such as garam masala, Baharat, and *ras el hanout*, and those dreamt up by a spice blender. Examples could range from a chicken seasoning to a steak rub or a stir-fry spice. Similarly, spice merchants fall into two main groups: artisan spice companies, that either market through their own retail outlets and online, and those Fast Moving Consumer Goods (FMCG) companies that sell through major supermarket chains.

One has to acknowledge that it is almost impossible to categorically state what is exactly in an authentic spice blend. Dozens of spice sellers in a Moroccan souk make their own version of *ras el hanout*, a spice blend known as 'top of the shop' and considered by many to be the pinnacle of spice blends, generally containing over twenty ingredients.[16] Consider a *ras el hanout*, bulked out with onion powder, salt, and free-flow agents, or one that simply contains seven spices plus salt.[17] Is that still a credible blend? Is it ethical for a major spice company to call a spice blend an Australian Bush Spice Seasoning, when it contains: 'Salt, Rice Flour, Sugar, Onion 12%, Garlic 9%, Pepper 7%, Paprika, Celery Seed 2.5%, Nutmeg, Oregano, Marjoram, Parsley, Rosemary, Vegetable Oil, Lemon Myrtle 0.5%, Capsicum, Wattle Seed 0.5%, Colour (Paprika Oleoresin)'?[18] How does this enhance the credibility of an emerging opportunity for native Australian ingredients, and the flow-on benefits to indigenous communities to financially benefit from native produce awareness, with only 1% native Australian ingredients, contributing no discernible impact on the ultimate taste?

Of greatest concern is the number of non-herb or spice ingredients that are used in many seasonings, which appear on supermarket shelves in the herb and spice category. Can these really be classified as herbs and spices?

Touching briefly on herb and spice pastes, such as Tandoori Paste, these are possibly the most obvious example of how a product is marketed in such a manner as to completely hoodwink the consumer. A famous brand of Tandoori Paste has these ingredients:

> Water, Rapeseed Oil, Durum Wheat Semolina, Salt, Sugar, Acidity Regulators (Acetic Acid, Citric Acid), Ground Cumin (2.5%), Ginger Purée (2.5%), Chilli Powder (2%), Mustard Powder, Ground Ginger, Ground Coriander Seeds, Ground Cinnamon, Garlic Powder, Ground Paprika, Onion Powder, Ground Fenugreek Seeds, Colour (Paprika Extract), Ground Celery Seeds, Stabilisers (Guar Gum, Xanthan Gum), Ground Black Pepper, Ground Turmeric.[19]

Note that ingredients are listed in descending order by weight!

In the mid-1990s I was involved in consumer research focus groups on attitudes toward and perceptions of herb and spice pastes. Believe it or not, these products – that are mostly water, oil, salt, sugar, food acids (for preservation) and only small quantities of spices – were perceived as fresher than dried herbs and spices, as they were wet, and in glass jars! When one thinks how easy it is to make a paste at home, the marketing of these pastes, and the advertising hype that implies their freshness, is fundamentally dishonest on the part of the FMCG food manufacturers making these products.

Let's now look at the most common ingredients in herb and spice blends/seasonings and try to understand the rationale for their inclusion. Table A summarizes a list of non-spice ingredients commonly found in blends from FMCG companies in Australia,

Ingredient	E#	AU	UK	USA	30	% Included
Salt	E201	8	7	14	29	97%
Sugar		8	2	7	17	57%
Flavour		4	3	8	15	50%
Spices (no individual listing!)		0	1	12	13	43%
Silicon dioxide	E551	0	3	5	8	27%
Citric acid	E330	3	3	1	7	23%
Rice flour		6	0	1	7	23%
Yeast extract		1	1	4	6	20%
Corn maltodextrin		0	1	3	4	13%
Vegetable oil		3	0	0	3	10%
Calcium stearate	E482	0	0	2	2	7%
Chicken flavour		2	0	0	2	7%
Dextrose		0	0	2	2	7%
Di-sodium inosinate & Guanylate	E626+E630	0	0	2	2	7%
Tricalcium phosphate	E451	0	0	2	2	7%
Calcium silicate	E552	0	0	1	1	3%
Canola oil		0	1	0	1	3%
Cellulose	E460	1	0	0	1	3%
Colour Amonia Caramel	E150c	0	1	0	1	3%
Corn flour		1	0	0	1	3%
Corn starch		0	0	1	1	3%
Extracts		1	0	0	1	3%
Maize flour		1	0	0	1	3%
Malted barley flour		0	0	1	1	3%
Potato starch		0	0	1	1	3%
Propylene glycol	E477	0	0	1	1	3%
Riboflavin (colour)	E101	0	0	1	1	3%
Soybean oil		1	0	0	1	3%
Total non-spice or unlisted spice:		40	23	69	132	
Average proportion across brands:*		4.4	3.3	4.9	4.4	

*Average shown above, to show each country relative to others, due to different sample sizes.

Table A: Summary of non-spice ingredients in FMCG spice blends sold in major supermarkets. Total surveyed: 30 blends.

the United Kingdom, and the United States. In Australia, 3 brands and 9 blends were surveyed; in the UK, 3 brands and 7 blends; in the USA, 5 brands and 14 blends. The USA is by far the largest market in the world for FMCG products. The first column shows the name of the non-spice ingredient, and also when an ingredient listing simply states 'Spices', with no information about what those spices are. The second column lists the E number (EU codes for specific additives) when applicable, with the third, fourth and fifth columns showing the number of times the ingredients occurred in the blends surveyed. The sixth column adds up each country to show a total for that ingredient followed by the percentage of occurrence.

Top of the list is salt, found in 97% of the products surveyed, and in many instances the first ingredient (meaning largest amount by weight). Salt makes food taste good, but why so much? On average, herbs and spices used in spice blends have a wholesale cost to a food manufacturer somewhere between US$8.00 and $16.00 per kilo, for the most common herb and spice ingredients. Salt, on average, costs less than US$0.20 per kilo. Therefore, bulk your blend out with a cheap, heavy ingredient to lower the cost, and ignore the resulting high risk health implications for consumers.[20] Although salt is as essential to life as water, human consumption of salt in processed foods far exceeds what are considered to be safe levels of consumption.[21] Of particular concern are vegetable and herb salts that give the impression that they are a healthy option, when salt is the first ingredient.[22]

Next on the list, coming in at 57% of products surveyed, is sugar (and dextrose at 7%). Given the global concerns about sugar consumption expressed by health professionals, one hardly needs to elaborate here.[23] Again, sugar is cheaper than most herbs and spices, and consumers become addicted to it when it is included in excessive quantities in processed foods.

Flavour! Goodness gracious, why add flavours, extracts, and colours to a blend of herbs and spices? Flavours, including natural, nature identical (a questionable descriptor), and artificial, are all concentrated and cost less than the real ingredient.[24] Food companies will tell you these are more consistent and safer due to the lack of potential pathogens. Yet they still use herbs and spices. Again, cost is the key driver.

Next is the 43% occurrence of listing 'Spices', but not listing what spices, unless they happen to be known allergens that must be declared. Is this to save space on labels, or simply a way to not tell consumers about items a consumer may not want, but that do not have to be mandatorily listed? Surely food companies should always list 100% of all ingredients.

Silicon dioxide at 27% is interesting. Along with Tricalcium Phosphate (7%), Calcium Stearate (7%), and Calcium Silicate (3%), these ingredients are what are known as free-flow agents. That is, they make the blend more free-flowing for packing on high-speed automatic packaging/filling machines. The added advantage is they help prevent clumping, something that happens when thousands of packs are made, then sit in a warehouse, followed by being shipped weeks or months after production, and finally end up on a supermarket shelf. A blend of herbs and spices that has been packed in an airtight pack should not have deteriorated if it has a few lumps in it.

Citric acid was found in 23% of surveyed blends. While citric acid occurs naturally, most citric acid used in food products is industrially manufactured. Citric acid imparts a harsh acidity to these blends when a more compatible ingredient would be natural lemon powder, amchur powder, or even sumac.

Rice flour, also at 23%, is used to help amalgamate the ingredients. At a significantly lower cost than most spices, it also helps to bulk out the blend economically. The downside is that rice flour binds up flavours to a certain degree, making the addition of extra flavours necessary. Other flours added for similar purposes and to assist in cost reduction are corn flour, corn starch, maize flour, potato starch, and malted barley flour.[25]

Yeast extract at 20% of surveyed blends is a food flavouring made from the same yeast used to make bread and beer. It's also added to some foods like soy sauce and cheese for a savoury flavour. The taste that yeast extracts create is sometimes referred to as umami. Although not a spice as such, yeast extract remains a legitimate way to add umami to a herb and spice blend.

Corn maltodextrin is added to improve the flavour by flattening sharp or dissonant flavour notes in some spices, while also enhancing density of taste on the palate and potentially extending shelf life.[26] Maltodextrin is a low cost and generally unnecessary addition if a herb and spice blend is well balanced with natural herbs and spices in the first place.

Oils, including vegetable, canola, and soybean, are generally added to overcome what is referred to as strata-ing, that is, a separation of ingredient particles of varying sizes, resulting in stratas, or layers, forming in the blend during storage and transportation, so it no longer looks homogenous. Oils also help to make a blend look glossy and appetizing. Sumac which has been adulterated with ground sumac seeds, citric acid, and artificial colour looks more natural with added oil.

Cellulose, an extender added to food products to assist free-flowing during packaging, may extend shelf life as an anti-caking agent.[27] Cellulose is cheap and bulks out spice mixes economically.

Di-sodium inosinate and guanylate is stronger than MSG.[28] It has basically the same effect, but it can be used in lower amounts and allows the manufacturer to avoid putting MSG on the ingredient list.

Propylene glycol is useful industrially, and may be a logical ingredient to add to products such as ice cream to enhance flavours, extend shelf life, and act as an emulsifier.[29] However, is this really necessary in a herb and spice blend?

Conundrum

One has to ask the question, 'What are the Perils of Popularity' for herbs, spices, herb and spice blends, and seasonings in 2020 and beyond? On the one hand they have become readily available, and cooks enjoy the convenience of these products to make less boring meals.

On the other hand, have these precious wonders of nature suffered the same fate as Pot-Pourri? Issues abound, from adulteration and lack of product knowledge by many food communicators to rogue traders and spice companies that value-engineer spice blends to reduce cost.

We are at risk of a time when no one remembers the original qualities of a spice blend like *ras el hanout*. Benchmarks for provenance, quality, and identity will be lost if we see a future when the artisan spice company has disappeared, a time when cooks can only source herbs, spices, and spice blends that satisfy commercial short-term interests in an ever-accelerating race to the bottom.

Those of us who care about such fundamental food integrity matters should embark on a consumer awareness campaign, so consumers will understand the importance of reading ingredient listings and reject products that are economical with the truth. Professional education institutions should also pay more attention to the proper evaluation of herbs, spices, and spice blends. When our daughter, undertaking a professional chef's course at a prestigious London institution, questioned the quality of the ground cumin seeds being used, she was told by the lecturer, 'It's only a spice, that doesn't matter.' Having grown up with spices, she was quite horrified at this response.

Food enthusiasts tend to emphasize the quality of meats, vegetables, and fruits; however the provenance, quality, and integrity of the herbs and spices used can make or break the end result. We should advocate for food educators to adopt a curriculum for herbs and spices, so food professionals know how to properly evaluate material. The curriculum would ideally cover key elements such as the roles of fresh and dried herbs – and why many spices have to be dried. Especially in an age where food safety and HACCP certifications are crucial, teaching should also cover the most appropriate criteria for storage and sanitation.[30] With such a curriculum, graduates of commercial cookery courses would be better informed and be able to properly evaluate herb and spice ingredients when they are better understood.

Food writers need to undertake thorough research on the herbs and spices they write about. They must be prepared to avoid hyperbole when describing spice experiences in exotic locations, as guests of charismatic farmers!

Notes

1 Ian Hemphill, *Spice Notes* (Sydney: Macmillan, 2000); *Spice Travels: A Spice Merchant's Voyage of Discovery* (Sydney: Macmillan, 2001); *The Spice and Herb Bible*, 3rd ed (Toronto: Robert Rose, 2014).
2 Harold McGee, *On Food and Cooking* (London: Hodder & Stoughton, 2004), p. 423.
3 'Smoked Paprika', *The Source Bulk Foods*, 2021 <https://thesourcebulkfoods.com.au/shop/cooking/smoked-paprika/> [accessed 23 March 2021].
4 Hemphill, *The Spice & Herb Bible*, p. 459.
5 For details of Sri Lankan cinnamon accompanied by a photo of cassia, see 'Cinnamon Sticks', *Spicewalla Brand*, 2021 <https://www.spicewallabrand.com/products/cinnamon-sticks> [accessed 23 March 2021].
6 Jane Black, 'When It Comes to this Ingredient, Believe the Hype', *The Wall Street Journal*, 8 November

2018 <https://www.wsj.com/articles/when-it-comes-to-this-ingredient-believe-the-hype-1541699428> [accessed 23 March 2021].

7   Isabella Beeton, *Mrs Beeton's Book of Household Management* (London: Chancellor Press, 1982 [1861]), p. 181.

8   'Food Recalled in Cancer Dye Scare', *BBC News*, 18 February 2005, <http://news.bbc.co.uk/2/hi/health/4277677.stm> [accessed 23 March 2021]

9   Xin-wei Li and others, 'Detection of Corn and Whole Wheat Adulteration in White Pepper Powder by Near Infrared Spectroscopy', *American Journal of Food Science and Technology*, 6.3 (2018), 114-17 <http://www.doi.org/10.12691/ajfst-6-3-5>

10 'Does Your Spice Rack Contain Fake Oregano?', *Choice*, 5 April 2016 <https://www.choice.com.au/food-and-drink/groceries/herbs-and-spices/articles/oregano-fraud> [accessed 23 March 2021]

11 'Saffron Alert', *HerbiesTV*, 5 November 2009 <https://www.youtube.com/watch?v=-7blOH_NmvU> [accessed 23 March 2021]

12 J.S. Pruthi, *Spices and Condiments: Chemistry, Microbiology, Technology* (New York: Academic Press, 1980), pp. 142-46.

13 John Humphries, *The Essential Saffron Companion* (Berkeley: Ten Speed Press, 1996), pp. 31-32.

14 Reay Tannahill, *Food in History* (New York: Penguin, 1988), pp. 162-64, 281, 292-95.

15 Pat Willard, *The Secrets of Saffron* (Boston: Beacon Press, 2001), p. 201.

16 Diana and Paul Von Welanetz, *The Von Welanetz Guide to Ethnic Ingredients* (New York: Warner Books, 1987), p. 615.

17 'Ras el Hanout', *East India Spice Company* <https://cdn.shopify.com/s/files/1/0253/7242/6294/products/70g_BlackPouch_RaElHanout_1080x.jpg?v=1573302286> [accessed 30 March 2020].

18 'Masterfoods Seasoning Bush Spice', *Woolworth's*, 2021 <https://www.woolworths.com.au/shop/productdetails/355473/masterfoods-seasoning-bush-spice> [accessed 23 March 2021]

19 'Tandoori Curry Paste', *Sharwood's*, 2021<https://www.sharwoods.com.au/our-ranges/pastes/tandoori-curry-paste> [accessed 23 March 2021]

20 'Self-Regulation Leaves Bad Taste as Food Industry Fails to Drop the Salt', *The George Institute for Global Health*, 9 January 2020 <https://www.georgeinstitute.org/media-releases/self-regulation-leaves-bad-taste-as-food-industry-fails-to-drop-the-salt> [accessed 23 March 2021].

21 Hemphill, *Spice Notes*, p. 353; see also 'The Future of Salt Reduction and Lowering Population Blood Pressure', *Blood Pressure UK*, 30 September 2020 <http://www.bloodpressureuk.org/news/news/the-future-of-salt-reduction-and-lowering-population-blood-pressure.html> [accessed 23 March 2021].

22 'Herbamare Original', *A. Vogel* <https://www.avogel.co.uk/food/products/herbamare/> [accessed 23 March 2021].

23 'The Sweet Danger of Sugar', *Harvard Health Publishing*, 5 November 2019 <https://www.health.harvard.edu/heart-health/the-sweet-danger-of-sugar> [accessed 23 March 2021].

24 Codex Alimentarius Commission, 'Discussion Paper on Flavouring Agents', *FAO*, October 2004 <http://www.fao.org/tempref/codex/Meetings/CCFAC/ccfac37/FA37_15e.pdf> [accessed 23 March 2021].

25 'Barley Flour', *Wikipedia*, 21 March 2021 <https://en.wikipedia.org/wiki/Barley_flour> [accessed 23 March 2021].

26 Joana Cavaco Silva, 'What Is Maltodextrin and Is It Safe?', *Medical News Today*, 11 July 2018 <https://www.medicalnewstoday.com/articles/322426> [accessed 23 March 2021].

27 Mariam Reimer, '15 Food Companies That Serve You "Wood"', *The Street*, 2 March 2011 <https://www.thestreet.com/opinion/cellulose-wood-pulp-never-tasted-so-good-11012915> [accessed 23 March 2021]

28 'Disodium Guanylate', *Wikipedia*, 25 February 2021 <https://en.wikipedia.org/wiki/Disodium_guanylate> [accessed 23 March 2021].

29 Elise Mandl, 'Propylene Glycol in Food: Is This Additive Safe?', *Healthline,* 2 March 2018 <https://www.healthline.com/nutrition/propylene-glycol> [accessed 23 March 2021]

30 'The Essential Guide to HACCP', *Safe Food Alliance*, 2020 <https://safefoodalliance.com/food-safety-resources/haccp-overview/> [accessed 23 March 2021].

The Road That Spices Travel is No Longer Silk

Peter Hertzmann

Standing in the giant Wukuaishi Wholesale Spice Market in Chengdu, surrounded by multi-bushel-size bags of chilli peppers, I could easily believe that modernity has done little to alter the basic concepts of the spice trade. For more than two millennia, Chengdu was the eastern terminus of the Southern Silk Road to India and a secondary, eastern terminus for the Silk Road to the Middle East.[1] Neither route was a 'road' in the modern sense of the word, but 'a stretch of shifting, unmarked paths across massive expanses of deserts and mountains' along which people, animals, and goods could travel.[2] Spices were just one of the precious items transported in one direction or the other, and the ancient – some dating to the writing of the Hebrew bible – overland routes would over time give way to other routes as transportation improved and regional politics changed.[3] The prevalent spices of the modern Chengdu market originated in the New World a few hundred years ago. The spices of the Silk Road days are now simply a footnote.

173

Roman Times

By the start of the common era, the Mediterranean coasts were already a major trading region that also included South-East Asia (i.e. Malaysia, Java, and the Spice Islands), China, India, Africa, Arabia, and Persia. After silk from China, spices were a principal commodity of Roman imports from these other regions. The culinary spices included cinnamon, cassia, saffron, turmeric, cloves, nutmeg, ginger, and long and round pepper.[4]

Since spices were first gathered, the degree and type of adulteration, whether happenstance or intentional, have been an issue. Spices, by their nature as dried organic matter, innately have a low water activity level and cannot support the growth of most bacteria, mould, or fungus. Should a spice become slightly moist, mould and fungus may contaminate it.[5] Improper handling or storage could damage a spice at any point from gathering to use. Intentional adulteration was another issue.

Spices were a valuable commodity in the Roman Empire.[6] Although there are claims of a rare specimen selling for 1000 denarii per pound, the prices of common spices were more reasonable. Per Pliny, the price of long pepper 'is fifteen denarii per pound, while that of white pepper is seven, and of black, four'.[7] If the spice merchant could reduce his expenses by supplementing his product with a bit of a less expensive item, he certainly could choose to do so. 'Long pepper is very easily adulterated with

Alexandrian mustard'; '[p]epper is adulterated with juniper berries, which have the property, to a marvellous degree, of assuming the pungency of pepper'; cinnamon was probably adulterated with cassia, which could easily be one-third the price; and cassia in turn could be 'adulterated with storax, and, in consequence of the resemblance of the bark, with very small sprigs of laurel'.[8]

The Middle Ages

By the Middle Ages, the trade routes extended well north into France and Britain. In England, the 'Spicers' were mostly dealing with spices for medicinal purposes. 'Pepperer' was the term self-adopted by the merchants who imported a range of goods from the Mediterranean region that included spices. In 1180, the Pepperers formed London's first mercantile guild – an act for which they were fined 16 marks since they failed to get a license from the King prior to organizing.[9] Before long, the Pepperers took over the 'Grocers' and became the Grocers Company or Guild.[10] The Grocers were placed in charge of the Great Beam and the Small Beam, the official standards for weighing, by Henry III. The guild's members were appointed 'weighers' by the Crown.[11] As can be seen in Table 1, the prices that spices brought required accurate weight.[12]

The guild established the profession of 'garbelers', the first public food inspectors in England. 'Garbel', from an old Arabic word meaning 'to sift, or select', was the process of detecting and removing impurities and adulterants from spices and similar products, and certifying to their purity. In 1316, the Lord Mayor of London prohibited grocers from 'facing' the bale 'so as to make the end of the bale contain better than the remainder of the bale'.[13]

Also in 1316, the grocers established their own ordinances pertaining to the quality of merchandise, including spices such as saffron, alum, ginger, and cloves, in that different batches couldn't be mixed. They also promulgated measures against adulteration, reinforced the Lord Mayor's decree against 'baling', and prohibited underweighting either outright or by adding water to make the spices heavier.[14] In the 1440s, '[b]y a charter of Henry VI., confirmed by Charles I., the wardens of the Company, or their deputies, could, like modern excisemen, enter druggists', apothecaries', and confectioners', as well as grocers' shops, and impose fines, and even imprisonment, for deceits; always seizing the spurious articles'.[15]

In Nuremberg in 1444, the penalty for violating the rules was a bit stiffer, when a spice merchant was punished for adulterating saffron by burning him at the stake using the adulterated saffron as part of the fuel. Another trio of miscreants was reportedly buried alive in saffron![16]

In 1453, the fall of Constantinople, the point where overland trade routes traversed from the Orient to the Occident, seriously stifled commerce because the Ottoman Empire greatly increased tariffs and limited trading nations.[17] Attempts to find a westerly route to the Spice Islands at the end of the century were unsuccessful, but they did result in a new source of previously unknown spice varieties. Some might say

Spice	Price per Pound	Year(s)
Pepper	1s. 1s. 6d. 1s. 10d. 2s. 6d.	1290 1337 1340 1350
Cinnamon	1s. 10d. avg	1264 to 1399
Mace	4s. 7d. avg	1264 to 1399
Ginger	1s. 6½d. avg	1264 to 1399
Saffron	4s. 9½d. to 14s. 7½d.	1300s

Work	Wages	Year(s)
Master Mason	4s. per week in summer; 3s. 4d. per week in winter	1377
Woman Field Labourer	1d. per day	1310 to 1320
Carpenter	1 to 1½d. per day 2 to 3d. per day	1317 1388

Table 1. Selected prices of spices compared to selected earnings of labour. Note: In the 1300s, there were 12 pence (d.) to a shilling (s.).

the 'discovery' of allspice, capsicum peppers, and vanilla from the Americas more than made up for finding no shortcut.[18]

Queen Elizabeth established the (British) East India Company in 1601 in an attempt to break the Dutch and Portuguese monopoly of the spice trade, but it would be a number of years until the first ship sailed to challenge their dominance.[19] In 1602, the Dutch, following two profitable sea expeditions to the East Indies at the end of the previous century, created the United East India Company by consolidating existing trading companies. It was their attempt to further monopolize the sea lanes to India and the Spice Islands.[20] Now, the spice-trade route went from traveling mostly overland to traveling mostly by sea.

175

The 1800s

In 1793, the German chemist and pharmacist Frederick Accum set up a laboratory in London. He made the identification of adulterated products and the identification of their guilty producers his life's work. Starting in 1798, he began a series of short postings in *Nicholson's Journal* detailing his work.[21] His magnus opus was published in 1820: *A Treatise on Adulterations of Food and Culinary Poisons.*[22]

Accum's section headings are suggestive of the spices he addressed, including 'Counterfeit pepper, and method of detecting it', 'White Pepper, and method of manufacturing it', 'Poisonous cayenne pepper, and method of detecting it', 'Adulteration of cinnamon, and method of detecting it', and 'Adulteration of mustard'.[23] The section on black pepper is as follows:

That factitious pepper-corns [*sic*] have of late been detected mixed with genuine pepper, is a fact sufficiently known. Such an adulteration may prove, in many instances of household economy, exceedingly vexatious and prejudicial to those who ignorantly make use of the spurious article. I have examined large packages of both black and white pepper, by order of the Excise, and have found them to contain about 16 per cent of this artificial compound. The spurious pepper is made up of oil cakes (the residue of lintseed, [*sic*] from which the oil has been pressed), common clay, and a portion of Cayenne pepper, formed in a mass, and granulated by being first pressed through a sieve, and then rolled in a cask. The mode of detecting the fraud is easy. It is only necessary to throw a sample of the suspected pepper into a bowl of water; the artificial pepper-corns fall to powder, whilst the true pepper remains whole.

Ground pepper is very often sophisticated by adding to a portion of genuine pepper a quantity of pepper dust, or the sweepings from the pepper warehouses, mixed with a little Cayenne pepper. The sweepings are known, and purchased in the market, under the name of P. D. signifying pepper dust. An inferior sort of this vile refuse, or the sweepings of P. D. is distinguished among venders by the abbreviation of D. P. D. denoting, dust (dirt) of pepper dust.[24]

A number of other authors quickly joined Accum's parade. Much of what they wrote seems to match, or copy, what he earlier wrote.[25] A decade or two later, authors greatly expanded the numbers of items being adulterated and provided the scientific methods necessary to determine the adulteration.[26] The outcome of the 'Lancet Committee' was the 'Adulteration of Food and Drugs Act' passed in England in 1860, but it was ineffective and much ignored. Parliament created a Select Committee to write an effective law. The earlier law was repealed, and a new law replaced it in 1875.[27]

Early Twentieth Century

Starting in the 1880s, the Division of Chemistry of the United States Department of Agriculture began issuing its multivolume, multiyear *Bulletin 13* which centred around the adulteration of food and how to detect it. Part 2 specifically addressed 'Spices and Condiments' and greatly increased the number of spices identified and their possible adulterations.[28] Over the sharp objections of industry, an anti-adulteration law was passed in the United States in 1906.[29] Adulteration of spices was not specifically mentioned in the law, but it did address food purity in general.

The law was weak, but it was a start. After passage, much time was spent in the courts debating whether individual products were adulterated or misbranded by the producer for some reason other than intention. Other common issues to address included whether a package was filled sufficiently or contained the stated quantity of contents.[30] The 1906 Act redefined adulteration in terms of economics and introduced the concept of misbranding. Per the law, misbranding included misleading ingredients, incorrect weight or measure, and the failure to state the inclusion of narcotics.[31] Misbranding would go on to become the major reason for product recalls in modern times.

Within a decade after the passage of the 1906 Act, the law was strengthened by changing the method of inspection from inspecting at the point of purchase to inspecting at the point of production, the source of the potential violation. When the producer was also the seller, as was common leading up to the turn of the twentieth century, inspecting at a retail level was sufficient. Now, with factories spewing out products and shipping them across the country, it was more efficient to inspect at the factory before a batch of product was dispersed around the country.[32]

The 1930s

After numerous attempts to amend the 1906 Act and after five years of negotiations in the 1930s, the 1906 Act was repealed and a new, more extensive act replaced it in 1938.[33] The new law: 1) widened the prohibition against economic adulteration; 2) mandated the establishment of food standards; 3) prohibited any false or misleading statement on food labels or in advertising; 4) required imitation food to be labelled as such; 5) required foods be labelled with specific information such as the name and address of the manufacturer, the net quantity of contents, the name of the food, and the statement of ingredients, and authorized the FDA to require the labelling to reveal all facts material to any other representations made for the product; and 6) prohibited any container that was made, formed, or filled so as to be misleading.[34]

By the time Franklin Roosevelt signed the act on 25 June 1938, much of the Silk Road had been replaced by sea lanes. Where overland trading was still carried out, camels and horses were replaced by trucks. What at one time could take much of a year to move from supplier to customer, now took only a few weeks. Most of the eastern end of the Silk Road was now a war zone, and soon most of the western end would be one, too.

Today (in the US)

The 1938 law has been amended and expanded many times since it was first enacted, but as codified in the United States Code, the Federal Food, Drug, and Cosmetic Act is still the current law.[35] From the law, federal regulations were, and still are, drafted by various departments or agencies of the government. Most fall under the purview the Food and Drug Administration under Title 21 of the Code of Federal Regulations.

Much of the federal regulation of spices comes under the same non-specific parameters as other food items – in particular, the general sections dealing with adulterated and misbranded foods – but there are a few sections that specifically refer to spices. Section 101.22 titled 'Foods; labeling of spices, flavorings, colorings and chemical preservatives' is part of the general section dealing with labelling. The important paragraphs of the section are:

> (2) The term spice means any aromatic vegetable substance in the whole, broken, or ground form, except for those substances which have been traditionally regarded as foods, such as onions, garlic and celery; whose significant function in

food is seasoning rather than nutritional; that is true to name; and from which no portion of any volatile oil or other flavoring principle has been removed. Spices include the spices listed in 182.10 and part 184 of this chapter, such as the following:

Allspice, Anise, Basil, Bay leaves, Caraway seed, Cardamon, Celery seed, Chervil, Cinnamon, Cloves, Coriander, Cumin seed, Dill seed, Fennel seed, Fenugreek, Ginger, Horseradish, Mace, Marjoram, Mustard flour, Nutmeg, Oregano, Paprika, Parsley, Pepper, black; Pepper, white; Pepper, red; Rosemary, Saffron, Sage, Savory, Star aniseed, Tarragon, Thyme, Turmeric.

Paprika, turmeric, and saffron or other spices which are also colors, shall be declared as 'spice and coloring' unless declared by their common or usual name.[36]

Any item identified as a spice need not be listed separately in the label's ingredient list. The generic listing of 'spices' is sufficient.

(h) The label of a food to which flavor is added shall declare the flavor in the statement of ingredients in the following way:

(1) Spice, natural flavor, and artificial flavor may be declared as "spice", "natural flavor", or "artificial flavor", or any combination thereof, as the case may be.[37]

Section 182.10, mentioned the quotation above, is a much more extensive list of 'Spices and other natural seasonings and flavorings' generally recognized as safe (GRAS) 'for their intended use'. The GRAS designation was introduced as part of the Food Additives Amendment of 1958, an amendment to the Federal Food, Drugs, and Cosmetic Act of 1938.

Congress recognized that many substances intentionally used in a manner whereby they are added to food would not require a formal premarket review by FDA to assure their safety, either because their safety had been established by a long history of use in food or by virtue of the nature of the substances, their customary or projected conditions of use, and the information generally available to scientists about the substances.[38]

In all, 83 separate items – from alfalfa seed to zedoary – considered to be either spices or flavourings are listed. Because Standards of Identity, as mandated by the 1938 Act, have never been established for spices, thirty-seven are further described in the Compliance Policy Guide.[39]

In accordance with 21 CFR 110.110 Current Good Manufacturing Practice in Manufacturing, Packing, or Holding Human Food, the FDA has issued a Food Defect Levels Handbook that 'establish[es] maximum levels of natural or unavoidable defects in foods for human use that present no health hazard'.[40] Individual spices are among the items listed in the Handbook (see Table 2).[41]

In 1974, Congress established a federal program to stop the spread of noxious weeds. The program has been revised twice since its inception.[42] Although federal and state weed lists contain hundreds of species, two species have been the emphasis of enforcement: onionweed (*Asphodelus sp.*) and dodder (*Cuscuta sp.*). The countries most likely to export spices containing noxious weed seeds are India, Pakistan, Turkey, Egypt, and China. If noxious weed seeds are found in a shipment, the options for treating and reconditioning imported spices are grinding them to a mesh size that devitalizes the noxious weed seeds, or heat-treating them to devitalize unwanted seeds, which also may damage the volatile oils of the spices.[43]

The importation of spices into the United States is no longer a matter of transferring cargo from the source to the destination. The Public Health Security and Bioterrorism Preparedness and Response Act of 2002 set a requirement that the FDA receive prior notice of food importation.[44] This requirement was modified by the Food Safety Modernization Act of 2011.[45] In May 2013, the FDA published a final rule, 'Information Required in Prior Notice of Imported Food'.[46] Essentially all food brought into the

Product	Defect (Method)	Action Level
Pepper, Whole (Black & White)	Insect filth and/or insect-mold (MPM-V39)	Average of 1% or more pieces by weight are infested and/or moldy
	Mammalian excreta (MPM-V39)	Average of 1 mg or more mammalian excreta per pound
	Foreign matter (MPM-V39)	Average of 1% or more pickings and siftings by weight
	DEFECT SOURCE: Insect infested – post harvest and/or processing infestation, Moldy – post harvest and/or processing infection, Mammalian excreta – post harvest and/or processing animal contamination, Foreign material – post harvest contamination SIGNIFICANCE: Aesthetic, Potential health hazard – mammalian excreta may contain salmonella	
Pepper, Ground	Insect filth (AOAC 972.40)	Average of 475 or more insect fragments per 50 grams
	Rodent filth (AOAC 972.40)	Average of 2 or more rodent hairs per 50 grams
	DEFECT SOURCE: Insect fragments – post harvest and/or processing insect infestation, Rodent hair – post harvest and/or processing contamination with animal hair or excreta SIGNIFICANCE: Aesthetic	

Table 2. Sample listing from 'Food Defect Levels Handbook'. 'MPM' indicates the Macroanalytical Procedures Manual standardized method of macroscopic analysis. 'AOAC' indicates the AOAC International standardized method of analysis.

United States, except that brought in personal baggage for personal use, is subject to the prior notice rules.[47]

The 2002 Act also had provisions for administrative detention of imported foods; requirements for the registration of any factory, warehouse, or establishment of an importer that manufactures, processes, packs, or holds food; and requirements for the maintenance of all records relating to the manufacture, processing, packing, distribution, receipt, holding, or importation of the food.[48]

In 2007, Congress directed the FDA to establish a Reportable Food Registry.[49] The Registry is an electronic portal for reporting when there is a reasonable probability that the use of, or exposure to, an article of food will cause serious, adverse health consequences or death. Reports may be submitted by responsible parties and by public health officials. The FDA reviews and assesses the information submitted and issues an alert or notification if deemed necessary.[50]

The Food Safety Modernization Act of 2011 introduced a number of clauses that indirectly affected spices.[51] Possibly, the most important is the Foreign Supplier Verification Program (FSVP).[52] Since most spices are imported, the FSVP directly effects spice importers. As of this writing, the FDA has only issued a Draft Guidance for how to comply with the FSVP.[53] The key requirements of the resulting rule are 1) who is covered by the rule; 2) the application of hazards analysis; 3) evaluation of food risk and supplier performance; 4) supplier verification; 5) corrective actions if something goes wrong; 6) exemptions to the rule; and 7) insuring that each, unique facility has a Data Universal Numbering System (DUNS) number.[54]

The U.S. Environmental Protection Agency is responsible for setting the maximum levels and tolerances of residual agricultural chemicals (pesticides, herbicides, fungicides, rodenticides etc.) on any imported spices, but enforcement is the responsibility of the FDA.[55] The FDA maintains a Pesticide Residue Monitoring Program that annually tests a broad range of imported and domestic commodities for approximately 700 pesticide residues.[56] Curiously, the actual inspection is the responsibility of the Animal and Plant Health Inspection Service, a division of the United States Department of Agriculture.[57] The European Commission also maintains a pesticides database for reference when importing spices into that region of the world.[58]

Today (in the Rest of the World)

Much of the rules concerning the spices throughout the remainder of the world are codified in a collection of international food standards, guidelines, and codes of practice called the Codex Alimentarius. The Codex was created and is maintained by the Codex Alimentarius Commission. The Commission is the 'governing organization' of the Joint FAO/WHO Food Standards Programme, a body of the United Nations.[59] The United States is a participant in the Codex Alimentarius, and thus much of the information is similar for both entities.

In addition to government organizations regulating the spice trade, there are regional trade associations that represent their member companies before the government bodies. The European Federation of the Trade in Dried Fruit, Edible Nuts, Processed Fruit & Vegetables, Processed Fishery Products, Spices and Honey (FRUCOM); American Spice Trade Association (ASTA); European Spice Association (ESA); and India Pepper and Spice Trade Association (IPSTA) are examples of these advocacy organizations.[60] Many of these organizations also produce their own standards for members to abide by.[61]

The Silk Road is no more. Explorers are no longer looking for shorter routes between the customer and the supplier. Freight forwarding companies direct the movement of spices by land, sea, and air. Although any spice not meeting international standards is termed adulterated, intentionally adulterated spices are rare. And, spices are for all consumers, not just the rich.

Notes

1   Yang Juping, 'The Relations Between China and India and the Opening of the Southern Silk Road During the Han Dynasty', *The Silk Road*, 11 (2013), 82-92; Valerie Hansen, *The Silk Road: A New History* (Oxford: Oxford University Press, 2012), p. 7; The actual term 'Silk Road' only dates to 1877, the year Baron Ferdinand von Richthofen, a German geographer in China, coined the phrase in his five-volume atlas (Hansen, p. 6).

2   Hansen, p. 5.

3   Exodus 30.23. The term 'sweet cinnamon' is found in most translations of this bible verse; Clifford A. Wright, 'The Medieval Spice Trade and the Diffusion of the Chile', *Gastronomica*, 7 (2007), 35-43 (pp. 36-37).

4   Michael Loewe, 'Spices and Silk: Aspects of World Trade in the First Seven Centuries of the Christian Era', *Journal of the Royal Asiatic Society*, 103 (1971), 166-79 (pp. 173-76).

5   Larry R. Beuchat, 'Influence of Water Activity on Growth, Metabolic Activities and Survival of Yeasts and Molds', *Journal of Food Protection*, 46.2, 135-41.

6   James F. Bush, 'Adulteration of Food and Other Natural Products in Ancient Rome', *Food and Drug Law Journal*, 57 (2002), 573-602 (p. 577).

7   C. Plinius Secundus, *The Natural History of Pliny*, trans. John Bostock and H.T. Riley, 6 vols (London: George Bell & Sons, 1857), VI, p. 112, (bk. XII, ch. 14). For comparison, a legionnaire's annual salary was 300 denarii (Lesley Askins and Roy A. Adkins, *Handbook of Life in Ancient Rome* (New York: Facts on File, 1994), p. 77).

8   C. Plinius Secundus, p. 113; Bush, p. 578; C. Plinius Secundus, p. 141 (bk. XII, ch. 43).

9   Pamela Nightingale, 'The London Pepperers' Guild and Some Twelfth-Century English Trading Links with Spain', Bulletin of the Institute of Historical Research, 58 (1985), 123-32 (pp. 123-24).

10   F. Leslie Hart, 'A History of the Adulteration of Food Before 1906', *Food and Drug Law Institute*, 7 (1962), 5-22 (p. 8). The Worshipful Company of Grocers of London still exists to this day (<https://grocershall.co.uk/> [accessed 12 April 2020]).

11   T.D. Whittet, 'Pepperers, Spicers and Grocers – Forerunners of the Apothecaries', *Proceedings of the Royal Society of Medicine*, 61 (1968), 801-06 (p. 802); Hart, p. 8.

12   James E. Thorold Rogers, *A History of Agriculture and Prices in England* (Oxford: Clarendon Press, 1882), I, pp. 256, 258, 273-74, 278, 627-31.

13   Hart, pp. 8-9.

14   Whittet, p. 803; Peter Barton Hutt and Peter Barton Hutt II, 'A History of Government Regulation of Adulteration and Misbranding of Food', *Food, Drug, Cosmetic Law Journal*, 39 (1984), 2-73 (p. 27).

15   John Timbs, *Curiosities of London* (London: Longmans, Green, Reader, and Dyer, 1868), p. 397.

16   Hart, p. 10.

17 Steven Runciman, *The Fall of Constantinople 1453*, Canto edn. (Cambridge: Cambridge University Press, 1990), p. 164.

18 Louis E. Grivetti, 'Herbs, Spices, and Flavorings', *Nutrition Today*, 51 (2016), 194-97 (pp. 195-97).

19 Hart, p. 12.

20 Robert Parthesius, *Dutch Ships in Tropical Waters: The Development of the Dutch East India Company (VOC) Shipping Network in Asia 1595–1660* (Amsterdam: University Press, 2010), pp. 34-35.

21 Hart, p. 14.

22 Frederick Accum, *A Treatise on Adulterations of Food and Culinary Poisons, Exhibiting the Fraudulent Sophistications of Bread, Beer, Wine, Spirituous Liquors, Tea, Coffee, Cream, Confectionery, Vinegar, Mustard, Pepper, Cheese, Olive Oil, Pickles, and Other Articles Employed in Domestic Economy, and Methods of Detecting Them* (London: Longman, Hurst, Rees, Orme, and Brown, 1820).

23 Accum, pp. XXII, XXIV.

24 Accum, pp. 284-86.

25 James Cutbush, *Lectures on the Adulteration of Food and Culinary Poisons: The Detection of Poisons in General and of Adulterations in Sundry Chemical Preparations, &c. used in Medicine and the Arts, with a Means of Discovering Them: and Rules for Determining the Purity of Substances* (Newburgh, NY: Ward M. Gazlay, 1823); *Deadly Adulteration and Slow Poisoning or, Disease and Death in the Pot and the Bottle* (London: Sherwood, Gilbert and Piper, 1829); A. Bussy, *Traité des moyens de Rrconnaitre les falsifications des drogues simples et composées* (Paris: Thomine, 1829); *The Domestic Chemist: Comprising Instructions for the Detection of Adulteration in Numerous Articles Employed in Domestic Economy, Medicine, and the Arts* (London: Bumpus & Griffin, 1831).

26 Lewis C. Beck, *Adulterations of Various Substances used in Medicine and the Arts, with the Means of Detecting Them* (New York: Samuel S. and William Wood, 1846); Arthur Hill Hassall, *Food and Adulterations; Comprising the Reports of the Analytical Sanitary Commission of 'The Lancet' for the Years 1851 to 1854 Inclusive* (London: Longman, Brown, Green, and Longmans, 1855); Jesse P. Battershall, *Food Adulteration and its Detection with Photomicrographic Plates and a Bibliographic Appendix* (New York: E. & F.N. Spon, 1887).

27 W.D. Bigelow, 'The Development of Pure Food Legislation', *Science*, n.s. 7 (1898), 505-13 (p. 510).

28 Clifford Richardson, *Foods and Food Adulterants* (Washington: Government Printing Office, 1887).

29 U.S. Pub. L. 59-384, 34 Stat 768 (1906).

30 Hutt and Hutt, pp. 55-61.

31 U.S. Pub. L. 59-384, 34 Stat 768 (1906), pp. 770-71.

32 W. R. M. Wharton, 'ITS Inspection Evolution', *Food, Drug, Cosmetic Law Quarterly*, 1 (1946), 348-60 (pp. 357-58).

33 U.S. Pub. L. 75-717, 52 Stat 1040 (1938), 'Federal Food, Drug, and Cosmetic Act'.

34 Hutt and Hutt, p. 62.

35 21 USC Chap. 9.

36 21 CFR 101.22 (a)(2).

37 21 CFR 101.22 (h)(1). This is further clarified in the FDA Compliance Policy Guide CPG Sec 525.650 Labeling of Seasonings.

38 Mike Saltmarsh, *Essential Guide to Food Additives*, 4th edn (Cambridge: Royal Society of Chemistry, 2013), p. 73.

39 'CPG Sec 525.750 Spices – Definitions', U.S. Food and Drug Administration <https://www.fda.gov/regulatory-information/search-fda-guidance-documents/cpg-sec-525750-spices-definitions> [accessed 16 April 2020].

40 'Food Defect Levels Handbook', U.S. Food and Drug Administration <https://www.fda.gov/food/ingredients-additives-gras-packaging-guidance-documents-regulatory-information/food-defect-levels-handbook> [accessed 16 April 2020].

41 'Macroanalytical Procedures Manual (MPM)', U.S. Food and Drug Administration <https://www.fda.gov/food/laboratory-methods-food/macroanalytical-procedures-manual-mpm> [accessed 16 April

2020]; *Official Methods of Analysis*, 21st edn (Rockville, MD: AOAC International, 2019).

42 U.S. Pub. L. 106-224, 114 Stat 358 (2000), 'Agricultural Risk Protection Act of 2000'.

43 *Noxious Weed Seeds in Spices – Information Resources* (Washington, DC: American Spice Trade Association, 2018), p. 2.

44 U.S. Pub. L. 107-188, 116 Stat 594 (2002), 'Public Health Security and Bioterrorism Preparedness and Response Act of 2002'.

45 U.S. Pub. L. 111-353, 124 Stat 3885 (2011), 'FDA Food Safety Modernization Act'.

46 78 FR 32359, 'Information Required in Prior Notice of Imported Food', Docket No. FDA-2011-N-0179.

47 *Prior Notice of Imported Food Questions and Answers (Edition 3): Guidance for Industry* (Rockville, MD: Office of Regulatory Affairs, 2016), p. 23. Found within FDA Docket FDA-2011-N-0179.

48 U.S. Pub. L. 107-188.

49 U.S. Pub. L. 110-85, 121 Stat 823 (2007), 'Food and Drug Administration Amendments Act of 2007'.

50 *Draft Guidance for Industry Questions and Answers Regarding the Reportable Food Registry as Established by the Food and Drug Administration Amendments Act of 2007 (Edition 2)* (Rockville, MD: Office of Regulatory Affairs, 2010), p. 2. Found within FDA Docket FDA-2009-D-0260.

51 U.S. Pub. L. 111-353.

52 21 CFR 1.500-1.514. Although published in the Code of Federal Regulations, the Foreign Supplier Verification Program is not a 'regulation' created by a law passed by Congress but a 'rule' established within the Executive Branch to comply with a law, in this case the Food Safety Modernization Act (FSMA), Pub. L. 111-353. It is published in the Code as Subpart L under Part 1 General Enforcement Regulations. The rule was also published in the Federal Register (v. 80, no. 228, 27 November 2015, pp. 74226-352) under FDA Docket FDA-2011-N-0143-0370.

53 *Foreign Supplier Verification Programs for Importers of Food for Humans and Animals: Guidance for Industry* (Rockville, MD: Office of Regulatory Affairs, 2018). Found within FDA Docket FDA-2017-D-5225.

54 'FSMA Final Rule on Foreign Supplier Verification Programs (FSVP) for Importers of Food for Humans and Animals', U.S. Food and Drug Administration <https://www.fda.gov/food/food-safety-modernization-act-fsma/fsma-final-rule-foreign-supplier-verification-programs-fsvp-importers-food-humans-and-animals> [accessed 16 April 2020]

55 40 CFR 180.

56 'Pesticides', U.S. Food and Drug Administration <https://www.fda.gov/food/chemicals-metals-pesticides-food/pesticides> [accessed 18 April 2020].

57 7 CFR 319.56-3.

58 'EU Pesticides database', European Commission <https://ec.europa.eu/food/plant/pesticides/eu-pesticides-database/public> [accessed 18 April 2020].

59 'Codex Alimentarius', Codex Alimentarius Commission <http://www.fao.org/fao-who-codexalimentarius/> [accessed 18 April 2020].

60 'European Federation of the Trade in Dried Fruit, Edible Nuts, Processed Fruit & Vegetables, Processed Fishery Products' <https://frucom.eu/>; 'American Spice Trade Association' <https://www.astaspice.org/>; 'European Spice Association' <https://www.esa-spices.org/>; 'India Pepper and Spice Trade Association' <https://ipstaindia.com/> [all accessed 18 April 2020].

61 For Example: *Clean, Safe Spices* (Washington, DC: American Spice Trade Association, 2017); *European Spice Association Quality Minima Document* (Brussels: European Spice Association, 2018); *TURMERIC Post-harvest Operations* (Rome: Food and Agriculture Organization of the United Nations, 2004).

Captain James Cook, Scurvy, and the Use and Misuse of Herbs

Heather Hunwick

'To some, scurvy was a toxin that rose up from the sea or fell down out of the atmosphere, seeping into the timbers of a ship then infecting the bodies of the sailors, suffocating, dry-drowning them.'

– Peter Moore, 2018[1]

The Age of Exploration unleashed a fearful manifestation of an ancient disease, scurvy. More technologically advanced ships capable of increasingly longer voyages would see scurvy emerge as 'one of the earliest occupational diseases'. By one estimate it accounted for over one million shipboard deaths from 1600 to 1800.[2] As expressed by the historian Kenneth J. Carpenter, scurvy 'is probably the nutritional deficiency disease that has caused the most suffering in recorded history'.[3]

In this year 2020, the 250th anniversary of Captain James Cook's landing in Botany Bay in the *Endeavour,* it is timely to review Cook's role in the saga of scurvy. Some recent scholars have tended to malign Cook in this regard, but care is needed when assessing eighteenth-century actions from current perspectives and knowledge. This paper will focus on just one aspect of scurvy on which so much has been written, the place of beers and ales as antiscorbutics in Cook's day, including spruce beer, a beverage he favoured. It will examine more specifically the tendency at the time to add herbs, broadly defined, to beers to enhance their antiscorbutic properties, and their use and misuse in pursuit of that end. To do so requires contextualization of the role of food, drink, and medication in the seventeenth and eighteenth centuries when they were often one and the same.[4]

The incidence of scurvy had been steadily worsening since 1700 with the increasing numbers and durations of maritime voyages. The British Admiralty was under mounting pressure to find a cure. Many prevalent theories, such as moist air and poor ventilation as causes, had not yet been fully discredited, but attention was increasingly turning to ships' 'victualing'. The Admiralty needed effective antiscorbutics; they should be cheap, stable for at least a year, portable, and sparing of water. It was a formidable task to limit choices to those they most favoured from amongst the babble of claims from vested interests and other influential parties. Cook's first voyage in the *Endeavour* and his subsequent two voyages into the Pacific provided opportunities to evaluate and report on several reputed antiscorbutic remedies. While Cook was at pains to accommodate the Admiralty's directions, as a seasoned mariner he had his own views.

Cook, as did some others, knew scurvy could be kept at bay or even cured with a diet of fresh fruits, vegetables, and meat. At the time it was inconceivable that scurvy stemmed from the lack of a micro-nutrient, and even more that it was at risk of destruction by then-usual food-preservation methods. Humoral doctrine – philosophical, not empirical – still dominated medical practice as it had for centuries, and its more senior adherents had the ear of the Admiralty. As put by Sir James Watt, 'This led to a blunderbuss approach to antiscorbutic treatment which confused the issue by failing to differentiate a true antiscorbutic from the remedies of longstanding tradition.'[5] The isolation of vitamin C was only accomplished in the early twentieth century, and even now its full role in human metabolism is not completely understood.[6] Spruce beer well-illustrates the many subtleties involved in seeking a cure in a world where biochemistry as we understand it lay far into the future.

Cook was no stranger to the 'pestilence of the sea'. During the Seven Years' War his ship, the *Pembroke*, when it reached Halifax in 1758, 'had so many sick on board that it took no part in the military action of Wolfe against the French'.[7] The town itself was much affected by outbreaks of scurvy. Founded a mere decade previously, Halifax, like most raw seaports and military towns, had a powerful thirst. Supplies of the beverage favoured by the lower classes, beer/ale, were limited because both the war and the harsh climate restricted supplies of grains suitable for brewing. But spruce trees and molasses were both abundant, so locally brewed spruce beer, wherein molasses rather than malt provided the sugars essential to fermentation, soon filled the gap. The *Halifax Gazette* in 1754 carried an advertisement by one Frederick Becker for 'choice spruce beer at five shillings a barrel or two pence a gallon', well below the price of rum offered in the same advertisement. Cook must have been aware of the popularity of spruce beer. Whether he believed it also had antiscorbutic benefits is not known but it seems plausible, as sentiments to that effect were widespread.

Some early settlers in northern parts of Canada certainly valued spruce-based drinks. In 1752, one Thomas Pichon wrote from Cape Breton Island that the inhabitants of Port-Toulouse 'were the first that brewed an excellent sort of antiscorbutic of the tops of the spruce-fir'. Peter Kalm, the Swedish-Finnish botanist who travelled widely in North America from 1748 to 1751, found the French in Canada largely drank spruce beer 'which, as they use no malt liquor, is their only drink, except wine brought from France which is pretty dear'.[8] Kalm noted that the botanists referred to the kind of spruce used as black spruce (*Picea mariana*). These brewed spruce-based drinks were likely local adaptations of long-established Baltic beers. Independently, antiscorbutic drinks based on the leaves and bark of certain local trees were known to at least some indigenous New-World cultures. When his expedition was trapped in ice in the St Lawrence River some 200 years earlier, Jacques Cartier saw his scurvy-afflicted crew dramatically restored to health by use of such a drink. Nevertheless, while sometimes described as a beer or even spruce beer, the historical account is clear: it was not fermented and more likely an infusion.

In August 1764, in Newfoundland to continue surveying the island's coast, Cook severely injured his right hand. As a result, 'the men, employed at ship tasks and "brewing of Spruce

Essence" – brewing "spruce beer", that is – grew a little restive, and even the excellent Peter Flower, Cook's senior hand, was with two others "confin'd to the Deck for Drunkness and Mutiny'". In 1765 Cook returned, and during an overhaul '[t]here was time to brew spruce beer again', and in the following year he notes similarly 'Here she was hauled ashore for scrubbing, and beer was brewed'.[9] Independently, in 1766 Joseph Banks, then just 23, joined an expedition to Newfoundland and Labrador. In early spring he noted how 'the Country is Covered with wood fir is the only Tree which can yet be distinguished of which I observed 3 sorts Black Spruce (*Picea mariana*) of which they Make a liquor Called Spruce Beer'.[10]

Settlers in Newfoundland in pursuit of cod had long relied heavily on spruce beer: 'Before the use of this beer was found at Newfoundland, the men were sickly, scorbutick, &c. but now there is no country where they are more healthy.'[11] Banks considered it a very common liquor of the country along with the popular 'chowder' and included his 'receipt' as 'Perfectly as I can get it':

> Take a copper that Contains 12 Gallons fill it as full of the Boughs of Black Spruce as it will hold Pressing them down pretty tight Fill it up with Water Boil it till the Rind will strip of the Spruce Boughs which will waste it about one third take them out & add to the water one Gallon of Melasses Let the whole Boil till the Melasses are all dissolved take half a hogshead & put in nineteen Gallons of water & fill it up with Drink from this Liquor in itself Very weak are made three Kinds of Flip Cald here Callibogus, Egg Calli and King Calli the first.[12]

186

In Cook's time England enjoyed two broad styles of 'spruce beer'. The older was a black beer commonly associated with Danzig, the main port of Prussia, a country called 'Sprewse' by Chaucer.[13] The popular 'Sprossenbier' (shoots beer), inevitably translated into English as 'spruce beer', was defined as a healthy beer made of the shoots of white spruce (now *Picea glauca*) and useful for scurvy.[14] In his 1787 encyclopedia, Krünitz calls Braunschweiger Mumme the king of the German beers. It was shipped to England, Holland, and even East India,[15] and by 1719 a London alehouse was selling 'Right Brunswick Mum, and Spruce-Beer, Wholesale and Retail.'[16] Meanwhile, the North American style described earlier, already highly popular throughout the New World, was a growing import into London. Its availability derived from the invention in North America of 'essence of spruce'.

Sea Scurvy and Land Scurvy

While the Admiralty's concern was scurvy as a seagoing malady, the disease had been known for centuries if not millennia. In 1679, Maynwaringe noted, '[t]he Scurvy is properly said to be endemical in most of our Northern Countries, that border upon the Baltic Sea, or adjacent to the German Ocean: As Denmark, Swedland, Norway, Ffrisland, Holland, England etc.'[17] Whether a series of particularly harsh winters and late springs may have increased the incidence of scurvy in England and Wales as the seventeenth century progressed – a period coinciding with the depths of the Little Ice Age – 'or merely indicated a greater awareness of its presence, is not known'.[18] By 1685

Thomas Tryon noted the condition was 'of late Years become an Epidemical or almost general Disease amongst English people'.[19]

It was generally believed 'sea scurvy' and 'land scurvy' were two different conditions until well into the eighteenth century. At the time humoral theory saw ill health as an imbalance in one or more of the four humours; in the case of scurvy the affected organ was the spleen. Correcting dietary treatments for the two conditions were distinct: 'For "hot," "alkaline," "sea" scurvy, cooling acidic foods such as oranges and lemons were advocated; "cold", "acid", "land" scurvy, in contrast, could be treated by the "hot" antiscorbutic plants such as scurvy grass, brooklime, and the cresses'.[20] Such herbs featured widely in contemporary medical texts and herbals. Carpenter refers to at least nine Dutch or German physicians between 1560 and 1600 who described the curative value of scurvy grass (*Cochlearia officinalis*) and watercress (*Nasturtium officinale*), or 'infusions of them'.[21] One of the earliest English references, in a 1568 herbal, added a third herb, brooklime (*Veronica beccabunga*).[22] In England in 1596 William Clowes published a manual of advice for both military and sea surgeons which described treating two sailors recovering from 'scorby'. Along with other practices of the day, he also included 'as their standard drink [...] new ale which had had scurvy grass, newly picked and bruised in a stone mortar, steeped in it for two days together with cinnamon and ginger'.[23] While guided by humoral practices, pragmatism ruled, and if appropriate he and others were increasingly prepared to employ long-standing empirical remedies.

With the dietary deprivations of long winters, particularly in more northern regions, '[s]pring purges, scurvy ales and diet drinks were all part of a normal, albeit seasonal diet'.[24] Few had access to professional physicians, so diagnosis and prescription were largely in the hands of lay practitioners such as apothecaries and surgeons, often women. Weyer, in *A Profitable Treatise of the Scorbie*, referred to the 'familiarly knowne' infusions of 'noble matrons'.[25] Herbals and household recipes, whether oral or written, were relatively similar, typically calling for large quantities of the favoured three herbs, sometimes augmented with others such as fumitory and dock root. These common herbs were crushed or pressed, infused into beer/ale for some days (occasionally into wine or milk), and then one or more doses (draughts) a day were administered for perhaps several weeks. The quantities, lengthy infusion times, and prolonged treatment arguably combined to confer some antiscorbutic effect. While none of these herbs are particularly high in vitamin C (their contents ranged from 40 to 100 mg per 100 grams, comparable to its concentration in fresh orange or lemon juice), typical recipes, such as those in the Appendix, administered as specified should have at least served as preventatives. These antiscorbutic herbs retained an important role across the sixteenth, seventeenth, and eighteenth centuries.[26] Scurvy ales, in short the 'cure', taken along with regular meals, was appreciated even if their preventative values were uncertain.

The Problem with Beer

Beer/ale and cider, the essential beverages of the British lower classes, were considered safer than water and milk, and widely believed to have medicinal value. The weaker 'small' beer was also the standard drink for seamen, their ration a gallon a day; for them it was a food, a welcome respite, and part of a healthy sea diet. Nathaniel Hulme, in his *A Proposal for Preventing Scurvy in the British Navy* published in 1768, called beer 'a noble drink for seamen' and noted that 'ships [...] have been observed to fall into the scurvy much sooner, after this wholesome liquor was expended, than while it was continued to be drunk'.[27] As this small beer had poor keeping qualities and occupied more space than spirits, with just a month's supply taken on board, Cook soon had to begin substituting it with other fermented liquors. Another approach was to brew beer while at sea. To that end the Admiralty specified two types of 'inspissated juice' to allow beer to be made on Cook's later voyages – but given the way they were prepared it is doubtful they, or the beer made from them, had any antiscorbutic values. Perhaps increasingly convinced this was indeed the case, and encouraged by long-established claims for its medicinal values, as will be seen, Cook made his favoured spruce beer wherever spruce or fir or their analogues were available.[28]

The reputation of sprossenbiers added to popular belief in the health benefits of beers more generally. In Hamburg in 1684, Johann Lange noted the health effects of the fir against scurvy and spoke of Danish and Swedish references to it as the 'Scharbocks-baum' (scurvy tree). In his 1787 encyclopedia, Krünitz described one recipe for Braunschweiger Mumme: brewed initially from wheat malt and small beans and left to ferment, then the inner bark of fir or birch or fir shoots were added. Another group of herbs and seeds were added, perhaps as flavourings, after the beer had fermented for a while.

Although fermented liquors and some fermented foods were long believed to have antiscorbutic values, Nathaniel Hulme called for caution in his treatise of 1768, highlighting the limitations of beer at this time. In his proposal to the Navy he cited the extensive empirical experience in favour of infusions of herbs into the daily ration of beer or any other liquor. He reasoned 'for if a handful of scurvy grass, eaten three times a day, will cure the scurvy, so in like manner will its juice if pressed out and drunk [...] the juice likewise of oranges or lemons'. He added that 'though good sound small beer [...] is an excellent antiscorbutick liquor [...] it is not found sufficient of itself to prevent the disease' so should be 'daily impregnated with the same quantity of the juice and sugar' [of lemon or orange or fresh greens].[29]

Sensible to the dilemma of supplying beer and the fresh herbs and/or their 'juices' to infuse on long voyages, he too turned to '[t]he antiscorbutick power of the fir'.[30] He even gave Banks his recipe for making spruce beer with molasses and leaves or wood shavings from the spruce or fir, plus variants using other conifers. James Lind, in his celebrated treatise published in 1753, held that infusions of pines and firs were effective antiscorbutics, but when fermented into spruce beer, were even more so.[31] This claim stemmed from the contemporary belief that scurvy was a symptom of putrefaction (the decay of various organs of the body) that fermentation inhibited. As noted earlier, Cook likely attributed such benefits to spruce beer, even though, as some have suggested more than two centuries later, he had 'probably had not heard of Jacques Cartier [...] or the Indian remedy'.[32] At issue was whether he, or anyone else for that matter, was right. It comes down mainly to fermentation.

Table 1 below, prepared by the biochemist Hughes, shows the destruction of vitamin C as the ingredients of spruce beer progress from untreated spruce leaves to stored product.

	Vitamin C content (mg/100g or mg/100 ml)
Untreated spruce leaves*	55
Aqueous infusion	14
After fermentation	<0.5
After storage for 14 days	0

*There is considerable seasonal variation in the vitamin C content of conifers: the vitamin C content of *Pinus sylvestris* needles is 65 mg/100g in late October, increasing to 120 in early spring. The spruce leaves used in the fermentation experiment were gathered during late November.[33]

Table 1: Changes in vitamin C concentration during preparation and storage of spruce beer.

How is ascorbic acid destroyed during fermentation of beer, as Hughes illustrates? Ascorbic acid is the most fragile (labile) of the vitamins. It is also an antioxidant (in other words, a reducing agent), destroyed by the oxidants with which it reacts. These include atmospheric oxygen, abetted by certain enzymes (oxidases) often encountered in fermentation. With the benefit of knowledge gained over the last century we now know that metals, particularly copper, can greatly speed up (catalyse) oxidation reactions, as can light and heat. Conversely, where no oxidants are present, then boiling, fermentation, and storage will be less damaging to ascorbic acid. A quick boiling to drive oxygen from the liquid can have a positive impact even as prolonged boiling can be destructive, and it also helps if there are other powerful antioxidants present, notably the class of compounds termed flavonoids, common in most fresh fruits and vegetables.[34] Therefore, if a concoction is boiled in a copper vessel open to the air in broad daylight or fermented without excluding air, any ascorbic acid originally present will soon be lost.

As is well known, by scrupulously collecting fresh greens, fruit, and meat, and insisting his crew partook of these, Captain Cook kept scurvy largely at bay in all his voyages into the Pacific. It was on his second South Seas voyage, on the *Resolution*, that he encountered circumstances prompting him to recall the alleged antiscorbutic properties of his old favourite, spruce beer. Arriving at Dusky Sound in New Zealand on 27 March 1772 after 117 days without landfall, perhaps because his sailors were showing more signs of scurvy than he was ready to acknowledge, he spent the next six weeks taking every opportunity to secure fresh foods: greens and fish, even seals. The conifers of Dusky Sound, although entirely unrelated to north American firs, being members of southern-hemisphere families: *rimu* (*Dacridium cupressinum*) and *miro* (*Prumnopitys ferruginea*), sufficiently resembled them to prompt Cook to use them to brew spruce beer according to his favourite recipe.[35]

Andreas Sparrman, a Swedish naturalist who joined the *Resolution* at Table Bay, agreed with others, finding the resulting beverage 'refreshing to our tired bodies tainted with scurvy'. After a small amount of rum or arrack has been added, with some brown sugar it was apparently referred to as kallebogas, after a similar mixture in North America, a reference which takes us back to Banks' time in Newfoundland.[36] But while no doubt refreshing, any antiscorbutic benefits apparent from the ship's extended layup in Dusky Sound could not have derived from the 'spruce' beer prepared to his recipe.[37] Ironically, had local plants, including an abundant herb Cook referred to as lambs quarters (probably the widespread *Tetragonia tetragonoides*, now commonly referred to as New Zealand spinach), been added as fresh infusions to the finished beer, it may well have proved beneficial.

Conclusion

Beers and ales, including spruce beer, for centuries were held to have antiscorbutic properties. But as this paper sets out, the addition of herbs was not sufficient to convey these benefits, whatever the appeal of the beers themselves. The herbs' content of vitamin C soon succumbed to prolonged boiling, particularly in the favoured copper kettles and cauldrons of Cook's times, and to fermentation, particularly in open vessels. The struggle against scurvy at sea in particular spanned centuries, even as long-standing traditional remedies consistently pointed to the value of herbal infusions, which involved treating their vitamin C content far more gently. In many ways Cook obtained his benign results throughout his three long voyages in spite of the conventional 'scientific' wisdom, by exercising the courage of his convictions borne of his own experiences, yet still remaining on the best of terms with his superiors.

History reminds us that long ocean-going voyages were known to many other cultural groups including Incas, Polynesians and Chinese, who like the North American Indians did not have the benefits of modern nutrition science. As argued by the anthropologist Levi-Strauss, 'primitive' cultures were masters of the 'logic of the concrete'. Knowledge was derived from sense perception, which ensured balanced diets in the harshest conditions. Their understanding was gained through trial and error over time immemorial: 'By undertaking extended sea voyages, westerners ventured out into an unknown biotrope to which they needed to adapt.'[38] Time, technology and science – and the potato – were eventually successful.

Appendix

The Countess of Arundel's drink for the Scurvy:

12 little handfuls	fumitory (*Fumaria officinalis*)
12 little handfuls	scurvy grass (Spoonwort, *Cochlearia officinalis*)
3 little handfuls	brooklime (*Veronica beccabunga*)
6 little handfuls	watercress (*Rorippa nasturtium-acquaticum*)
3 gallons	strong beer or ale

Clean and stamp the herbs. Put them in a bag and hang them in the ale until it is stale (about a week). Remember to close up the container of ale.

Drink a good draught in the morning [about a pint], fasting an hour after, another an hour before dinner, and another half an hour before you go to bed […] Use it three weeks or a month together.[39]

From the Countess of Kent:

A Medicine very good for the Dropsie, or the Scurvy and to clear the bloud.
Take four gallons of Ale, drawn from the tap into an earthen Stand, when the
Ale is two dayes old, then you must put in of Brook-lime, of Water-cresses, of
Water-mints with red stalkes, of each four handfuls, half a peck of Scurvy grasse,
let all these be clean picked, and washed, and dried with a cloth, and shred with
a knife, and then put into a bag, then put in the Ale, and stop it close, so that it
have no vent, stop it with Pie paste; the best Scurvy grasse groweth by the water
side; it must be seven days after the things be in before you drink it.
   Take two quarts of water, and put in four ounces of Guaicum, two ounces of
Sarsaparilla, one ounce of Saxifrage, put it in to a Pipkin, and infuse it upon the
embers for twelve houres, and then strain it, and put it into the Ale as soon as it
hath done working, this being added makes the more (?).[40]

Acknowledgements

I wish to express appreciation for inspiration from an earlier paper by Dr Andrea Cast.

Notes

1   Peter Moore, *The Endeavour: The Ship and the Attitude that Changed the World* (Sydney: Vintage
    Australia, 2018), p.164.
2   R.E Hughes, 'The Nutrients – Deficiencies, Surfeits and Food-Related Disorders, IV.D.8, Scurvy', in
    Cambridge World History of Food, ed. by Kenneth F. Kipple and Kriemhild Conee Ornelas (Cambridge:
    Cambridge University Press, 2000), pp. 988-1000, (p. 989).
3   Kenneth J. Carpenter, *The History of Scurvy and Vitamin C* (Cambridge: Cambridge University Press,
    1986), p. vii.
4   Andrea Cast, 'For Your Health: Medicinal Drinking in Seventeenth-Century England', *Culinary
    History*, eds A. Lynn Martin and Barbara Santich (Brompton, SA: East Street Publications, 2004), pp.
    55-66 (p. 62).
5   Sir James Watt, 'Medical Aspects and Consequences of Cook's Voyages', in *Captain James Cook and His Times*,
    ed. by Robin Fisher and Hugh Johnston (Vancouver: Douglas & MacIntyre, 1979), pp. 129-57 (p. 135).
6   Joan M. Woodhill and Silvia Nobile, 'Vitamin C (L-Ascorbic Acid and Dehydro-L-Ascorbic Acid):
    A Contribution to the Captain Cook Bicentennial Celebrations', *The Medical Journal of Australia*, 1
    (1971), pp.1009-14.
7   Egon H. Kodicek and Frank G. Young, 'Captain Cook and Scurvy', Notes and Records of the Royal
    Society of London, 1 (1969), 43-62 (p. 43) <https://www.jstor.org/stable/530740> [accessed 2 October 2019].
8   Martyn Cornell, 'A Short History of Spruce Beer Part Two: The North American Connection',
    Zythophile, 20 April 2016 <http://zythophile.co.uk/2016/04/20/a-short-history-of-spruce-beer-part-
    two-the-north-american-connection/> [accessed 13 August 2019].
9   John C. Beaglehole, *The Life of Captain James Cook*, Vol. IV (London: A. and C. Black Ltd, 1974), pp.
    80-81, 83, 87.
10 A.M. Lysaght, *Joseph Banks in Newfoundland and Labrador, 1766: His Diary, Manuscripts and Collections*
    (London: Faber and Faber, 1971), p. 120.
11 Nathaniel Hulme, *Libellus de natura, causa, curationeque scorbuti, To which is annexed, A proposal for
    preventing the scurvy in the British navy* (London: Thomas Cadell, 1768) <https://onesearch.library.uwa.

edu.au/permalink/61UWA_INST/1vk1d8f/alma99545860702101> [accessed 5 May 2020].

12 Lysaght, p. 139. A mixture of 'spruce beer' and rum, callibogus was apparently a popular drink in Newfoundland. The addition of an egg would make a traditional English drink called 'a flip'.

13 Martyn Cornell, 'A Short History of Spruce Beer Part One: The Danzig Connection', *Zythophile*, 20 April 2016 <http://zythophile.co.uk/2016/04/20/a-short-history-of-spruce-beer-part-one-the-danzig-connection/> [accessed 11 September 2019].

14 Johann Cristoph Adelung, *Grammatisch-Kritisches Wörterbuch der-hochdeutschen Mundart: mit beständiger Vergleichung der übrigen Mundarten, besonders aber der oberdeutschen* (Wien: Bauer, 1811).

15 Johann Georg Krünitz, *Oeconomische Encyklopädie, oder allgemeines System der Staats-, Stadt-, Haus-und Landwirthschaft in alphabetischer Ordnung* (Brünn: 1787).

16 Cornell, Danzig.

17 Everard Maynwaringe, *Morbus Polyrhizos et Polymorphaus. A Treatise of the Scurvy* (London: 1665), Preface.

18 Hughes, p. 990.

19 Thomas Tryon, *The Good Housewife Made a Doctor: Or Health's Choice and Sure Friend* (London, 1692), p. 253.

20 Hughes, p. 993.

21 Carpenter, p. 34.

22 Hughes, p. 993.

23 Carpenter, p. 35.

24 Cast, p. 63.

25 Johann Weyer, *A Worthy Treatise of the Eyes….Together with a Profitable Treatise of the Scorbie*, trans. by W. Bailey (London, 1587?), pp. 25-28.

26 Hughes, p. 993.

27 Hulme, p. 10.

28 Brett J. Stubbs, 'Captain Cook's Beer: The Antiscorbutic Use of Malt and Beer in the Late 18th Century Sea Voyages', *Asia-Pacific Journal of Clinical Nutrition*, 12 (2003), 129-37 (p. 135).

29 Hulme, pp. 11, 23.

30 Hulme, p. 91.

31 Carpenter, p. 229.

32 Kodicek and Young, p. 43.

33 R.E. Hughes, 'James Lind and the Cure of Scurvy: An Experimental Approach', *Med Hist*, 19 (1975), 342-51.

34 John J. Durzan, 'Arginine, Scurvy and Cartier's "tree of life"', *Journal of Ethnobiology and Ethnomedicine*, 5.5 (2009) <http://dx.doi.org/10.1186/1746-4269-5-5>

35 James Cook, *The Journals of Captain James Cook on His Voyages of Discovery, II. The Voyage of the Resolution and Adventure, 1772-1780*, ed. by J.C. Beaglehole (Cambridge: Cambridge University Press, 1961), p. 137.

36 Kodicek and Young, 55.

37 Hughes, p. 348.

38 Mathieu Torck, *Avoiding the Dire Straits: An Inquiry into Food Provisions and Scurvy in Maritime and Military History of China and wider East Asia* (Weisbaden: Harrassowitz Verlag, 2009), p. 50 <https://www.jstor.org/stable/j.ctvc16gb0.10> [accessed 15 May 2019].

39 W.M., *The Queens Closet Opened: Incomparable Secrets in Physick, Chirurgery, Preserving, Candying, and Cookery; as They Were Presented to the Queen* (London: 1656), pp. 169-70.

40 Elizabeth Grey, *A Choice Manuall for Rare and Select Secrets in Physick and Chyrurgery: Collected and Practised by the Right Honourable, the Countesse of Kent*, ed. by W.I. Gent (London 1654). p. 30.

A Journey Back in Time Taste: Herbs and Spices in Medieval German Cuisine

Helmut W. Klug, Christian Steiner, Fritz Treiber,

Julia Eibinger, and Astrid Böhm

Introduction

The kitchen of the Middle Ages as we know it today only provides a small insight into the cooking traditions of this epoch. Depending on the historical discipline, the beginning and end of the epoch vary to a great extent. For our convenience we frame 'the Middle Ages' with the dates 500 to 1500. The starting point is meant to suggest that the influence of the ancient Roman Empire on contemporary cooking has passed; the end point marks a distinct shift in cookbook production when printers discovered that these books can be sold very easily (the first German cookbook was printed 1485). Their craft had a serious impact on this text type. Nevertheless, the core characteristics of medieval cooking – humoral dietetics and cooking conform to Ordinary Time – still affected the kitchens of the following centuries. The social background of medieval recipes is always and exclusively the upper class, the religious and secular nobility as well as rich townspeople. Although we do have information, albeit second-hand, on the alimentation of peasants and the poor, we do not have cooking recipes that relate to that social class.

This paper focuses on German-language cooking recipes, the corpus of which comprises 60 recipe collections with approximately 6000 recipes, that have been recorded in handwriting between 1350 and 1500. They convey characteristics of medieval and early modern cooking from the tenth to the seventeenth century. This paper gives a short introduction to the herbs and spices used in medieval German cooking recipe texts, and we discuss the role herbs and spices played in the kitchen of that time. In this paper we focus on a select few collections that have been recently edited and semantically enriched to provide a proof of concept for an experimental research method into the flavour of medieval cooking. In that context we want to provide flavour profiles not only for medieval dishes but also for the kitchen of humours by applying Digital Humanities research methods.

Medical and Dietetic Background

Leaving the obvious alimentary effect aside, medieval cuisine was intensely focused on dietetics and health care. In the Middle Ages food and drink were believed to be one of the primary sources for maintaining health. In this context *regimina sanitatis* literature summarizes ancient lore on the properties of drink, food, and cooking.[1] The underlying concept was the theory of humours: it described the whole universe by setting all things within a gradation system of the primary qualities cold, warm, dry, and moist.[2] It was the core of medieval western medicine and was handed down in the beginning through clerics and monasteries, and later through the medical personnel of that time. The roots reach back into antiquity, but the peak of philosophical discourse on this topic lies in the Middle Ages. Within the framework of monastic medicine in the early Middle Ages, ancient Mediterranean traditions were extended to include European-Alpine ones. In the High and Late Middle Ages, the influence of Arabic teachings on medicine, which by then were already scholastic discussions, increased greatly and spurred these thoughts.

Medieval thinking was profoundly dominated by Christianity, and this was especially true for everything concerning humans and the nature surrounding them: four elements ruled the macrocosm, i.e. the world surrounding us. Hildegard von Bingen, a nun who took very individual paths in her occupation with monastic medicine, explained: 'God also created the elements of the world. They are in humankind, who lives with them. They are called fire, air, water and earth. These four basic elements are so closely connected and bound together that none can be separated from the others. Thus, they hold so closely together that one can call them the basic building blocks of the cosmos.'[3] The theory of the elements was therefore also applied in the medieval understanding of man: the ground rule was the idea that the human organism itself and the substances beneficial for its healing could be described with the same qualities. Human beings – as all things in nature – were understood as microcosms within the macrocosm. They were thus the image of the elementary world on a reduced scale. Eventually a consistent theorem emerged that interlinked medical lore with socio-economic-religious systems to an overall philosophy of a whole period.[4] So, for example, foreign and expensive spices were more suitable ingredients for upper class clerics and nobility, whereas local herbs were hardly ever used in food preparation of the rich.[5]

The main concern of this medical theory was to stay healthy through constant prophylaxis especially in the fields of the *sex res non naturales,* and to work on a balanced household of humours. The mix of humours in a person was strongly related to internal (gender, age, etc.) and external (time of the day, season of the year, etc.) factors. Dietetic texts suggested ways to temper foodstuffs to provide better food tolerance in respect to the complexion of the eater. Cooking recipes did follow the humoral theory, but in general this information is hidden in the cooking instructions, or in the properties that ingredients add to a food, only sometimes accentuated through an author's remark.

The role of the medieval chef was to prepare meals that support the health of his master and sometimes even his guests. However, he was also meant to provide good food.[6] Around 1350 Konrad of Megenberg, a well-known religious and economic author of his time, explained the rules of keeping house. He detailed the areas of responsibility for each member of the household, therefore also for the cook, who took care of various

194

dietetic aspects in context with preparing and even serving the food.[7] In order to provide balanced food, a cook had to know about the complexion of the eater and about humoral theory, which provides gradations (the 1st degree indicates the lightest, the 4th or 5th degree destructive or even lethal effect) for the primary qualities of foodstuffs, cooking processes, etc. Herbs and spices were potent means to alter the humoral status of foodstuffs.[8] Similar to an equation, the primary properties of foodstuffs and preparation methods complemented each other as well as the humoral profile of the eater.

Herbs and Spices in the Middle Ages

The culinary culture of the Middle Ages evolved in a continuous process from Roman and ancient eating habits.[9] Unfortunately, we can only trace these culinary developments from the most recent Roman to the oldest medieval traditions, because, due to a nearly 1000-year gap in cooking recipe tradition, we lack the necessary evidence. Nevertheless, a comparison of the oldest medieval recipe collections from France and Italy with the collection attributed to the Roman Apicius clearly shows a distinct change in the use of herbs and spices: while the use of pepper and cumin declines, ginger and saffron are used more frequently.[10] Like Apicius' recipes, the oldest surviving medieval recipes present an extraordinarily creative cuisine, which prefers to emphasize changes in taste, colour, and form of the basic ingredients. It often claims a surprise effect which manifests itself especially in so-called 'show dishes', as a central feature of these is the use of luxurious herbs and spices as they emphasize a certain level of social standing. The late medieval recipe collections demonstrate that food has long since left behind the purpose of a purely life-supporting process and that the entertainment value, which targeted all available senses, must be seen as an equal, if not more important, factor.

195

If one wanted to describe the aroma of the food of the medieval upper class, the only valid comparison would be the cuisine of the Middle East, in which comparable spices are still preferred today.[11] At the same time, however, the rumour must be contradicted that the taste of medieval food developed from contact with Arabs in the course of the Crusades: it is the product of a continuous development, and eastern spices had long been known from medical recipes. Arab contacts were only relevant in regard to the spice trade until European merchants directly dealt with Asian sellers.[12] The high prices resulting from the long transport routes and the surcharges of the innumerable middlemen turned spices into luxury items that could only be purchased by rich households. There, spices were not only used for flavouring food:

> Spices soothed and cheered, creating a refined environment of taste and comfort. They could be consumed in edible form or breathed as perfume or incense. The odor of spices wafted through houses fumigated with burning aromatics, as a kind of predecessor to aromatherapy. Churches were also permeated by the odor of resinous spices, especially frankincense, used in the celebrations of the Christian liturgy.[13]

The use of spices can be interpreted as a means of representation, but this is less evident in the quantity than in the varieties of spices used. Saffron, for example, ranks at the upper end of this scale, due to its costly production, while pepper – especially in the late Middle Ages – was a comparatively cheap spice used throughout all classes; its role as a means of payment certainly contributed to this. To balance this, new varieties of pepper were imported, such as long pepper (*Piper longum*), Malaguet pepper (*Aframomum melegueta*), or cubeb pepper (*Piper cubeba*), and offered to the richest as correspondingly luxurious products. Generally, a larger selection of spices can be assumed for rich households than for less wealthy ones.[14] Above all that, foreign spices added a certain amount of mystery and adventure to a dish.[15]

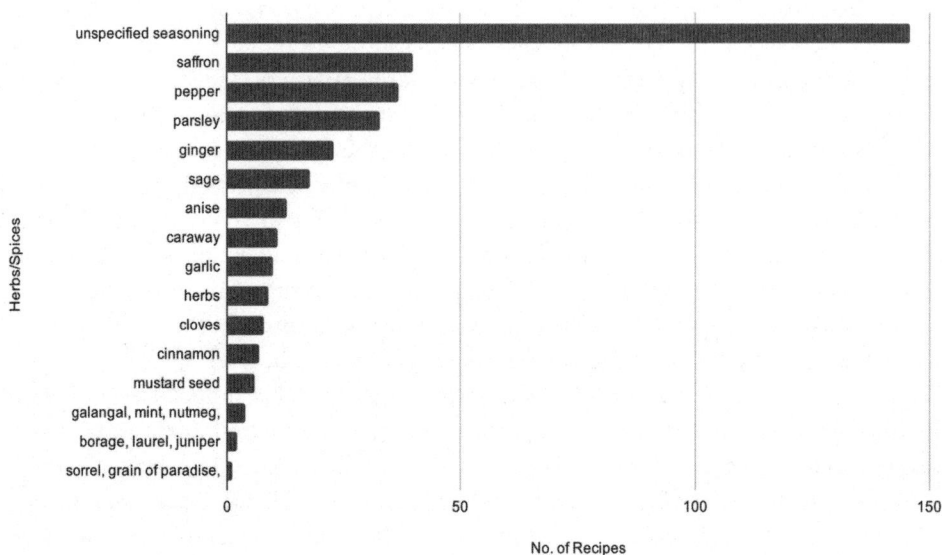

Chart 1: A list of Spices used in German medieval cooking recipe collections.[16]

Research on a corpus of 6 select recipe collections that hand down 365 German cooking recipe texts from the late medieval period provides an interesting overview of medieval flavouring habits.[17] A little less than 10% of the recipes do not contain any seasoning instructions at all. In the majority of recipes, about 40%, adding herbs and spices is only implicitly required, the standard phrase for implicit seasoning is 'season it well'. A result of this study is that implicit flavouring instructions generally refer to pepper, ginger, cinnamon, and cloves. Saffron (10.13% of total flavouring instructions in 10.96% of the recipes) is the most called for spice and primarily used for colouring, closely followed by pepper (9.37%, second most common spice in 10.14% of the recipes). Other but less frequently used spices are ginger (5.82%), cloves (2.03%), cinnamon (1.77%), and galangal (1.02%). Domestic herbs and spices, however, are mentioned with a distinctly lower frequency. Although parsley is the third most common spice (8.35%), it is only used in 33 (9.04%) recipes, and it is used to colour food green rather than for aroma. Sage, aniseed, caraway, garlic, or unspecified 'herbs' are called for even less frequently. All in all, the use of imported vs. domestic spices is well balanced (123 vs. 119) when the unspecific flavouring instructions are left out of the equation. If we do assume that unspecified flavourings generally refer to imported spices, these are used in more than two-thirds of the recipes.

Research Background

In the international research project *CoReMA*, located at the University of Tours, France, and the University of Graz, Austria, we are researching possible connections of medieval French and German cuisines.[18] The aim of the project is, for the first time, to transcribe all medieval German, French, and Latin manuscript recipe collections before 1500 and describe them with codicological metadata. The texts are semantically enriched with information on text composition, ingredients, tools, and dishes. This data, especially the combination of ingredients, will be the basis to learn about recipes common to both cuisines and their possible migration.

The basis for the enrichment is normative data that is tied into the linked open data cloud via Wikidata. Launched in 2012 to establish a common knowledge base and provide structured data for all of the different languages in Wikipedia, Wikimedia Commons, and other foundation projects, Wikidata has evolved into a multi-disciplinary, machine-readable, centralized and linked knowledge hub used for ever increasing use cases, especially within the Life Sciences.[19] The emphasis of this datahub is on the creation of abstract semantic web concepts and on the normative structuring of the data, both of which create access points from different research angles. Therefore, annotating the historical texts with reference numbers from Wikidata provides not only the possibility to compare the content of different language texts but additionally opens a door into the world wide web of linked open data. The interconnection of different databases via these numbers creates a nearly infinite web of knowledge.

For the *CoReMA* project we make use of data from different ontologies and databases as well as transformed data from books into databases.[20] For the present article we use the Wikidata reference numbers to link to databases holding information on the aroma molecules of various foodstuffs.[21] This provides us with access to big data repositories, containing data that complements our small sliver of knowledge. The use cases of these databases normally lie in scientific big data research or economic purposes that mostly aim at quantitative content analysis. This data has already been successfully used in studies that compare the flavour of different cuisines.[22]

The aroma of foodstuff is generally composed from hundreds of different aroma molecules, but there are only a few key flavour molecules that dominate the flavour of an ingredient, while other molecules add to and round off the aroma of a certain ingredient.[23] To focus on that qualitative aspect we have built our own database on the basis of the modernist cookbooks by Vierich/Vilgis *Aroma* and *Aroma: Gemüse*, which

197

provide these main flavour molecules, and the different databases.[24] The combination of different resources aims at the completeness of the data and also allows for better data curation. While the verbal description of the individual molecules makes an aroma summary of the foodstuff or dish possible, the flavour groups provide the means to calculate the flavour profile.

Group	Group name	Flavour description
1	aliphatic compounds	waxy, green, mushroomy, fruity
2	linear sulfur nitrogen compounds	sulfurous, cabbage, onion, horseradish notes
3	acyclic terpenes	citrus, fruity, floral
4	cyclic terpenes	balsamic, camphor, woody
5	sesquiterpenes	dark, heavy-floral
6	aromatic compounds	deep and aromatic
7	phenols, phenolderivates, phenylpropanoids	Cinnamon, Nutmeg and co.
8	heterocyclic compounds, hydrocarbons, amides, macrocycle	roast flavours
9	trigeminal stimulus	no aroma

Table 1: Distinct flavour groups and their verbal flavour description.[25]

198

Our resource holds information on herbs and spices relevant to medieval cuisine. It lists the main aroma molecules of ingredients, verbally describes the molecule's flavour profile, and relates the molecules to eight distinct flavour groups (Table 1). In these groups, aromatically and chemically related flavour molecules are gathered. Following the verbal description, flavour groups 1-8 range from a light, volatile to a deep and dark aroma; group 9 collects molecules that stimulate the trigeminal nerve with hot, warm, cold, or astringent sensations. The group characteristics allow a short, summarizing description of an ingredient: parsley smells grassy-green, citrus fresh with a warm aromatic undertone (Table 2). The visualization of the flavour profile shows that parsley aroma spikes into three different directions, an emphasis lies on acyclic terpenes, a citrus, fruity, floral odour (Chart 2). With this information we are not only able to name the predominant flavours of a dish and to describe the aroma with a suitable vocabulary, but we can also use the distinct flavour groups to visualize the aroma of ingredients on a radar chart to get a better grasp on the positioning of an ingredient or dish within these nine flavour poles.

Calculating Flavour of Medieval Dishes
In respect to historic cuisines, our research into a description of food aroma is highly experimental. Although we believe that our approach towards the aroma of medieval food focusing on qualitative results can provide relevant findings, these cannot be

Ingredient	Wikidata	Flavour group	Flavour group aroma	Molecule	PubChemID	Vierich/ Vilgis	FooDB	FEMA
parsley	Q65522500	1	waxy, green, mushroom, fruity	(Z)-HEX-3-ENAL	6428782	green-grassy		
parsley	Q65522500	3	citrus, fruity, florid	1,3,8-P-MENTHADIEN	176983	grassy-spicy		
parsley	Q65522500	3	citrus, fruity, florid	LIMONEN	440917	orange, terpen-lemon	mint, lemon, citrus, orange, fresh, sweet	citrus, mint
parsley	Q65522500	6	deep, aromatic	MYRISTICIN	4276	spice, warm, balsamic	balsamic, spice, warm, woody, balsam	

Table 2: Tabular flavour profile of parsley.

generalized or reviewed without certain constraints. The most obvious of these is the fact that we have no access to medieval ingredients and their historic aroma profile, which can be assumed to differ greatly from modern ones. It may well be only the aroma of herbs and spices that has not substantially changed over the centuries. Another constraint is how to deal with flavour in a medieval context, as we have only sketchy knowledge on how medieval man perceived flavour: While in the scholastic domain taste/flavour/odour were regarded as rather abstract aspects of humoral theory, there nevertheless are positive and negative references to flavours and odours in literary texts.[26] German cooking recipe texts do not refer to the flavour of food at all. An additional, albeit temporary, drawback is that at the moment our database on the flavour of medieval cooking ingredients only holds a selection of medieval ingredients (certain herbs and spices, for which the relevant data was available) – vegetables, meat, dairy products, etc. are missing. Furthermore, the data available only describes the fresh, unprocessed ingredients; the influence of cooking processes is not incorporated. We are able to calculate with the most fragrant ingredients but at the moment we can only work with select recipes.

All in all, these factors have to be duly noted, but they will not prevent interesting findings to questions that have not been asked this way before. We must stress that we do not aim at creating historic flavour profiles! Our foremost aim is to produce a modern flavour profile to add information to select research questions. An additional goal is to possibly gain another distinct factor for recipe comparison between different cuisines – this may be the cuisines of Germany and France, but it might also support the characterization of different recipe collections.

Our flavour profile is an abstraction of food sensorics: the aim is a visual characteristic of a food or foodstuff, since the results are not derived from a tasting process but calculated from the data in our database. The underlying assumption, which is also used in aroma pairing, is that flavour molecules from a distinct flavour group add up and their characteristic aroma intensifies.[27] The result of the calculation will be a distinct positioning of an ingredient within the eight flavour groups, or respectively, on the eight-axis radar chart.

Analysis

Question: How Are the Flavour Profiles of Medieval Herbs and Spices Distributed on a Radar Chart?

Our flavour database holds 44 ingredients, the majority of which (38) are herbs and spices. A rather even distribution on the flavour chart was to be expected (Chart 3). Nevertheless, there is a distinct spike towards balsamic, camphor, and woody aroma not only in count but also in herbs and spices containing flavour molecules from group 4. Interestingly, similar evidence comes from contemporary literature or the bible, which praise the aroma and virtues of the spikenard as a queen of herbs.[28] *Nardostachys grandiflora* is an herb native to the Himalaya region, substitutes in Europe were valerian spikenard (*Valeriana celtica*), valerian (*Valeriana officinalis*) and also spike lavender (*Lavendula latifolia*). All three have a pungent, musky, balsamic, medicinal odour. The results of this analysis strongly correlate with information from very divergent sources. We take this as an indicator for the potential of this analysis. Considering the constraints listed above, this way of looking at historic food indeed provides new insights.

200

Question: How Can We Describe the Flavour of the Humours?

Herbs and spices are generally used for adjusting the humoral properties of food, either as ingredients in a dish or as ingredients in sauces that are served alongside the main dishes. The radar chart proves the fact that most herbs and spices are humorally warm and dry (Chart 4). It also shows that this category is distributed nearly evenly in the flavour groups but surprisingly, there is a very intense flavour spike at group 4 and only a moderate one at group 9; there are no flavours from group 2. The first describes the pungent, musky, balsamic, earthy odour discussed above, the second groups molecules that trigger a trigeminal stimulus, which in this case most likely is the hotness of certain spices. Herbs and spices with warm and moist prime qualities tend to the more volatile flavour groups with a distinct spike to group 1: waxy, green, mushroom flavours (Chart 5). Only very few herbs and spices in the database are cold and dry (Chart 6). The flavour sensation with these lies on a trigeminal stimulus (group 9). There are no cold and moist herbs or spices in our database. It is very illustrative that the different prime qualities can be associated with distinct flavour profiles.

Question: What Is the Flavour Profile of Select Medieval Recipes?

For this we have selected four diverse recipes containing ingredients that are documented in our database. As expected, the visualization of the recipes produced also very diverse

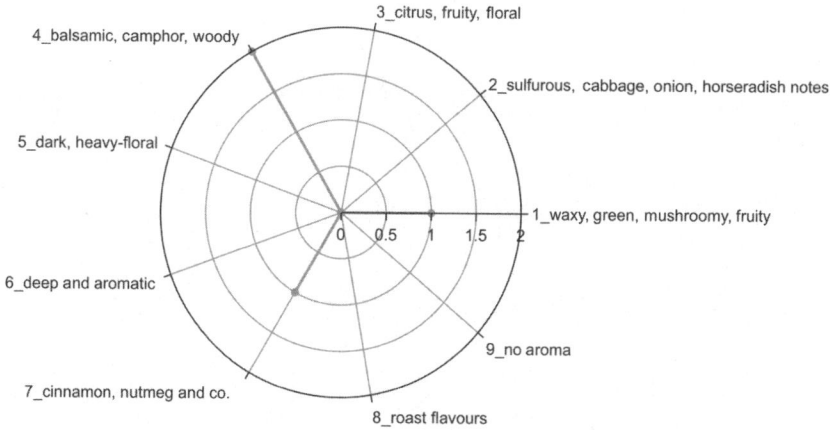

Chart 2: Flavour profile of parsley as radar chart.

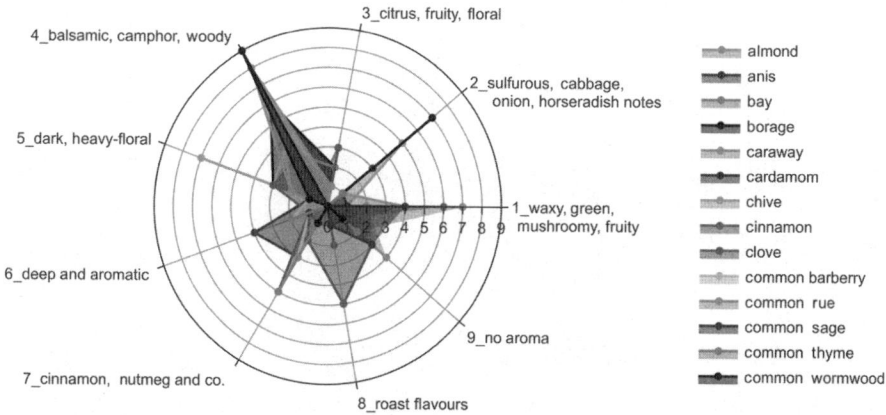

almond
anis
bay
borage
caraway
cardamom
chive
cinnamon
clove
common barberry
common rue
common sage
common thyme
common wormwood

Chart 3: Flavour profiles of all medieval herbs and spices in our database.

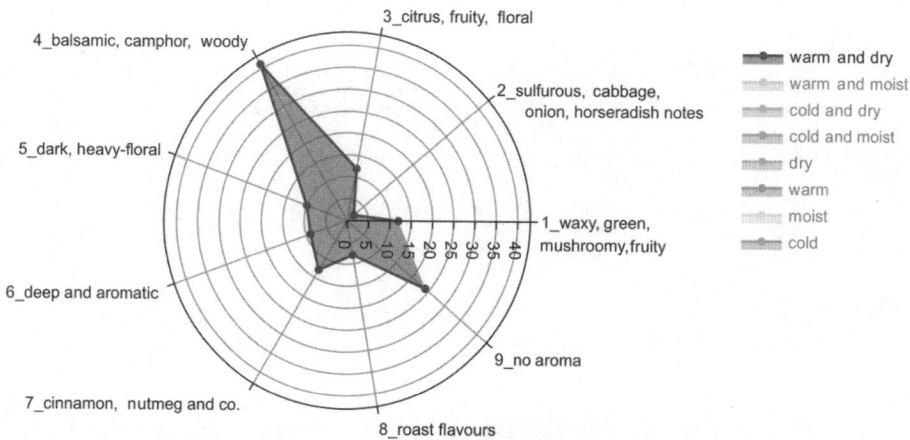

warm and dry
warm and moist
cold and dry
cold and moist
dry
warm
moist
cold

Chart 4: Flavour profiles of the humoral primary quality warm/dry.

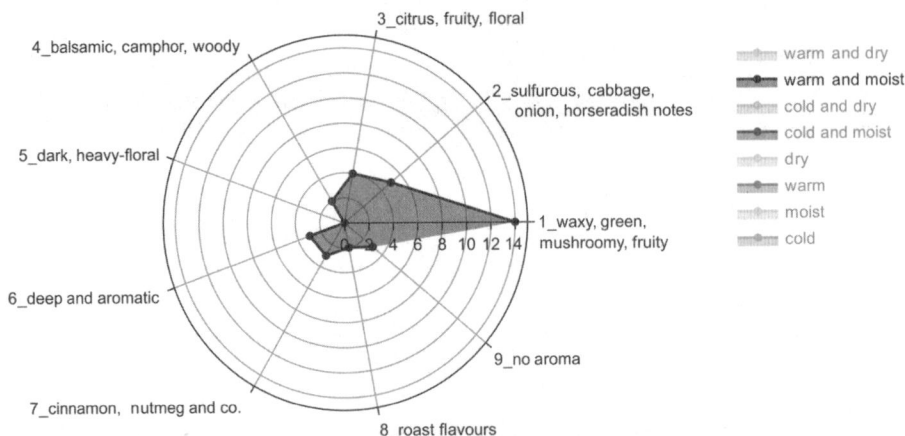

Chart 5: Flavour profiles of the humoral primary quality warm/moist.

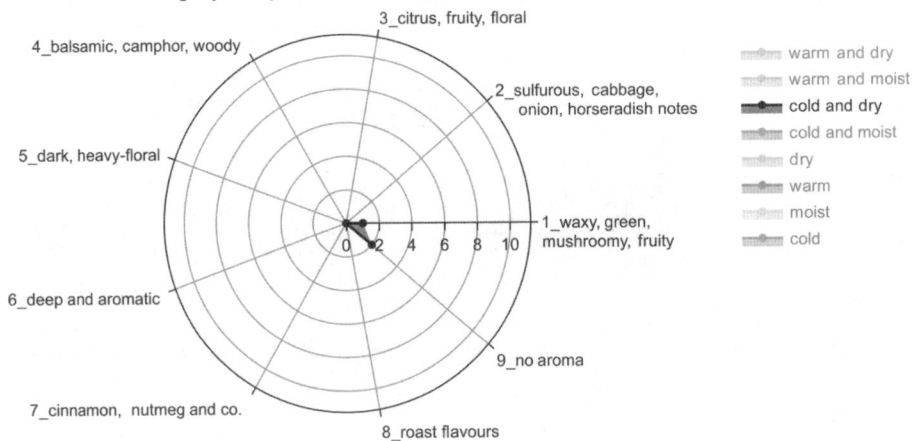

202

Chart 6: Flavour profiles of the humoral primary quality cold/dry.

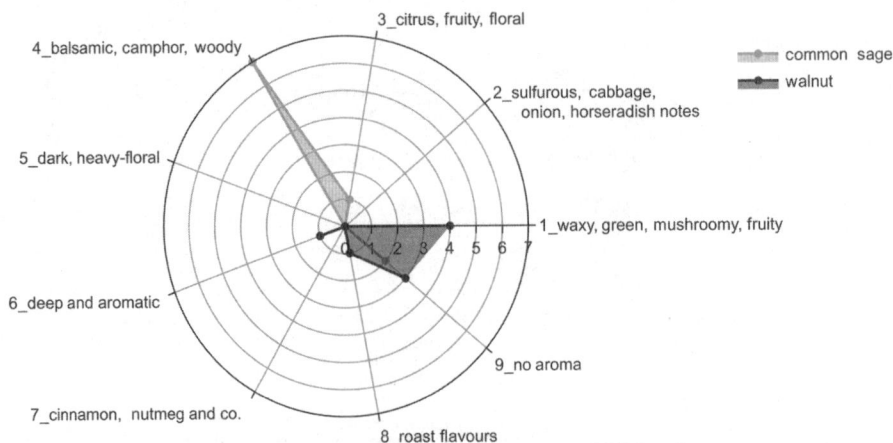

Chart 7: Flavour profile of select recipe 'Sauce of Sage and Walnut'.

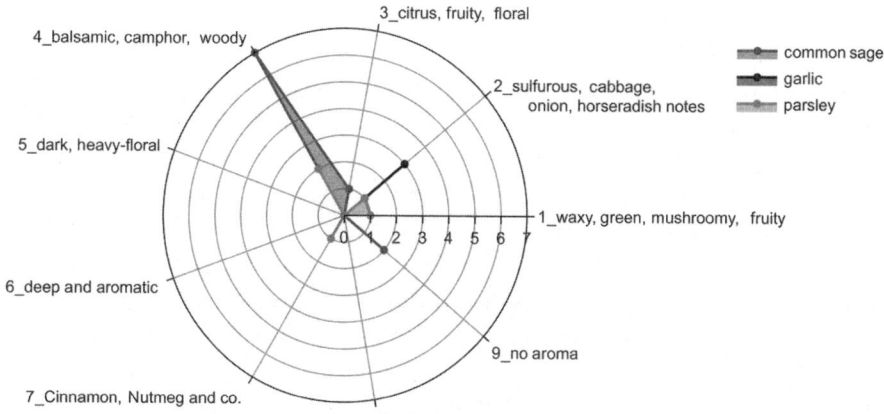

Chart 8: Flavour profile of select recipe 'Sauce of Sage, Garlic, and Parsley'.

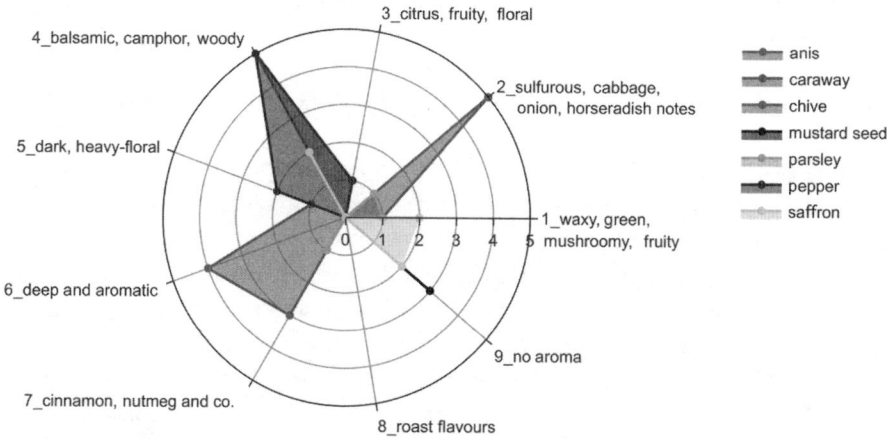

Chart 9: Flavour profile of select recipe 'Mustard Sauce'.

203

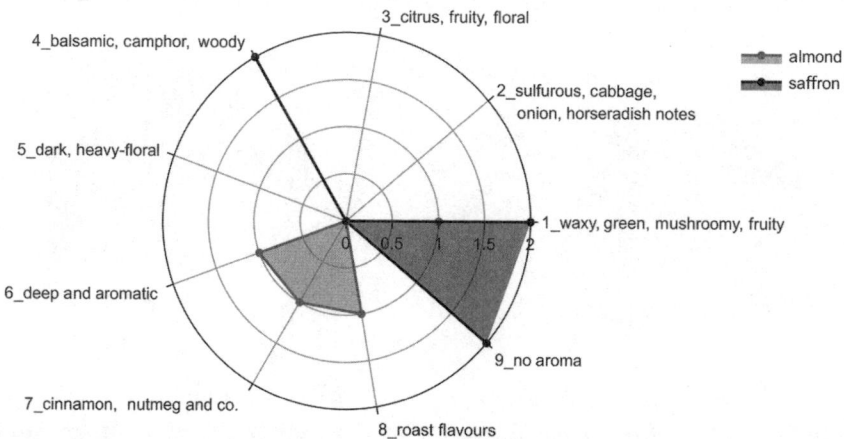

Chart 10: Flavour profile of select recipe 'Hedgehog of Almonds'.

flavour profiles. Three recipes are for sauces (sage, garlic, mustard), one recipe is for a main dish, a so-called 'almond hedgehog'. The flavour profiles for the sauces have extreme spikes towards different flavour groups: the sage-walnut-sauce (Chart 7) has slight aromatic (group 6), green (group 1) notes and spikes towards the inevitable balsamic notes (group 4). The garlic sauce (Chart 8) has, of course, sulfurous (group 2) flavour but spikes again towards the balsamic notes (group 4). A very interesting flavour profile can be attributed to the mustard sauce (Chart 9): it shows moderate, and evenly distributed but pronounced spikes towards four flavour groups (2, 4, 6, 9). The almond recipe (Chart 10), in contrast, has a rather evenly distributed flavour profile of deep aromatic to roast flavour notes (groups 6, 7, 8) that are accompanied by waxy, green (group 1), balsamic and camphor notes (group 4).

The data can not only be used to visualize the distribution of flavour, but it can also be the basis to provide a vocabulary to talk about these recipes. Charts 11 and 12 show the word-cloud visualization of the flavour profiles for the mustard recipe and the 'Hedgehog of Almonds'.

Question: *Can the Flavour Profile of the Ingredients Be Used for a Comparison of Recipe Collections?*

The 60 medieval recipe collections hand down c. 6000 recipe texts: only a moderate percentage of these are individual recipes, the others are textual variations of base recipes. The working assumption for a comparison of recipe collections would be that they hold many similar recipes, thus naming similar ingredients from which a similar flavour profile can be calculated. A comparison of two collections (Bs1, Chart 13, and Gr1, Chart 14), that hold nearly the same number of recipes, and that are known to hand down similar recipes, produced a surprising result: Bs1 is much richer in the use of herbs and spices. This is especially obvious for group 2 where Gr1 only has onion and Bs1 onion, garlic, and horseradish. The differences may be explained with the different social background of the collections: Gr1 probably was collected and written down in

204

Chart 11: Word-cloud visualization for the flavour profile of the recipe 'Mustard Sauce'.

Chart 12: Word-cloud visualization for the flavour profile of the recipe 'Hedgehog of Almonds'.

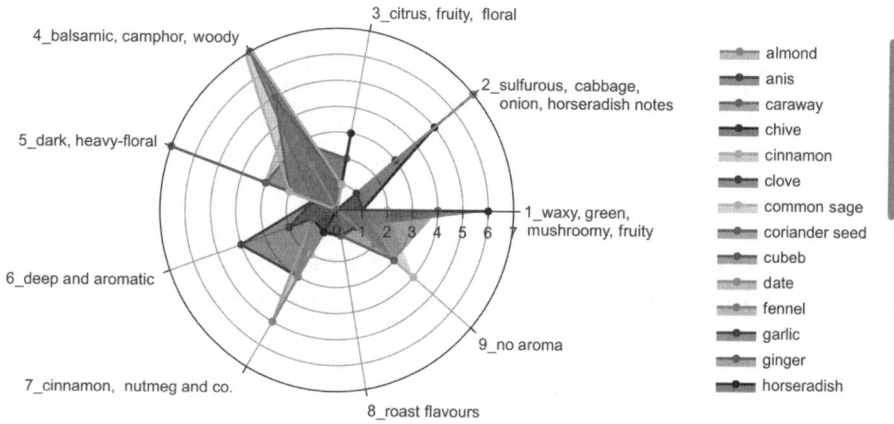

Chart 13: *Flavour profile of the select recipe collection Bs1.*

Legend (Chart 13): almond, anis, caraway, chive, cinnamon, clove, common sage, coriander seed, cubeb, date, fennel, garlic, ginger, horseradish

Axes: 3_citrus, fruity, floral; 2_sulfurous, cabbage, onion, horseradish notes; 1_waxy, green, mushroomy, fruity; 9_no aroma; 8_roast flavours; 7_cinnamon, nutmeg and co.; 6_deep and aromatic; 5_dark, heavy-floral; 4_balsamic, camphor, woody

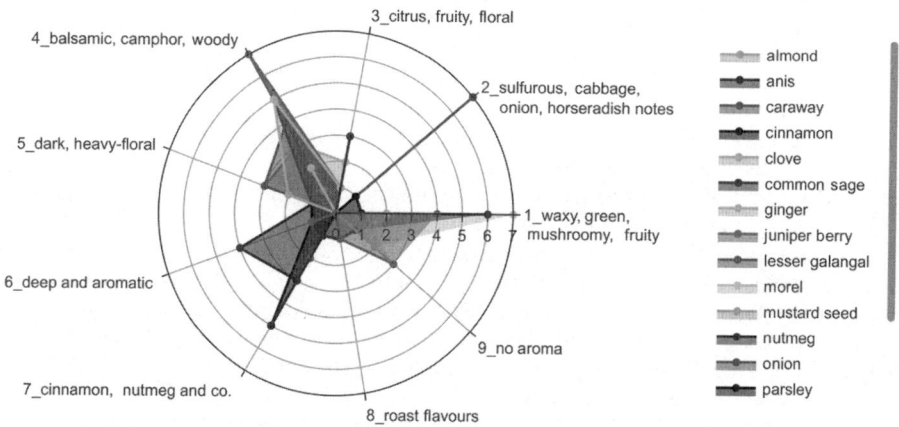

Chart 14: *Flavour profile of the select recipe collection Gr1.*

Legend (Chart 14): almond, anis, caraway, cinnamon, clove, common sage, ginger, juniper berry, lesser galangal, morel, mustard seed, nutmeg, onion, parsley

Axes: 3_citrus, fruity, floral; 2_sulfurous, cabbage, onion, horseradish notes; 1_waxy, green, mushroomy, fruity; 9_no aroma; 8_roast flavours; 7_cinnamon, nutmeg and co.; 6_deep and aromatic; 5_dark, heavy-floral; 4_balsamic, camphor, woody

205

a rural monastery, but Bs1 is attributed to the personal chef of Ulrich V., Count of Württemberg. The results of this comparison are also highly promising for verifying existing theories on cooking recipe collections, but they are also bound to open up new research questions.

Conclusions, Perspectives

The analysis of the humours, select recipes, and recipe collections provides compelling insights into these medieval cultural sources. A flavour profile of the herbs and spices grouped by their humoral attributes yields distinct differences aligned to their primary qualities. Although we will not be able to describe the flavour of medieval dishes, the flavour profiles of herbs and spices named in the recipes allow us to draw comparisons with other historic, in our case literary, sources. Satisfactorily, the results strongly overlap. The comparison of the flavour profiles of select recipes, as well as the comparison of the profiles calculated for recipe collections, hint at a great potential of this research method. The different visualizations of the flavour profiles allow a differentiated approach towards texts and collections that is not only a verbal comparison of ingredients but that is driven by visual impressions.

The proof-of-concept analysis has clearly shown the potential of our approach of calculating flavour profiles to get more insight into historical cooking recipes. Therefore, the next steps will be the expansion of our flavour database and a general alignment of our data so that we will be able to analyse more recipes. Additionally, we want to implement an automated service for recipe comparison in the context of our project website.[29]

Notes

1   Melitta Weiss Adamson, *Medieval Dietetics: Food and Drink in 'Regimen Sanitatis' Literature from 800 to 1400* (Frankfurt a. M.: Lang, 1995).

2   Helmut W. Klug and Karin Kranich, '*Ursprung und Grundlagen der mittelalterlichen Temperamente-Medizin*', in '*Man nehme.*': *Kochbücher und ihre Rezeption im Laufe der Jahrhunderte* (Graz: Steiermärkische Landesbibliothek, 2016), pp. 137-70.

3   CC 2,37ff. Wighard Strehlow and Gottfried Hertzka, *Hildegard of Bingen's Medicine*, trans. by Karin Anderson Strehlow (Santa Fe, NM: Bear, 1988), p. xx.

4   Allen J. Grieco, 'Medieval and Renaissance Wines: Taste, Dietary Theory, and How to Choose the 'Right' Wine (14th-16th centuries)', *Mediaevalia*, 30 (2009), 17.

5   Massimo Montanari, *Medieval Tastes: Food, Cooking, and the Table: Arts and Traditions of the Table: Perspectives on Culinary History*, trans. by Archer Brombert (New York: CUP, 2015), pp. 29-30f, 173; Christopher M. Woolgar, 'Feasting and Fasting: Food and Taste in Europe in the Middle Age', in *Food: The History of Taste*, ed. by Paul Freedman (London: Thames & Hudson, 2007), pp. 163-95 (p. 180).

6   Bridget Ann Henisch, *The Medieval Cook* (Woodbridge: Boydell Press 2009).

7   Konrad von Megenberg, *Yconomica*, ed. by Sabine Krüger, 3 vols, Monumenta Germaniae Historica: Scriptores, 10 (Stuttgart: Hiersemann 1973-1984), I (1973) pp. 192-94 (Part 5, Book 1) (pp. 192-93).

8   Ria Jansen-Sieben, 'From Food Therapy to Cookery-Book', in *Medieval Dutch Literature in its European Context*, ed. by Erik Kooper (Cambridge: CUP, 1994), pp. 261-79 (p. 273f.); Klug and Kranich, pp. 127-28.

9   Bruno Laurioux, 'Spices in the Medieval Diet: A New Approach', *Food & Foodways*, 1.1 (1985), pp. 43-75 (pp. 61-66); Helmut Hundsbichler, '*Nahrung*', in *Alltag Im Spätmittelalter*, ed. by Harry Kühnel (Graz: Styria, 1984), pp. 196-231 (p. 205).

10   Robert Maier, *Der Liber de Coquina: Herkunft und Nachwirkung des ältesten erhaltenen Kochbuchs des europäischen Mittelalters* (2012), slides 28-29 <https://www.academia.edu/1723548/Der_Liber_de_Coquina> [accessed 2 April 2021].

11   Paul H. Freedman, *Out of the East: Spices and the Medieval Imagination* (New Haven: Yale University Press, 2008), p. 25; Christopher M. Woolgar, 'Food and the Middle Ages', *Journal of Medieval History*, 36 (2010), 1-19 (p. 8).

12   Montanari, pp. 6, 118.

13   Freedman, p. 5.

14   Laurioux, p. 52.

15   Freedman, pp. 89-90, 133-34.

16   Colour versions of all charts presented in this paper can be found at: https://gams.uni-graz.at/o:corema.dissem.ofs2020.

17 Helmut W. Klug, *"gewürcz wol Vnd versalcz nicht': Auf der Suche nach skalaren Erklärungsmodellen zur Verwendung von Gewürzen in mittelalterlichen Kochrezepten'*, *Medium Aevum Quotidianum*, 61 (2011), 56-83.

18 Project *'Cooking Recipes of the Middle Ages: Corpus, Analysis, Visualisation'*; Austria: PI Helmut W. Klug, fwf grant no. I 3614, France: PI Bruno Laurioux, ANR grant no. ANR-17-CE27-0019-01.

19 Some of these projects are SNOMED-CT (Systematized Nomenclature of Medicine – Clinical Terms), MeSH (Medical Subject Headings), UMLS (Unified Medical Language System) and FMA (Foundational Model of Anatomy) etc.

20 For data from different ontologies and databases, see FoodON <https://foodon.org/>; Wikidata <https://www.wikidata.org/>; *MPS: Portal der Pflanzen des Mittelalters / Medieval Plant Survey: Repository*, ed. by Helmut W. Klug, technical director Roman Weinberger (2008-2020), <http://medieval-plants.org/>. For transformed data from books into databases, see Friedemann Garvelmann, *Pflanzenheilkunde in der Humoralpathologie* (München: Pflaum, 2009); Thomas A. Vierich and Thomas A. Vilgis, *Aroma* (Berlin: Stiftung Warentest, 2012); Thomas Vierich and Thomas A. Vilgis, *Aroma Gemüse* (Berlin: Stiftung Warentest, 2017).

21 FooDB <https://foodb.ca/>; FlavourDB <https://cosylab.iiitd.edu.in/flavordb/>; Vierich/Vilgis, *Aroma*; Vierich/Vilgis, *Gemüse*.

22 Anupam Jain, N. K. Rakhi and Ganesh Bagler, *'Spices Form the Basis of Food Pairing in Indian Cuisine'* (submitted 12 Feb 2015) <arXiv:1502.03815>; Kush R. Varshney and others, *'Flavor Pairing in Medieval European Cuisine: A Study in Cooking with Dirty Data'* (submitted 30 July 2013) <arxiv:1307.7982v1>

23 Vierich/Vilgis, *Gemüse*, p. 37; Jia-Wei Yan and others, 'The Aroma Volatile Repertoire in Strawberry Fruit: A Review', *Journal of the Science of Food and Agriculture*, 98.12 (September 2018), pp. 4395-4402 <https://www.doi.org/10.1002/jsfa.9039>

24 Vierich/Vilgis, *Aroma*.

25 Vierich/Vilgis, *Gemüse*, pp. 12-18.

26 Grieco, pp. 24-25; Freedman, ch. 3; Woolgar, Feasting, p. 168; David Howes and Constance Classen, *Ways of Sensing: Understanding the Senses In Society* (London: Routledge, 2014), p. 43.

27 Vierich/Vilgis, *Gemüse*, p. 99.

28 The hero Gawan is treated with an ointment of spikenarde in Wolfram from Eschenbach's *Parzival*; the herb is named in the *Song of Songs*.

29 *CoReMA – Cooking Recipes of the Middle Ages*, ed. by Helmut W. Klug with Astrid Böhm and Christian Steiner <hdl.handle.net/11471/562.10>

The Chilli Diaspora: Unravelling Evidence from Sixteenth-Century Botanicals

Michael Krondl

Today, the planet produces and consumes more dried chilli (*Capsicum spp.*) than all other spices combined, over four million tonnes in 2018, yet before Columbus's fateful trip, chillies were limited to a narrow tropical and subtropical strip of the Western Hemisphere.[1] Upon his return it was only a matter of decades before botanists, apothecaries, and even blue-blood amateurs were cultivating the little shrubs across Europe, not so much as a foodstuff but as an exotic curiosity. The plant's popularity rode on a wave of enthusiasm for horticulture set in motion by Europe's global expansion. The botanical *Wunderkammern* have long gone, but we have scores of herbals and botanicals, in hundreds of editions and translations, to document the period's gardening frenzy. These texts are both a treasure load of valuable insights and a sinkhole of misinformation and misdirection. My ambition here is to sort out the fool's gold from the real thing.

Gardens and Herbals

The sixteenth-century enthusiasm for gardening has been widely documented.[2] Networks of plant enthusiasts, especially in Italy and the Low Countries, sought out the most exotic specimens, sending each other seeds, bulbs, and even dried samples with growing instructions enclosed. Gardeners tended to be interested most in plants producing unusual blooms, or, in the case of chillies, their colourful and varied pods. The era's greatest chilli enthusiast was the Italian botanist and Capuchin friar Gregorio da Reggio (d. 1618) who wrote a mini-treatise on the subject describing a baker's dozen varieties. He too focused on each plant's appearance, not its flavour. Herbalists widely understood the pods to be edible and assigned them to the same pharmacological category as black and long pepper, yet they too seemed mostly interested in the plants as exotic curiosities. And elite cuisine had no interest whatsoever in the incendiary spice.

The Southern (Hapsburg) Netherlands was especially renowned for its gardens. The aristocratic Charles de Saint Omer (1533-1569), now mostly known as the patron of the famed Flemish botanist Carolus Clusius (1526-1609), had a garden that Lodovico Guicciardini described as 'admirable with an infinity of excellent plants'.[3] He compared it favourably with a nearby garden owned by the Antwerp apothecary Peeter van Coudenberghe (1517-1599) and counted some 400 exotic plants under cultivation.

Notably, both gardens included capsicums: Clusius gave Saint-Omer seeds of a 'Brazilian Pepper' in 1566 that apparently flowered that autumn, and Coudenberghe evidently had a similar variety growing in his vegetal menagerie. Clusius's compatriot and fellow botanist Matthias de Lobel (1538–1616) insisted that the region exceeded all others in horticultural matters, claiming that more flora was grown there than in any other place not excluding 'ancient Greece, spacious Spain, the whole of Germany, England and France, and even Italy which is so well cultivated'.[4]

The collectors of exotica benefited from the proximity of Antwerp, the Hapsburg empire's main northern port and the hinge of a global trading network. Portuguese *naus* arrived here from east and west loaded with black pepper and sugar and other tropical stuffs, possibly including Brazilian peppers. The port is a stone's throw from England, France, and the Rhine, but its tendrils extended across the Hapsburg realms from Vienna to Naples to Madrid and farther, to the newly-occupied lands in the Americas.

It's perhaps no wonder that some of the century's most notable botanists hail from here, not only Clusius and Lobel but also Rembert Dodoens (1517-1585). All mentioned chillies in their botanical works and were, in turn, cited (sometimes with attribution but often without) in other botanists' work. In England, John Gerard's 1597 *Herball* mostly just copied Dodoens on the topic, while the 1633 reprint added information and illustrations lifted from Clusius.[5]

The mania for exotica and its documentation was Europe-wide. The Spanish physician Nicolas Monardes (1493-1588) had his own garden in Seville to cultivate American arrivals and documented capsicums and their commonplace use in Andalusia in an herbal devoted to New World plants.[6] Several Italian naturalists described chilli peppers, most notably Pietro Andrea Mattioli (1501-*c*.1577), but also Castore Durante (1529-1590), the above-mentioned friar Gregorio da Reggio, and, intriguingly, Pietro Antonio Michiel (1510-1576), in a manuscript that was only published in 1940.[7] Worth mentioning here is that neither the *converso* physician Garcia de Orta (1501-1568) nor his colleague Cristóbal Acosta (*c*.1525-*c*.1594), both based in India, mentioned the spice in their herbals.

The first botanist to mention the spice was the Tubingen-based Leonhart Fuchs (1501-1566), and was consequently one of the most commonly quoted authorities on the subject. Authority was important. One of the challenges that European scholars faced when confronted with flora and fauna that had no classical antecedents was how to categorize them. Thus, Fuchs insisted that Pliny had called this American native *siliquastrum*, or *piperitis*, names that stuck for generations. The German doctor also postulated that it was the same plant as Avicenna's *Zinziber caninum*, another point of confusion for decades to come.[8] The era's enthusiasm for plants created a continent-wide market for the botanicals.

Fuchs' Latin original was rendered into Dutch, German, Spanish, and French. Mattioli's books were even more popular, appearing in Latin, Italian, German, Czech, French – close to 300 editions in all prior to 1650.[9] The texts were often recycled, as were the illustrations. Images from Fuchs's 1545 octavo editions show up in Dodoens's

Leonhart Fuchs, Läbliche Abbildung und Contrafaytung aller Kreüter [...] in ein kleinere Form auff das aller artlichest gezogen *(Basel: Michael Isengrin, 1545). Left: 425.* Capsicon rubeum & nigrum. Roter and brauner Calecutischer Pfeffer. *Middle: 426.* Capsicum oblongius. Langer Indianischer Pfeffer. *Right: 427.* Capsicon latum. Breyter Indianischer Pfeffer.

Crüydeboeck (1554) and the English translation, *Nievve Herbal* (1578); Turner's *New Herball* (1551-1568); and as late as the 1633 edition of Gerard's *Herball*.[10] When the original plates were unavailable, a copy would do. The chilli images in the 1590 edition of Mattioli's *Kreutterbuch* show an unmistakable similarity to Fuchs's 1545 plates.[11] Sometimes several images might be combined into one. In a feat of graphic taxidermy Hieronymus Bock's *Kreüter Buch* (1546) includes an image of a pepper plant that blends all three varieties illustrated in Fuchs's octavo.[12]

The Garden of Babel

If illustrations are an unreliable guide to understanding who knew what when, etymology is even more epistemologically fraught. As Fuchs's attempt to slot capsicums into then-extant taxonomy demonstrate, names are as likely to confuse as to elucidate.

The earliest Spanish sources sometimes use the Arawak *axi* or Nahuatl chilli (chile, chili) but more typically Europeans came to use a variant of the word pepper, usually with some modifier to distinguish it from the South Asian spice. Fuchs offers the Latin names *piper Hispanum, piper Indianum*, and *piper ex Chalicut* (Spanish, Indian, or pepper from Calicut), in German *Chalecutischer* or *Indianischer Pfeffer* (Calicut or Indian pepper).[13] The Indian and Spanish monikers make sense given the plant's origin; Calicut a lot less so.

This seeming link to the South Asian emporium has led several writers, most notably Jean Anderson, to conclude that Fuchs, residing in Western Germany, was sourcing his peppers in India. Perhaps Fuchs really did believe that capsicums were related to Pliny's cardamom (*siliquastrum*) and thus were native to the Malabar coast. A more plausible explanation, though, is that *chalecutischer* (also *calecutischer*) was used in a generic way for all things exotic at the time.[14] The modifier does keep showing up in botanicals throughout the century, especially those penned by non-German speakers. Germans, though, sometimes call it *Teütscher* (German) *Pfeffer,* presumably with the full understanding that it wasn't native to Germany. The 1662 Czech translation of Mattioli refers to it as '*Pepř Indyánký kterémuž wuobec Turecký říkagý*' ('Indian pepper which is called Turkish').[15] The later term is repeated in later editions and entered German as well. A 1604 Hapsburg register of tariffs lists something called Turkish or Moravian pepper.[16] A little earlier, Johann Coler reports seeing 'Turkisch Pfeffer' in Frankfurt and described it as 'red pods harvested after Michaelmas', a convincing description of capsicums. So, does that mean that chilli peppers arrived in Central Europe via the Ottoman Empire? Or was it yet another version of *calecutischer*, meaning exotic and strange? Or, as I would suggest, is it a data point too ambiguous for any definite conclusion? Coler also points out that, in Vienna, *Turkischer Pfeffer* referred to the best-quality black pepper imported from Venice.[17] Moreover, the Czech equivalent, *turecký pepř,* was a synonym for *piperát,* that is pepperweed (*Lepidium latifolium*).[18]

In English and French, the etymology is somewhat less disobliging. Here, the most common appellation was Ginnie (as Gerard spells it) or *poivre de Guinée,* and it is perfectly

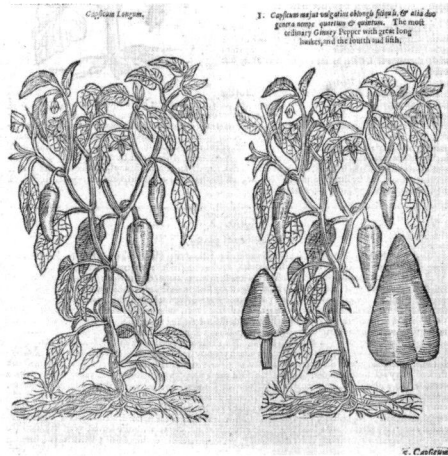

Eucharius Rösslin, Kreuterbuch von natürlichem Nutz *(Frankfurt: Egenolff, 1550), n.p.* Teustcher oder Indianischer Pfeffer. Siliquastrum. Piperitis. *Note how the publisher combined the three images from Fuchs' 1545 octavo edition, see p. 210.*

John Parkinson, Theatrum Botanicum *(London: Thomas Cotes, 1640), 356.* Capsicum longum. Capsicum majus vulgatius oblongis siliquis. *Note the virtually identical illustrations in Gregorio da Reggio, see p. 212.*

possible that capsicums reached English and French entrepots from Brazil via Portuguese ports on the West African coast. Gerard says 'these plants are brought from forren countries, as Ginnie, India and those parts, into Spaine and Italy; from whence wee have received seede for our English gardens'.[19] Dodoens noted the use of *Brasilien peper* for chillies, perhaps because Antwerp served as an outlet for Portugal's tropical commodities.

To confuse the matter further, by the late 1500s, Portuguese visitors started to reference plants resembling capsicums as 'malagueta', something the Brazilians do to this day. The actual malagueta, or grains of paradise (*Aframomum melegueta*), is an African spice unrelated to capsicums. In Italy, the terminology is more transparent. Durante uses the descriptive name *pepe cornuto* (cone shaped), as well as *pepe d'India*. Michiel adds that commoners called it *pepere rosso* (red) as well as *pepe hispano* or *indiano*. By the mid-seventeenth century, a Bosnian-Italian dictionary translates *pepe d'India* as 'paprika' (as well as well *Papar çrregleni*, 'red pepper') for the first time.[20]

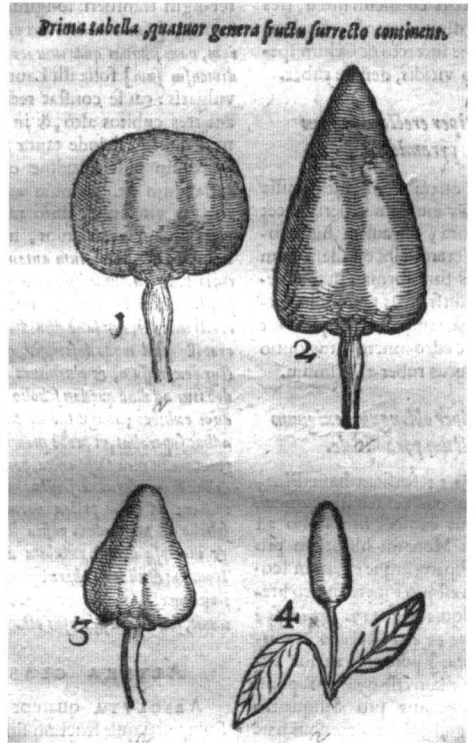

Gregorio da Reggio, "Piper Americanum" in Carolus Clusius, Curae posteriores *(Antwerp: Plantiniana Raphelengii, 1611), 97. 1.* Piper rotunda maius surrectum*; 2.* Piper oblongum erectus maius pyramidale*; 3.* Piper erectum minus pyramidale*; 4.* Piper oblongum, exiguum erectum pyramidale.

Vectors of Diffusion

Even if etymology is a maze of dead ends, the botanicals are hardly useless. They are one of very few sixteenth century sources that pinpoint chillies' presence and use across Europe. Even so, the reader needs to tread carefully to distinguish unacknowledged citations from eye-witness testimony.

In Europe, capsicums were noted soon after Columbus's return. The papal vice-chancellor, Ascanio Sforza, mentioned receiving seeds from Spain as early as 1492.[21] According to Fernández de Oviedo y Valdés, writing in 1535, 'It [had been] brought to Spain and Italy where it is considered a very good spice, and it is very healthy, and appreciated everywhere it can be found; and merchants and others send for it from Europe, and search it out to eat and enjoy it.'[22]

A lively system of correspondence crisscrossed the continent, trading information and seeds across Europe so that by the mid-sixteenth century, living plants were observed in countries as widely separated as Italy, Hungary, Moravia, the Southern Netherlands and even England. While not always dependable, the herbals hint at the chronology of this diffusion. As books were updated, authors, editors, and translators inserted new information, thus offering some indication of their arrival.

Mattioli's texts serve as a particularly clear example of this, since his writing extends over decades, and his work documented the presence of chillies in several locations. His 1540 commentary on Dioscordides did not mention capsicums, but the expanded 1544 edition featured both peppers and tomatoes.[23] Can we surmise that these American natives had become more common? Peppers showed up again after the Sienese physician had relocated to the court of Ferdinand II in Prague. The 1562 Czech language translation, *Herbarz, ginak Bylinář* adds several seemingly eyewitness details, presumably inserted by the translator Tadeáš Hájek: 'Indian pepper which is generally called Turkish pepper is also [like marsh pepper] common with us'. This seems plausible since others also mention chilli's presence in the Czech crownlands. The following year's German translation, also published in Prague, seems less reliable. Here the entry begins, 'the Indian pepper is newly arrived in German lands, it is grown fresh. It is grown in planters and herb gardens'.[24] Was it? Fuchs, writing twenty years earlier writes that it was 'found almost everywhere in Germany now, planted in clay pots and earthen vessels'. Did the translator just adapt the information from Fuchs? A posthumous 1590 German version of Mattioli's herbal published in Frankfurt, retains the remark about the pots and about chilli's recent arrival, even though the rest of the text is now quite different. Jarringly, this printing replaces the lovely illustration from the Prague editions with a copy of Fuchs's ubiquitous octavo woodcuts. This version was then translated into Czech in 1596, and now claimed that the chilli is 'common and well known' in both the Czech and German lands. Given the Fuchs precedent, my tendency here would be to ignore the German-language comments but to credit the Czech observations.[25] In part, this is because there are several other data points substantiating Mattioli's (or his translators') remarks about the commonness of capsicums in Bohemia and Moravia. Clusius, for one, recalls having 'seen [the pepper plant] grown in the greatest abundance, in the 1585th year of Christ, in the suburban gardens of the famous city of Brno in the March of Moravia; and the farmers made a considerable profit from it, since the common people used it frequently'.[26] In a 1578 letter, the Flemish botanist also confirms that peppers were growing in the Szalónak (now Stadtschlaining) garden of Count Boldizsár Batthyány, some 200 kilometres south of the Moravian capital. The Hungarian count was one of the region's notable amateur horticulturalists and a frequent recipient of Clusius's letters and specimens. The most solid corroboration, however, comes from archaeologists, who found pepper seeds they dated to the sixteenth century in Prague and in Brno.[27] This sort of multidisciplinary proof does not exist in other European locations.

Nonetheless, the case of England shows that the botanicals have some merit in establishing chronology. The English botanist John Turner (1508?–1568) does not include

213

chillies in *Libellus de re herbaria novus* (1538) but does mention them in an expanded English language version from 1548. Nonetheless, he pretty much just quotes Fuchs, adding that in English the spice is called 'Indishe pepper' (presumably only by those who had read the German botanist!). Turner adds the not very credible comment: 'The herbe groweth in certejne gardines in Englande.'[28] He skips over the subject altogether in his magnus opus, *A New Herball* (1551-1568), thus giving the impression that chilli wasn't very common in Albion. The next time it makes an appearance, other than in works of translation – such as Dodoens's 1570 London edition – is in John Gerard's 1597 *Herball*. Gerard cribs most of his description from Dodoens but then adds several informative details. He expands on the Fleming's warning on 'the great care and diligence' necessary to grow the semi-tropical plant and, helpfully, tells the reader that it is on sale 'in the shoppes at Billingsgate'.[29]

Gerard's comment is one of the very few references to a market for capsicums. Bock, writing in the Rhineland-Palatinate, mentions that some German merchants used it to adulterate black pepper.[30] As mentioned above, it was also on sale in Frankfurt and was possibly taxed by the Hapsburgs. Given such sparse references, it seems that its role as a trade good was marginal at best.

A Taste for Spice

From a pharmacological perspective, the botanists generally lumped capsicums in with black pepper. Depending on the authority, in the Galenic system it was hot to the third or fourth degree. Nonetheless, there was some scepticism about just how edible it was. Dodoens thought it 'dangerous to be often used or in to a great a quantitie: for this pepper hath in it a certayne hidden evyll qualitie, whereby it killeth Dogges, if it be given them to eate'.[31] Gerard ascribed to it a 'malitious qualitie, whereby it is an enemie to the liver & other of the entrails'.

Southern European consumers were more enthusiastic. Oviedo y Valdés claims that the Conquistadors picked up the taste from the natives, noting: 'the Christians [...] use it as much as the Indians, because not only is it a very good spice, it adds a good taste and warms the stomach; it is a healthy thing, though rather hot in taste'.[32]

The Portuguese naturalist, Gabriel Soares de Sousa, made much the same point in Brazil a half century later remarking that the Portuguese ate certain chillies 'in imitation of Indian custom'. They would apparently grind the dry peppers, mix the powder with salt, and use it to season both fish and meat, He adds that this salt 'displeases no one'.[33] By this point, peppers were already cultivated in Portugal as Clusius reported during a visit in 1564-65.[34]

The Iberian taste of chillies is corroborated by Monardes. After explaining its medical qualities, he points to its culinary attributes:

> All the sortes are used in all manner of meates and potages for that it hath a better tast then the common Peper hath. Beaten in peeces, and cast into the brothe it is an excellent sauce, they doe use it in al thinges that the aromatike spices are used in,

214

which are brought from *Maluco*, and *Calicut*. It doeth differ from that of the East Indies, for that costeth many ducates; and this other doth cost no more but to sowe it, for that in one plant you have spice for one whole yere, with lesse hurt and profite.[35]

This points to the two primary uses of the spice: for food and for medicine. The Italian botanist Castore Durante gave a recipe that even combined the two. After mentioning that it was used in 'all the sauces (*condimenti*) and foods because it is of better taste than common pepper', he gave directions to make the nutraceutical more digestible, instructing the reader to grind up the whole pod including the seeds, stir these into dough and make a *pan biscotto* out of it.[36]

As Monardes made explicit, capsicums were considered a poor person's substitute for black pepper, or occasionally for saffron. A rare early elite recipe using chillies, here mixed into chocolate, appeared in Antonio Colmenero's *Curioso tratado de la naturaleza y calidad del Chocolate* (1631). After warning of the medical risks of chocolate drinking, he nonetheless gave detailed instructions on how to make it, explaining that in Mexico the preference was for the hot 'Chilparalagua' (elsewhere spelled 'Chilpaclagua') chilli whereas in Spain they preferred the broad, milder *pimientos de España*.[37] Another early recipe, this time for a chilli-seasoned main dish called 'Spanish-style' pork, shows up in a Czech manuscript attributed to a minor noblewoman dated to 1645. Here, pork chops are smeared with cloves, garlic, and 'Turkish' pepper, then marinated, smoked, and finally braised.[38] In Spain itself the first collection of chilli recipes came a century later in another manuscript also written by a woman, the Andalusian Calvillo de Teruel's *Libro de apuntaciones de guisos y dulces* (1740).[39] Almost a quarter of her recipes include *pimentón*, indicating how ubiquitous this 'Indian' pepper was now in southern Spain.

215

In the Wake of the *Naus*

Yet what of India itself? Numerous scholars have insisted that chillies reached the coast of Malabar in the first decades of the sixteenth century and were even re-exported to Europe. I remain highly sceptical. A stronger case might be made for Africa.

For the Gulf of Guinea, the records are not as clear-cut as for Europe or America, but there is at least some evidence that chillies had been adopted by the late 1500s. The Cape Verdean writer André Alvares d'Almada described 'a sort of pepper which climbs up trees like ivy, and grows in little bunches like the flower of the grape when it is opening to form a bunch. In these parts this pepper is called *mantubilha*: it burns like pepper and dyes like saffron'. Some South American chillies do climb, and both pungency and dyeing effect are certainly chilli-like. Admittedly the indigenous Ashanti pepper (*Piper guineense*) answers this description as well, though its use as a dye is not documented elsewhere.[40] Less ambiguous is Manuel Alvares's roughly contemporary description of French sailors being tortured by a Sierra Leone potentate by rubbing their eyes with 'red malaguetas, which are a kind of pepper'.[41]

However, for India, there isn't even this fragmentary evidence. Certainly, basing any

Indian connection on the *Calecutischer* moniker is a non-starter. Scholars have cited Mattias Lobel's 1576 statement that 'in our memory, [the pepper] has been brought from Goa and the shores of Calicut'.[42] Given that the Portuguese had lost Calicut almost fifty years earlier, at least half of that statement is improbable. I don't doubt that he believed that chillies were arriving from the subcontinent, it is just that neither the botanists on the ground in South Asia nor any visitors remark on the spice's presence. Neither the very thorough Garcia de Orta nor the more lackadaisical Cristóbal Acosta mention the spice, writing in the 1560s and 1570s respectively.[43] If it was so widely distributed in Portugal's Indian territories, why would both Goa-based botanists have ignored it? Similarly, John Huyghen Van Linschoten, having spent six years in Portuguese India in the 1580s, describes all the types of pepper available on the Malabar coast, including a cheap form of black pepper called camorin, but makes no mention of capsicums.[44] It is only in the 1670s that Hendrik van Rheede describes it in the East Indian context.[45]

There are, however, at least three other local mentions worth examining. K.T. Achaya points to a composition by the South Indian poet Purandaradasa from the sixteenth century that supposedly refers to chillies: 'I saw you green, then turning redder as you ripened, nice to look at and tasty in a dish, but too hot if an excess is used. Savior of the poor, enhancer of good food, even to think of [the deity] is difficult'.[46] There are two problems with this verse: the first is that black pepper, like chilli, starts out green and ripens to red; the second, as Divva Schäfer has pointed out, is that the poet's work wasn't codified until the nineteenth century. She is also sceptical of a 1649 mention by Fray Sebastien Manrique of a green-pepper-laced pickle served to him at the home of a Mughal notable.[47] Schäfer suggests that he is referring to green peppercorns rather than chillies, but the context is too ambiguous to say anything definitive.[48] Given van Rheede's reporting, it is almost certain that chillies were present in South Asia by this point, but whether they would have been used in elite Mughal cookery seems less likely. The third bit of evidence comes from the Tibetan herbal, *The Blue Beryl*, a classic text of the Tibetan medical tradition from the late-seventeenth century, which tells us that 'Capsicum (*tsi-tra-kas*) increases digestive warmth of the stomach and is the supreme medication for the alleviation of oedemata, haemorrhoids, animalcules, leprosy and wind'. The spice is elsewhere also supposed to alleviate diseases of phlegm and prolong the lifespan.[49] All this points to a relatively late date for the widespread adoption of what is today's Asia's favourite spice.

So how did chillies get there? Even if there is no proof tracing the vectors of the plant's diffusion, I think it's possible to assemble a working hypothesis by looking at the context of sixteenth-century long-distance trade in both the Atlantic and Indian oceans, the basis for the so-called Columbian exchange of foodstuffs between east and west.

Historians have identified a number of nodes that anchored sixteenth-century transoceanic trade routes. In Europe these included Lisbon, Cadiz (the port of Seville), and Antwerp; in the West Indies there were Cartagena, Havana, Santo Domingo, and Veracruz (depending on the commodity); in Brazil, São Salvador da Bahia; in Africa the Cape Verde Islands and São Tomé; and in Asia, not only Goa, but Malacca located in the eponymous straights, as well as Manila, the destination of the so-called Manila galleon originating in Acapulco.

In the tropics, the most critical nodes for Columbian exchange were the Portuguese Cape Verde Islands off the Western tip of Africa and São Tomé in the Gulf of Guinea. There is good sixteenth-century documentation that American yams (*Dioscorea spp.*), peanuts, pineapples, sweet potatoes (*Ipomoea batatas*), and manioc (*Manihot esculenta*) were transferred from Brazil to the Atlantic islands and then in turn to the African mainland.[50] The ubiquity of so many New World plants would argue for the presence of chillies as well. Eventually several of these New World plants made the voyage to India as well, but how quickly did this occur?

Whereas in Spain, chillies were an inexpensive stand-in for pepper, and maybe saffron, why would Indians, but especially South Indians, pick up the taste for chillies? They certainly weren't a cheap substitute for black pepper in a place where the berries grew wild in the Kerala hills. Moreover, I am not convinced by the cavalier statements of Western scholars that Indians changed the profile of their cuisine the moment chillies arrived.[51] There were other factors in play on the Malabar coast, though. Pepper may have been free for the picking, but it was also something you could sell, an internationally-traded commodity; it was quite literally money that grew on trees – or vines at any rate. Several visitors to the Malabar coast report that the poor people there did not eat black pepper (*Piper negrum*) but rather an inferior kind called canarins (possibly named after Kanara, a community south of Goa). Linschoten described it as looking like buckwheat, writing, 'it is of an ashe colour, and holow within, with some smal kernels in eating tasteth and heateth like other pepper, yet it is used onely by the poore people', adding that it was not commodified like black pepper.[52] Perhaps the locals found the New World pepper more to their liking than this poor man's substitute for real pepper? Or it may have insinuated itself into the local culinary culture more slowly, through the native wives of Portuguese settlers or the Indian cooks of missionaries. Or perhaps it was first inserted into local medical practice before entering the cuisine. Or all of the above. As unsatisfying as the answer is, all we can do for now is speculate.

Conclusion

As this paper has demonstrated the research on the distribution of the world's most popular seasoning is far from complete. While published botanicals and travellers' reports are of enormous value, they do not provide an adequate explanation of why culinary cultures around the world shift and change with the arrival of foreign ingredients. This is especially true when the ingredients serve virtually no nutritional value and thus are no more than carriers of culinary culture. It is easier to explain the adoption by the Portuguese of an easily-grown staple like maize, or manioc by West Africans, than the acceptance of a foreign food stuff that induces pain orders of magnitude greater than any local ingredient. Moreover, chillies present an additional explanatory challenge since they enter cuisines under the radar of cookbooks. They are, in other words, not an elite fashion that can be periodized like, say, the sixteenth-century Italian fad for cinnamon sugar. Yet if we can understand the adoption of chillies, perhaps we can better explain the formation of non-elite foodways.

There are number of potential avenues of further research. There may be ships' manifests that list supplies taken on board. These certainly exist for the Dutch East India Company. Another potential source of information are letters, especially those sent by Portuguese Jesuits between Brazil, Portugal, and India. There was certainly medical interest in the plants, so a further analysis of plant use in both European and Indian medicine could provide further context for capsicums worldwide distribution. Once we have those, perhaps we will finally understand the taste for the world's most popular seasoning.

Notes

1   FAO 2018 figures are: 4,164,594 tonnes dried chillies, 732,524 tonnes black pepper and 2,837,472 tonnes miscellaneous spices ('FAOSAT', FAO, 2020 <http://www.fao.org/faostat/en/#data> [accessed 15 May 2020]).

2   A good overview, mainly focused on Clusius, is provided by Florike Egmond, 'Clusius and Friends: Cultures of Exchange in the Circles of European Naturalists', in *Carolus Clusius: Towards a Cultural History of a Renaissance Naturalist* (Amsterdam: Royal Netherlands Academy of Arts and Sciences; Chicago: University of Chicago Press, 2007), pp. 9-48.

3   Florike Egmond, *The World of Carolus Clusius: Natural History in the Making, 1550-1610* (Milton: Taylor & Francis, 2010), 17.

4   Egmond, p. 11.

5   Compare Rembert Dodoens, *A Nievve Herball* (London: Gerard Dewes, 1578), p. 634 to John Gerard, *The Herball* (London: John Norton, 1597), p. 292; and Carolus Clusius, *Curae posteriores* (Antwerp: Plantiniana Raphelengii, 1611), pp. 95-107 to John Gerard, *The Herball Or Generall Historie of Plantes* (London: Adam Islip Ioice Norton and Richard Whitakers, 1633), pp. 92-93.

6   Nicolás Monardes, *Dos libros* (Seville: Sebastian Trugillo, 1565), folio 44-45.

7   Pietro Antonio Michiel, *I cinque libri di piante dal codice Marciano*, ed. Ettore di Toni (Venice: C. Ferrari, 1940), p. 370.

8   Leonhart Fuchs, *De historia stirpium commentarii insignes* (Basel: Michael Isengrin, 1542), p. 731. Pliny describes *siliquastrum* or *piperitis*, as 'a kind of pepper' from southern India with seeds in 'small pods [...] such as we see in beans'. (*Silisqua* is Latin for pod.) See Barbara Pickersgill, 'Spices', in The Cultural History of Plants (New York: Routledge, 2012), p. 158.

9   'Mattioli, Pietro Andrea 1501-1577, *WorldCat Identities* <https://worldcat.org/identities/lccn-n81007084/> [accessed 30 May 2020].

10   Both Latin and German octavo editions of the 1545 *De historia stirpium* utilize identical woodcut plates. The former was printed by Michael Isingrin; the latter by Johann Bebel.

11   *Kreutterbuch* (Frankfurt: Johann Feyerabend, 1590), p. 182.

12   *Kreüter Buch* (Strasburg: Wendel Rihel), p. 350. As best as I can determine, there are only three sets of original capsicum illustrations in the sixteenth century: the Fuchs illustrations, which were in turn based on drawings by Albrecht Mayer; the drawing in Michiel's unpublished manuscript; and Gregorio da Reggio's extensive illustrations first published in Clusius's *Curae posteriores*.

13   Fuchs, p. 731.

14   Perhaps the best-known example of 'calecutisher' used in this way is in series of woodcuts created for Maximilian I depicting South American natives carrying stalks of maize! See Christian Feest, "'Selzam

Ding von Gold Da von Vill Ze Schreiben Were": Bewertungen Amerikanischer Handwerkskunst Im Europa Des Frühen 16. Jahrhunderts', Pirckheimer Jahrbuch, 1992, pp. 105–26.

15 Bock, Kreüter Buch, p. 350; Eucharius Rösslin, Kreuterbüch (Frankfurt: Christian Egenolph, 1550), p. 213; Pietro Andrea Mattioli, Herbarz, Ginak Bylinář (Prague: Melantrych, 1562), p. 156.

16 Underschidlicher so wohl zu Wasser als Landt (Johann Jacob Mayr, 1681), pp. 27, 61.

17 Johann Coler, Calendarium perpetuum (Wittenberg: Helwig, 1603), chap. 34; this is presumably the same as the earlier 1591 edition, which I have not seen.

18 See Hadrianus Junius, Nomenclator qvadrilingvis Boemicolatinograecogermanicvs (Veleslavín (Prague): M. Danielis Adami, 1598), pp. 96, 110.

19 Gerard, pp. 292-93.

20 Castore Durante, Herbario nuouo (Rome: Iacomo Bericchia, & Iacomo Tornierij, 1585), p. 344; Michiel, I cinque libri di piante dal codice Marciano, 370; Jakobus Mikalia, Blago jezika slovinskiga illi slovnik u komu izgorarajuse rjeci slovinske Latinsi, i Diacki (Loreto: Baptistam Seraphinum, 1649), 4p. 02.

21 Otto Gecser, 'Some Like It Hot: Piquant Taste between the Middle Ages and Modern Times Why', in My Favourite Things: Object Preferences in Medieval and Early Modern Material Culture, ed. by Gerhard Jaritz and Ingrid Matschinegg (Zurich: LIT, 2019), p. 96.

22 Gonzalo Fernandez Oviedo y Valdez, Historia general y natural de las Indias (Madrid: Imprenta de la Real academia de la historia, 1851), p. 275.

23 Pietro Andrea Mattioli, Libri cinque della historia, et materia medicinale (Venice: Niccolo Bascarini, 1544), p. 7.

24 Herbarz, Ginak Bylinář, p. 156; New Kreüterbuch (Prague: Melantrich, 1563), p. 217.

25 Kreutterbuch, p. 182; Herbář Aneb Bylinář (Prague: David Adam, 1596), p. 178. That said, both these versions include the original comment that you need to be careful not to touch your eyes when handling chillies, something that would only come from hand's-on experience.

26 Clusius, Curae posteriores, p. 104.

27 Michal Preusz and others, 'Exotic Spices in Flux: Archaeobotanical Material from Medieval and Early Modern Sites of the Czech Lands (Czech Republic)', Interdisciplinaria Archeologica VI.2 (2015), 223-36. Several authors also point out the presence of a chilli in Giuseppe Arcimboldo's Vertumnus (1591), meant to depict Rudolf II. While the Italian painter did spend time in Prague, the portrait was painted in Milan, so the Prague connection may be meaningless.

28 The Names of Herbes (London: John Day & Wyllyam Seres, 1548), p. 43.

29 The Herball, or, Generall Historie of Plantes, p. 292.

30 Gecser, p. 99.

31 A Nievve Herball, or, Historie of Plantes, p. 634.

32 Oviedo y Valdez, p. 275.

33 Gabriel Soares de Sousa and Francisco Adolfo de Varnhagen, Tratado descriptivo do Brazil em 1587 (Rio de Janeiro: Typographia Universal de Laemmert, 1851), p. 176.

34 L'Écluse, Exoticorvm libri decem, p. 341.

35 Nicolás Monardes, Joyfull Newes out of the Newe Founde Worlde (London: W. Norton, 1580), p. 20.

36 Castore Durante, Herbario nuouo (Rome: Iacomo Bericchia & Iacomo Tornierij, 1585), p. 344.

37 Antonio Colmenero de Ledesma, A Curious Treatise of the Nature and Quality of Chocolate (London: J. Okes, 1640), p. 6.

38 Čeněk Zíbrt, Staročeské umění kuchařské (Prague: Dauphin, 2012), p. 406.

39 Ana Vega Pérez de Arlucea, 'María Rosa, una cocinera andaluza del siglo XVIII', Las Provincias, 29 June 2018 <https://www.lasprovincias.es/planes/maria-rosa-cocinera- 20180629004018-ntvo. html?ref=https:%2F%2Fwww.google.com%2F> [accessed 30 May 2020].

40 Andre Alvares Almada, Tratado breve dos rios de Guine' do Cabo Verde, 1594 reprint, (Porto: Diego Köpke, 1841), p. 77.

41 Manuel Alvares, Ethiopia Minor and a Geographical Account of the Province of Sierra Leone, trans. by P.E.H. Hair ([Liverpool]: Dept. of History, University of Liverpool, 1990 [c. 1615]), 230.7 <https://

search.library.wisc.edu/digital/AJ7WGQHU5WJOJZ8N/pages> [accessed 30 May 2020].

42 Matthias de l'Obel, *Nova stirpivm adversaria* (Antwerp: Christophorum Plantinum, 1576). Several modern authors allude to another early source claiming the Portuguese brought 'Pernambuco' pepper from the Spanish West Indies to Goa. The origin of this seems to be George Watt, *The Commercial Products of India* (London: John Murray, 1908), p. 265, who cites the 1605 edition of Clusius, *Atrebatis exoticorum*, as his source. While the page cited does mention a *Capsicum brasilianum* (not 'brazilianum' as Watt writes), there is no mention of Pernambuco or Goa whatsoever.

43 Garcia de Orta, *Coloquios dos simples e drogas da India*, Reprint of 1563 edition., vol. 1, 2 vols. (Lisbon: Imprensa Nacional, 1891); Cristóbal Acosta, *Tractado de Las Drogas, y Medicinas de Las Indias Orientales* (Burgos: Martin de Victoria, 1578).

44 Jan Huygen van Linschoten, *The Voyage of John Huyghen Van Linschoten to the East Indies,* Vol. II (London: Hakluyt Society, 1885), p. 74.

45 Hendrik van Reede tot Drakestein and others, *Hortus Indicus Malabaricus* (1678-1679) (Amsterdam: Johannis van Someren & Joannis van Dyck, 1678), vol. v.1-2, p. 110.

46 Achaya, *A Historical Dictionary of Indian Food* (New York: Oxford University Press, 1998), p. 42.

47 Sebastião Manrique, *Itinerario* (Rome: F. Caballo, 1649), pp. 329-30.

48 Divya Schäfer, 'Exotic Tastes, Familiar Flavours: Transcultural Culinary Interactions in Early Modern India', in *HerStory. Historical Scholarship between South Asia and Europe: Festschrift in Honour of Gita Dharampal-Frick*, ed. by Rafael Klöber and Manju Ludwig (Books on Demand, 2018), p. 50. Plausibly, she cites as evidence the use of pimienta (black pepper) here rather than *pimiento* (capsicum). Contemporary dictionaries do point to a gender change in process in the seventeenth century, though the sources are inconsistent.

49 Yuri Parfionovich and Gyurme Dorje, *Tibetan Medical Paintings: Illustrations to the Blue Beryl Treatise of Sangye Gyamtso (1653-1705)*, ed. by Fernand Meyer (New York: H.N. Abrams, Inc., 1992).

50 Mendes Ferrão, '*Intercâmbio de Plantas Nos Séculos* XV *e* XVI', *Revista de Ciências Agrárias,* 36.2 (2013), pp. 258-66.

51 Jean Andrews is typical, writing: 'The new spice was welcomed by Indian cooks who, accustomed to pungent black pepper and biting ginger, produced hot, spicy foods. The Mesoamerican pepper provided more heat with less grinding and expense. It grew readily and fruited abundantly in a sympathetic environment. The easily cultivated and naturalizing *C. annuum* var. *annuum* was a welcome addition to the native spices, whose restrictive cultural requirements and high costs put them in a luxury category. Into the curries they went' (*Peppers: The Domesticated Capsicums* (Austin: University of Texas Press, 1995), p. 199).

52 Linschoten, p. 74.

'Good Old Things': The Transformation of Wild Herbs from Common Sustenance to Aristocratic Luxury in Early Modern England

Gina Rae La Cerva

During the early modern period in England, wild herbs were indistinguishable from vegetables. They were gathered from the nearby fields, woods, and hedgerows for daily pottages. Since the majority of people still lived near wild landscapes, it was common practice to make a meal with what was free-growing and easily at hand: plantain and mallow, dock and nettles, ivy-leaved toadflax, skirret, succory, hyssop, watercresses, sorrel, savory, borage, bugloss, purslane and chervil, pea shoots, samphire, scurvy grass, beach mustard, arrow grass, and the buds of elders, clary, and alexanders. One hundred herbs to add to the pudding. But by the dawn of the Enlightenment period, wild herbs began gracing the tables of the wealthiest gourmands. The transformation from common greenstuff to elevated ingredient dovetails with the rise in botany. Motivated both by scientific curiosity and a desire to bring long forgotten flavours back to the table, botanists searched out new plant specimens to study, often relying on the poor country women who intimately held this knowledge from their own use of wild herbs in the kitchen.

In the early sixteenth century, wild herbs were such a common element of the average person's diet, and considered a standard part of peasant tradition, that they were rarely mentioned in much detail or with any special concern. It is possible that upper-class households also found free-growing herbs to add to their meals, but menus and cookery books rarely mention greenstuff, much less do any distinguish between 'wild' and 'cultivated' plants. Another difficulty in understanding the role of herbs in early modern diets is that some authors interchanged the words 'vegetable' and 'herbs'.

In fact, most descriptions of herbs were found in medical herbals printed for pharmacological, rather than culinary, uses. In the previous centuries, many monasteries had extensive medicinal gardens. Monks produced numerous herbal manuscripts by hand, many of which were based on texts first created in classical antiquity, such as the *De materia medica*, a five-volume encyclopedia about herbal medicine written in the first century by the Greek physician Dioscorides. But until the printing press was developed, these handmade books remained rare and inaccessible to the ordinary person. Most herbal knowledge was therefore kept alive as folk medicine, handed down from mother to daughter.

With the invention of the printing press in the fourteenth century, a great number of books could be easily produced, and ancient herbals became more accessible than ever before. Theophrastus's *Enquiry into Plants* (*Historia plantarum*), written sometime between 350 BC and 287 BC, was first translated into Latin in 1483 and is one of the earliest examples of an attempt at systemic biological classification. It describes plant structure, reproduction, and growth habits, and carefully distinguishes between plants found in the woods, growing wildly, or cultivated as crops.

The fuzzy distinction between wild herbs as foodstuff or as medicine comes in part because of the prevalence of humoral theories of health, which derived from ideas dating back to classical Greece and China and gained prominence in the Medieval Period. The universe was believed be made of four elements that needed balancing within the body. Eating certain foods was a way to change the balance of these humours. Intertwined with these beliefs was that of the Doctrine of Signatures, which first appeared in Western thought with the ancient Greeks and Romans. It was believed that every being bore some mark of God, whether hidden or invisible, and with this indication one could discern where they fit within God's natural hierarchy. According to the idea of the Great Chain of Being, plants and animals were linked in a vertical chain, with the value and placement of each species directly related to the identifying marks found within their signatures. Plants with common emblems – their shapes and colours, habits and locations – were more related. These signs were a gift from God, such that we might know the natural order and allowing mankind to discover Nature's curative powers: it was a mirror to our infirmities.

According to this kind of sympathetic medicine, the medicinal power of herbs was not inherent in their buds and leaves, but lay in their complementary resemblance to human needs and desires. If a flower looked like an eye, it could treat eye infections. If the petals were triangular or flesh-coloured, like the human heart, the plant would remedy ailments ranging from chest-pains to heartbreaks. The roots of the plant mandrake resembled a miniature person, and, like a spirit double, was believed to hold the power of anesthetics. It was also a cure for sterility and the collapse of passion. Needless to say, it became extremely sought after, leading to widespread poaching, fraud, and counterfeiting – perhaps the first example of the black-market trade in wild products.

Not only did nature fit within God's hierarchy, but social class did as well, and therefore appropriate diets also mirrored a natural hierarchy. Bulbs and roots were considered the lowest because they grew directly in the soil, whereas fruit growing on the tops of trees was more noble in character. Birds were at the top of the animal kingdom and this high position suggested they were a more appropriate food for the higher classes of society. The further food was from the earth, the more delicious it was meant to taste.

As the Renaissance progressed, there was increasing interest in herbal texts from the classical period. Herbals were translated and published in the vernacular languages, rather than Latin as was common among treaties of other types of knowledge at the time, so that they might be more generally accessible. By the sixteenth century, knowledge of flowering plants had greatly increased, but their study was still tinged with magic and superstition. As a result, the accuracy of the information in herbals varied. For instance, *The grete herball*, published in 1526, contained a series of woodcut images derived from illustrations made in the previous century. Many of the same woodcuts were repeated for entirely different plants, with little relevance to their descriptions. The visuals thus functioned primarily as decoration.

But as interest in anatomy and medical drawings increased, some authors went to great efforts to depict plants with a similarly high degree of accuracy. In his herbal *De historia stirpium commentarii insignes* (*Notable Commentaries on the History of Plants*), first published in Switzerland in 1543 and known as the 'New Herbal' in the English version, Leonard Fuch describes 400 wild plants first identified in ancient texts. The illustrations were drawn in nature by the botanical illustrator Albrecht Meyer, then cut into wood by a master engraver. The level of attention to detail meant that noblemen could use the book for plant identification. Pietro Duodo, an Italian Renaissance diplomat, included this book in his gentleman's traveling library, a collection of 90 works in 133 volumes which he hoped would be a portable source of information, encompassing all the knowledge available at the time.

Around this time, William Turner published the first part of his *New herball, wherin are conteyned the names of herbes* (1551), with beautiful woodcuts, primarily copied from Fuch's book. The treatise was published in three parts beginning through the second half of the sixteenth century. As one of the first systematic surveys of England's plants, it became a touchpoint for the transition of herbal knowledge away from its association with magic, superstition, and religion and into the realm of the scientific.

223

Perhaps most interesting to our understanding of the culinary uses of wild herbs was that Turner's book includes the 'vertues of every herbe' and the location of local plants.[1] This combined with it being written in English rather than Latin meant that what had once been in the domain of apothecaries was now more accessible to the general population. He identifies modern names and plants from classical herbal descriptions, such as those found in Pliny and Dioscorides, and delineates between wild and cultivated varieties. For example, 'Wild mynte […] looketh more whitish than the garden mynte doth, and it hath a very strong savour'.[2] Wild mint was considered 'hotter and drier' under humoral definitions, and so it was not recommended for the diverse culinary and medicinal purposes that garden mint could be used for. However, the leaves could be powdered for an anti-poison.

Turner was not the only writer to point out that wild herbs were of much stronger flavour than their domesticated counterparts. The botanist John Parkinson (1567-1650), who began his career in a London apothecary before becoming the apothecary to James I and eventually the Royal Botanist to Charles I – and thus straddled this shift from herbalism to science – was particularly interested in delineating herbs that were of use in kitchens. His motivations appeared to be more in service to expanding general knowledge of plants rather than strictly culinary: he makes note of kitchen uses 'very sparingly' as he does not desire to write 'a treatise of cookery, but briefly to give a touch thereof'.[3] He describes Dutch and Flemish immigrants using strongly flavoured herbs, such as tarragon and chervil, and notes that French immigrants liked salad herbs with a stronger flavour than the English.

There is a botanical explanation for the fact that wild herbs are often stronger in flavour: plants growing wildly tend to exist in harsher environments with less water and nutrients than herbs grown domestically. This stress causes wild plants to produce more of the volatile compounds that produce flavour. Additionally, as herbs were domesticated, they were often selected to be less pungent in favour of other characteristics, such as ease of transplanting or other growth habits that made them suitable to gardens.

In early botanical descriptions we begin to see a picture of the use of wild plants as foodstuffs by poor citizens, practices which had likely been occurring for centuries but was not of concern until it became relevant to the domains of science. People regularly gathered wild leeks, Clove gillyflowers, annual mercury, chickweed, the leaves of ground elder, cresses, burnet, skirret and the leaves of wild strawberries, violets and primroses, moss and colewort, nosesmart, peppergrass, pea shoots, cowslip and goatsbeard, buttercup, yarrow and rampions, rye-grass, pennyroyal, and smooth hawksbeard. The strong, bitter flavours of these wild herbs seemed to define the lives of the poor who ate them as a matter of survival. But, given how nutrient-dense and flavourful wild herbs are, in some instances the poor likely enjoyed superior meals to the rich.

As botany became increasingly in vogue for upper-class couture naturalists, there was a frenzy of plant collecting, a sort of friendly competition between quasi-professionals to see who could seek out the most interesting wild plants to bring into potherb gardens for cultivation and study. These ardent plant collectors, finding exotic potherbs in other countries or out in the wilds of their own backyards, developed into a network of wealthy men who traded specimens with each other for their own trials, and eventual published treaties. Botanists were further elevated if they discovered a new wild plant that could be added to the dinner table, even if that herb had been known to the poorer classes for centuries.

As they went out to the hedgerows and woods looking for rare edible curiosities, they were clearly motivated by a foodie sensibility. Parkinson was enamoured with the sweet parsley in the Italian ambassador's London garden. He writes about 'those that take delight in eating of herbs', and describes plant collectors as 'those whose curiosity searcheth out the whole work of nature to satisfy their desires'. Indeed one of the arguments against deforesting Bernwood Forest in Buckinghamshire during the reign of James I came from the University of Oxford, which adamantly feared it would destroy the wild herbs growing there, which were considered to be its 'blessed commodities'.[4]

Indeed, flavour and culinary usage were very intertwined with these botanical studies. As botanists began to more systematically describe plants in the mid-seventeenth century, edible wild herbs were prevalent in their studies. On occasion, some botanists even indulged in eating the specimens they were collecting! The famed William Coles suggests that 'if you have forgotten a cucumber on your picnic then pick wild salad burnet', a wild herb that looks like parsley and has the subtle taste of cucumber. Coles spent much of his time in the fields watching country people gather herbs, and then added what he found to his plant identification schematics. He described how and where many edible wild plants grew, including purslane, nettle tops, watercresses, 'black potherb' (alexanders or black lovage), and the buds of alders. It is evident that he enjoyed his time with country folk, observing their practices and genuinely admiring their use of foraged foods. 'There is not a day passeth over our heads but we have need of one thing or other that groweth within their circumference,' he wrote admirably. Indeed, food seemed to require such wild-sourced herbs to have any flavour. He continues, 'We cannot make so much as a little good pottage without herbs, which give an admirable relish and make them wholesome for our bodies.'[5]

As in previous centuries, herbs – and particularly wild herbs with their more potent flavours – held both culinary and medicinal properties, characteristics which were not considered separate. William Langham, in his *Garden of Healthe* (1579) writes about hundreds of plants – from wild caraway to cotton weede to fleawort – detailing both their medicinal and culinary uses. Cole writes about nettles as both a delicious food and a blood purifier. Purslane and sorrel were both cleansing and anti-scorbutic. The use of a still became increasingly popular in upper-class manor houses for the creation of herbal oils and essences for both medicinal and culinary purposes. John Partridge detailed precise instructions on how to gather wild herbs for the still in *Treasuries of Hidden Secrets* (first printed in 1573, and then reprinted over the next 75 years). Do not wash them, he admonished, just wipe them dry. In 1640, Lord Howard of North paid his brewer to put herbs in his beer. In his cookbook *The accomplisht cook*, Robert May has a recipe for Metheglin, a flavoured mead, made with 'field herbs' such as wild thyme, mint, rosemary, fennel, angelica, hyssop, burnet, agrimony. In another for a broth against consumption, he recommends, 'Violet leaves, wild tansie, succory-roots, large mace, raisins, and damask prunes boil'd with a chicken and a crust of bread'.[6] Other broths required 'sweet herbs' or herbal possets made up of some combination of balm, borrage, endive, tamarisk, harts-horn, yellow sanders, blessed thistle, burage, savory, pennyroyal, fumitory, or marigold flowers. Others required 'cool herbs' such as violet leaves, strawberry leaves, and bugloss.

This period was also a time of experimentation in cuisine, especially for vegetables, as more and more exotic varieties were brought home to England from the colonies and medieval superstitions about the unsavoury and dangerous quality of vegetables disappeared. Fresh wild herbs became a staple of both upper-class and middle-class cookbooks and party menus. Linnaeus describes the 'sweetish, with a slight aromatic, warm pungency' of *Eringium* leaves (likely sea holly) for salads, and it was fashionable to comfit the roots.[7] Samphire growing along the seacoasts (Sir William Petre at Ingatestone in Essex liked it pickled), wintercress in the cold months and young purslane gathered along country paths in spring (the Countess of Kent was a fan), and water houseleek pulled from the fens were all eaten in this period. Sorrel, chervil, and parsley in soups and sauces lent an acidity that paired well with fatty meats. Pigweed

225

was used as a potherb and the stems were pickled in salt and vinegar for use in winter salads. Broom buds were pickled too.

In salads, wild herbs abounded. Sow-thistle, wild hyssop, and jack by the hedges (*Alliaria*) added flavourings. Sir Kenelm Digby ate borage and bugloss, sorrel and chervil. Gerard Markham was fond of succory and the leaves of wild violets. John Evelyn wrote an entire treatise on salad called *Acetarua: A Discourse of Sallets* (1699), citing numerous wild herbs as ingredients. Robert May has recipes for 'grand sallets' requiring 'knots of buds of sallet herbs, buds of pot-herbs, or any green herbs, as sage, mint, balm, burnet, violet-leaves, red coleworts streaked of divers fine colours, lettice, any flowers'.[8] Edible flowers were a vital element at any fancy dinner. The blossoms of borage, bellflowers, rampions, marigolds, hopbuds, violets, lily flowers, alexander buds, lavender, primroses, cowslips, rose, hawthorn and peony were used for flavour and colour. Clove gully flowers preserved in sugar and vinegar were served in winter salads.

The loss of flavour that occurred when these plants were grown in gardens was generally accepted for the convenience, but it was agreed that if a chef wanted stronger flavours herbs should be found out in the wild. Wild mustard grew all over much of the country and was particularly celebrated in Tewksesbury and Wakefield.[9] May has a recipe for a flavouring cake that could be taken along for use anytime: mustard mixed with honey, cinnamon, and vinegar, then dried in the sun.

By the turn of the eighteenth century, land-use changes associated with enclosure, and legislation that encouraged farmers not to let their fields go fallow, were making it increasingly difficult for poor people to source local wild herbs. In the year 1694, William Westamount bemoaned the disappearance of the ladythistle, a wild spring herb, to over-harvesting, writing, 'as the world decays, so doth the use of good old things and others more delicate and less virtuous brought in'. Wild herbs began to occupy a realm of nostalgia, just before they were forgotten. This process fits in well with what Ken Albala calls 'a dialectic of culinary styles', whereby we can see a recurring pattern of cuisines shifting between complexity and simplicity. Each new aesthetic period borrows from the previous one, thus incorporating and reinterpreting older elements into a new evolution.[10]

As the Enlightenment took root, plant schematics and classification became firmly established, and medicine increasingly moved away from strictly herbal cures. For botanists, the focus was less on uses of plants and much more on totalizing systems for organization. The government promoted the cultivation of cereal production, in part to free up labour for the Industrial Revolution, and the general population was urged to eat more grains, rice, peas, and root vegetables – particularly those with high proteins as a substitute for meat. Theophilus Lobb, in his 1763 book *Primitive Cookery*, recommends the poor eat cardoons – a kind of thistle and the wild version of the globe artichoke – fried and buttered, as they could be found abundantly in ditches and hedges.[11]

Botanical treaties contained less and less mention of the virtues of wild plants in either culinary or medicinal uses, although in 1783 Charles Bryant tried to combine the two areas in his *Flora Dietetica: Or History Of Esculent Plants, Both Domestic And*

Foreign, which describes milk thistle (lady's thistle) as one of the best wild edibles. But generally for the upper class, gardening inventions extended growing seasons, and new exotic vegetables and herbal varieties combined with improvements in crop breeding meant reliance on and interest in local herbs was a quickly fading fashion.

We are today experiencing a resurgent interest in foraging for wild herbs. At the same time, we are facing a frightening global wild plant extinction: we have lost nearly 600 species in the past 250 years. Understanding the history of our relationship to wild herbs – how they have been associated with both poverty and luxury – is necessary if we are to stem the tide of loss. Perhaps reviving a taste for these diverse wild herb species will spur us to conserve the landscapes in which they are sourced, and that the taste of the wild will reconnect us to the common nourishment we have forgotten.

Notes

1   William Turner, *A new herball, wherin are conteyned the names of herbes in Greke, Latin, Englysh, Duch, Frenche, and in the potecaries and herbaries Latin: with the properties degrees, and naturall places of the same* (London: printed by Steven Myerdman and sold by John Gybken, 1551), Prologue <https://tile.loc.gov/storage-services/service/rbc/rbc0001/2016/2016english36423/2016english36423.pdf> [accessed 30 March 2021].

2   William Turner, *A new herball, Parts II and III*, ed. by George T.L. Chapman, Frank McCombie, and Anne U. Wesencraft (Cambridge: Cambridge University Press, 1995), Prologue <https://books.google.com/books?id=ouWABJeOC4MC&pg=PA451&lpg=PA451&dq=Wild+mynte&source=bl&ots=7ejzlBbnIM&sig=ACfU3U3Ouay8uRibLOnlNsm1NTFRCNzh-A&hl=en&sa=X&ved=2ahUKEwje3eu96uHpAhUYWsoKHb2hAvkQ6AEwAH0ECA0QAQ#v=onepage&q&f=false> [accessed 30 March 2021].

3   John Parkinson, *Paradisi in Sole Paradisus Terrestris, or, A Choise Garden of All Sorts of Rarest Flowers with their Nature, Place of Birth, Time of Flowring, Names, and Vertues to Each Plant, Useful in Physic or Admired for Beauty: To which is Annext a Kitchin-Garden Furnished with All Manner of Herbs, Roots, and Fruits, for Meat or Sauce Used with Us, with the Art of Planting an Orchard... All Unmentioned in Former Herbals* (London: Methuen, 1904 [1656]), p. h <https://archive.org/details/paradisiinsolepaooparkrich> [accessed 30 March 2021].

4   Joan Thirsk, *Food in Early Modern England: Phases, Fads, Fashions, 1500-1760* (London: Hambledon Continuum, 2007), pp. 70, 290, 211

5   William Coles, *The Art of Simpling. An Introduction to the Knowledge and Gathering of Plants. Wherein the Definitions, Divisions, Places, Descriptions, Differences, Names, Vertues, Times of flourishing and gathering, Uses, Temperatures, Signatures and Appropriations of Plants are methodically laid down* (London: printed by J.G. for Nath. Brook, 1656).

6   Robert May, *The accomplisht cook or, The art & mystery of cookery* (London: printed for Obadiah Blagrave, 1685), pp. 487, 742.

7   Robert Hogg, *The Vegetable Kingdom and Its Products: Serving as an Introduction to the Natural System of Botany, and as a Textbook of All the Vegetable Substances Used in the Arts, Manufactures, Medicine, and Domestic Economy: Arranged According to the System of De Candolle* (London: W. Kent, 1858), p. 380.

8   May, p. 321.

9   Thirsk, p. 315.

10 Ken Albala, 'Toward a Historical Dialectic of Culinary Styles', *Historical Research*, 87.238 (November 2014), pp. 581-90.

11 Theophilus Lobb, *Primitive Cookery: Or the Kithen Gareden Display'd, containing a Collection of Receipts for Preparing Great Variety of Cheap, Healthful and Palatable Dishes without either Fish, Flesh or Fowl* (London: 1763).

Just Mad About Saffron:[1] A Note on Jewish Memory and Pharmacology

Joshua Lovinger

Medical teaching strongly influenced medieval notions of good taste and table etiquette. Humoralism informed recipes, the appropriateness of food combinations, the construction of dishes and sauces, and the order of courses. Physicians and apothecaries were not in the kitchen, but their lessons provided answers to who should eat what and when. The healthy, no less than the ill, were to consume a diet fitted to their individual temperaments and place in society to achieve a healthy balance of the four humours: yellow bile, black bile, phlegm, and blood.[2] The application of insights from medical and culinary history to the classic medieval texts of Jewish law and custom (halakah[3]) is still in its infancy, but careful reading can illuminate new dimensions of Hebrew texts and Jewish ritual practices. Here we uncover the background of one such obscured and then forgotten custom from Provence.[4]

This custom relates to the Jewish festival of Šavu'ot and is found in *Kol Bo*, an anonymous compendium of Jewish law and custom from the late thirteenth to early fourteenth century. The section on Šavu'ot contains a culinary interlude. Šavu'ot, also known as the Feast of Weeks or Pentecost, begins seven weeks (or fifty days) following the beginning of Passover. Passover, Šavu'ot, and Sukkot comprise the biblical pilgrimage festivals, when Jews travelled to the Temple in Jerusalem to pray and offer sacrifices specific to each festival. Passover and Sukkot also involved practices outside the Temple, such as eating unleavened bread (*maṣṣah*; pl. *maṣṣot*) and bitter herbs at the Passover *Seder* and dining in temporary booths (Lev 23:42) and reciting a blessing over the four species (Lev 23:40) on Sukkot, but Šavu'ot did not. Both before and after the destruction of the Temple in 70 CE, Šavu'ot was marked only by general prescriptions to abstain from labour, to rejoice with festive meals, and to recite holiday prayers as on Passover and Sukkot.[5] In the Talmudic period (70-*c*.500 CE), Šavu'ot became associated with the date of the revelation at Mount Sinai, but only in the medieval period were unique Šavu'ot rituals developed that involve specific foods.

A Cryptic Culinary Custom

Kol Bo (lit. 'Everything within'), a Provençal halakic work, mentions three culinary customs unique to Šavu'ot, each followed by its presumed rationale(s). The author seemed sure of the reasons behind the first two, though he was less certain about the third, proffering two guesses.

גם נהגו לאכול דבש וחלב בחג שבועות, מפני שהתורה נמשלה לדבש וחלב, כמו שכתוב
"דבש וחלב תחת לשונך".
ונהגו בכל ישראל גם כן לשום במצה זפרן, והטעם לפי שמשמח הלב.
גם נהגו הנשים לעשות בשבועות לחם ארוך, ולו ארבע ראשים. ונראה לומר כי נמצא המנהג
זכר לשתי הלחם הקרב בעצרת. או אפשר מפני מזל תאומים המשמש בסיון⁶.

[1] It was also customary to eat honey and milk on the holiday of Šavuʿot because
the Torah is compared to honey and milk, as it is stated (Cant 4:11): 'Honey and
milk are under your tongue'.

[2] And it was customary among all of Israel to also place in the maṣṣah saffron.
And the reason is because it gladdens the heart.

[3] The women also had the custom to make on Šavuʿot an elongated bread
with four heads. And it seems to be because the custom is in remembrance of
the two bread loaves which were offered [in the Temple] on 'Aṣeret [= Šavuʿot].
Alternatively, it is possible that [the custom] is because the constellation of
Gemini serves in [the month of] Sivan [within which Šavuʿot falls].

Forms of the first and third of this series of practices were still well-known in later
centuries.⁷ (The first is the reason contemporary Jews bake cheesecakes for the holiday.)
We will focus on the second, the use of saffron in maṣṣah. The custom is enigmatic.
Maṣṣah is the prototypical symbolic food of Passover, not Šavuʿot. And the Bible labels
this unleavened bread a 'bread of affliction' (Deut 16:3), not what one would expect
to 'gladden the heart'. Moreover, where does one obtain unleavened bread six weeks
after Passover? (Notably, while there are lengthy discussions in Jewish legal literature of
maṣṣah baking before Passover, none exist regarding Šavuʿot.)

Also, the formulation of *Kol Bo* provides no detail about how the saffron is eaten
with the maṣṣah. Is it baked in to season the dough or applied afterward in a glaze?

Finally, unlike the two other customs, the author hints at the widespread geographical
distribution of eating maṣṣah with saffron by describing it as 'customary in all of Israel'.
However, other contemporary Provençal scholars who mentioned festive Šavuʿot dishes
did not allude to the use of saffron and maṣṣah.⁸

Further details regarding this custom can be found where the passage is repeated in
the *Orḥot Ḥayyim* (lit. 'Pathways of life') of R. Aaron ha-Kohen of Lunel (c.1260-1330).⁹
Kol Bo was an initial version of R. Aaron's *Orḥot Ḥayyim*, likely composed before 1295
and the 1306 expulsion of the Jewish community from France. In his revised version
finished on Majorca, *Orḥot Ḥayyim*, R. Aaron includes the contemporary Catalan
halakic opinions he encountered travelling through Spain.¹⁰

ונהגו לאכול דבש וחלב ביום ראשון, מפני שנמשלה התורה לדבש וחלב, כמו שנאמר 'דבש
וחלב תחת לשונך'.
גם נהגו הנשים לישות לחם, ולו ארבעה ראשים כזה [ ] ונראה שהוא זכר לשתי הלחם, או
מפני מזל תאומים שמשמש בסיון.
גם נהגו שמצניעין ממצות של פסח, וטובלין אותו במי הזעפראן שמשמח את הלב.

[1] And it was customary to eat honey and milk on the first day [of Šavuʿot]

because the Torah is compared to honey and milk, as it is stated (Cant 4:11): 'Honey and milk are under your tongue'.

[2] The women also had the custom to knead a bread with four heads, like so [ ]. And it seems to be in remembrance of the two bread loaves on Šavuʿot or because the constellation of Gemini serves in Sivan.

[3] It was also the custom to save from the Passover *maṣṣot* [for Šavuʿot] and they would dip it in saffron waters, for it gladdens the heart.[11]

In this revised version, R. Aaron changed the order of the customs, demoting the use of maṣṣah with saffron to last. He also deleted that the custom was spread among 'all of Israel'. Among the Jews of Iberia the custom was unknown; it must have seemed less universal. But R. Aaron did clarify some aspects of the practice – the maṣṣah used was saved specifically for this Šavuʿot custom from those baked for Passover; also, the saffron was not baked in the maṣṣah, but the maṣṣah was dipped in a liquid seasoned with saffron (making fifty-day-old stale maṣṣah more palatable).[12]

At the close of the fourteenth century, R. Samuel b. Mešullam of Gerona (b.1335) was the last medieval Jewish authority to refer to this custom from *Kol Bo* and *Orḥot Ḥayyim*. He used a similar linguistic root to describe the maṣṣah saved from Passover for Šavuʿot (צנע, to hide or save), but he described the custom in several new forms.[13]

מנהג הוא להצניע מן המצות של פסח עד חג השבועות, זכר למצות שהוציאו ממצרים, שאכלו מהן עד שירד המן.

ויש אומ׳ שהמנהג לרמוז כי שבועות הוא עצרת של פסח, כמו ששמיני של חג הוי עצרת מסוכות. וטובלין המצות במי זעפראן ובדבש, ואוכלין, ומשגרין לאוהביהם.

וטעם הזרעפאן [צ״ל זעפראן] מפני שמשמח.

וטעם הדבש מפני שנתנה בו תורה שנמשלה לדבש, שנא׳ ׳דבש וחלב תחת לשונך׳.

[1] It is a [or: the] custom to save from the Passover *maṣṣot* until the holiday of Šavuʿot, in remembrance of the *maṣṣot* that they took out of Egypt, which they ate until the manna fell.

And some say that the custom is to hint that Šavuʿot is the *ʿaṣeret* [= closure-festival] of Passover, just as the eighth day of *Ḥag* [= eighth day of Sukkot, i.e. *Šemini ʿaṣeret*] is the *ʿaṣeret* of Sukkot.

[2] And they would dip the *maṣṣot* in saffron waters and in honey and eat [it], and send [it] to their loved ones.

And the reason for the saffron is because it gladdens.

And the reason for the honey is because the Torah, which is compared to honey, was given on it [Šavuʿot], as it is stated (Cant 4:11): 'Honey and milk are under your tongue'.[14]

Omitted were the specially-shaped holiday breads. And the author conflated the two other customs – honey (without milk) was now joined to consuming maṣṣah with saffron on Šavuʿot. He understood the focus to be maṣṣah; the saffron and honey were accoutrements. R. Samuel b. Mešullam viewed eating unleavened bread on Šavuʿot as the conclusion of Passover, an idea already found in the biblical commentary of the Catalan exegete

Naḥmanides (1194-1270) to Lev 23:36. However, gifting this maṣṣah to others is novel.

Later generations, encountering this custom through printed texts instead of living tradition, did not know what to make of it. They wedged the custom into pre-existing culinary structures. In Eastern Europe, where saffron featured prominently in popular Slavic pastries known as kołacz and in Easter breads, Jews kept the saffron to flavour leavened cakes and ḥallah breads and dropped the maṣṣah.[15] The custom was thus rendered less distinctive for Šavu'ot, as Eastern European Jews baked ḥallah breads with saffron (and occasionally raisins) for Sabbaths and other holidays as well.[16] Yiddish authors of fiction set in Russia and Poland more frequently described saffron loaves for Purim.[17] However, in North Africa, where there was a centuries-old custom to eat or bake maṣṣah on Šavu'ot as a talisman against scorpion bites, Jews reading *Kol Bo* assumed it referred to that known custom and dropped the saffron.[18]

Herbal Lore and Reading R. Aaron

Determining the origin for the custom described by R. Aaron requires dissecting his concise rationale, conveyed in only three words in *Kol Bo*, לפי שמשמח הלב, 'because it gladdens the heart'. His reasoning – which does not change between *Kol Bo* and *Orḥot Ḥayyim* – is not conjecture, unlike his explanation for the baking of special holiday breads; regarding the use of maṣṣah and saffron he is certain: 'it' gladdens the heart. 'It' cannot refer to maṣṣah, the Bible's 'bread of affliction'. Maṣṣah is discussed ad nauseum in other halakic works without any inkling of a gladdening effect. Nor is it likely that 'it' refers to combining unleavened bread and saffron, which does not appear earlier in Jewish literature (nor elsewhere). The rationale specified by R. Aaron is driven by saffron only, so our understanding of this enigmatic Provençal custom must focus on this costly spice.

There were no biblical or talmudic antecedents leading R. Aaron to link saffron with gladdening the heart. Saffron, made from the dried stigmas of *Crocus sativus,* is a hapax legomenon in the Hebrew Bible, appearing only in Cant 4:14 amongst a list of other fine spices: 'Nard and saffron, fragrant reed and cinnamon, with all aromatic woods, myrrh and aloes – all the choice perfumes.' Saffron's pleasant scent may have fostered its inclusion in the incense offered in the Temple, but only as one of many ingredients.[19] While the Hebrew root used in *Kol Bo* for joyfulness (שמחה|smḥ) is connected to the heart in numerous scriptural verses, only one relates to spices, with none singled out as causing elation.[20] ('Oil and incense *gladden the heart*, and the sweetness of a friend is better than one's own counsel' (Prov 27:9).)

If earlier Hebrew literature did not ascribe unique properties to saffron, what served as R. Aaron's source and what did he mean by 'gladdening'?

The passages in *Kol Bo* and *Orḥot Ḥayyim* were likely understood by contemporaries but misinterpreted by later readers because the expression 'it gladdens the heart' was actually a *terminus technicus*; it was not merely a borrowing from similar biblical phrases. Originally it did not simply mean a substance which induces happiness through pleasant scent or taste alone. Thirteenth-century Provence was the home not only of R. Aaron and Jewish legal scholars, but also of a flourishing movement involved in Arabic-to-Hebrew translation of philosophical and scientific texts.[21] The Hebrew root (שמח|smḥ) was used by contemporary Jewish translators for Arabic *mufriḥ*, which indicated that the ingredient had the properties of an exhilarant or a cardiac remedy.[22] R. Aaron was drawing upon medical terminology in describing the use of saffron as a cardiac exhilarant, indicating that the rationale for the Šavuʿot custom related to pharmacologic characteristics of saffron.

Classical Greek and Roman medical works did not mention this characteristic of *Crocus sativus*. While Pliny and Dioscorides devoted sections of their works to saffron, suggesting pharmacologic applications – Dioscorides noting that it was an aphrodisiac and Pliny that saffron 'is extremely useful in medicine' – neither connected the herb to either the heart or to joyfulness.[23] Surprisingly, saffron is scarcely mentioned in the gargantuan Indian medical encyclopedias either.[24]

Among many of the earliest physicians writing in Arabic there was no mention of saffron in connection with the heart. In Baghdad, the capital of the Abbasid Caliphate and the centre of medical study in the Islamic Golden Age, a leading Syriac Christian physician, Yuḥannā Ibn Māsawayh (Mesue; d.857) listed saffron as 'good for the liver and stomach, similarly for all the humors' with no mention of cardiac effects.[25] A century later, in the Northern African centre of Qayrawān, the Jewish physician and philosopher Isaac b. Solomon Israeli (c.855-c.955) followed Ibn Māsawayh in his *Liber dietarum particularum* in declaring that saffron strengthened the stomach and opened obstructions in the liver.[26] He, too, made no mention of the heart.

However, one of their contemporaries had a different view. In his *Comprehensive Book of Medicine*, Rhazes (al-Rāzī; 854-c.925-935) quoted a ninth-century Christian physician, Qusṭā ibn Lūqā (d.912), who asserted that saffron gladdened the heart.

Interestingly, Rhazes warned of dangers from saffron's elating effect. Dioscorides had cautioned against overuse of saffron ('poisonous when an amount of three *drachmai* is drunk with water'). Rhazes, though, cited authorities stating that saffron mixed with wine could provoke excessive, dangerous laughter (contrary to Pliny, who claimed that saffron could mitigate the effects of alcohol (*Historia naturalis* 21:81)).[27]

Cardiac effects and cautions regarding saffron triggering dangerous laughter became commonplace in subsequent medical herbal literature, displacing staid presentations on saffron by Ibn Māsawayh and Isaac Israeli. Among the most prominent (both dependent upon Rhazes) were those of Pseudo-Serapion, in his book of botanical simples, and Avicenna (Ibn Sīnā; d.1037), in both his *On Cardiac Remedies* and *Canon of Medicine*, Latin translations of which served as the primary medical textbooks in Western Europe until the early modern period.[28]

In the Provence of R. Aaron, the dietary works of Isaac Israeli were considered authoritative, included in the 1309 curriculum of the medical school at Montpellier. But, the chief teacher there, Arnold of Villanova, translated Avicenna's *On Cardiac Remedies* and wrote a commentary on the anonymous but popular thirteenth-century *Regimen Sanitatis* of Salerno, both of which linked saffron with the heart and happiness.[29] The

232

Canon, On Cardiac Remedies, and Arnold's *Regimen* were closely studied by Provençal Jews, as surviving Hebrew translations attest. These works emphasized the connection of saffron to joy; as a result, Hebrew and Latin writings through the Renaissance referred to saffron as an antidote for melancholy.[30]

Thus, R. Aaron recorded a custom to consume maṣṣah with saffron on Šavu'ot, due to saffron's widely known property as a pharmacologic stimulant to induce joyfulness on the holiday.

Kol Bo: A Medieval Miscellany, Its Sources, and Culinary Traditions

But why would an antidepressant be necessary on Šavu'ot? Jewish law prohibits fasting or mourning and requires that one rejoice on all festivals – not just on Šavu'ot. The context of this custom in *Kol Bo* and *Orḥot Ḥayyim* may provide some clue.

Though R. Aaron's books cite thirteenth-century Provençal works, they also draw on Northern European materials. The percentage of the latter is even higher in *Kol Bo* (where our custom already appears), as that work includes less from Spanish scholars (R. Solomon ibn Adret and R. Yom-Tov b. Abraham of Seville) whom R. Aaron encountered after exile from France. Rather, late thirteenth-century German and Northern French scholars R. Me'ir of Rothenberg and R. Pereṣ of Corbeil are among the most cited authorities.[31] Furthermore, after the organized portion of this code there appears a miscellaneous collection of legal decisions from Franco-German authorities.[32]

This food custom, as we have seen, occurs as one of three culinary practices for Šavu'ot. While the combination of maṣṣah with saffron is not found in earlier texts, the first custom on the list, 'to eat honey and milk', is. The legal decisions of R. Avigdor b. Elijah ha-Kohen (d. *c*.1275), reflecting exegetical methods of the German Pietists and their doctrines, refer to the consumption of dairy products (but not honey) on Šavu'ot. It seems that the custom was already widespread; many people were asking about its source.[33] Even before R. Avigdor, we find mention of dairy products (again, without honey) on Šavu'ot in a comment of R. Ele'azar b. Judah of Worms (d.1238) in the name of an even earlier German authority.[34] (Honey is likely omitted solely because the halakic question involves only the consumption of milk – and dairy products – in proximity to meat. Honey could be eaten with either dairy or meat.) The earliest witnesses here to the consumption of dairy on Šavu'ot date from a century before R. Aaron and stem from the traditions of Ashkenaz (German Jewry). And there is further proof for this origin.

Šavu'ot, commemorating the giving of the Torah, was the traditional date for initiating Jewish elementary education in Ashkenaz. R. Ele'azar b. Judah of Worms recorded this practice: 'It is the custom of our ancestors to sit the children down to study (the Torah for the first time) on Šavu'ot because that is when the Torah was given.'[35] As part of this initiation, children would begin instruction with the book of Leviticus and would be fed cakes, kneaded with honey and milk.[36] As G. Oberlander has noted, the custom for all – adults too – to eat foods containing milk and honey on Šavu'ot mimics the educational rite for children, and marks the holiday as a time of renewal of Torah study for all Jews.[37] Versions of these Ashkenazic rituals were transmitted in *Kol Bo* and *Orḥot Ḥayyim* too.[38]

It would be reasonable, then, to consider that the other two culinary customs listed in the series in *Kol Bo* and *Orḥot Ḥayyim* are likely of Ashkenazic origin as well.

Memory of Šavuʿot in the Middle Ages

If the use of saffron on Šavuʿot to induce happiness stems from Ashkenaz, then its employment on this festival alone becomes more understandable. In Ashkenaz the Jewish community would be prone to melancholy during this period. Without the addition of a pharmacologic stimulant, they would find it difficult to rejoice on the holiday. The massacres of Rhineland Jewry during the First Crusade in 1096 had occurred around the time of Šavuʿot, and histories and liturgies from that era emphasize the proximity to the festival; the chroniclers focused upon reversing the holiday's normally celebratory atmosphere to one of mourning.[39] The receipt of the Torah at Sinai was contrasted with the desecration of Torah scrolls and Jewish sancta at the hands of the marauding Crusaders and the local populace. In Cologne, R. Eliezer b. Nathan recounted that '[t]he foe destroyed the synagogue and removed the Torah Scrolls, desecrating them and casting them into the streets to be trodden underfoot. *On the very day that the Torah was given, when the earth trembled and its pillars quivered,* they now tore, burned and trod upon it – those wicked evildoers regarding whom it is said: "Robbers have entered and profaned it"'.[40] The preparation of the Israelites for the giving of the Torah at Sinai was transformed into the preparedness of the Rhineland Jews to lay down their lives to avoid the baptismal font. R. Solomon b. Samson, commenting on the murder of R. Qalonymos the Pious, draws this and similar comparisons: '*On the very day that the Lord had said to his people [Exod 19:1], 'Be prepared for the third day,'* on that day they prepared themselves, extended their throats, and offered up their sacrifice, a sweet savor unto the Lord. On that day eleven hundred holy souls were slain for the sake of the Great Name of Him Who is One in the world, besides Whom there is no god.'[41] On the Sabbath preceding Šavuʿot, it became the custom to read the names of the many martyrs. When later massacres occurred, more names were recorded in the communal *Memorbucher* and then added to the public recitation.[42] R. Abraham Klausner (d. 1407/08) and his disciples recorded that Rhineland Jews would recite the prayer *ʾAv ha-Raḥamim* ('Father of Compassion') on the Sabbath before Šavuʿot. The prayer laments 'the holy congregations who gave their lives for the sanctification of the Name' and beseeches God to exact retribution. R. Jacob Moellin (d.1427) recorded that the Jews of Mainz in the early fifteenth century were still fasting on the third of Sivan (three days before Šavuʿot) to commemorate the destruction of the city's Jewish community on that day in 1096.[43]

No wonder then that thirteenth-century Jews needed pharmacological assistance to fulfil the biblical mandate to rejoice on Šavuʿot.[44]

Disappearance of the Custom

But the use of saffron with maṣṣah on Šavuʿot soon disappeared. Where did this custom go?

Shortly after R. Aaron composed *Kol Bo*, a question regarding the permissibility of saffron was addressed to the greatest Jewish law respondent of the thirteenth century,

R. Solomon ibn Adret (known as Rašba, d.1309/10) in Barcelona. The inquirer had heard that Rašba prohibited the use of saffron sold by gentile merchants and wished to confirm whether this was the case, inasmuch as his own teachers in the north had permitted it. Rašba confirmed the rumour. Though he noted that 'immeasurable' fields of saffron crocuses were being planted locally in Catalonia in his day, merchants commonly falsified saffron by dyeing additives with non-kosher wine, mixing it into the portion sold to increase its weight. Merchants also used strands of dried ox meat to mimic the red saffron threads and add bulk to their product.[45]

Disquietude over the permissibility of saffron was more acute on Passover when mixtures of flour and water, other than maṣṣah, were prohibited for fear that the mixture would become impermissibly leavened (ḥameṣ). Flour dyed red through the addition of wine or similar reddish coloured liquids was also added to the saffron being sold.[46] Ancient authorities like Pliny, Dioscorides, and Isidore of Seville were also worried about saffron adulteration, given the product's expense, so this was not a uniquely Jewish problem.[47] Therefore, Rašba personally would not use saffron, except for that purchased as the crocus stamens were being harvested. Nor was he alone – he asserted that 'the pious ones' of Barcelona acted similarly.[48]

Though Rašba's inquirer was from the Northern French school, whose authorities often turned to their own decisors, the recent deaths of the preeminent Jewish scholars of that region had left a vacuum of local authoritative voices.[49]

While Rašba's colleague, R. Asher b. Yeḥi'el, who had emigrated from the Rhineland to Toledo, seems to have not shared his concerns over saffron adulteration, the Austrian Jewish scholars farther east did.[50] They even pointed out an additional issue: the use of sourdough (prohibited on Passover) to revive the colour of saffron that had dulled during miles of transport. Interestingly, they noted that Rhenish Jews – like R. Asher b. Yeḥi'el – were lenient on the matter.[51] But the strict view held by the majority following Rašba later predominated and was included in the sixteenth-century codes that became authoritative even for Rhineland Jewry.[52] In essence, strict legalistic concerns over non-kosher meat, unleavened bread on Passover, and prohibited wine overrode a local folkway.

These rulings made continued observance of the custom of eating maṣṣah with saffron on Šavu'ot near-impossible. Rašba's rulings were controlling for many of the Jews of Provence.[53] Saffron was typically harvested in the autumn; even if the spice was permitted year-round with the exception of Passover this would prove to be a problem. If Jews had to dispose of their stores of the year's spice prior to Passover in the spring, they would be unlikely to have any saffron left over for use on Šavu'ot. And so the living custom faded away, leaving only faint echoes in these medieval texts.

Notes

1   Donovan Leitch, 'Mellow Yellow' (Epic, BN26239, 1967).
2   On this culinary-medical link, see Ken Albala, *Eating Right in the Renaissance* (Berkeley: University of California Press, 2002), pp. 243-45.
3   Transliteration of Hebrew and Arabic (with some exceptions) follows the style guide from *Aleph: Historical Studies in Science and Judaism.*

4   Provence refers here to the territories on both sides of the Rhône. (Technically, the Mediterranean coast to the west of the Rhône was Septimania, later Languedoc, while east of the Rhône was Provence *sensu strictu*.) See Isadore Twersky, 'Aspects of the Social and Cultural History of Provençal Jewry,' *Journal of World History*, 11.1 (January 1968), 10 (n. 1).

5   See e.g. Simcha Fishbane, 'In the Absence of Ritual: Customs of the Holiday of Shavuot,' in *The Impact of Culture and Cultures Upon Jewish Customs and Rituals: Collected Essays* (Brighton: Academic Studies Press, 2016), pp. 126-61.

6   *Kol Bo*, Vol. III, ed. by David Abraham (Jerusalem: Feldheim, 1992), cols. 218-19, §52.

7   See e.g. Gedaliah Oberlander, "אכילת מאכלי חלב בחג השבועות", *Or Yisrael*, 32[8.4] (Sivan, 2003), 104-20; David Golinkin, 'Why Do Jews Eat Milk and Dairy Products on Shavuot?' *Responsa in a Moment*, 10.7 (June 2016); Eliezer Brodt, 'The Mysteries of Milchigs,' *Ami Magazine* (12 May 2013), 89-93. For Šavu'ot baked goods: Daniel Sperber, *Minhage Yisra'el*, Vol. III (Jerusalem: Mossad ha-Rav Kook, 1994), p. 139 (n. 69); Antonius Margaritha, *Der gantz Jüdisch glaub* (Augsburg: Heynrich Steyer, 1530) (no pagination; s.v. 'Pfingsten'); Johann Buxtorf, *Jüden Schul* (Basel: Sebastian Henricpetri, 1603), p. 450 (ch. 15); R. Joseph Juspa Han, *Yosef 'Omeṣ* (Frankfurt-am-Main, 1723), p. 106b, §854.

8   Qalonymos b. Qalonymos of Arles (1286-c.1328) notes those who gathered honey and milk and who baked uniquely shaped breads in advance of Šavu'ot; Jacob b. Abba Mari Anatoli (thirteenth century) describes the custom to eat dishes with honey and milk. See Qalonymos b. Qalonymos of Arles, *'Even Boḥan,* ed. by A.M. Habermann (Tel Aviv: Machbaroth Lesifruth, 1956), p. 34 (describing 'ladder'-shaped breads, different-sounding from those in *Kol Bo*); Jacob b. Abba Mari Anatoli, *Malmad Hatalmidim* (Lyck: M'kize Nirdamim, 1866), p. 121b.

9   He was originally from Narbonne (Judah D. Galinsky, 'Of Exile and Halakhah: Fourteenth-Century Spanish Halakhic Literature and the French Exiles Aaron ha-Kohen and Jeruham b. Meshulam,' *Jewish History* 22.1-2 (2008), 81-96). 'Rabbi' is abbreviated R. throughout.

10 Šelomoh Z. Havlin, "לעניין הספרים 'כלבו' ו'ארחות חיים': מחקר לזיהוי מחבר ספרים אלו, כתבי היד שלהם ומהדורותיהם", in *Orḥot Ḥayyim: Inyane Šabbat*, ed. by S.Y. Klein and Y Klein (Merkaz Šapira': 'Or 'Eṣyon, 1996), pp. 41-68.

11 R. Aaron ha-Kohen of Lunel, *Orḥot Ḥayyim* (Florence, 1750), p. 78a.

12 In commentaries on the Passover laws, contemporary Provençal scholars, R. Manoaḥ of Narbonne (thirteenth to fourteenth century) and R. Menaḥem Me'iri of Perpignan (1249-1316) mention seasoning Passover maṣṣah with saffron after it had been baked (following R. Abraham b. David of Posquières (d.1198)), but the prescribed (and not incidental) use of saffron with maṣṣah that R. Aaron details was clearly on Šavu'ot alone. See R. Menaḥem Me'iri, *Bet ha-Beḥirah: Pesaḥim*, ed. by Joseph Klein (Jerusalem, 1967), p. 115; R. Manoaḥ of Narbonne, *Sefer ha-Menuḥah* (Jerusalem: Pardes, 1957), p. 15, §20.

13 Ya'aqov Šemu'el Spiegel, "הקדמת החיבור וסדר ליל פסח לר' שמואל ב"ר משולם ירונדי בעל אהל מועד", *Moriah*, 21.10-12 (1998), 6-15.

14 NLI film no. F53333. Printed (with minor variations) as R. Samuel b. Mešullam of Gerona, *'Ohel Mo'ed* (Jerusalem, 1886), p. 107a.

15 See e.g. R. Yeḥi'el Miḳl Epstein, *Aruḵ ha-Šulḥan* O.Ḥ. 494:5; Isaac b. Mordecai Lipiṣ, *Seder Maṭ'amim* (Warsaw, 1890?), p. 34b, §160; John Cooper, *Eat and Be Satisfied* (Northvale, NJ: Jason Aronson, 1993), p. 195. This was facilitated by a pseudocorrection in the reprinting of an eighteenth-century work through which many scholars encountered the *Kol Bo*'s text (*Ḥoq Ya'aqov* of R. Jacob Reisher).

16 For ḥallah dough mixed with saffron, see e.g. R. Israel Isserlein, *Terumat ha-Dešen*, no. 189; R. Moses Isserles, *Darḵe Mošeh Y.D.* (Sulzbach, 1692), p. 96d (326:2); R. Moses Isserles, *Šulḥan 'Aruḵ Y.D.* 326:1; Edward Fram, *My Dear Daughter* (Cincinnati: HUC Press, 2007), pp. 276-77, §112. Only in a 'thrice-blessed wonderland' would people eat ḥallah with saffron on a weekday (Isaac Dov Berkowitz, 'The Last of Them', in *Yiddish Tales*, trans. by Helena Frank (Philadelphia: JPS, 1912), p. 567.)

17 A few examples include I.L. Peretz, *The Book of Fire: Stories*, trans. by Joseph Leftwich (New York: Yoseloff, 1960), p. 431; idem, "המגגנ", in: *Sefer ha-Mo'adim*, ed. by Yom Tov Levinsky, Vol. 6 (Tel Aviv, 1959), p. 257; Sholem Aleichem, *Tevye's Daughters*, trans. by Frances Butwin (New York: Crown, 1949), p. 113; idem, בחול ובמועד, trans. by Aryeh Aharoni (Tel Aviv: Sifriyat Po'alim, 1997), p. 395; Isaac Bashevis

Singer, *The Family Moskat: A Novel,* trans. by A.H. Gross (New York: Farrar, Straus, Giroux, 2007), p. 191; idem, *The Manor and The Estate,* trans. by Joseph Singer & others (Madison, WI: University of Wisconsin Press | Terrace Books, 2004), p. 120; Isaac Bashevis Singer, *Meshugah,* trans. by the author & Nili Wachtel (New York: Farrar, Straus, Giroux, 1994), p. 164.

18 Anonymous, *Ḥemdat Yamim,* Vol. 3 (Constantinople, 1735, reprint Jerusalem: Maqor, 1970), p. 60d; R. Ḥayyim Joseph David 'Azulai (1724-1806), *Lev David* (Livorno, 1789), pp. 76a-b.

19 Baraita in bKer 6a. Saffron does not appear on the brief list of incense ingredients at Exod 30:34 (or Sirach 24:15).

20 Particularly within the sapiential books (e.g. Ps 4:8, 19:9, 105:3; Prov 15:13, 15:30, 17:22, 23:15).

21 For a list of these, see Mauro Zonta, 'Medieval Hebrew Translations of Philosophical and Scientific Texts: A Chronological Table', in *Science in Medieval Jewish Cultures,* ed. by Gad Freudenthal (Cambridge: Cambridge University Press, 2011), pp. 17-73.

22 Gerrit Bos, *Novel Medical and General Hebrew Terminology from the 13th Century: Volume 4* (Leiden: Brill, 2018), p. 51, s.v. "התקשרות", quoting Hebrew translations of Avicenna's book on cardiac remedies; Maimonides, *On the Elucidation of Some Symptoms and the Response to Them...,* trans. by Gerrit Bos (Leiden: Brill, 2019), pp. 61-62, 99, ll. 14-15; p. 62, n. 122. See also Gerrit Bos, *A Concise Dictionary of Novel Medical and General Hebrew Terminology from the Middle Ages* (Leiden: Brill, 2019).

23 Pliny, *Natural History* 21:17 and 21:81. Dioscorides, *De materia medica,* trans. by Lily Y. Beck (Hildesheim: Georg Olms-Weidmann, 2017), p. 23 (1:26). Saffron does not appear in Galen's *De alimentorum facultatibus.*

24 Their teachings had significant influence on the early Arabic medical works; see Oliver Kahl, *The Sanskrit, Syriac and Persian Sources in the Comprehensive Book of Rhazes* (Leiden: Brill, 2015), pp. 7-28. There are scant references to saffron in *Caraka-Saṃhitā, Súsruta-Saṃhitā,* and *Bhela-Saṃhitā.*

25 Martin Levey, 'Ibn Māsawaih and His Treatise on Simple Aromatic Substances: Studies in the History of Arabic Pharmacology I', *Journal of the History of Medicine and Allied Sciences,* 16.4 (October 1961), 403. A cardiac effect is also absent in the passage from Ibn Māsāwayh in Pseudo-Serapion, De simplicibus medicinis (Strasbourg: Georgius Ulricher, 1531), p. 120.

26 *Omnia opera Ysaac* (Lyons: Bartholomeus Trot, 1515), Part I, fol. 130c.

27 *Continens Rasis,* Vol. II | *Seconda pars continentis Rasis,* ed. by Hieronymus Surianus (Venice: Bernardus Benalius, 1509), 37:1:241, fol. XXIvb-XXIIra – '*Dixit Costa: crocus letificat cor...*'; also qtd. in Pseudo-Serapion, p. 120.

28 Pseudo-Serapion, p. 119, s.v. 'Constan.)'; see also Matthaeus Sylvaticus (d.ca.1342, Salerno), *Pandectae medicinae* (Lyons: Theobaldus Paganus, 1541), fol. 107vb. Latin: Avicenna, *Liber Canonis...* (Basel: Ioannes Heruagios, 1556), p. 206 (2:2:129). English: Avicenna, *Al-Qānūn fī'l-Tibb,* Book II, trans. by Maulana A.H. Farooqi, trans. (New Delhi: Jamia Hamdard, 1998), pp. 241-42.

29 Patricia W. Cummins, 'A Salernitan Regimen of Health,' *Allegorica,* 1.2 (Fall 1976), 92-93, ll. 223-24. Some had different versions of the text.

30 On saffron in the Middle Ages, see Luise Bardenhewer, *Der Safranhandel im Mittelalter* (Bonn: P. Hauptmann, 1914) and Maria Tscholakowa, '*Zur Geschichte der medizinischen Verwendung des Safran* (crocus sativus),' in *Kyklos: Jahrbuch des Instituts für Geschichte der Medizin an der Universität Leipzig,* 2 (1929), 179-90.

31 *Orḥot Ḥayyim,* Part II, ed. by M. Schlesinger (Berlin: M'kize Nirdamim, 1902), pp. 638-55.

32 Cyrus Adler and M. Seligsohn, 'Kol Bo,' *Jewish Encyclopedia,* Vol. VII (New York: Funk and Wagnalls, 1916), pp. 538-39.

33 *Perušim u-Pesaqim le-R. Avigdor Ṣarfati,* ed. by I. Hershkovitz (Jerusalem: Maḵon Harere Qedem, 1996), p. 478, §§595-98. Ephraim Kanarfogel, *The Intellectual History and Rabbinic Culture of Medieval Ashkenaz* (Detroit: Wayne State University Press, 2013), pp. 360-61, 472-77.

34 Simcha Emanuel, ed., *Rabbi Elazar Vormsensis / Oratio ad Pascam* (Jerusalem: Mekize Nirdamim, 2006), pp. 39-40, 110.

35 *Sefer ha-Roqe'ah ha-Gadol* (Jerusalem, 1960), p. 164, §296, trans. in Ivan G. Marcus, *Rituals of Childhood: Jewish Acculturation in Medieval Europe* (New Haven: Yale University Press, 1996), p. 26. Gedaliah Oberlander, p. 106 (n. 17).

36 *Maḥzor Vitry,* ed. by S. Hurwitz, Vol. II (Nürnberg: I. Bulka, 1923), pp. 628-29, §508.

37 Gedaliah Oberlander, pp. 106-07; compare M.M. Honig, in Daniel Sperber, *Minhage Yisra'el,* Vol. VII

(Jerusalem: Mossad ha-Rav Kook, 2003), p. 398.

38 Ivan G. Marcus, p. 33.

39 Shlomo Eidelberg, *The Jews and the Crusaders: The Hebrew Chronicles of the First and Second Crusades* (Hoboken: Ktav, 1996), p. 23, 28-29, 49. For the Hebrew texts, see A.M. Habermann, ed., *Sefer Gezerot Aškenaz ve-Ṣarfat* (Jerusalem: Taršiš, 1946) and Eva Haverkamp, ed., *Hebräische Berichte über die Judenverfolgungen während des Ersten Kreuzzugs* (Hannover: Hahnsche Buchhandlung, 2005).

40 Eidelberg, p. 85

41 Eidelberg, p. 44.

42 See Siegmund Salfeld, *Das Martyrologium des Nürnberger Memorbuches* (Berlin: Leonhard Simion, 1898), pp. 5-10.

43 R. Abraham Klausner, *Sefer ha-Minhagim*, ed. by S. Spitzer (Jerusalem, 2006), p. 120, §131; R. Jacob Moellin, *Sefer Maharil: Minhagim*, ed. by S. Spitzer (Jerusalem, 1989), p. 159, 243-44; R. Zalman Yent, *Minhagim / Seder Treviso*, appended to R. Isaac Tyrnau, *Seder ha-Minhagim*, ed. by S. Spitzer (Jerusalem, 2000), p. 171; Israel Elfenbein, ed., *Sefer Minhagim de-Be Maharam…* (New York, 1938), p. 29; *Maḥzor mi-Kol ha-Šanah Šalem ke-Minhag ha-'Aškenazim* (Tobias Foa: Sabbioneta, 1557), p. 128b; R. Solomon b. Judah Lebuš of Lublin (d.1591), *Pisqe u-Še'elot u-Teshuvot Mahareš mi-Lublin*, ed. by Isaac Herskovitz (Brooklyn: n.p., 1988), p. 3, Pisqe Mahareš mi-Lublin §11.

44 Jews may not have been alone in utilizing the stimulant properties of saffron in a liturgical context. Volker Schier, noting astonishingly large amounts of saffron donated to a South German Birgittine monastery in the sixteenth century, speculates that nuns used saffron as a stimulant to enable long days of singing during Lent (see Schier, 'The Cantus Sororum: Nuns Singing for their Supper, Singing for Saffron, Singing for Salvation', in *Papers Read at the 12th Meeting of the IMS Study Group Cantus Planus, Lillafüred/Hungary 2004, Aug. 23-28*, ed. by László Dobszay (Budapest, 2006), pp. 857-70; Schier, 'Probing the Mystery of the Use of Saffron in Medieval Nunneries', *The Senses and Society* 5 (2010), 57-72; Corine Schleif and Schier, *Katerina's Windows: Donation and Devotion, Art and Music, as Heard and Seen in the Writings of a Birgittine Nun* (Pennsylvania University Press, 2009)).

45 Wine produced by gentiles was prohibited. Without meat having undergone proper preparation per kosher laws these dried threads would be prohibited.

46 The prohibition of eating ḥameṣ on Passover was far more severe than consumption of Gentile wine or improperly prepared meat. The former was biblical in origin; its penalty was death by Divine decree. For reviews of saffron adulteration in Hebrew sources, see Zohar Amar, *Book of Incense* (Ramat Gan: Bar Ilan University, 2002), pp. 112-17; Abraham Ofir Shemesh, 'Food Deceptions and Falsifications in the Ancient Food Industry and Their Legal Ramifications according to Rabbinical Literature,' *JLAS* XVIII (2008), 244-62.

47 Dioscorides; Pliny; *The Etymologies of Isidore of Seville*, trans. by S.A. Barney and others (Cambridge: Cambridge University Press, 2006), p. 350 (XVII.9.5).

48 R. Solomon ibn Adret, *Responsa* 1:133 and 4:88.

49 R. Me'ir of Rothenberg was imprisoned in 1286 and died in 1293, followed by the martyrdom of his pupil R. Mordecai b. Hillel in the Rindfleisch pogroms in 1293. (R. Me'ir of Rothenberg had also corresponded with Rašba.) R. Pereṣ of Corbeil too had recently passed, prompting his younger brother, R. Joseph b. Elijah, to address this query about saffron to Rašba.

50 R. Asher b. Yeḥi'el, *Responsa* 24:6.

51 R. Ḥayyim b. Isaac 'Or Zarua', *Pisqe Halakah shel R. Ḥayyim 'Or Zarua'*, ed. by I.S. Lange (Jerusalem, 1972), p. 80; R. Šalom of Neustadt, *Hilkot u-Minhage Mahareš*, ed. by S. Spitzer (Jerusalem, 1997), p. 18, §31; pp. 25-26, §46; R. Jacob Moellin, p. 133; R. Isaac Tyrnau, p. 43; R. Joseph b. Moses, *Leqet Yošer*, Vol. I: O.Ḥ., ed. by Jacob Freimann (Berlin, 1903), p. 75.

52 This view of R. Šalom of Neustadt was cited in R. Moses Isserles, *Šulḥan 'Aruk O.Ḥ.* 467:8; *Maḥzor mi-Kol ha-Šanah Šalem ke-Minhag ha-'Aškenazim* (Tobias Foa: Sabbioneta, 1557), p. 74a. See also R. Elijah b. Moses de Vidas (sixteenth century) *Toṣa'ot Ḥayyim* (Amsterdam: Immanuel Benveniste, 1650), p. 24b, §48.

53 But see Pinchas Roth, 'Regional Boundaries and Medieval Halakhah: Rabbinic Responsa from Catalonia to Southern France in the Thirteenth and Fourteenth Centuries', *JQR* 105.1 (Winter, 2015), 72-98.

Stone Curry: *Parmotrema perlatum* as a Secret Spice in Indian Food

Priya Mani

A lichen found its way into a curry, quietly.

A very curious spice, *Parmotrema perlatum*, called stone-flower, is an immensely popular 'secret spice' in spice blends or masalas throughout the Indian subcontinent (Figure 1). It is a lichenized fungus of the Parmeliod family (Parmeliaceae). Lichens, by their very classification on the cusp of the plant and animal kingdoms, are fascinating.[1] The stone-flower has broad, curled foliage, typical of foliose lichens; grows in large round mats with a wrinkled surface; and are light grey-green on the upper surface and dark, purplish-black on the underside.

It is known as stone-flower in English. Other vernacular names include *shipal, shaileya, shilapushpa* (Sanskrit), *kalpasi* (Tamil), *pathar phool* (Hindi), *dagad phool* (Marathi), *chaileyam* (Malayalam), *Shaiba, ushnea* (Arabic). All mean flowers that grow on stone. But as its name and many vernacular forms suggest, stone-flower may not grow only on stones. Nayaka, Upreti, and Khare assert that it grows in the Nilgiris and Palani Hills in India.[2] *P. perlatum* prefers well-lit, neutral to somewhat acid-barked

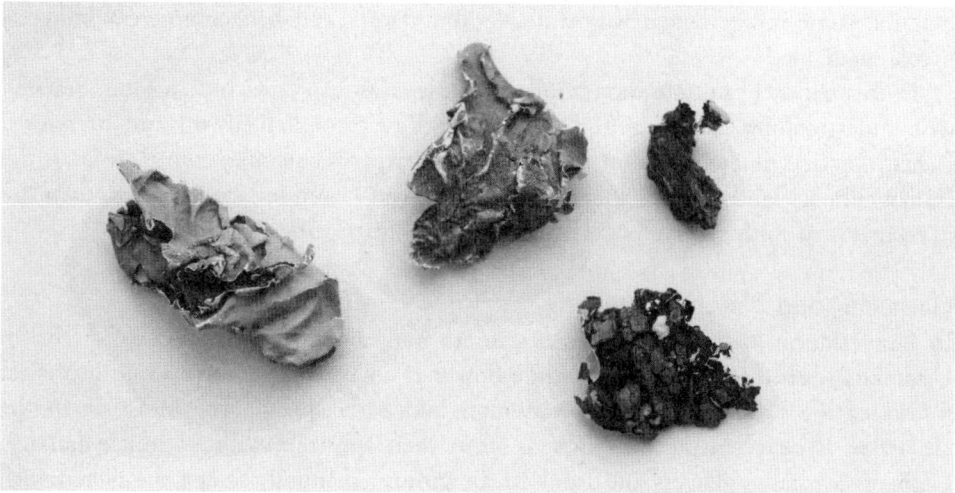

Figure 1. Stone-flower. Botanical name: Parmotrema perlatum; *binomial name:* Parmotrema chinense.

239

broad-leaved trees and sometimes siliceous rocks and coastal rocks where illumination is moderate to good.[3] Its presence indicates open, thinned-out forests with more sunlight.[4] Goyal, Verma, and Sharma suggest that the vernacular forms for stone-flower like *pathar phool, kalpasi, chaileyam*, and *shilapushpa* could refer to its traditional therapeutic action on *ashmari* (urinary stone) in the Ayurvedic system of Indian medicine.[5]

A literary review of ancient uses of stone-flower traces back to the *Atharva Veda* (1500 BC), *Susruta Samhita* (1000 BC), and several *Nighantu* (AD 1100-1800); the identification of Sanskrit names refers to several species of Parmelioid lichens such as *P. cirrhata* and *P. perforata, P. sulcata.*[6] They are substances of great medical interest across other practices of natural medicines like Unani and Siddha and appear under the vernacular name *Charilla* (syn. *Chadillo, chhadila*) for various diseases and disorders.

The Tamils have long known the stone-flower for its therapeutic use. The *Supplement to the Pharmacopoeia of the King and Queen's College of Physicians* (1856) notes:

> Among the indigenous diuretics, none, perhaps, deserves more attention than the *Kalpasi* of the Tamuls, which Ainslie has identified with the *Lichen rotundus* of Rotter?. This lichen grows plentifully on the rocks in some parts of Southern India, and is met with in a dry state in most of the medicine bazaars of the Peninsula […] . [It has] alleged diuretic properties for which it is in high repute among the natives […].[7]

In his *Materia Indica* (1826), Ainslie notes that '*Kull pashie* (Tam.) *Puttir ka pool* (Hind.) […] *Ratipanchi* (Tel.) […] possess a peculiar cooling quality' and is used to 'prepare […] a liniment for the head.'[8] Ainslie, however, seems to have recorded the lichen name erroneously: his description and use match the general knowledge on stone-flower. The *Travancore Gazette* lists it as one of the herbs collected for sale corroborating the fact that the stone-flower lichen was available abundantly and had commercial value as herbal medicine.[9]

In this paper, I examine the use of stone-flower as a spice in Indian food. Starting with understanding, gathering, and material handling through fieldwork and interviews, I then describe its contribution to flavour with experiments and eventually map the Indian culinary landscape for the use of stone-flower – from infusion styles to their use in recipes – to study its practice with prospects for the future.

Gathering and Material Handling

In conversation with masala manufacturers and wholesale suppliers of herbs in Uttarakhand, India, I learnt that stone-flower is collected from temperate broadleaf forests of the Himalayas mainly in winter and early spring. The moisture in the air makes it easier to pick the lichens from their substrate without much damage. Gatherers, usually villagers and local ethnic groups, manually scrape the lichen with a sharp knife-like tool from the lower branches of oak trees, trunks, and fallen limbs. Many factors control the prices such as availability, weather, labour, and demand,

and cooperatives help regulate them. Women sort and clean the lichens by hand. They visually inspect them before grading, then separate them using vibrators and air-dry the lichen. Stone-flower picked at higher altitudes have larger foliage and a higher percentage of aromatic compounds and are graded as higher quality with more commercial value. Workers seal the lichens in ten-kilogram (about twenty-two pounds) bags in dry rooms and sell them to large masala manufacturers. The highest grades are exported to the Middle East. In recent years, India has imported stone-flower from Tanzania and Nigeria to meet the demands of the booming domestic herbal medicine industry. As of this writing, the imported product is of satisfactory quality at better prices, offering traders better margins.

Humans have consumed lichens mainly as sources of carbohydrates, although the complex carbohydrates in lichens are not easily broken down in the human digestive tract and have an acrid taste. Lichens are boiled in an alkaline medium like wood ash to remove acidic compounds before preparation and consumption. It is crucial to note the omission of this step in the case of stone-flower, presumably due to the small quantities consumed as a spice.

India has a vast domestic market for spice blends. Brands such as Everest Spices, MDH, Badshah, Catch, Rajesh, and Ramdev masalas dominate the northern states. Bedekar, K-Pra, and Hathi hold sway in the western region while regional favourites like Priya Masala in Andhra, MTR in Karnataka, and Aachi Masala in Tamil Nadu dominate the south. A systematic scan of their product packaging shows the use of stone-flower in many of their blends. The lack of a common vernacular name contributes to the many variations that appear, such as lichen flower, black stone-flower, and stone-flower lichen. They are fairly expensive, selling at INR 450 per kilogram (May 2020) at wholesale markets in Uttarakhand, and online retail shops sell it for twice as much. In Indian bazaars, lichens sold by the name *Charilla* typically consist of a mixture of two or more species of Usnea, Parmelia, Ramalina or Heterodermia and are widely used in the herbal products industry. For domestic use, stone-flower retails in small packages weighing 10-50 grams.

As a dry-store cupboard ingredient, the lichen is light and voluminous. The surface is sturdy but with a delicate, fabric-like quality that does not crumble between your fingers but tears easily. Some pieces may still have wood from the substrate which does not matter in a masala. In its dry state it has little smell, sometimes mildly warm and woody. Alone, it is flavourless, accompanied by a very dry mouthfeel making it almost impossible to eat by itself. It is stored dry in an airtight container and stays usable for a long time.

Understanding the Contribution to Flavour

I have taken stone-flower out of its known context in spice blends and experimented by using a series of conventional cooking techniques – soaking, steaming, and frying, in addition to dry grinding – to scrutinize its contribution to gustation, perception, and acceptance.

Soaked

A couple of pieces of stone-flower were soaked in filtered water and left undisturbed for twenty-four hours. The soaking liquid turned a clean pink. The lichen appeared hydrated and stable but had not changed in colour. Prolonged soaking had not weakened it, and they were still tough to eat.

The smell developed over the soaking period. At about two hours of soaking, the smell was ripe with a dewy petrichor. There was a mild spicy note, reminiscent of cold green tea. At twenty-four hours, the smell was very aromatic, dense, and woody. If one is familiar with Indian cuisine, it was not difficult at this point to feel a 'masala' like smell emanating from it.

At this point, the lichen was incredibly sweet to taste with a very bitter aftertaste. On repeated testing, the bitter aftertaste seems to remain. The soaking liquid mirrored this taste experience.

Steamed

The soaked pieces were then placed on a clean muslin and steamed at 100°C for ten minutes. Now the lichen pieces looked lighter and were moister and delicate to touch. They were not fragile and displayed structural stability. The aroma was denser, displaying a bright 'masala' note. It did not taste sweet at all, which was surprising and counterintuitive.

Frying

I fried the steamed pieces immediately in hot oil at 130°C. The pieces stopped bubbling in oil after about fifteen seconds and were removed and drained on a kitchen towel. The air was filled with a fantastic, heavy, aroma immediately likened to a 'masala' smell.

On tasting, the lichen had attained shattering crispiness with a very delicate, intriguing mouth feel. It did not taste sweet but fell short of my mind's expectations set off by its intense aroma. I dressed a few pieces with sea salt and tasted it. The salt instantly brought out its flavour. The lichen had a mushroom flavour, but one peculiarly its own for dense and sapidity of savour. It was rich and full of umami, tasting wonderful as a snack.

Wood remnants stuck to some of the lichen pieces do not fry well and taste undesirable.

The Recipes

Nandita Godbole, in her novel *Ten Thousand Tongues: Secrets of a Layered Kitchen* (2018), writes of the stone-flower and its appetizing flavour and the satiety it offered to a dish:

Bapu and Ratanlal settled to eat their dinner before the women. Ratanlal liked the spice, and though he was craving a meat preparation, it would be an inconvenient request at such a late hour. The misal was a stew of matki (Turkish beans or moth beans), cooked down with onions and spices. They could taste the heat of the black pepper, the nuttiness of dried coconut and the unmistakable dagad phool, a lichen popular in this region. The lichen gave the stew a meaty aroma. A pot of well-made misal stewing in a kitchen sent out invisible messengers, its aromas inviting strangers and friends alike as it floated out into the streets; it made even the most satiated diner hungry.[10]

The journey mapping the use of stone-flower as an ingredient in food has been fascinating. Two main patterns evolve:

1. The first is dietary choice – its use in the vegetarian kitchen and the non-vegetarian one.
2. The second is cultural – its use in Muslim kitchens across the Indian subcontinent and in regional kitchens influenced by the Marathas. The foods of Pakistan, Nawab-influenced Uttar Pradesh and Nizam-influenced Hyderabad, are examples of the former. The foods of Maharashtrian Brahmins – the communities of Saoji, Kolli, Pathare Prabhu, and Saurashtrians of Thanjavur and Chettiars of Karaikudi and Pudukkottai – are good examples of the latter.

Before I show the vast range of regional cuisines that use the stone-flower as a star ingredient, I must highlight that, in India, people have different expectations of food cooked by home cooks and professional cooks, though both are respected and unique. A divisive opinion extends to the kind of food cooked in these two contexts. Professional cooks are expected to know secret techniques and add secret spices to make a dish taste addictively good. Stone-flower is undoubtedly one of those secret spices seen more in the professional cook's spice box than in the home. The sheer diversity of the human palette has given every cuisine such innumerable variants that 'authenticity' is open to interpretation.

243

Stone-Flower in the Muslim Kitchen

The street cooks of Lucknow (*nanbhais*) cater to the family table, each specializing in a dish to produce products unparalleled in the home kitchen. From this culture comes the spice blend *potli* masala, or *sachet d'épices*. The stone-flower, known here as *pathar phool*, is a star secret ingredient. Its ambiguous form and lack of aroma protect its stealthy presence in the cooks' domain. Imtiaz Qureshi, the famous proponent of Mughlai cuisine and progenitor of the most prominent Mughlai chefs in India today, relates his early days as a cook in Lucknow when he would carry his secret spices in a small pouch and not disclose them to other cooks. Competition was stiff, and plagiarism was rife.[11]

In Lucknow, a variation of the *potli* masala, called *Lazzat-e-taam* or 'that which enhances the taste of food', is the signature masala used in Awadhi cuisine. Stone-flower is mixed with fragrant vetiver roots and rose petals and other typical Indian spices. A *pansari*, or traditional spice and herb dealer, would sell this masala. *Lazzat-e-taam* is typically added to ground meat and kneaded, then allowed to rest before being fashioned into kebabs and cooked. A *korma* such as *Awadhi ghost korma* or *Lucknawi korma* calls for the masala as a final addition to the preparation.

In Hyderabad, cooks use another variation of the *potli* masala. Unlike other commercially available spice blends, most of the spices in a *potli* masala are packed whole, accompanied by a small sachet of ground spices, the ingredients of which are unclear, thus keeping the secret intact: stone-flower is a crucial ingredient. The contents are boiled in water to make a strong decoction that is added to the gravy as it cooks. *Nihari*, a slow-cooked stew of meat and marrow; *shorba*, a meat-based broth; and *paya*, a variety of foods cooked with trotters, all call for *potli* masala. Blooming the stone-flower in water instead of hot oil is a distinct difference from the typical use of spices in the subcontinent.

The Muslim kitchens of Hyderabad prepare *bhojwar* masala with stone-flower, peanuts, and coconuts for stuffed dishes such as *baghara baingan*, stuffed aubergines; *mirchi ka salan*, stuffed banana peppers in a sauce; and *mahi gosht*, a meat-based curry. When used in a rub, stone-flower is sometimes mixed with chickpea flour to prevent it from turning the food black.

The use of stone-flower in *biryani*, an aromatic rice dish with meat, fish, or legumes, is ubiquitous in the Muslim kitchens of the subcontinent. Stone-flower is so important in imparting that defining, restaurant-style '*biryani*-flavour' that it is also called *biryani* flower. Some people only know it by that name!

The Muslims of Pakistan and Bangladesh use a variation of the *potli* masala too. But interestingly, it is not known or used among the Bohra Muslims or Moplahs of Kerala.

Stone-flower in the Maratha Kitchen

The *Rasachandrika* (1943) uses stone-flower, known here as *dagad phool*, in its recipe for *amti* masala, a traditional spice mix of the Saraswat Brahmin community. Various simmered lentil preparations like *varan* and its namesake dish *amti* use the *amti* masala. It is added to the cooked dal and simmered to finish.

Gravies like *patal bhaji*, a dish of colocasia leaves, peanuts, and split garbanzo, and *sukki bhaji*, made of radishes, use *amti* masala together with tamarind and boiled vegetables and is allowed to simmer for a few minutes before finishing. *Upkari*, a dry stir-fry often made with banana flowers, uses *amti* masala and powdered jaggery as a finish to the dish.[12]

Narayani Nayak (1953) recording the traditional cuisine of Maharashtrian Brahmins outlines the meticulous preparation of *goda* masala, a traditional mix with stone-flower in copious quantities. It contributes to the characteristic dark colour and deep, aromatic taste.[13]

Goda masala is often confused with *kala* masala, another regional variant, which is a topic of much debate. Nevertheless, stone-flower is unanimously considered both the star and the secret ingredient in both.

Koli masala of the Konkan fisherfolk uses stone-flower, slow-roasted in a warm clay pot. The stone-flower is cooled and ground into a powder with other spices. Cooks add the *koli* masala to hot oil after frying ginger, garlic, or onion pastes.

Soumitra Velkar from the Pathare Prabhu community gives us a recipe for their *sambhar* masala where stone-flower is an essential spice. Poppy seeds, dry chillies, bengal gram, and wheat are roasted in a little oil while all the other spices including stone-flower are just ground (neither roasted nor toasted). The word *sambhar*, he explains, comes from 'sam' meaning equal, referring to equal parts of grains, spices, and coriander-cumin seed, and 'bhar', meaning quantity, making the role of the stone-flower remarkably prominent here.[14] The Pathare Prabhu *sambhar* masala is different from the Tamilian masala of the same name.

Mutton Rassa, an essential dish of the Saoji community in Nagpur, who have set up eateries across the region, uses stone-flower, dry-roasted along with other spices, then ground into a fine paste using water, added to hot oil, and sauteed to release the aroma.

K-Pra, a wildly popular spice manufacturer in Pune, Maharashtra, lists stone-flower on their ingredients lists for many blends like *goda* masala, *kolhapuri* masala, *malvani* masala, and *misal* masala. Some of their more famous, pan-Indian dishes like *pav bhaji*, *chana* masala, and *garam* masala also include stone-flower.

The traditional masala from Goa, Xacuti, also calls for stone-flower in some versions.

Michael Swamy in *East Indian Kitchen* (2010) gives us a traditional recipe for *East Indian Bottle* masala with stone-flower supplying the paramount flavour. The masala is hand-pounded and includes buds of the ironwood tree and *Artemisia vulgaris,* typical of the Western Ghats.[15] The *East Indian Cookery Book* (1981) uses bottle masala in thirty-four of its recipes, including ones for much-loved dishes like duck *moile* and prawn *lonvas*.[16]

Yet the most popularized use of stone-flower is in Chettinad cuisine, known here as *kalpasi*. Here it is added, early in the cooking process after clove, cinnamon, star anise, and kapok buds have been bloomed in hot oil. Chicken, lamb, and seafood dishes popular among the Chettiars make use of the stone-flower. Talking to professional cooks, I understood that it is used sparingly due to the intensity it imparts. Some families may simply not enjoy this and hence instruct cooks not to include any.

The Chettiars have absorbed many ingredients, cooking styles, and flavours from Burma, Cambodia, and Malaysia, where they secured trade connections. Many Chettiars strongly believe they have borrowed the use of stone-flower from these cultures, like star anise from China, but I have not found any references to or evidence for this claim.

The NPCS Board of Food Technologies outlines recipes for commercial manufacturing of masalas. The stone-flower features in many recipes in substantial quantities.

- *Goda* masala calls for 500 grams (1.1 pounds) of stone-flower in all three variations of its 1000 kilograms (2204.6 pounds) blend with cloves, cinnamon, black pepper, and cassia buds, or 0.05%.
- *Shahi biryani* masala uses 2 kilograms (4.4 pounds) of stone-flower in its recipe for 1000 kilograms (2204.6 pounds), or 0.2%

- *Garam* masala, a ubiquitous spice blend uses copious quantities of stone-flower. A 1000 kilograms (2204.6 pounds) batch needs 30 kilograms (66.1 pounds) of stone-flower, or 3%.[17]

Infusing the stone-flower in the cooking liquid is also common in Saudi Arabia and Libya. The stone-flower, known as *shaiba* leaves, is infused in meat stews and casseroles like *Mofatah al dajaj, Albokary*, and *Saha wa Aifa*. In Libya, *shaiba* leaves are an important ingredient in *Tbeikhet 'Eid*, a stew of lamb and chickpeas, and in *Sharba*, a Libyan soup.

While the medicinal references of stone-flower are many, it has been difficult to isolate an instance in history when it found its way into cuisine. We depend on oral traditions, lore, and memory in the absence of cookbooks, making the story complicated. Over the last few decades, the use of stone-flower has become prevalent among cooks in the subcontinent as a secret additive to their masalas, increasing the lichen's demand.

Did the medicinal use of stone-flower among the Tamils inspire its culinary use in Chettinad? Could it have been possible that the Maratha rulers of Thanjavur learnt this and spread it through the Deccan? Or could it be the Marathas who foraged it in the Western Ghats and shared its culinary use with the Tamils? How is it that the stone-flower finds a ubiquitous use in the meat dishes of Muslim India – from Lucknow to Hyderabad and beyond to Pakistan and Bangladesh?

246   But I should refrain from the temptation to find a pattern, connect the dots, and present a monocentric story to you. The history of food is not always straightforward.

Elsewhere in the Indian subcontinent, there is a more diverse use of lichen in food. The Limbu and Rai communities of Nepal consume at least three lichen species, *Everniastrum cirrhatum, E. nepalense*, and *Parmotrema cetratum*, as a delicacy and bulking agent rather than as a spice. Ethnobotanists regard the Limbu and Sherpa ethnic groups as the most lichenophilic in the region. *Sargyangma*, a kind of sausage made up of minced pork, lichens, pork's blood, eggs, fat, and spices, is their most popular dish.

How Can This Understanding Help Us in New, Different Uses for The Stone-Flower?

The stone-flower is used in salty, savoury dishes. In the Indian subcontinent, it is quite common to find spices like cardamom, clove, cinnamon, saffron, star anise, pepper, nutmeg, and garlic to play a role in both salty and sweet recipes. It seems thought-provoking that the stone-flower does not find itself used in a sweet rendition.

The inclusion of stone-flower at different stages of cooking has an imminent impact on its flavour. Cooks use stone-flower in specific flavour dispersion techniques in India:

1. Addition to hot oil, so the spice infuses its aromatic compounds into the oil, allowing for its fat-soluble flavour compounds to infuse rapidly in the oil, which then forms the base of a gravy (for example in Chettinad). As the rest

of the cooking process follows, the potent and pungent spicy notes become undertones. One smells the aroma first but tastes it last.

2. Sun-drying, toasting, and hand-pounding the stone-flower into an aromatic masala with longer shelf life. It is added to the cooking liquid, which on careful simmering keeps the aroma and flavour as top notes (for example, *goda, kala,* and *bhojwar* masalas).

3. Wet grinding of the roasted spice for immediate use or shorter shelf life (for example in Sao's Mutton Rassa). A braised approach to blooming the watery paste in oil intensifies the infusion.

4. Steeping the spice in the cooking liquid (stew, broth, curry pastes) in two ways – infusing it at an appropriate time in the cooking process offers profound control to achieve the desired flavour and making a decoction allowing for more developed, deeper flavours (for example, Hyderabadi *potli* masala.)

The role of stone-flower in a dish is not as a significant taste but rather a taste enhancer – bringing depth to the plethora of spices already in the mix. Many people refer to it as the 'meaty taste', which makes me wonder if it behaves the same way as umami in the dish? Lichens do synthesise amino acids, one of which is glutamate, and this could contribute to this flavour. Savoury combinations heighten the umami experience.

Chef Izzat Hussain suggests a stone-flower marinade for Kalpasi Tikka. It is an exciting and novel way to taste the stone-flower in the company of just a few spices and a simple cooking technique. Stone-flower mixed with equal quantities of black pepper, long pepper, and cloves with apple cider vinegar tenderizes the paneer for about 30 minutes before they are coated with roasted gram flour and chargrilled.[18] The lack of any fat on the paneer singed the spices, so I added a little oil to the marinade before repeating. The fat vastly improved the finish; the spices now roasted in oil and the resulting dish tasted novel and fantastic! The stone-flower aroma shone, cutting the piquancy of the peppers and pungency of the cloves. The aroma that fills the air reminded me of a garam masala.

In a different take from most recipes using stone-flower, I came across an interesting recipe for a dessert that used stone-flower. Chef Mukesh Rawat served Chettinad chocolate at the Hilton, Chennai where he infused chocolate with stone-flower. I tried recreating the dish, but the lack of a complete recipe left me clueless about the desired finish. To make a 100-gram bar of chocolate, I chose a single estate, Indian origin cocoa with 70% cocoa. I fried a few small pieces of stone-flower in cocoa butter and mixed it with the melted chocolate, poured into moulds, and set dotting some pieces with sea salt. On tasting, the chocolate tasted chiefly of itself: high-quality chocolate with bright, fruity notes. But the pieces specked with a grain of salt had a deep, robust, aromatic aftertaste that lingered long after eating the chocolate. The use of stone-flower in sweets and desserts is undoubtedly a new area for exploration.

Such new uses require continued availability, of course. In 1986, Moxham wrote that 'despite the large number of lichens processed, their abundance in the preferred collecting areas and reasonably rapid growth seem to indicate that conservation measures are not necessary at the moment, although transboundary air pollution may be a long-term threat'. However, by 1997 Shah documented the need for protection and conservation of lichens in India because of their intense exploitation, complaining that conservation has not received the desired attention. In 2010, Upreti and others declared stone-flower to be rare and threatened due to overexploitation. Like most lichens, they are sensitive to air pollution. The lichens used in India grow at rates from 5 mm/year to about 2 cm/year for the most rapidly growing leafy (foliose) lichens.[19]

The spice industry is global in its cultivation and consumption. Today, commercial farming of most spices is at scale. Lichens are naturally occurring and cannot be farmed. They are deeply affected by the environment, which makes them natural bioindicators of air pollution. With global air quality deteriorating and threatening to wipe out sensitive ecosystems around the world, the rapid depletion of lichen habitats is a cause for concern.

Putting the focus on the use of lichens as a spice emphasizes our relationship with spices from time immemorial. Our insatiable curiosity for the exotic leads to an unheeded approach to cultivation and commercial exploitation. If such blundering consumption is not checked in time, it will result in extinction.

Acknowledgements

I would like to thank Mr Murli Raman, who helped me with remote fieldwork in India by contacting various spice manufacturers and wholesale dealers; Mrs Annam Senthil Kumar of Annamcooks.blogspot.com and Mrs Kalyani Ilango, who advised me on foods of the Chettiars; and Dr Arjun Kumar Ravi, who helped me with analyzing gas chromatography of *P. perlata* for taste-enhancing umami compounds.

Notes

1 Angus Stevenson, *Oxford Dictionary of English* (Oxford University Press, 2010). Lichens are composite plants consisting of a fungus that contains photosynthetic algal cells. Their classification is based upon that of the fungal partner, and the algal partner is either green algae or cyanobacteria.

2 Sanjeeva Nayaka, Dalip Kumar Upreti, and Roshni Khare, 'Medicinal Lichens of India', in *Drugs from Plants*, ed. by P. Trivedi (Jaipur: Avishkar Publishers, 2010), pp. 24-25.

3 Udeni Jayalal and others, 'The Lichen Genus Parmotrema in South Korea', *Mycobiology*, 41.1 (2013), 25-36 (p. 31) <http://dx.doi.org/10.5941/MYCO.2013.41.1.25>

4 Dalip Kumar Upreti, Rajesh Bajpai, and Sandeep Nayaka, 'Lichenology: Current Research in India', *Plant Biology and Biotechnology*, 1 (2015), 272 <http://dx.doi.org/10.1007/978-81-322-2286-6_10>

5 Parveen Kumar Goyal, Santosh Verma, and Anil Kumar Sharma, 'Pharmacological and Phytochemical Aspects of Lichen *Parmelia Perlata*: A Review', *International Journal of Research in Ayurveda & Pharmacy*, 7 (2016), 102-07 (p.102) <http://dx.doi.org/10.7897/2277-4343.07138>

6 Kumar Kaushal and Dalip Kumar Upreti, '*Parmelia* spp. (lichens) in Ancient Medicinal Plant Lore of India', *Economic Botany*, 55 (2001), 458-59 <https://doi.org/10.1007/BF02866567>

7 Edward J. Waring, 'Notes on Some of the Indigenous Medical Plants of India', *Supplement to the Pharmacopoeia of the King and Queen's College of Physicians in Ireland, MDCCCL* (Dublin: Smith

Hodges, 1856), pp. 70-71.

8   Sir Whitelaw Ainslie, *Materia Indica; Or, Some Account of Those Articles which are Employed by the Hindoos and Other Eastern Nations, in Their Medicine, Arts, and Agriculture* (London: Longman, 1826), vol. 2, p. 170.

9   *The Travancore Government Gazette* (Trivandrum: Kingdom of Travancore, 1901-1925).

10 Nandita Godbole, *Ten Thousand Tongues: Secrets of a Layered Kitchen* (Roswell, GA: Turmeric Press, 2018) (Kindle edition).

11 Moeena Halim, 'Nawab of the Kebab', *India Today*, 29 February 2016 <https://www.indiatoday.in/magazine/food-drink/food/story/20160229-kakori-house-bandra-kebab-chef-imtiaz-qureshi-ishtiyaque-828497-2016-02-17> [accessed 20 May 2020].

12 *Rasachandrika: Saraswat Cookery Book* (Mumbai: Mangalore Trading Association, 1943), p.1.

13 Narayani Nayak, *Cookery Craft* (Mumbai: Mangalore Trading Association, 1953), p. 23.

14 Soumitra Velkar, *The Prawnickles of Velkar* <https://soumitravelkar.com/> [accessed 20 May 2020].

15 Michael Swamy, *The East Indian Kitchen* (Westland Limited, 2010); Beverley Ann D'Cruz, "How Mumbai's Masalawaalis Make a Single Spice from 30 Ingredients: Bottle Masala Is Impossible to Find in Stores', *Atlas Obscura*, 20 September 2019 <https://www.atlasobscura.com/articles/bottle-masala> [accessed 23 March 2021].

16 *East Indian Cookery Book* (Mumbai: The Bombay East Indian Association, 1981).

17 *Handbook on Manufacture of Indian Kitchen Spices (Masala Powder) with Formulations, Processes and Machinery Details*, 2nd edn, rev. by NPCS Board of Food Technologists (New Delhi: NIIR Project Consultancy Service, 2018), pp. 110, 111, 113, 129.

18 Chef Izzat Hussain, *Izzat ka Khana: Mughlai Cuisine Recipes* (Chennai: Notion Press, 2018), pp. 22, 44, 46 (Google ebook).

19 Sanjeeva Nayaka and Dalip Kumar Upreti, 'Status of Lichen diversity in Western Ghats, India', *Sahayadri E-news*, XVI (2005) <http://wgbis.ces.iisc.ernet.in/biodiversity/sahyadri_enews/newsletter/issue16/main_index.htm> [accessed 23 March 2021].

Cinnamomum Zeylanicum: Continuing Voyages of Discovery

Jennifer Moragoda

The Mother of All Cinnamon

> As a fruit is better in one country than in another, so the cinnamon of Ceylon is better than all others.
>
> – Garcia da Orta (1563)[1]

The praises of *Cinnamomum zeylanicum* have been sung by poets, and many strange tales have been devised to obscure its true geographical source. The Portuguese historian Barros (1552) referred to Sri Lanka as 'the mother of all cinnamon', while to the Dutch colonial administrators cinnamon was 'the bride around whom everyone danced'. As its long-familiar botanical name reflects, it has been synonymous with the island of Ceylon to which it is endemic. As of 2019, Sri Lanka accounted for 90% of the world's supply of *C. zeylanicum*, and it is acknowledged to produce the finest quality of cinnamon worldwide.

Though several attempts were made to introduce seedlings smuggled out from the island to other subtropical countries spanning the globe by Portuguese, Dutch, French, and British traders during the seventeenth to the eighteenth centuries, most ended in failure for reasons that will be touched upon later. Presently, Madagascar and the Seychelles are the only other countries which cultivate *C. zeylanicum* on a commercial scale.

The somewhat unfortunate botanical re-designation of *C. zeylanicum* as '*Cinnamomum verum*', though linguistically severing its exclusive association with the island, implicitly undergirds its standing as the 'true' cinnamon and alludes to the perplexing etymological spin-offs and confusion that continues to exist between the identities of Sri Lankan cinnamon and the 'cassia cinnamons', namely *C. burmanii*, *C. cassia*, and *C. loureiroi*.[2] In the spice trade, these species grown respectively in Indonesia, China, and Vietnam are commonly referred to as 'cassia', while *C. verum*/*C. zeylanicum* is referred to as cinnamon. The cassias share very similar characteristics, having an assertive spicy punch and aroma (due to their high content of cinnamaldehyde), a much more robust flavour with anise-like overtones, and sometimes a slightly bitter taste. This differs markedly from the more delicately nuanced bouquet and spicy, sweet, slightly citrusy taste of *C. zeylanicum*. Thus, cassia is largely used in beef or pork dishes in China and Vietnam. Inexpensive Indonesian cassia (*C. burmanii*) is the most commonly used cinnamon in the United States. It is famously utilized by commercial bakeries in cinnamon buns.

The aroma is piped out to tempt passersby; the intense cinnamic fragrance, like the top notes of perfume, abruptly reel them in. The subtle depths of true cinnamon are best enhanced by its pairing with sugar, on neutral canvases such as rice puddings, chocolates, egg custards, and biscuits. However, it works in more complex savoury settings too, for instance in Mexican *moles*, which brilliantly bring together the holy trinity of cinnamon, chocolate, and chillies. In fact Mexico is the largest consumer of Sri Lankan cinnamon worldwide. It might be said that cinnamon is to cassia what cognac is to brandy.

Regrettably, in many countries including the US no commercial protection or distinction is afforded to *C. zeylanicum*, and true cinnamon and cassia alike are permitted to be labelled under the generic catch-all 'cinnamon'. This further muddies the distinctions between the two for unwary buyers, particularly if the spice is sold in powdered form which renders visual identification difficult. This leads to some unfortunate confusion for consumers and competitive disadvantages for Sri Lankan exporters, particularly as the three cassias can be two to six times cheaper than *C. zeylanicum*. Fortunately, the steeper price of *C. zeylanicum* has not deterred demand. While Sri Lanka contributes only 10% of the world's total output, it is the highest grossing producer of all cinnamon and cassia worldwide.[3] Seen in this light, *C. zeylanicum* is indeed the gold standard of all 'cinnamons'.

An impressive number of historical references to both cinnamon and cassia – both helpful and confounding – exist through the ages. In the case of *C. zeylanicum*, an extensive coterie of administrators, cosmopolitan travellers, botanists, sociologists, agriculturalists, and research scientists have enlightened us on almost every aspect of this subject. However, the general public remains unaware of the differences between the two, and even among scholars cassia quills are sometimes mistakenly represented as Sri Lankan cinnamon. Within its brief confines, this paper sets out to acquaint the reader with *C. zeylanicum* and to present selected glimpses into its remarkable saga. The narrative will hop to various points in its history, exploring the somewhat misty beginnings of mother cinnamon, when knowledge of its true source was limited to a small number of intrepid traders from the ancient world; moving onto its middle period in the sixteenth through the mid-nineteenth centuries, cinnamon's heyday as the island's most valuable export that coincides with the 450 years of European occupation; and onto cinnamon's post-colonial present. These snapshots will hopefully give a brief idea of the long historical links and influence of cinnamon on Sri Lanka's fortunes and its strong association with the island.

The Importance of *Terroir*

C. zeylanicum, a perennial tropical evergreen, is a highly adaptable and hardy plant that can thrive under a wide range of tropical conditions. It flourishes in the wet zone on the southwestern quadrant of the island. From time immemorial, cinnamon was gathered from the trees that grew rampantly in the lush jungle. Then in 1770, over 100 years into their 150-year occupation, the Dutch VOC finally discovered it could be cultivated.

They believed the silver sands of the coastal lands around Negombo and Colombo produced the finest cinnamon. It was in these areas that they and later the British established the island's first large scale cinnamon plantations, though little cinnamon is grown there any longer. Cinnamon is now largely cultivated in areas south of Colombo in the Kalutara, Galle, and Matara districts, and more inland in the Ratnapura district. Recently, the latter district has been identified by some experts to have the most ideal conditions for producing 'Alba', the highest grade of cinnamon (Figure 1).

Beyond *terroir,* the quality of cinnamon is maximized through proper cultivation practices and ultimately depends on the experience and skills of the cinnamon peelers of the *Salagama* community, who have been exclusively tied to this traditional caste occupation for an unbroken period of over five hundred years. Before this, their original caste occupation was the weaving of fine cloth. One can speculate whether the manual dexterity required in weaving contributed to their skill as peelers.

Cinnamon and Cassia – Some Differences

Cinnamaldehyde, the major compound contained in both cinnamon and cassia barks, accounts for their similarity in taste. *C. zeylanicum* contains 65-80% cinnamaldehyde and 5-10% eugenol, along with at least 90 compounds and over 50 very minute unidentified ones. These aromatic flavouring compounds synergistically combine to produce the distinct overall organoleptic qualities associated with Sri Lankan cinnamon. In comparison, cassia bark can contain up to 95% cinnamic aldehyde, accounting for its assertively spicy bite.[4] Cinnamon's soft, thin bark can be readily broken off from the quill and is easily masticated, unlike cassia, which is hard and woody. Importantly, in recent years scientists have flagged warnings on some cassias for their significant coumarin content, which is potentially harmful to the liver. In contrast, true cinnamon contains only trace elements of coumarin.[5]

The physical differences between cinnamon and each of the cassias can be best appreciated by comparing their quills side-by-side. Cinnamon quills are characteristically a yellowish to a light reddish brown in colour and have a smooth texture. As only the inner portion of the cinnamon bark is used, the quills can be cut in thin layers, and

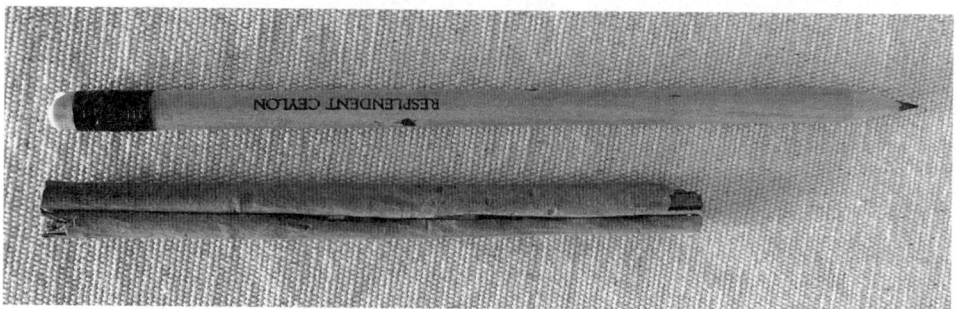

Figure 1. Alba grade C. zeylanicum *(author's photo).*

Figure 2. C. zeylanicum *quills (Dominic Sansoni/ThreeBlindMice).*

compactly rolled, and when pressed, the quill is somewhat pliable. The two inwardly curved edges of the quill meet to form the seam. A sectional view reveals that the quills are stuffed with several concentric layers of irregular pieces of cinnamon (Figure 2). In stark contrast, the cassia quills have a darker reddish-brown colour and consist of a single thick outer layer of rough, hard bark, formed into a hollow pipe with similarly inwardly curling edges (Figure 3).

253

Sri Lanka classifies its cinnamon into four main grades and several sub-grades based on the diameter of the quill, the extent of brownish blemishes (known as foxing), the quill length, and the number of 1050 mm length quills per 1 kilogramme. The finest grade of Sri Lankan cinnamon quills, Alba, is rolled almost as thin as a pencil, and in colour is an unblemished yellowish brown (Figure 1).[6]

While cassia is often sold in broken pieces and in powdered form, 95% of Sri Lankan cinnamon is sold in 3-6-inch lengths as in the quill form it best displays its unique qualities and can be easily distinguished from cassia. Adulteration and inauthenticity are easier to camouflage in powdered form and there are cases where cassia powder is flagrantly mislabelled as Sri Lankan cinnamon powder.

Harvesting and Processing Methods

In Sri Lanka cinnamon is harvested twice annually. The selected branches are cut at the base, bundled, and transported back to the peeling shed. There, usually within the next day, the rough outer bark is scraped off before the intricate process of extricating the inner bark: first rubbing the branch with a metal rod to help detach the inner bark before it is peeled off with a special curved knife (Figures 4 and 5). It is dried for several hours, during which the peel begins to naturally curl inwards along both long edges. Then, a suitable peeled strip is stuffed with layers of smaller off-cuts and broken pieces known as featherings and quillings as well as pieces of the outer bark known as chips (Figure 6), before another segment is joined to it and similarly filled. When enough segments have been added to form a length of 42", the quill is carefully shaped and rolled by hand, and trimmed if necessary. The experienced peeler knows how to maximize the quality potential of each individual shoot and is capable of peeling uniformly thin layers from the cinnamon branch, selecting appropriately sized pieces to fill the casing, and rolling the quills into a thin compact quill of uniform diameter. The skills of the peeler can make the difference between a lower- and higher-grade cinnamon (and a higher profit differential).

Cinnamon trees are first harvested after 1-2 years and so resemble a tall shrub, while cassia trees are typically raised for 10-20 years before they are first harvested. Thus their bark layer is significantly thicker, harder, and heavier than that of cinnamon. The peel does not require such care in removing and can be done in situ; the bark from both the main trunk and the branches are harvested. Due to its hard, thick peel, cassia quills are left hollow. Cinnamon's comparatively more elaborate and specialized peeling processes result in its high price tag, with labour costs comprising 60% of the total production cost in Sri Lanka, and reflects the critical importance of the cinnamon peelers. In fact, the limited success in cultivating *Cinnamomum zeylanicum* outside of Sri Lanka is largely due to the lack of peeling expertise. The *Salagama* community has managed to hone its skills over generations, their lives closely governed by the seasonal cycles of cinnamon.

254

Figure 3 (left). Cinnamomum cassia *quills from China: note the thicker peel and hollow casings (author's photo). Figure 4 (right). Peeling off the outer cinnamon bark (Senuri Gamage/Savour Route).*

The Cinnamon Isle – Geography is Destiny

Ceyllam [...] is a thing of such importance in India [...] on account of the advantages this island possesses: the first [...] the fine cinnamon [.... It lies] in the track of all the ships of Malaca and Bymgalla [Bengal] none being able to pass without being seen and known of in that part. [Y]our principal residence ought to be there, since it seems that there you are in the centre of everything.
  – Letter from King Manuel to D. Francisco de Almeida (1506)[7]

At the scent of this cinnamon, the kingdom loses its people.
  – Anonymous Portuguese poet[8]

Positioned at the crossroads of the ancient world, Sri Lanka, the birthplace of *C. zeylanicum*, had an importance that belied its size. Strategically situated at a convenient midway point where the two maritime silk routes converge, and on the doorstep of the vast emporium of India, this small island nation has been simultaneously blessed and cursed by its geography. Its natural riches further added to its allure as an entrepôt and territorial acquisition.

The perimeter of the island is ringed by a plethora of excellent and safe harbours approachable to vessels plying the Indian Ocean from all directions. In earlier times, it had the particular advantage of two seasonal monsoons, the first in the fall blowing northeasterly, and the second in the summer southwesterly, alternately propelling ships either towards its shores or back, depending on their direction of travel. The first mariners were perhaps blown off course mid-journey in storm-swept seas. As the island came into sight, they must have experienced relief and disbelief at the unexpected sighting of the

255

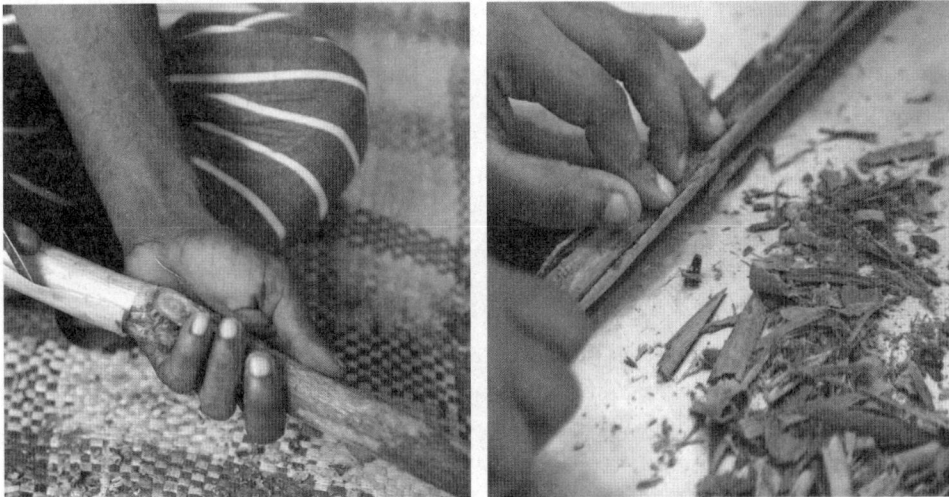

Figure 5 (left). Peeling the inner bark (Luxshmanan Nadaraja/WildLight). Figure 6 (right). Filling the quill with layers of featherings and chips (Senuri Gamage/Savour Route).

lush, verdant shores of this tropical paradise, with the spectacular Adam's Peak emerging from the distance as the island drew into view. It would have been serendipity, indeed.

Even before Ptolemy literally put Sri Lanka on the map, the island was attracting traders from neighbouring and more distant lands. Though the source of the world's best cinnamon would become an open secret to Arab, Indian, and Chinese traders, it was only after the arrival of the Portuguese to west India in 1498 that awareness began to register on European traders that Ceylon was the source of this most esteemed of all 'cinnamons' – which fetched exorbitant prices in markets back home. Beginning in the early sixteenth century, this realization culminated in the competitive scramble to wrest control of this highly prized spice and to seize possession of this island. Not content to peacefully compete in the island's pre-existing trade, which by then was dominated by Muslim and Arab traders, the Portuguese, Dutch, and British, each in turn, managed to wrest the monopoly over Sri Lanka's cinnamon and to control the busy trade route passing between its northwestern shores and the Malabar and Coromandel coasts of India with their valuable trade settlements. The period of European colonization (1505-1948) expanded the market and improved the cinnamon enterprise, but at great human cost. The existence of cinnamon could be said to have changed the orbit of Sri Lankan history.

The Cinnamon Puzzle

> The woods are their apothecaries [...] The cinnamon tree [...] grows wild in the Woods as other Trees, and by them no more esteemed.
>
> – Robert Knox (1681)[9]

Many contemporary observers have debated about when Sri Lankan cinnamon first reached the outside world and how the island was first identified as the source of true cinnamon. Some ask, if it reached the Red Sea ports as far back as biblical times, how could its source have been kept a secret for so long? Copious travellers' accounts of the early period, written by the most astute observers of the ancient world, extol the pearls, gems, ivory, tropical woods, and elephants of Ceylon, but they are reticent about cinnamon until around the tenth century. There is little mention of cinnamon, so widely valued beyond its shores, in local epigraphical or written sources of this highly literate island (with the distinction of possessing the oldest and longest spanning chronicle in the world, the *Mahavamsa*) nor did cinnamon become a trope in traditional or court poetry. Although many other indigenous trees are frequently depicted, it features neither in the richly pictorial Buddhist temple wall paintings of the southwestern coastal belt where cinnamon flourished, nor in the traditional Buddhist temple art of the Kandyan highlands, where the first wild cinnamon species are believed to have originated, although many other indigenous trees are frequently depicted. However, the term *kurundu* (Sinhala for *C. zeylanicum*) is prevalent in the names of villages and rivers in several regions of the island.[10]

Deliberate obfuscation, myriad discrete trade networks, widespread markets, a broad range of qualities and forms of both cinnamon and cassia, and geography may account for this confusion – that surprisingly exists to a certain degree still. Its absence in the local imagination may be more straightforward. The attitude of the rural islanders towards *kurundu* is easily understood in light of the well-stocked tropical paradise that surrounded them. Before nature's supremacy was overturned by the laws of supply and demand, *C. zeylanicum* proliferated like a weed in the lowland hills of the island. In addition, there were innumerable valuable wild medicinal herbs, trees, fruits, and plants available to the ecologically minded islanders. It is not unusual under these circumstances for inhabitants living at a distance from the ancient urban centres and principal ports located in the northern portion of the island not to have regarded *kurundu*, at least initially, as anything of special value. If they had, they might not have imagined its astronomical value in the wider world beyond their shores.

The Moroccan Berber traveller Ibn Battuta provided some additional clues. In 1344, Battuta arrived to the island in the northwest coastal town of Puttalam, which lies further north of Chilaw, the upper boundary of the natural habitat of *C. zeylanicum* that extends to Dondra, the southernmost point of the island. He also later journeyed to the southern port of Galle, among other places. In a brief passage he gives a somewhat fantastical account that bears some interesting elements. Battuta relates that 'the whole of [the island's] coasts are covered with cinnamon trees brought down by torrents and heaped up like hills on the shore', and he claims that traders from Malabar and Coromandel would take these away without payment but would later give presents of cloth and other items to the king.

The reference to cinnamon trees being brought down by torrents may have an element of truth. Numerous rivers cross cinnamon country, emptying into estuaries at several points along the western coastline, providing a convenient means of transporting cinnamon to the seashore. Furthermore, Battuta seems to describe an established barter trade arrangement with the outside world built on trust, and a shorthand explanation of the internal feudal traditions that obligate subjects to provide services (*rajakariya*) or to forgo a portion of the natural produce in return for land tenure. In addition, cloth was indeed one of the most valued items of trade from the Indian coast from the earliest times.[11] Was Battuta's description based on a second-hand account that may have gotten a bit lost in translation?

A Well-Kept Secret

> From Ceylon they bring a great deal of good cinnamon, which costs them very little money, while the sailors without any money collect wild and bad cinnamon in the woods.
>
> – Garcia da Orta (1563)[12]

As alluded to above, it seems highly possible that cinnamon initially found its way out of the country from one of the numerous remote harbours which dot the cinnamon coast.

Any of these points would have provided convenient access for obtaining cinnamon. In early times, it is likely that foreign traders would have loaded cinnamon from Sri Lanka's southern rather than its then bustling northern ports, continuing onwards to ports in Malabar, such as Cochin and Calicut and beyond. According to Ravindran, 'the Assyrians and Babylonians were in close contact with the Malabar Coast where they purchased spices including cinnamon, and their route that stretched to China may have included other ports on the way'.[13] Calicut was an important export point for Muslim and Chinese traders; Ceylon's cinnamon was widely available there.

The significant price differential between both places was an incentive for traders from the east or from Red Sea ports to collect cinnamon directly from the source, bypassing middlemen. By the thirteenth century, the locus of central political power on the island began to shift southwards, and by the fifteenth century Kotte, located conveniently amidst cinnamon country, became the island's principal kingdom, while westwards-oriented Colombo became the kingdom's chief port. The kingdom derived its greatest profits from cinnamon and Muslim traders controlled the trade until the Portuguese displaced them and gradually seized control of the cinnamon trade after their arrival in 1505. They located their main administrative headquarters there, as did their Dutch and British successors.

Northern and Eastern Ports

Moving back in time, the ancient Buddhist kingdom of Anuradhapura, which reigned from the third century BCE until the tenth century CE, was located inland in the north central dry zone of the island. Its main port, the bustling entrepôt of Mantota, lay off its northwestern coast. It and the several other harbours in the northern third of the island also had ancient connections with regional port cities along the nearby Malabar and Coromandel coasts.

While demand for cinnamon appears to have been greater in countries further to Sri Lanka's west, the prestige products most desired by the South Indian kingdoms were primarily Sri Lanka's elephants, famed for their singular intelligence, and the exquisite pearls fished off its northwestern coast in the Gulf of Mannar. The relatively low demand for Sri Lankan cinnamon within India, that continues to the present day, is natural given that cinnamon leaves (*tejpat*) and Indian cassia bark (*C. tamala*), along with a plethora of other indigenous spices, were used in cuisine and medicine since ancient times, as confirmed in Kautilya's *Arthashastra*. The Sanskrit terms used to designate both cassia and cinnamon were derived from the Persian word '*darcini*' or 'Chinese tree or bark' most likely indicating the early introduction of cassia into Northern India by Persian traders along the Central Asian caravan route.[14]

In the seventeenth and eighteenth centuries, the remote northeastern harbours of Trincomalee and Batticaloa served as the 'back door' into cinnamon country for many traders. It was here in 1602 that the Dutch sea captain Joris van Spilbergen made contact with the King of Kandy Vimala Dharmasuriya. The former was on a mission to seek permission to trade in cinnamon. Once the king's suspicions were allayed, he apologized for not having very much cinnamon on hand, confiding that he had laid waste to his supply and had forbidden any peeling of it to spite the Portuguese.[15] The Dutch eventually assisted the Kandyan king in ridding him of his enemy in 1656, but a mere twenty-one years later they had fallen out with the Kandyan king. The Frenchman L'Estra, who arrived off the coast of Batticaloa in 1677, recorded smelling the fumes of cinnamon being burned by the local inhabitants – this time to take revenge on the Dutch, who had forcibly occupied the island and were making great profits from its sale.[16] Indeed, the Dutch themselves regularly destroyed their own supplies of cinnamon to keep the supply down to maintain high prices. In 1744, Heydt noted that at times one-half to one-third of the cinnamon harvest was destroyed to keep prices artificially high.[17] The Dutch profit on cinnamon sold in one particular year was a stunning 2,278,451 guilders.[18] If we take the figures provided in the secret report sent by Dutch Governor Schreuder to Amsterdam in 1756 as a rough indication, an estimated 321,626 to 482,440 lbs might have been burnt in a single year. Heydt describes in great detail the annual spice bonfire he witnessed in Colombo that had the atmosphere of a 'church fair'. Unwanted spices were piled into a massive heap measuring about 100 feet long by 24 feet wide and 4 feet high that would burn continuously over the course of 2-3 days.[19]

The Cinnamon Peelers

> Superintendent of the cinnamon peelers: principal qualifications required: honesty, unselfishness, wisdom, and justice.
>
> – from the instructions of Governot Rijckloff van Goens, Sr. (1656-65)[20]

> Eight eggplants, but nine taxes.
>
> – Sinhalese proverb[21]

During the middle chapters in the history of Sri Lankan cinnamon, the *Chalia* community (in latter times better known as the *Salagama*), would come to play a central role in the cinnamon enterprise, a role which they still largely inhabit in modern times. Tradition states that their ancestors were invited by the Sinhalese ruler to settle in his kingdom to revive the art of fine weaving in the thirteenth century. However, in a later period they fell out of favour with the king, were banished to lowland villages, and allowed to stay on in the island only if they would take up the work of cinnamon harvesting and peeling. From this time onwards, cinnamon and the *Salagama* community were inextricably linked. The actual work of peeling was carried out by one section of the caste, comprising about one-third of its numbers. The higher-ranking members served as headmen of their villages, overseers, and soldiers. The work was dangerous and gruelling, particularly when the cinnamon was gathered from the jungles, and involved walking great distances, camping in disease-infested jungle for extended periods, and lugging heavy loads of cut branches to a central point for peeling.

Endemic disease, wild elephants, and attacks by the forces of the Kandyan king were some of the common perils they faced. The mortality rate was high.

During these twice-yearly excursions, drums had to be constantly beaten to drive away wild elephants and other animals in the teeming jungle, including snakes that hid beneath the undergrowth. The European colonizers were completely dependent on the labour, knowledge, skills, and management of the *Salagama* and did all they could to keep the community on good terms, since they were the most valuable cogs in their money-making machine. As a mark of their efforts to gain the allegiance of this group, the Dutch emulated Kandyan court customs, creating an annual ceremonial occasion known as the *paresse* to flatter and impress them. The entire contingent of the *Chalias* travelled by foot to Colombo where they assembled according to rank and village on the lawn terrace of the Governor's residence with its magnificent view of the sea to report to him and his council members before they began the season's work.[22] Beyond all the pomp and pageantry though, a grimmer reality prevailed. The cinnamon peelers led a meagre existence and were exploited by both foreign and local officials in this lucrative trade. The *Chalias* often rebelled against the many injustices and deprivations they suffered, sometimes allying themselves with the Kandyans when conditions became unbearable.

New Beginnings – Cinnamon Reclaimed

The British gained complete control of the island in 1815. Shortly thereafter, towards the mid-nineteenth century, profits on cinnamon for the first time began to tumble after the then British colonial government shortsightedly killed the industry through several misjudged policies. This gave a leg-up to cassia in western markets which until then had exclusively imported Sri Lankan cinnamon. When it lost its lustre, cinnamon was abandoned, and the British focussed their attention on coffee cultivation, the next big thing. Vast expanses of virgin forest in the southern hills and central mountains of the island were carved up. This cleared the way for the local Sinhalese elite, including members of the upper echelons of the *Salagama* community, to take ownership of this industry. In fact, in modern times, its largest exporters are members of the *Salagama* community.

The turning away of colonial interest and the abolishment of draconian governmental proscriptions on growing or cutting down cinnamon (earlier punishable by death), along with other reforms, helped restore some normalcy and freedom. Today, 70-80% of the industry is comprised of smallholders, and cinnamon is commonly found even in the home gardens of cinnamon peelers. Many peelers continue to lead an itinerant lifestyle, contracted by smallholders to peel their crop. Their economic position has vastly improved as they can command from 33% to 50% of the selling price, or at least twice the average wage rate when paid by the day. The skills of the peelers are in ever greater demand as the industry is booming, but their numbers are falling. The social stigma connected with this occupation still exists to a certain degree, and the younger generation prefer to pursue white collar jobs. As the prestige of cinnamon has risen locally and internationally, and as this industry has been reshaped and reimagined, the *Salagama* peelers are finally starting to gain well-deserved respect for their central role in the preservation of one of Sri Lanka's most iconic natural products.

Particularly in the past decade, cinnamon has been taken forward and upgraded by a new generation. As part of the Geographic Indicator (GI) initiative, and in an effort to promote best practices and attract outsiders into this occupation, the local cinnamon industry set up the Cinnamon Training Academy. The government has also created the 'Pure Ceylon Cinnamon' trademark, which has been registered so far in its four largest markets, Mexico, the US, Peru, and Colombia.

Although the industry has found its way again, with the traumas of the past growing more remote in shared memory, the scarcity of peelers to meet the growing demand for Sri Lankan cinnamon may pose a stumbling block. The skill of the peeler is the critical determinant in the production of high-quality cinnamon. Should this expertise disappear, the finest grades of cinnamon may become a thing of the past.

Notes

1   Garcia da Orta, 'Fifteenth Colloquy: Cinnamon,' in *Colloquies on the Simples & Drugs of India by Garcia da Orta (Lisbon, 1895) by the Conde de Ficalho*, trans. by Sir Clements Markham (London: Henry Southern & Co, 1913), pp. 118-37 (p. 124).

2   At the International Botanical Congress in 2011, the Code of Botanical Nomenclature (ICN) for *Cinnamomum zeylanicum Blume* was officially designated as *Cinnamomum verum*, based on a narrow technicality, although the former name has been in wide use since 1666. However, the ruling allowed the term *C. zeylanicum* to be used as a synonym. For a detailed discussion, see Jayasiri Lankage, 'Botanical Name of the Ceylon Cinnamon Plant' <https://www.srilankanspices.com/download/lank-age.pdf> [accessed 4 April 2021].

3   Mordor Intelligence, *Cinnamon Market Growth, Trends, and Forecast 2019-2024* (Hyderabad: April 2019).

4   See U.M. Senanayake and R.O.B. Wijesekera, 'Chemistry of Cinnamon and Cassia', in *Cinnamon and Cassia: The Genus Cinnamomum*, ed. by P. N. Ravindran, K. Nirmal-Babu, and M. Shylaja (London: CRC Press, 2004), pp. 80-120 (p. 104).

5   For instance, see F. Woehrlin and others, 'Quantification of Flavoring Constituents in Cinnamon: High Variation of Coumarin in Cassia Bark from the German Retail Market and in Authentic Samples from Indonesia', *Journal of Agricultural Food Chemistry*, 58 (2010), 10568–10575. It is the author's hunch that bark age may be a significant factor in cassia's higher coumarin content.

6   See Classification for Quills ISO 6535:1997 (SLS 81:2000).

7   D. Ferguson, 'The Discovery of Ceylon by the Portuguese in 1506', *Journal of the Ceylon Branch of the Royal Asiatic Society*, 19.59 (1907), 284-400 (p. 333).

8   Michael Krondl, *The Taste of Conquest: The Rise and Fall of the Three Great Cities of Spice* (New York: Ballantine Books, 2007), p. 184.

9   Robert Knox, *An Historical Relation of the Island of Ceylon* (London: Richard Chiswell, 1681), p. 16.

10 Jayasiri Lankage, 'Cinnamon, Tree that Gave the Name to the Country and Changed the Course of History', *Cinnamon Academy Sri Lanka* <http://cinnamonacademy.lk/2016/10/16/cinnamon-tree-that-gave-the-name-to-the-country-and-changed-the-course-of-history/> [accessed on 1 June 2020].

11 *Ibn Battuta: Travels in Asia and Africa 1325-1354*, trans. by H. A. R. Gibb, 3rd edition (London:

Routledge & Kegan Paul, 1953), p. 254.

12　Da Orta, p. 123.

13　P.N. Ravindran, ed., *Black Pepper: Piper Nigrum* (Boca Raton: CRC Publishers, 2000), p. 5.

14　Hūšang Aʿlam, 'Dārčīnī', *Encyclopedia Iranica*, 15 November 2011 <https://iranicaonline.org/articles/darcini> [accessed 4 April 2021].

15　François Valentijn, *François Valentijn's Description of Ceylon*, ed. by Sinnappah Arasaratnam (London: Hakluyt Society, 1978), p. 290.

16　Francois L'Estra, *Relation ou journal d'un voyage aux Indes orientales* (Paris: Estienne Michelle, 1677), p. 125.

17　Johann Wolfgang Heydt, *Heydt's Ceylon: Being the Relevant Sections of the Allerneuester Geographisch- und Topographischer Schau-Platz Von Africa und Ost-Indien, Etc. Etc., Wilhermsdorff, 1744*, trans. by R. Raven-Hart (Colombo: Ceylon Government Information Department, 1952), p. 31.

18　Lodewijk Wagenaar, *Cinnamon and Elephants: Sri Lanka and the Netherlands from 1600* (Amsterdam: Rijks Museum, 2016), p. 152.

19　Heydt, pp. 148-49.

20　Rycklof van Goens, *Instructions from the Governor-General and Council of India to the Governor of Ceylon, 1656-1665*, trans. by Sophia Pieters (Colombo: H.C. Cottle, Government Printer, 1908), p. 42.

21　John M. Senaveratna, *Dictionary of Proverbs of the Sinhalese* (Colombo: Times of Ceylon, 1936), p. 14.

22　See Lodewijk Wagenaar, 'The Apparition of the Cinnamon Peelers: Dutch Colonial Presence in Eighteenth-Century Ceylon and its Reflection in Non-Literary Prose' in *Shifting the Compass: Pluricontinental Connections in Dutch Colonial and Post-Colonial Literature*, ed. by Jeroen Dewulf, Olf Praamstra, and Michiel van Kampen (Newcastle upon Tyne: Cambridge Scholars, 2013), pp. 112-27.

What Does Prestige Taste Like? The Divorce of Saffron from its Cultural Context

James O'Donnell

Saffron flowers dread the rain. It was thus out of necessity that my partner and I, weary and drenched, went back to our field to reattach the protective cover over the blooms. For millennia, the flowers have grown in arid climates, yet they patiently flourished on our farm in upstate New York. Late October is saffron's peak blooming season. Out of frozen soil resiliently comes a pale white stem, which slowly reveals a tightly wound violet bud. Within a night the flower then opens, presenting three ruby red stigmas like a gift, which must be meticulously separated from the flower itself by hand, then carefully dried and packed. Our saffron, both the edible flowers and stigmas, were destined for elite kitchens across New York City, where we watched decorated chefs touch and taste the gossamer petals with the sincere wonder of a child.

But most of them had absolutely no idea what to use it for.

One celebrated chef took a whole flower and dunked it in a teacup of hot water. We all stood around, looking at it, the colour of the water unchanging and without aroma, feeling underwhelmed. Others experimented with preserving it: drying, fermenting, candying. Others went about things the traditional way, drying just the red stigmas and using them as a spice. Meanwhile, the flowers kept blooming, and we kept harvesting, unsure of what sort of culinary delights they would end up in. Nonetheless, every drop off of flowers was welcomed with awe, photos, and a feeling of decadence. We would ask the crew: do you know what you're using them for yet? Responses were mixed, but unsure. After going door to door with our flowers, to some of the top restaurants, led by mostly white chefs, we would receive the same response: magical, beautiful, wonderful…but how do we cook with them?

Some of the results were delicious. More often, though, they were confusing. We thought we were taking on an innovative agricultural experiment: a prestigious, globetrotting ingredient could be grown right on our farm. What we really did was divorce an ingredient from the practices, people, and knowledge that created it, and expected it to stand alone. What biases led us to bring this ingredient to chefs with no cultural ties to the spice, rather than to chefs with the tools to actually use it? What led us to grow it in the first place, when it's never been a part of either of our culinary upbringings? Where did we go wrong?

Journalist Navneet Alang writes about our modern era of the global pantry, 'when a succession of food media-approved, often white figures have made an array of international ingredients approachable and even desirable to the North American mainstream – the same mainstream that, a decade ago, would have labeled these foods as obscure at best and off-putting at worst'.[1] Examples of this global pantry include ingredients like turmeric, tahini, and gochujang, which are increasingly placed ad-hoc in recipes from more white-centred cuisines. They've become steadily incorporated into mainstream dishes, but only in a slow, precise pace. To the cooks who feel a cultural tie to these ingredients, it can feel as if they are taboo until the white-led media broadcasts that they're 'safe' to cook with.

Alang explains that the inherent problem is not about who can or cannot use a given ingredient. Instead, the more pressing question is, 'whether, say, a person of color could have also made a stew featuring chickpeas and turmeric go viral. Aren't both the perceived novelty and the recipe's "virality" tied to the whiteness of its creator?'[2]

For saffron, there seem to be two cultural realities. One surrounds the areas where it is grown: northeastern Iran, Herat province in Afghanistan, the Abruzzo region of Italy, Kashmir. These regions have vastly different methods of growing and harvesting saffron, as well as distinct ways of using it in dishes and recipes, but, still, the changing of the seasons can be mapped to the saffron fields. The spice finds its way into regional cuisine, cultural memory, iconography, livelihoods.

White American home cooks live in the second reality, one where saffron is commodified, exported, removed from its agricultural roots, its recipes, farmers, and cooks, and bottled indifferently on the shelf with a high price tag. What's left is just a feeling, one of luxury, decadence, and fanciness. We can't exactly pinpoint where this feeling comes from or what it tastes like, but there is a cachet. It hinges on inequality and exoticism. An American home cook perusing recipes online to use their saffron for will find little about the flavour itself. Instead, the food media uses words like 'elegance', 'polish', 'elevate', 'precious', 'luxurious', or 'elusive'. In this reality, saffron feels almost secondary to the act of eating, but instead acts as an accessory, confirming a feeling of superiority and wealth. This second reality is what we felt when we stood in those kitchens with those chefs; we felt underwhelmed because we clung to the prestige of saffron without any greater cultural association to it. We didn't do the work of bringing a culinary background to understanding the spice, but we didn't need to: it was performative. But when it's merely performative, it isn't delicious.

The spice trade has juggled these two realities pretty well. It's created an $880 million industry off of a product that many white consumers have little idea what to do with but who sense its elegance and purchase accordingly.[3] How did we get here? How has the industrial spice trade divorced saffron from its cultural context, and what are the consequences?

To set the scene, we must recall the intentions of the spice trade to begin with. Although spices have been consumed and traded since 6000 BC, the sale of spices in the fifteenth and sixteenth centuries drove unprecedented wealth to traders (though not to the agricultural regions that actually grew them). The fact that this era occurred right at the transition period in Europe between feudalism and capitalism comes as no coincidence. Clifford A. Wright explains:

> Although the ancient Greeks, Romans, Indians, and Arabs had actively traded spices, it was not until the slow dissolution of feudal structures in western Europe in the late Middle Ages and the rise of a bourgeoisie associated with the creation and accumulation of capital in certain city-states that spices took on a far more significant role than simple culinary use would suggest.

He goes on to say that cookbooks for the elite required exorbitant amounts of spices, far beyond what would seem to be necessary from the perspective of flavour. As Wright notes, 'Wealthy Europeans consumed spices in such extraordinary quantities during these centuries that the demand drove up prices. Yet it remains unclear how the spices were used. Although enormous amounts of spices featured in cooking, the volume of the trade was so great as to suggest that they may also have been hoarded like gold.' It is much more likely, then, that spices carried currency, saffron included. The 'budding capitalists' that Wright refers to took enormous risks, establishing complex supply chains and leveraging colonial power to make riches as middlemen. Indeed, much of the violent colonial exploration by European powers in the fifteenth and sixteenth centuries was done in direct attempts to control the lucrative spice trade. The increase in scale was dramatic: 'When Vasco de Gama sailed for India in 1497, the annual imports of black pepper to Europe were about two million pounds; by 1506 that figure had risen to about three million pounds, and in 1570, to about six million pounds.'[4]

265

Little has changed in the spice trade today. Profits are centred around the traders, not the farmers. Producers have few choices of who to sell their product to and little equity in the supply chain, leading to poor trade conditions and stagnant wages. The commodity spice trade is built on stale product, poor conditions, and inequality.

As the spice trade has commodified saffron, the original uses and applications of the spice have been obscured to unfamiliar consumers. In the literature around saffron's history there is remarkably little about cooking. The spice is thought to have originally been domesticated in Crete, and Jo Day describes, in great detail, the use of saffron as a motif in clay tablets, jars, and paintings in Crete dating back to 3000 BC which showcased saffron being used to heal wounds.[5] Researchers say that saffron was also used as pigment throughout the Persian Empire. The spice finds its way into myth, such as the Hellenic story of Crocus and Smilax. Medicinal uses varied: the spice was toasted, ground, or steeped and applied in a variety of different mediums to treat medical issues from urinary tract to gastrointestinal pains. The petals and stamens were used in dyeing fabrics as well, and there are claims that wealthy Romans used the spice in baths, ceremonies, wines, potpourri, and religious offerings. The spice was blended into skin products and perfumes, as well as teas. While it appears in historical recipes, it seems there were far broader uses other than cooking.[6]

How has the saffron industry adapted to an American market less reliant on myth, traditional medicine, and ceremony? Lior Sercarz is an Israeli chef, spice blender, and the founder of La Boite, a spice company based in New York City that sells spices to elite chefs and home cooks. He admits to not growing up around the spice and to being generally confused at the reverence some hold for it. He explains, 'I use a bit at home. Floral, savory, slightly piney. Is it worth the cost? I'm not sure.'

Cooking with saffron is an art in subtlety and patience. The spice requires infusions and time: it is not a potent additive that can be easily thrown into an existing dish. But for many cooks, the draw is not deliciousness, but prestige. Lior openly confirms, 'It's like caviar, or foie gras. If someone's paying for it, I love it.'

If saffron has been divorced from its uses in medicine, perfume, and dyeing fabrics, it's no wonder why American home cooks have trouble understanding the spice. But what about the chefs and cuisines that do hold it as a gastronomic icon, who steward the ingredient to its full potential? For this, turn to Persian cuisine: take *gheymeh nesar,* where lamb shoulder is slowly braised with pistachios and almonds in a saffron broth, or *shole zard*, a floral pudding of starchy rice simmered with saffron and rosewater. Or, the iconic *tah-dig*, a rice dish where the bottom layer is caramelized and browned, while the top is beautifully steamed with the aroma of saffron. In many of these dishes, the use of saffron is part flavour, part colour, part celebration.

266

As the industry grows, there are many attempts to automate the task of separating stigmas from flowers. I spoke to engineering students from the University of Pennsylvania who spent a year researching, designing, and engineering a machine to automate the separation of saffron stigmas from their flowers. This physically demanding task involves a significant amount of the workforce in growing regions. They landed on the topic after considering a number of other agricultural automation projects, from harvesting table grapes to using drones to count the number of apples in an orchard. The team successfully built a prototype of a machine that could take in saffron flowers, and spit out just the stigmas, all while beating the cost of human labour by operating at less than $5100 per acre.

I asked the team member I spoke to if he ever cooked with saffron, to which he said no. None of the team members had any agricultural experience, but they thought there was a huge automation opportunity given the high price of saffron. I asked hypothetically, how do you think American cuisine would change if we had access to more affordable saffron, given that it's less familiar to many home cooks? They weren't sure, but they were certain it would transform the saffron economy. Their goal was to have saffron grown domestically, in the United States, just like my partner and I were doing. Except it would be larger, and more profitable, and compete with the saffron coming in from Iran.

Through the modern lenses of agribusiness, neoliberalism, and capitalism, the group's logic is sound. If there's demand for something, it follows to grow it where it's cheapest, and sell it where it's most valued. I didn't have a good reason for why they were wrong, except I remembered standing in the kitchen, with chefs who had no cultural knowledge of, understanding of, or relation to the spice, and wondering what to do with it. Is a cheaper ingredient a win if consumers have no cuisine that supports it? How can we honour the cultural transmission that happens through cooking if we continue to divorce ingredients from their origins? What sort of jumbled, confused global cuisine is industrial agriculture bringing us towards?

I harken back to our decision to grow saffron in the first place. It somewhat embodies the same complexities of the global pantry. Where did our desire come from? It certainly was not from a place of honouring a shared cultural heritage. It did, though, come from a place of curiosity, of loving food, of respecting the honour and dignity in agriculture, but sometimes that is not enough. Why did we market the product to mostly white chefs who we had worked with in the past? Why did we think culinary magic would happen when the participants had little overlap with the cultural identity of the ingredient?

On the topic of cooking with ingredients outside one's culture, writer Priya Krishna explains, 'I love that people's pantries are getting more global, but I do hope that when people cook with them, they take the time to educate themselves about the origin of these ingredients, rather than treating them as ingredients in a vacuum, divorced of their context.'[7] There is much to lose by treating these ingredients in a vacuum. We have work to do in stepping aside, honouring the agricultural roots, power struggles, and wisdom behind the ingredients we grow and cook with. This work will make us better cooks and farmers, but more importantly preserve the sovereignty of regional cuisines.

267

Notes

1   Navneet Alang, 'Alison Roman, Bon Appetit, and the Global Pantry', *Eater,* 20 May 2020 <https://www.eater.com/2020/5/20/21262304/global-pantry-alison-roman-bon-appetit> [accessed 22 March 2021].

2   Alang.

3   'Saffron Market Size, Share & Trends Analysis Report by Application, 2020-2027', *Grand View Research*, April 2020 <https://www.grandviewresearch.com/industry-analysis/saffron-market> [accessed 22 March 2021].

4   Clifford A. Wright, 'The Medieval Spice Trade and the Diffusion of the Chile'. *Gastronomica*, 7 (2007), 35-43 (pp. 36, 35, 39).

5   Jo Day, 'Crocuses in Context: A Diachronic Survey of the Crocus Motif in The Aegean Bronze Age', *Hesperia: The Journal of the American School of Classical Studies at Athens*, 80 (2011), 337-79.

6   P. Willard, *Secrets of Saffron: The Vagabond Life of the World's Most Seductive Spice* (Boston: Beacon Press, 2002).

7   Qtd. in Alang.

'A Spice of Idolatry': Seditious Spices and Ginger Anxieties in Jonson's *Bartholomew Fair*

Taylor Parrish

Ben Jonson's riotous city comedy, *Bartholomew Fair* (1614), has long attracted critics invested in the depiction of material culture in Jacobean theatre. However, this work has not been much examined from the interdisciplinary perspective of literary food studies, despite the author's significant interest with culinary trends and the politics of eating. Thus, Jonson's engagement with the cultural politics surrounding the use of spices has not been analyzed. But, as I identify in this paper, a thorough understanding of how 'exotic' seasonings function in Jonson's work enriches our understanding of how spices and spiced foods were perceived in the author's historical moment. Focusing on the character Joan Trash and the gingerbread she sells at the fair market, I explore how Jonson's play establishes how 'hot' spices were gendered in the Jacobean period due to their association with women's health and the Protestant anxiety that exotic seasonings could tempt consumers into adultery. I consider how *Bartholomew Fair* comments on women's cookery and domestic labour, concluding with a consideration of the seditious power spices like ginger possessed in the hands of the female huckster. In this paper, I argue that Joan Trash and the multiple levels of anxiety both she and her gingerbread inspire offer commentary on how spices, as well as the women who used these seasonings in their cooking and those who sold spiced goods, were perceived as possessing a dangerous amount of influence in Jacobean England.

Prior to the gingerbread-woman's first appearance in Act Two, *Bartholomew Fair* begins with a conversation between Littlewit, the London proctor, and his pregnant wife, Win-the-Fight, about the festival at Smithfield. Having written a puppet play that will be featured at the fair, Littlewit genially persuades his wife to feign a craving for the roasted pork served at Smithfield, so that the couple will be permitted to attend the fair, despite the reservations of Win's strict Puritan mother, Dame Purecraft, who pronounces the roasted pig a 'foul temptation'.[1] But, not wishing to deny her daughter the roasted pork she craves, she concedes to go with the pair to the festival, accompanied by the reverend Rabbi Zeal-of-the-Land Busy, who consoles Dame Purecraft with assurances that the group 'may be religious in the midst of the profane'.[2] As the first Act establishes, food and the politics of eating are central to *Bartholomew Fair*; the roasted pork Win is promised quite literally sets the stage for the comedy. However, as the fairgoers progress through the festival, it is quickly apparent that some foods, like the roasted pork, can be rendered acceptable by Puritan rationalizations while others cannot.

Though Joan Trash features in several moments of *Bartholomew Fair*, by far her most memorable scene is the confrontation with Busy in Act Three. After the group sates their hunger (and Win's fictitious craving) on the roasted pork sold by the pig-woman, Ursula, Littlewit encourages his wife to 'long to see as well as taste' the pleasures of the festival, so that the group can attend the fair market.[3] However, Busy is quickly overcome by the sheer volume of hobby-horses and trinkets for sale and declares the whole market an abomination, a veritable nest of 'apocryphal wares'.[4] In a sanctimonious speech which directly satirizes the rhetoric used by Puritans in their public denunciations of excess and temptation, Busy enacts the trope of the 'Puritan-at-the-Fair' and begins to sermonize against the market vendors.[5] He quickly fixates on Joan Trash and the gingerbread she is hawking and is motivated by a pious fervour to enter into the following exchange:

TRASH   And what's my gingerbread, I pray you?
BUSY   The provender that pricks him [the Beast of Revelations] up. Hence with thy basket of popery, thy nest of images, and whole legend of gingerwork. [...] I was moved in spirit to be here this day in this Fair, this wicked and foul Fair and fitter may it be called a Foul than a Fair – to protest against the abuses of it, the foul abuses of it, in regard of the afflicted saints that are troubled, very much troubled, very exceedingly troubled, with the opening of the merchandise of Babylon again, and the peeping of the popery upon the stalls, here, here, in the high places. See you not Goldylocks, the purple strumpet, there, in her yellow gown and green sleeves? The profane pipes, the tinkling timbrels? A shop of relics! [...] And this idolatrous grove of images, this flasket of idols, which I will pull down –
Overthrows the gingerbread.
TRASH   O my ware, my ware, God bless it!
BUSY   – in my zeal, glory to be thus exercised.[6]

This altercation locates Trash's gingerbread at the zenith of Busy's outrage at the fair and contains multiple levels of Puritanical indignation. As Elyssa Cheng explains, Busy associates the gingerbread, moulded to represent St. Bartholomew, with Catholicism and the perceived worship of idols; Puritans of the period were particularly intolerant of all reminders of the 'popish' sect.[7] But, as I will identify, anti-Catholic sentiments account for only a portion of his outrage at her wares. This passage is critical to my analysis of Trash's gingerbread and the relationship it had to Jacobean understandings of spices, women's health, and Protestant theology.

A comprehensive analysis of this scene must first be situated within the Early Modern understanding of the critical relationship between food and the Protestant eater. As Madeline Bassnett observes, a person's relationship to food in Jonson's moment was positioned at the crossroads of sustenance, health, and spiritual security; a person's choice of food was often considered within the landscape of all three of these considerations. Further, Protestants of the period emphasized the necessity of what Bassnett describes as 'temperate dining', a sober, disciplined relationship to nourishment that strictly avoided gluttony and kept Providence in mind when eating. As she describes, 'What one ate and how one ate it was key to managing and maintaining not only physical but also spiritual well-being, which supported individual virtue and a healthy relationship to God.'[8] Jonson's work reflects this sentiment when Busy directs how his companions should consume Ursula's roasted pork at the fair: 'with a reformed mouth, with sobriety and humbleness; not gorged in with gluttony or greediness'.[9] It is significant that Busy emphasizes consumption, particularly in the public space of the fair, must be sombre and measured to align with Protestant temperance; it is clear that he subscribes to the understanding that eating is an expression of one's devotion to God. Even in the fictitious space of Jonson's play, consumption and rituals of eating have profound implications. The Protestant relationship to food and eating is important because, while it is clear the roasted pork can be rationalized for godly eaters, Trash's gingerbread cannot be integrated into the diet of the elect.

Food's ability to impact a person's bodily health and spiritual wellness is rendered additionally complex in *Bartholomew Fair* when one considers the social position of spices necessary for Trash's gingerbread. Spices such as cinnamon, nutmeg, ginger, and pepper in Jonson's moment were considered 'exotic' goods because of their 'mysterious origins' and association with racialized 'heathen lands'.[10] Although Peter Lloyd asserts that these spices in the period 'were as symbolic as they were functional' because of their ability to convey wealth and status, I believe Stefan Smith's argument for the inclusion of seasonings like ginger and pepper in Early Modern cuisine is more compelling; spices were purchased and eaten because consumers enjoyed their flavours, in addition to, rather than because of, their social significance.[11] As prices for ginger and other foreign seasonings dropped in London markets after 1600 they became more fiscally accessible and started appearing in middle-class household records, in addition to those of the gentry.[12] Gervase Markham's *The English Huswife* (1615), a domestic manual published the year after Jonson's play, attests to the use of foreign seasonings over the Jacobean period.[13] In his gingerbread recipe, Markham recommends the use of several imported seasonings in this 'Banquet Fare' recipe, to include cinnamon, aniseed, liquorice, and, naturally, ginger, under the assumption that these goods would be readily attainable by upper- and middle-class women.[14] As the critical ingredients became more available for a wider class of Britons, foods like gingerbread correspondingly increased in popularity.

Spices like ginger and others needed in the production of gingerbread thus implied multiple associations in Jonson's period, consistent with their rising accessibility and usage in the private sphere of wealthy and middle-class households. However, an increase in the availability of spices served only to elevate the anxiety of strict Protestants concerned with the impact foods could have on the body, and, by extension, the soul, of the god-fearing Englishman. This suspicion, borne from the Protestant understanding of eating as a religious act and the imperative for temperance, quickly evolved into critical censure.

270

Indeed, as both Bassnett and Gitanjali Shahani comment, spices and their use in English cuisine could not be divorced from their association with 'heathen lands'.[15] Signifying both as foreign and as hedonistic indulgences, exotic spices like ginger could not be incorporated into the Protestant logic of virtuous eating.[16] As Shahani describes, '[spices'] incorporation into the English diet were accompanied by pervasive anxieties about mixing and mingling with foreign entities.'[17] Bassnett notes that Protestants of the period were encouraged to prize native herbs and turn away from foreign seasonings because of the belief in God as the 'ideal local supplier'. Virtuous eating required the consumer to first trust in God to provide and to eat only that which had been offered, in order to invest the body in inward virtue which would lead to the expression of outward faith. The belief that God had provided the English all they could require for sustenance (body and spirit) ultimately motivated parsons and more spiritual physicians to recommend their neighbours avoid spices like ginger and cinnamon altogether, lest they endanger their standing with the almighty. Ingesting products from un-Christian territories, for sustenance or style, would put the English at fatal risk, according to the strict Protestant worldview of temperance and reliance on God in all matters.[18] Busy's destruction of Trash's gingerbread in Act Three thus reveals the pervasive anxiety of Jacobean Puritans surrounding both the easy access of foreign goods for the London fair-goer and the impression that the consumption of foreign spices could negatively affect one's relationship to God.

But while the Puritan Busy is certainly the loudest in expressing his concerns about Trash's gingerbread and the potential impact it could have on the wayward consumer, he is not the only character to insult her goods. Leatherhead, the puppet master and toy-vendor, also comments on Trash's wares, revealing the concern that spices could produce ill-health in the Jacobean consumer. Jealous of Trash's booth, he looks on with disdain at her gingerbread, commenting that her wares are likely made with: 'stale bread, rotten eggs, musty ginger and dead honey'. Leatherhead pulls no punches in his assessment of Trash's gingerbread, suggesting that her ingredients could only produce the effect of a thoroughly disgusting product that could make the consumer ill.[19] But despite Leatherhead's concern that Trash's gingerbread might have the potential to induce ill-health in the consumer, records show that spices such as the 'musty ginger' were formative among medical treatments of the period, as Shahani notes. Part of the appeal of exotic spices in the Early Modern period was their potential as medicinals, an important connection in my consideration of Trash's gingerbread and her use of spices in *Bartholomew Fair*.[20]

The relationship between culinary trends and the consumption of food for one's health in the Jacobean period takes on additional significance when one considers that gingerbread spices were prescribed by physicians, particularly in matters of women's health.[21] As Jennifer Evans has investigated, spices were frequently used in the treatment of irregular menstruation and couples' struggles with conception and fertility.[22] Under the Galenic understanding, spices like ginger, cinnamon, and pepper were classified as 'hot' and were thus useful in scenarios in which the body had become unbalanced by cool humours.[23] In her chapter 'Provoking Lust and Promoting Conception', Evans describes the common practice of prescribing: 'compound remedies contain[ing] cinnamon, saffron, candied nutmeg, candied ginger and eryngo' and heavily spiced 'hot foods' for women perceived to be barren.[24] These seasonings prevented frigidity which, accordingly: 'robbed the body of its ability to experience sexual pleasure and its ability to conceive'. Though physicians believed heat was necessary for both parties in the conception of a child, the woman's cooler body (under humoral understanding) was typically seen as the barrier to successful conception in the event of infertility. As Evans observes, spices like ginger and cinnamon served as aphrodisiacs and 'seed provokers' in that they promoted lust by heating a woman's body and warming her womb, simultaneously encouraging intercourse and improving her ability to conceive.[25] 'Hot' spices, like those used in Trash's gingerbread, were gendered in the Jacobean period by their association with fertility, pregnancy, and menstruation and their perceived proximity to the female body.

The gendered connotation spices possessed in Jonson's moment can be particularly seen in Busy's references to the Beast of Revelations when abusing Trash's gingerbread in Act Three. While Leatherhead's hobby-horses are associated with the Beast's belly, lungs, and tail, it is telling Trash's gingerbread is sexualized in Busy's rant about the sinful indulgences of the fair market.[26] Describing Trash's goods as the 'provender that pricks him up', Busy's telling word choice associates her gingerbread with phallic stimulus, an appraisal which is not inconsistent with the use of 'hot foods' as aphrodisiacs to promote fertility.[27] In considering the spices used to make Trash's gingerbread in the historical moment of Jonson's writing it is critical to return to my earlier analysis of the Protestant concept of temperate eating and the implications this has for Jonson's work. Busy's outrage at the gingerbread stall is motivated by the belief that certain dietary choices had great impact on an individual's spiritual and bodily health. Because strict Protestants viewed food as the vehicle for greater virtue, gingerbread and other 'hot' foods could be perilous if consumed outside of the confines of marital intimacy between a husband and wife.[28] Busy thus views Trash's goods as a powerful aphrodisiac which will lead good Christians into debauchery, as this examination of the historical context demonstrates. Though his rage is styled as humorous in Jonson's comedy, it is consistent with the belief that exotic spices had the ability to erode Christian virtue.[29]

While Busy's rage at the gingerbread is certainly suggestive, it is noteworthy that his anger is not only directed at the gingerbread, but also extends to Trash herself. The presence of gingerbread in Jonson's work is rendered additionally significant when one considers the woman selling it and the implications this has for how market women were perceived in their historical moment. Busy's anger at the presence of Trash is highly indicative of how market women were perceived as the dealers of exoticized goods. Spices were gendered in Jonson's historical moment, both for the reasons I have already explored in their use in health and fertility and, as Shahani argues, the fact that women were the primary medium by which gingerbread and other such spiced goods were able to circulate in English society.[30] Bassnett notes that the English housewife and domestic servant were, somewhat predictably, the primary site of anxiety for strict

Protestants who viewed women as dangerous harbingers of foods which could provoke an individual into lust or other sins, potentially divorcing Christians from God. Rather than succumb to the temptations of exotic spices like ginger, Puritans like Busy encouraged the women of their communities to be content with native English herbs like basil, rosemary, and thyme, in order that women might 'improve the godliness of her broader community', with the understanding that native herbs were all the godly Englishman required for virtuous eating.[31] As Bassnett describes, the English housewife was encouraged to look only to 'the provision of her own yard' for fear that the fruit of her labour would put their community in danger of committing spiritual transgressions if they used seasonings beyond what God had placed around them.[32]

As this analysis suggests, a women's ability to influence her broader community through the cooking and baking she performed had vast implications for how her role was perceived within greater English society. This inherent anxiety about women's production within the domestic sphere and their ability to influence matters beyond the home with their cookery becomes additionally complicated in *Bartholomew Fair* when Trash's character is considered within the public sphere of the market. In our first introduction to the gingerbread woman in Act Two, Leatherhead scathingly refers to her as a 'lady o' the basket' before telling her to begone lest she drive away his customers.[33] Trash, unwilling to give up the ground she paid for in order to sell her gingerbread at the market, quickly asserts her equal right to the space by exchanging a series of jabs with the trinket-dealer, and the two settle into sharing the space in relative harmony, hawking their respective wares in tandem.[34]

Leatherhead's description of Trash's identity as a 'lady o' the basket' is crucial to her character and position within Jonson's work. Referenced by other characters as 'good mother Joan' and 'goody Joan' at various intervals when her aid is requested by other market vendors in Acts Two and Three, Joan Trash is specifically associated with the domestic sphere by these references.[35] However, Leatherhead's reference to her basket in Act Two labels her a 'huckster', a seller of small goods. Huckstering required individuals to obtain small goods for quick sale then hit the cobblestones and peddle their wares from a basket, often loudly proclaiming the goods for sale, a practice which Trash herself displays in the promotion of her stall: 'Buy any gingerbread, gilt gingerbread!'.[36] As David Pennington has explored, huckstering in the Early Modern period was an occupation predominately taken up by women, especially widows, who lacked other means to support themselves and their families.[37]

The identification of Trash as a huckster is essential to my reading of Jonson's work, as it sees her aligned with the strikingly public sphere of the fair market generally, in addition to the domestic space that her gingerbread denotes. As a huckster (and therefore, presumably, a widow), Trash would have enjoyed an independence unavailable to married women, whose movements into the public sphere were not necessarily endorsed unless accompanied by her husband.[38] However, this freedom of movement and the illegal sale of small goods also associated the female huckster with sexual availability, as Marion Wynne-Davies has argued.[39] This connotation sheds additional light on the comments

Busy makes about Trash before smashing her ginger wares in Act Three. In addition to condemning her as a merchant of profanity, Busy also denounces her as a harlot in his reference to her as 'Goldylocks, the purple strumpet'.[40] Busy thus aligns huckstering with prostitution, an association that directly maligns her practice of selling gingerbread on the streets of the London market.[41] While there is no indication in Jonson's work that Trash sells her body along with her bread (which in itself is noteworthy, given the ample display of sex work at other intervals in the play), Busy collapses the distinction in his evaluation of Trash and her position in the public sphere of the market.

But while this association certainly accounts for Busy's suspicion of Trash herself, it does not quite account for the outrage that prompts him to overthrow the whole gingerbread stall. This action, I would argue, is directly tied to the problematic discourse surrounding huckstering, spices, and the anxiety that the domestic sphere had considerable ability to affect the public, godly sphere in Jonson's period. Though hucksters commonly sold goods like oranges, fuel, and other produce, Trash's sale of the gingerbread she has made makes her unique even among members of her community.[42] Few hucksters peddled wares they themselves produced and, though the act of selling goods on the street saw them undeniably sexualized, their connection to the domestic sphere was effectively distanced. Trash, in selling the wares she produces herself, maintains her connection to the private sphere of the domestic home, which is essential in my reading of Jonson's work. As I have earlier described, Protestant leaders were deeply uncomfortable by the possibility of English women using exotic spices that could induce sinful temptation in their cookery; the prospect of a street-walking huckster selling exotic wares with the potential to induce lust and lasciviousness is enough to make Busy positively apoplectic.[43]

Joan Trash's gingerbread stall at the fair market in *Bartholomew Fair* offers a productive opportunity to examine the cultural perception of spices in the Jacobean period. The tension across the play where Trash and her wares are concerned is significant when one acknowledges the influence of theatre and literary works in Jonson's historical moment. Theatre in the Jacobean period, as today, functioned not only as a critique of dominant society, but also as a mirror which reflected shifting cultural values and perspectives. Though Busy is certainly the loudest critic of Trash and her gingerbread, it is noteworthy that other characters also express anxiety over the potential effects her products could have on fair-goers. The multiple instances of apprehension where Trash and her gingerbread are concerned reflect a cultural preoccupation and apprehension about the influence of spices in English society. In Busy's view, at least, Trash's gingerbread belies the danger of the fair: the exotic (and erotic) spices in Trash's wares might induce god-fearing Englishmen to forget their prayers and descend into immoral, lustful debauchery. For Busy, the gingerbread cannot be allowed to remain because of its potential to upset the Christian order of Protestant society. As Jonson's play demonstrates, 'hot' spices were not without their controversy (despite their popularity as ingredients), particularly when one considers the rising support Puritans and their strict, temperate ideology garnered in the decades leading to the English Civil War; over the next century spices like ginger and cinnamon decreased significantly in popularity in part because of these cultural shifts.[44] Simultaneously, as I have argued, Jonson comments about the disruptive potential of women's participation in the emerging capitalist market by styling Trash as a huckster of illicit and illegal spiced goods. Joan Trash and her gingerbread thus serve as a reminder for conservative and strict Protestants of the impact women could have on their community through their domestic arts, should they choose ingredients that have the potential to disrupt the Christian order.

Notes

1   Ben Jonson, *Bartholomew Fair*, ed. by Michael Jamieson, 3rd edn. (London: Penguin Books, 2004), I. 5. 135-60.
2   *Bartholomew Fair*, I. 6. 72.
3   *Bartholomew Fair*, III. 6. 12.
4   B*artholomew Fair*, III. 4. 52.
5   *Bartholomew Fair*, III. 6. 52. Kirsty Milne attributes the writing of Jonson and several of his contemporaries to the creation of the 'Puritan-at-the-Fair' trope that outraged militant Protestants of the period. As she describes, this trope situated a Puritan in an English fair in order to mock the stereotypical displays of Calvinist-fuelled outrage at the merry-making and indulgence on display. Jonson's Puritan character, Busy, described as a former baker-turned-minister, contributed to the formation of this trope ('Reforming Bartholomew Fair: Bunyan, Jonson, and the Puritan Point of View', *Huntington Library Quarterly*, 74 (2011), 289-308 (pp. 290-92)).
6   *Bartholomew Fair* 3.6 66-68, 78-90, 92-95
7   Elyssa Y. Cheng, 'It's All for Sale': Market, Theatre, and Flesh Trade in Ben Jonson's Bartholomew Fair', *Tamkang Review*, 47 (2017), 117-32 (p. 125).
8   Madeline Bassnett, *Women, Food, Exchange, and Governance in Early Modern England* (London: Palgrave Macmillan, 2016), pp. 108-09, 114-15, 109. Bassnett's reflections on food's importance in the humoral (Galenic) system of health are significant. As she writes: 'each person began life with a particular combination of the four qualities – hot, cold, moist, and dry – and the four humours – black bile, yellow bile, blood, and phlegm. Foods, which themselves contained distinctive mixtures of the qualities, affected the state of the humours and therefore the body as a whole [.... I]t was important to eat the right foods, at the right time, and in the right order, as any misstep could induce disorders, leading to the production of less-than-desirable humours and blood-borne spirits (natural, vital, and animal) that governed the body, mind, and soul [...] drawing the unfortunate thinker into confusion and possibly sin' (pp. 108-09).
9   *Bartholomew Fair*, I. 6. 65-67.
10 Gitanjali Shahani, 'The Spicèd Indian Air in Early Modern England', *Shakespeare Studies,* 42 (2014), 122-37 (pp. 122-23).
11 Paul Lloyd, *Food and Identity in England, 1540-1640: Eating to Impress* (New York: Bloomsbury, 2015), p. 119; Stefan Smith, 'Demystifying a Change in Taste: Spices, Space, and Social Hierarchy in Europe: 1380-1750', *The International History Review*, 29 (2007), 237-57 (pp. 239, 241); Ken Albala, 'Spices and Garnishes', *The Banquet: Dining in the Great Courts of Late Renaissance Europe* (Urbana-Champaign: University of Illinois Press, 2017), pp. 56-72, (p. 56).
12 Lloyd, pp. 120, 126-27. The declining price of ginger, particularly in the first decades of the seventeenth century, occurred due to a confluence of events in the global spice trade. As Jonathan Eascott notes, the East India Company was unable to obtain large quantities of spices at the source due to the vicious tactics of the Dutch VOC in the Indian Ocean (*Selling Empire: India in the Making of Britain and American, 1600-1830* (Chapel Hill: University of North Carolina Press, 2016), pp. 28-30). However, despite the apparent lack of access to Indian ginger from EIC channels, Bethany Aram notes that London enjoyed a steady supply of Caribbean ginger from Spanish colonial exploits, having smuggled ginger plants out from under the Portuguese in the 1580s. Until the year after the publication of *Bartholomew Fair*, Caribbean ginger was five

times less expensive than Indian ginger and is likely the primary reason ginger was increasingly accessible ('Caribbean Ginger and Atlantic Trade, 1570-1648', *Journal of Global History*, 10 (2015), 410-30 (p. 413)).

13 Albala, p. 64.

14 Markham, Gervase, *The English Huswife*, 14th edn. (London: University of London, 1683), p.107.

15 Shahani p.123; Bassnett pp. 112-13.

16 Smith, p. 251.

17 Shahani, p. 122.

18 Bassnett, pp. 111-12, 108-09.

19 *Bartholomew Fair*, II. 2. 8-9.

20 Shahani, p. 123.

21 Shahani, p. 123.

22 Jennifer Evans, 'Provoking Lust and Promoting Conception', *Aphrodisiacs, Fertility, and Medicine in Early Modern England* (Martlesham: Boydell and Brewer, 2014), pp. 87-130 (p. 87); Jennifer Evans, '"Gentle Purges Corrected with Hot Spices, whether the Work or Not, do Vehemently Provoke Venery"; Menstrual Provocation and Procreation in Early Modern England', *Social History of Medicine*, 25 (2011), 2-19 (pp. 9-11).

23 Albala, p. 58; Bassnett, pp. 108-09.

24 Evans, 'Provoking Lust and Promoting Conception', pp. 91, 96.

25 Evans, '"Gentle Purges"', pp. 7, 92, 93.

26 Evans, '"Gentle Purges"', pp. 63-65, 67-68.

27 *Bartholomew Fair*, III. 6. 67 (my emphasis). An examination of the etymological history of 'prick' reveals the use of this term to indicate: 'A thing which serves as a stimulus, prompt, or incitement; a spur, an incentive' in the Jacobean period, in addition to the bawdy association with phallic symbolism more common in contemporary use ('Prick', Def. 9b and 12c., *Oxford English Dictionary Online* (Oxford: Oxford University Press, 2020)).

28 Shahani, pp. 123-24; Evans, 'Provoking Lust and Promoting Conception', pp. 90-91.

29 *Bartholomew Fair*, III. 6. 67.

30 Shahani, p. 126.

31 Shahani, p. 124; Bassnett, p. 110.

32 Bassnett, pp. 111-112.

33 *Bartholomew Fair*, II. 2. 3.

34 *Bartholomew Fair*, II. 2, 12-25; 84-145.

35 *Bartholomew Fair*, II. 5. 156, III. 4. 84-85.

36 *Bartholomew Fair*, II. 2. 32; David Pennington, 'Taking it to the Streets: Hucksters and Huckstering in Early Modern Southampton, circa 1550-1652', *The Sixteenth Century Journal*, 39 (2008), 657-79 (pp. 665-66).

37 Pennington, 'Taking it to the Streets', pp. 660, 664.

38 David Pennington, '"Three Women and a Goose make a Market": Representations of Market Women in Seventeenth-Century Popular Literature', *The Seventeenth Century Popular Journal*, 25 (2010), 27-48 (p. 37).

39 Marion Wynne-Davies, 'Orange-Women, Female Spectators, and Roaring Girls: Women and Theatre in Early Modern England', *Medieval and Renaissance Drama in England*, 2 (2009), 19-26 (p. 20). Regrate laws in the Early Modern period technically prohibited huckstering, as the parcelling of bulk items into smaller wares was perceived as a threat to shopkeepers and permanent markets (Wynne-Davies, p. 22). However, as Pennington notes, this practice often went unenforced, provided the huckster did not interfere with established commerce; even when hucksters were fined, the amount was negligible. The fact that leet officials turned a blind eye to the practice of huckstering, especially when the huckster charged was a widow, suggests an awareness that these women often had few options for supporting their families after the death of their husbands ('Taking it to the Streets', pp. 672-74).

40 *Bartholomew Fair*, III. 6. 84-86.

41 *Bartholomew Fair*, III. 6. 88-89.

42 Pennington, 'Taking it to the Streets', p. 661.

43 Shahani, pp. 124-26; *Bartholomew Fair*, III. 6. 78-87.

44 Smith, pp. 249-51.

İsot: The Pepper on Hot Rooftops

Tuba Şatana

İsot refers to pepper in Şanlıurfa, Turkey. It is the foundation of the city's cuisine as well as its chief commodity. *İsot* is a serious subject in Şanlıurfa, filling discussions about how many kilos of pepper should be bought to be dried, how many days it should be left drying on the rooftops, and how the division of labour and pay for workers is unequal.

İsot is turned into its spice form through traditional methods. This paper tells the story of *isot* in Şanlıurfa: the traditional methods of making *isot*, the use of *isot* in the kitchen, and the rich culture created around the spice. Giving necessary details about this age-old process, the paper focuses on how *isot* has become not only a simple product but a word that almost cultishly defines the whole city. The final test of the finished product comes when kneading the world-famous *çiğköfte,* an essential preparation for the local culture of *misafirperverlik*, hospitality.

İsot is the bread and butter of Şanlıurfa.

Şanlıurfa

The South-Eastern Anatolia Region of Turkey, part of the Fertile Crescent and upper Mesopotamia, has been the cradle of civilizations and the crossroad of cultures for centuries. This region still reflects the wisdom of its ancient heritage, but today it is also home to one of the largest hydroelectric, irrigation, and development projects in the world. Known as GAP, the South-Eastern Anatolia Project is located in the Euphrates and Tigris Rivers basins and the Upper Mesopotamia plains. GAP covers three million hectares of agricultural land. This project has contributed to the economic and social development of the region, and incomes and the local population's quality of life have notably improved in recent years.[1]

Agriculture still forms the basis of the provincial economy in Şanlıurfa, and almost half of Turkey's fresh red pepper is harvested in Şanlıurfa. Although pepper is not a commercial product of the city like cotton, corn, and red lentils, *isot* plays the central role in the city's culture and cuisine. Şanlıurfa's cuisine is based on wheat, sheep meat, fat, and *isot*. The preferred fat, another local delicacy, is *Urfa yağı*, clarified butter. Şanlıurfa is known for abundance and hospitality, and the city is said to be spiritually blessed. The area's traditional generosity shows when its residents invite guests into their homes, to gather around their tables.

İsot

İsot means pepper in Şanlıurfa. *İsot, ısıot,* and *ısot* refers to fresh pepper or dried chilli flakes with heat similar to cayenne; etymologically, *issi ot* is pepper, and the word is used generally for red pepper and pepper in Şanlıurfa.[2] The word refers to fresh pepper, to dried whole pepper, to the dried spice, and to pepper paste.

Although tomatoes and peppers have a huge impact on local cooking, the history of the cultivation of pepper is blurry and need more study. The first mention of red pepper, the *capsicum annuum* native to the Americas, was in the eighteenth century in the kitchen register accounts of Ottoman palaces.[3]

In homes all around Turkey, people prepare for winter in various ways, such as making *salça,* tomato paste; drying peppers; making *tarhana;* drying *yufka* bread; drying grapes, apricots, and nuts; making fruit leather; and pickling various things. Preparations vary from city to city due to the products that grow natively and shape local cuisines. In Urfa, making *isot* dominates the winter preparations, followed by making *frenk suyu,* tomato paste.

İsot is enjoyed fresh when in season, as well as when it is dried and pounded as a spice, dried whole for stuffing, and turned into paste. Dried *isot*'s colour varies from red to almost black according to individual preferences of each household.

Dried purple *isot* smells nutty, like liquorice, and once tasted it feels like eating the sun, with a warm feeling surrounding you. The pepper should not be too salty, too oily, or too black, but just perfectly balanced in taste and texture: *ipek gibi,* like silk.

278

Outside of Urfa, the word *isot* evokes purple-coloured dried pepper, varying from the integrity of its meaning at its source. While shopping for spices in Istanbul, if you ask for *isot,* you will be offered the darkest coloured, almost blackish dried chilli flakes, and if you are presented with red chilli flakes you think you are scammed. This belief reflects a lack of authentic information about what *isot* means and what *isot* really is.

İsot Cultivation and Harvest

Pepper seedlings are usually planted in the fields at the beginning of May. The first flowering of the pepper starts around July, followed by the first green pepper crop at the beginning of August. The pepper continues to blush on the plant, turning red after fifteen days, and then the red pepper crop starts and continues until the end of October. This average yearly cycle in the open fields – not in greenhouses – changes depending on the weather conditions. The first green peppers are consumed fresh, and the red peppers are turned into dried pepper and paste.

Most of the people working in the fields are women – sometimes even children – but the heavy workload, like lifting big sacks of pepper, is done by men. If you own a field and want to harvest the crop, you call the middleman locally called *Çavuş,* sergeant, and ask him for workers. He provides workers, like a temporary agency, taking his cut from their daily wages. The workers have no social security or insurance; they just receive a daily wage. *Çavuş* usually works with the same workers, as well as the same owners of the fields, based on reciprocal trust built up from previous business. The people *Çavuş* works with usually have very low incomes, or no income at all, and they are generally women with children: the wages they earn might be for pocket money or kitchen supplies or might even comprise their whole income. Working in the fields, under the frying sun, is the only option for unskilled and unqualified workers, as the work does not require any special harvesting skills, and often their children work alongside them in the same conditions. Unfortunately, this remains the ugly truth in the poor rural countryside.

Some Urfa families that own land have large families so they do not need to hire workers but can harvest their own peppers.[4]

One of the more crowded cities in South-East Turkey, people come to Şanlıurfa from the villages for better working conditions, and in recent years also there has been a refugee population from Syria too.

Choosing the Right *İsot* for Drying and Making Paste

Customers who do not have land for their own pepper crop buy their pepper from the wholesaler.

Once *Urfalı*, the locals, want to make their own *isot*, they search for the right kind of *isot*, starting from the seed, looking for heirloom peppers. Fields with alluvial soil rich with manure are preferable, especially around Cülab suyu and in the wetlands around Edene and Diphisar, but also around Sultantepe, Hancağız, Kaene, Germuş, and Paşabağı. *Urfalı* who go to the wholesale market ask the sellers about where and how the *isot* was grown.[5]

279

Many locals simply categorize *isot* as long or round. More detailed categories include: *kiraz biberi*, small and round cherry pepper; *kalem biberi*, thin and long; *çarliston biber*, conical with a pointy end; and *dolmalık biber*, a thin-fleshed bell pepper used for stuffing.[6] There are many tricks for choosing the right kind of pepper: most importantly, they should be the same size, not too big or too small. The middle size is the most fruitful for yield and for taste. The small ones are not easily deseeded, and the big ones are not as delicious as the middle-sized ones.

In each house, discussions might last for days about how many kilos to buy and which pepper to choose. The men of the house wander around the wholesalers, trying to balance their budget with the pepper variety they seek. Everyone hopes they buy the right ones: once bought and dried there is no turning back, and only then can they taste it to see if this was indeed the right kind of *isot* for the household.[7] As this process shows, *isot* has a personal story based on each family's preferences. Depending on the number of family members, each household might buy between 100 kg and 600 kg fresh pepper to turn into spice.

In the past, locals might buy some peppers early to test which was the most delicious pepper, but this is not a common method anymore. They would dry a sample and knead *çiğköfte* with it. If the crop from that specific field was delicious, then they knew that was the *isot* they sought.[8]

Then the city turns red. On rooftops, courtyards, balconies, and fields, peppers are layered everywhere to be baked by the sun. Starting from the middle of August, as you walk down the empty streets in Şanlıurfa, a scent hangs in the air. If the scent had a colour, it would be red too. That scent makes your eyes water and your nose run: all a part of the *isot* making. The urban architecture is based on the climate: houses are protected from the sun and the heat, so domestic lives are not visible from the street, but the smells and noises are everywhere.[9]

Making Traditional *İsot* and *İsot Reçeli*

Making your own *isot* is traditional in Urfa, and the process tells a lot about each family and their traditions.

One of the most laborious steps of drying *isot* is deseeding the peppers and cleaning out the veins. Huge amounts of pepper require a lot of hot and spicy work, so this step is often outsourced. This job is done *imece usulü*. It is communal work, hard work, but it also allows people to come together. A circle of women deseeds peppers while singing, gossiping, and drinking tea. After deseeding, they put the peppers back in the sack and return them to their owners. The majority of the households that still prepare their own *isot* keep the seeds for the next year.

Some families pay others to prepare *isot* for their household, following their specific instructions.[10] Families that cannot make their own *isot*, or have it made for them, rely on sellers known for good finished products, though buying *isot* is hardly preferable for real locals. When buying from a shop, there is no bargaining on the price when the *isot* is good, because everyone knows how difficult and time-consuming it is to make. Low-income families buy their *isot* from the market, where the shops offer low prices per kilo. Regardless of how it is made or where it is purchased, every household in Urfa, from the underprivileged to the wealthy, has *isot*, uses *isot*, and loves *isot*. When it comes to *isot*, everyone talks the same language.

Mrs Adile Buluntu Akkuş, a member of one of the oldest and most reputable families in Şanlıurfa, told me about her method of making dried *isot* and pepper paste: 'We used to make *isot* from 600-700 kg pepper, distribute it to our friends and family, not anymore. Nowadays, we consume 30 kg of *isot* spice per year. We used to pound it in *dibek*, pestle and mortar, made from a black stone, *karataş*.' She describes drying *isot* in the shade, a less common and more meticulous method:

> Deseed them, divide the pepper into 6 pieces, wash and drain them thoroughly. Layer them on the clean muslin cloth. I turn them upside down, every once in a while, to prevent them from sticking to each other and moulding, as well as sticking to the cloth. After two days, I put them in the plastic bags for another two days, not more. But, I do not put them in the direct noon sun, but in the afternoon and keep them in the nylon bag till the next morning, take them out from the bags, layer them to air out and dry, then repeat the process one more day.

We do not like dark purple or black colour, it is not preferred in my household.

I remember my mother using the special pepper bags, she used to sweat the peppers in those cotton bags, but not more than two days, just to give it a purple colour. The dark purple, blackish pepper was not preferred before. I remember my father telling my mom to throw the blackened dried peppers away, stating it is inedible. After the process, those pepper bags were washed and dried, and placed back till next year. The people started using nylon bags about 35-40 years ago, before that it was cotton bags.

After taking them out of the bags, I let them dry until crisp. The pepper pounded in *dibek,* a big pestle and mortar, made of black stone, we prefer this because if you put the peppers in bags and pound them with *tokmak,* mallet on the stone, the pepper sticks to the bags, so we do not prefer pounding in the bag. After the pounding, put the chilli flakes in the *kalbur,* sieve the pepper, and your *isot* is ready. You add a little salt and a little olive oil of high quality for preservation.[11]

Dried *isot* has a colour palette from red to black. The longer the pepper is left under the sun, the blacker it gets. Each family has their own preference and their own colour palette. Every colour has a customer, and each home has different colours of *isot* for their use.

So why does purple seem preferred? The common thought I gathered from interviews is that *isot* used in *çiğköfte* should be the same colour as the meat that is used. It is important for *çiğköfte* to have a homogeneous colour: the pepper should be invisible. In the past, the meat for *çiğköfte* came from gazelles, and it was a dark pink, but now most often meat comes from Awassi sheep, particularly from the inner leg, which again has a darkish pink colour. Purple *isot* mixes perfectly with bulgur and sheep's meat. Indeed, a common colour in Urfa is purple: the locals love to wear a purple shawl-like garment on their heads, like the preferred colour of *isot*. Purple means prosperity.

The locals distinguish bad *isot* from good by its smell. A well-prepared *isot* smells of pepper – Mrs Akkuş says, '*mis gibi biber kokar*', smells beautifully of pepper – whereas bad *isot* smells rancid, like vinegar and mould.[12] Good *isot* should also have a homogenous colour. Whether red or purple, different shades of colour reflect an uneven drying process; even colouring means that someone watched the *isot* carefully, paying utmost attention.

İsot reçeli literally translates as pepper jam: luscious, spicy, and sweet, it is one of the most prestigious products of the city. Mrs Akkuş's method contains a boiling period, as she puts it, '*bibere göbek attırmak*', making the pepper belly dance for just a couple of seconds before it is dried under the sun:

I grind the fresh pepper in the mincemeat machine; this releases all the juice of the pepper then wait for its first boil. I use a small amount of *Bursa* pepper too, mildly spicy, to cut down the spiciness a notch and give the paste smooth eating, otherwise it will be so hot, as poison. Then I pour the boiled peppers in trays

281

adding a little salt for preservation. The paste is then cooked under the sunlight, on the rooftop. The pepper mixture in the trays needs to be stirred frequently. *İsot reçeli*, slowly cooks under the Urfa sun, in a week. Its water evaporates, leaving the pepper a sun-kissed aroma, emphasizing the sugar content in the pepper, its unique taste. It has a very pleasant taste.[13]

İsot reçeli is also used in stews and enjoyed as a spread – often with oregano, olive oil, and walnut – as well.

Mrs Zehra Avşaroğlu mentioned that the veins of the peppers are dried in some households; fiercely spicy and eaten plain or used in mezzes, they are just exquisite.[14]

İsot in Şanlıurfa Cuisine

As a staple, *isot* is always on the table, from breakfast to dinner, and not a day passes without it.

On the street, breakfast finds the working class hanging around neighbourhood bakeries, waiting for the fiercely hot pepper to come out of the oven to be gulped down with freshly baked *dırnaklı ekmek* flatbread while sipping tea. Breakfast at home might be fried eggplants, *isot*, Urfa cheese, and herbs that vary from family to family.

İsot has many tones on the colour palette, and that variety of colours is used in the kitchen. *İsot* is a significant ingredient, since pepper shows itself in meals, that is, its colour changes that of the food with its own, whether red, purple, or black.

Fresh *isot* is also widely used in stews, called *güveç* after the earthenware pot they are cooked in, especially during summer months, when tomatoes and eggplants are in season and most delicious. Both *domates güveç*, tomato stew, and *patlıcan güveç*, eggplant stew, made with the local sheep's meat, *İvesi* or Awassi, always have fresh *isot* in common. *İsot dolması*, stuffed peppers, are a delicacy.[15] *Tepside isot dolması*, stuffed *isot* served on a tray, is a dish preferred by *esnaf,* small business owners, in the summer months. Like many dishes, this one might be sent to the neighbourhood bakery to be cooked in its wood-burning oven and then enjoyed with hot bread. *İsot Çömleği*, made with pomegranate juice, tomatoes, local sheep meat, *isot*, and clarified butter takes about six hours from start to finish, and of course its most distinctive ingredient is *isot*.

In restaurants, *bostana*, made with fresh *isot*, purslane, tomatoes, and onion first chopped then mashed, is a regularly served juicy salad. Charcoaled pepper and flatbread are the first things brought to your table in every kebab restaurant. Every table has its own spice bowl filled with *isot*, and if customers like it, they quickly ask where it is from and are directed to the seller at the *İsotçu Pazarı*, where they might buy a couple of kilos or the whole stock. The *İsotçular Pazarı* is the main market for *isot* shopping. The *isot* is displayed out in the open, in open bags, a sight for sore eyes. The locals do not buy *isot* without tasting it, and so they do not prefer packed *isot*. One consideration is where the *isot* was made; they avoid *isot* made in parts of the city called *pinti,* dirty, because of the conditions in which the dried pepper is prepared. The most important thing is the

282

taste of the end product, but they also seek the right colour, and sometimes less spicy *isot* might be bought for the children. If customers like the product, they sometimes buy the whole sack.[16]

Other common dishes made with *isot* include:

- *Ağzı açık*, an open-faced fried pastry with mincemeat topping, and *lahmacun*, mincemeat-topped flatbread, both with *isot* in Urfa.
- *Urfa Ciğer Kebabı*, cooked after *isot* is sprinkled on, is a charcoal-grilled liver kebab savoured for breakfast and throughout the day. Part of the street food culture, the liver stalls go on 24/7 scattered on the streets around the city. Sitting on stools at small tables, customers use their own personal cutting boards and knives to work up an appetite assembling and garnishing peppers, onion, and *isot* on skewers to be charcoal-grilled.
- *Urfa Eşkili* is a green pepper pickle made from all kinds of local grapes grown in Şanlıurfa, including *Azezi, Çiloreş, Tahannebi, Hatunparmağı, Hönüsü, Kabarcık, Horoz Karası, Sergi Karası, Tilgören, Sultani Çekirdeksiz,* and *Oğlak Karası,* but red grapes are also used in *Oğlak Karası*. In the past, families with vineyards used to prepare *urfa Eşkili* to share with their neighbours as well as to serve to their guests at home.[17]
- *Çiğköfte, çikifte*, literally raw meatballs, kneaded with bulgur and spices, with *isot* forming one-third of the mixture, is the famous, definitive final test of the finished product.

283

Many of the dishes in the region, including *Çiğköfte, Urfa Ekşili, Lahmacun, Ciğer Kebabı, İsot Çömleği,* and *Kazan Kebabı* have received Geographical Appellation Registration Certificates approved by the Turkish Patent Institute.[18] While all of these include *isot* as a crucial ingredient – and although *isot* is one of the key elements cited as part of the justification for certification – *isot* itself is not yet recognized in this way.

İsot and Urfa Folkways

İsot has a moral role in the city's culture as well as a crucial part in its cuisine. It is the talk of the town.

Way back, when a girl was ready for marriage, the groom's parents would investigate the bride-to-be based on her skill in making *isot*: whether she was interested in *isot*, if she was good at making and drying it, whether her *çiğköfte* was delicious. The son's mother would inspect her accomplishments, because *isot* was like a hidden message, a code of whether she was eligible to care for their precious son. The decision provided the answer of whether she was the right bride. The *isot* told them if her work is neat and clean. If the *isot* was delicious, she knew her way around the kitchen.[19]

Traditionally, Turkish mothers might warn misbehaving children by threatening to put pepper in their mouths, but that threat doesn't work with kids in Urfa: they never understand why that might be a bad thing because they eat *isot* all the time.

There are many local phrases and sayings involving *isot*.[20] Some include:

- *İsot kırmak*: to deseed *isot* and clean the veins
- *İsot çıkarmak*: to make dried *isot* from fresh
- *Terletme*: to sweat, referring to the sweating process that takes place in nylon bags
- *Biber sofrası*: the cotton fabric for drying peppers on, on the rooftops or wherever the household dry their peppers
- *Kesim*: the yield
- *Döğmeç ekmeği gibi kıtır kıtır*: the pepper should be as dry as the local *yufka* bread used in a local dish called *döğmeç*
- *Her şey iste bizden, biber isteme*: ask about anything but pepper
- *İyi isodun hırsızı çok olur*: good *isot* has many thieves
- *İsotsuz hayatın tadı olmaz*: without *isot*, life has no taste
- *Urfalının derdi ağzı yakan biber değil, lezzetli bir isot yemektir*: an *Urfalı* wants to eat delicious *isot*, not have his mouth burnt
- *Sıra geceleri*: *Sıra* means turn, and *sıra* nights happen by turns. When there was no entertainment in the city, men gathered to chat, to get together, and to teach the young ones about local traditions. There are three kinds of *sıra gecesi*, one with alcohol, one with religious chanting, and one with entertainment by the young ones. There are a lot of caves around Urfa, and the men clean up a cave to hold *sıra gecesi* there. *Çiğköfte* has the seat of honour on those nights. Traditionally women do not go out at night, so when the men have *sıra gecesi*, the women either gather in their houses or just stay home.[21]

Aşık İbrahim Karabulut's epic *Yurdu Gezelim*, which has fourteen verses on food and travelling in Turkey, also mentions pepper along with the famous Arabian horses: 'Throw me some pepper from Urfa, get one swarthy, one red' combining pepper and horses in the same line:

> '*Urfa'dan biber at sana bana*
> *Birin yağız birin al alalım gel.*'[22]

Urfa is known for its bards and singers, including singing poets like Tenekeci Mahmut, Hacı Nuri Hafız, Halil Hafız ve Kadir Güzel, and others, because the voices of the local men are said to be improved because of the *isot* they eat.[23]

All of these values lose their voices as *isot* travels outside the city borders, where unfortunately it becomes known merely as a purple-coloured dried chilli.

Notes

1   Ministry of Industry and Technology, 'Southeastern Anatolia Project Regional Development Administration', GAP, 2015 <http://www.gap.gov.tr/en/> [accessed 13 April 2021].

2 Türkçe Sözlük, *Ali Püsküllüoğlu* (Istanbul: Doğan Kitap, 2005), p. 872; '*İsot*', *Nişanyan Sözlük: Çağdaş Türkçenin Etimolojisi*, 2021 <https://www.nisanyansozluk.com/?k=isot&lnk=1> [accessed 13 April 2021]; *1939'dan günümüze Yazılı Kaynaklarda Yemek Kültürü Terimleri Sözlüğü*, ed. by Nilhan Aras, (Istanbul: MSA Yayınları, 2013), p. 311.

3 Özge Samancı, 'Vegetable Patrimony of the Ottoman Culinary Culture', in *Proceedings of the Fourth International Congress of Ethnobotany*, ed. by Füsun Ertuğ (Istanbul, Efe Yayınları, 2006), pp. 565-570 (p. 567).

4 Interview, Mehmet Girgin (landowner and farmer from Urfa, agricultural engineer (M.Sc)), Istanbul, age 48.

5 Mehmet H. Özal, *Özellikleri ve Güzellikleriyle Çiğköftemiz* (Istanbul: Özlem Kitabevi, 1997), pp. 56-59.

6 Özal.

7 Mehmet Saraç, *Canlarına Değsin* (Istanbul: Everest Yayınları, 2009), pp. 10-11.

8 Interview, Mrs Zehra Avşaroğlu (housewife), Urfa, age 63.

9 *Yurt Ansiklopedisi: Türkiye, İl İl, Dünü, Bugünü, Yarını*, ed. by Yücel Yama, 11 vols. (Istanbul: Anadolu Yayıncılık A.Ş. 1982-84), 10: *Tekirdağ-Tokat-Trabzon-Tunceli-Urfa-Uşak-Van-Yozgat-Zonguldak*, ed. by Cenap Nuhrat, p. 7436.

10 Avşaroğlu.

11 Interview, Mrs Adile Buluntu Akkuş (housewife), Urfa, age 60,

12 Akkuş.

13 Akkuş.

14 Avşaroğlu.

15 Avşaroğlu; Akkuş.

16 Mustafa Hakkı Aydoğdu and others, 'Şanlıurfa İsot Biberinin Pazarlama Kanallarındaki Durum Tespiti: Satıcılar Örneklemesi', *Harran Tarım ve Gıda Bilimleri Dergisi*, 20.4 (2016), 290-300 <https://wwww.doi.org/10.29050/harranziraat.282270>

17 'Urfa Eşkili – Şanlıurfa', *Türkiye Kültür Portalı* <https://www.kulturportali.gov.tr/turkiye/sanliurfa/neyenir/urfa-eskili> [accessed 15 April 2021].

18 Türkiye Cumhuriyeti Sanayi Teknoloji Bakanliği, *Türk Patent ve Marka Kurumu*, 2014 <https://www.turkpatent.gov.tr/TURKPATENT/> [accessed 15 April 2021]

19 Akkuş; interview, Prof Dr Ferit A. Atasoy (academician), Urfa, age 51.

20 Akkuş; Atasoy.

21 Akkuş.

22 *Halil İbrahim Sofrası*, ed. by Ali Abbas Çınar (Istanbul: Kitabevi, 2005), p. 58.

23 Mehmet Saraç *Canlarına Değsin* (Istanbul: Everest Yayınları, 2009), p. 21.

Season with Money, Prestige, and 'Civilization': Culinary Herbs and Spices in Colonial Congo (1885-1960)

Eva Schalbroeck

Colonial Congo did not witness largescale production of herbs and spices for culinary use. Nonetheless, they give telling insight into Belgian colonials' attitudes towards the Congolese surroundings and society, and their own role and identity. This paper firstly considers herbs and spices as reflections of the prevailing discourse built upon rationality, isolationism, and the Belgian Catholic 'civilizing mission'. It also examines them as 'witnesses in spite of themselves', elements which unintentionally revealed things which ran counter to that same narrative.[1] Accordingly, it shows how examining herbs and spices can help us to gauge the various, often contradictory, ways in which Belgian colonials dealt with unfamiliar surroundings.

Financial and Scientific Footnotes

Colonialism in the Congo does not conjure up images of colourful and fragrant spices and herbs, like the British, Portuguese, and Dutch imperial endeavours do. It is, rather, generally associated with excessive violence and racism, plunder, aggressive evangelization, disingenuous humanitarian and scientific ideals, and a chaotic decolonization. From 1885 until 1908, Léopold II, King of the Belgians, privately owned and exploited the Congo. The violent extraction of rubber and forced labour condoned under the rule of this self-proclaimed 'civilizing genius' sparked a worldwide wave of humanitarian protest. In 1908, Belgium took over the Congo and implemented reforms to root out the worst atrocities. However, as the new colonial power lacked funds and personnel, a radical economic policy overhaul did not occur.

Harsh capitalism and developmentalism relying upon minimally compensated and generally coerced Congolese labour remained the norm. Agriculture – based upon the often-obligatory cultivation of cash crops such as coffee – always played second fiddle to the hugely lucrative mining industry. Christianity and basic education were the cornerstones of the 'civilizing mission', mainly embodied by Belgian Catholic missionaries. Their Protestant counterparts, generally Americans and British, were minority figures who initially received no state funding. This reflected Belgium's fear of external influences in the Congo. Science largely revolved around 'rationalizing' the colonial and missionary endeavour, namely making them more efficient and especially more profitable. After an unplanned and chaotic decolonization in 1960, the Democratic Republic of Congo (DRC) still mostly appears in the news under the keywords 'violence', 'poverty', and 'disease'.

Thus, although the narrative of colonial Congo is generally told in the starkest terms with regards to the Leopoldian episode, similarities can be discerned between the Belgian and Leopoldian period. This rings particularly true for colonial thinking. From 1885 until 1960, colonial minds were geared towards rationality, capitalism, and the Christian 'civilizing mission'. In an enterprise carried out by the state, missions, and large companies, there were few straightforward incentives for an active and profound engagement with herbs and spices. Nonetheless, colonials and missionaries did encounter a wide variety, including cinnamon, ginger, cloves, mace, cayenne pepper or pili-pili, tamarind, pepper, vanilla, nutmeg, and various green herbs (generally described as 'fine herbs'). In the sources, most references are made to the last four types. Varieties of these herbs and spices were spread from the Americas and Asia to the African continent by European, African, and Arab traders and travellers, often via Zanzibar or Madagascar. Central Africa also had a large variety of endemic 'wild' varieties, in particular of pepper and vanilla.

Colonials thus did not introduce any herbs and spices into the Congo, but – usually haphazardly, occasionally systematically – worked with what they found. Nutmeg nuts, from trees growing along rivers, were collected by hand. Similarly, pepper shrubs growing on trees in the tropical forest were harvested when and where colonials and Africans with good climbing skills encountered them. Vanilla was more actively cultivated in 'vanilleries' in the Mayombe, Bas-Fleuve, and Kasai regions and in botanical gardens, such as the one in Eala, just outside of Coquilhatville (Mbandaka).[2] Once picked and dried, the vanilla was transported in small glass tubes.[3] It usually ended up in perfume or confectionery and desserts. Finally, thyme, parsley, and laurel were also cultivated.

Growing herbs and spices was a time-intensive activity done by a handful of people, rather than by big, state-supported enterprises. As it was a labour-intensive activity, the men involved, mostly settlers, missionaries, botanists, and businessmen, presumably worked together with their Congolese servants, cooks, labourers, and mission pupils. Due to the complicated nature of the work, the relatively good working conditions, and the personal collaborations, it most likely did not involve forced labour. Some of the herbs and spices were sold locally; others were exported at relatively low tariffs. The Belgians, known for beer, chocolate, and hearty stews, were, however, not big consumers of spices and herbs. Most Belgian dishes could be made with the 'panier traditionnel' (traditional basket), which consisted of about a dozen herbs and spices, including pepper, nutmeg, cinnamon, cloves, juniper, thyme, laurel, and vanilla. While the Dutch ate *speculaas* with spices cheaply imported from their colonies, the Belgians ate *speculoos*, a cookie with lots of sugar, but without the expensive spices.

The Belgian spice and herb diet did not really change during the colonial period. Furthermore, the Congo was not the only place where the Belgians could get their already limited '*panier*'. In the heart of Europe, Belgium was firmly embedded in extensive trade networks. For the Belgians, the Congo did not have the same meaning the Indies had for the Dutch. Herbs and spices were thus only produced on a small scale during colonial rule: no colonial returned from the Congo as a rich man by growing herbs and spices. Indeed, in statistical surveys of the colonial economy, herbs and spices are mentioned under the 'rest' heading; anonymous extras in a rather meagre economic story. They, however, do regularly crop up in cookery manuals, propaganda, and ethnographic and botanical works, sources which suggest an alternative, meatier story. Herein, herbs and spices are enhancers, supporting the main message the source conveys and the narrative of the rational, capitalist, and Belgian Catholic 'civilizing mission'. They also unintentionally reveal particular sentiments and motives at odds with this narrative.

Herbs and Spices as Enhancers and Spoilers
Exploration, Development, and Being Belgian

Until 1900, the few Belgians and other Europeans in the Congo were engrossed with exploring, surviving, and setting up the colonial administration, economy, and mission. Although getting hold of herbs and spices was not a priority, they featured regularly in travel accounts, guidebooks of world fairs held in the metropole, and publications aimed at the Belgian public. These served to give the mother country a glimpse of the colony as well as to convince the Belgians of the righteousness of the colonial endeavour. In effect, herbs and spices concretized an abstract message about a distant enterprise which did not keep most Belgians awake. *Le Congo Belge en images* (*The Belgian Congo in Images*) contained evocative descriptions of how the unpopulated land between rivers was 'covered with nutmeg nuts' due to the abundant nutmeg trees.[4] This underpinned the idea of the Congo as an unexplored country, bursting with natural riches, which the Congolese had failed to exploit.

This booklet also mentioned how men like David Livingstone, the famous British explorer, missionary, and doctor, wrote down in his travel notes the question 'who planted the nutmeg trees in Katanuta?'.[5] This elucidated the colonial ambition to develop the region's natural riches 'in collaboration' with the Congolese. The guide of the Tervuren Section of the Brussels International Exhibition of 1897 mentioned how certain Congolese ethnic groups added vanilla to brews made with coffee and cocoa beans, noting the resemblance to the habits of the Belgians' pre-modern ancestors: social Darwinism explained with a spiced drink.[6] Consternation about how the Congolese were ignorant about what 'real' pepper was – because they preferred the *Solanacaea* pepper over *Piperaceae* pepper – subtly but clearly remined readers about the nature of 'colonial collaboration': the 'superior' Belgian 'fathers' guided the 'inferior' Congolese 'children'.

Certain references to herbs and spices, however, somewhat muddled this easily digestible story. Gustave Oppelt, a writer of operas and historical works, knew how to liven up his work and did so too when contributing to the Tervuren guide. He almost boastingly explained how markets where herbs and spices were traded, such as those in Oudjiji and Nyangué on the banks of Lake Tanganyika, were attended by up to 3000 people.[7] Implicitly, he conveyed the idea that the Congolese could perfectly well cultivate herbs and spices and sell them regionally without 'external help'. In fact, they had been doing so for centuries. *Le Congo Belge en images* also devoted considerable attention to British explorers and missionaries, like Verney Lovett Cameron, the explorer who encountered a 'bed of nutmeg trees that was 40 to 50 metres long'.[8] Although these men had supported the Leopoldian endeavour, they remained Protestant and British, those associated with the downfall of King Léopold. Nonetheless, their herb and spice trophies somewhat contradictorily featured in celebratory histories of the Belgian Catholic endeavour.

Finally, 'the East', generally associated with 'the Arab slave trade', loomed large in propaganda. Another famous British traveller, Richard Burton was described finding a 'good-smelling heavy sample' of nutmeg in Uswi, north of Unyamwési. He ostentatiously claimed it was 'really superior to the product from Zanzibar'. It was also reported that 'in Maniema and Urua, there is a [red] pepper [...] the size of a marble [...] which is so strong that the Arabs – who eat pepper by the handful – cannot stomach it'.[9] The explicit reassurance that the spices and herbs found in the Congo were as good, if not better, than those found in 'the East' – traditionally known for them – was at odds with confident statements about how the Belgians singlehandedly defeated the 'barbaric Arabs'.

Herbs and spices not only buttressed and undermined conceptions about exploration and development, but also those concerning 'Belgian food'. Due to the relative economic insignificance of herbs and spices, there are no systematic overviews of the types and quantities early colonials consumed. Documentation on food prices gives an idea – or at least of what it was believed administrators should or could eat. In the *Bas-Congo* (Kongo Central), they paid 0.20 francs for salt, pepper, and oil, the only 'condiments' deemed necessary to turn strong Portuguese wine, fresh meat, butter, eggs, and tinned vegetables – not unlike the things they would eat in Belgium – into a couple of meals in 1899.[10] *Le Congo Belge en images* explained to Belgians in Belgium who were curious or concerned about what their compatriots in the Congo ate that it was perfectly possible to grow 'Belgian' fruit, vegetables, and herbs in the colony. It contained a testimony of a colonial who had successfully made a 'classic', a salad of tomatoes and mayonnaise; not a dish known for its unusual herb and spice mix.

By eating 'proper' Belgian food, colonials not only wanted to maintain their connection with their own country. They also believed that this was paramount to remaining healthy in a climate considered unsuitable for their bodies. Such fears were not unique to Belgian colonialism or colonialism in the nineteenth and twentieth centuries in general. Similar fears prevailed during, among others, the Spanish colonization of the Americas, as examined by Rebecca Earle.[11] Belgian colonials' concerns thus unwittingly echoed century-old 'classic' fears, somewhat counteracting all their talk about modernity and progress.

The administrators in question were generally single men who stayed in the Congo for only a few years. They were not encouraged to bring their wives or start a family. Often 'boys', male servants, did their cooking and washing. In some cases, colonials took on a '*menagère*', denoting both a housekeeper and a mistress; another potential cook.

Whether administrators were giving orders to their 'boys' and '*menagères*' or cooking for themselves over a bush fire, they were forced to properly think about cooking – ideally something flavoursome – for the first time in their lives. Albert Page, a former colonial agent, sensed a gap in the market and wrote *Guide pratique de la cuisine au Congo*.[12]

This sensible booklet contained no less than four pages of recipes with a very Belgian staple: the potato. Among others soufflés, galettes, and mash could all be made with just four 'condiments': pepper, thyme, parsley, and laurel. This booklet showed colonials how to put the theory of 'eating Belgian' in practice. The dish '*pommes de terre á la Bangala*' (Bangala – another word for Lingala, a Congolese language – potatoes) contained precisely the same herbs and spices as most of the others. One of the few recipes which required a spice which could have come from Congolese surroundings was the familiar '*crème à la vanille*'. Although these last dishes strongly resembled Belgian ones, they hinted at adaptability and pragmatism, something generally not so loudly advertised.

Scientific Rationality, Prestige, and Curiosity

From 1910 onwards, Belgian colonial rule expanded, something most visible in the growing network of schools, hospitals, and companies. This was facilitated by the boom of 'colonial sciences', such as botany. Various botanical exploration trips were undertaken, while botanical gardens and agricultural schools mushroomed in Belgium and the Congo. Despite having never set foot in the Congo, Émile De Wildeman was considered an expert on Congolese plants and thus also herbs and spices. Between 1912 and 1931, he headed the Botanical Garden of Brussels, which was connected with the one in Eala.[13] Gardens in Belgium and the Congo exchanged information and specimens with those in other countries and colonies, such the garden of Buitenzorg in Java (the Dutch Indies) and Kew in Great Britain.

During this period, Belgian interest in herbs and spices in the Congo notably increased. Shifting conceptions of the 'civilization mission' in part explains this. Initial ideas about erasing the 'primitive' and 'worthless' Congolese society and rebuilding it according to 'superior' Christian and European norms gave way to the 'guardianship model' from 1918 onwards: colonials and missionaries believed that Congolese surroundings could serve as the basis of colonial society, given that they were 'improved' according to European norms. This compromise between acknowledging Congolese culture and seeing all its aspects through European-tinted glasses is particularly visible in histories, herbaria, and ethnographic works. A history of the missionary endeavour in the Congo in a Catholic periodical mentioned that the pepper trade between Central Africa and Europe had existed since the fifteenth century, until the Portuguese king forbade it out of fear of competition.[14]

Herbaria included meticulous notes on how Europeans thought particular spices were called in the many languages spoken in the Congo. Pepper, for example, was called '*embongwa*' in the Bambesa region. The Mongwandi called it '*gbomboli*'. In the Lingala dialect, it was known under various names including 'boloko, bololoko, and pilipili'.[15] In his 'descriptive sociological' work about the Baluba (Luba) people, Scheut missionary

Father Pierre Colle noted that this ethno-linguistic group in the centre and south of the Congo was not too keen on herbs and spices. Although '*exitants*' (stimulating and sexually arousing things) like pili-pili or cayenne pepper were abundant in the region, the Baluba did not use them, according to Colle. Colle and the creator of the herbarium presumably interacted with people from the described tribes, but they did not actively collaborate with them or acknowledge their insights. Actively encouraging Congolese culinary habits was considered a bridge too far.

The Belgians' interest in herbs and spices also grew simply because they, now ruling the Congo rather than just exploring it, looked at their surroundings differently: after the conquering, came the taming, or at least the ambition to. The neat, orderly overview of the 'wild' African flora in the garden of Eala embodied their efforts and wishful thinking. During the interwar period, scientific ideas about rationality peaked. Botanists, including De Wildeman, too were preoccupied with figuring out how crop cultivation could be done in the most economical and thus most profitable manner. He compared different types of 'African' peppers and vanilla and their degree of *piperine* and *vanilline* to find out whether they could replace or substitute 'common' pepper and vanilla plants. As sophisticated as his chemical analyses and classifications looked, he presumably also spent considerable time tasting and smelling the pepper and vanilla. He concluded that, in spite of the complicated procedure to pollinate, grow, harvest, and conserve vanilla – the plant required a lot of care, specific growing circumstances, and a good dose of luck – doing so in the Congo was practically feasible.

Actually selling and exporting the spice, however, was a whole different matter. De Wildeman wondered whether the 'Congolese pepper' could be acknowledged as an equivalent of the 'original' one, to ensure it would stand a chance on the market. He also condemned vanilla manipulations, which, according to him, resulted in overly expensive products with an inferior taste and health consequences.[16] Although De Wildeman was interested in the culinary aspect of the matter, his thinking was in line with the prevailing economic focus. But why then did he spend so much time racking his brains about a crop with a yield that paled in comparison to, say, that of cotton in an endeavour in which making money was the prime rationale? Men like De Wildeman found in examining these complex and hard-to-grow herbs and spices some form of prestige, which they felt they – in spite of international recognition – did not receive from the state.[17] In these studies, he could also give free reign to particular interests. De Wildeman was fascinated by the habit of certain ethnic groups of seasoning their food with the ground aromatic bark of the *Xylopias* tree.[18] He was also not too prudish to mention the aphrodisiacal reputation of vanilla. Finally, he boasted that 'special specimens', such as vanilla and pepper plants, could only be seen in 'his' garden.[19]

A similar story goes for certain missionaries. Although they perpetually complained about being short on staff and funds, some, like the White Fathers in Baudouinville (Moba) still found time to cultivate one of the most time-consuming spices: vanilla. Although missionaries emphasized their evangelizing zeal, they too did not shy away from the adventure and prestige

291

associated with growing a vanilla that would rival the so-called 'best' Mexican variety. Thus, while debates about pepper and vanilla fitted in with notions of scientific rationality, the plants in question were also objects of personal curiosity and prestige.

Exchange, Isolationism, and Fusion Cuisine

The Belgian colony not only survived the Second World War relatively unscathed, but also saw its economy expand. After this very international episode, the Belgians reaffirmed their policy of splendid isolation. Although they conceded to funding Protestants and Catholics on equal terms, they emphasized the Catholic nature of the colonial endeavour. Legal reforms were part of Belgian colonials' efforts to 'reward the war effort' of the Congolese. *Evolués* ('evolved Congolese'), the term for the new middle-class Congolese, could get their so-called 'higher-developed status' certified. Eating and seasoning food like a Belgian was part and parcel of their efforts to 'be like the Belgians'. In *foyers*, urban domestic training centres, Congolese middle-class women were taught how to make Belgian food, which seemed rather grey and bland in comparison to what they were used to.[20] Not all colonials, however, believed food was a viable route into 'European civilization'. Sacred Hearts missionary Gustaaf Hulstaert, for example, accused *evolués* 'unable to financially afford a European lifestyle' of 'putting on a show': 'they only dressed and dined like Europeans when these came to visit'.[21]

From the 1940s onwards, the Belgian population in the Congo visibly expanded. More administrators stayed longer and brought their wives and families. According to popular works, some ventured into 'traditional Congolese cuisine', such as *poulet moambe*. This chicken stew with tomato, onion, and palm nuts was usually served with finely cut cassava leaves and baked cooking banana or plantain.[22] It generally contained pepper, occasionally some nutmeg and laurel, but its distinctive taste came from pili-pili. Presumably, this so-called typical dish was many Belgian colonials' first encounter with this spice. They most likely got the recipe from their Congolese cooks or perhaps from one of the Congolese women in the *foyers*. In practice, there was thus room for exchange in places where in theory a one-sided 'civilizing mission' took place. Whether colonials stayed true to the recipes, tried other dishes, or whether this was all just some '*plaisanterie*' remains an open question.

These 'experiments' fitted in with the careful exchange and exploration – whereby colonials stayed on 'their side' of the racial divide – which had characterized Belgian colonial rule so far. Profound knowledge of African herbs and spices was never considered a means of attaining an 'insider status' or of 'going native', like in the Dutch East Indies. This was also true of indigenists, those who proposed utmost respect for and study of African culture. Hulstaert, for example, was an expert on Mongo language and culture, but barely mentioned food. 'Real Congolese', according to him, 'can serve you a cup of coffee with sugar (but no milk), rice, potatoes, and bananas'.[23]

The *Livre de cuisine du Congo* (*Book of Congolese Cuisine*) is the biggest surprise – both to Belgian colonials and readers today. It does not contain Congolese dishes, as its title seems to suggest.[24] Alongside recipes which Belgian colonial women would have recognized, there were some unfamiliar recipes. These included 'Savoury Pudding', made with salt, pepper, and fine herbs, and 'Freshly Made Ravioli' with nutmeg. Last but not least is an 'Indian Delicacy with Cheese', a mixture of mango, cheese, eggs, fine herbs, bread, macaroni, raisins, seasoning, and curry powder, steamed for no less than four hours and served with, of all things, cheese sauce. That this booklet is a translation of something originally written by a British woman, presumably the wife of a Protestant missionary, clarifies much of the culinary confusion. Presumably, this booklet catered to their own community, as well as British women elsewhere in Africa.

It remains unclear who took the initiative to translate this booklet into French. Were the British keen to tap into a new audience of Belgian women who had little colonial culinary resources at their disposal? Or did the Belgians hastily translate it to avoid poorly fed Belgian bodies? Whatever the motives behind this translation, the references to curry powder and British recipes do pertinently reveal the holes in the 'Belgian bubble': it was impossible to keep the Congo free from 'foreign influences', in spite of the authorities' strenuous efforts, in part due to economic development. It remains hard to tell how many people actually cooked these recipes.

Nonetheless, they show that there is a fair chance that Belgians in the Congo not only tried on new fashions more quickly than Belgians in Belgium, but presumably also tasted curry powder before those they had left behind. Growing Belgian usage of herbs and spices reflected a growing genuine interest in the Congolese environment, as well as the allure and the perceived threat of the world beyond it, which had increasingly come into reach. The result was not the recreation of 'authentic' dishes, as done today. Rather, is was fusion cuisine *avant la lettre,* foreshadowing the weird dishes 1980s cuisine would produce.

Postcolonial Leftovers

Herbs and spices are generally not seen as part of Belgium's colonial legacy, like curry spices are associated with British rule. While it is possible to eat the spicy *poulet moambe* (and other dishes) in Brussels and Antwerp, on the whole Belgium does not have an equivalent of the British curry culture. Similarly, typical Belgian dishes have not really found entry in Congolese cuisine. That Belgian tastes became more multicultural mainly due to cheaper travel and labour migration from Maghreb countries and Turkey, rather from its former colony (like in Great Britain and the Netherlands) partly explains this. But perhaps 'leftovers' – inspired by Ann Laura Stoler's concepts of 'debris' and 'decay' – offers a way to better think about how people have dealt with the remains of colonial rule, remains which do not always have a fixed form.[25]

Decolonization was hasty, chaotic, and at times violent. From one day to the next, most colonials were evacuated. Especially for children this was a traumatic experience, one which they are only now putting into words. The daughter of a former administrator stated, 'I never digested the flight from the Congo (in 1960). I was born there and experienced the nicest years of my youth there. The Congo still lives in my memories and I want to return if I ever get the chance. Especially the smell I will never forget, the sweet smell of vanilla.'[26] For her, recalling the smell of vanilla was a very powerful, visceral way of giving place to her unspoken sense of loss.

For the Congolese side of the story, it is more productive to think about what does not remain. Various recent press pieces decry that too few people consume and know of regional herbs and spices. During colonial rule, indigenous practices and knowledge were discouraged. Flora was either deliberately destroyed or indirectly damaged by colonial economic development. The introduction of new crops also impinged upon the ecosystem long after 1960. Also, a lack of interest and investment from the DRC government, instability due to armed conflict, and infrastructural and economic problems – elements which have colonial roots – are cited as culprits.[27] Some deploy the same 'recipe'. Although the efforts of Spiritan Father Lucien Favre to help the Baka people in northern Congo harvest wild pepper stem from religious motives, and are backed by UNICEF and a charity, one cannot help but smell a colonial waft.[28]

Others creatively repurpose the leftovers. Sandrine Vasselin Kabonga, belonging to the Congolese diaspora in Belgium, sells pepper from Kivu, her home region, in Europe. Rather than replicate postcolonial structures, she deliberately chose to sustainably harvest and export the pepper with Congolese directly affected by conflict. Her mission statement rings: 'revealing African treasures' helps to avoid the further loss of ancestral knowledge. Even in this uplifting tale, there is more than meets the eye. Her website also contains a personal story about the discovery of a jar of pungent pepper which 'summoned up the smell' of her home region. The pepper is not only sold online, but also sits along the Himalayan pink salt in Michelin starred restaurants and luxury food markets.[29] The website furthermore highlights how all spices are grown locally and organically and produced in an artisanal manner. While these are genuine and legitimate concerns, they also speak to ideas currently in vogue among those most inclined to buy the spices, namely chefs and 'foodies'. The Instagram-look of the website, rather than a 'traditional African' theme, is also smart marketing. Even when the aims of cultural and culinary exploration and making money are reversed in the pecking order, they remain inherently bound up.

Conclusion

Which herbs and spices Belgian colonials did or did not consume is in itself interesting. Nonetheless, we should also take herbs and spices seriously as reflections and shapers of overall attitudes and ideas. They allow us to see prevailing concerns about rationality and 'Belgian food for Belgian bodies', and their basis in colonial power structures and racial divides, from a different angle. By taking the sources' dominant and implicit messages together, we best understand the wide range of motives and contradictions involved in making sense of an unfamiliar environment, either because a person left their home country for a colonial career or a missionary vocation or because colonialism profoundly tainted someone else's home country. These are not hidden, but neither are they addressed. Accordingly, herbs and spices, elements which might have been overlooked from a purely economic perspective, can help us to see colonialism in the Congo in less stark and in more vivid terms.

Notes

1   Marc Bloch, *The Historian's Craft* (Manchester: Manchester University Press, 1954), p. 51.
2   Émile De Wildeman, *Notices sur des plantes utiles ou intéressantes de la flore du Congo* (Brussels: Veuve Monnom, 1905), p. 329.
3   *L'agriculture au Congo Belge et au Ruanda-Urundi de 1948 à 1952* (Brussels: Ministère des Colonies, 1954), pp. 149-50, 155.
4   *Le Congo Belge en images* (Brussels: Lebègue, 1927), p. 114.
5   *Le Congo Belge en images*, p. 114.
6   Théodore Masui and Charles Liebrechts, Guide de la Section de l'Etat Indépendant du Congo à l'Exposition de Bruxelles-Tervuren en 1897 (Brussels: Veuve Monnom, 1897), p. 170.
7   Gustave Oppelt, *Léopold II – roi des Belges, chef de l'État Indépendant du Congo* (Brussels: Hayez, 1885).
8   *Le Congo Belge en images*, p. 114.
9   *Le Congo Belge en images*, p. 114.
10   Joseph Plas and Victor Pourbaix, *Les sociétés commerciales Belges et le régime économique et fiscal de l'Etat Indépendant du Congo* (Brussels: Lesigne, 1898), p. 40.
11   Rebecca Earle, *The Body of the Conquistador: Food, Race, and the Colonial Experience in Spanish America, 1492-1700* (Cambridge: Cambridge University Press, 2012).
12   Albert Page, *Guide pratique de la cuisine au Congo* (Antwerp: Van Nylen, 1909).
13   De Wildeman, *Notices*, p. 120.
14   De Wildeman *Notices*, p. 120.
15   'Piperaceae', *Flore du Congo Belge et du Ruanda-Urundi* (Brussels: Institut National pour l'Etude Agronomique du Congo Belge, 1948), I, p. 17.
16   De Wildeman, 'Sur les Poivres Indigènes du Congo. Note Préliminaires', *Bulletin des Séances de l'Institut Royal Colonial Belge*, 2 (1931), 346; De Wildeman, *Notices*, pp. 1-32, 120-49.
17   Myriam Mertens and Guillaume Lachenal, 'The History of "Belgian" Tropical Medicine from a Cross-Border Perspective', *Revue Belge de Philologie et de Histoire*, 90.4 (2012), 1249-72.
18   Émile De Wildeman, *Les plantes tropicales de grande culture* (Brussels: Castaigne, 1908), 21.
19   De Wildeman, *Notices*, p. 121.
20   Nancy Rose Hunt, 'Domesticity and Colonialism in Belgian Africa: Usumbura's Foyer Social, 1946-1960', *Signs*, 15 (1990), 447-74.
21   Gustaaf Hulstaert to Alexis Kagame, 14/08/1946, Centre Aequatoria (Mbandaka, DRC), Correspondence Gustaaf Hulstaert, Special Correspondence, X. Kagame, Box. 64-65, Film 22, CH 4.5.
22   Jan Raymaekers, *Congo: de schoonste tijd van mijn leven: getuigenissen van oud-kolonialen in woord en beeld* (Antwerpen: Van Halewyck, 2009), p. 120.
23   Hulstaert to Kagame, 21/10/1944, 14/08/1946, and 02/06/1947, Aequatoria.
24   Clare Willett, *Livre de cuisine du Congo* (Saint-Savin: Librairie Raimbeau 1942).
25   Ann Laura Stoler, 'Imperial Debris: Reflections on Ruin and Ruination', *Cultural Anthropology*, 23.2 (2008), 191-219.
26   *Herinneringen aan Congo*, ed. by Fred Herckens e.a. (Antwerp: Garant, 2006), p. 47.
27   Muriel Devey Malu-Malu, 'Bassin du Congo. L'Afrique des Epices Méconnues', *Makanisi* <https://www.makanisi.org/bassin-du-congo-lafrique-des-epices-meconnues/> [accessed 30 November 2020].
28   *Report Activities Père Lucien Favre* <https://sod3452258127386e.jimcontent.com/download/version/1539183392/module/7693730356/name/nouvelle%20lucien%20pour%20le%20site.pdf> [accessed 30 November 2020].
29   Muriel Devey Malu-Malu, 'Misao, ce poivre sauvage du Kivu qui séduit des chefs étoilés', *Le Point Economie* <https://www.lepoint.fr/economie/misao-ce-poivre-sauvage-du-kivu-qui-seduit-des-chefs-etoiles-13-02-2018-2194671_28.php#> [accessed 30 November 2020].

'This is all very well, but where in Ireland can you get fresh tarragon?' Myrtle Allen and Herbs: Towards the Creation of an Irish Food Identity

Regina Sexton

In February 1966, Myrtle Allen of Ballymaloe House in East Cork, enticed readers of her food column, 'Cookery', in the *Irish Farmers Journal* (*IFJ*) with a description of casserole-roasted chicken. Her instruction to bake the chicken with tarragon and butter in a covered casserole with the resultant juices thickened with a teaspoon of flour and a quarter pint of cream to make a sauce, is '[t]he best and simplest way I know for cooking a broiler'. However, for many of her readers, this best way of cooking chicken would remain beyond reach. Fresh tarragon was not widely available in Ireland, Myrtle Allen's seedsmen 'smugly crossed it off' her list year after year, and her 'precious sprig propagating in [her] garden' was brought to her by a 'foreign friend'.[1] In the absence of tarragon, as evident in Myrtle's question, 'where in Ireland can you get fresh tarragon?', she gave a more detailed recipe for 'casserole roasted chicken' where the elusive 'foreign' herb is replaced with a bouquet garni.

This glimpse into Irish cookery in the mid-1960s can be viewed as a rich micro-image of a culinary culture in the process of change, and Myrtle Allen, an unpretentious farmer's wife with six young children, would through her cookery, writings, and activism come to question and shape Irish food culture in the latter half of the century. This paper will discuss her relationship with herbs as a case study of a community and a food culture in flux.

Viewed through her engagement with herbs, this exploration marks the first detailed analysis of Myrtle's contribution to the formation of a modern food identity for Ireland.[2] It argues that examining Myrtle's relationship with herbs elucidates the food philosophy of a gentle but driven woman who was at once ahead of and very much of her time in an era of considerable change in Ireland. This analysis provides a contextual background from which to map the extension, reception, and impact of her philosophy in domestic and international communities of food producers, chefs, and consumers. This research relies heavily on Myrtle's papers: following her death on 13 June 2018, the author examined and assessed Myrtle's extensive personal archive in advance of the Allen family's bequest of the collection to University College Cork. This body of kitchen, restaurant, and personal papers revealed that herbs were a consistent feature of her writings, reflections, and practices, and this paper provides the first insight into aspects of the content and nature of her papers, which are now being catalogued.[3] This discussion is confined largely to Myrtle's work in the 1960s, based on early menus from Ballymaloe House, her journals of food writing, and her food articles in the *IFJ*.

Myrtle's relationship with herbs evolved steadily as she built her relationship with food through her cooking, her cookery classes, her food writing, and her food activism. The relationship built tentatively, with her early recipes and menus noticeably herb-shy: the opening night menus for the House dining room, The Yeats Room, are typical of their time and without distinctive character. Subsequently, a slow-building profile for herbs is evident as the menus evolved to accommodate a growing customer base: an early booklet of menus from 1964 features routine meat/fish and herb-pairings: herb butter for steak, rosemary with lamb, and Ballycotton plaice in herb butter (Figures 1 and 2).[4] To this point her engagement with food is shaped by inherited family styles of cookery and her early but brief cookery training. Her childhood food culture aligned to typical middle-class trends: her mother's handwritten books record recipes for plain, substantial savoury dishes where herbs, predominantly the trio of thyme, parsley, and bay, are used in set if not mandatory ways to flavour soups, stews, and assorted savoury

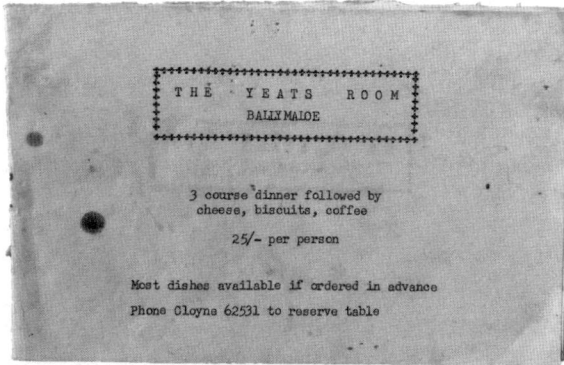

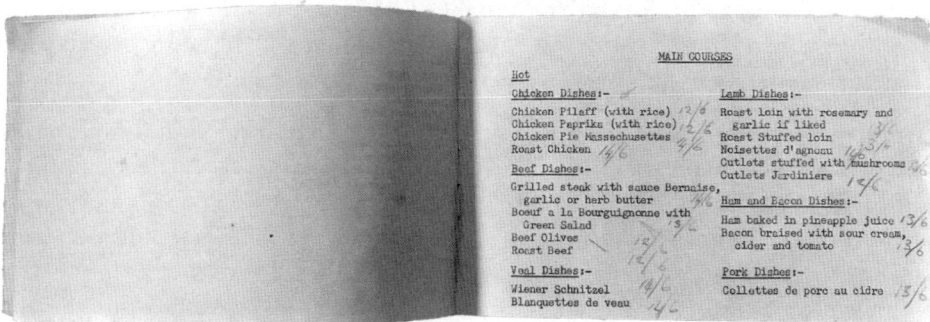

Figure 1 and 2: Small booklet of menus detailing the courses and meals served in the opening season of The Yeats Dining Room at Ballymaloe House, Co. Cork. 1964. By kind permission of Ballymaloe House and Special Collections & Archives, Boole Library, University College Cork.

dishes.[5] The only herb treated individually is parsley, which plays multiple roles as a dish flavouring, as a decorative item, and in the ever-present parsley sauce. Amongst the handwritten recipes, a single scrap newspaper cutting advises to 'make more use of mint'. In Myrtle's childhood food culture, herbs played secondary roles in repetitive and customary ways. Equally, her unconventional cookery training did little to develop curiosity to unlock herbs' potential. Myrtle's unstructured, brief training conformed to contemporary trends with a nod to received notions of the superiority of French cuisine. Here she describes the events that led to a life in the kitchen:

> I myself, have practically no training in cooking. After school (Frensham Heights, Surrey and Newtown School, Waterford) I took some elementary lessons in cookery at the Cork School of Commerce and I spent a week before the restaurant opened in the Cordon Bleu School in London. I was very young and unable to cook when I got married but learned in my own kitchen with my husband's products [and] various books (Philip Harben's "The Way to Cook" gave me the first grasp of the subject). […] A restaurant was always on our minds so in May 1964 we started timidly in our own dining room to serve the food we produced and offer the type of dinners which one might expect in any similar large private country house in Ireland.[6]

As a self-directed cook, her evolving and intrinsic sense of food connected directly to her experiential learning and reflective practice, and was influenced directly by her marriage to a farmer and by her immersion in a community of small local producers and fisherman:

> My husband has quite an extensive farming and fruit growing concern. This included a wide range of products, mushrooms, cucumbers, apples, tomatoes, a variety of field vegetables, milk, cream, home grown veal, eggs and so on. We live in a fertile farming area. What we do not produce ourselves we can pick up for free at the moment […] watercress from the local streams, quality fat geese from my neighbours, fresh fish from the small fishing village of Ballycotton, excellent meat from the local butcher who fattens and kills his animals locally.[7]

As a progressive and innovative vegetable grower, Myrtle's husband, Ivan, hosted regular visits of European commercial horticulturists to his east Cork farm. At these gatherings, Paddy O'Keeffe, editor of Ireland's farming newspaper the *IFJ*, experienced Myrtle's cooking for family and visiting agricultural advisors. Table talk revealed her food philosophy: that food and meals should be simple, varied, tasty, and within the budget of a farmer's wife. With the Farm Home Pages section in mind, O'Keeffe invited Myrtle to write a series of cookery articles: the first, published on 28 July 1962, details that the column is 'by a farmer's wife for farmers' wives'.[8] By late 1964, Myrtle had a media platform that voiced opinion not only on cookery but also on contemporary agricultural policy and a rapidly changing Irish food system. The Ballymaloe kitchen and The Yeats Dining Room gave her space to put a physical shape on an evolving food philosophy increasingly untouched by the rigidly formulaic approach taken by cookery training institutions.

Unburdened by such training, she began to develop an increasingly critical and reflective approach to ingredients and cookery styles. Her journals from the period often consider a dish or an ingredient in multiple temporal and spatial settings. Contemporary food developments are mulled over, framed against their impact on local producers, many of whom were her kitchen suppliers. Her past is revisited sometimes to prompt revision of what would become her guiding principles for choosing, sourcing, and cooking ingredients. One journal entry recalls a class in the time of rationing, 'The French Lesson': wondering about the French term 'gourmet', she remembers thinking 'how funny to have a special name for him, we thought, with the reality of porridge & stew ahead and only the dream of a rasher & egg'. This comparative interplay between outside and home/internal food cultures, with its implied tension between a higher order of what was considered good food and a lower order of simplicity embodied in porridge and stew, would reshape her ethos on food. On consideration she constructs her own definition of a gourmet:

> Who's a gourmet anyway? I believe the man who relishes a floury Irish spud carefully chosen for quality, grown & picked in his own garden, cooked in its jacket and served to him fresh from the pot with a shake of salt and a knob of golden butter – he is an Irish gourmet and no one from Paris to New York & back again can tell him a thing about quality + flavour in food. The thing about a gourmet is that he is not a snob, but what he eats must be perfect in quality and perfectly cooked, be it an egg, a loaf of soda bread, pâté foie gras or a bottle of wine or even a cup of tea.[9]

A developing critical voice considered food at its most elemental level. In an *IFJ* article, 'Picnic Packs', she revisits the topic of the carefully chosen and cooked potato and reiterates the claim that no more than three ingredients can deliver a memorable, if not visceral, gastronomic experience. For a seaside picnic she suggests bringing cold meats, salad, and a pot of scrubbed uncooked potatoes: 'Cooked in salt water on the strand & eaten with butter, I tell you, this is the spud of your life.'[10]

Myrtle's maturing food philosophy emphasized three key factors: quality, taste, and deliberately simple cooking techniques, where quality was defined in accordance with how, where, and by whom ingredients were produced or reared.[11] Her aim was to support a short food chain with anything not produced at home procured locally and wild foods in season collected for the kitchen. In this context, farm vegetables and the herb garden defined the House's food style, as herbs emerged as leading players in a distinctive Ballymaloe cookery style. In another journal entry, she acknowledges their importance: 'Freely available outdoors, I will soon be able to pick masses of herbs and rhubarb so they should form the backbone of our menus.'[12] And beyond the importance of herbs in directing cookery style and in framing taste, Myrtle also understood the role

299

of mixed herbage in grazing pastures in determining the taste profile of meat and dairy produce. In a statement that has come to embody Myrtle's relationship with food, she sketches a story about the butter she bought from the local farmer. Implicit in the detail is the message that diverse grasslands produce pleasant, site-complex flavours (Figure 3): 'I bought a few pounds of fresh butter from my neighbours, "That butter you sold me had a marvellous flavour", I said. "Ah yes" was his reply "that field always made good butter". But nobody cares about flavour any longer, not to that degree. My heavens, where are we going.'[13]

Recognizing the interconnectedness of environmental factors, agricultural methods, and human endeavour also drew Myrtle to Mr. Cuddigan, the butcher in the nearby village of Cloyne, who grazed and finished his animals on mixed-herb grasslands. As a farmer's wife knowledgeable in the intricacies of food production, Myrtle was well-positioned to appreciate Wendell Berry's statement that 'eating is an agricultural act', and she located herself in the system to act as an agent delivering recipes and dishes chosen for quality and taste based on production pace and sense of place.[14] In effect, her cooking was not a single act but rather an expression of community. In this environment, rather than cultivating the cult of Ballymaloe chef for herself, she remained the consummate but humble professional cook. In the *Observer Magazine*, Sue Arnold noted that Myrtle placed the quality of ingredients above the work of the cook: 'good food has very little to do with cooking and everything to do with good ingredients. Of course, she appreciated being in the food guides, but what those inspectors should really be doing was checking the raw materials, not the consistency of the sauce or the size of the dining room'.[15]

Thus far this descriptive narrative of one woman's development of a food philosophy based on home and community food production and her support of traditional farming methods (with herbs playing a central role in both kitchen and field) could be viewed as merely a local expression of a general style encountered in many country house enterprises. In a present-day context, we recognize the elements of Myrtle's approach – local food in season, slow production methods, quality defined by alignment to the ethics of sustainable production and responsible consumption – as the

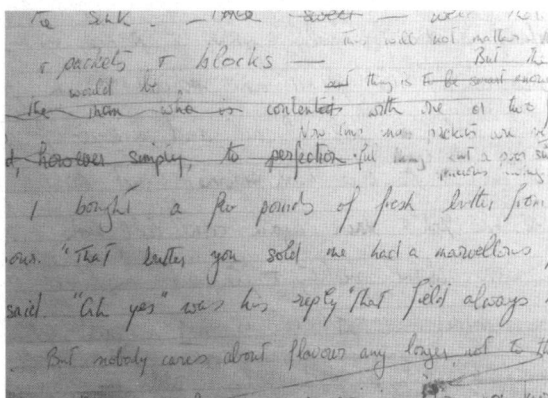

Figure 3: 'That field always made good butter.' The famous line that illustrates Myrtle Allen's intuitive understanding of the importance of herbs to ingredient quality. By kind permission of Ballymaloe House and Special Collections & Archives, Boole Library, University College Cork.

300

main tenets of an alternative food system that operates at a distance from mainstream practice. However, retrospection, presentism, and the relatively recent maturation of such discourses, whether public, populist, or academic, detract from the novel, dissenting, and eccentric nature of Myrtle's mindset in 1960s Ireland.

The decade saw Ireland break with its obsessive attachment to inward gazing and embrace a more liberal and outward engagement with the world. Multidimensional changes encouraged by cheap overseas travel, increased education opportunity, and an emerging youth culture – intensified by the establishment of a state television service in 1961 – ruptured a 'hermetically sealed national culture'.[16] And while Ireland did not stand apart from its British and European neighbours in experiencing this quickening social change, the particularities of Irish economic conditions following the establishment of the Free State left Ireland especially welcoming of outside influences.[17] The economic policy of protectionism and isolationism disadvantaged farmers' ability to access markets and good prices, while the economic slump after World War II left the country depressed by emigration, unemployment, and migration from rural areas to cities. The drive towards economic liberalization and departure from protectionism in the First Programme for Economic Recovery (1958-63) improved international trade and inward investment, which in turn disrupted not only the jaded ambition toward economic independence but also the ideologies of cultural self-sufficiency. Added to the mix was a steady progression of the rural electrification scheme which from 1946 transformed Irish rural life. And, in the background, the Treaty of Rome sought to secure food and stabilize markets by increasing productivity through applying scientific and technological innovations to agricultural practice and food production.

301

In this climate of transformation, an older order of agricultural and dietary practice was enthusiastically replaced with the objects of technological innovation and the products of science: a process which marked the post-Famine period but accelerated in this new era of rapid change and prosperity. For a certain rural demographic, electricity brought the electric cooker to rural homes, moving cooking from open hearths to hobs and ovens. A burgeoning tourism industry afforded rural communities opportunities to generate income by offering guest house accommodation and farmhouse meals. This kaleidoscope of change clashed with the vested interests of the tourism industry that was best served by presenting an old-world Ireland resplendent with thatch cottages and stews cooked over open fires. Many of the tensions associated with change played out in the pages of the *IFJ*, and as its food writer Myrtle often assumed roles of commentator, educator, and soundboard responding to changes in Irish food culture. Two examples illustrate her observations and reflections:

> As the standard of living goes up one kind of food takes a back seat while another becomes popular [...]. In the fish line, I'm sad to see cod, pollack, mullet and even bream out while plaice, sole and salmon enjoy all the front seats.[18]

An English visitor toured the west before calling on us some years ago. The scenery was marvellous, but not the food! 'Why serve fish fingers when they overlook the sea? Why tinned vegetables, can they not grow fresh ones? Why no cream when the hotel has its own milking herd? Rashers and eggs for 17 meals for a stay of 10 days!' he wailed.[19]

Consequently, her writing often becomes didactic as she supplies menu options for guest-house owners: simple ways to prepare fresh fish and advice to use fresh herbs to improve the taste quality of dishes. Her instruction for pairing roast chicken with fresh herbs – 'The following method for roasting a chicken in butter in a gentle oven demonstrates best how herbs transform an ordinary dish into something very delicious' – falls in with her frequent recommendations to include more fruit and vegetables in meals.[20] The imagined offerings that the typical Irish farmhouse might offer to foreign guests, as outlined below, sets up the purity of Ireland as a haven of respite for those whose food cultures were denigrated by industrialized food production:

Ireland has been 'found' by the holiday makers [...]. Most of our guests come from industrial areas where they are restricted physically by urban and industrial development. Their food is anything but 'farm fresh' [–] most of it will have travelled many miles from its origin – they will expect fresh cream and milk from the cow, and their children will dream of collecting eggs from the henhouse. They will expect homemade scones and soda bread and good country butter if it can be made or bought; freshly caught fish if the coast is near and they will also expect that rarest of commodities on an Irish farm – fresh vegetables and fruit.[21]

Myrtle's attention to the restricted range of fruits and vegetables in the Irish diet is important as a new iteration of a recurring discourse that linked the lack of diversity and a deficiency of vegetables and fruits to an underdeveloped food culture. From the late eighteenth century onwards, individuals, groups, and government agencies advocated for greater dietary diversity to safeguard against the insecurities inherent in the potato-dominated diet of small farmers and the poor. Cultivating a food garden to produce vegetables, fruit, pulses, and herbs brought nutritional benefit and stretched more expensive food items. The role of herbs in facilitating these sound domestic economy measures is a theme consistently expounded in allegorical, fictional, and government reports. The increased attachment to commercial goods – tea, white baker's bread, sugar, cheap fats, and fruit spreads – filled the debates and action responses of social reform movements and government directives in the post-Famine period, while the realities of extreme nutritional deficiency in urban and rural areas concerned both the Congested Districts Board and the Departments of Agriculture and Education in the early decades of the Free State. The lack of diversity and a propensity to consume poor commercial products above fresh fruits and vegetables was linked not only to the economic health of the nation but also to its social health and the strength of its moral character.[22] Bell and Watson detail the explicit paternal responsibility taken by the Department of Agricultural and Technical Instruction in encouraging labourers to develop 'a potentially idyllic lifestyle, in which the garden [or urban allotment] played a crucial role and if the opportunity to betterment was wasted it could be integrated into lifestyle choices by education and leadership.[23] The humble herb, therefore, was a means to economic, social, and moral betterment with potential to offer a sense of fullness and meaning to rural and urban labourers' lifestyles.

That advocacy for fruit, vegetable, and herb consumption should continue in Myrtle's polemics indicates the minor role herbs played in mainstream Irish dietary patterns; there was little interest in growing beyond the thyme, parsley, sage (and maybe a bit of bay) trio. The Irish traditional farm concentrated on livestock production on a commercial basis with high economic value assigned to meat and milk, leaving women concerned with keeping fowl for meat and eggs as domestic butter-making for the home and market declined. With the farm concerned with fluctuating prices for milk and meat, and women exercised by the redesign of rural homes to accommodate electricity and indoor plumbing, growing herbs was not a priority. In rural areas, 'herbs' was the collective term used for plants with medicinal properties. Therefore, for the rural population that made up Myrtle's readership in the *IFJ*, herbs did not enter their routine culinary activities: to expect chicken cooked with tarragon was foolhardy at best and at worst decidedly elitist in its disconnect with the realities of rural life. The tarragon sprig brought to Myrtle by a 'foreign' friend would remain foreign to the culinary rhythms of Irish rural life. And while Myrtle's intention was to suggest culinary betterment and sensory enjoyment by using a particular herb, the clash of values dramatized in the example of chicken with tarragon versus the chicken with a bouquet garni seems a microcosm of the divergent engagements with outside influences that characterized Ireland in this decade of change. The tensions between the traditional and the new, the local and the global, in the context of Irish agriculture and food production were played out through the pages of the *IFJ*. These tensions extended far beyond the example of herb chicken to illustrate the conflicting aspirations and values attending food as ingredient and food as market commodity, most especially at a time when the marketability of Irish produce was crucial in planning Ireland's succession to membership of the European Economic Community. In this environment, that a commentator might recommend the merits of an herb brought by a 'foreign friend' while at the same time exalting a potato cooked in sea water to an audience actively displacing an old food order with a new one typifies how multiple meanings attached to food complicated and unsettled a sense of identity.

Away from the pages of the *IFJ*, Myrtle moved to integrate herbs more fully in her cooking in the House. By the late 1960s, she had become increasingly reliant on the herb garden, detailing in a journal entry that 'I become more dependent on my herb garden... Fennel, lemon balm and marjoram grow luxuriantly for us. The tarragon patch also yielded a good crop annually, although friends tell me that it will not grow in the Dublin area'. Fish that she had seen fall from favour were included on House menus with pollack, cod, or ling with cream and bay leaves becoming regular offerings. Grey sea mullet with *maître d'hôtel* butter and Ballycotton dab in herb butter are listed when available from the boats at Ballycotton, while plaice in butter and herbs was a House regular alongside the chicken with tarragon. These herb-rich meals were offered in the dining room alongside dishes based on traditional ingredients that were well-known to *IFJ* readers: elderflowers, elderberries, blackberries, carrageen moss, eel, mackerel, home-made black puddings, watercress, whortleberries, cockles and mussels, and oatmeal. These ingredients were strong representatives of a rural Irish pattern of consumption that balanced home-produced or gathered foods with shop-bought commercial product. Little if any had market value, and, while relished for their individual taste and cooking qualities, their connection to customary practice or their status as wild and free ingredients rendered them poor foods relative to the perceived sophistication of commercial goods. But at Ballymaloe, whortleberries with carrageen moss sat equitably with smoked mackerel with *fines herbes,* roast lamb duxelles, and *potage bonne femme.* These inclusive menus were not designed to acknowledge the hegemony of French cookery nor to recreate a refined and diluted version of tradition. Indeed, recreating tradition was never Myrtle's objective, and the decision to serve traditional Irish food came largely as 'a response to the demand from foreigners'. Ingredients were chosen based on her principle to seek out the best quality ingredients and to spotlight their tastes with simple kitchen treatment. But as she pointed out 'simplicity is difficult', and preserving the integrity of the ingredient necessitated adherence to a more complex ethical food and cookery philosophy.[24] The approach was unlike the practice of many of her industry contemporaries, and her outsider status was compounded further by gender, by her lack of professional training, and by her reluctance to follow kitchen and food fashions. In effect, her wildly unfashionable stance made her highly fashionable, if not a curiosity, especially to outside commentators as the intrinsic integrity of her work ethic was recognized and validated by the most acclaimed international food writers and food guides.

Inside Ireland, the reaction to her work prompted a re-think of the ill-informed stereotyping of Irish food, much of which was the product of self-derision and insecurity linked to the 'serf-mentality' inherited from a colonial past.[25] The inferiority of Irish food culture in all its real and imagined complexities and the perceived fragility of an Irish food identity was subject to interrogation and reinterpretation as received opinion was questioned against the external validation of Myrtle's cookery and food philosophy. The success of her alternative approach supported local food movements and encouraged communities of chefs and producers to become active practitioners in the formation of a new food identity for Ireland through their work in producing speciality and artisanal produce. Myrtle's construction of a new value system gave creative space to reform, refine, and reshape a food identity for Ireland. This dynamic process of reformation illustrates well Arjun Appadrai's assertation that 'food [...] is a marvelously plastic kind of collective representation' that makes the process of tradition-making and remaking fluid, dynamic, and mutable.[26] Her thinking enabled that process. It also informed a number of external food movement organizations, notably Euro-Toques, and she served

304

ARDSALLAGH GOAT'S CHEESE
LOCAL HONEY AND ROCKET LEAVES

POACHED WILD SALMON, GARDEN PEAS, CHERVIL,
AND HOLLANDAISE SAUCE

ROAST RACK AND LEG OF EAST CORK LAMB
WITH SWEET MARJORAM AND SHANAGARRY BABY CARROTS

A SALAD OF LEAVES FROM THE BALLYMALOE GARDEN
BALLYCOTTON NEW POTATOES

STRAWBERRY AND ELDERFLOWER JELLY
CRUSHED STRAWBERRIES AND CREAM
ELDERFLOWER GRANITA, PISTACHIO LANGUES DE CHAT

CORK FARMHOUSE CHEESE
FROM THE ENGLISH MARKET

Figure 4: Myrtle Allen passed away on 13 of June 2018, the day before Cork City Council hosted a banquet in the Long Room in the Crawford Art Gallery to mark the visit of HRM The Prince of Wales and The Duchess of Cornwall. This menu was prepared by a Ballymaloe team and it had strong herb elements paired with local produce. Rory O'Connell was head chef for the evening and after the dinner he sent out a simple tweet, 'Think we did Cork and Mrs Allen proud tonight' (@rorysfood, 14 June 2018).

as inspiration for Claus Meyer in his formation of the New Nordic Cuisine Movement.[27]

Myrtle Allen can be described as a culinary contrarian who disturbed the received value systems applied to food and cookery in Ireland in the second half of the twentieth century. Foremost in her food philosophy was the maintenance of the flavour of ingredients and their presence in a finished dish. The status she assigned to ingredients, be they defined as staple, wild, or traditional, was determined by her self-designed principles outside of accepted mainstream food and culinary norms. In this new frame of thinking, herbs played an integral part in achieving her food and culinary ambitions. She not only recognized the synergetic culinary relationship between herbs and lead ingredients in dishes, but she also advocated for their transformative power in creating distinct taste profiles of meat and dairy produce from animals grazed on 'old pastures full of herbs and particularly with trefoil', which in turn gave ingredients local character and identity.[28] At times, as in the case of chicken with tarragon, her thinking was at odds with economic, social, and cultural imperatives that underpinned the character of Irish food culture, especially in a time of transition and change.

305

It would be unwise to hold that herbs and herbs alone directed Myrtle's work; rather it can be argued that her relationship with herbs illustrates her independent thinking which connected ingredients in the kitchen to the broader infrastructural complexities of food systems. This independence of mind placed her outside the spirit of her time. As a counterforce, she created a new food and cooking model that inspired new ways of thinking that in time led to a more nuanced consideration of the slippery question: what is Irish food?

Notes

1   Description of tarragon chicken taken from Myrtle Allen, *Irish Farmers Journal* [hereafter *IFJ*], 19 February 1966, p. 43.

2   Using Myrtle Allen's first name throughout this paper is a deliberate choice of the author and the Allen family. It reflects the affection with which she is held in Irish food and culinary communities, where the familiarity inherent in the use of her first name expresses both respect and endearment for her work and memory.

3   This research is undertaken with the permission and approval of the Allen family. The author also wishes to express gratitude to the Boole Library, University College Cork for their permission to use and reproduce material from the Myrtle Allen Archive.

4   Cork, University College Cork, Special Collections & Archives [hereafter Cork], uncatalogued MS Allen, booklet of menus for the initial season of The Yeats Room Restaurant, Ballymaloe House.

5   Cork, uncatalogued MS Handwritten Recipe Book of Elsie Stroker dated October 1901, pp. 58, 110, 114.

6   Cork, uncatalogued MS Allen, The Baberton Spiral Notebook, I (handwritten orange spiral notebook I, unpaginated and undated).

7   Cork, MS Allen, Barberton Notebook I.

8   Allen, *IFJ*, 28 July 1962.

9   Cork, uncatalogued MS Allen, The Baberton Spiral Notebook 2 (handwritten orange spiral notebook I, unpaginated and undated).

10 Cork, MS Allen, Baberton Notebook I.

11 For more detail, see Myrtle Allen, 'Notes on Tastes and Flavours in Practical Cookery', in *Taste: Proceedings of the Oxford Symposium on Food & Cookery 1987*, ed. by Tom Jaine (London: Prospect Books, 1988), pp. 17-24.

12 Cork, uncatalogued MS. Allen, red handbook notebook.

13 Cork, MS Allen, Baberton Notebook 2.

14 Wendell Berry, 'The Pleasures of Eating', in *What Are People For?* (Berkeley: Counterpoint, 1990, rpt. 2010), p. 147.

15 Sue Arnold, 'How Paris Got into an Irish Stew', *The Observer Magazine*, (n.d.), p. 7.

16 J.J. Lee, *Ireland 1912-1985: Politics and Society* (Cambridge: Cambridge University Press, 1989), p. 204.

17 For a comprehensive economic history of the Irish Free State and Irish Republic, see Andy Bielenberg and Raymond Ryan, *An Economic History of Ireland since Independence* (New York: Routledge, 2013).

18 Allen, *IFJ*, 26 March 1966, p. 27.

19 Allen, *IFJ*, 12 March 1966, p. 29.

20 Cork, uncatalogued MS Allen, foolscap journal of food writings.

21 Allen, *IFJ*, 5 March 1966.

22 For discussion of post-Famine nutritional decline and dietary anxieties see Ian Miller, *Reforming Food in Post-Famine Ireland: Medicine, Science and Improvement 1845-1922* (Manchester: Manchester University Press, 2014).

23 Jonathan Bell and Mervyn Watson, *Rooted in the Soil: A History of Cottage Garden and Allotments in Ireland since 1750* (Dublin: Four Courts Press, 2012), pp. 46-47.

24 Cork, MS Allen, foolscap journal.

25 Lee, p. 204.

26 Arjun Appadurai, 'GastroPolitics in Hindu South Asia', *American Ethnologist*, 8.3 (1981), 494-511 (494).

27 See Ann Cahill, 'Legacy Food Special: Northern Star', *Business Post*, 2 June 2012 <https://www.business-post.ie/legacy/food-special-northern-star-fafb178f?auth=registered> [accessed 13 May 2020].

28 Allen, 'Notes on Taste', p. 17.

The Geopolitics of Saffron and the Puzzles of Saffron Arithmetic

Richard Warren Shepro

Spanish saffron from La Mancha commands the highest prices in the world, but Iran produces over 90% of the world's saffron. Spain today is considered the world's second largest exporter of saffron solely because it imports nearly half of the world's production – purchased from Iran – which exporters in Spain then channel to the rest of the world as a Spanish product. Does this tell us that saffron is really a commodity? Or is there a reason for saffron from certain places to be highly prized and priced accordingly? The statistical puzzles of saffron arithmetic lead us to broader questions relevant throughout the food world, such as: what makes a food from a particular place so special that governments should reward its makers with a special designation or monopoly?

Saffron is vital to the cooking of the Middle East and parts of South Asia. In Europe and North Africa, it is essential: in *paella* in Spain, and key to important dishes in Italy (*risotto Milanese, chiusoni...*), France (*bouillabaisse, mouclade...*), and in North Africa (many couscous dishes and *tagines...*). Although the extreme medieval taste for spices other than pepper largely disappeared from European food in the seventeenth century, saffron remained significant, a status that has continued to this day.[1]

Where does saffron come from? Botanically, the answer is clear. Saffron comes from the female reproductive organ (pistil) of a lovely purple autumn flower, *Crocus sativus*, the saffron crocus. Each bloom's pistil contains three stigmas (pollen receptors) which are attached to the style, the stalk that connects the stigmas to the ovary. The stigmas are red, the style is whitish or yellow (Figure 1). Saffron filaments, or threads, are the dried stigmas. They can be sold as separate threads, or with the three stigmas still attached to a part of the style, which some say adds complexity to the flavour, although nowadays most premium saffron contains almost exclusively red threads.[2]

Figure 1: Saffron crocus, La Mancha, Spain. Photograph: Azafrán de la Mancha.

Geographically, the answer is like the solution to a puzzle. In 1986, it was reported that Spain 'satisfies 70% of the world's demand for saffron'.[3] Two decades later, Iran produced over 90% of the world's saffron.[4] It is natural to wonder how such a momentous shift could happen, particularly at a time when Iran's role in international commerce has been so restricted by boycotts and sanctions. Certainly, as Spain has emerged from its economic isolation under Franco's long regime, there been a shift away from agricultural products, but not nearly enough to cause a shift of this magnitude. On the contrary, new agricultural cooperatives have been established in Spain, there is government promotion of saffron from La Mancha as the finest saffron in the world, and in 2001 the European Union awarded its coveted 'Protected Designation of Origin' (PDO) status (like that for *Reggiano Parmigiano* cheese and for Champagne) to Spanish saffron grown in La Mancha that meets certain standards (Figures 2 and 3).[5]

This specially designated La Mancha saffron appears to command the highest saffron prices in the world.[6] Even generic saffron is incessantly referred to as the most expensive spice in the world.[7] In cost per kilogram that is accurate, but in terms of cooking expense it is an arithmetic myth. A minuscule quantity flavours a lot of food or liquid. Many cooks, conscious of its cost but also mindful that too much saffron can make a dish bitter, count out each saffron thread – often with tweezers – and as a rule of thumb employ five or six threads for each person their dish will serve (one gram of saffron generally contains from 160 to over 400 filaments).[8] Others, with accurate scales, suggest 0.02 grams per serving. Even considering the high cost of purchasing tiny quantities of a spice in a supermarket, those proportions amount to only about 15-40 Eurocents per serving, far less if the saffron is purchased in larger quantities, and one well known merchant suggests the cost would be only 0.4 cents per serving if only people would steep their saffron long enough in liquid to release the full flavour. One could bankrupt oneself on a surfeit of fresh truffles or caviar because they are foods, not flavourings; that would be hard to do with saffron. So saffron is not actually expensive. But it is precious, and handling it carefully is a sound idea.[9]

The far greater arithmetic puzzle is found in saffron production and sales numbers released by economic reporting agencies. Compiling and analyzing international trade statistics is far from an exact science, fraught with difficulties of comparing different

Figures 2 & 3: Saffron and discarded petals, La Mancha, Spain. Photograph: Azafrán de la Mancha.

reporting systems and levels of accuracy and honesty. However, all variations of the relevant statistics reveal that Iran is indeed the producer of almost all the world's saffron, that about half of Iran's saffron is exported to Spain (dwarfing Spain's own production), and, astonishingly, that the total amount of saffron that Spain exports is about the same as what it imports from Iran.[10] According to the Ministry of Industry of Spain, in 2010 Spain produced only 1500 kilos of saffron, but almost 190,000 kilos were exported from Spain and labelled in some way as Spanish.[11] In many years the sum of the reported saffron exports attributed to Iran and to Spain significantly exceeds the total world production.

The inescapable conclusion is that Spain is considered the world's second largest exporter of saffron solely because it re-exports nearly half of the world's saffron, purchased from Iran – which Spanish exporters then channel to the rest of the world as a Spanish product. The trade statistics are not corrected for double counting: the same saffron is counted as an Iranian export when it leaves Iran, and again when it leaves Spain. Iranian saffron is repackaged, relabelled, and re-exported as 'packaged in Spain', 'selected and packed in Spain', or sometimes even 'produced in Spain'. Trading saffron through Spain allows Iranian producers to achieve higher prices and to minimize the effects of boycotts and sanctions – through legal means or not.

Medieval trade routes and Muslim expansion led to a taste for saffron in the foods of Spain and Italy, and the Crusades and maritime routes took it to England and France. Saffron's spread throughout the world was fast and vivid, like the spread of the saffron's evocative colour when submerged in warm liquid. The expansion was not simply in terms of use, as with most spices from exotic lands, but in cultivation as well. Other costly imported spices required special growing conditions not found in Europe, but *Crocus sativus* can grow in any temperate climate. Cultivation in Britain became significant enough that by the 1540s the market town in Essex known as Magna Walden and Chipping Walden had changed its name to Saffron Walden, with saffron the chief crop sold.[12] Plans were laid for cultivation of saffron in Ireland.[13] It became an important crop in France and was grown in North America.

For some reason, over subsequent centuries saffron production has essentially retreated to the locations where it was grown in the early Middle Ages: Spain, Kashmir, and, overwhelmingly, Iran. By 2005, Iran was producing 94% of the world's saffron, exporting 82% of the world's supply and consuming 12%, and this market share has continued. There has been some expansion to new areas as well, but none significant in terms of world production.[14] It can be easy for the high price of saffron to lead people to expect easy money is to be had, forgetting the labour and distribution costs and the difficulty of scaling production to compete effectively. A recent thoughtful plan to grow saffron in Rhode Island, the smallest US state, is intriguing but the promise 'that farmers in the Northeast stand to make a lot of money' is far from assured.[15]

Labelling

Knowing where saffron comes from depends, in the first instance, on labels. Food labelling

309

laws generally have three principal goals. First, there is a public health component. The impetus for many purity laws throughout the world was to protect the public from adulterated, dangerous, or even poisonous products. The best saffron is sold in filaments, each filament a stigma, and even with less expensive ground saffron where adulteration is more plausible but appears to be rare, there is rarely a public health concern. At a broader level, accurate labelling protects the consumer. Labels should be honest and not mislead people. Finally, following the model of *Reggiano Parmigiano* and Champagne, there is protection for growers or producers of products that have achieved a special reputation for goodness or quality that also protects consumers who know that they want, for example, the highly prized *lentilles de Puy* and not just a generic green French lentil.

Labelling laws and regulations for food are exceedingly complex, often involving multiple and sometimes overlapping regulatory schemes. Where international trade is involved, they become even more complex, often involving treaties and arcane principles of international law. Much of the Iranian 'Spanish' saffron winds up in the United States, which is the largest consumer of saffron but technically only the third largest importer of saffron (after Spain, by far the largest, and then Hong Kong which, like Spain but on a smaller scale, 'exports' most of what it 'imports', probably for similar reasons but without a historical connection to saffron production). The US has an array of laws and regulations that create a scheme known as 'COOL': Country of Origin Labelling regulations. These rules have many peculiarities, but there is currently no US legal requirement for a reseller to disclose a spice's country of origin to end users.[16] US customs regulations do require declaration of the country of origin of products imported for commercial purposes, but after importation no rule requires that information as to spices to be repeated. In the end, in the US, if a spice is marked as having come from a particular country it is done either for marketing reasons or by a merchant who feels it is important for customers to know.

Much of this remarketing may have been legal under EU law. There are many details and exceptions ('loopholes') in the law of labelling of agricultural commodities, and as a practical matter tracing origin can be difficult. Careful phrasing such as 'packed in Spain' may be accurate even if designed to mislead. (Sales in the US are generally not subject to EU law.[17]) It was formerly legal in the EU for sales simply to identify the name of a Spanish shipping company on labels, regardless of where an agricultural product came from. However, national legislation in Spain has been revised to address labelling, and EU labelling continues to evolve, and it can take some time for enforcement to keep up with legal changes.[18] Finally, it is worth remembering that although the prices are high the volume of saffron sales worldwide is small and may only rarely attract the attention of law enforcement officials.

The sale of so much Iranian saffron through rebranding in Spain is not simply a matter of getting a higher price because of the prestige of Spanish saffron. It is also a way for Iranian producers to sell saffron when transparent exports from Iran are politically difficult, especially if the goal is to sell the saffron in the United States. The United States has imposed forms of trade sanctions on Iran at various times since 1979, lifting them under the Joint Comprehensive Plan of Action ('Iran Nuclear deal') in 2015. At that moment, Iran appeared poised to rejoin the community of nations.[19] With the chaos that ensued after the United States withdrew from this agreement in 2018 and reimposed a complete ban on Iranian imports, the export potential for overt Iranian exports changed yet again. With a treaty still in force with Europe, but unilateral sanctions imposed by the United States, Iranian producers face difficult decisions and continue to come up with 'creative' solutions. United Nations trade sanctions on Iran have always been less severe and do not affect saffron. Spain (despite recent US opposition) has bilateral trade agreements with Iran. Despite Iran's dominant world position in saffron production, the saffron trade is minuscule compared to Iran's oil and other industries so the saffron trade has not figured in trade negotiations. However, it is implausible that the US could import as much saffron as it does without most of it coming indirectly from Iran.

An additional connection between Spain and Iran in the saffron market is that Spanish businesses have invested in production in Iran, and introduced more modern technology, particularly controlled drying at low temperatures as is done in La Mancha.[20]

Saffron Quality and Protected Designations

Saffron quality can be measured. There are quality standards, different from country to country, but all based mainly on measurable attributes such as the length of threads, the depth of the colour, the power to colour a liquid. Spain sorts its saffron into four categories based on colouring power: the top is coupe (all stigmas cut from the style so that everything is red), then Mancha (still high quality), and finally Rio and Sierra (more brownish than red). The Iranian system categorizes saffron in a different way, with Sargol (all red, but sometimes just the tips of the filaments), Nigin (all red, longer filaments, often called neguine, using a French version of the word because France has significant bilateral trade with Iran), Super Nigin (still longer filaments, the most expensive), Pushal (similar to Mancha, with the three stigma still attached to the style), and lower grades that include large amounts of style.

A more recent approach to grading is laboratory analysis based on an ISO standard that sets minimum measurement levels for a number of characteristics, mainly for three chemical components: picrocrocin (flavour and bitterness), crocin (colour), and safranal (aroma).[21] Many saffron producers advertise based on these ISO measurements, particularly the measurement for colouring power.

Separate from these ratings are the official geographical recognitions – the PDOs – and other governmental support, and Spanish saffron from La Mancha is not the only saffron in the EU to achieve such a recognition. There is now a separate PDO for saffron from Munder, in Switzerland, and for Krokos Kozanis, in Greece. To achieve these recognitions, Switzerland and Greece had to demonstrate to the EU that there was something unique about them. Other saffron is highly prized, and two venues – Kashmir, an ancient venue, and Afghanistan, a new one – deserve special attention.

Saffron from Kashmir has been famous from antiquity but achieved its own protected legal status in May 2020 (Figure 4).[22] This is not the PDO received from the EU by Spain, Switzerland, and Greece, but something granted by the government of India, which has a legal status outside India only to the extent it is protected by international agreements.[23] The impetus for Kashmiri producers to seek protected status seems to have been that the price of Kashmiri saffron had fallen by nearly 50% as Iranian saffron became dominant.[24] This status was achieved a few years after a professor of marketing studies in Kashmir argued that the crisis in the Kashmir saffron industry would be best addressed by developing a better 'branding strategy', emphasizing high quality, providing employment for women (Figure 5), and cracking down on Iranian saffron being sold as Kashmiri, a 'spurious trade [that] runs in crores'.[25]

Figure 4: Saffron crocus in Kashmir, India. Photograph: Kashmir Kesar Kingdom Pvt. Ltd.

Afghanistan has become, fairly suddenly, the third largest exporter of saffron, which means that it is actually the second largest producer since Spain's production is so small. Its nascent industry has achieved high quality and is charging very high prices; its distributors have produced beautiful marketing campaigns based in part on the noble idea that saffron will help the country overcome its dependence on opium production – a tall order indeed: Afghanistan is to the opium market what Iran is to saffron, generally thought to produce 90% of the world's supply, and UN estimates suggest opium to be a $4 billion market while saffron production worldwide is $390 million.[26]

This emphasis on geographical origin and ISO laboratory analysis are in some ways antithetical to each other. The ISO parameters are based on the idea that it is possible to tell quality by measuring the strength of certain components. ISO analysis does not address origin, and some well-respected merchants assert it is more objective and never identify the source of their saffron. Although some geographical designations require quality measurements to be met, the awards based on geography depend more on history, *terroir*, and perceptions of quality developed over centuries. The two ideas are starting to converge in a new field of 'food authenticity testing' that uses spectroscopy and statistical analysis to confirm geographical origin and detect fraud. These digital-fingerprint techniques have been used to analyze the origin of wine, olive oil, coffee, and now saffron.[27] So far, analysis of this sort has consistently verified the authenticity of La Mancha PDO saffron – and also confirmed that much that is simply labelled as 'Spanish' or 'Packed in Spain' is not.[28]

Conclusion

The statistical puzzles of saffron arithmetic and the subterfuge it reveals lead us to broader questions relevant throughout the food world. What makes an agricultural product grown in a certain place so special that we should take special note of it? Should governments reward the makers or growers of such products with a special designation that increases their profits and gives them a sort of monopoly? If so, do we do so in the name of gastronomy, or in service of a public that craves information? And are these questions of quality genuine, or are they the subject of lore? Can the quality be measured, as the ISO ratings suggest, or is the issue so complex that it can only be sensed in a kind of connoisseur's gestalt?

Or are some products, even if rare and precious, really commodities, where once a certain level of quality is achieved most specimens are roughly the same and there is no need for anyone to be a connoisseur?

With regard solely to saffron, does massive mislabelling without consumer revolt tell us that saffron is really a commodity? Are the proponents of pure ISO testing and an indifference to geographical origin correct? Is there still a reason for La Mancha saffron to cost twice the price of the next 'best'?

In the world of cheese, or wine, there are specially protected products whose distinctiveness is evident, and these products deserve special appreciation and attention. No one would confuse *Parmigiano Reggiano* with *Comté* cheese. However, both of those cheeses have competitors that in a blind tasting could easily be confused: a young *Parmigiano Reggiano* with an older *Grana Padano*, for example, or *Comté* with *Gruyère*. In the wine world, there have been tests and criticisms of whether connoisseurship is real.[29] With an ingredient such as saffron that is cooked with many other ingredients, is it possible that anyone can really tell whether best quality La Mancha saffron PDO has been used in a paella or whether the dish is 'adulterated' with an equally famous saffron from Kashmir, or with a carefully selected Iranian saffron that is marketed as 'packed in Spain'?

313

Figure 5: Saffron harvest, Mashad, Iran. Photograph: David Vanille, Sélection d'épices.

The trade in saffron provides a peculiar and probably beneficial form of consumer choice, although outright mislabelling should not be allowed. A connoisseur can buy saffron based on pedigree and geographical assurance (PDO), or buy it with no indication of origin from a merchant who stakes his reputation on an ISO certificate. Part of the magic of saffron, perhaps, is that the fragrance and colour it imparts when skilfully used can blend together with memories and a sense of history and geography. Saffron from a special place can create an unforgettable experience, but other saffron may also, quite apart from the question of where it came from. Pondering the ancient history of saffron and the fluid worldwide movement of both spices and people in our modern world, I am particularly struck by the endorsement of Iranian saffron in this portion of the 2019 poem, 'Saffron', by a young American poet and biologist of Iranian descent, Amir Safi:

> My mother picks up the pestle and mortar and does to saffron what the clerics have done to her country / pours in steaming water till the liquid in the bowl becomes the Caspian swallowing the sun / it smells like a home I have not returned to in 10 years / saffron / pound for pound/ the most expensive spice in the world / worth more in its weight than gold / if customs found it, they would surely throw it away / but my grandmother is a high-stakes smuggler / her currency is my mother's joy / every time she visits, she brings some in her luggage / and my grandmother always comes through / and … approaches me with the same enthusiasm I had as a boy catching a fish / holds the small packet between her thumb and her index finger and says / you cannot find saffron this good in America, Amir / you cannot find saffron like this anywhere, but Iran /and this is where I learn the limitations of the American dream / that you cannot find here what you already have …[30]

And the same could be said of saffron from La Mancha, or Kashmir, or perhaps even, if the circumstances are right, of threads of Iranian saffron taken from a little tin covered with pictures of nineteenth-century Spain and the carefully chosen words 'Genuine Pure Saffron' and 'specially selected and packed in Spain', surrounded by a saffron-coloured cellophane wrapper to which (perhaps after customs has been cleared) someone has affixed a small official-looking seal that says 'Genuine Spanish Saffron'.

Notes

1   See Paul Freedman, *Out of the East: Spices and the Medieval Imagination* (New Haven: Yale University Press, 2008), pp. 216-23.
2   John Humphries, *The Essential Saffron* Companion (Berkeley: Ten Speed Press, 1996), p. 29.
3   Susan Linee, 'A Pound of Saffron is Worth a Bounty: In Spain, Growing This Expensive Spice Helps Maintain a Good Life', *Los Angeles Times*, 23 November 1986.
4   M. Ghorbani, 'The Efficiency of Saffron's Marketing Channel in Iran', *World Applied Sciences Journal*, 4 (2008).
5   The foundation that administers the mark Azafrán de la Mancha sets out the history of the appellation and provides information on the nineteen packagers allowed to use the designation (<https://doazafrandelamancha.com/en/pdo-management.html#timeline> [accessed 5 March 2021]). The PDO designation, the most rigorous of the EU food classification schemes, has a different name in each of the twenty-three EU languages (European Commission, 'Quality Schemes Explained <https://

ec.europa.eu/info/food-farming-fisheries/food-safety-and-quality/certification/quality-labels/quality-schemes-explained_en> [accessed 5 March 2021]). The term PDO is also used to refer more generally to include similar schemes around the world.

6   At wholesale pricing. The highest-priced saffron in the world may be the generic saffron powder sold in tiny amounts in envelopes. In the US these can cost $8 for three 120 mg portions (about $20,500 per kilo). It's better to buy a full gram of good quality saffron filaments for about the same $8 ($8000 per kilo). One gram of fully certified La Mancha saffron of the highest quality can be had for $18 ($18,000 per kilo). Because packaging is a large part of the cost in small quantities that same La Mancha saffron sells for $10,000 per kilo in a somewhat larger tin.

7   Saffron is generally considered a spice but occasionally an herb.

8   Claudia Roden notes this practice in *The Food of Spain* (London: HarperCollins 2011) though with her long experience prefers to rely on 'a pinch'.

9   While writers have referred to saffron as 'worth its weight in gold' for many centuries, my Symposium presentation showed a chart of recent representative per kilo prices of selected luxury goods (in US dollars), compared with costs *per serving* of the same products:

Per kilo		*Per serving*	
Saffron	$18,000	Saffron	$0.90
Madagascar vanilla bean	$1,769	Madagascar vanilla bean	$6.25
Fresh Périgord black truffle	$1,441	Fresh Périgord black truffle	$72.00
1985 Château Margaux	$967	1985 Château Margaux 15cl	$150.00

10   Except as otherwise cited, the statistics I have relied on are compiled by UN agencies that can be analyzed in different ways with the assistance of statistical databases such as statista.com. As of this writing, the latest compiled statistics are for 2017. There is more limited compiled data for 2018.

11   Eva Cavero, 'El azafrán español tiene trampa', *El Pais*, 30 January 2011 <https://elpais.com/diario/2011/01/30/sociedad/1296342004_850215.html> [accessed 9 March 2021].

12   The name remains today, although saffron is no longer grown there. A detailed history is contained in Braybrooke, Richard Griffin (Baron), *The History of Audley End. To which are appended notices of the town and parish of Saffron Walden in the county of Essex* (London: S. Bentley, 1836).

13   *An account of saffron the manner of its culture and saving for use, with the advantages it will be of to this kingdom* (Dublin: A. Rhames, 1732).

14   There are revivals of production in parts of France, the US, Greece, and other areas.

15   Jessica Fu, 'Saffron Is the World's Most Expensive Spice. Why Don't We Grow It Ourselves?' *The Counter,* 11 November 2019 <https://thecounter.org/saffron-northeast-university-of-rhode-island-iran/> [accessed 9 March 2021].

16   For example, butchers and fish markets are not required to reveal the country of origin of their meat or fish, but full line grocers are.

17   Occasionally there are special agreements with the US, such as the agreement that the US will not allow sparkling wine producers to use the term 'Champagne' unless they had a pre-existing use.

18   'Los análisis confirman el fraude del azafrán', *Levante*, 19 January 2016 <https://www.levante-emv.com/sociedad/2016/01/19/fraude-azafran/1368027.html> [accessed 9 March 2021]

19   Naomi Duguid's 2016 book, *Taste of Persia: A Cook's Travels Through Armenia, Azerbaijan, Georgia, Iran and Kurdistan* (New York: Artisan), reflects the optimism of that time and depicts an exciting quest to find saffron fields near Mashad, in eastern Iran, where most of Iran's saffron is produced.

20   Lukas Huss, 'The Case Study of Saffron from La Mancha PDO', *Current Issues of Protected Geographical Indications 2016,* p. 11.

21   International Organization for Standardization, Standards ISO 3632-1 (2011) and ISO 3632-2 (2010) which replaced earlier standards from 1980 and 1993. See <https://www.iso.org/obp/ui/#iso:std:iso:3632:-1:ed-2:v1:en> and <https://www.iso.org/standard/44526.html>

22   Hemant Singh, 'Kashmiri Saffron given GI Tag: Know what is Geographical Indication (GI) Tag?' *Jagran Josh*, 7 May 2020 <https://www.jagranjosh.com/general-knowledge/what-is-the-meaning-of-

geographical-indication-tag-to-kashmiri-saffron-1588680149-1> [accessed 9 March 2021].

23 There is some international protection through the membership of the World Trade Organization, which hotly debates the details of geographical name protection but does not have the power the EU has over its member states. See, for example, the example of basmati rice, in Estelle Biénabe and Delphine Marie-Vivien, 'Institutionalizing Geographical Indications in Southern Countries: Lessons Learned from Basmati and Rooibos,' *World Development*, 98 (October 2017), 58-67 <https://doi.org/10.1016/j.worlddev.2015.04.004>. Outside the EU, geographical name protection quickly gets far weaker but even more complicated than within the EU. The Lisbon Agreement of 1958 has few signatories. A newer initiative, the 2015 Geneva Act of the Lisbon Agreement, has even fewer. The protections it provides are administered by the World Intellectual Property Organisation (WIPO) in Geneva. The EU and a few other countries, including North Korea, joined the Geneva Act group in February 2020. The US opposes the process.

24 Chander Mohan, 'Kashimiri Saffron Gets GI Tag', *Krishi Jagran*, 2 May 2020 <https://krishijagran. com/agriculture-world/kashmiri-saffron-gets-gi-tag/> [accessed 22 March 2021].

25 Natasha Saqib, 'Geographic Indication as a Branding Tool for Saffron', *International Journal of Management and Social Science Research Review*, 1.11 (May 2015), 22. Aside from saffron arithmetic, there is a fascinating quality to the traditional Indian numbering system under which a 'lakh' is one hundred thousand, written as 1,00,000, and a 'crore' is one hundred lakhs, written as 100,00,000.

26 See, for example, Stephanie Glinsky, 'Afghanistan: Herat's Opium Fields Make Way for Saffron', *The National*, 4 July 2019 <https://www.thenational.ae/world/asia/afghanistan-herat-s-opium-fields-make-way-for-saffron-1.882342> [accessed 24 March 2021] and Mujib Mashal, 'Hashim Aslami Has Just One Word for Afghan Farmers: Saffron', *The New York Times*, 26 April 2019. The World Bank has promoted this initiative ('Saffron: A Major Source of Income and an Alternative to Poppy', *World Bank*, 19 January 2015 <https://www.worldbank.org/en/news/feature/2015/01/20/saffron-major-source-income-alternative-poppy> [accessed 24 March 2021]), but it is controversial. Most saffron harvesters in Iran and Afghanistan are women or, according to some reports, children. When Kashmir recently obtained a special geographical designation from India for its saffron, it argued that the designation would increase demand and accordingly create more jobs for women. The jobs do provide some opportunity, but harvesting and cleaning saffron happens only during the autumn. These are seasonal jobs, hardly transformational when the owners of saffron businesses are almost always men. Giulia Minoia and Adam Pain are highly suspicious of the argument that harvesting saffron improves the lot of women in Afghanistan ('Saffron: The social relations of production', *Secure Livelihoods Research Consortium Working Paper 48*, August 2016 <https://securelivelihoods.org/wp-content/uploads/WP48_Saffron_The-social-relations-of-production.pdf?> [accessed 24 March 2021]).

27 M.J. Martelo-Vidal and M. Vázquez, 'Advances in Ultraviolet and Visible Light Spectroscopy for Food Authenticity Testing', in *Advances in Food Authenticity Testing*, ed. by Gerald Downey (Cambridge: Woodhead Publishing, 2016), pp. 35-70; Josep Rubert and others, 'Saffron Authentication Based on Liquid Chromatography High Resolution Tandem Mass Spectrometry and Multivariate Data Analysis,' *Food Chemistry*, 204 (1 August 2016), 201-209 (p. 201) <https://www.sciencedirect.com/science/article/abs/pii/S0308814616300048> [accessed 24 March 2021]. See also R. Consonni and others, 'NMR Spectroscopic Studies in Saffron Authenticity and Quality,' in *Magnetic Resonance in Food Science: Defining Food by Magnetic Resonance*, ed. by Francesco Capozzi, Luca Laghi, and Peter S. Belton (London: The Royal Society of Chemistry 2015), pp. 65-76.

28 Rubert and others. There are also reports of adulteration involving substitution of parts of the crocus that are not saffron, or stigma from other flowers, particularly with powdered saffron.

29 See, for example, the statistical study by Roman Weil, 'Analysis of Reserve and Regular Bottlings: Why Pay for a Difference Only the Critics Claim to Notice?', *Chance*, 18.3 (Summer 2005), 9-15, and the famous statistics article by Orley Ashenfelter, 'Predicting the Quality and Prices of Bordeaux Wines', *The Economic Journal*, 118.529 (June 2008), 174-184.

30 *Michigan Quarterly Review*, 58.2 (Spring 2019) <https://sites.lsa.umich.edu/mqr/2019/04/saffron/> [accessed 24 March 2021] (punctuation as in the original).

316

Pepper and Paradox in the Roman Imagination

Jeremy Simmons

It is probably safe to say that Pliny hates pepper. A world away from the ancient pepper plantations of Malabar, in the Mediterranean metropolis of Rome, the first-century encyclopedist Pliny the Elder passes judgement on the purchase and consumption of the Indian spice throughout his monumental *Natural History*. While describing the maritime routes from Egypt to southwestern India, Pliny bemoans the loss of Roman capital from the spice trade: 'indeed, the voyage is made every year [...] a worthy subject, since in no year does India drain our empire of less than 50 million *sesterces*' (*Nat. Hist.* 6.26.101). When treating the botanical properties of black pepper later in his work, Pliny reveals that he cannot fathom why the plant is so popular in Rome: 'to think that its only pleasing quality is pungency and that we go all the way to India to get this [...] both pepper and ginger grow wild in their respective countries, and yet here in Rome we buy them by weight, as if gold or silver' (*Nat. Hist.* 12.14.29).

The exchange of spice for specie has long been used to define an extensive web of overland and maritime connections between the Mediterranean world and the Indian subcontinent. At the high point of this interregional commerce in the first century CE, commodities imported via the Indian Ocean, such as spices, gemstones, ivory, and textiles flooded Mediterranean markets. References to pepper far outnumber other Indian Ocean products in the works of first-century poets and historians, suggesting its wider presence within the literary fabric of the Roman world; in fact, Pliny returns to pepper throughout his encyclopedia with a frequency rarely extended to other items, on no fewer than forty-five occasions. The increased consumption of pepper during Rome's first century under the emperors corresponds nicely to that of other commodities from outside Italy, such as Spanish wine and olive oil – a moment when Roman Italy stops exporting surplus and leans heavily on importation to sustain the million-man city at the heart of the empire.

But why is Pliny so angry about pepper? It is not a problem with seasonings in general, as we see with the author's treatment of salt, without which 'civilized life is impossible' (*Nat. Hist.* 31.41.88), as well as a variety of herbs from the traditional Roman garden. Pliny's frustrations with pepper stem from a fixation within the broader Roman cultural imagination, an obsession with an allegedly corrupting force: *luxus*, or 'luxury'. Over the last two decades, there has been a growing scholarly interest in better understanding the consumption of aromatic products vis-à-vis their frequent designation as 'luxuries' (e.g. Dalby 2000; Parker 2002; van der Veen 2003;

Fitzpatrick 2011; Cobb 2013; Evers 2017; Cobb 2018; Mayer 2018; Simmons 2020). Importantly, products in and of themselves cannot achieve social meaning – say, of luxuries – without the context of their consumption; luxury is a relative characteristic, not an absolute one. Such a conclusion should encourage us to further interrogate ancient criticism like Pliny's and search for other ways in which pepper was consumed beyond the 'luxurious'.

This paper explores how pepper consumption resonated within the Roman literary imagination and challenges its label of 'luxury'. In doing so, it focuses primarily on Roman literary texts written between roughly 30 BCE and the early third century CE, at times juxtaposing them to works that approach pepper from more technical perspectives, such as Pliny the Elder's encyclopedia and compilations of culinary and medicinal recipes. In the course of its analysis, this paper also goes beyond Roman pundits, to the material evidence of pepper consumption, the intellectual frameworks of connoisseurs, and the sensory experience of ancient consumers. When viewed in combination, these interwoven narratives reveal the ambiguities in the social valuation of pepper beyond the tropes of 'luxury'. Once we acknowledge the literary distortion of pepper which we encounter in texts, we can better understand the larger 'consumerscape' of ancient Rome – a combination of economic factors, cultural mandates, and intellectual discourses that served as the underlying context for consumption and, in turn, informed consumer behaviour.[1]

Before we proceed, some technicalities: ancient Roman authors focus primarily on black pepper, called *piper* in Latin or *peperi* in ancient Greek, which was cultivated in the coastal hills of ancient Malabar – this is the modern *Piper nigrum* L., which graces most of our tables today alongside granulated salt. While a spice called 'pepper' was known to Greek writers as early as the fourth century BCE, it appears that these older treatments dealt with what we today call 'long pepper', a plant native to northern India (ancient *piper longum* or *peperi makron*; modern *Piper longum* L). 'Long' and 'black' pepper are conflated in the Roman period, and, based on the ancient testimony, most authors erroneously viewed these distinct spices to be different fruit stages of the same plant (Simmons 2020: 290). As a result, intellectuals in the ancient Mediterranean understood both types to possess similar characteristics, such as heat and pungency. These properties are of immense importance, as they dictate not only the multivalent functions of the spice in Roman society, but also serve as the characteristics that enter intellectual discourse, whether through banter or outrage.

Pig and Pepper

The ubiquity of pepper surely prompted its presence in Roman literature of the first century CE. As a caveat, many Roman writers regularly experienced the world of the *convivium*, or banquet, and thus our literary sources tend to focus on pepper's role in elite contexts – and criticism of it. Arguably the most famous example is Trimalchio's dinner in the *Satyricon*, a satirical novel by Petronius. At this parody feast, much of the food contains pepper, including fig-pecker in peppered yolk and a peppery *garum*, or fish sauce; the host's wife also distributes additional ground pepper for guests from a boxwood mill (*Sat.* 33.8, 36.3, 74.5). Heavily peppered dishes factor among the over-the-top elements of a meal sponsored by new money, in this case, the freed slave Trimalchio. As a result, pepper is implicated in broader charges of luxuriousness through a form of *reductio ad absurdum*, in comically exaggerated form.

But further sources point to pepper's indispensable application in the culinary realm. In Apicius's *The Art of Cooking*, the main surviving source for the Roman culinary arts, pepper appears in the vast majority of recipes, whether during preparation or as a final garnish (see Grocock and Grainger 2006). Heavily peppered dishes of peacock and flamingo point to its use in the *convivium* (*De re coq.* 2.2.6, 6.2.21, 6.8.14, 7.2.1, 8.1.9-10, 8.7.2, 8.8.1, etc.), but pepper is also an ingredient in more popular drinks and condiments, including spiced wines and various *garum* sauces (e.g. *De re coq.* 1.1-2, 1.31, 1.33). Peppered dishes are served throughout the satirical *Epigrams* of the Flavian poet Martial, with their economic extremes marked by a boar on the one hand and beets on the other (*Ep.* 7.27.7-8, 13.5, 13.13). The former would have been immensely expensive given its Caledonian proportions, but the beets are part of the humbler fare of the 'workman's lunch', the *prandia fabrorum*.

Roman authors provide strong evidence for a much wider application of the spice than just in the refined dishes of the *convivium*. In the fictional banquet of Petronius's novel, a joke underpins this culinary necessity. As the diners prepare to tuck into yet another grand hog, Trimalchio scolds a cook for not gutting the pig and comments on the slave's forgetfulness: 'you'd think he'd only left out pepper and cumin!' (*putes illum piper et cuminum non coniecisse*; *Sat.* 49). While some of the diners expect the enslaved chef to be punished, a glib Trimalchio equates the mistake to the omission of pepper, a more common case of culinary carelessness. Even Pliny the Elder, perhaps biting his lip, admits that it is now commonplace in Roman cooking, despite the former reliance on kitchen gardens for seasonings (*Nat. Hist.* 19.19.58-59).

Pepper's ubiquity is met by the rhetoric of distaste. In the passages at the start of this paper, Pliny cannot understand why anyone would import something all the way from India merely for its pungency – a collective error amounting to an annual trade deficit of 50 million *sesterces*. Pliny's logic has more recent incarnations, from eighteenth-century intellectuals wrangling with increased British consumption of tea (e.g. Simon Mason's *The Good and Bad Effects of Tea Consider'd*, 1745) to those currently who decry the loss of American capital to global trade. Determinations such as Pliny's arise from simplifying macroeconomics for rhetorical effect, but also from competing notions of value. Taste and virtue are often like oil and water; Pliny can chastise consumer and culture simultaneously, writing off the plant and all those who partake of it.

The beauty of such moralizing is how reductive it can be. For one thing, moralists often engage in an intellectual conflation of 'economic luxuries' – that is, commodities whose consumption increases proportionally to personal income – and the cultural perceptions of 'luxury' behind Roman literary treatments of pepper. This conflation is especially dangerous since we rely on sources like Pliny for precious attestations of pepper's price during the Roman period, which is needed to make any substantial claims about its availability. Moreover, Roman medical authorities, including Celsus, Dioscorides, and Galen, single out the merits of pepper in numerous prescriptions and dietary recommendations. I have pointed out elsewhere how peppered foods prescribed in these texts, from spiced wine and *garum* to various porridges, have medicinal benefits even for healthy individuals, from aiding in digestion to treating snakebites and malaria. Tellingly, medical writers often state that pepper can be added to bitter substances such as wormwood or lupin to make a medicament more palatable or pleasurable, with the medicinal benefits of the spice being incidental (Simmons 2020: 313-14). Taste, in fact, has much utility.

Charges of luxury involving spices like pepper often focus on exorbitant quantities being consumed in single instances, such as Martial's pepper-encrusted boar or Trimalchio's thoroughly peppered feast. Indeed, the elite may have distinguished their consumption of pepper from that of the wider population through excess, along with other elements of *habitus* discussed below. From these fictional representations, the modern reader may conclude that there was too much pepper in Roman cuisine – though not all consumers would have heaped on the spice, a fact conveniently ignored in these literary treatments. Apicius's cookbook, while containing convivial favourites, also preserves recipes for more accessible porridges and sauces, the sort sold by urban food vendors (Garnsey 1991: 85; Grocock and Grainger 2006: 23; Holleran 2012: 140-46). When we step back from the distortions of satire, we can imagine more sparing use by other members of the urban population, as suggested in previous scholarship (van der Veen 2003: 407, 412; Cobb 2018: 534; Simmons 2020: 303-04). The workman's lunch of beets stands as an alternative to pig and pepper.

All of this is to say that consumers had more diverse motivations than those presented in Roman literary take-downs, which often oversimplify to galvanize blame. Some consumers may well have gone whole hog, but others probably tried to get products on the cheap regardless of quality; still others likely overpaid according to hierarchies of value held by moralizers, such as Martial's Sextus, who considers pepper to be worth more than its weight in silver (*Ep.* 10.57). But even if we take Pliny's limited price data at face value, there is growing scholarly consensus that black pepper could be purchased as an occasional 'economic luxury' by a wider portion of the population than previously assumed (e.g. Mrozek 1975, Corbier 1985, Rathbone 2009, Cobb 2018, Mayer 2018, and Simmons 2020). This cautious optimism is bolstered by archaeological discoveries of pepper in non-elite contexts at the Italian city of Herculaneum, reflecting its wider presence in civilian life (Rowan 2017). Despite moralizing warnings, people consumed pepper anyway – probably more people than punditry would lead us to believe.

In fact, the moralizers present their own set of contradictions. Painstaking application of moralizing logic may best be reflected in a satire of the first-century author Persius. In a particularly striking passage (*Sat.* 6.21), Persius renders the image of a miser, who 'sprinkles sacred pepper himself over his platter' (*ipse sacrum irrorans patinae piper*), rather than having a slave do it for him, a common practice of the *convivium*. This is an exemplary use of the loaded adjective *sacer* ('sacred') – pepper is simultaneously *awesome* and *awful*, possessing the epithet of a willing or forfeited dedication to the gods. 'Sacred pepper' (*piper sacrum*) reflects latent literary anxieties practiced by a fictional consumer: pepper's delicious flavour will overpower in convivial proportions; the value of its taste should be weighed against that of coin; and the urge to satisfy human desires must beware the insidiousness of decadence. It questions the growing compulsion for Romans to partake of imports like pepper instead of 'making do' with simple pleasures, as Persius's persona suggests (*utar ego, utar*; *Sat.* 6.23-24) – the hallmark remedy to 'luxury' – despite the inherent wealth needed to engage in this humbler form of gratification. A life of moralizing leads only to paradox.

Facts and Figurines

By interrogating some of the literary characterizations of pepper, we begin to see that the spice defies universalizing charges of 'luxury' by pundits like Pliny. Pepper graced fine food and costly medicaments but was also included in popular foodstuffs like wine and fish sauce (Meyer 1980: 410; Garnsey 1991: 85; McLaughlin 2010: 143). Pepper in and of itself is not luxurious; rather, consumption carries with it associated practices, which contribute to what Pierre Bourdieu has described in the context of *habitus* and articulations of status (Bourdieu 1984).[2] Thus, as much as this paper seeks to point out the literary distortions through which we encounter pepper, it also attempts an archaeology of the practices surrounding its consumption – factors like connoisseurship and accoutrement, which differentiated the consumer experience. Such factors present their own paradoxes worthy of exploration.

321

While excessive peppering, the sort found at Trimalchio's banquet, is criticized, satirists mock more discerning connoisseurs as well. In one instance from his *Satires*, Horace describes a chance encounter with Catius, a gourmand who expounds on his culinary discoveries: 'I was the first to serve up wine lees and fish paste, white pepper and black salt sifted on to dainty little dishes' (*hanc ego cum malis, ego faecem primus et allec,* | *piper album cum sale nigro* | *incretum puris circumposuisse catillis*; *Sat.* 2.4.73-75). White pepper, a more processed and exclusive form of black peppercorns, has a milder flavour than the black variety, and thus, while it does occasionally appear in Apicius's recipes, it most often gets prescribed in medicines. Horace's caricature inverts the standard colours of each condiment and social expectation, and the joke lands only if the audience understands the exclusivity of white pepper in culinary contexts, if not its ridiculous use therein.[3]

The consumer knowledge demonstrated by Horace's gourmand had a practical application – namely, mitigating asymmetric information between vendors and consumers. In the absence of regulation, crafty entrepreneurs could add adulterants, such as juniper berries, to their wares, additions difficult to discern with the naked eye. Accordingly, rigorous procedures developed, recorded by medical writers like Dioscorides and Galen, to pick the best pepper (e.g. visual inspection, flotation, taste tests; Simmons 2020: 308-09). Such frameworks of knowledge empowered consumers to make informed choices and are essential for the development of certain behaviours of consumption, such as connoisseurship. They also reflect that taste in and of itself had particular criteria – good black pepper was thought to taste 'pungent' while still maintaining good mouth feel. These criteria, though arbitrary, allowed for knowledge of true taste to be hoarded and even weaponized against supposedly less discerning palates: for instance, the medical writer Galen takes an opportunity to call out those who think the spice is 'astringent' rather than 'pungent' (*SMT.* xii.162K), and even Pliny knows what pepper should taste like, discrediting the ordinary view that likens its flavour to all-heal (*Nat. Hist.* 19.62.187).

Connoisseurship of this commodity, as with all commodities, thus rests squarely upon the curation and consumption of larger corpora of knowledge.[4] References to the Indian spice, peppered throughout the texts of the Classical corpus, contribute to knowledge-building enterprises of medical writers like Celsus and Galen. The spice-filled dialogue in the *Learned Banqueters* of Athenaeus reveals this doubling of consumption – not only do the diners at a Greco-Roman banquet partake of heavily peppered dishes (including a very large pig), but their spicy meal prompts them to display their literary chops by quoting from memory every Classical Greek reference to *peperi*, from Aristotle to the punchlines of Attic comedy (*Deipno.* 2.66d-f). Detested as it may be by Pliny, pepper must be included within his encyclopedia, which allegedly contains 20,000 facts drawn from 2000 volumes; Pliny states that 'it's not books, but warehouses that are needed' for all these factoid treasures, among which pepper must be counted (*Nat. Hist.* pr. 15-18).

But, in another paradoxical twist, pepper also possesses a tenuous, if antithetical, relationship to Roman literary production in the minds of its writers. Take Catius in Horace's *Satires*: his incessant language of discovery, being the 'first' (*primus*) to find novel uses for white pepper, recalls and effectively replaces the self-professed aim of so many Latin didactic poets who claim to be the 'first' to pursue their literary projects.[5] Moreover, several Roman poets lament the reuse of paper containing poetry – moth-eaten, grubby, and forgotten – to wrap pepper and other aromatics in the urban marketplace. Horace provides the most vivid description at the ironical end of his *Epistle* addressed to the emperor Augustus; after listing the poets of the Latin literary tradition and the benefits of the profession, he humbles himself, foreseeing an unceremonious death for his poetry, hauled off to the street where they sell incense and pepper wrapped in useless paper (*Epis.* 2.1.264-70). Bad poetry thus meets bad ends, but even good poetry can suffer this fate. Martial advises his little book of *Epigrams* to find a new owner quick, lest it be rushed off to a soot-filled kitchen, where its papyrus would meet a similar demise (*Ep.* 3.2.2-5; see also Statius *Silv.* 4.5.29-36). In these instances, pepper stands as an existential threat to literary production; a zero-sum game is afoot.

322

Literature is one thing, but pepper also entered Latin idiom. Slang uses of the word *piper* appear in the conversation between freedmen in Petronius's novel to describe someone as hot-tempered – *piper, non homo*, 'he's pepper, not a man' (*Sat.* 44.6) – and in an epigram of Martial to describe a thieving hand as 'peppery' (*piperata manus*, *Ep.* 8.59.4; see Parker 2002: 60). These *hapax legomena* might represent the flirtatious language of the *convivium* or more common expressions; in either case, they reflect how pepper gave rise to metaphors based on its properties of heat which then changed the texture of banter. In these instances, we find impressions of this commodity on language and cultural literacy, a way in which consumption ripples beyond a purely economic act into a larger cultural phenomenon. Pepper thus fills the storehouses of knowledge and even spices up the Latin language, but it also threatens the world that projects like the encyclopedia or satire seek to tame.

Beyond connoisseurship, other elements of *habitus* develop for pepper at the *convivium*, namely the use of particular utensils. *Piperatoria*, or silver peppershakers, were used to distribute pepper at the table. Several examples survive from antiquity, including two from Pompeii's House of the Menander, in the shape of a shell and shipping amphora respectively (Guzzo 2006: 191-224). As expensive items, *piperatoria* further defined the consumption of pepper, couching an increasingly available product in an additional trapping of status articulated through precious metal. The numerous shapes of these figurines, while participating in another instantiation of connoisseurship – that of the silverware collector – also contributed to a playful, multisensory dining experience, the sort on display in Athenaeus. Pepper, shipped all the way from India, could reach its final destination in an amphora of silver, the fodder of wit and pleasure.

323

But peppershakers, as with other elements of *habitus*, depended upon elements of human subjugation. *Piperatoria* would have been handled by slaves, human agents integral to the multisensory experience fostered by these objects. Slaves and freedmen often possessed names based on spices as well, like Pepper or Cinnamon, instances where the tastes of the master's *convivium* become markers of enslavement.[6] We should not forget that the forgetful cook in Petronius's novel almost faces savage punishment in front of the diners – here, physical violence regularly wielded against the enslaved is leveraged to articulate the grand surprise, that the apparently ungutted pig actually contains cooked sausages in place of entrails. Diners at marvellous or mundane *convivia* did not necessarily ponder the larger consequences of their consumptive acts or the human capital behind its production. Objects like the 'Sleeping African Slave' *piperatorium* (British Museum 1889, 1019.16), whose exhausted subject is shackled and pierced in the head for sprinkling pepper – a sinister delight for slave-owners born of spice, silver, and servitude – remind us that the study of consumption dovetails with a history of oppression.

However, the connection between spice and subjugation lies elsewhere in the Roman imagination through the petty ethics of luxury – namely, that free Romans themselves were enslaved to their own desires. This is best demonstrated by Pliny the Elder's tirade against what he calls the 'theft of factories' (*officinarum furta*; *Nat. Hist.*

13.2.17). In an extensive passage, Pliny takes a firm stance against promoting foreign medicines in Rome, claiming that the deceit of profiteers causes unknowing customers to rely on mysterious concoctions from Arabia and India – it is through one of the arts that Roman conquerors are conquered (*Nat. Hist.* 24.1.4-5; see also 22.56.117-18). Although Pliny does not keep his word, citing many peppery remedies, his underlying argument is clear: that the voracity of Roman consumers is the unmaking of empire.

Foreign and Familiar

An environmental conundrum at the heart of this particular anxiety demands further interrogation: despite Roman familiarity with pepper, the spice was cultivated in foreign reaches beyond Roman control. It was widely believed in Greco-Roman scientific thought that unique environmental conditions in India not only promote prodigious plant growth, but also transfer heat to exotic flora, which exude fragrant smells and pungent tastes (Simmons 2020: 282-83). Thus, pepper had to be imported from India, a region well beyond Roman hegemony – and Rome had no hope of gaining control over its production. Therefore, by Pliny's moralizing logic, every purchase of pepper undermines the certainty of an empire without end.

Roman authors offer some ways over this intellectual hurdle. One solution involves a rereading of the Plinian paradigm of wasteful empire. The voracious demand of Roman consumers becomes a boon for the empire in the *Encomium of Rome*, a second-century oration by Aelius Aristides. Here, Roman demand for Indian products strips the aromatic trees in India bare and results in almost a Roman monopoly – Rome does rule the whole world, not through iron, but with gold and silver (*Orat.* 14.200). Another solution is cultivating the literary landscape to accommodate the spice. Mythical descriptions of pepper cultivation in the Roman world can be found throughout Roman literature. Most famous is Trimalchio's pepper-growing estate (Petronius *Sat.* 38), what Peter Garnsey has rightly described as a 'travesty of the ethic of self-sufficiency' to be espoused by Roman villa-owners (1999: 24). Martial too describes his window-box in one of his *Epigrams*, hinting at the prospect of raw peppercorns (*Ep.* 11.18.8-9).[7] In these fictions, the economic imperialism at the heart of Pliny's anxieties and Aristides's praise morphs into an ecological one, a violation of the natural order through which the foreign becomes familiar.

However, pepper consumption altered the familiar environments of urban landscapes in more tangible ways, especially in Rome. Most relevant were the so-called *Horrea Piperataria*, the state-built 'pepper-warehouses' along the Via Sacra commissioned by the emperor Domitian (Piranomonte 1996: 45). The warehouses, whose remains have been found under the Basilica of Constantine, have been estimated to have been as large as the later structure, with a capacity of 5800 tons of spice (McLaughlin 2010: 144). Certain individuals, most notably the physician Galen, were given clearance to select the choicest varieties of aromatic products for their wares, but the warehouses may have also served as the locus for auctioning merchandise (Evers 2017: 58-61). Pepper was also available to consumers outside the *horrea*: likely candidates include the shops of the *Vicus Unguentarius* and *Vicus Turarius*, the so-called 'perfume quarters' of the city. Other retailers for pepper and peppered products in the city include *tabernae* ('shops') and the *stationes* ('stations') of foreign traders situated along the Via Sacra (De Ligt 1993: 29; Terpstra 2013: 137 ff.).

Rome also exported certain habits to the provinces. The city's million-man market accelerated the larger Mediterranean economy; the volume of spending at the capital and the movement of people in and out of the city spread habits to a wide range of consumers throughout a network of 'feeder' towns – places like the Bay of Naples – and along the military frontiers (see Hopkins 2000). Archaeobotanical remains attest to this directionality of supply, with pepper discoveries not only at Pompeii and Herculaneum, but also along the German frontier and in Britain; documentary sources also record pepper along the frontiers, including papyri from Egypt, wooden tablets from Vindolanda, and a lead plaque from the Roman outpost at Trier (Schwinden 1983: 22; Kučan 1984: 51-56; Cappers 2006: 114; Evers 2017: 72-74). As individuals with coin purses at the end of supply lines, legionnaires could obtain these goods perhaps more easily than others in the provinces. Nevertheless, the provincial elite partook of the spice much as those in Italy did; in fact, some of the finest silver *piperatoria* hail from Britain (e.g. those of the Hoxne Hoard, British Museum 1994,0408.33-36), forged during the twilight hours of Roman rule. Thus, pepper consumption encapsulates the paradoxical push and pull of empire, all the while stirring up associated anxieties for those who stood to gain the most from it.

325

Peppery Paradoxes

Pepper forms paradoxes in the Roman imagination. It simultaneously reflects Roman dominance through market forces and its defeat by them; it defines Roman refinement while remaining foreign to a canonical Roman way of life as a harbinger of destructive 'luxury'; it stands outside the reach of the average Roman in quantities used for banqueting, but more meagerly peppered fare appears far more attainable; one must know about pepper and its qualities to be sufficiently urbane, even if it is the bane of moralizing tropes and even literature itself. Across these various takes, a sort of reductive reasoning prevails for rhetorical effect, a conflation of function and commodity regardless of context, intent, or the identity of the consumer. Standing two-millennia removed, we can understandably take these interwoven, even convoluted factors for granted at first glance. Rather than demonizing forms of consumption as 'luxurious', we ought to recognize their complexities and appreciate the choices of individuals whose lives were transformed by moments of connectivity.

Acknowledgements

I would like to thank Sally Grainger, Susan Weingarten, and Raymond Sokolov for their insightful comments on my paper and for the lively discussion on the topic during the 2020 OFS V-Symp 'Spices in Antiquity' panel. I would also like to thank James Zetzel and my colleagues at the American Academy in Rome for their thoughtful suggestions on an earlier version.

Notes

1   For the concept of 'consumerscape' in the context of Classical Athens, see Davidson 2012: 25.
2   I am indebted to Sally Grainger's V-Symp discussion of Bourdieu in relation to ancient spice consumption.
3   Many thanks to Sally Grainger for pointing out a similar inversion between *faex* and *allec* (pers. comm.).
4   A striking parody of this hunger for exotic knowledge can be found in Aulus Gellius (*Noc. Att.* 9.4). For more, see Woolf 2011: 81-84.
5   For the *primus* motif, see Volk 2002.
6   For the evidence from Asia Minor, see Robert 1963: 177-85.
7   See also Columella, the first-century agronomist, who describes Rome as blossoming with aromatics (*Rust.* 3.8.4-5).

References

Bourdieu, P. 1984. Distinction: *A Social Critique of the Judgement of Taste* (Cambridge: Harvard University Press)

Cappers, R. T. J. 2006. *Roman Foodprints at Berenike: Archaeobotanical Evidence of Subsistence and Trade in the Eastern Desert of Egypt* (Los Angeles: Cotsen Institute of Archaeology)

Cobb, M. A. 2013. 'The Reception and Consumption of Eastern Goods in Roman Society', *Greece and Rome*, 60.1: 136-52

—— 2018. 'Black Pepper Consumption in the Roman Empire', *Journal of the Economic and Social History of the Orient*, 61.4: 519-59

Corbier, M. 1985. 'Dévaluations et évolution des prix (Ier-IIIe siècles)', *Revue Numismatique*, 6.27: 69-106

Dalby, A. 2000. *Dangerous Tastes: Spices in World History* (Berkeley: University of California Press)

Davidson, J. 2012. 'Citizen Consumers: The Athenian Democracy and The Origins of Western Consumption', in *The Oxford Handbook of the History of Consumption*, ed. by F. Trentmann (Oxford: Oxford University Press), pp. 23-46

de Ligt, L. 1993. *Fairs and Markets in the Roman Empire* (Amsterdam: Gieben)

Evers, K. G. 2017. *Worlds Apart Trading Together: The Organisation of Long-Distance Trade between Rome and India in Antiquity* (Oxford: Archaeopress)

Fitzpatrick, M. P. 2011. 'Provincializing Rome: The Indian Ocean Trade Network and Roman Imperialism', *Journal of World History*, 22.1: 27-54

Garnsey, P. 1999. *Food and Society in Classical Antiquity* (Cambridge: Cambridge University Press)

Grocock, C. and S. Grainger. 2006. *Apicius: A Critical Edition* (Totnes: Prospect Books)

Guzzo, P. G. (ed.). 2006. *Argenti a Pompei* (Milan: Electa)

Holleran, C. 2012. *Shopping in Ancient Rome* (Oxford: Oxford University Press)

Hopkins, K. 2000. 'Rents, Taxes, Trade and the City of Rome', in *Mercati permanenti e mercati periodici nel mondo romano: Atti degli Incontri capresi di storia dell'economia antica* (Capri 13–15 Ottobre 1997), ed. E. Lo Cascio (Bari: Edipuglia), pp. 253-68

Kučan, D. 1984. '*Der erste römerzeitliche Pfefferfund- nachgewiesen im Legionslager Oberaden*', *Ausgrabungen und Funde in Westfalen-Lippe*, 2: 51-56

Mayer, E. E. 2018. '*Tanti non emo, Sexte, piper*: Pepper Prices, Roman Consumer Culture, and the Bulk of Indo-Roman Trade', *Journal of the Economic and Social History of the Orient*, 61.4: 560-89

McLaughlin, R. 2010. *Rome and the Distant East: Trade Routes to the Ancient Lands of Arabia, India and China* (London: Continuum)

Meyer, F. 1980. 'Carbonized Food Plants of Pompeii, Herculaneum, and the Villa at Torre Annunziata', *Economic Botany*, 34.4: 401-37

Mrozek, S. 1975. *Prix et rémunération dans l'Occident romain, 31 av. n.è.-250 de n.è.* (Gdansk: Societas Scientiarum Gedanensis)

Parker, G. 2002. '*Ex oriente luxuria*: Indian Commodities and Roman Experience', *Journal of the Economic and Social History of the Orient*, 45.1: 40-95

Piranomonte, M. 1996. '*Horrea Piperataria*', in *Lexicon Topographicum Urbis Romae,* vol. 3 (Rome: Quasar), pp. 45-46

Rathbone, D. 2009. 'Earnings and Costs: Living Standards and the Roman Economy', in *Quantifying the Roman Economy: Methods and Problems*, ed. A. K. Bowman and A. Wilson (Oxford: Oxford University Press), pp. 299-326

Robert, L. 1963. *Noms indigènes dans l'Asie-Mineure gréco-romaine* (Paris: A. Maisonneuve)

Rowan, E. 2017. 'Bioarchaeological Preservation and Non-Elite Diet in the Bay of Naples: An Analysis of the Food Remains from the Cardo V Sewer at the Roman Site of Herculaneum', *Environmental Archaeology*, 22.3: 318-36

Schwinden, L. 1983. '*Handel mit Pfeffer und anderen Gewürzen im römischen Trier*', *Funde und Ausgrabungen im Bezirk Trier*, 15: 20-26

Simmons, J. A. 2020. 'Pepper Consumption and the Importance of Taste in Roman Medicine', *Ancient Society*, 50: 277¬-324

Terpstra, T. 2013. *Trading Communities in the Roman World* (Leiden: Brill)

van der Veen, M. 2003. 'When Is Food a Luxury?', *World Archaeology*, 34.3: 405-27

Volk, K. 2002. *The Poetics of Latin Didactic: Lucretius, Vergil, Ovid, Manilius* (Oxford: Oxford University Press)

Woolf, G. 2011. *Tales of the Barbarians: Ethnography and Empire in the Roman West* (Malden: Wiley-Blackwell)

327

The Wild Yuzu: Japan's Little Treasure

Aiko Tanaka

Figure 1. The imperfect beauty of the wild yuzu.

In Western Japan lies a mountain range that stretches from just outside the city of Osaka all the way to Kyoto, and within these mountains grows the wild yuzu. Its deep, fresh flavour and scent has long been loved by the nation's people as it complements the simple tastes of the Japanese palate. Historically, yuzu seeds were shared from farm to farm and home to home, and yuzu trees were once a common sight in home gardens. Hardy by nature and requiring little maintenance, the yuzu can withstand temperatures as low as -7 degrees Celsius, and therefore it was once common practice for farms of all types (barring those in the far north of Japan where the winters are too brutal for even the yuzu) to have at least one fruit-bearing tree for the household's consumption. Yet in modern Japan, while yuzu is still marketed commercially by large corporations through condiments such as yuzu vinegar or yuzu pepper, the fruit in its natural form is now rarely used in home cooking and the number of organically grown wild yuzu trees is sadly on the decline.

Yuzu's Introduction to Japan

The yuzu is a fruit with a long history. With origins in China, it is believed that the first yuzu seeds were brought to Japan during the Nara Period (710-794 AD) by Buddhist monks and scholars who crossed the sea carrying seeds and foods previously unknown to that island nation: garlic, chives and tea, to name just a few. Most of these edible plants were too strongly flavoured to find a following in a country where the native people were used to a diet of fish, seaweed, and locally available vegetables. Yet the yuzu, with its small, fruit-bearing trees that could thrive even in cold temperatures, were a welcome addition. The fruit itself has a thick, uneven skin, large seeds, and can range in size from five centimetres (two inches) in diameter to the size of a small grapefruit. Grown from seed, it takes the yuzu tree about eighteen years to produce its first fruit, and fifty years or more for its fruit to reach its full maturity and flavour.

Yuzu in Japanese Cuisine

The taste of fresh yuzu may be an important element of Japanese traditional food culture, but, due to the thickness of the peel and the oversized seeds, each fruit produces

Figure 2. A comparison of yuzu to other citrus shows the thickness of the peel and oversized seeds.

only a slight amount of juice when pressed, presenting a unique dilemma when used as an ingredient. Only 10% of a yuzu is made up of juice. Therefore, it is generally the peel which is used in cooking. As it is very high in tartness and fragrance, a little goes a long way. Yuzu zest can be added to soups, hot pots, and teas; used as a topping for fish or vegetables; or it can be treated in the same way as lemon or orange zest to add flavour to cakes and other desserts. When dried, it becomes a spice or is mixed with pepper to make the popular *yuzu-koshou*. The juice or extract appears as a main ingredient in the condiment *yuzu-ponzu*, which is used in much the same way as vinegar but can also be consumed as a stand-alone dipping sauce for meat and vegetables.

Yuzu's taste has been described as 'not quite a lemon, not quite an orange'.[1] In fact, its flavour is quite indescribable. Although primarily known as a winter fruit, it can be eaten year-round. Its colour, ranging from vivid green in summer to golden yellow in autumn and winter, is representative of the seasons, an ever-important aspect of Japanese meals. Yuzu is often found as a garnish and occasionally they are hollowed out and used as natural dishes. Since the peel is so prized in Japanese food culture for its lustrous colour and imperfect beauty, great care is taken to hand pick the yuzu so as not to damage them during harvesting. This is not so much the case in other Asian countries where yuzu is grown as they are used in those regions for making teas and jams, thereby rendering the peel insignificant and allowing for harvest using machinery or by simply shaking the trees till the fruit falls to the ground.

330

Figure 3. The height of wild yuzu trees is a challenge when harvesting.

Yuzu as Medicine

Yuzu are rich in vitamins and antioxidants. They contain three times more vitamin C than the common lemon and are rich in flavonoids and collagen which rejuvenate the skin. The presence of the soluble fibre pectin in yuzu can lower blood sugar levels by slowing the digestion of sugar and starch.[2] It is said that the fragrance alone can aid in the process of digestion and relaxation. Since ancient times, the Japanese have enjoyed floating whole yuzu or yuzu peels in their baths, called *yuzu-yu*. It is in this way that the people of old warded off winter flus and cold.

The *ukiyo-e* wood block artist Katsushika Hokusai (1760-1849), well-known for works such as 'The Great Wave' and his depictions of Mount Fuji, was known to have been a devotee of yuzu for medicinal purposes. It is said that in his late sixties he suffered from a 'middle wind' (possibly referring to a cerebral hemorrhage), but was cured by the regular use of *yuzu-kusuri*, or yuzu medicine.[3] According to his personal records, yuzu peel stewed in saké until thick and drunk with hot water was just the thing for beating illnesses. One would like to think that Hokusai's devotion to yuzu contributed to his longevity, as he lived until the ripe age of 89, quite unusual for those times.

The Wild Yuzu of Osaka

In the town of Minoh on the outskirts of Osaka there grows a species of wild yuzu whose trees can measure up to ten metres (over thirty feet) in height and which have thrived in those mountains since the first seeds were planted nearly 1300 years ago. While most commercially produced yuzu are cultivated via grafting, the wild variety are grown purely from seed and tend to be larger in size. At this time there are only around 5000 such trees left in existence within Japan. The few yuzu farming families which still remain in the northern Osaka region have for generations devoted themselves to the propagation and protection of this rare tree.

The remaining wild yuzu trees of Japan owe their existence to these hard-working farmers who have practiced traditional, organic farming methods for centuries. Their year-round loving attention, and abstinence from the heavy use of chemical fertilizers and pesticides so prevalent in commercial Japanese agriculture, have helped the wild yuzu to thrive in a pure state for the past millennium. In an attempt to avoid food loss, a number of these farmers have turned their focus to independent research on how best to market the yuzu by promoting its value not only as a fragrant ingredient, but also as a medicine and cosmetic as it has been used since ancient times.

Another influential figure in the promotion of Minoh's wild yuzu is the independent researcher Eiko Okayama, a local resident who over the past decade has developed a business around yuzu as a natural conditioner for healthy skin and as an alcohol-free disinfectant. An industrial-academic collaboration between Okayama and Osaka University has examined yuzu's antibacterial properties and found it to be effective.

The Future of Yuzu

While the yuzu will likely never disappear from Japanese cuisine, it faces some obstacles in this modern era. In 1964, the year in which Tokyo played host to the summer Olympics, the Japanese government implemented an active importation plan of lemons from the United States. Through this and the importation of other so-called 'Westernized' foods, they hoped to shift to a post-war economy of swift growth based on that of the United States. According to Japan's Ministry of Agriculture, Forestry, and Fisheries, the nationwide harvest of yuzu fruit in the year 2016 (the most recent public figures) yielded 26,000 tons, with only 1000 tons being of the ungrafted, naturally grown variety.[4] In contrast, the year 2017 saw the import of 53,000 tons of lemons into Japan in addition to those grown domestically.[5]

Figure 4. Yuzu peel was once a common garnish in Japanese home cooking.

The ready availability of low-cost lemons and other foreign citruses has resulted in a decline of yuzu consumption for the average person. It is now rarely used in home cooking and is mostly found only at traditional restaurants. Finding yuzu in a supermarket these days can be a bit of a challenge. This is why Minoh city, the home of the aforementioned wild yuzu, is making an effort to promote and educate the public about this local treasure through their fanciful city mascot and events such as the annual Yuzu Festival, the organization of a volunteer picking team, and by using locally-sourced yuzu as an ingredient in public school lunches.

It is my belief that food educators in Japan such as myself must all do our part to further promote the many uses of this amazingly adaptable fruit, in order to ensure that the yuzu will be around for generations to come.

Homemade Yuzu-Ponzu

Ingredients:
500 ml pure yuzu juice (or a mix with other citrus juices)
500 ml Japanese soy sauce

50 g dried bonito fish flakes (katsuobushi)
30 g dried kelp (kombu)

Combine the bonito flakes and kelp with the soy sauce and refrigerate for two to three days. When ready, drain the liquid and discard the kelp and bonito flakes. Combine with the yuzu juice. Store for up to three months in the refrigerator.

Easy Yuzu Pickles

Ingredients:
¾ carrot
½ Japanese radish (daikon)
½ cucumber
1 celery stalk
4 Japanese ginger (myouga)
200 ml rice vinegar
200 g sugar
freshly squeezed juice of 2 yuzu
peel of 1 yuzu
dash of salt

Cut all vegetables and the yuzu skin into thin matchsticks. Mix together the vinegar, sugar and salt in a saucepan and bring to a boil. Once boiling, add the yuzu juice and vegetables. Lower the heat and simmer gently for 20 to 30 minutes. Chill and serve.

Yuzu Pound Cake

Ingredients:
220 g flour
1 tbsp baking powder
4 eggs
220 g sugar
100 ml cream
100 g unsalted butter, melted
1 tbsp brandy (optional)
zest of 3 yuzu

Beat together the sugar and egg till creamy. Mix in the cream, butter, and yuzu zest. Sift together flour and baking powder in a separate bowl. Combine wet and dry ingredients until just moistened. Bake in a lined pound cake tin at 180 degrees Celsius for 25-30 minutes. Brush with brandy while still warm.

Notes

1   Vivian Morelli, 'The Zesty World of Yuzu', *NHK World Japan,* 18 December 2017 <https://www.nhk.or.jp/dwc/food/articles/108.html> [accessed 11 May 2020].

2   Joanne Slavin, 'Fiber and Prebiotics: Mechanisms and Health Benefits', *Nutrients,* 5.4 (22 April 2013), 1417-35 <http://www.doi.org/10.3390/nu5041417>

3   Kyoshin Iijima, *Katsushika Hokusai Den* (*The Biography of Katsushika Hokusai*) (Tokyo: Iwanami Shoten, 1999).

4   Japan Ministry of Agriculture, Forestry, and Fisheries, *Survey of the Production Dynamics of Specialty Fruit Trees (2016)* <https://www.maff.go.jp/j/heya/kodomo_sodan/0305/06.html> [accessed 26 January 2021]

5   Global Agricultural Information Network, *United States Department of Agriculture's Citrus Annual,* 26 December 2019, p. 13.

Ambiguous Aromatic Umbellifers and Other Obscure Characters: On the Intricacies of Recreating China's Culinary Past

Robban Toleno

In China's thirteenth century, a poet compiled 104 rustic and unusual recipes. Now, seven centuries later, I am translating the collection into English and attempting to recreate the dishes. Some recipes use wild plant ingredients with names that puzzle even Chinese scholars working on the collection. Too often, scholars interpret Chinese plant names purely based on evidence in written records, but many botanical identities are obscured behind layers of confused nomenclature. A single plant might have many popular names and a single popular name might refer to a number of different plants. Botanical knowledge of China's past and present is a field teeming with synonyms – and would-be synonyms that appear on investigation to be false matches. Historical Chinese recipes often use names that have not remained current over the centuries and across different regions. Combine this vagueness of terminology with complications arising from differences between editions, as well as the provisional state of modern botanical knowledge, and you have a recipe for botanical confusion.

My solution to the difficulty of determining botanical identities for plants in China is to diversify the sources of evidence. On the basis of two sample recipes from the collection, I argue that practice – the testing of hypotheses through recipe recreation – has an important augmenting role in researching China's culinary past, because of limitations in printed materials for understanding plants in Chinese history. Only by testing hypotheses can we refine our theories on historical plant ingredients and rediscover the value of these old Chinese recipes. Furthermore, culinary recreations have the advantage of manifesting differences between versions of a recipe in ways that help us understand recipe interpretation as a process of history.

Updating and Preserving China's Diverse Culinary History

Historians sometimes take the view that projecting modern botany back into history is anachronistic and pointless. I cannot agree. This view turns history into an ultimately unknowable Platonic space disconnected from the experiential realities of our historical connections with plants. China's past is a living root, not a sterile museum exhibit. At stake in the work of explaining the cultural history of plants in China is the diversity of culinary practices that helped shape Chinese civilization. The Chinese maintain an astonishing level of culinary diversity, but some of their cultural and ecological diversity has come under threat from the modernizing of industry and agriculture, as I have personally witnessed in the last three decades.

Reasons for discontinuity in the use of certain plants for food in China include, in deep history and now, the challenge of properly identifying plants and transmitting information on how they are edible to younger generations. Some of this knowledge has been shared orally across generations. There are also several genres of writing, such as materia medica (*bencao*), agricultural texts (*nongshu*), and recipe collections (*shipu*), that have provided a literary foundation of botanical knowledge that has been evolving for at least two millennia. This foundation of knowledge is in literary Chinese, a form of Chinese that differs from modern Mandarin much as Chaucer's writing differs from modern English. The evolution of China's botanical knowledge entered a new stage in the twentieth century, with the institution of modern botanical conventions and efforts to graft modern botany onto the rootstock of premodern botanical knowledge.

The provisional nature of historical Chinese botanical knowledge is not unique. Worldwide, the foundations of botanical knowledge are still in development; botanical nomenclature continues to evolve as botanists gain new insights into plant phylogenesis. Plant identities are often not as accurate as we assume. Interpreting plant identities in Chinese history involves multiple naming systems: historical Chinese plant terms, modern Chinese plant terms, different binomial nomenclature ascribed to Chinese plant names by different botanists as equivalency hypotheses, and common names for plants in English. These knowledge domains are still being aligned. We need to further clarify, say, whether a Chinese plant name signified one *Artemisia* species and not others. This work is ongoing and important for the survival of China's ecological and cultural diversity. One cannot protect that which is not known.

The *Shanjia qinggong* Recipes: Foods of Rural Intellectuals in Medieval China

I first came upon the recipe collection *Shanjia qinggong* 山家清供 (*Pure Offerings of Rural Households*) while exploring the history of food in China during my doctorate. Compiled by the poet LIN Hong 林洪 (fl. 1224-1263), this is one of the best preserved early recipe collections from China, holding a prominent place in Chinese food history. The collection intrigued me. In the Song dynasty (960-1279), China experienced a cosmopolitan cultural flourishing, developing a restaurant culture with complex cuisines in urban areas, and yet here was a recipe collection celebrating rustic vegetable dishes.

Lin Hong is said to have passed the imperial exams, but does not seem to have held public office. He travelled around China to visit intellectuals in their private academies and official posts, inquiring about the foods that he was served and writing down notes that he later compiled into this collection of recipes and anecdotes. By the Southern Song dynasty (1127-1279), woodblock printing techniques were well enough developed to allow even lesser-known scholars to publish small works. Lin Hong probably published his recipe collection through a clan school that issued imprints of texts for local circulation and for use as textbooks (called *jiashu keben*).[1]

Around the end of the Yuan dynasty (1271-1368) and beginning of the Ming (1368-1644), Lin Hong's recipe collection was picked up for inclusion in a large anthology of texts called the *Shuofu* 說郛 (*The Outer Wall of Learning*), helping to preserve it. At the end of the sixteenth century, the scholars ZHOU Lüjing 周履靖 (1549-1640) and CHEN Jiru 陳繼儒 (1558-1639) produced an edited version of Lin Hong's recipe collection for the anthology *Yimen guangdu* 夷門廣牘 (*Extensive Documents of the City*), substantially altering some of the text. The various editions available today appear to mostly derive from these two streams: the *Shuofu* edition that is likely closer to Lin Hong's original, and the heavily edited *Yimen guangdu* edition.[2]

I am translating both the older *Shuofu* edition from the Hanfenlou 涵芬樓 library collection (HFL) and the *Yimen guangdu* edition (YG), in order to compare them. The latter has clarifications and details for recipes that may constitute a valuable contribution toward understanding the recipes. Or, perhaps Zhou and Chen's editing corrupted Lin Hong's culinary intentions? Until the editorial changes are better understood, we cannot easily judge the relative value of these editions, so this comparative work enters into my analysis of each recipe.

The individual recipes of the *Shanjia qinggong* remain poorly understood even in China, despite a recent resurgence of interest in this collection. Due to difficulties of language and the opacity of Lin Hong's explanations, those of us working on these recipes must grapple with problems of how to properly identify ingredients or interpret a dish. Scholars who have published on this collection, such as WU Ke in China and the Japanese scholar NAKAMURA Takashi, often disagree on the identities of plants in the recipes.[3] I am unaware of any Western scholarship on this collection that has delved into the details of the recipes, but pioneering Sinologists who worked to identify plants in Chinese historical sources, including G. A. Stuart, Bernard E. Read, Berthold Laufer, Edward H. Schafer, and Frederick J. Simoons, all struggled with botanical identification and nomenclature, leaving many points of uncertainty in our knowledge of plants in Chinese history.[4] Even the impressive *Dictionnaire Ricci des plantes de Chine* has led me to some confused results when trying to identify plants that Lin Hong features in his recipes.[5]

With no fully authoritative reference for identifying plants in Chinese history, I find that I must use a combination of tools and strategies in order to avoid pitfalls in translating Lin Hong's centuries-old recipes. My methods involve using a small library of reference books in Chinese, Japanese, English, and French, in combination with searches of plants in China's historical writings. After identifying possible matches, I check online sources to clarify binomial nomenclature, sorting through superseded synonyms. Online tools in Chinese help me conduct virtual ethnobotany forays into the uses of plants in Chinese society, providing images and text that can support or

337

undermine my working hypotheses. Finally, I take my hypotheses to the kitchen, trying out recreations of the recipes with actual herbs and spices. The palate can be a harsh critic, but it is also an excellent teacher.

Below, I discuss examples of plant confusion to illustrate how the practice of recreating historical recipes supports my work of translation. The test kitchen for historical recipes is a laboratory for continuing the work of clarifying China's botanical history, complementing what can be done with literary sources. A recipe translation is, after all, merely a hypothesis, the proof of which is in the pudding.

Ambiguous Aromatic Umbellifers

Yuguanfei 玉灌肺 (*Jade-Filled Lung*), recipe #35, is a faux-meat recipe from Chinese imperial kitchens that has a kind of morbid brilliance. It looks like head cheese, all gelled and meaty, but is entirely plant-based. If it were to appear in English on a restaurant menu, it might be called 'vegan stuffed-lung'. It mimics in appearance a steamed dish of stuffed lungs that was cooked in medieval China, and its name, literally 'jade-poured lung', reflects this origin.[6] The two editions differ somewhat:

[HFL:] Mung bean starch, fry-bread, sesame, pine nut, walnut, and *shiluo*. Powder these six, stir together, pour into a rice pot, steam until cooked, cut into the appearance of pieces of lung, and serve with a jujube sauce. Now, as in the past, the imperial name [for this dish] is 'court-favoured jade-filled lung'. You want it to be served as no more than a vegetarian dish. From this [dish], we [can] see the intention of the imperial court to celebrate frugality and dislike killing. How, then, could it be appropriate for rural dwellers to be extravagant [by eating meat]?

眞粉、油餅、芝麻、松子、胡桃、蒔蘿。六者為末，拌和，入甑，蒸熟，切作肺樣塊，用棗汁供。今後苑名曰 '御愛玉灌肺'. 要之不過一素供耳。然, 以此見九重崇儉, 不嗜殺之意. 居山豈宜侈哉?

[YG:] Mung bean starch, fry-bread, sesame, pine nut, walnut (remove skins). Add a little *shiluo*, white sugar, a little 'red yeast' ground into powder. Mix it together, put it in a rice pot, and steam until cooked. Cut it to appear like pieces of lung and serve it with a spicy sauce. Now, as in the past, [...(as above)]

真粉、油餅、芝麻、松子、核桃去皮，加蒔蘿少許，白糖紅曲少許，為末拌和，入甑蒸熟，切作肺樣塊子，用辣汁供。今後...

Both versions of the recipe are flavoured with the herb *shiluo* 蒔蘿, a plant that the great Sinologist Berthold Laufer identified in 1919 as 'cummin' (*Cuminum cyminum*) or caraway (*Carum carui* or *carvi*) in his study *Sino-Iranica*, asserting this on the basis of compelling linguistic evidence and arguing that previous observers who had identified it as fennel (*Foeniculum vulgare*) were mistaken.[7] Edward Schafer later suggested that *shiluo* may actually refer to dill (*Anethum graveolens*).[8] Modern botanical information

338

from China sides with Schafer on this point, and dictionaries now define *shiluo* as dill, but historians must be cognizant of the sometimes irregular use of plant names in history. It would be easy to dismiss Laufer's argument as erroneous, but he was likely correct that *shiluo* was not fennel, as some people had suggested. He reasoned that *shiluo* is a Chinese transliteration of Sanskrit *jīra* coming from Middle Persian *žīra* or *zīra*, meaning cumin (*jeera*) in India. Laufer's view is reasonable in light of the philological evidence, but it seems that another transliteration, *ziran* 孜然, prevailed for denoting cumin, while *shiluo* came to denote dill. How these foreign transliterated words entered into usage in China is a complex historical problem; we cannot assume that botanical identities were always clear to historical actors who used these terms.

Still, loan words do provide important points of reference for China's botanical lexicon, which is rich in synonyms. Common names for plants in China are sometimes loosely applied and can denote more than one plant. For example, *shiluo* was sometimes called *xiaohuixiang*, 'small *huixiang*'. 'Huixiang' literally means 'returning aroma', referring to an aftertaste, a fragrance that lingers after swallowing. Today, *xiaohuixiang* usually denotes fennel, as does *huixiang*, without the diminutive. Just as there was in the popular vernacular a 'small' *huixiang*, there was also a 'large' one: *dahuixiang* 大茴香, star anise, also called *bajiao* 八角, 'eight horns'. In contrast with star anise, which grows as a tree and has large seed heads, both dill and fennel are small plants with small seeds, hence their sharing, at times, the diminutive *xiao*. Dill's other common name, *tuhuixiang* 土茴香, 'rustic' *huixiang*, was also shared with fennel. The differences between dill and fennel have sometimes been overlooked in China, leading to occasional conflation of the two plants.

Common names for umbellifers are an ongoing source of confusion in China. Search Google in Chinese for *dahuixiang*, and one finds, along with mention of star anise, websites aiming to clarify for Chinese home cooks the different names of umbellifer spices and herbs. Some people today use the 'small' and 'large' comparison not for star anise and fennel, but to differentiate fennel and dill as herbs, due to differences in the stature of each plant. Furthermore, the seeds of cumin, being small, can also be called *xiaohuixiang* (along with dill and fennel), though it is more readily differentiated by its loan-word name, *ziran*. Loan-word names thus serve as helpful clues regarding plant identities, but as we saw with the Chinese transliteration of spice names from Sanskrit and Middle Persian, such linguistic borrowings do not necessarily lead to a coherent botanical identity with a philologically clear lineage across languages.

With confidence in the identity of my thirteenth-century Chinese ingredient somewhat dampened, I puzzled over its role in the recipe. Use of the loan word helps reduce the likelihood that fennel or cumin was intended, and most scholars seem to agree that it should be dill.[9] There is no indication in the recipe, however, on whether to use dill as herb or spice. Nakamura states that the seeds are to be used.[10] A recent Chinese effort to recreate the recipe also uses dill seed.[11]

Testing this hypothesis that dill seed was intended, I went on to systematically test,

339

also, dill foliage, cumin seed, fennel seed, and fennel foliage. Furthermore, I tested both the older recipe (HFL) and the version of this recipe that was altered by Zhou and Chen in the late sixteenth century (YG). The older recipe calls for the ingredients to be ground up and mixed, then steamed, sliced, and served with a jujube sauce. This recipe thus has a granular texture, into which *shiluo* is integrated for flavour. I found that dill foliage, fennel foliage, cumin seed, and fennel seed were all plausible, each differing in aroma and texture. Only dill seed seemed a definite fail; it was too hard to pulverize in my mortar, cooked up as unsightly dark specks in the meaty mass, and had relatively poor flavour.

In recreating *Yuguanfei* from Zhou and Chen's recipe, I found that the intention was an artful realism: a mock meat coloured pink by the addition of 'red yeast rice' (rice cultured with the mould *Monascus purpureus*). Using the delicate green tips of dill foliage creates in the cooked dish lacing black lines that are suggestive of small blood vessels, supporting the illusion that the dish is made from meat. The delicacy of dill foliage is perfect for this role; fennel foliage is also possible, though thicker. Seeds, especially of dill, are too coarse and fail to preserve the smooth, marbled aesthetic of this version of the recipe. Zhou and Chen's recipe is served with a spicy sauce, probably mustard.

This case of ambiguous umbellifers illustrated for me how Zhou and Chen's recipe departs significantly from that of the HFL edition, adding a layer of creative interpretation. Because even Lin Hong may have been interpreting this recipe from hearsay, and because cumin, fennel, and dill were sometimes confused in China, attempting to reach a definitive answer on which umbellifer to use may be futile. Cooks in Chinese history probably would have used what they had on hand, gravitating toward the ingredients that they preferred. And despite the views of some scholars, dill seed was probably not a favourite for either version of the recipe. The context of the use of an ingredient matters, and dill seed is uncompelling in this context.

Eating Fleabane and Mugwort in Search of *Peng*

Penggao 蓬糕 (*Peng* Rice Cake), recipe #59, is a steamed rice cake flavoured with a plant called *peng* 蓬, the identity of which has perplexed me for almost a year. Lin Hong says to pick tender *baipeng* 白蓬, 'white' *peng* plants, cook them, mash them, mix in rice flour, and then steam the mixture until fragrant:

> (Wait for the rice to boil. Take *peng* mixed with wheat flour and cook it into rice. This is *peng* rice.)[12] Pick tender plants of white *peng*, cook and finely mash them, mix with rice flour [YG: and sugar]; cook with steam until fragrant. Privileged sons of this generation know the importance of deer antler and stalactite, but do not know to eat this, which is in fact a great tonic. How can people [ignorantly] treat rural foods as vulgar? The Min area (Fujian) has the grass *bai*[13] (barnyard grass) [which is used similarly].

蓬[米+燕]糕俟飯沸，以蓬拌麵，飯煮：蓬飯
采白蓬嫩者，熟煮細搗，和米粉，蒸熟，以香為度。世之貴介子弟知
鹿茸、鍾乳為重而不知食此，實大有補，詎可以山食而鄙之哉！閩中
有草稗。[14]

In the case of this recipe, differences between the two editions are minimal, so the primary question revolves around the botanical identity of the plant *peng*.[15] Historical references on *peng* do not point us toward a firm identity, but they do provide some clues. Li Shizhen (1518-1593), compiler of the important Ming-dynasty medical text *Bencao gangmu* 本草綱目 (*Compendium of Materia Medica*), pointed out that '*Peng* plants are not a singular type'. He illustrates how '*peng*' appears in the names of a good number of plants as different as wild rice (*diaopeng*), a kind of cereal grain (*shupeng*), yellow water-lily (*huangpeng*), and the plant 'yellow *peng* weed' (*huangpengcao*) or 'flying *peng*' (*feipeng* 飛蓬), which is 'akin to lamb's-quarters [or] mugwort' 藜蒿之類.[16] Neither he nor anyone other than Lin Hong seems to know what is meant, however, by 'white *peng*'.

Several botanical reference works agree that the most ancient and basic botanical identity of *peng* in Chinese history is *feipeng* ('flying *peng*'), identified by the Japanese botanist KANŌ Yoshimitsu as *Erigeron acer*.[17] This identification is credible, but overconfident in designating a species, since there are dozens of *Erigeron* species in China that put out small flying seeds in a similar manner and which include '*feipeng*' in the name.[18] The genus *Erigeron* is constituted by a group of similar plants, commonly referred to as fleabanes in English and *feipeng* in Chinese.

341

In his pioneering work on Lin Hong's collection, the Chinese scholar Wu Ke interprets 'white *peng*' as *feipeng*.[19] To gain insight on this hypothesis, I decided that the daisy fleabane (*Erigeron annuus*), which grows in my area and is edible, was probably similar enough to Chinese fleabanes to allow for some initial testing of its potential in the historical recipe. In early spring, fleabanes push up tender shoots with light green foliage and fuzzy stems that stand out from the surrounding vegetation; the light colouring could be the meaning of 'white' in the recipe. The soft shoots are a little bitter, but if cooked thoroughly they have a flavour similar to artichoke, with a pungent aroma that lingers on the nose. Fleabane seems a plausible match for the Chinese recipe, save for three points: 1) The plants I tried were not very fragrant, despite the distinctive aroma when eaten – yet the recipe calls for the cakes to be steamed 'until fragrant'; 2) I find little information on the use of fleabane as an edible plant in China; and 3) I have yet to see fleabane described in Chinese medicine as a tonic (having a restorative or invigorating effect).

Perhaps stumped by the problem of identifying white *peng*, some scholars chose to merely repeat Lin Hong's name for the plant without a modern identifier.[20] Others settled on another hypothesis: that the plant is a '*hao* 蒿', an *Artemisia* species from a group of plants known in English by the common names mugwort and wormwood.

There is a long history in China of confusing *peng* with *hao*, as both fleabanes and mugworts are common weeds of similar stature that flourish in open areas around villages and agricultural fields.[21]

The underside of mugwort is covered in hairs and has a whitish sheen; some species have whitish coloration all over the leaves, top and bottom. That this group of plants is widespread, common, has white coloration, has a distinctive fragrance, and appears in culinary applications across East Asia makes it a compelling second candidate.

Nakamura adopts this hypothesis, treating the plant in question as an East Asian mugwort that is common in Japan.[22] Indeed, the Chinese character 蓬 (*peng*) is read 'yomogi' in Japanese, having been adopted in Japan to refer to the mugwort *Artemisia princeps*, which is used there as a culinary ingredient in such foods as *daifuku mochi*, small glutinous rice cakes stuffed with sweetened bean paste (the green version being called *yomogi mochi*). The cultural practice in Japan of using mugwort as a flavouring in glutinous rice seems to run parallel with this old recipe from China. In Chinese, *Artemisia princeps* is called *kuihao* 魁蒿, the 'great' or 'chief' *Artemisia*. In Korea it is known as *ssuk* 쑥 and used in a wide variety of foods including rice cakes, noodles, and stews.[23]

I tested Lin Hong's recipe using *Artemisia vulgaris*, common mugwort, which has an appearance and fragrance similar to common East Asian mugworts (I have tasted several in different parts of China and in Japan). While the flavour and fragrance were pleasant enough, the fibrous texture of the leaves had the mouthfeel of cotton. The fibres are masked when mixed into glutinous rice, but can be a problem in other types of rice flour. One option is to use only the green juice, but the recipe does not suggest this.

Perhaps some *Artemisia* species are less fibrous and more fragrant than others? Looking deeper into *Artemisia* use in China alerted me to the diversity within this genus. The Chinese botany site *eFlora* lists 230 species and varieties of *Artemisia*![24] My search for culinary uses of these turned up some important points. Among the species, I found *louhao* 蔞蒿 (*A. selengensis*), which is discussed as a vegetable in recipe #34 of Lin Hong's collection: 'Its leaves are like those of *ai* 艾, white in colour. It can be steamed as a vegetable.'[25] *Louhao* is cultivated commercially in China and has foliage similar to other *Artemisia*, such as *ai* (*aihao* 艾蒿, *A. argyi*). To the casual observer, the *Artemisia* species that we refer to as 'mugwort' or 'wormwood' cohere as a group; likewise in China for *hao*. If Lin Hong was familiar with the appearance of *Artemisia* plants such as *louhao* and *ai*, why would he refer to a similar plant as *peng*? *Ai* is one of several *Artemisia* species celebrated within Chinese medicine and could also be a candidate for *peng*, if not for the awkwardness of it appearing elsewhere in Lin Hong's collection.

Still another explanation gets around the problems with fleabane and mugwort. A recipe in Lin Hong's collection, #57 *Dongting yi*, 'Confection of Dongting Lake', calls for *peng*, though not white *peng*. Chinese authors of a recent book of historical recipes argue that the plant in question should be either *Artemisia argyi* (*aihao*) or *Pseudognaphalium affine* (*shuqucao* 鼠麴草, 'mouse koji plant').[26] They point to the

342

tradition of making *qingtuan* 青團 (青糰), 'green rice cakes', for the Qingming tomb-sweeping festival of spring. *Qingtuan* vary by region. Balls of sticky rice are coloured green with plant juices and stuffed with a sweet or savoury filling. Mugwort juice is often used to colour and flavour the cakes, but other plants are also used.

We may never know, from textual information alone, whether Lin Hong meant for people to use fleabane, mugwort, *Pseudognaphalium*, or some other plant. Trying all possibilities could yet help us recover the flavours of China's past.

Conclusions

The work of translating Lin Hong's thirteenth-century collection of recipes entails grappling with problems of botanical identification. Literary sources are crucial for gathering clues, but irregularities in our knowledge of China's culinary past call for research methods that include ethnographic information and practical application of hypotheses through recreations of historical recipes. By bringing historical recipes out of the study and into the kitchen, we engage in a process of recipe-interpretation that parallels that of historical Chinese actors. When the obscure characters in books fall short, the palate can yet reinvigorate our knowledge of the verdant characters of the field.

Notes

1 NAKAMURA Takashi, *Chūgoku no shokufu* (Tōkyō: Heibonsha, 1995), p. 24. Surnames of East Asian authors supplied in caps for first mention.
2 Nakamura 24.
3 LIN Hong, *Shanjia qinggong,* trans. (to Mandarin) by WU Ke (Beijing: Zhongguo shangye chubanshe, 1985); Nakamura.
4 Rev. G. A. Stuart, *Chinese Materia Medica: Vegetable Kingdom* (Shanghai: American Presbyterian Mission Press, 1911; repr. Taipei: Southern Materials Center, 1987); Bernard E. Read, *Chinese Medicinal Plants From the Pen Ts'ao Kang Mu* 本草綱目. *A.d. 1596: 3rd. Edition of a Botanical, Chemical and Pharmacological Reference List* (Peking: Peking Natural History Bulletin, 1936; repr. Taipei: Southern Materials Center, 1936); Berthold Laufer, *Sino-Iranica: Chinese Contributions to the History of Civilization in Ancient Iran: With Special Reference to the History of Cultivated Plants and Products* (Chicago: Field Museum of Natural History, 1919); Edward H. Schafer, *The Golden Peaches of Samarkand: A Study of T'ang Exotics* (Berkeley: University of California Press, 1963); Frederick J. Simoons, *Food in China: A Cultural and Historical Inquiry* (Boca Raton: CRC Press, 1991).
5 Francine Fèvre and Georges Métailié, *Dictionnaire Ricci des plantes de Chine* (Paris: Association Ricci, 2005).
6 Uyghurs in Northwestern China still make a stuffed-lung dish using actual lung: *öpkä hesip*, called *mian feizi* 面肺子 in Chinese. Thanks to Fuchsia Dunlop for bringing this to my attention.
7 Laufer, p. 383.
8 Schafer, p. 148.
9 See for example Wu (trans.), *Shanjjia qinggong*, p. 44; Lin Hong, *Shanjia qinggong*, ed. by ZHANG Yuan (Beijing: Zhonghua shuju, 2013), p. 74; and the following two citations.
10 Nakamura, p. 73.
11 XU Li, ZHENG Yasheng, and LU Ran, *Song yan* [*Delicacies of the Song Dynasty*] (Beijing: Xinxing chubanshe, 2018), pp. 101-03.

12 This interlinear note after the recipe title gives a recipe for cooked, flavoured rice (like risotto). In the *Yimen guangdu* edition, the editors have moved this note to the end.

13 *Echinochloa crus-galli* (L) Beauv.

14 HFL edition, with a note from the YG edition on sugar.

15 There is an archaic and unidentified character in the title of this dish in the HFL edition, but this is likely a clarification of the type of rice cake and not botanical information. The later YG edition adds sugar to the recipe, which is the primary difference.

16 Li Shizhen could be, alternatively, pointing to a particular species of mugwort, if this is read as a single composite plant name: *lihao*, a synonym of *louhao* 蔞蒿, *Artemisia selengensis*. See *Bencao gangmu*, second grain section ('*gu zhi er*' 穀之二), 18th item.

17 KANŌ Yoshimitsu, *Shokubutsu no kanji gogen jiten* (Tōkyō: Tōkyōdō shuppan, 2008), pp. 297-98.

18 The Chinese Plant Names index *eFloras* (<http://www.efloras.org>) counts thirty-nine species, the Chinese names for which mostly end in -*feipeng*.

19 Wu trans., *Shanjia qinggong*, p. 70, n. 4.

20 See for example Zhang (ed.), *Shanjia qinggong* (2013), p. 122; Lin Hong, *Shanjia qinggong*, ed. by FEI Yong (Tianjin, China: Baihua wenyi chubanshe, 2019), p. 161. SONG Siwei's illustrated *Shanjia qinggong: guren de yazhi shenghuo* (Nanchang, China: Jiangxi meishu chubanshe, 2018), p. 120, inexplicably changes the plant name in the Mandarin translation to *bailian* 白蓮, 'white lotus'.

21 See for example Li Shizhen's comments at the start of this section and Kanō, p. 298.

22 Nakamura, p. 110.

23 Based on internet research. See, for example, images associated with Korean 'mugwort cooking': 쑥 요리.

24 Search 'Artemisia' at <http://www.efloras.org>.

25 *Ai* is now identified as *A. argyi*, but it may have been ambiguous in history, sometimes serving as a synonym for the larger category of *hao* (mugworts). See Fèvre and Métailié, pp. 3-4, 166.

26 The latter plant, in the family *Asteraceae* along with fleabanes and mugworts, is fuzzy, white, and fragrant (Xu, Zheng, and Lu, pp. 57-59).

344

A Twenty-First-Century Spice: A Journey to Madagascar and the Promise and Peril of the Wild *Tsiperifery* Pepper

Amy B. Trubek, Eric Bishop-von Wettberg, and Maya Moore

The quest for spices is a story both global and particular; here, three American researchers – an anthropologist, a plant ecologist, and a conservationist – go on a journey to Madagascar to understand a wild pepper with an unusual flavour (the *tsiperifery* pepper, wild harvested from a vine in the genus *Piper* thought to be endemic to Madagascar's rainforests), witnessing the early consequences of these realities in this singular place. As is so often the case, this is a story of both promise and peril, for the plant, the people involved in its domestication and production, and for the natural forests where the plant is grown. But this story, because it is about a potentially new spice for global trade, is very twenty-first century. It is a story in the making and also a story concerning various possible futures – for a plant, people, and a place.

Madagascar, the world's fourth largest island, has a long, complex engagement with the spice trade. So many of the trade-offs involved in the global spice trade are made manifest in Madagascar. This is a story told in many areas of the globe after the Columbian Exchange and the emergence of the modern spice trade. However, due to Madagascar's long geographic isolation, there are unique elements: there are over 11,000 species of vascular plants documented on the island, of which more than 80% are endemic (Callmander and others 2011). Among them is *tsiperifery* – a remarkable and mysterious pepper new to the global culinary scene.

In this essay, we explain the significance of the plant from the point of view of botany, cultivation, domestication, culinary and medicinal uses, and subsistence livelihoods; explore why spice exporters, conservationists, and development agents have turned their attention to this spice; share the perspectives of those interested in making it part of the global spice trade; and speculate on its future – from domestication to distribution.

Introduction

How did it all begin? This decision to go to Madagascar. Amy came late to the idea. Initial conversations started between Maya Moore, a Food Systems PhD student who has worked on conservation and community development in Madagascar for over a decade, and Eric Bishop-von Wettberg, an expert in crop domestication and conservation genetics. During a graduate seminar, their mutual admiration for the unparalleled biodiversity of plants (and animals) found on this amazing island nation emerged. Maya presented on the case of a wild pepper in the genus *Piper* found in (increasingly compromised) Malagasy rainforests. There was an immediate sense of shared possibility: Eric loves a good never-been-domesticated story, and Maya plans to carry out her dissertation research at the intersection of conservation efforts and farmer livelihoods in Madagascar. Fortunately, there was a small grant opportunity at the University of Vermont for transdisciplinary research efforts. Why not go and find out more about the plant, the people, and the possibilities? But they needed one more collaborator to fulfil the expectations of the grant – transdisciplinary research recasts and reframes and thus requires multiple perspectives.

Amy's interest in taking this long trip, which involved eighteen hours in an airplane, several airports, and multiple stops at passport control, was primarily professional (though she confesses to a lifelong fascination with this place due to its relationship to evolutionary history). The promise of the plant and the pepper, endemic to such an unusual natural environment, was too good to pass up.

Amy has been enthralled with the consequences of the Columbian Exchange and the colonial rush to move plants desired by Europeans for their flavour and aroma to far-flung outposts for decades. As is the case with many budding food studies scholars of her generation, Sidney Mintz's book *Sweetness and Power* was a touchstone; his articulation of the push and pull between production and consumption before, during, and after colonialism shaped her scholarship. She has taught about this push and pull to culinary students, university undergraduates, and graduate students specializing in food systems. Never tiring of the topic, she often thought about Madagascar, with its long and complex engagement with the global spice trade. And there was a personal connection; her father's family owned a chemical company that made synthetic flavours and fragrances, including vanilla.

So, we became a team (with Maya as our fearless trip leader). Together, our trio – Amy, trained as an anthropologist and chef and now a food scholar; Eric, educated as an ecologist with a long-standing involvement in plant domestication and genetics; and Maya, a Malagasy-speaking former Peace Corps volunteer learning how to combine conservation and food systems – set out to engage with 'real world' actors across the supply chain. What could we find out about the desire for this pepper apparently sparked from a specialized group of food aficionados? How did this desire connect to plant domestication and what were the implications for farmer livelihoods?

We put together an itinerary that would allow us to travel up and down the eastern half of the island, witnessing the deforested landscape outside our Sprinter windows; going into rainforest preserves to see lemurs; visiting with farmers, spice traders, and conservationists; and sharing many memorable meals. We wanted to know about the plant, but we also wanted to know more about the emerging export market, who was involved in sourcing it and moving it from the rainforest to the nation's capital and then ultimately beyond (especially to France, which the Malagasy have sarcastically

346

nicknamed 'Sweet Mother'). From farmers and NGOs to spice exporters and plant scientists, we learned how each are playing their own role and hold individual hopes for the pepper: to improve their livelihoods, to conserve the rainforest, or to add new pizzazz to their spice business portfolio.

There is so much to say about this unforgettable experience, but here is the main point: we completed our journey with the shared realization that this story is not romantic but humbling. The human desire for variety in our diet has transformed landscapes and shaped political, economic, and cultural destinies for centuries, and in all cases (including this one) what transpired cannot be cast within the frame of the hero (or heroine) myth. Instead, this is a cautionary tale.

The Place: Madagascar, Spices for Others

The global spice trade defines the modern human experience, past, present, and future. The desire for the tastes provided by them – the fruit of the black pepper vine and the allspice tree, the inner bark of the cinnamon tree, the flower bud of the clove tree, the seed pod of the vanilla vine, the seed of the cacao tree, the seed (nutmeg) or seed coat (mace) of nutmeg trees, the root of the ginger and turmeric plants – have propelled civilizations, justified colonialism, inspired plantation production systems, precipitated complex trade networks and concomitant trade conflicts, expanded cuisines, transformed sensory experiences, and on and on.

The story of spices in Madagascar is a story told in many areas of the globe after the Columbian Exchange and the emergence of the modern spice trade. However, due

347

The pepper as packaged and sold for export (photo credit: Floribis).

to the island's long-term isolation, there are unique elements: it is also a biodiversity hotspot, with 90% of all its animals and plants endemic to the island, from the iconic lemurs to *ravinala* (traveller's palm) and baobab trees. Madagascar is also one of the world's least developed countries with close to the entire population engaged in subsistence activities and 76% living on less than $1.90 per day (World Food Programme 2020). Thus, a persistent tension exists between the uniqueness of Madagascar's natural heritage and the market logics of growing and selling tropical spices and other desirable foods (vanilla, cacao, and coffee among others).

Many of these tensions are as long-lived as the first plantings of vanilla, coffee, and cacao over a century ago. Vanilla came from Mexico by way of La Reunion in the 1840s; cloves, native to the Maluku Islands of Indonesia, were first introduced onto Madagascar's St. Marie island even earlier (Danthu and others 2014), even though Madagascar would not be fully colonized by the French until 1894. But because the *tsiperifery* vine is thought to be unique to the island and has never been domesticated or grown in plantations, this is also a story about very contemporary preoccupations: conservation of rainforest, protection of biodiversity, resilience of livelihoods, and models for development.

Madagascar is known as a modern day 'spice island', with a location identified by the European colonists to have the right set of conditions for growing highly desired spices such as clove, vanilla, and more, at a large scale for export to Europe and beyond. Interestingly, even today, visitors to Madagascar observe that the traditional cuisine does not use these spices, or many others either. Indeed, beyond the use of a very hot pepper sauce (*sakay*) and some ginger, Malagasy dishes are usually flavoured with salt (copiously) and the occasional addition of a bit of black pepper or curry powder – the latter most certainly introduced by the *karana*, an Indo-Pakistani migrant population – both of which come in small, red cardboard boxes produced in the capital by the spice company TAF Products Madagascar. It is possible that the relative blandness of the native Malagasy diet lies in the long history of relying primarily on rice as the main carbohydrate staple of the diet, as well as the main livelihood of the people. Or it may be that export crops were never incorporated into the cuisine 'of this place and people' by those engaged in growing and harvesting them; these were simply flavours understood to be valuable to others.

Most spices grown commercially in Madagascar today were domesticated elsewhere and introduced (even coconut, which has made its way into classic Malagasy dishes like *poulet au coco*, was brought to the island), beginning with the colonial plantations that began in the nineteenth century. The process has been to bring the plants to the island, to create efficient means of producing their desirable aspects (the pods, the buds, the seeds, the pulp, etc.) through the use of cheap local (and originally forced) labour, and then to export those parts of the plant across the globe. Over time, a broader range of spices have arrived in Madagascar and have been grown commercially for export. These include cacao, cinnamon, turmeric, ginger, black pepper, and *baie de rose*.

The *tsiperifery* pepper is the first new spice to be introduced to the Madagascar export market in nearly a century. But unlike other spices grown in Madagascar, it is thought to be native and has never been cultivated or domesticated. Though it was documented by British botanists in the 1890s as one of 4000 'economic plants' native to Madagascar, it was not actively pursued commercially until the latter part of this decade. At the moment, all of the *tsiperifery* currently being exported, or sold in-country to foreign tourists and expats, is still being collected from the rainforest.

We learned that, in the past, local people collected the pepper opportunistically when they went into the forest and used it, not only as a medicine, but also to season some dishes. They used fresh, green berries to season *ravitoto* (a popular dish made of pounded manioc/cassava leaves) or cooked bananas. Since realizing its 'value' to the outside world, locals told us that they have discontinued using it in this manner. They do still use it as a traditional medicine – leaves and stem made into a tea and drunk as a cough medicine.

It is not entirely clear just when and why the *tsiperifery* pepper was again 'discovered' and elevated to a desirable spice for those seeking sensory uniqueness, leading to this rush to source – and possibly domesticate – it to sell to tourists in Madagascar and to gourmets around the globe. As the story goes, some *tsiperifery* pepper was brought to France and shared at the annual *Salon de Gastronomie,* an international agro-food exhibition in France where chefs gather in search of new flavours. However the wild pepper actually found its way to the attention of chefs in France, francophone Canada, and more widely in the West, those who encountered it were 'wowed' by its aromatic properties, the same ones used as plant defences against herbivores in its native rainforest habitat.

Today, the three-star Michelin chef Anne-Sophie Pic sells *tsiperifery* in her line of spices. Master French chocolatier Francois Pralus famously incorporated *tsiperifery* into his 2013 *Bûche de Noël*. And the pepper has gained attention in the US as well; celebrity chef Wolfgang Puck has included it in his recipes. Lake Champlain Chocolates

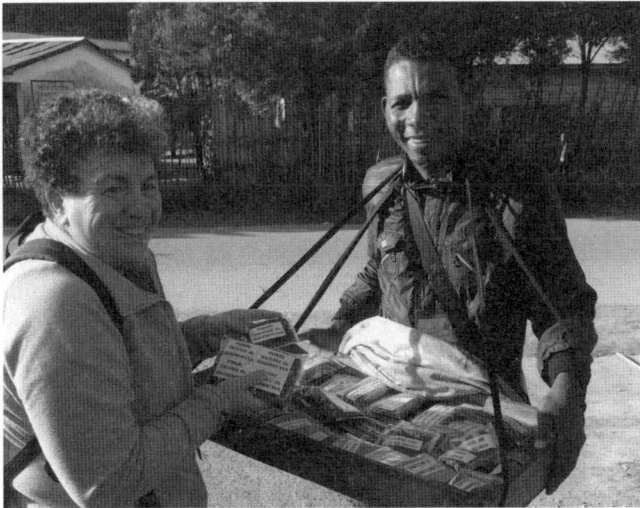

Selling the pepper to tourists.

in Burlington, Vermont, who initially came by the pepper by way of Montreal, even created a *tsiperifery* chocolate bar (now discontinued).

Ultimately, as the spice export trade from Madagascar has become increasingly competitive, with more and more companies owned and operated by well-connected foreigners because it is so lucrative (especially for vanilla), these actors seem to be looking for ways to 'spice up' their repertoire. Adding another pepper to the other pepper and pepper-like species that they export (black pepper *Piper nigrum, baie de rose*), increases their edge on the European and American markets. Therefore, we suspect that it may have been expatriate spice traders, named *Zanatany* (French born in Madagascar who maintain feet in both worlds), who were behind the re-introduction of the spice to European sensibilities – after all, someone had to ship it to France and present it at the *Salon de Gastronomie*. Thus, although this is the first new spice plant to emerge from Madagascar in a century (if not ever), the power and the glory went to middlemen, not the planters and harvesters (as was the case in pre-colonial and colonial eras).

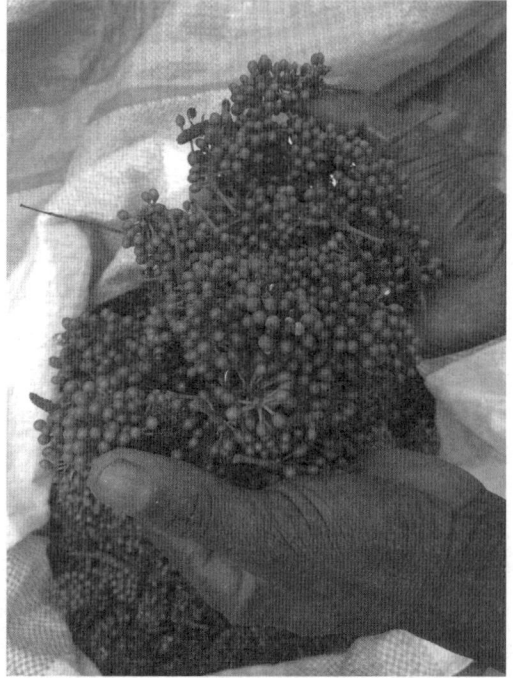

Harvesting the pepper.

350

The Plant: To Domesticate or Not?

The current means of obtaining the peppercorn is by foraging in the forest. However, to go beyond the everyday subsistence needs of those living in or around the natural habitat of the plant and forage for export is not sustainable (Razafimandimby and others 2017). This is because, like most Pipers, *tsiperifery* is a vine which can grow up to twenty metres high in the rainforest canopy, making the berries difficult to harvest without cutting down the entire vine or the tree that it grows upon. It also occurs at low density in the wild.

But there is another idea afloat in Madagascar – why not try to create a plantation system, the model used for cacao and other globally desired flavours? Efforts to domesticate *tsiperifery* are now underway, aiming to select for some of the traits found in black pepper, such as hermaphrodism and a bush stature. Domesticating *tsiperifery* could make it easier to grow in plantations and potentially reduce impacts on forests (since theoretically fewer people would be entering them to cut down *tsiperifery* vines and tutors). But such efforts face significant biological challenges due to the complex nature of crop domestication.

We encountered confusion around how to propagate the *tsiperifery*. Like other species in the *Piperaceae*, wild pepper is dioecious – having separate male and female plants. This trait complicates seed set in plantations, as males are necessary but difficult to identify prior to flowering. Similar to date palms, papayas, and hops, most wild black peppers, as well as long peppers (*Piper longum*, another cultivated *Piper* that was known in antiquity and likely gives the genus its name based on the Sanskrit word *Pippali*), occur in separate male and female forms; only the females produce the peppercorns, but males must be nearby for pollination to occur. Black pepper, however, through its long cultivation history, has been domesticated in ways that make it easier to grow. For starters, it has been selected for hermaphrodism (Nair 2004: 280). Cultivation becomes much easier at large scale when all individuals produce fruit, which allows for plantation landscapes (Nair 2004).

We met with the team of Malagasy researchers who are leading the national efforts to study *tsiperifery* (unusually, all three of the PhD-level researchers were female in a nation where access to higher education is still very limited, especially for women). For these researchers, the first step had been to map the distribution of the wild resource. They are part of the team that documented how the pepper grows from the northern tip of the island down to the southeast, all along the eastern rainforest corridor.

Their next step is to work out the relationship of the wild Malagasy pepper to related species by means of DNA sequencing. There is still uncertainty about how the pepper arrived in Madagascar, as it appears to be more closely related to the mainland African species than to *Piper borbenense*, another pepper found on La Reunion (e.g. Weil and others 2020). Furthermore, they have identified four different morphotypes, which suggests either genetic diversity or differential responses to Madagascar's incredibly complex landscape. Further genetic testing will be needed to determine this relationship.

Finally, they have also established a living collection at an agricultural research station to the east of the capital. One of the researchers has established multiplication by seed, which means that they harvested seed from plants. Having a supply of seeds, preferably from a living collection (thus not from the forest), is a basis for any breeding program. It is also an essential resource for determining if any variation in flavour of the pepper is due to either genetic differences or differences in location.

351

Remarkable as the local researchers and conservationists are, there is no infrastructure for DNA sequencing in Madagascar. Partnerships with responsible researchers abroad are needed for training and for access to research infrastructure. In addition, to determine the uniqueness of the Malagasy *tsiperifery* pepper, it must be compared to other peppers from La Reunion and mainland Africa. However, in order to do so, plant material must be allowed to be shipped beyond Madagascar's borders. When we inquired about getting material under the standard material transfer agreement to grow at our university for teaching and research to complement efforts in Madagascar, it quickly became apparent that this would not be possible.

A concern that looms over the sharing of live plant material and tissue for sequencing is a long history of Western biopiracy. Perhaps the most famous example of biopiracy is the acquisition of rubber from Brazil by the British. During the 1870s, the British were able to take rubber seeds from the Brazilian Amazon back to the Royal Botanic Gardens, Kew, ultimately leading to the establishment of massive British rubber plantations across the Malayan peninsula without any benefits being returned to Brazil.

Today, researchers in Madagascar are better protected from biopiracy, due to several international agreements. The Convention on Biological Diversity (CBD), the Nagoya Protocol to the CBD, as well as the International Treaty on Plant Genetic Resources for Food and Agriculture provide standardized means for foreign researchers to access materials and for benefit sharing with the countries providing materials. Although the Nagoya Protocol has a framework for access and benefit sharing, Madagascar is not yet equipped to participate in it. Even getting DNA, which is not currently covered by the Nagoya Protocol (von Wettberg and Khour, 2020), so that we could contribute to the needs for sequence data, was impossible. Unfortunately, the frameworks, as well intentioned as they are, have stifled research, without similar impacts on multinational exporters who seem to be able to obtain any material they desire if production demand can be met.

The People: Foraging, Growing, and Selling *Tsiperifery* to Meet Demand

In our travels to learn more about the plant, the peppercorns, and those engaged with thinking about it as a new spice for the global market, there emerged a visible tension as to the model for the future of this spice. Could it remain a wild and foraged spice, propagated on family farm plots, or should it become a domesticated crop produced in larger, and perhaps even sun-grown, plantations? Neither approach, we learned, was ideal.

A consortium of conservation and development NGOs, agronomists, and spice export companies was created to support smallholder farmers who incorporate wild pepper into their pre-existing agroforestry plots. The spice export companies were looking for sufficient supply to meet new-found demand, conservation organizations were hoping to employ yet another strategy for protecting the diminishing rainforest (90% is thought to have been lost), and development organizations were keen to aid farmers in diversifying their holdings to augment their income and raise their standard of living. None seemed to consider the implications for connecting peasant farmers to the vagaries of the global market, and the possible vulnerabilities that might arise; the potential of a cash income was understood to be a 'win-win'.

The consortium began providing technical assistance to farmers on how to identify and collect the pepper, aiding them in obtaining harvesting permits for initial stock (which must be collected from the forest) and supporting their efforts to incorporate and strengthen their cooperatives. We spoke to people involved with the consortium, who then introduced us to those involved in planting and harvesting. We visited one such farmer's cooperative situated about ten hours by car southeast of the capital at the foothills of Ranomafana National Park. This cooperative had been approached by the consortium to initiate trials to grow *tsiperifery* in the understory of their agroforestry fields. To develop beyond an occasional foraging system for the pepper, the farmers received training to create a more organized system of planting, harvesting, and fermenting it. The goal was to create a supply for national and international markets.

The farmers that we met with seemed interested in the project, though not overly motivated – more *laissez-faire,* particularly since the initial spice exporter had already lost interest. The cooperative of farmers simply could not produce the quantity of pepper required for a robust supply chain. The farmers had also been instructed to construct bamboo ladders to reduce the need to cut down the high-growing pepper vine, but they shared with us that they felt that these ladders were too cumbersome to carry into the forest and too slippery and dangerous to climb. There was a disconnect between the farmer's knowledge, needs and concerns, and the goals of the consortium.

The president of the cooperative, however, remained motivated. He had personally received a phone call from another spice company, and other people had come to him looking to buy pepper cuttings; he had even been approached by an NGO that wanted to get involved and apparently planned to plant a lot of pepper. He also seemed to be running his own side business through personal connections to the capital, as he admitted to purchasing and selling green berries from other unincorporated collectors, who had undoubtedly harvested it from the forest, and using the know-how that he had received through the training to dry it.

Others in the cooperative seemed sceptical as to the worth of adding the pepper to their existing cash crops, such as vanilla. Furthermore, they had heard stories of a nearby village being contracted to collect the blue seeds of the *ravinala* traveller's palm (*Ravenala madagascariensis*), wild ginger, and the seed of the Ramy tree for the French fashion house, Christian Dior, and the project had not gone well. Thus, they recognized the fickleness of the market and the challenges of working in a cooperative and with international buyers and middlemen. Their pepper vines were scattered few and far between among their other fruit trees, sometimes growing on the same tree as a vanilla vine. At the level of the forest floor (so to speak), people were wary.

353

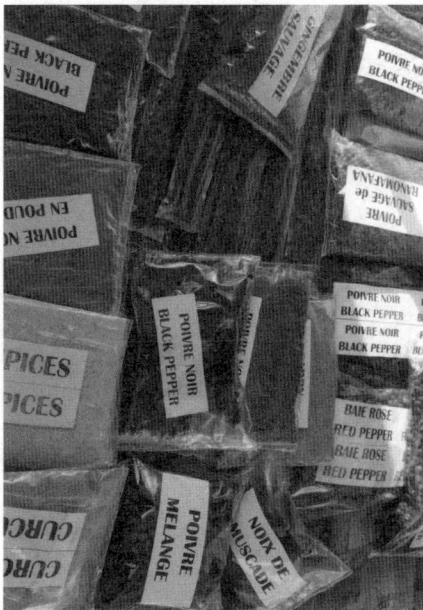

Packets of peppers and spices.

A growing trend among conservation organizations has been to promote cash cropping, particularly using shade-grown agroforestry techniques, among smallholder farmers. The rationale is that such new endeavours would provide more ready access to cash and move the farmers beyond their traditional slash and burn agricultural techniques. In return, there would be reduced pressure on forests and enhanced biodiversity. However, there has been little to no evidence that this conservation strategy actually works. In fact, there are instances in which increased demand for a product that is still being wild harvested has led to overexploitation of the resource. Without careful planning, the result could be more local people going into the forest and harvesting unsustainably.

Since there is currently no certification program for wild pepper, purchasers have no way to trace whether it was harvested sustainably. At the gates to Ranomafana National Park, a young Malagasy entrepreneur operates a small family restaurant out of which he also sells spices, including *tsiperifery*, which he purchases locally. He is certain that the pepper was collected somewhere nearby, though he is unsure if it came from within the park boundaries or the forest surrounding the protected area. He is unaware that just down the road a local conservation organization is working with farmers to try and domesticate the pepper.

Even spice exporters that pride themselves on sourcing sustainably are exporting *tsiperifery* that has been harvested from the wild, because right now no supply exists from cultivated and domesticated plants. As we have shared, there is already evidence of them losing interest in working with farmer cooperatives that were unable to produce the amount of pepper that they required – thus, they inevitably return to purchasing from local collectors to meet their demand. Without an integrated system along the supply chain to explicitly incorporate community values rather than solely commodity crops for national and global markers, this will never be a sustainable system.

Our second visit was to a Malagasy-French businessman's plantation well-situated just a few hours to the east of Antananarivo (along Route National 2, the major trucking route that links the capital to the primary port of Toamasina). The vast swath of land (10,000 hectares), obtained by his grandfather after Madagascar gained independence from the French in 1960 and French-occupied land was returned to the people, was now divided among his descendants. He had experimented with growing the pepper in the shade starting in 2013 and is now interested in planting his pepper seedlings out in full sun because the pepper in the forest understory was taking too long to grow. His location, with easy access to both the capital and the port at Toamasina, as well as financial capital, make it probable that he will control the market if he is able to successfully propagate this pepper on his hilly, already deforested land. But what of the smallholder cooperative in Ranomafana? Can they compete with a well-connected European-educated businessman who speaks both French and English?

Conclusion

Understanding the *tsiperifery* plant, we realized, was crucial for a successful transition from occasional indigenous collection to the reality of a globally desired and distributed spice. Trial and error would not benefit the plant, the people, the rainforest, or the nation. As researchers, we now acknowledge the power of contextual knowledge. A better understanding of the plant, the practices, the organization of power and control over distribution, and the already existing relationships across the system seems the best way to address the current *ad hoc* approach.

Spice traders and NGOs are already starting to lose momentum with the domestication project. In some instances, retailers have already moved on to the next taste. Funds for research are also increasingly difficult to access. The Nagoya Protocol has complicated international partnerships that might facilitate access to research funds. However, diversifying the spice trade has benefits, in terms of protecting against disease outbreaks in other species, creating an agricultural system more resilient against climate change, and diversifying sources of income for smallholder farmers. There are ways to integrate the knowledge about the plant, the practices, and the organization of the global spice trade to reduce other pressures on Madagascar's unique and threatened forests. But much work remains to be done before that happens.

Ultimately, we each came away with our own concerns. Maya was worried that without a certification program, the global demand would drive more harvesters into the forest, potentially leading to exhausting the resource. Eric did not see a way for the DNA work to happen without assistance from the outside, and, ironically for a crop that is being exported, foreign researchers are unable to export living plant material for propagation to study it. Amy worried that the fickleness of the culinary world would mean chefs would move on to the next best thing.

We also all shared a concern: any new spice species is still a wild plant, though it might be planted and protected by people. There are so many possible (and unintended) consequences to making it the object of culinary attention. Wild harvest or domestication and widespread cultivation is but one of a series of decisions that will have cascading effects for the plant, the people engaged with it, and the natural environments where it will thrive. The promise of a lucrative, yet also harmless, transformation of a wild plant to a luxury flavour has not been borne out by history. Why and how would it happen in this case?

355

References

Callmander, M. W. and others. 2011. 'The Endemic and Non-Endemic Vascular Flora of Madagascar Updated', *Plant Ecology and Evolution*, 144.2: 121-25.

Danthu, P. and others. 2014. 'The Clove Tree of Madagascar: A Success Story with an Unpredictable Future', *Bois et forets des tropiques*, 320.2: 83-96.

Hobbes, J. and A. Dolan. 2008. *World Regional Geography*, 6th ed. (Belmont, CA: Cengage Learning).

Madagascar (2020). World Food Programme, www.wfp.org/countries/madagascar

Mintz, S. 1984. *Sweetness and Power* (Boston: Beacon Press).

Nair, K.P. 2004. 'The Agronomy and Economy of Black Pepper (Piper nigrum L.) – The "King of Spices"', *Advances in Agronomy*, 82: 273-392.

Razafimandimby, H. and others. 2017. 'Tsiperifery, the Wild Pepper from Madagascar, Emerging on the International Spice Market whose Exploitation Is Unchecked: Current Knowledge and Future Prospects', *Fruits*, 72.6: 331-40 <https://doi.org/10.17660/th2017/72.6.1>

Royal Botanic Gardens, Kew. 1890. 'Economic Plants of Madagascar', *Bulletin of Miscellaneous Information*, 1890, 45: 200-15 <https://www.doi.org/10.2307/4118422>

von Wettberg, E. and C.K. Khoury. 2020. 'Access to Crop Digital Information and the Sharing of Benefits Derived from Its Use: Background and Perspectives', *Plants, People, Planet*, 2.3: 178-80.

Weil, M. and others. 2020. 'Quality, Typicity and Potential Valorization of Piper borbonense, a Poorly Known Wild Pepper from Reunion Island', *Fruits*, 75.3: 95-103.

The Curious Case of Asafoetida

Sharmila Vaidyanathan

Introduction

In one of her recent interviews, cookbook author and food writer Madhur Jaffrey reminisced about her early food struggles in a foreign land. Having moved to London in 1955, Jaffrey longed for the familiar flavours of her homeland, a memory she aptly conveyed using the following lines: 'There is this pea-green smog that comes in at 3 o'clock and you see nothing. This was just after the War, and the food was simply awful. I was dreaming of *hing jeere ki alu* or *bhara hua karela* while having some watery cabbage mess or transparent roast beef at the canteen.'[1] When it comes to spice-infused Proustian memories about Indian food one would expect to encounter a homage to the local street food *chaat* that is flavoured with a mishmash of spices, or a fiery curry that contains a homemade spice blend. Instead, Jaffrey was seeking the comfort of a spice that is also called the stinking resin, India's umami bomb, and Devil's Dung – asafoetida or asafetida. *Hing jeere ki alu* that she mentions here is potatoes spiced with cumin and asafoetida.

Asafoetida or *hing* as it is commonly known in Hindi is a dried latex obtained from the taproots of perennial herbs which mainly grow in Afghanistan and Iran. By itself, asafoetida is not something one would dream of bringing close to their food, owing to its strong aroma. The minute a tiny amount of the spice is introduced to hot oil as part of the tempering this revulsion is put to the test as asafoetida transforms the whole dish, lending a unique umami flavour. Asafoetida is not fiery like red chilli, warm like garam masala, or exotic like saffron. Google images of Indian spices and you will see vibrant shades of yellow, red, green, and black represented by turmeric, chilli powder, cardamom pods, and whole pepper. The lacklustre asafoetida does not make an appearance in these multicoloured canvases. Yet, in communities where it is used, the spice is essential and possibly even irreplaceable. This is why its journey to becoming a fitting ingredient deserves a special mention. Although several medicinal benefits of asafoetida have also been recorded, this paper will focus on the role of asafoetida as a spice.

Divided into four parts, the paper explores the history of asafoetida and its entry into the kitchens of India. It also looks at asafoetida from an agricultural point of view, before outlining the culinary and cultural implications of the spice in Indian cooking.

And Then There Was Asafoetida

To understand asafoetida, one would have to take a step back and learn about an altogether different herb – silphium. A favourite among Greeks and Romans, silphium was literally loved to death. When the Greeks colonized the ancient city of Cyrene, in modern-day Libya, they encountered the herb in 631 BC. Silphium soon became a star of the region, widely used as a vegetable, condiment, and as feed for animals. It also had a range of medicinal benefits. So much was the herb revered that coins from the region have its inscription imprinted on them.[2]

So what happened to silphium? The herb disappeared from the landscape entirely by the first century AD. Despite having strict rules in place, silphium was repeatedly harvested and overgrazed, its popularity as a contraceptive not helping. In her comprehensive article on silphium, science journalist Zaria Gorvett notes that the herb could have either gone extinct or is possibly hiding in plain sight as a weed. Nevertheless, silphium's decline brought a 'stinky' yet reasonable substitute, asafoetida, into the picture.[3]

In the blog *Tavola Mediterranea,* archaeologist and award-winning food blogger Farrell Monaco recreates the Apician recipe of Parthian Chicken using asafoetida. Monaco explains that even though silphium is listed as an ingredient, the name of the dish suggests that it was probably made using asafoetida. The alternative resin from Parthia, modern-day Iran, was a cheaper substitute.[4] The discovery of asafoetida dates back to 328 or 327 BC when Alexander's soldiers found it in Afghanistan and thought they found silphium. They used the herb to digest raw horse meat.[5]

Hing Diaries

After the end of the Roman empire, asafoetida's mention seems to be limited to its medicinal use in the European region.[6] Monaco writes, 'Some of these dinner recipes tell me that Romans enjoyed cooking with wine and spices that literally hit the sinus cavity with a wallop when you're heating them together in a broth over a flame. Ajwain, asafoetida, vinegars, wines, cumin and ground pepper pack a powerful punch....'[7] If I were to read the last sentence in isolation, I would think that she was talking about Indian food, barring the wine of course. Ajwain or carom, cumin, ground pepper, asafoetida – add lentils, coconut, a few vegetables, and you have just made a South Indian *kootu*, a thick gravy often eaten with rice. After Roman food, it looks like asafoetida decided to continue its legacy in a similar atmosphere – in the company of bold flavours.

With the source of asafoetida being geographically close, it comes as no surprise that the spice entered India at some point. The Ayurvedic treatise *Kashyapa Samhita*, one of India's oldest texts on medicine, mentions that asafoetida was imported to India from Afghanistan.[8] Ayurvedic principles form the foundation for Indian food. Over time, Asian, European, and Persian influences have also left their imprints. Asafoetida stands at the intersection of all of these factors.

In his definitive guide to Indian food, K.T. Achaya writes that meat dishes spiced with asafoetida are mentioned in the Indian epic *Mahabharata* which documents events that possibly occurred in the eighth century BC.[9] Epics apart, there are several historical references that provide a glimpse into asafoetida's presence in Indian food. In *Manasollasa*, a twelfth-century compendium written by a king of the Western Chalukya dynasty (spread over southern and central India), there is a recipe for fish scrotums roasted in fire and cooked in hot oil along with cardamom, rock salt, pepper, and asafoetida.[10] *Ain-i-Akbari*, a book that records the third Mughal emperor Akbar's (AD 1555-1605) administration and the culinary practices of the time, mentions that foods were spiced with large quantities of saffron and asafoetida. So much was asafoetida used during the period that European visitors to the country complained about the pungent spice.[11] Asafoetida is also mentioned in the sixteenth century, in Portuguese physician and herbalist Garcia de Orta's notes: 'All the Hindus who can afford it buy it to add to their food. The rich Brahmins, and all the Hindus who are vegetarian eat a lot of it.'[12]

Garcia de Orta's stay in India coincides with the Vijayanagara Empire in south India. Records from the era indicate that foods were seasoned using clarified butter and spices such as cumin, fenugreek, mustard, pepper, and sesame seeds. Many digestive spices were commonly used during this period.[13] Asafoetida is not mentioned here, even though de Orta noted that it was used as a seasoning sauce among Brahmins and Hindus. The spice was probably a part of the digestive ingredients. Surprisingly, the seasoning in south Indian food remains the same even today. Asafoetida also made its way to the Anglo-Indian tables. During the colonial era, post hunting or *shikar* as it is known in Hindi, cooks would often stir up flavourful sauces that included chillies, cayenne pepper, asafoetida, and wine to accompany the meat.[14]

Bringing Asafoetida Home

While cooks in colonial India added asafoetida to their sauces, the first colonial capital of the country, the city of Calcutta (Kolkata) had its own interesting link to the spice. In the nineteenth century, many businessmen from Afghanistan came to the city to sell *hing*, dry fruits, and attar or perfume. Known as *kabuliwalas* in common parlance – people from the Kabul region – they went door to door, making asafoetida easily available.[15] As the legend goes, it was a *kabuliwala* who gave the founder of Laljee Godhoo & Co (India's most popular asafoetida brand) the inspiration to set up an industry to manufacture the edible spice.[16]

India receives its asafoetida in the crude form from Afghanistan, Iran, Uzbekistan, and Kazakhstan.[17] The perennial herbs from which the dried latex is obtained belong to the *Ferula* genus. There are several species in this genus spread across Europe, Central Asia, and North Africa. Asafoetida gets its name from *Ferula assafoetida*, an important species in this family. Although many commercial varieties of the plant exist, the most important source of the spice is *F. assafoetia* Linn., which grows in Iran and Afghanistan.[18]

Different varieties of asafoetida exist in the market, based on the country of origin and the way the spice is obtained from the plant. As someone who uses asafoetida in her cooking almost every day, I have never made an attempt to purchase a brand that provides a so-called superior quality of the spice, nor do I know how to identify one. I seek some solace in the fact that *hing* dealers in the busy Delhi markets are not aware of the different varieties either. When food writer Marryam Reshii enquired about the number of *hing* types they dealt with, they gave her an exaggerated number of seventy-four, which Reshii later clarifies, in her book *The Flavour of Spice*, is definitely not true. Based on provenance, the best asafoetida to have on the shelf is Kandhari, sourced from Afghanistan, followed by the Iranian variety, and the asafoetida that is obtained from the Herat region of Afghanistan.[19]

The process of obtaining asafoetida from the *Ferula* plant is not that easy. When the plants are four to five years old, before the onset of flowering, the foliage around their carrot-like roots is removed. The living roots are laid bare with the stem cut out and incisions are made. The resin produced is collected in pits dug in the soil. The slicing of the roots and collection of resin is repeated for a few weeks until no more resin is obtained. The exudate is then processed for the crude form of the spice.[20]

Nestled in the hill station of Palampur in the northern Indian state of Himachal Pradesh is the Institute of Himalayan Bioresource Technology. Here, scientists are taking the first steps to initiate asafoetida cultivation in India. Dr Ashok Kumar, a senior scientist at the institute working on this project, informs me over a phone call that they imported the planting material or seeds from Iran. He explains that even though there are many wild varieties of the *Ferula* genus growing in India in the Himachal region, like *Ferula jaeschkeana*, the goal of this project is to propagate the commercial variant. To facilitate conducive growing conditions, cultivation trials are being conducted in the mountainous Lahaul and Spiti regions of the state. Dr Kumar adds that since India is so reliant on the import of asafoetida, growing the plant in-house will aid farmers and consumers.

Not much is known about asafoetida as an agricultural crop. In source countries, asafoetida is also obtained from plants growing in the wild, which is why substantial data is not easily available. In the *Handbook of Herbs and Spices*, the former executive director of the Spices Board of India, C.K. George, explains that import data on asafoetida is not well organized. Data obtained by him for the years between 2005 and 2010 show that import quantities are often erratic.[21] The asafoetida that is imported is made more palatable by blending it with flour and edible gum. This diluted form is called compounded asafoetida. Despite these impediments, asafoetida is easily available in the Indian stores. While fifty grams of the popular brand is priced at about eighty rupees, some of the more niche brands sell about ten grams of *hing* chunks for more than three hundred rupees – almost four times the price of the regular brand.

India also exports processed asafoetida. When New York-based cookbook author and television personality Padma Lakshmi showed her Instagram followers how to make an Indian raw mango curry, I saw her reach for the same brand that I use in my kitchen in India. One of her viewers was quick to ask about the spice. 'Many devout orthodox Brahmins and Jains don't eat onions or garlic so they'll only use asofatida [*sic*]. It gives the same sulphuric flavor. Use it sparingly,' Lakshmi wrote in response.[22]

Onion, Garlic, Asafoetida

What Lakshmi elucidates in her response is essentially the crux of asafoetida's use in Indian food. The spice seems to have become an unintended player in caste-system-induced food prohibitions. The ancient Vedic society was one divided based on four castes – the brahmins or priests, kshatriyas or warriors, vaishyas or traders and agriculturists, and sudras or service workers. As Colleen Taylor Sen elaborates in *History of Food in India*, the *Dharmasutras* or ancient texts written as extensions of the Vedas dictated how people should function within their respective castes. These rules included dietary restrictions as well. Onion and garlic were prohibited for Brahmins as they were considered aphrodisiacs.[23]

Ayurveda also classifies foods as *Rajasic, Tamasic,* or *Sattvik* – based on how they impact the body on consumption. The goal, in essence, is to consume *sattvik* foods, which do not disturb the body or its functioning, and are conducive to one's spirituality.[24] Onion and garlic are considered *rajasic* and *tamasic*, owing to their pungent nature. It is said that such foods promote negative emotions like anger, anxiety, and lethargy.

Apart from Brahmins, Lakshmi also mentions Jains in her response. Jainism is a religion rooted in *ahimsa* or non-violence that believes that everything in nature is alive. In terms of food, this belief translates into stricter rules beyond avoiding meat. The rules of Jainism prohibit the consumption of vegetables that grow underground, as pulling plants from their roots is essentially killing them. Onion and garlic are again shunned, here because of the added prohibitions of this religion.[25]

In essence, asafoetida fills both culinary and cultural voids. Owing to the presence of sulphur compounds, the spice provides an experience similar to consuming onion and garlic. If the traditions outlined above had not changed over time, then that's all there would be to the story of asafoetida. Instead, asafoetida has managed to mark a strong presence in Indian food despite changing culinary preferences and a shift to a diet that is becoming more global. I have no better way to explain this than to look into my own family.

My mother was raised in an orthodox Brahmin family in the state of Tamil Nadu in south India. Although onion and garlic had already become regulars in my grandmother's kitchen, they were prohibited on auspicious days like Tuesdays and Fridays, and on festival days. Foods were spiced mainly with green and red chillies, and flavoured using coriander seeds, cumin seeds, and pepper. Every time oil was heated for tempering, asafoetida made its way into it. The quintessential garam masala was not a part of my grandmother's cooking. After her marriage, my mother moved to the northern part of India, where she was exposed to flavours a lot different from her mother's kitchen. Garam masala found its way into our home, and my school lunches often included both south Indian and north Indian variants, making them an equal part of my upbringing. Asafoetida continued to be a part of our south Indian dishes, especially the *Sambhar* – a thick soup-like dish with vegetables cooked in tamarind juice, lentils, and a spice blend called *sambhar* powder. I grew up seeing both *sambhar* powder and garam masala renditions on the table.

I moved to the United States for a brief period in my mid-twenties, expanding my food dictionary further. I experienced familiar foods in a new form, and new foods in a familiar form. When I moved back to India, along with *sambhar* powder and garam masala, my kitchen cupboards were also populated with pasta seasonings and herbs. As always, asafoetida sat in the corner of the shelf.

Pat Caplan explains these changes in her research that explores the veg/non-veg food divide in the city of Chennai (formerly Madras) in south India. As Caplan notes, food habits among the middle class are now influenced not just by the inherent rules of caste, but also by interactions with people within a society, especially in an urban set-up.[26] Earlier, interactions were limited, and people rarely ventured outside their castes, making changes in diets sparse. But with changing times and exposure to information, we see these rules adapting to the new world. For example, Caplan shows how eggs were introduced in Brahmin families as a way to improve nutrition for the children.[27]

Despite these shifts, and having access to the original experience, asafoetida continued to hold its position in the kitchen: an important reason being that changes were not adopted all at once. Some families continued with traditional food practices. For example, Caplan writes that when she offered 'pialo' (pulao or pilaf) to a mixed caste group, one Brahmin woman refused the food on account of the presence of onions, while another did not have an issue with the dish.[28] Although Caplan attributes this to the food being cooked by her housekeepers, such discrepancies exist even today in some families.

While the example of the Tamil Brahmin community denotes asafoetida's role in a strictly vegetarian construct, there are some Brahmin communities where meat is allowed, but the onion-garlic rule stands. The most prominent example of this is Kashmiri food from the Jammu & Kashmir province in northern India. The cuisine of the region is divided into two major types – the Kashmiri Pandit cuisine and the Kashmiri Muslim cuisine. In *Multiple Flavours of Kashmiri Pandit Cuisine,* Annapurna Chak explains that asafoetida became a way to distinguish between the two. While the Hindus used generous amounts of asafoetida and yoghurt, the Muslims used onions and garlic. She elaborates that the Pandits mainly ate mutton, while chicken, eggs, onions, and garlic were prohibited. Along with asafoetida, cardamom, cinnamon, cloves, and dried ginger were used to spice the gravies. These rules have now become flexible, and to represent this change, her book includes recipes that use onions, garlic, and asafoetida as ingredients. She also provides a chicken version of *Rogan Josh*, a mutton-based gravy, and uses asafoetida for seasoning, thus establishing that the plates are now open.[29]

The first-ever cookbook published in India in 1831 was called *Pakrajeswar*. Written in Bengali under the guidance of the king of Burdwan, a region in the state of West Bengal, recipes in *Pakrajeswar* had a strong Mughal influence to them, and were mostly non-vegetarian. They included meat like mutton and fowl. One notable aspect of the cookbook was that there was no mention of onion and garlic in any of the recipes, even though Mughal recipes did use them in their mutton preparations. A note at the beginning of the book clarified that onion and garlic were not listed in the ingredients as they were hardly consumed. It was only in 1879 that a Bengali cookbook published by an unnamed author introduced onion and garlic in the written form, indicating that they were considered acceptable then.[30]

Similar to the Kashmiri Pandit community, the Bengali Brahmins consume meat, but as shown by their earlier cookbooks, onion and garlic were avoided. In her analysis of Portuguese influence on Bengali food, Colleen Taylor Sen breaks down these rules on how certain kinds of fish, venison, and game were allowed, but mushrooms (along with onion and garlic), beef, duck, and boar were not allowed. She also gives a glimpse of the spices that were used in Bengali cooking until the twelfth century – mustard seeds, poppy seeds, long pepper, and asafoetida.[31] Utsa Ray highlights that asafoetida was included by Bipradas Mukhopadhyay, who published a periodical of recipes called *Pak Pranali* in 1883 and a Bengali cookbook *Soukhin Khadya-Pak* in 1889. As seen by the years of publication, this was after onion and garlic had already found their way into Bengali cookbooks.[32] Over a phone call, Dr Ray explained that Mukhopadhyay's mention of asafoetida is significant as he tried to incorporate new ingredients and vegetables in Bengali food through his recipes, though this does not mean that asafoetida was absent prior to him mentioning it in his recipes.

Bong Mom's Cookbook is a popular blog and cookbook by Sandeepa Mukherjee Datta which provides a peek into modern Bengali kitchens. Here, flavours decide what goes into a dish rather than prohibitions. Datta is a New Jersey-based engineer who decided to document the recipes of her home state – West Bengal.[33] For example, while discussing the recipe of a red lentil soup, Datta says one can influence flavours in the lentils by adding the quintessential Bengali five-spice or onions or fenugreek seeds or asafoetida.[34] In stark contrast to the historical cookbooks, Datta's blog and cookbook have generous mentions of onion, garlic, and asafoetida and make allowances for improvisation where needed.

While these nuances are interesting to note, they do not mean that the prohibitory rules have completely vanished from India's culinary landscape. In another popular Bengali food blog, I find the recipe for *Niramish Alu'r Dum* which is described as the 'Bengali "vegetarian" curried winter potatoes' (*niramish* means vegetarian). As the dish is made without onions and garlic, the writers share that it can be used as an offering to God.[35] The potatoes are spiced with asafoetida among other spices. Datta also explains in her blog that strict vegetarianism is practised by Bengali widows; a restriction that is observed in many vegetarian communities as well where they consume food without onion and garlic.[36] Additionally, in many communities, food that is prepared after a death in the family is devoid of onion, garlic, and, in some cases like the Tamil Brahmins, even asafoetida.

The above examples go to show the role asafoetida plays in communities that are strictly vegetarian and in communities that are predominantly vegetarian but have some allowances for meat consumption. Does this mean asafoetida by itself is not a favoured ingredient? Well, in seeking the answer we find ourselves in Kolkata again eating the asafoetida-flavoured fried pastry – *Hinger Kochuri*. Interestingly, the origins of this dish will take you to north India. Immigrants who moved to Kolkata for trade introduced this pastry which has somehow become synonymous with the place of arrival.[37] Asafoetida is also a crucial part of the pickling process. The recipe for the Mango *Hing* pickle, for example, requires just four ingredients; raw mangoes, salt, red chilli powder, and asafoetida. Of course, it goes without saying that asafoetida adds a dash of magic while seasoning any dish. When the popular Indian food magazine, *Goya Journal,* asked fourteen women across different communities to name an ingredient crucial to their cuisine, a respondent from the Sindhi community (people who migrated from the Sindh region of Pakistan) mentioned asafoetida. The spice makes all the difference to their chickpea gravy and aids in digesting it.[38] That's asafoetida in a nutshell. Its addition to many lentil-based dishes may be due to its digestive properties, but one simply cannot ignore the flavour contribution.

Perhaps the most fitting use of asafoetida is in the preparation of the famous *Chhappan Bhog* at the Jagannath Temple in Puri, Odisha (a state in eastern India). The fifty-six-course meal (*chappan* in Hindi is fifty-six) offered to the deity is then served to at least 10,000 people, on a daily basis. 'All of the ingredients for these fifty-six dishes are local,' writes Varud Gupta in his book *Bhagwan ke Pakwaan: Food Of The Gods.* 'Food of the Gods' is a lesser-known moniker for asafoetida. Since no onions and garlic are used in this elaborate preparation, asafoetida makes its way into the sacred temple kitchens to fulfil its role.[39] The food is eaten by people across communities.

Conclusion

363

In many ways, the study of asafoetida's culinary journey is a study of contradictions. Brought in as a replacement for the ancient herb silphium that was known to be a contraceptive, asafoetida found itself in Indian cuisine as an alternative to ingredients that were considered aphrodisiacs. First used to digest raw horse meat, the spice later played a crucial role in caste-based food prohibitions, while also providing a fitting solution for strict norms of vegetarianism. The ingredients asafoetida was brought in to replace are now widespread in Indian kitchens. Yet, asafoetida remains an essential spice for its medicinal value and its culinary contributions. Just for this never-give-up spirit, asafoetida deserves a special mention in dialogues about Indian spices.

Acknowledgements
Special thanks to Sally Grainger, Dr Ashok Kumar, Pritha Sen, Marryam H. Reshii, Dr Utsa Ray, and Chef Auroni Mookherjee for generously sharing their knowledge with me.

Notes
1   Anusua Mukherjee, '"I Am an Actress who Acts the Part of a Cook": Madhur Jaffrey', *The Hindu*, 4 April 2020 <https://www.thehindu.com/society/i-am-an-actress-who-acts-the-part-of-a-cook-madhur-jaffrey/article31247433.ece> [accessed 6 April 2020].

2   Chalmers L. Gemmill, 'Silphium', *Bulletin of the History of Medicine,* 40.4 (1966), 295-313 (pp. 299, 305).

3   Zaria Gorvett, 'The Mystery of the Lost Roman Herb', *BBC Future,* 2 September 2017 <https://www.bbc.com/future/article/20170907-the-mystery-of-the-lost-roman-herb> [accessed 19 March 2020].

4   Farrell Monaco, 'Apicius' Parthian Chicken and Vegetable Dinner with a Red Wine Tracta Sauce', **Tavola Mediterranea,** 21 September 2017 <https://tavolamediterranea.com/2017/09/21/apicius-parthian-chicken-vegetable-dinner-red-wine-tracta-sauce/ > [accessed 19 March 2020]

5   Andrew Dalby, *Food in the Ancient World from A to Z* (London: Routledge, 2003), p. 29.

6   Andrew Dalby, *Dangerous Tastes: The Story of Spices* (Berkeley: University of California Press, 2000), p. 111.

7   Monaco.

8   C.K. George, 'Asafoetida', in *Handbook of Herbs and Spices,* ed. by K. V. Peter (Cambridge: Woodhead Publishing Limited, 2012), p. 151.

9   K.T. Achaya, *The Illustrated Food of India A-Z,* 2nd edn (New Delhi: Oxford University Press, 2014), p. 11.

10 Nalini Sadhale and Y.L.Nene, 'On Fish in Manasollasa (c. 1131 AD)', *Asian Agri-History,* 9.3 (2005), 1-12 (p. 5) <https://www.asianagrihistory.org/pdf/articles/fish_article.pdf> [accessed 30 March 2020].

11 Lizzie Collingham, *Curry: A Tale of Cooks and Conquerors* (London: Vintage Books, 2006), pp. 28-29.

12 Dalby, Dangerous Tastes, p.111.

13 Jyotsna Burde, 'Food and Food Habits in Vijayanagara Times', *Kamat Research Database,* 2020 <http://www.kamat.com/database/articles/vnagar_foods.htm> [accessed 24 April 2020].

14 Collingham, p 125.

15 Poulomi Banerjee, '125 Years of Tagore's Kabuliwala: Here's What Life Is Like for the Community Today', *Hindustan Times,* 29 June 2017 <https://www.hindustantimes.com/india-news/in-search-of-tagore-s- kabuliwala/story-JgtSdmfJpoPKKVokebwYwN.html> [accessed 24 May 2020].

16 Shailesh Menon, 'Meet the Hing Kings, who Brought the Spice to India over a Century Ago', *Economic Times,* 27 March 2018 <https://economictimes.indiatimes.com/industry/cons-products/food/meet-the-hing-kings-who-brought-the-spice-to-india-over-a-century-ago/articleshow/63471891.cms?from=mdr> [accessed 15 March 2020].

17 Menon.

18 George, p 152.

19 Marryam H. Reshii, *The Flavour Of Spice* (Gurgaon: Hachette Book Publishing India, 2017), p. 193.

20 George, pp. 157-58.

21 George, p. 153.

22 Padma Lakshmi, *@padmalakshmi,* 24 April 2020 <https://www.instagram.com/p/B_XwIImhBap/ > [accessed 25 April 2020].

23 Colleen Taylor Sen, *Feasts and Fasts: A History of Food in India* (New Delhi: Speaking Tiger Publishing, 2016), pp. 78-81.

24 Achaya, pp. 221, 247, 265.

25 Sen, *Feasts and Fasts,* p. 53.

26 Pat Caplan, 'Crossing the Veg/Non-Veg Divide: Commensality and Sociality Among the Middle Classes in Madras/Chennai', *South Asia: Journal of South Asian Studies,* 31.1 (2008), 118-42.

27 Caplan, p.128.

28 Caplan, p. 135.

29 Annapurna Chak, *Multiple Flavours of Kashmiri Pandit Cuisine* (Bloomington, IN: Partridge Publishing, 2015), pp. XVI, 196.

30 Utsa Ray, *Culinary Culture in Colonial India: A Cosmopolitan Platter and the Middle-Class* (Delhi: Cambridge University Press, 2015), pp. 63-64.

31 Sen, 'The Portuguese Influence on Bengali Cuisine', in Food on the Move: Proceedings of the Oxford Symposium on Food and Cookery, 1996, ed. by Harlan Walker (Devon: Prospect Books, 1997), p. 291.

32 Ray, 'Eating "Modernity": Changing Dietary Practices in Colonial Bengal', *Modern Asian Studies,* 46.3 (2012), 703-29 (pp. 709-13).

33 Sandeepa Mukherjee Datta, *Bong Mom's Cookbook* (2020) <http://www.bongcookbook.com/>

[accessed 27 March 2020]; Datta, B*ong Mom's Cookbook Stories From A Bengali Mother's Kitchen* (New Delhi: Harper Collins Publishers India, 2013) <https://www.amazon.in/Kindle-eBooks/b?ie=UTF8&node=1634753031> [accessed 23 April 2020].

34 Datta, *Bong Mom's Cookbook Stories From A Bengali Mother's Kitchen*.

35 Saptarshi Chakraborty and Insiya Poonawala, Niramish Aloo Dum, *Bong Eats* (Updated 2020) <https://www.bongeats.com/recipe/niramish-aloo-dum> [accessed 3 May 2020].

36 Datta, 'Aloo Phulkopir Dalna with Chingri – and Food Tales of Bengali Women', *Bong Mom's Cookbook,* 28 May 2013 <http://www.bongcookbook.com/2013/05/chingri-aloo-phulkopir-dalna-and-food.html> [accessed 27 March 2020]

37 Sandip Roy, 'Mithai-Turned-Mishti: The Story Of Kolkata's 'Non-Bengali' Sweets', *Huffpost,* 27 October 2019 <https://www.huffingtonpost.in/entry/mithai-turned-mishti-non-bengali-sweets_in_5db46d3ee4b006d4916f8bf5> [accessed 28 April 2020].

38 Anisha Rachel Oommen and Aysha Tanya, 'Mum's the Word', *Goya Journal,* 8 May 2016 <https://www.goyajournal.in/blog/mums-the-word> [accessed 2 May 2020].

39 Varud Gupta and Devang Singh, *Bhagwaan ke Pakwaan: Food Of The Gods* (Gurgaon: Penguin Random House India, 2019), p. 99.

Herbs and Spices in the Court Cuisine of Medieval Cyprus: Food in the Cyprio-Gallic Style

William Woys Weaver

This paper represents a distillation of themes discussed in my yet-to-be published book tentatively called *The Sugar Kingdom: Cyprus and the Transformation of Medieval Cuisine*. While that text encompasses several hundred pages with numerous illustrations, my discussion here will focus on herbs and spices, how they were used (or not) by different levels of society, and what has been gleaned from roughly thirty-six years of research into the unique culinary culture that evolved on Cyprus during the Middle Ages.

Cyprus was not a sideline player in the medieval politics of the Mediterranean. While the Lusignan Kingdom was established by Crusaders in 1192, and while religion and the recovery of Jerusalem have long been central themes of Crusader Studies, Cyprus was also party to Europe's first experiment in colonial expansionism. The colonizing of the Levant for economic gain and the vast wealth accrued by transforming sugar into a market commodity set the stage for new social dynamics and a new type of international cuisine dubbed *viand de Chypre* distinctive to the Lusignan Court yet widely imitated in Europe. This hybrid aristocratic culture, blending Byzantine Greek with French, resulted in a new Creolized dialect called Cyprio-Gallic with vocabularies only used in insular texts. It is not clear when this language died out, but after 1489 with the dissolution of the monarchy by the Venetians, Italianization profoundly altered the island's cultural profile.

Cypriot historians have generally categorized the period 1191 to 1374 as the Lusignan golden age and that is essentially the same time frame for this presentation (Nicholaou-Konnari and Schnabel 2005). During this golden age Cyprus became the spice emporium for Silk Road trade with Famagusta serving as the great clearing house for all things coming out of Asia (Jacoby 1984). After the fall of Acre (modern Akko in Israel) and the collapse of the Kingdom of Jerusalem in 1292, the Pope published a Bull forbidding direct trade with Islam; all Silk Road goods were required to pass through Cyprus to pay for the expense of repelling the Muslim threat. Thus, Cyprus became well-supplied with exotics associated with Silk Road commerce, including fine Chinese porcelains.

The documentation of this trade arrangement and lists of specific trade goods moving through commercial channels are massive and much too large to enumerate here. This includes court documents, merchant records and accounts, diaries of religious pilgrims, tax lists, and, quite surprising, an impressive body of culinary material, much of which has been misidentified by previous medieval historians unfamiliar with the peculiarities of Cyprio-Gallic cuisine – more on that shortly.

Foremost among the records dealing with spices are the travel accounts gathered and published in the continuing series *Excerpta Cypria*, merchant records like *The Zibaldone da Canal* (Dotson 1994), the market tax records of the kingdom dating from about 1250 (Coureas 2002), and a vast archive of Genoese notary records and bills of lading for both Ayas in the Armenian Kingdom of Kilikia and its sister port Famagusta in Cyprus. These Genoese documents are being edited and gradually published by medieval historian Laura Balletto, a tedious endeavour since the records are commonly written in medieval Genoese dialect incorporating colloquial commercial terms borrowed from Greek or Armenian. All the same, we now have a clear picture of what was being bought and sold, but how much of it ended up on Cypriot tables? Furthermore, there is a missing link in this chain of exchange because the most important trading partner with Cyprus was Ancona due to Cypriot alliances with the Dukes of Milan (Visconti family in particular), and very little research has been undertaken on Ancona trade records, or even what if any Cypriot materials may lurk in their local archives.

Thus, for information on the herbs and spices used in medieval Cypriot cuisine, we must turn to several other types of surviving records as well as historical ethnography. Culinary documents from the period reveal to us what may have been consumed, whereas historical ethnography can suggest cultural continuities that survive even today. *367* In both instances Cyprus is fortunate especially since many Byzantine or medieval foods and preparation techniques have been recorded in the mountain villages within living memory. In fact, there are ancient foodways that survive only in Cyprus: for example, rusks made with chickpeas and the widespread use of pickled terebinth as part of the fish *mezé*. However, culinary documentation is complicated because it has survived in fragmented form, yet several sources have emerged with clear references to herbs and spices and their uses as interpreted according to Cyprio-Gallic style (this term refers both to the language and the indigenous culture associated with it).

Aside from plentiful Byzantine sources framing the traditional and rather conservative nature of food and foodways as practiced by the Cypriot Greek gentry, several books of a medical-dietary nature are known to have existed in the Lusignan Royal Library. One of them is called the *Canones* of Pseudo-Mesue which was translated into Latin from Arabic (or quilted together from several Arabic sources) sometime between 1260 and 1290 and which is now attributed with convincing evidence to a Syrian Christian named John of Damascus (Lieberknecht 1995). The material on herbs and spices is exacting and there are even recipes for making jams and jellies as medical remedies.

Another non-culinary text is a Cypriot Greek work (exact title to be determined) devoted to dietetics taken to Italy in 1463 by Cypriot nobleman Hippolito Nacci (a courtier of exiled Queen Charlotte de Lusignan) and then embedded in the

Renaissance cookbook *De honeste voluptate et valetudine*. That highly tangled but also well-documented exposé was taken up in my essay for *Court and Performance in the Pre-Modern Middle East* (Weaver 2017). The original book written in Cypriot Greek survives in a private collection which is not at this time accessible to scholars. Alas, I might add.

Now for the culinary texts. These are the sources in which we learn first-hand how herbs and spices were utilized, although in medieval terms, the flavour profiles are not always clear since many texts are either highly corrupted, or else they represent a type of kitchen shorthand only understood by practicing cooks in that period. None of the documented court cooks employed in the Lusignan kitchens could read or write (there were two kitchens, one for the king and one for the queen – they also dined separately). It was the assignment of the royal cook (a noble 'white-collar' bureaucrat) to act as kitchen executive with the ability to communicate the content of written recipes to the hands-on cooks (mostly Cypriot Greeks or Greek slaves from Asia Minor). He was also expected to communicate with the royal physician to determine how to interpret the recipes according to medical advice. This interpretation was based on botanical medicine, thus the Galenic role of spices and local herbs fell into place as royal humours required. The abundant use of saffron is a case in point. It is not a common herb in Greek or Cypriot cookery, yet in terms of Byzantine dietetics it was considered a cordial, a stimulant for the heart and the circulation of blood. For this reason, saffron figured often in Byzantine court cookery because it was a traditional health supplement for emperors.

This health-food emphasis on saffron appeared in several recipes in the *Libellus de arte coquinaria* (Digest from the Art of Cookery), a medieval text edited and published in 2001 by Constance Hieatt and Rudolf Grewe under the sub-title 'An Early Northern Cookery Book', though I must pause to point out that the Hieatt-Grewe edition of this manuscript is so totally off the mark that it demands a new edition. The title itself indicates that this work was condensed from something larger and older. Furthermore, internal evidence (terms used only in Cyprio-Gallic) indicate that this text was originally composed not in northern Europe where it was translated into several languages, but rather in Cyprus, probably at Famagusta since Famagusta measures appear in some of the recipes.

Contrary to the conclusions of Hieatt and Grewe, it appears that the *Libellus* was originally composed in Cyprio-Gallic sometime before 1300, and then translated into Latin about 1315-1316. The Latin translator was not Cypriot and was unfamiliar with Cypriot foodways (and cookery in general). This shortcoming emerges in the Latin itself and the awkward way in which Cyprio-Gallic was Latinized. For example, the Cypriot word *ygali* (goat milk yoghurt) was rendered into Latin as *caleus*, which is phonetic gibberish. The Cyprio-Gallic word for apricots (*hrosomilles*, from demotic Cypriot *chrysomelo*) was rendered into Latin as *Jerusalem*. There are ample clues of this sort in over half of the recipes. I have devoted an entire chapter in my book to similar textual evidence; it is much too extensive to include here.

Once the true nature of the *Libellus* began to reveal itself other related texts or fragments of related texts began to fall into place as documents of Cyprio-Gallic cuisine. Taken together, there are about seven culinary texts, some of which may trace to Byzantine cookbooks now lost. On that point, there is enough circumstantial evidence to suppose that there was a pre-existing Byzantine source on hunt cookery, since the *Libellus* is the first medieval cookbook to include recipes in the 'hunter style'. This culinary fiction employed chicken in place of real game although the recipe was intended to replicate the rusticity of men eating in Homeric simplicity around a campfire. The primary herb is garlic. Naples ramps (*Allium neopolitanum*) and great headed leeks (having garlic-like bulbs) can be harvested in the woods of Cyprus, so they are symbolic of living off the land, one of the underlying philosophical points of the noble hunt. Another aspect of hunt cookery was the intentional elimination of the feminizing elements of court cuisine. All forms of imported spices were dropped in favour of local wild-harvested herbs. Mastic berries took the place of black pepper, sumac took the place of imported saunders (red sandalwood), and the berries of sweet laurel were used like juniper berries in sausages and game marinades.

This brings us to the stark contrast between urban and rural cookery in medieval Cyprus. While the kingdom was divided into bailiwicks and then sub-divided into feudal manors, the landowners generally lived in the cities, especially in Nicosia and Famagusta. Their estates were managed by petty bureaucrats, so the grand feasting associated with Cypriot court life occurred in urban palaces. For this reason, the urban markets were structured much like those in Constantinople, with a high degree of specialization not found in Europe. Even the royal court supplied its kitchens from the open market; this tended to concentrate luxury foods and imports into the hands of merchant elites, the very same sort of well-off households that may have used the *Libellus* as a guide for good living. What is clear from the *Libellus* is that it was not intended as a royal cookbook: it did not contain those kinds of dishes – *aphraton* (mousse) for example – and the costly spices and sugar used at the *haute court*. However, it was exotic enough to northern Europeans to represent in their eyes the fabled lifestyle of the East. Thus, the *Libellus* was a talisman, a passport into the world of the medieval imagination.

369

The oldest known exotic spice imported to Cyprus was Ceylon cinnamon. Italian archaeologist Maria Rosaria Belgiorno uncovered a Bronze Age perfume factory at Pyrgos-Mavroraki, and several of the jars contained chemical traces of cinnamon (2004). Even in the Middle Ages, Cyprus remained a centre for perfume production, so the fine line between flavour and aroma was effectively blurred. Perfumed food was part of the courtly dining experience, amplified by using spice mixtures derived from Byzantine tradition. These spice mixtures were styled *poudre douce* or *poudre forte* in Cyprio-Gallic or *artima glyki* (sweet) and *artima apsi* (hot, spicy) in Byzantine Greek. Hot spiciness mimicking Capsicum peppers was achieved by combining equal parts ground ginger and ground white pepper.

Perfuming was further amplified by using ambrette or musk mallow (*Hibiscus abelmoschus*), which was locally grown – it thrives in the climate of Cyprus, but while the Greek serfs may have raised it for their overlords, ambrette did not figure in village cookery. Ambrette is what is known as a 'botanical cognate' because it could be used interchangeably with highly expensive spikenard (*stakhos*) imported from India. Like almond milk, spikenard defined the courtly cuisine of Constantinople perhaps as much for its status as for its perceived medical virtues according to Galenic doctrine. But also, like ambrette, spikenard blurred the distinctions between flavour and aroma, since it transformed the taste of food into perfume.

This sensuous and highly sensory approach to cookery was appreciated at the Cypriot court and was a feature of many dishes prepared as *viands de Chypre*. Spikenard roots or ambrette seeds were soaked overnight in boiling water or wine, then pulped the following day, and strained through coarse silk. The resulting musky 'milk' was then incorporated into recipes. Italian traveller Nicolo Martoni observed in 1394 that the Cypriot nobility used musk liberally in their cookery, even in breadcrumb soup (Cobham 1908). The *Libellus* features a recipe for breadcrumb soup because breadcrumbs were considered more easily digestible than coarse grains or even flour. That recipe is coloured yellow with saffron and was meant to serve as a more healthful and delicate alternative to *trachanas*, a peasant gruel made with cracked wheat and fermented goat's milk. Indeed, one is tempted to call the *Libellus* recipe faux *trachanas* because the texture and flavour are similar, aside from the spices. This is the kind of panada served in urban palaces while the villagers ate *trachanas* with mint, since mint

370

Figure 1 (left). 'Bark saffron' (phloiós tou krokou) was a colloquial medieval term for dried, sliced turmeric due to its visual appearance resembling shreds of bark. Figure 2 (right). Green jujubes are shown here pickled in sweet-sour syrup spiced with star anise. Photos by William Woys Weaver.

was considered an aid to digestion (Weaver 2002).

The *Libellus* also mentions a spice called 'bark saffron', a term that confounded Hieatt and Grewe because it is a little-known colloquial commercial term for turmeric, or as written in Byzantine Greek *phloiós tou krokou*. Turmeric was introduced into Byzantine cookery via Persia and was commonly used to 'gild' food or sauces, especially sauces that were served in the form of ornamental arabesques dabbled over the surface of pies, puddings, and tarts. Turmeric was called 'bark saffron' because the corms were sliced and dried, thus resembling shavings of bark (Figure 1). Their commercial origin was India which played an oversized role in Cypriot court cuisine.

For many years I maintained a long correspondence with the late Indian food historian K.T. Achaya (refer to Achaya 1994 in the bibliography). My interest focused on better understanding the nature of the spice trade with Cyprus especially since Indian merchants (many of them Nestorian Christians) resided in both Nicosia and Famagusta. They even built a Nestorian church in Famagusta which survives today as a picturesque ruin. The Cypriot-Indian connection is deep-rooted and figures in some of the food terms employed in medieval Cypriot Greek.

For example, guinea fowl were called 'Indian hen' (*kotopoulo yiahni*) and tamarind was called 'Indian carob'. Even today taro is called 'Indian tuber' (*kolokassi yiahni*). The insular Cypriot perception that anything exotic and foreign came from India was perhaps strengthened during the early Byzantine period when Cyprus figured in the brisk trade between Alexandria and Constantinople, a period when Indian goods were reaching Egypt via the Indian Ocean (De Romanis and Tchernia 1997). Yet this perception of India was also muddled to some extent because Chinese cinnamon (cassia) was thought to be the bark of Indian bay leaf (*Cinnamomum tamala*) and cassia buds were thought to be the berries of the same plant, hence all three were called *malabathrum* in medieval merchant records.

371

Perhaps the most important contribution of the Indian traders in Cyprus was their importation of Indian rice and rice flour, which figured in the cookery of the royal court but not in the cuisine of commoners – or in the *Libellus* for that matter. These same merchants also introduced a rare Himalayan onion called the St. John's Onion or Royal Shallot which was propagated by the Order of St. John of Jerusalem and disseminated to their hospices in Europe. Since it is a rare triploid its chemistry is unique and straddles the line between garlic and leek, with the health benefits of both. It is mentioned in one of the recipes in the *Libellus* as the 'red onion' because the inner skin turns wine red when exposed to sunlight.

The list of exotic herbs and spices imported to Cyprus is large and not everything can be correlated with specific Cypriot uses. However, this list would include cloves, rhubarb, ginger, pepper, long pepper, cubeb, cardamom, star anise, red anise, tamarind, rock alum (for pickling), saunders (red sandalwood), and dragon's blood, a resin from an East Indian palm tree. Long pepper (*Piper longum*) was used extensively in marinades and pickles and even to flavour traditional *garos* (fish sauce) used by the Cypriot

Greek gentry. Cubebs were often employed to 'flourish' (decorate) ornamental dishes brought to the table as culinary entertainments. Cardamom was combined with native Cypriot *rigani* (*Origanum dubium*) to create a new flavour that does not resemble either ingredient. Likewise, star anise was combined with cardamom to 'warm' the humours of green jujubes, as shown in Figure 2. Jujubes were only found in aristocratic gardens so that fact alone equated them with courtly cuisine. The unripe fruit was valued for its apple-like flavour which was improved when pickled in honey vinegar.

Like the mystery spice created from cardamom and *rigani*, Ceylon cinnamon was combined with native cumin, especially in dishes called *yiachni* (Figure 3). They consisted of sautéed vegetables that were then sweated quickly in *saltsaria* (chafing pans). This preference for combining cinnamon and cumin has remained a feature of Cypriot cookery that distinguishes it from mainland Greece. And while it is often treated as a typical Cypriot flavour profile, the origin of this combination traces to Galenic medicine, since both ingredients are warm and dry and were thought to strengthen the heart. In short, this was an alternative way to imitate the perceived medical effects of saffron.

The essence of medieval Cypriot cuisine is defined by the island's *terroir*. And not surprising due to its isolation from the mainland, Cyprus developed a rich biodiversity that has shaped local diet since ancient times. Cyprus is the only place claiming twenty-three species of oregano (Padulosi 1997), and most of them are used in local

372

Figure 3 (left). Arkopeponia yiachni *is made with sautéed wild melons, chopped walnuts, walnut oil, and toasted pine nuts flavoured with cumin and cinnamon. The silver spoon and serving dish are medieval. Figure 4 (right). Quince paste (*kydonopasto*) flavoured and coloured with sumac could also contain chopped nuts, in this case, chopped pistachios. Photos by William Woys Weaver.*

cookery. Furthermore, there are many other botanical species unique to the island, and they cannot be replicated with substitutes because their flavours and textures are one of a kind. This would include the island's native oregano endemic to the Troodos Mountains; Cape Greko Mustard which combines characteristics of lettuce and rocket; and St. Hilarion Kale, a succulent cabbage resembling broccoli except that it grows on rocky mountainsides. While overharvesting has now threatened many of these unique food plants, other indigenous herbs are better documented in the medieval record.

For example, sumac was used extensively in both savoury and sweet dishes. Red sauce (*Kokkinosaltsa*) was normally served French style at court with spit-roasted meats while *grouta tou soumaki*, sumac-flavored *chalvas* (soft candy) made with barley starch and honey or low-grade cane syrup, was one of the inexpensive sweets sold village to village by street vendors. By contrast, quince paste (*kydonopasto*) was considered a luxury food since it was made with sugar and thus it often figured as a gift-food for dinner guests to take home after a meal. Such food distributions were considered a social requirement of the nobility and are still practiced today at Cypriot weddings. The addition of sumac to quince paste was only one of many flavour variations (Figure 4).

Likewise, camelina (also called Gold of Pleasure) provided the basis for mustard-like Camelina Sauce served with game, while the oil of camelina seeds was commonly substituted for olive oil during periods of fasting. The Roman Catholic court could consume olive oil as well as fish when fasting while Greek religious canon forbade it. Thus, the dietary practices of medieval Cyprus were highly nuanced according to one's religious profession, with the added complication that due to shared obsessions for holy relics, it was commonplace for Cypriots regardless of ethnic background, economic situation, or religious persuasion to partake in the religious observances of their neighbours. In this way, urban cuisine became quite cosmopolitan in character while the plant-based diet of the Greek rural poor followed highly localized patterns based on *terroir* and Byzantine tradition.

References

Achaya, K.T. 1994. *Indian Food: A Historical Companion* (Delhi: Oxford University Press)

Belgiorno, Maria Rosaria. 2004. *Pyrgos-Mavroraki: Advanced Technology in Bronze Age Cyprus* (Nicosia: Archaeological Museum)

Cobham, Claude. 1908. *Excerpta Cypria: Materials for a History of Cyprus* (Cambridge: Cambridge University Press)

Cortese, Arabella (ed.). 2020. *Identity and Change in Ancient Cilicia* (Wiesbaden: Ludwig Reichert Verlag/ Mitteilungen zur Spätantiken Archäologie und Byzantinischen Kunstgeschichte)

Coureas, Nicholas (trans.). 2002. *The Assizes of the Lusignan Kingdom of Cyprus* (Nicosia: Cyprus Research Centre)

De Romanis, Federico and Andre Tchernia (eds.). 1997. *Crossings: Early Mediterranean Contacts with India* (New Delhi: Manohar Publishers)

Dotson, John E. 1994. *Merchant Culture in Fourteenth Century Venice: The Zibaldone da Canal* (Binghamton, NY: Medieval & Renaissance Texts and Studies)

Grewe, Rudolf and Constance B. Hieatt. 2001. '*Libellus de arte coquinaria*': *An Early Northern Cookery Book*

(Tempe: Arizona Center for Medieval and Renaissance Studies)

Jacoby, David. 1984. 'The Rise of a New Emporium in the Eastern Mediterranean: Famagusta in the Late Thirteenth Century', in *Μελεται και Ψπομνιματα 1* (Nicosia), pp. 145-79.

Lieberknecht, Sieglinde (ed.). 1995. *Die Canones der Pseudo-Mesue: Eine mittelalterliche Purganten-Lehre* (Stuttgart: Wissenschaftliche Verlagsgesellschaft)

Nicholaou-Konnari, Angel and Chris Schnabel (eds.). 2005. *Cyprus: Society and Culture 1191-1374* (Leiden: Brill)

Padulosi, Stefano (ed.). 1997. *Oregano: Proceedings of the IPGRI International Workshop on Oregano* (Rome: IPGRI)

Weaver, William Woys. 2002. 'The Origin of Trachanás: Evidence from Cyprus and Ancient Texts', *Gastronomica,* 2.1: 41-48.

——. 2017. 'The Court Cuisine of Medieval Cyprus: Food as Table Theatre', in *Court and Performance in the Pre-Modern Middle East*, ed. by Maurice Pomeranz and Eveyln Birge Vitz (New York: New York University Press)

374

Food for the Soul: The Rabbis' Cinnamon

Susan Weingarten

Andrew Dalby's excellent book *Siren Feasts: A History of Food and Gastronomy in Greece* suggests that in the ancient Greek world 'spices were not used predominately for food' but to make perfumes, perfumed oils, medicines, and aromatic wines, and only later and less ubiquitously to flavour food. Ancient Jewish sources confirm Dalby's impression for other parts of the ancient Mediterranean world: in the Bible, spices are smelled, not eaten. When and how did this change? Dalby notes an increasing use of spices in Roman times mentioned in the pages of Athenaeus and the Apicius collection. From here their use in food escalates, leading to the massive use of spices in Europe in the Middle Ages, with worldwide trading and even wars over these desirable commodities.

This paper looks at Jewish sources written by rabbis from Late Antiquity up to the Modern period in order to trace some parts of the journey of spices from fragrance to food. Scholars have already noted some of these developments, but I bring new material and interpretations in the light of rabbinical sources.[1] I take one particular spice, cinnamon, as a paradigm.

Cinnamon is a fragrant spice made from quills, rolled-up and dried pieces of the inner bark of the tree *Cinnamomum zeylonicum* growing in Ceylon, today's Sri Lanka.[2] It seems to have been traded to ancient Palestine from very early times: most scholars accept the identification of biblical Hebrew *qinamon* with what we call 'cinnamon' today.[3] *Cinnamomum zeylonicum* is often confused with cassia, *Cinnamomum cassia*, although there are two different words for them in Hebrew which appear separately in various lists of spices. Hebrew / Aramaic *qetzia* (or *qida*) has been proposed as the origin of the word 'cassia'. The quills sold today as 'cinnamon' are usually cassia in practice, and it is often unclear to which plant ancient sources are referring. Later Jewish sources are even more confused, as they bring biblical *qaneh*, translated as *calamus*, 'sweet reed' or 'cane', into the equation. This appears to be another scroll-like aromatic, whose name reminded the European rabbis of *canelle,* the French for cinnamon, although, as with cassia, all these terms are cited in the Bible as separate entities. There was also a spice named *qilufa*, literally 'stripped', which was taken by some rabbis as the stripped bark of cinnamon and / or cassia. Four of these terms appear separately in one list, together with other spices, while cinnamon as such is sometimes referred to as *qinamon bosem*, where *bosem* refers to the word for spice or perfume. Was this a fifth (or sixth) sort? I do not propose a solution, but note that whereas ten different kinds of cinnamon are described by the Swiss scholar Johann Scheuchzer in his eighteenth-century *Physica sacra,* modern botany identifies 275 species.[4]

The traditions of rabbinic cinnamon begin with the Hebrew Bible, where cinnamon appears three times: in Exodus, Proverbs, and the Song of Songs. In Exodus 30.23 it is one of the ingredients of the perfumed oil used to anoint the High Priest himself, one of the 'chief spices' along with myrrh, sweet calamus, and cassia, in a base of olive oil: 'Take [...] the principal spices: of pure myrrh five hundred shekels and of sweet cinnamon half so much even two hundred and fifty shekels and of sweet calamus two hundred and fifty shekels. And of cassia five hundred shekels [...] and of olive oil a hin. And thou shalt make it an oil of holy ointment.' This concoction is so holy that it is forbidden to make it other than for a holy purpose – anointing the High Priest, the Tabernacle, or a God-appointed King. Anyone using it for another purpose, say later talmudic rabbis commenting on this, will be cut off from their people.[5]

In contrast, in Proverbs 7.17, cinnamon, myrrh, and aloes perfume the bed of the harlot who lies in wait at the corner for the young man devoid of understanding who goes after her 'as the ox goeth to the slaughter'. In contradistinction to the holiness of the first use, we now have a totally profane use for the spice, as an aphrodisiac in adulterous sex.

In the Song of Songs 4.14, cinnamon is also used in the context of making love, but here it is not adulterous, but merely erotic. The rabbis had few problems with the erotic in the proper context. When it came to the debate as to whether to accept the erotic poem that is the Song of Songs into the canon of the Bible, Rabbi Aqiva declared: All the writings are holy but the Song of Songs is the Holy of Holies.[6] Songs' lover and his beloved were allegorized by the rabbis as God and his beloved Israel. Later, Christian exegetes would see them as Jesus and his church.[7] The girl is a locked garden to which the lover is invited, in which we find spikenard and saffron, calamus and cinnamon, frankincense, myrrh and aloes, with all the chief spices. She is compared in the next verse to an orchard, *pardes,* the beginning of the links between spices and paradise in Jewish traditions.

Thus biblical cinnamon belongs to the whole spectrum of the sacred and the profane: it is an ingredient of the oil used to anoint the High Priest in the Tabernacle, and perfumes the bed of the lovers, traditionally King Solomon and one of his many wives, but allegorized by the rabbis as God himself with his bride the people of Israel. But Solomon is also credited with writing the book of Proverbs, and here cinnamon perfumes the bed of the harlot who lies in wait for the young man devoid of understanding.

So far we have concentrated on cinnamon as an aromatic, for these are the sources the rabbis continually refer back to, to give themselves the authority of the biblical text. There is no evidence of anyone actually eating cinnamon in the texts from Songs or Proverbs: it seems to have been used simply to perfume the woman – or the bed. But slowly we find gastronomic uses creeping in.

The first hint of this, appropriately perhaps, is in the Apocrypha, those texts not accepted into the canon of the Hebrew Bible but referring to many of its protagonists.

Figure 1. Synagogue mosaic, Hammat Tiberias. The square incense shovels with red coals appear twice, to the right of each candlestick. Wikimedia commons.

The book of Ecclesiasticus, the Wisdom of Ben Sirah, was long preserved only in Greek, but the Hebrew original turned up recently in the Dead Sea Scrolls. Here we find Wisdom herself perfumed with cinnamon and other spices – but also tasting sweeter than honey.[8] We will see other uses of cinnamon in the Pseudepigrapha later.

377

In the later midrashic literature, there seems to be a further reference to cinnamon with sexual connotations. The patriarch Abraham is compared to a cinnamon tree which grows better the more it is stripped and fertilized, in the context of begetting a child at the age of a hundred on his ninety-year-old wife, after he had long lost sexual interest or potency.[9] His potency, the midrash implies, was restored to him by his circumcision, like the stripping or pruning of the cinnamon tree. Cinnamon trees do indeed continue to be productive for fifty or more years, and this midrash seems to hint at aphrodisiac connotations.[10] However it is totally unclear whether such an aphrodisiac was smelled, eaten, or applied externally.

To return to the incense. The cinnamon and other spices which make up the priests' anointing oil are part of a recipe, which gives quantities. The rabbis of the Talmuds discuss this recipe, and add a further recipe for the incense used in the Temple (as opposed to the Tabernacle) along with instructions of what not to include, and a ban on trying to reproduce the Temple incense after the Temple was destroyed: this too was liable to the death penalty.[11] Synagogue mosaics contemporary with the Jerusalem Talmud include what appear to be representations of incense shovels (Figure 1).

Does this mean that incense was used in the late antique synagogue in spite of the ban? Incense was used at the conclusion of *symposia* in both Greek and Jewish contexts, together with scented water to wash hands. There seems to be no strong evidence for its use in synagogues, however, and it is possible that the shovels are depicted in the mosaics in memory of the incense in the Temple.[12]

Following the details of the anointing oil in the book of Exodus, we are given details of the spices to be compounded into the incense for the Tabernacle. There are only four of these, and they do not include cinnamon: *nataf, shahelet, helbona,* and pure *levona,* translated as *stacte*/balm, onycha, galbanum, and pure frankincense, although *nataf*/*stacte* has been translated as 'oil of cinnamon'.[13] It is very unclear indeed what these words represent in Hebrew, Greek, English, or any other language. The terms used in Exodus differ slightly from those in the Talmud. One of these is explained: balm/*tzori*, we are told, is called *nataf* in the Bible because it was a dripping (*n-t-f*) resin. The second in the list in Exodus is *shahelet*, while the Talmuds have *tsipporen*. What the connection (if any) between *shahelet* and *tzipporen* was, is unclear. *Shahelet* is translated in the Septuagint as *onycha*, the *operculum* of a sea snail, the shiny, hard, whiteish substance the snail uses to close itself in against attackers; it looks like a fingernail. Would this product of a non-kosher snail have been used in the holy oil, even though it was not for eating? Or is this why the talmudic text changes it for *tsipporen*, a word used both for fingernails and cloves, without explanation? Dalby has concluded that cloves as we know them, which grow in the distant Molucca islands, actually got to the Roman world, including ancient Palestine, around the turn of the first century CE.[14] The fact that the origin of many spices was so unclear may have been why it took so long for them to be used in Jewish cooking, as opposed just for smelling.

We have seen the biblical prescription for spices for the Tabernacle in the wilderness. By the time of the Jerusalem Temple which took its place, these four spices were clearly no longer enough. Josephus, the first-century Jewish historian who was himself once a priest serving in the Temple, tells us that he knew of thirteen spices and notes their significance. They come, he says, 'from sea and from land, both desert and inhabited', and signify that 'all things are of God and for God'.[15] Josephus does not specify which spices he is talking about (does the reference to 'sea' hint at the *onycha*/*operculum*? Or is he referring to trade routes?), but it is possible that the memory is preserved in a passage quoted in both Talmuds which gives details of the spices. The list begins with the biblical spices from the Tabernacle and then adds more. It is a little difficult to decide which of the ingredients make up the thirteen (some rabbis counted eleven or twelve), but this time they do include cinnamon and cassia, as well as *qaneh* and *qilufa*:

> Our Rabbis have taught: The compound of incense consisted of balm, *tsipporen*/cloves, galbanum and frankincense, each in the quantity of seventy manehs; of myrrh, cassia, spikenard and saffron, each sixteen manehs by weight; of costus twelve, of aromatic bark three, and of cinnamon nine manehs; of lye of Karsina nine qabs; of Cyprus wine three se'ahs and three qabs, though if Cyprus

wine is not available, old white wine may be used instead; of salt of Sodom the fourth of a qab, and a minute quantity of a herb that caused the smoke to ascend straight upwards / ma'aleh 'ashan. R. Natan says: Also a minute quantity of amber from the Jordan. If, however, honey is added, the incense is rendered unfit; while if one omits one of the ingredients, he is liable to the death penalty. R. Simeon ben Gamaliel said: Balm is nothing but a resin which exudes from the wood of the balsam-tree; the lye of Karsina was rubbed over the *tsipporen* in order to render it beautiful, and the *tsipporen* was steeped in the Cyprus wine to make it more pungent [...].[16]

The Jerusalem Talmud adds a comment attributed to the spice grinders of Jerusalem: if they had added honey, the whole world would not have been able to withstand the smell.

This text forms part of the Sabbath liturgy to this day, bringing a virtual memory of the Temple incense, including cinnamon, into the synagogue.[17] There is evidence from the rabbinic kabbalists of the Zohar in the sixteenth century that this passage was also read aloud at other times as a prophylactic against plague, recalling the incident in Numbers 16.46-48, when incense marked the arrest of the plague in the wilderness.[18] It has not proved noticeably effective against COVID-19 in 2020.

To return specifically to our cinnamon.

Classical authors have a wonderful hoard of stories, rumours, and pure inventions about cinnamon. Herodotus, the 'father of lies', as he was known in the ancient world, is the best:

379

The process of collecting the cinnamon is even stranger. In what country it grows is quite unknown. The Arabians say that the dry sticks, which we call *kinamomon*, are brought to Arabia by large birds, which carry them to their nests, made of mud, on mountain precipices which no man can climb. The method invented to get the cinnamon sticks is this: People cut up the bodies of dead oxen into very large joints, and leave them on the ground near the nests. They then scatter, and the birds fly down and carry off the meat to their nests, which are too weak to bear the weight and fall to the ground. Then men come and pick up the cinnamon. Acquired this way it is exported to other countries.[19]

Pliny, writing in Rome in the first century CE, rejects this story, but supplies another:

Those old tales were invented by the Arabians to raise the price of their goods. There is an accompanying story that under the reflected rays of the sun at midday an indescribable sort of collective odour is given off from the whole of the peninsula, which is due to the harmoniously blended exhalation of all those aromas, and that the first news of Arabia received by the fleets of Alexander the Great were these odours, wafted far out to sea.

All these stories are nonsense [...].[20]

Pliny then produces an account of bringing the cinnamon over vast oceans, but he (or his informers) so garbles his geographical terms that it took a long time before people understood the true origins of cinnamon in Sri Lanka and southern India.[21] But what is of interest to us here is the story of the fragrance of cinnamon filling the whole of the Arabian peninsula, and wafting to the fleets of Alexander. For there was a parallel story told in the talmudic sources.[22] They described the smell of the cinnamon growing around Jerusalem as filling the whole of the Land of Israel. Cinnamon, they wrote, was so common that goats (or camels) fed on it, and the sticks were used for fuel for the altars of the Temple. After the destruction of the Temple this ceased, and there remained only a tiny barleycorn of cinnamon in the treasury of Queen Tsimtsemai.[23] Other stories of Alexander the Great appear in the talmudic literature, and elsewhere, part of the traditions now called the Alexander Romance, so it is not surprising that the story of the Land of Cinnamon identified by its smell should be shared between Greeks and Jews. But whereas for the Greeks the exoticism of the cinnamon was a function of distance in space from the faraway land of Arabia, the Jewish sources imported the spice to the God-given Land of Israel, where anything was possible for the Almighty, including the growing of exotic plants. Here cinnamon is remote in time, rather than space: the late antique rabbis placed it hundreds of years earlier, in the time when God's Temple still stood, when all must have been right with the world.[24]

Other points of meeting between Greek and Jewish worlds over cinnamon come in the legends of the phoenix, the mythical bird which dies on a funeral pyre she builds herself and is resurrected. The phoenix built her nest with sticks of the spice, as related both by Herodotus and the early Jewish Pseudepigrapha.[25] In neither of these early traditions is cinnamon actually eaten: the Greek phoenix builds her nest with the sticks, while the Jewish phoenix (which eats manna from heaven and dew from earth) uses the spice in her funeral pyre. Spices were commonly used around the dead in antiquity to disguise the smell of decay.[26]

We have already noted the associations of cinnamon and other spices with the orchard paradise in the Song of Songs. The rabbis of late antiquity develop this association in a number of suggestive midrashim: when Adam was expelled from Eden and his return barred by an angel with a fiery sword, he wept, and the angel let him back for a brief time. He brought out seeds, to plant and feed himself, and spices, to feed his soul. Rabbis commenting on the last verse of the book of Psalms: 'Let every soul praise God', asked what does the soul enjoy that the body doesn't? The answer was smell.[27] Food in general was to feed the body; fragrances like cinnamon were food for the soul.

Another legend tells of Noah's dove, sent to find dry land as the Flood receded, which entered Eden: '"Why did you bring back an olive branch?" people asked her, "Why not sweet spices like cinnamon or balsam?" "Better the bitterness which comes from God," replied the dove, "than sweetness from any other source."'[28]

Spices, then, originate in Eden. Today, at the conclusion of the Sabbath, the second soul, which accompanies the Jew on the day of rest that is a foretaste of the

World to Come, departs, but the departure is made tolerable by smelling spices, including cinnamon.[29]

So how did cinnamon become a food, rather than just a fragrance? According to Theophrastus, the Greeks used it as a spice for wine: he was convinced that spices improved wine, but ruined food.[30] I have not found any record of this use in Jewish sources, where pepper is the preferred spice for wine.[31] We noted the problems of the use of *operculum* above, which may have led to its substitution by cloves because of its animal origin. There are also rabbinic discussions of musk in the Middle Ages, describing it as congealed blood of a deer.[32] Deer are kosher animals, but blood is forbidden in Judaism. Maybe the slow take-up by Jews of the practice of using spices in food is partly due to worries about the animal origins of some spices.

Unlike the dubious musk and *operculum*, however, cinnamon actually looked like a bit of wood or bark, and some rabbis specified that its blessing was that used for fragrances from trees. Whatever the reason, it is clear that it was used from talmudic times for chewing, if not for eating. This identifiable stage on the way from fragrance to food was paradoxically due to the definition of cinnamon as a non-food. Eating and drinking were forbidden on Jewish fast-days, but the rabbis were aware of the misery of a dry mouth during a fast. So they allowed people to chew dry pungent stuff to encourage the production of saliva: you could chew cinnamon as long as you spat it out afterwards! However, on the Day of Atonement this was forbidden, just in case you ingested some of the cinnamon by mistake: chewing and spitting out cinnamon was only permitted on minor, not major, fast-days.[33] Dalby notes that Indians and Chinese chewed cinnamon and other spices to sweeten the breath.[34] This may also have been a factor encouraging people to chew spices when fasting, when the breath may smell bad due to dehydration.

This in-between status of cinnamon as something not quite edible was underlined by the discussions as to what blessing was to be said over it: 'Our Rabbis have taught: It is forbidden to a man to enjoy anything of this world without a benediction, and if anyone enjoys anything of this world without a benediction, he commits sacrilege.'[35]

The rabbis of the third-century Mishnah record blessings praising God for different kinds of foods, which were categorized according to their origin.[36] For the fruit of the tree, one should say: 'Blessed are You, O Lord our God, King of the Universe, who creates the fruit of the tree' (although wine had its own special blessing). For produce from the earth you said: '[…] who creates the produce of the ground' (but bread and other foods made of grain had their own blessings). There was a general blessing for other foods, such as milk or cheese or eggs. Rabbi Judah said that no blessings were to be made over bad things, such as locusts. By the time of the Jerusalem Talmud, categorized blessings were added for fragrances: '[…] who creates fragrant trees', 'who creates fragrant herbs', 'who creates sweet-smelling oil', 'who gives a good smell to fruit' (this was said over especially fragrant fruit: citrons and quinces, and later over nutmeg), and a general 'who creates different kinds of fragrances'.

Later rabbis debated which of these blessings to apply to cinnamon. Should it be 'fragrant trees', as it is obviously not a herb?[37] Should they give up categorizing and use the all-inclusive 'different kinds of fragrances'?[38] These discussions continue into the Middle Ages, when we have the first rabbinical evidence of use of cinnamon as food. Among non-Jewish contemporaries in Europe, cinnamon was by now immensely popular, for example in cameline sauce, which stars in the fourteenth-century *Viandier*, so-called after its camel-colour, given to it by the ground cinnamon which was its main ingredient.[39]

This extensive medieval European use of cinnamon was problematic for the rabbis. We saw that the Talmud noted that after the Temple was destroyed only a tiny piece remained in the Queen's treasury – so how, they asked, could it be so common in contemporary Europe? They concluded that there must be problems of identification. *Canelle* could not possibly be referring to the same spice as the Talmud, according to R. Moses of Coucy in thirteenth-century France.[40] There are many discussions of terminology and identifications, often in Arabic and much garbled, which will not concern us here.

But the discussions of which blessing to say do show us that smelling cinnamon was predominantly giving way to chewing it (like pepper, cloves, and even liquorice) to moisten the mouth on fast days, to sweeten the breath, and to protect against toothache.[41]

A new use of cinnamon by Jews in medieval and later Europe was in the Passover food *haroset*. *Haroset* was a dip eaten in memory of the clay from which the Israelite slaves made bricks in Egypt. Wicked Pharaoh had given them straw for the bricks at first, but later demanded they supply it themselves.[42] The mixture represented the clay for the bricks, and spices in it represented the straw. Some rabbis specified that the spices in memory of straw should appear as long stringy bits – so cinnamon came in.[43]

Perhaps because of *haroset*, cinnamon became more generally used in food, as we see from the discussions of the blessings. Although it came from a tree, it was not a fruit, and was thus subject to the food blessing 'who creates the produce of the ground'. The fifteenth-century R. Jacob Landau (who moved from Germany to Italy) marks the transition: if you smell cinnamon, you bless 'over fragrant woods', if you eat it, it is 'produce of the ground'.[44] By the sixteenth century, food use was clearly well established, although there were still disagreements over blessings. Rabbi Mordekhai Yaffe of Prague writes that the blessing should be 'who gives a good smell to fruit', and adds the telling comment: 'because its most important use is not just to smell, but also to eat'.[45] The seventeenth-century Rabbi Hayim Benveniste in Constantinople stopped chewing cinnamon on fast days, because it was too enjoyable.[46]

Finally, in the nineteenth century, Rabbi Yehiel Mikhl Epstein in Lithuania actually gives us a recipe![47] He is discussing whether food made from grain or the compound used to flavour it constitutes the more important element in the food eaten: thus, he tells us, with *lekakh* (spice cake) it is the flour made from the grain which takes precedence over the spices, so the cake has the blessing 'sorts of grain'. He adds that there is a food in some places called *ingberlakh*, where you fry cinnamon with walnuts and almonds. Some people add *farfel* (pasta pieces) to this, and it depends which is the major component: if it is spices, you bless 'creates the produce of the ground', but if it's *farfel,* you bless 'sorts of grain'.

The name *ingberlakh* comes from *ingber,* ginger in Yiddish, but clearly he is reporting a local variant made with cinnamon.[48]

Notes

1   See for example A. Dalby, *Dangerous Tastes: The Story of Spice* (London: British Museum Press, 2000) and P. Freedman, *Out of the East: Spices and the Medieval Imagination* (New Haven: Yale University Press, 2009).

2   H. McGee, *On Food and Cooking: The Science and Lore of the Kitchen* (New York: Scribner, 2004), pp. 424-25.

3   Analysis of small ceramic flasks from eleventh-tenth-century BCE from Israel/Palestine has shown remains of cinnamaldehyde, a component of both cinnamon and cassia, in what seem to have been wine flasks (D. Namdar and others, 'Cinnamaldehyde in early Iron Age Phoenician Flasks Raises the Possibility of Levantine Trade with South-East Asia', *Mediterranean Archaeology and Archaeometry*, 12.3 (2013), 1-19).

4   *Physica Sacra* (Augsberg/Ulm, 1731) – Scheuchzer also includes an account of the biblical burning bush; M. Zohary, *Plants of the Bible* (Cambridge: Cambridge University Press, 1982), p. 202.

5   Babylonian Talmud (= BT) Keritot 5a. For a convenient brief explanation of the talmudic literature, see S. Weingarten 'Nuts for the Children: The Evidence of the Talmudic Literature', in *Nurture: Proceedings of the Oxford Symposium on Food and Cookery 2003*, ed. by R. Hosking (Bristol: FootWork, 2004).

6   Mishnah Yadayim iii,5.

7   Freedman, p. 77.

8   Ecclesiasticus 24.15-20.

9   Genesis Rabbah 46 and parallels.

10 Interestingly, cassia, if not cinnamon, has been reported to restore sexual function to aging male rats (S. Kumar, 'Efficacy of *Cinnamomum Cassia Blume* in Age-Induced Sexual Dysfunction of Rats,' *Journal of Young Pharmacists,* 5.4 (9 December 2013), 148-153 <http://www.doi.org/10.1016/J.JYP.2013.11.001>). Here too the research report does not specify how the cassia was 'administered' to the rats: as a smell, food, injection, or by external application?

11 BT Keritot 5a.

12 L. I. Levine, *The Ancient Synagogue: The First Thousand Years* (New Haven: Yale University Press, 2005), pp. 234, 306.

13 Webster's Dictionary, 1913 ed.

14 Dalby, *Dangerous Tastes*, p. 50.

15 *Jewish War* 5.218-19.

16 Jerusalem Talmud (=JT) Yoma 42d; BT Keritot 11a.

17 English prayerbooks cut the text. After mentioning soaking the *tsipporen* in wine, the talmudic source continues: 'In fact urine might well serve this purpose, but urine may not be brought within the precincts of the Temple because this is disrespectful.' Modern translators of the text clearly thought if it was disrespectful to bring urine into the Temple, it must also be disrespectful to even mention this in the synagogue, and they censored the English translation, leaving it in the Hebrew text, in what Gibbon famously called 'the decent obscurity of a learned tongue' (*Autobiography of Edward Gibbon,* ed. by Lord Sheffield (London, etc, 1907) p. 212). The reader may wonder whether urine was indeed efficacious in intensifying the smell. I have tried it on cloves (not on *operculum*): it does work quite well. But it is clear from this, if from nothing else, that these spices here were not for eating and as such are really out of our remit.

18 Numbers 16.46-48 [RV] = 17. 12-15 in other versions.

19 Herodotus 3. 110-111, qtd. Dalby, *Dangerous Tastes*, p. 37.

20 *NH* 12.87-88, tr. qtd. Dalby, *Dangerous Tastes*, pp. 37-38.

21 Dalby, *Dangerous Tastes*, p. 38

22 BTShabbat 63a; JTPeah 20a and parallels.

23 Queen Tsimtsemai is unidentified outside this story.

24 Another talmudic legend of Alexander has him visiting King Qetzia, or the king of Qetzia: the inhabitants brought Alexander gold as food instead of bread, as they thought he must have bread already, but would want gold. But spices play no part in the story, apart from the name: *qetzia* is the Hebrew for cassia.

25 For the phoenix in Herodotos, the *Apocalypse of Baruch*, and the *Exagogue of Ezekiel*, see R. Van den Broek, *The Myth of the Phoenix According to Classical and Early Christian Traditions* (Leiden: Brill, 1972).

26 See also John 19.32f.

27 BTBerakhot 43b.

28 Songs Rabbah 1, 4.

29 On spices and Eden in the Middle Ages, see Freedman, especially chapter 3: 'The Odours of Paradise'.

30 Theophrastus, *On odours*, 10.

31 *Qonditon* spiced wine is made of pepper, honey, and wine: see, for example, *Pesiqta deRav Kahana* 12. But note the probable evidence for cinnamon in wine at a much earlier period in Namdar and others above n.3.

32 Rabbeinu Bahaye: Comm. in Ex 30.23. Rabbinic sources unless otherwise noted are cited from the Bar Ilan Responsa database, version 24.

33 See for example *Sefer Raviyah* (Germany, *c*. twelfth century) Taanit, 861.

34 See also E.H. Schafer 'Rosewood, Dragon's Blood and Lac', *Journal of American Oriental Society*, 77 (1957), 129-36.

35 BTBerakhot 35a.

36 Mishnah Berakhot, chapter 6.

37 See for example *Shibbolei haLeqet* (Rome, *c*. thirteenth century) Seder Berakhot 160.

38 See for example *Orkhot Hayim* (*c*. fourteenth century) pt 1, Hilkhot Berakhot 38.

39 T. Scully, *The Art of Cookery in the Middle Ages* (Woodbridge: Boydell, 1995), p. 114. It could be bought ready-made in *c*. fourteenth-century Paris. See the recipe by Daniel Myers: 'Cameline Sauce', *Medieval Cookery* <http://medievalcookery.com/recipes/cameline.html> [accessed 15 March 2021].

40 *Sefer Mitzvot HaGadol* (*c*. thirteenth century) 167.

41 e.g. Rabbenu Yeruham (*c*. thirteenth-fourteenth century).

42 Exodus 5.6-11.

43 See for example J. Möllin (the Maharil: Germany, c. fifteenth century) *Sefer HaMinhagim*, ed. by S. Spitzer (Jerusalem: Jerusalem Institute, 1989), who says cinnamon and cassia should be added to *haroset* in the form of long strips, like straw. For other references, see S. Weingarten, *Haroset: A Taste of Jewish History* (New Milford: Toby, 2019).

44 *Sefer Agur* Hilkhot Berakhot HaPerot 275; 305.

45 *Levush* OH 216.3.

46 *Sheyarei Knesset HaGedolah* OH 567.3.

47 *Arukh HaShulhan* OH 212.8.

48 This recipe for Passover *ingberlakh* has crumbled *matzah* instead of *farfel*: 'Ingberlach: A Jewish Homemade Candy for Passover', *AZDaily*, 20 March 2014 <https://www.azcentral.com/story/life/food/recipes/2014/03/20/ingberlach-jewish-homemade-candy-passover-recipe/6660613/> [accessed 16 March 2021].

Lessons from the Chilli in China

Gerald Zhang-Schmidt

From their journeys through the Pacific around 1905, Austrian scientist-explorers Dr K. and L. Rechinger brought back a herbarium specimen of a *Capsicum frutescens* they had found on Upolu, Samoa. They annotated how it 'grows as a weed in the coconut palm plantations' and 'when ripe, the Chinese coolies eat it. Very hot'.

That the Rechingers even found a chilli worth botanizing, and added a cultural-culinary note, is surprising. It's a special bonus that there was a China connection. China is not often recognized as a place of particularly spicy food, at least not outside of particular provinces, but the country is one of the biggest growers and consumers of chilli. The chilli may have been discovered by Europeans because Christopher Columbus wanted to find black pepper, but its spread went very differently (cf. Halikowski Smith 2015). Black pepper, although declining in popularity, continued to be a trade good; one can find it in cargo manifests. The chilli must have travelled with the European 'explorers'. Sometimes, it may even have rushed ahead of them. It quickly superseded black pepper in everyday culinary importance around the world – but it did so as the spice of the poor, and especially of the non-European ethnic other. It grows easily almost everywhere, and people around the world seemed to have just been waiting for its pungency. Thus, most of the time, it was and is overlooked in its special cultural-culinary connections – even (or perhaps, especially) as it is such a screaming-hot spice to the uninitiated.

Now, various world cuisines are recognized for their spiciness, for example Mexican and Thai; there are also hints of a recognition that certain kinds of chilli peppers are necessary to give such 'ethnic' cuisines their authentic flavour (cf. Zewdie and Bosland 2001). Chinese cuisine is not well recognized as spicy – but some of its regional cuisines are. With this observation alone, one enters the realm of lessons that can be learned from a deeper engagement with the chilli peppers in China: the pungent character of certain cuisines; the role that different chilli peppers (and approaches to them) play in such spicy cuisines; and the relationship between spiciness, tastes, and diners that hint at a modernization amidst the popularization of spicy eating.

Lesson 1: Cuisines of the Chilli

The authenticity of a cuisine is a difficult topic. What makes it special and different from others, recognizable as itself, has been considered an element of cooking styles, preparations, ingredients, but especially aromatics, making them 'flavour principles' of the respective cuisines (as per Rozin 1983). Elisabeth Rozin only considered chilli peppers as one among many defining aromatics, but their role appears rather stronger – and more peculiar.

In China, as in so much of the world, the chilli arrived sometime between 1500 and 1700. Culinary mentions of it become common only in the nineteenth century (cf. Dott 2020), leading to claims that it is hardly traditional, although, as Dott argues, 'constructed authenticity does not require indigeneity' of a food (2020: 51). Whether the chilli is older or newer as a (major) ingredient, spiciness has been considered the defining characteristic of the Chinese cuisine(s) of the country's west, meaning the provinces up the Changjiang (Yangtze river) towards the Himalayas: Sichuan, Guizhou, and Hunan. Ancient texts from times long before the chilli's introduction already spoke of these areas' people as liking strong flavours. The cooking ingredients that were found in Hunan's Mawangdui tombs lend credence, at least, to the use of various stronger flavourings; they included ginger, scallions, and Sichuan peppers. *Mujiangzi* (also known as *shanhujiao* and *maqaw*, unripe fruits of *Lindera glauca* (Sieb. et Zucc.) Bl. or *Litsea cubeba* (Lour.) Pers.) also have traditionally been in culinary use in these areas and lend a certain pungency; Japanese cornelian berry (*shanzhuyu*, *Cornus officinalis* Torr. ex. Dur.) is also mentioned as an aromatic used before the chilli, but its taste is sour rather than pungent.

Once the chilli arrived, it established itself as such a determining flavour that it is seen as representative and necessary for the cooking styles of these provinces. The only question in most people's minds is how exactly the saying that 'Sichuan people aren't afraid of spiciness, Hunan people don't fear spiciness, Guizhou people are afraid of not having spiciness' is supposed to go (as there are different versions putting the people from those provinces into different hierarchies), similar to how it's either Sichuan or Hunan women who are the *lameizi*, the 'spicy girls' of China.

Lesson 2: Spicy Cuisines, but Spicy in What Way?

Attractive and easy as it may be to classify certain cuisines as spicy, this is too superficial by far. Although cuisines rich in chilli tend to be described only as spicy, there are differences not only in how spicy they are, but also in how they are spicy.

Sichuan with its *málà* flavour combining Sichuan peppercorn's numbingness and chilli's pungency is perhaps the best-known case of a cuisine being represented by a (distinct) spicy flavour. There are many more flavours and techniques employed by Sichuan cooking (*Chuan cai*). While this makes it a typical oversimplification to equate *málà* flavours with Sichuan cuisine (or Sichuan cuisine with nothing but *málà* flavour), this link is strong and well-recognized.

Hunan cuisine (*Xiang cai*) is similarly associated with the spiciness of chilli. Here, however, it is not – in fact, never (in the argument, not in reality) – a *málà* flavour one finds, but a *xin-la* or *xiang-la* 'fresh/pure' or 'aromatic' pungency.

Guizhou cooking is considered a part of the spicy 'West' of culinary China. Unlike the above two styles of cooking, however, it is not counted among the (eight) great cuisines. Quite possibly, the reason is the even greater influence of ethnic minorities in this province; Sichuan has greater acclaim as a more civilized province of high culture, Hunan a complicated but highly regarded status as home of 'provincial patriots' (as per Platt 2007). The cooking, similarly, is considered more refined in Sichuan, more rustically Chinese in Hunan, and wilder, with more than half of all recipes including chilli peppers and a typical – and to many authors, confusing – sour-spicy flavour in Guizhou (cf. Wang and others 2019).

Lesson 3: Cuisines of the Chilli, Used in Certain Ways

Different kinds of pungency come from different ways of using chilli, so that the mere description does not suffice. We also need to ask how the chilli is used and prepared.

In talking about Hunan's *xin-la* ('pure' spicy), gained through the use of fresh chilli, this difference was hinted at. Hunan cooking predominantly uses fresh chilli, green or red depending on the recipes in question. The importance of such chilli, freshly stir-fried, is perhaps best (or at least most amusingly) illustrated by the joke about the two typical dishes of Hunan: red peppers fried with green chilli and green peppers fried with red chilli. When it comes to preserved chilli, the same flavour (principle?) comes to the fore in Hunan's *duo lajiao* ('chopped chilli'), which is fresh chilli preserved in salt brine. Treated this way, it retains the fresh flavour that is sought after.

Sichuan cuisines' flavours are not only *málà*, and *málà* dishes themselves already differ from the spiciness of Hunan dishes in their use of dried chilli. Furthermore, the 'soul of Sichuan cuisine' is *Pixian doubanjiang*, the famous fermented paste of red chilli and broad beans (with salt and wheat). It gives a certain funk and an umami quality to dishes made with it; its spiciness is dialled down; the salt content is a challenge to cooks new to *doubanjiang*. Other flavour combinations are manifold, making it much more difficult to pin down a typical flavour of Sichuan cooking. (But then, perhaps the combination of the *málà* flavour being very special and easy to remember is the very reason why it would be emphasized out of a plethora of different flavours!)

Guizhou cooking's typical sour-spicy aroma is intimately related to the preservation of chilli. The taste is often attributed to a use of vinegar, but it actually derives from the chilli that is chopped and salted similarly to Hunan's *duo lajiao*, but then sour-fermented into *zao lajiao*. Guizhou cooking is also characterized by the use of *ciba lajiao*, a chilli paste made from rehydrated dried chilli that is pounded (or ground) and fried, giving it a somewhat sour-fishy flavour. (Guizhou cooking also uses *zhe'er gen*, the root of *Houttuynia cordata* Thunb., which is also fishy in aroma.)

This predilection for sour (fermented) aromas is often seen as influence of the Miao ethnic minority's traditions and tastes. Their best-known traditional dish is the 'sour soup' fish (*suantangyu*). Originally, it was made from a pure rice ferment; nowadays the more popular version is the red sour soup (*hong suantang*) which is fermented with tart

387

tomatoes and chilli. Either way, this sour ferment is also flavoured with the *mujiangzi* mentioned above and with Sichuan pepper, continuing this old tradition.

Thus, we see that certain (Chinese) cuisines are not only characterized by spiciness, but also by characteristic kinds of spiciness, and those in turn derive from different uses or preparations of chilli, the main component giving them their pungency.

In rather typical fashion for discussions of spicy cooking, the descriptions so far only spoke of chilli – but is that all there is to it?

Lesson 4: The Right Chilli(es) for the Cuisine

The chilli is not just a peculiar spice as a flavour principle of certain cuisines, where it is not easy to decide which cuisines are truly spicy, and where it needs further consideration of what sorts of spiciness, achieved through which preparations, are meant. It is also peculiar when it comes to the spiciness and the different kinds of chilli that give that spiciness.

Many recipes and discussions that mention chilli without any further distinction make it seem as if chilli were just a pungent spice without other distinguishing characteristics. It often sounds as if one could use whichever chilli one wants to use. At best, there tend to be mentions of getting a type of chilli that is not too pungent, for example.

In reality, one cannot only differentiate the levels of pungency, that is, how hot a chilli is. The sensory characteristics of chilli, as described by Guzmán and Bosland, encompass the '1) Development, 2) Duration, 3) Location, 4) Feeling, and 5) Intensity' of chilli peppers' heat (2017). Guzmán and Bosland also point out that 'it is critical to use the correct chile pepper when formulating a spicy Asian soba noodle dish or a Hungarian goulash product' as different characteristics are considered right for these respective culinary contexts, deriving from the chilli used in them (2017: 189). They do not mention the aromas aside from the pungency which can also be found in different kinds of chilli, and which (can) play a role in cooking.

The relationship between different types of chilli and different dishes and cuisines is not an easy one-to-one. In fact, it has proven a topic on which little clarity exists. Although few relationships have ever been considered, local cooks and eaters will quickly point out when something is not right, so that one cannot deny the existence of any relationship.

There is at least one case where the relationship appears to be straightforward: Sichuan cuisine, especially its *Pixian doubanjiang*, and the *erjingtiao* chilli. This particular type of chilli is the best-known in Sichuan and very popular in Sichuan cooking, thus held in high esteem. Producers of *Pixian doubanjiang,* especially, declare this chilli to be the one they use. It appears to be more of a type of chilli than a variety, however; there are different kinds of *erjingtiao* that differ in some characteristics (such as the size and thickness of the fruits).

Sichuan also uses other kinds of chilli such as the low-pungency *denglongjiao* ('lantern chilli'), which is nearly as broad as it is long (both just about an inch, 2.5 cm maximum); the smaller and spicier *zidantou* ('bullet chilli' with the name again describing the basic shape); and the small, mid-length, very spicy *mantianxing* and *qixingjiao* (the former's name does not have a usual or easy translation; *qixingjiao* is 'seven-star chilli').

The majority of these kinds of chilli, at least as they enter the chilli trade, are not actually grown in Sichuan (anymore), but in Guizhou (where they are also used). Other kinds of the upright-growing 'facing-heaven chilli' *chaotianjiao* (a category/type to which *mantianxing* and *qixingjiao* also belong), which are used all across China, are heavily cultivated in Zhecheng, Henan; still other chilli comes from cultivation in Xinjiang; and some is even imported from India.

One needs to draw distinctions between local chilli for local use, chilli that has entered wider trade (sometimes with a local pedigree being upheld), and chilli for the worldwide trade, as well as the characteristics that make these appropriate for different uses.

In Guizhou, aside from the chilli produced for trade (and its own culinary uses, including in the spicy oils made by Laoganma), many of them are considered to belong to Sichuan as much as to Guizhou, which also has typical kinds of chilli that are more local. The city Dafang, for example, produces *zhoujiao* or *jizhuajiao* ('wrinkled' or 'chicken claw' chilli); Huaxi, a suburb of the province's capital Guiyang, produces a *Huaxi lajiao* that has received a geographical protection of origin (even as it seems little known and used). Kaili, or at least the producers of *suantangyu* (the sour fish soup), grow a *laoshanjiao* ('old mountain chilli'). (The chilli seeds available in the USA as 'Thunder Mountain Longhorn' belong to this type, apparently.) By now, the variety used for the production of *suantang* is *laoshanjiao* 8-*hao* (number 8), developed from the original type, 1-*hao* (number 1). The latter is much thinner-fleshed, if similarly long, slender, and wrinkled, and thus less suited for fermentation, but preferred for making Guizhou's *laziji* (spicy chicken) and still grown as the traditional local type.

Hunan is a special case. In recent years, a Zhangshugang chilli (from a place of that name) has been marketed very successfully as a special type for frying as green chilli. The city of Hengdong also grows a special, yellow-ripening, chilli which has been marketed, for at least ten years already, as yellow tribute pepper. ('Tribute pepper,' *gong jiao*, is otherwise often heard as a moniker for the Sichuan pepper from Hanyuan, which is similarly marketed as having been a tribute to the emperor.) Most of the chilli used, whether imported or locally grown, of traditional stock or newly developed, however, is not differentiated by name. It is of a fitting type for Hunan cuisine, or it would not sell, but these fitting attributes are an implicit knowledge of its users, not of any formal criteria.

Lesson 5: It's Complicated and Up to Creativity – Except When Not

Which types of chilli have traditionally been used and are seen as essential or can easily be replaced with others is a matter of botany and the vagaries of history, of tastes and trade, and perhaps even of serendipity.

Historically, and with some continuation into the present, the right chilli was the type of chilli grown and used locally. This may seem like a matter of course, but it may point to an interplay between plant (spice) characteristics, growers' selection, and development of cuisines that is rather complicated. Did the chilli that happened to arrive in a place become the right one, shaping its eater's tastes? Or was a chilli only adopted when it fitted in with the desired flavour profile of a cuisine? How and why did *chaotianjiao* ('facing-heaven chilli') spread widely and get into general use for chilli pepper flakes, *erjingtiao* come to be produced more widely than in its 'native' Sichuan but still retain the link to this place, whereas other types like *Dafang zhoujiao* or *Huaxi lajiao* remain strongly rooted in their respective places, to the point where they have official recognition as local products?

In local home cooking with locally grown ingredients, people simply know the kinds of chilli they consider right; anything else is either a less-known exotic or an import that still fits. In China, one can still find many farmer's markets with local produce, and the local character of produce has some importance. Asking if a chilli is local, *bendi*, typically results in emphatic agreement (at least in Hunan, where I have done this regularly) as long as it is not an import from far away. This has gone to the point where the '*bendi*' character of chilli is so emphasized that it has ended up marking at least one accession of Chinese chilli in international gene banks, apparently having been misunderstood as the name of that chilli. Most of the time, such local chilli does not have any particular name. Rather, it is only addressed as green or red chilli, long or screw or facing-heaven chilli, dangerously hot or not too pungent. The emphatic claim that the chilli is local may also hide that the seeds may have come from a professional seed development company – and even chilli breeding in China, as it turned out in conversations with seed developers, is shaped by a concern for the locally fitting characteristics. (The explanation given to me was simple: if people did not like it, it would not sell.)

Only a few types of chilli are not only grown locally, but also marketed more widely. Such interaction with larger markets seems to have resulted in some types getting distinct names. In the extreme, seed developers have to label their different varieties. These names are hardly ever known except to the farmers and industrial users of special varieties, but these chilli are not just developed for higher yields and pest resistance, but also for certain flavours and uses.

Cooks have some leeway for creativity and preferences, of course. In fact, a seemingly simple aspect such as the typical pungency level of a cuisine can shift in line with customer expectations. Thus, Sichuan cooking outside of Sichuan has proven, even within China, to typically rise in levels of pungency the further away from Sichuan one gets. My first encounters with Sichuan food were in Beijing, and the *mapo doufu* there was spiced so strongly that it was hardly edible for anyone. In Chengdu, at the dish's birthplace, in contrast, it was always comfortably spicy. Marketing attempts have also played a role, as chilli makes it easy to declare a store as having the spiciest food in the world (and news outlets as well as social media appear to like these declarations).

Lesson 6: Modernization in Degrees of Spiciness

Levels of pungency lead to a final lesson in the spread and marketing of spicy foods that I found particularly noteworthy. (Full disclosure: This development comes from a company, Dezhuang, with which I have an affiliation: they were the main sponsor of my research into the chilli in China for the World Chilli Alliance.) Much of the rise of spicy eating, in China as well as around the world (certainly in the 'Western countries'), has been driven by young people with a more adventurous taste and by a certain machismo. Perhaps the benign masochism of which Rozin and Schiller (1980) spoke in regard to the chilli, the pleasure of safely going to one's limits, has been a driving force.

The challenge for the food industry has been that the spiciness of dishes and products is marked haphazardly, if it is marked at all. What is labelled as hot in Germany is mild compared to spicy products in the UK, and what is marked as hot in East Asia is more pungent still, with a greater range than anywhere else (cf. Kalsec 2019). In order to bring standardization into this area to make things easier for diners, Dezhuang, which produces spice mixtures especially for hot pot and operates chains of hot pot restaurants, developed a rating system for spiciness.

The research for these 'Li's Spicy Degrees' looked at the levels of pungency in hot pot bases by measuring their capsaicinoid content (that is, by determining their Scoville Heat Units) and correlated ranges of pungency with a wide variety of diner's impressions. From that, they grade foods as having a spiciness of 12, 36, 45, 52, 65, or 75 degrees. 'Slightly spicy' 12 degrees are, by the official description, for the 3% of people who do not eat chilli, such as children and the elderly; 'medium spicy' 45 degrees is suitable for the largest number (45%) of people; 75 degrees is only meant for the small number of people who like to challenge their limits.

This drive towards modernization and standardization in one of the few under-regulated areas of the otherwise highly regulated food industry, and in the area of chilli cuisines that are typically not even recognized as such, has been extremely interesting to see. Speaking as a fan of spicy eating, this drive holds potential to make pungent dishes more accessible to more people (held back by a fear of getting food that would be too hot to handle for them), even as the other typical and necessary characteristics of spicy foods (certainly in the case of hot pot flavours) are retained.

Final Thoughts

From cuisines that are distinctly spicy compared to others, to distinct kinds of pungency that differentiate such cuisines, arising from different uses of chilli and different types of chilli, into local agriculture and far-ranging trade, the pungency of the chilli is much more than just hot. It links old trade networks that spanned the globe and the poor who joined trading expeditions and were local farmers, who could not afford expensive spices but could bring and grow spicy chilli. It connects us to this past and to the present of remaining heirloom types of chilli, and to new agricultural and food-industrial modernization.

Chilli is also, prominent as its pungency has become among all the herbs and spices, the strangest among them all: It is easy to grow, easy to use and recognize and get burned by, easy to market in a social media world thanks to the extremes to which its pungency can go – and for the same reasons, it is fiendishly hard to recognize as a diverse spice, the diversity of which matters.

In that difficulty also lies the fun, the potential for exploration, out among the growers of the chilli and in our own gardens and kitchens.

References

Dott, Brian R. 2020. *The Chile Pepper in China. A Cultural Biography.* New York: Columbia University Press

Guzmán, Ivette, and Bosland, Paul W. 2017. 'Sensory Properties of Chile Pepper Heat – and Its Importance to Food Quality and Cultural Preference'. *Appetite,* 117: 186-190.

Halikowski Smith, Stefan. 2015. 'In the Shadow of a Pepper-Centric Historiography: Understanding the Global Diffusion of Capsicums in the Sixteenth and Seventeenth Centuries'. *Journal of Ethnopharmacology,* 167: 64-77.

Kalsec. 2019. *Spicy Perceptions. Hot and Spicy Food Industry Insights.* ebook

Platt, Stephen R. 2007. *Provincial Patriots. The Hunanese and Modern China.* Cambridge, MA, London, England: Harvard University Press

Rechinger, K. and L. 1905. '*Reisen ach den Samoa-Inseln*, No. 290, *Capsicum frutescens*', Natural History Museum of Vienna

Rozin, Elisabeth. 1983. *Ethnic Cuisine.* Lexington, MA: S. Greene Press

Rozin, Paul and Schiller, Deborah. 1980. 'The Nature and Acquisition of a Preference for Chili Pepper by Humans'. *Motivation and Emotion,* 4(1): 77-101.

Wang, Siyuan and others. 2019. 'Regional Pungency Degree in China and Its Correlation with Typical Climate Factors'. *Journal of Food Science,* 84.1: 31-37.

Zewdie, Y., and Bosland, Paul W. 2001. 'Capsaicinoid Profiles Are Not Good Chemotaxonomic Indicators for Capsicum species'. *Biochemical Systematics and Ecology,* 29: 161-69.

Contributors

Ken Albala is Professor of History at the University of the Pacific and the author or editor of twenty-five books on food.

Lauren Allen, a chef, artist, researcher, and writer, graduated from the master's program in Gastronomy at Boston University.

Volker Bach, a freelance translator and historical cooking instructor, is the author of *The Kitchen, Food, and Cooking in Reformation Germany* and the forthcoming *Das Landsknechtkochbuch*.

Scott Alves Barton teaches Food and Environmental Studies, and Anthropology at New York City universities. He has recently begun an embodied practice tied to issues of US enslavement, Sierra Leone-Lowcountry rice agriculture, and hospitality.

Nina Bauer is a historian who finds the subject of food to be the most fascinating subject of all, whether it is the cultural history of oysters, wartime cooking or food fraud through the ages. She has a Master of Arts in History and Museology from University of Copenhagen.

Janet Beizer, Professor of Romance Languages and Literatures at Harvard University, specializes in French literature and civilization. She is finishing a book called *The Harlequin Eaters: Leftovers and the Patchwork Imagination in Nineteenth-Century Paris*.

Eric Bishop-von Wettberg is Associate Professor of Plant and Soil Science at the University of Vermont.

Astrid Böhm is a research assistant at the Centre for Information Modeling at the University of Graz. She specializes in historical script and manuscript studies.

Voltaire Cang, an academic researcher based in Tokyo, writes about Japan's 'intangible' heritage, including food and other cultural traditions. He is finishing a book titled *Heritage and Identity in Japanese Food Culture*.

Marianne Jennifer Datiles is a doctoral researcher at the University College London School of Pharmacy.

Julia Eibinger works as a student assistant at the Centre for Information Modeling at the University of Graz. Her focus is on semantic annotation of medieval cooking recipes and data science.

Contributors

Rebecca Federman is a Managing Research Librarian at the New York Public Library, where she supports research in the humanities, social sciences, and culinary sciences.

Julia Fine, a Cambridge Trust and George Kingsley Roth scholar in the Centre of South Asian Studies at the University of Cambridge, is working on a dissertation delineating the environmental history of salt production in Bengal, with a particular focus on the Sundarbans.

Paul Freedman is Professor of History at Yale University. He is the author of *Ten Restaurants That Changed America* (2016) and *American Cuisine and How It Got This Way* (2019).

Alexandr Gorokhovskiy is a professional marketeer and drinks industry executive with more than 15 years of experience. His personal interest in the history of distilled alcohol has recently led him to embark on a PhD program at Utrecht University.

Binti Gurung has worked at Archives New Zealand in Wellington. She is currently researching the history of food in Nepal, as well as promoting ancient Nepali herbs, indigenous grains, and products in Kathmandu.

Michael Heinrich is Professor of Ethnopharmacology and Pharmacognosy at the University College London School of Pharmacy.

394

Ian Hemphill has been involved with herbs and spices since early childhood, and now owns an artisan herb and spice business in Australia. Ian is the author of *Spice Notes, Spice Travels, Spice Notes and Recipes*, and *The Spice & Herb Bible*.

Peter Hertzmann is an autodidactic polymath with a strong contrarian bent who likes to provide an alternative approach about all aspects of food. His three books are *Knife Skills Illustrated: A User's Manual*, *A Perfect Mouthful*, and *50 Ways to Cook a Carrot*.

Heather Hunwick is currently an Honorary Research Associate at the University of Western Australia. Her two most recent books are *Doughnut: A Global History* and *The Food and Drink of Sydney, a History*.

Helmut W. Klug works at the Centre for Information Modeling at the University of Graz. A senior post-doc researcher in digital humanities and food history, he is interested in the recipe as a cultural heritage object.

Michael Krondl is a food writer, culinary historian, cooking teacher, and artist. His books include *The Taste of Conquest: The Rise and Fall of the Three Great Cities of Spice* and *Sweet Invention: A History of Dessert*.

Contributors

Gina Rae La Cerva is a geographer, environmental anthropologist, and award-winning writer who has traveled extensively to research a variety of environmental and food-related topics.

Vivienne Lo is a Professor in the department of History and the convenor of the University College London China Centre for Health and Humanity. She also teaches the Ancient and Medieval history of China and has specialist modules in the History of Asian Medicine and Classical Chinese medicine.

Joshua Lovinger is a vascular neurologist based in New York. He has also completed graduate work in medieval and Jewish history, and is interested in the relationship between food, science, and Jewish law and custom.

Priya Mani, a designer and cultural researcher based in Copenhagen working to create gastronomical experiences, is particularly interested in the social interactions of making, presenting, and consuming food.

Mark McWilliams, Professor of English at the United States Naval Academy, has served as Editor of the Oxford Symposium on Food and Cookery since 2011.

Maya Moore, a PhD student in the Food Systems Program at the University of Vermont, has lived and worked in Madagascar for almost fifteen years. She is looking into the ways in which smallholder farmers in the tropics are experiencing changes in their environment.

Jennifer Moragoda resides at the geographic confluence of east and west in Sri Lanka, the cinnamon isle. Her many research interests include comparative cultures, textiles, gastronomy, and food history.

James O'Donnell is a forager, writer, and communications specialist based in New York. With a background in food and agriculture, his work focuses on the hidden labour that shapes our everyday world.

Taylor Parrish is a PhD Candidate in English at Tufts University. Her research focuses on the intersections between food, agriculture, hunger, and environmental justice in Anglophone literature.

Jessica M. Pigza is the Outreach & Exhibits Librarian for Special Collections & Archives at the University of California, Santa Cruz, where she curates exhibits and supports research on a broad range of topics related to the countercultural history of California's Central Coast.

Contributors

Tuba Şatana is a chronicler focusing on food culture and the city, the small establishments that make the city unique, and the people who make it happen. She is the founder and creator of Istanbul Food and Sapor Istanbul Food Symposium, lives in Istanbul.

Eva Schalbroeck is a historian of colonialism and missionary activity in Central Africa. She is also interested in the immaterial afterlife of this past. She studied at the KU Leuven and the University of Cambridge and is currently a lecturer at Utrecht University.

Regina Sexton, Lecturer and Programme Manager of the Postgraduate Diploma in Irish Food Culture at University College Cork, is a food and culinary historian, award-winning food writer, broadcaster, and cook. She writes about food and identity, tradition, and the Irish country house.

Richard Warren Shepro is both an international lawyer and a food scholar. He teaches at the University of Chicago and is the author of six Oxford Symposium papers. He is a former editor of the *Harvard Law Review*.

Jeremy Simmons recently received his PhD in Classical Studies from Columbia University. After a year at the American Academy in Rome and another at New York University, he will be an assistant professor in ancient history at the University of Maryland, College Park.

Charles Spence is the head of the Crossmodal Research Laboratory at the University of Oxford. His research focuses on how a better understanding of the human mind will lead to the better design of multisensory foods, products, interfaces, and environments in the future.

Christian Steiner is a research assistant at the Centre for Information Modelling in the Austrian Centre for Digital Humanities at the University of Graz, Austria. He is particularly concerned with methods of semantic modelling.

Aiko Tanaka is the president of Aiko Tanaka Culinary School in Osaka, founder of Food Activist Organization Japan, and co-founder of the Japan Food Studies Institute. Her primary focus is on spreading knowledge of Japanese cooking and promoting SDGs for a healthy future.

Robban Toleno earned a PhD in Asian Studies from the University of British Columbia for work on food and nourishment in the history of premodern Chinese Buddhism. He writes about human-environment interactions.

Contributors

Fritz Treiber is a molecular biologist at the Centre for Society, Science, and Communication at the University of Graz. He focuses on nutrition science and modern food myths.

Amy B. Trubek is a professor in food systems at the University of Vermont. Her research interests include the history of the culinary profession, globalization of the food supply, the relationship between taste and place, and cooking as a cultural practice.

Sharmila Vaidyanathan is a freelance writer from Bangalore, India. She writes about food entrepreneurship, sustainability and conservation.

William Woys Weaver received his PhD from University College, Dublin and is the author of fifteen books and hundreds of articles on foods and foodways.

Susan Weingarten is a food historian and archaeologist living in Jerusalem. She is the author of *Haroset: A Taste of Jewish History.*

Gerald Zhang-Schmidt is the educator and independent scholar behind the blog ChiliCult.